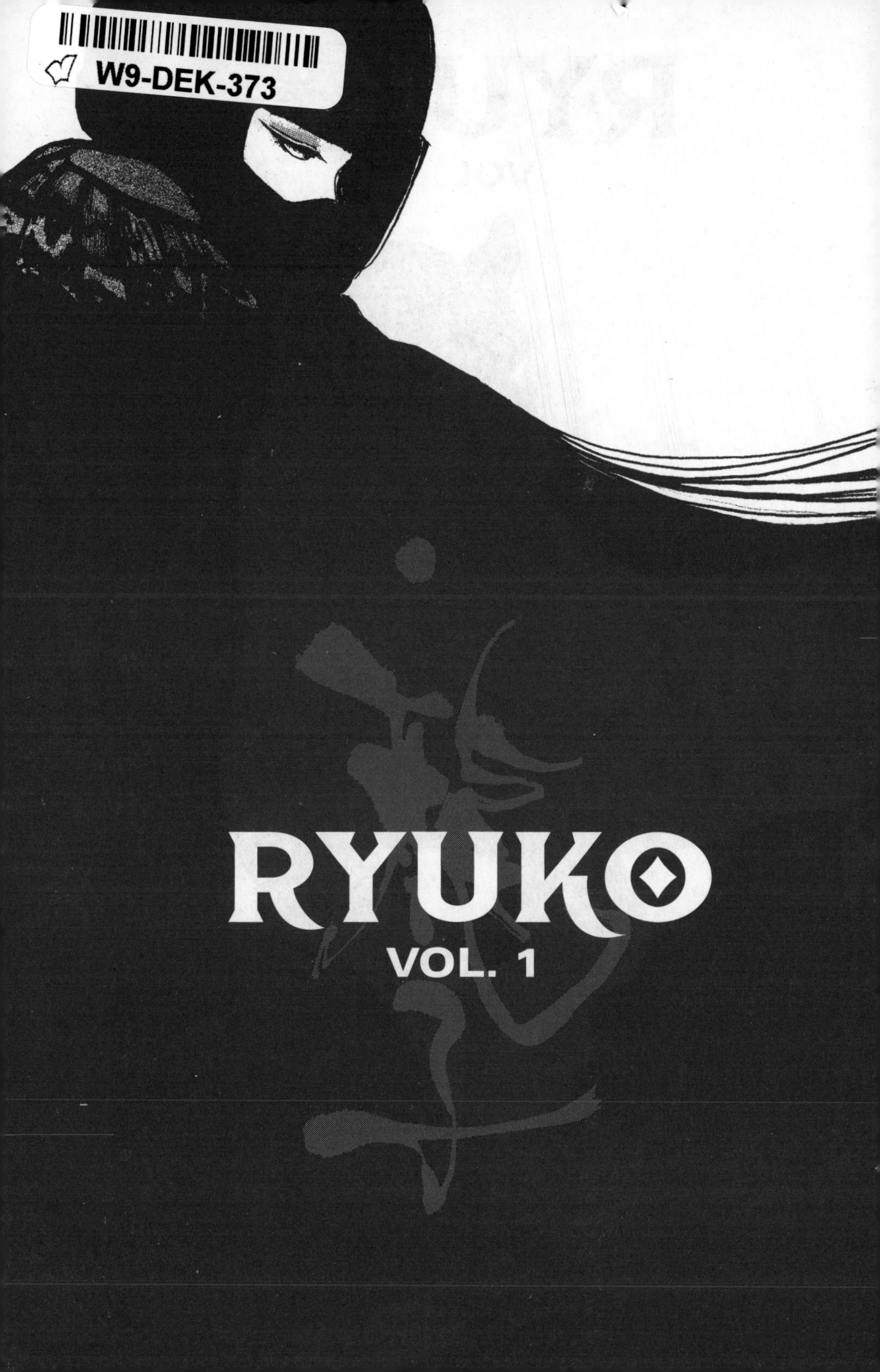
RYUKO
VOL. 1

RYUKO

VOL. 1

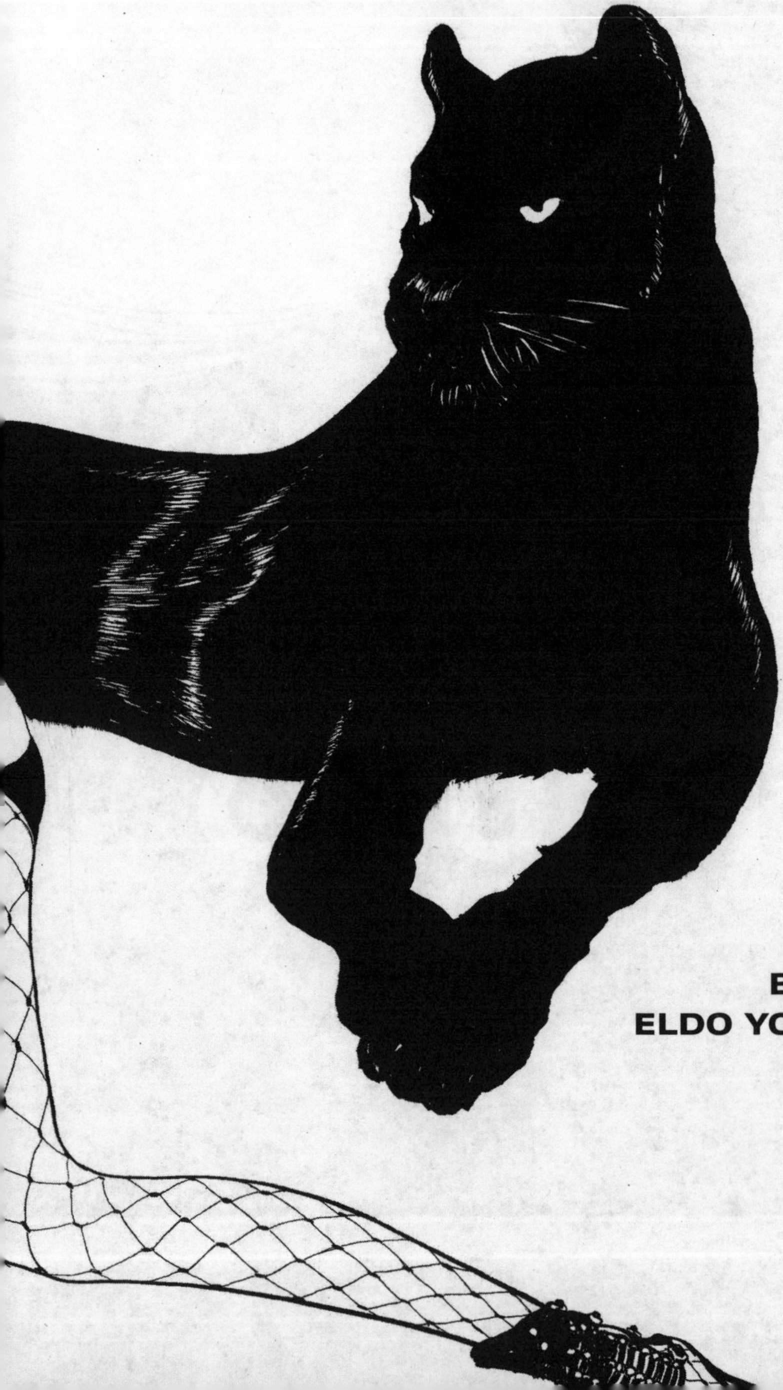

BY
ELDO YOSHIMIZU

Translation: Motoko Tamamuro and Jonathan Clements
This manga is presented in its original right-to-left reading format.

TITAN COMICS

Managing Editor Martin Eden
Contributing Editor David Leach
Designer Donna Askem
Art Director Oz Browne
Senior Production Controller
Jackie Flook
Production Controller Peter James
Production Assistant Rhiannon Roy
Sales & Circulation Manager Steve Tothill
Marketing Assistant Charlie Raspin
Publicist Imogen Harris
Senior Publicist Will O'Mullane
Senior Brand Manager Chris Thompson
Publishing Director Darryl Tothill
Operations Director Leigh Baulch
Executive Director Vivian Cheung
Publisher - Nick Landau

Ryuko Volume One.
© 2019 Eldo Yoshimizu. All rights reserved.
Published by Titan Comics, a division of Titan Publishing
Group, Ltd, 144 Southwark Street, London SE1 0UP, UK.
Titan Comics is a registered trademark of Titan Publishing Group Ltd.
The name *Hard Case Crime* and the Hard Case Crime logo are trademarks
of Winterfall LCC. Hard Case Crime Comics are produced with editorial
guidance from Charles Ardai.

10 9 8 7 6 5 4 3 2 1

First printed in India. July 2019.

A CIP catalogue record for this title is available from the British Library.

www.titan-comics.com

Chapter 1:
Father and
Daughter

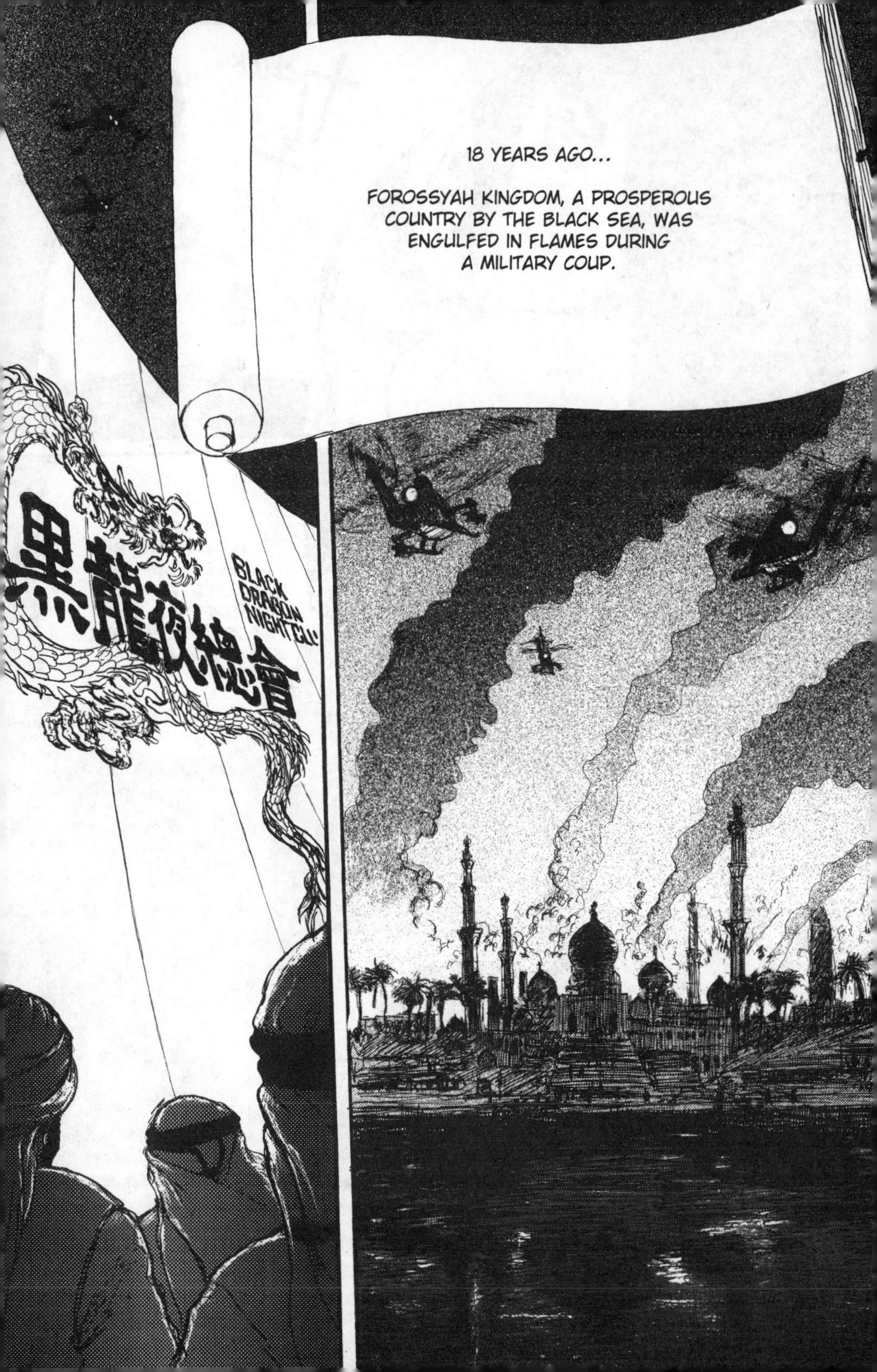
18 YEARS AGO...
FOROSSYAH KINGDOM, A PROSPEROUS COUNTRY BY THE BLACK SEA, WAS ENGULFED IN FLAMES DURING A MILITARY COUP.
黑龍夜總會
BLACK DRAGON NIGHTCLU

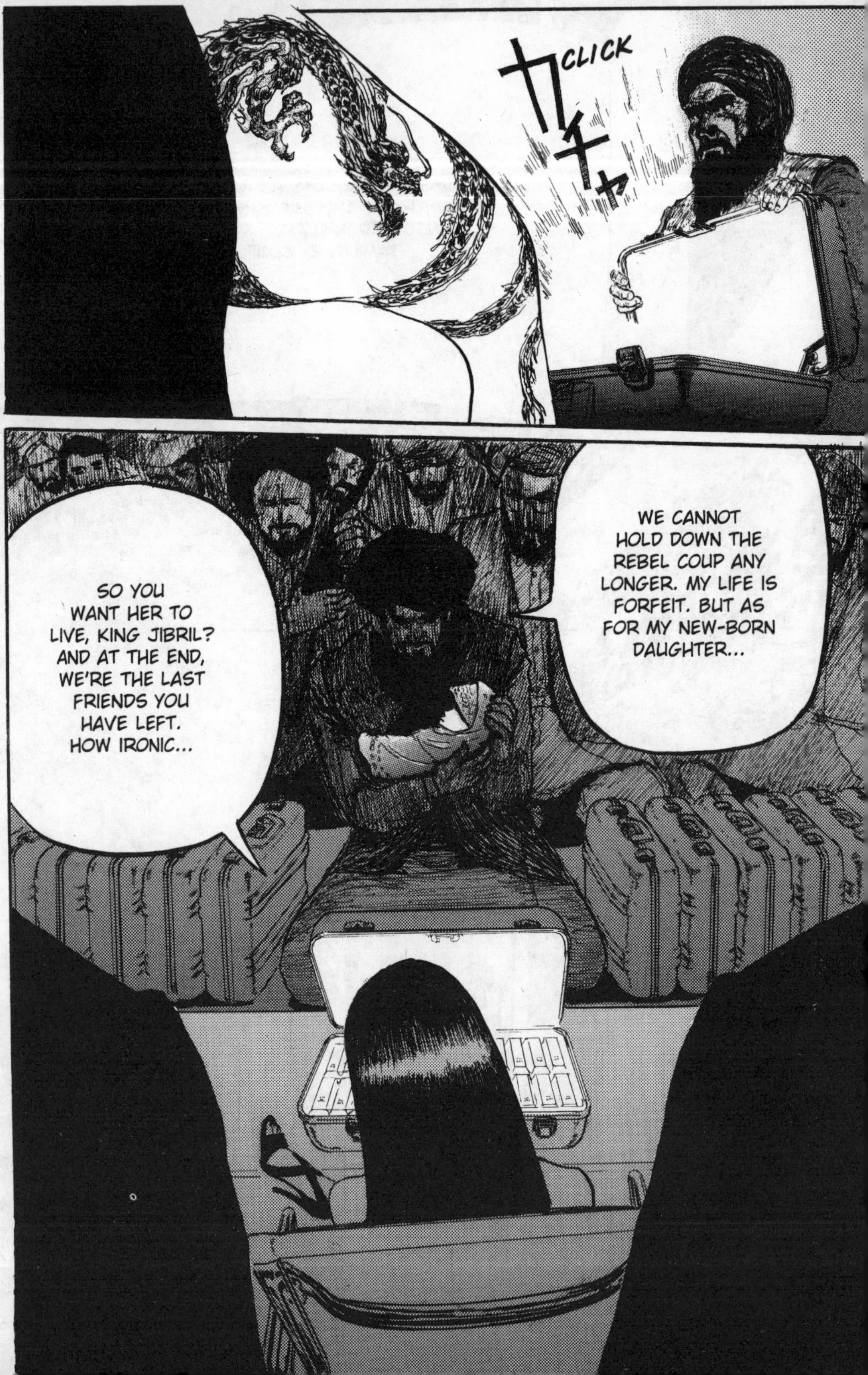
カチャ
CLICK
WE CANNOT HOLD DOWN THE REBEL COUP ANY LONGER. MY LIFE IS FORFEIT. BUT AS FOR MY NEW-BORN DAUGHTER...
SO YOU WANT HER TO LIVE, KING JIBRIL? AND AT THE END, WE'RE THE LAST FRIENDS YOU HAVE LEFT. HOW IRONIC...

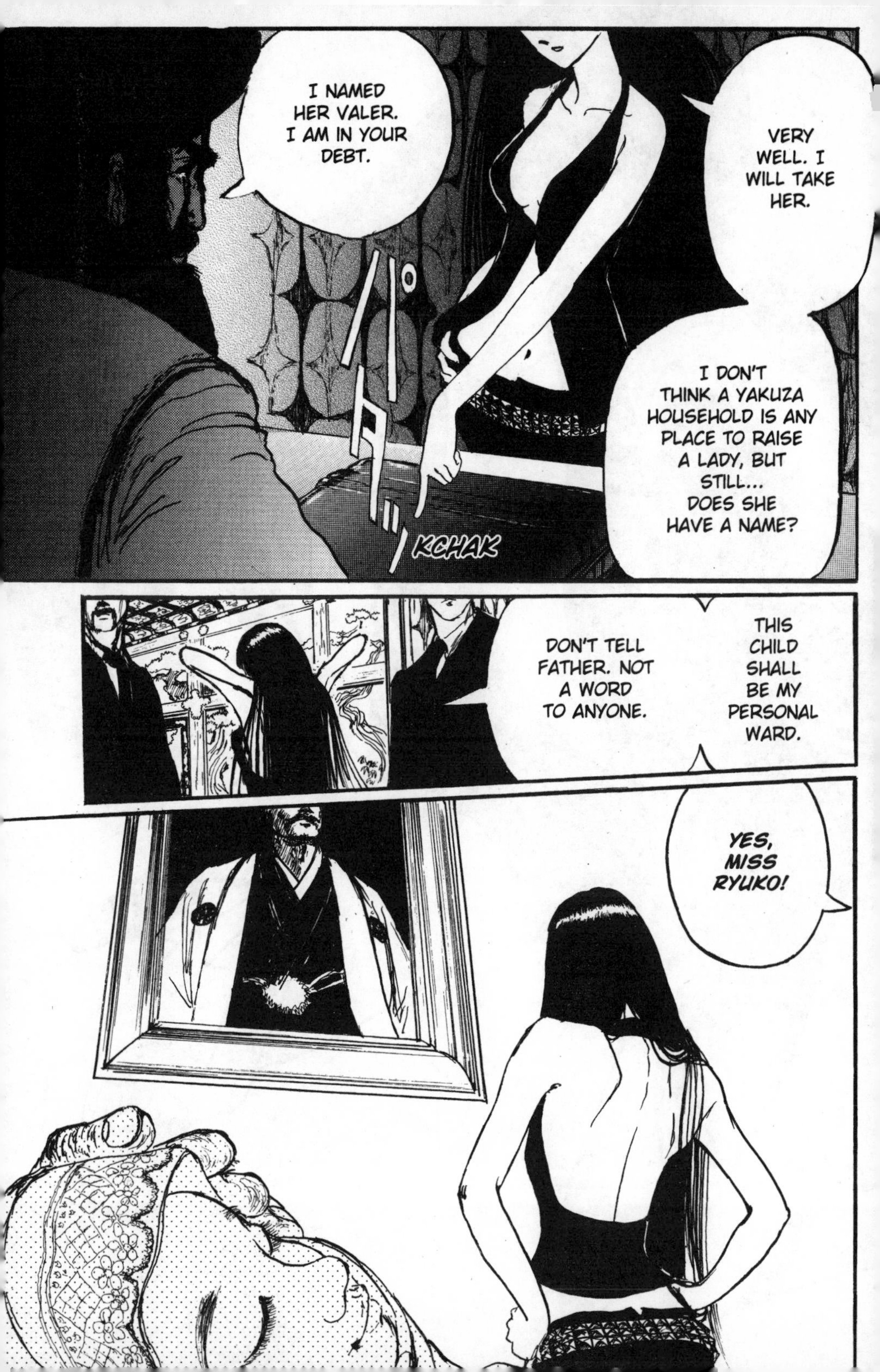
VERY WELL. I WILL TAKE HER.
I DON'T THINK A YAKUZA HOUSEHOLD IS ANY PLACE TO RAISE A LADY, BUT STILL... DOES SHE HAVE A NAME?
I NAMED HER VALER. I AM IN YOUR DEBT.
KCHAK
THIS CHILD SHALL BE MY PERSONAL WARD.
DON'T TELL FATHER. NOT A WORD TO ANYONE.
YES, MISS RYUKO!

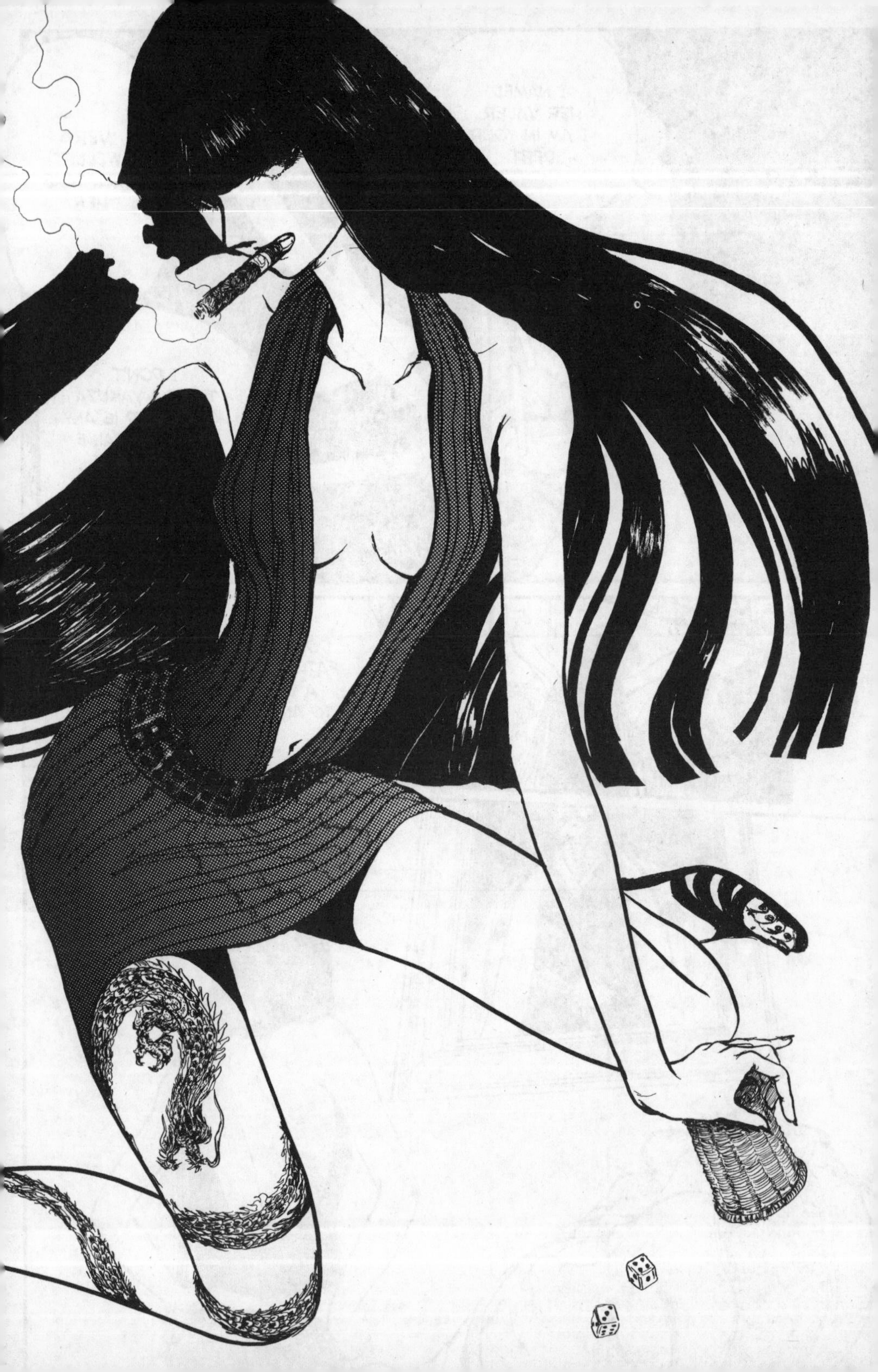

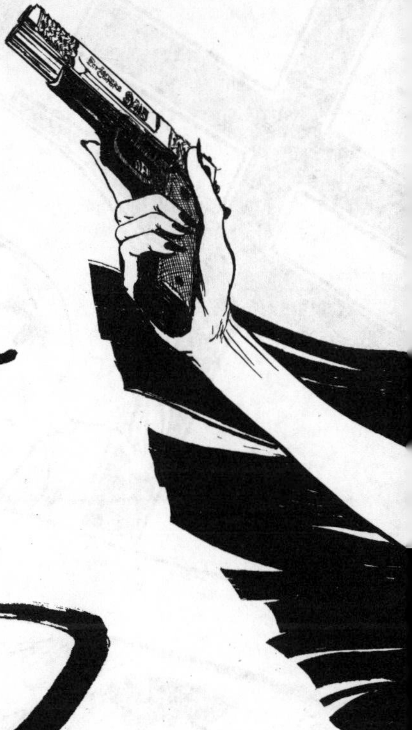

龍子

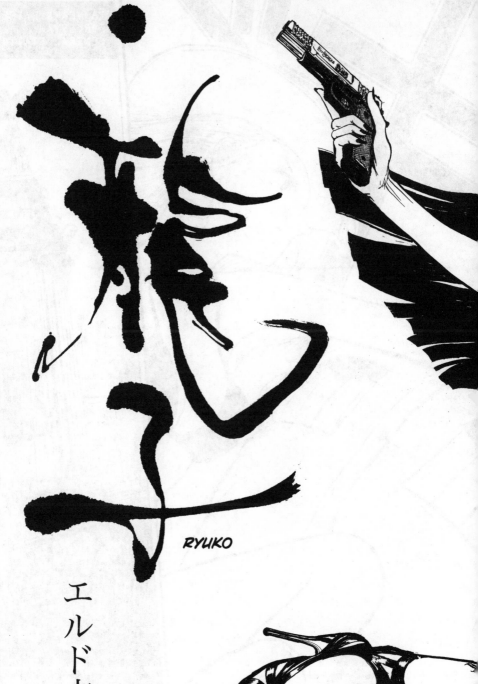

RYUKO

エルド吉水

ELDO YOSHIMIZU

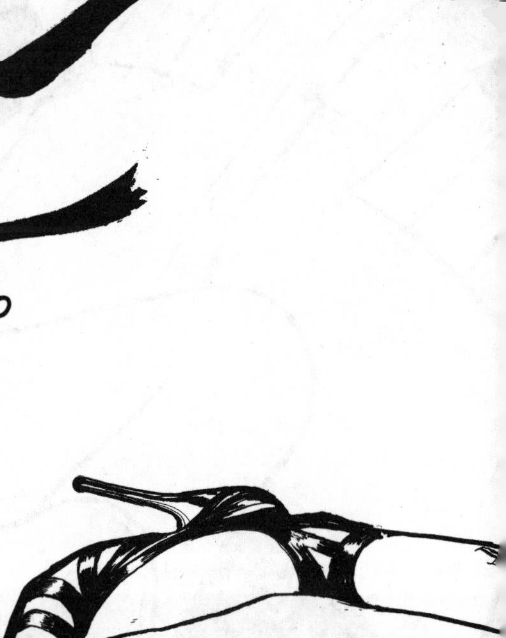

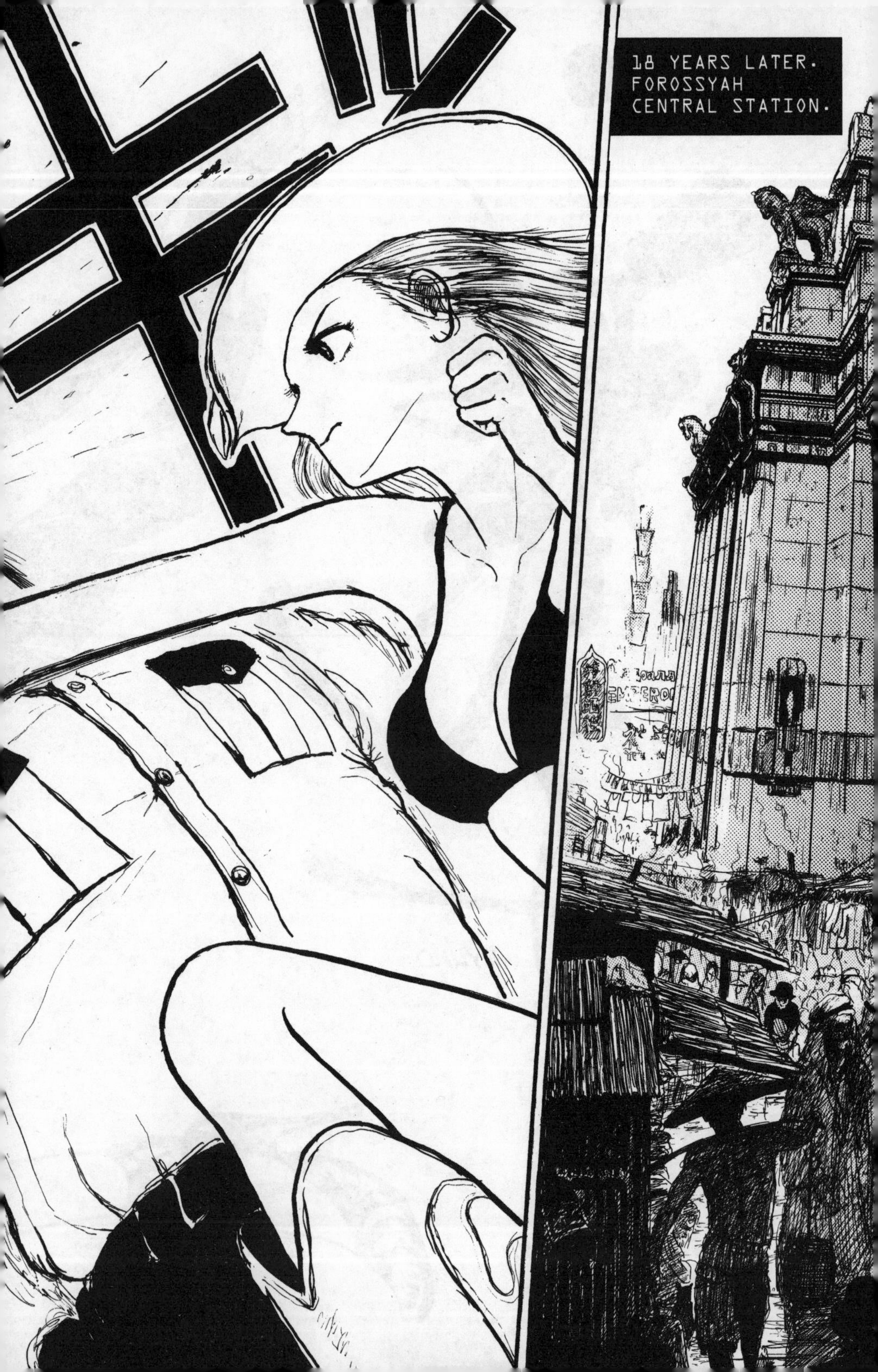
18 YEARS LATER.
FOROSSYAH
CENTRAL STATION.

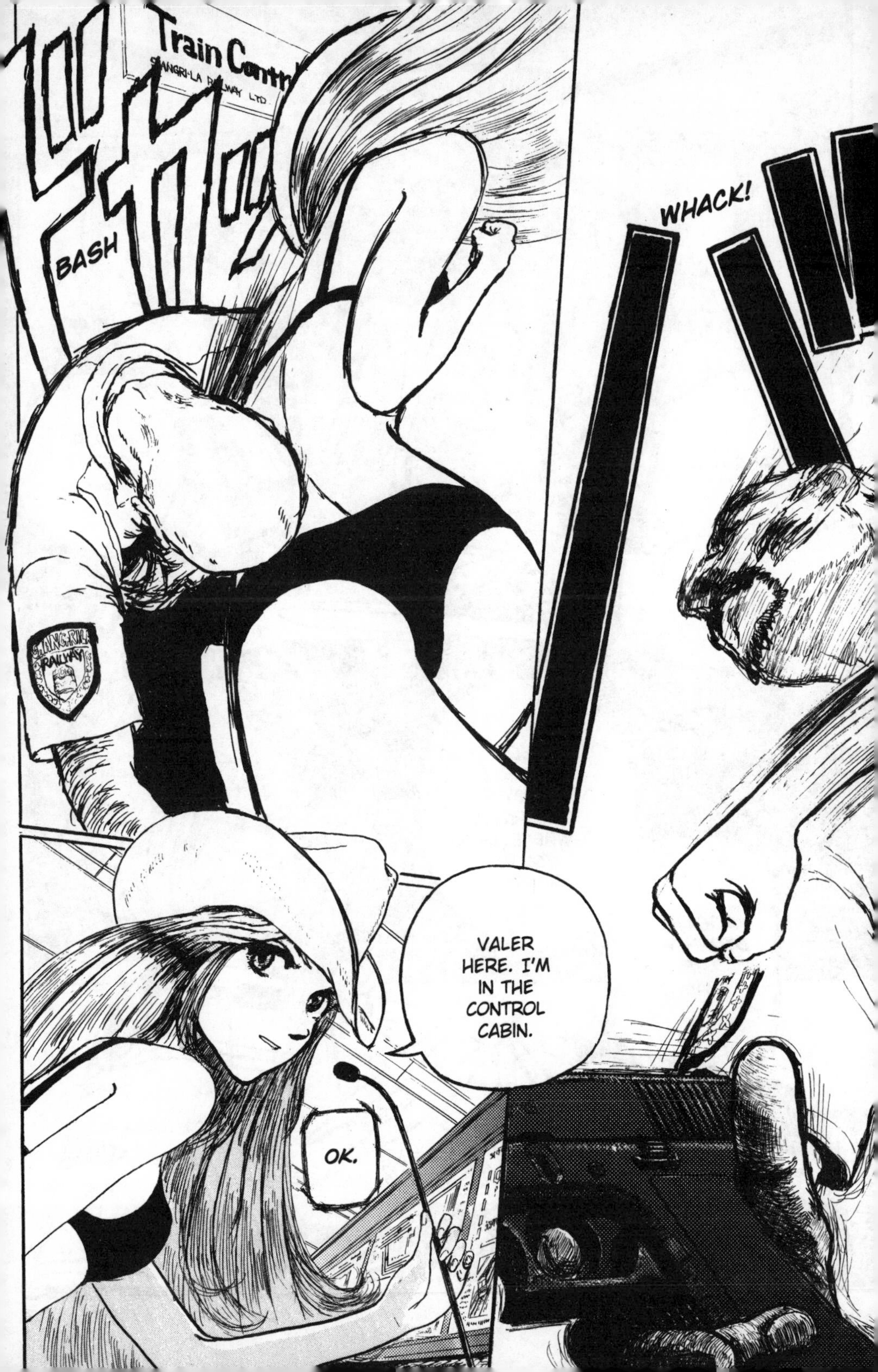
WHACK!
BASH
VALER HERE. I'M IN THE CONTROL CABIN.
OK.

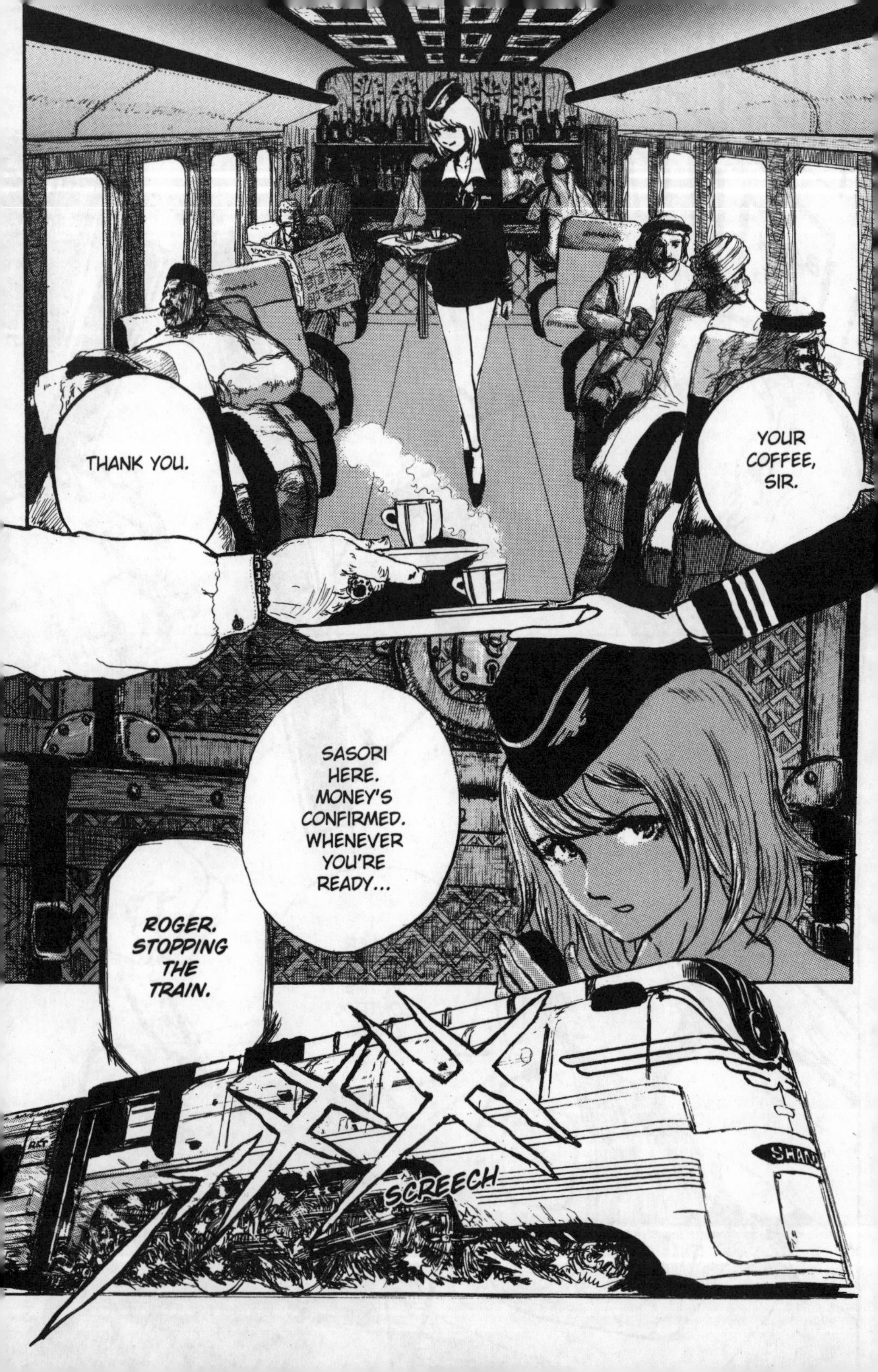
YOUR COFFEE, SIR.
THANK YOU.
SASORI HERE. MONEY'S CONFIRMED. WHENEVER YOU'RE READY...
ROGER. STOPPING THE TRAIN.
SCREECH

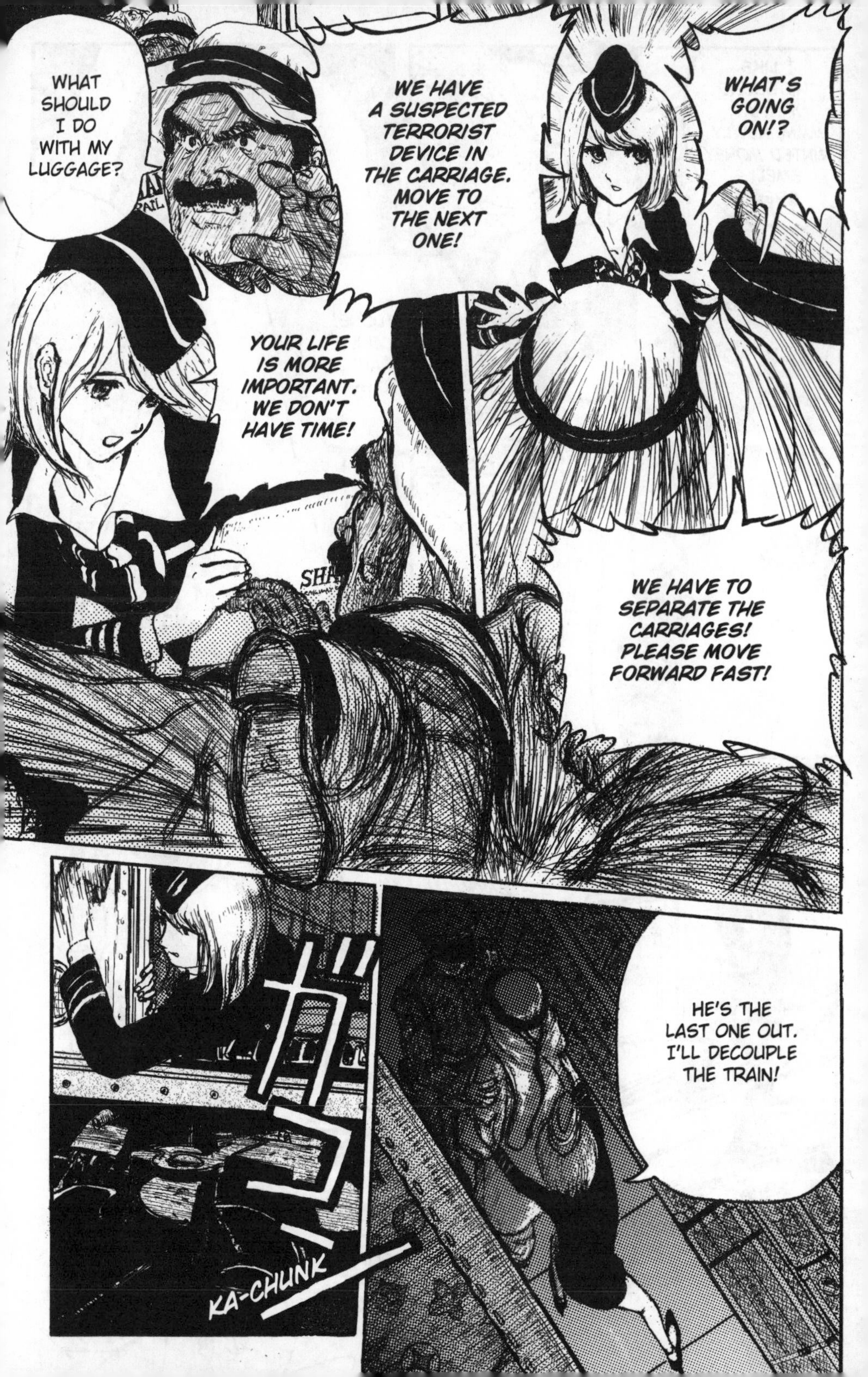
WHAT'S GOING ON!?
WE HAVE A SUSPECTED TERRORIST DEVICE IN THE CARRIAGE. MOVE TO THE NEXT ONE!
WHAT SHOULD I DO WITH MY LUGGAGE?
YOUR LIFE IS MORE IMPORTANT. WE DON'T HAVE TIME!
WE HAVE TO SEPARATE THE CARRIAGES! PLEASE MOVE FORWARD FAST!
HE'S THE LAST ONE OUT. I'LL DECOUPLE THE TRAIN!
KA-CHUNK

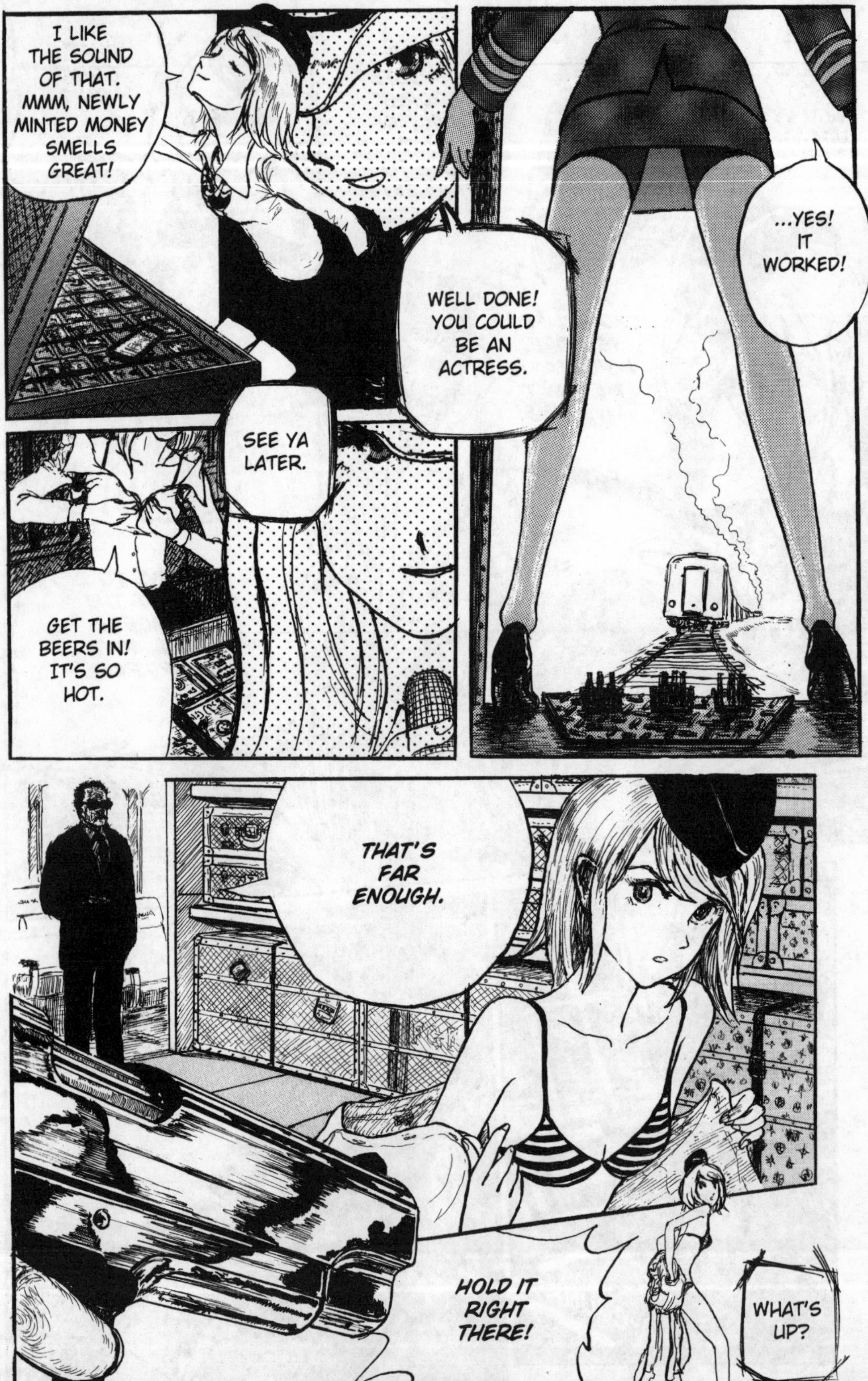
...YES! IT WORKED!
WELL DONE! YOU COULD BE AN ACTRESS.
I LIKE THE SOUND OF THAT. MMM, NEWLY MINTED MONEY SMELLS GREAT!
SEE YA LATER.
GET THE BEERS IN! IT'S SO HOT.
THAT'S FAR ENOUGH.
WHAT'S UP?
HOLD IT RIGHT THERE!

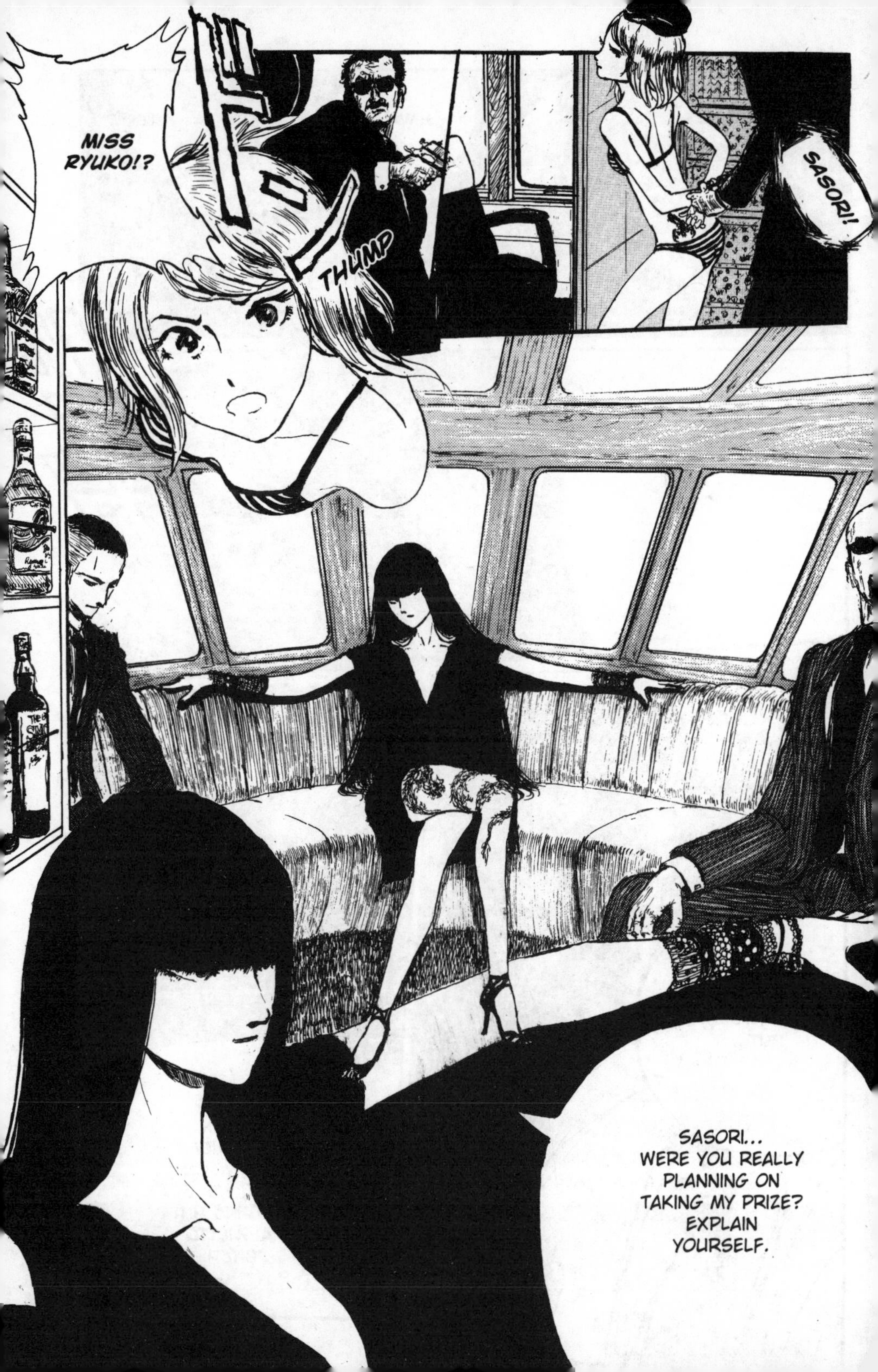
SASORI!!
THUMP
MISS RYUKO!?
SASORI... WERE YOU REALLY PLANNING ON TAKING MY PRIZE? EXPLAIN YOURSELF.

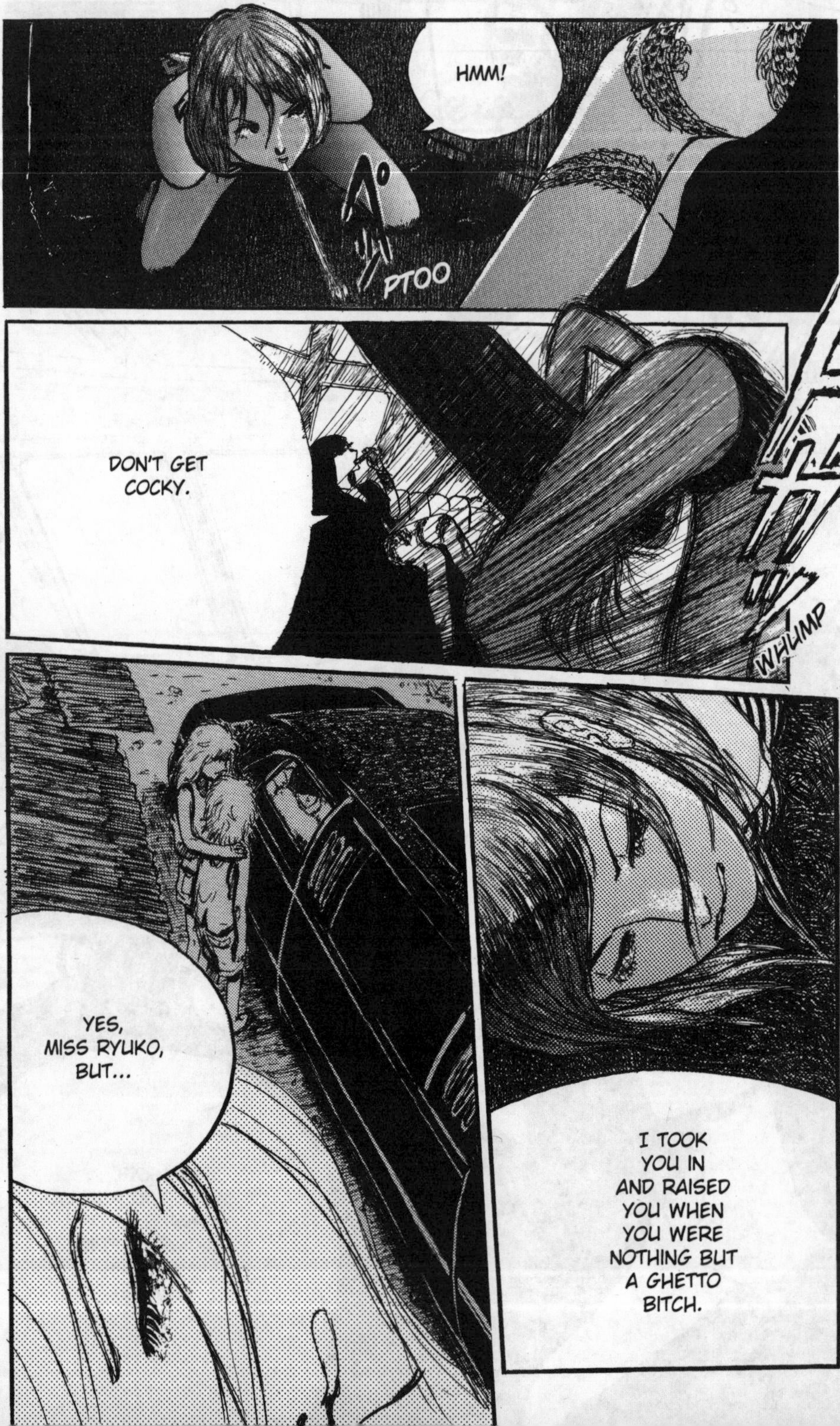
HMM!
PTOO
DON'T GET COCKY.
WHUMP
I TOOK YOU IN AND RAISED YOU WHEN YOU WERE NOTHING BUT A GHETTO BITCH.
YES, MISS RYUKO, BUT...

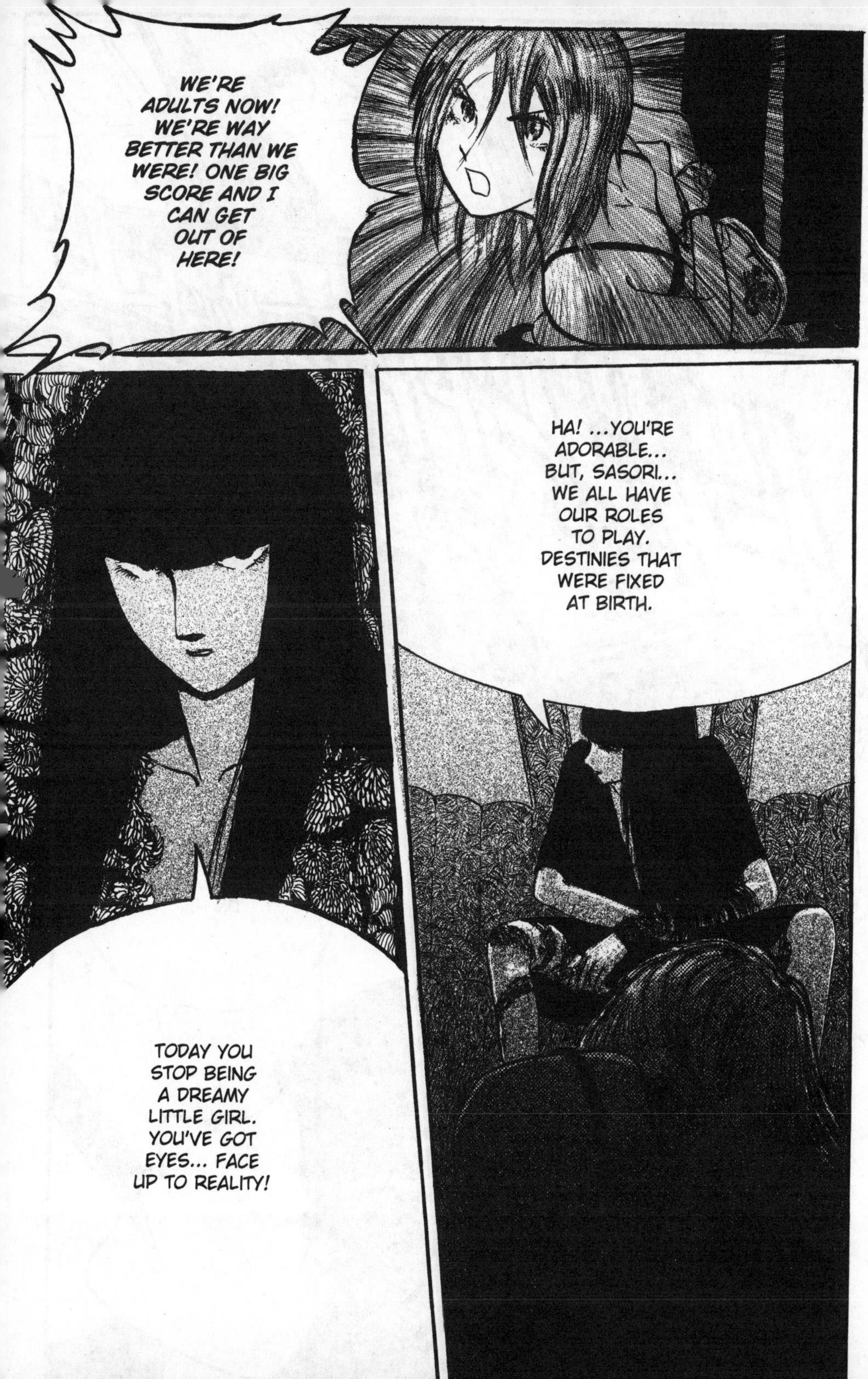
WE'RE ADULTS NOW! WE'RE WAY BETTER THAN WE WERE! ONE BIG SCORE AND I CAN GET OUT OF HERE!
HA! ...YOU'RE ADORABLE... BUT, SASORI... WE ALL HAVE OUR ROLES TO PLAY. DESTINIES THAT WERE FIXED AT BIRTH.
TODAY YOU STOP BEING A DREAMY LITTLE GIRL. YOU'VE GOT EYES... FACE UP TO REALITY!

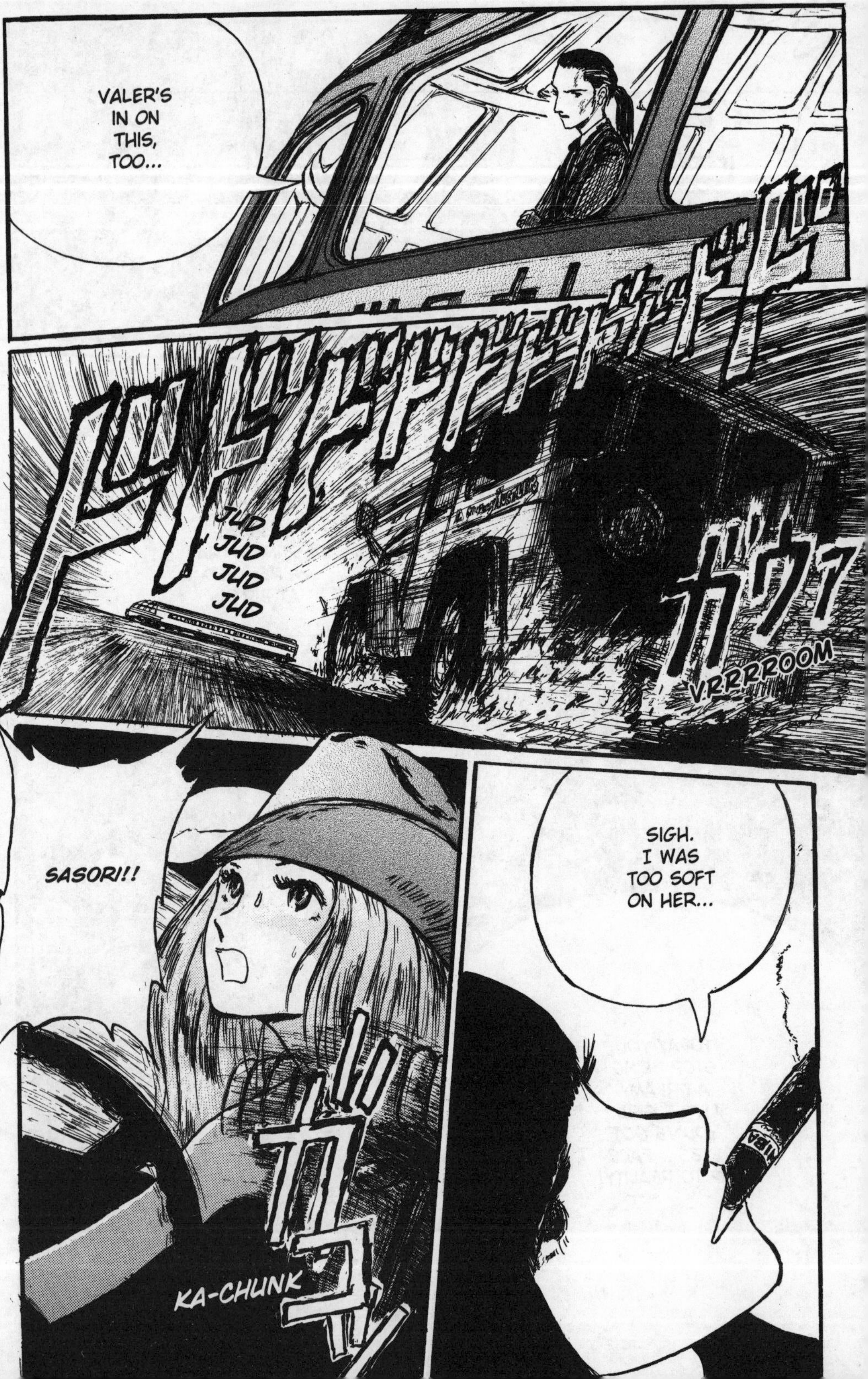
VALER'S IN ON THIS, TOO...
JUD JUD JUD JUD
V.R.R.RROOM
SIGH. I WAS TOO SOFT ON HER...
SASORI!!
KA-CHUNK

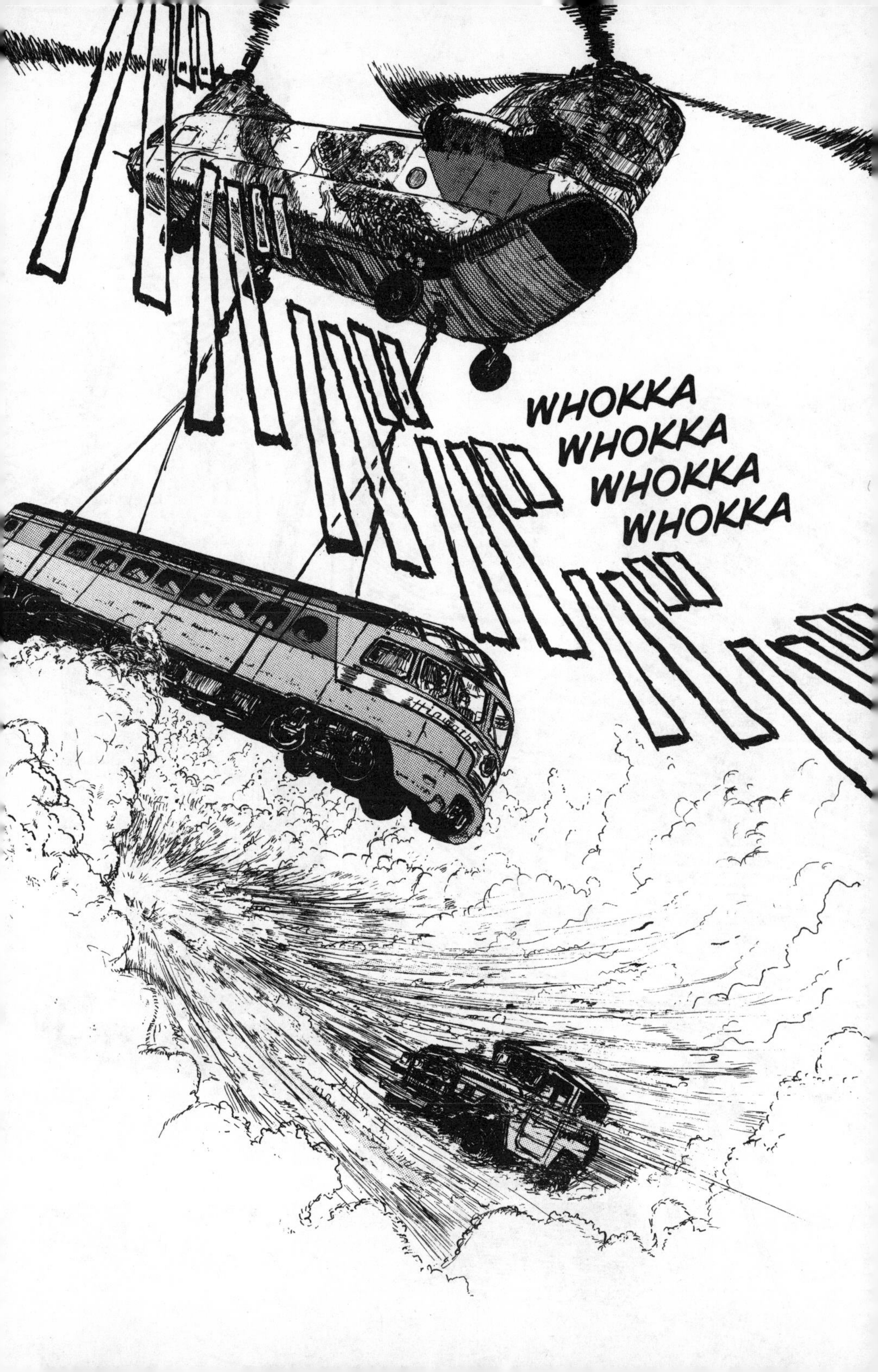
WHOKKA
WHOKKA
WHOKKA
WHOKKA

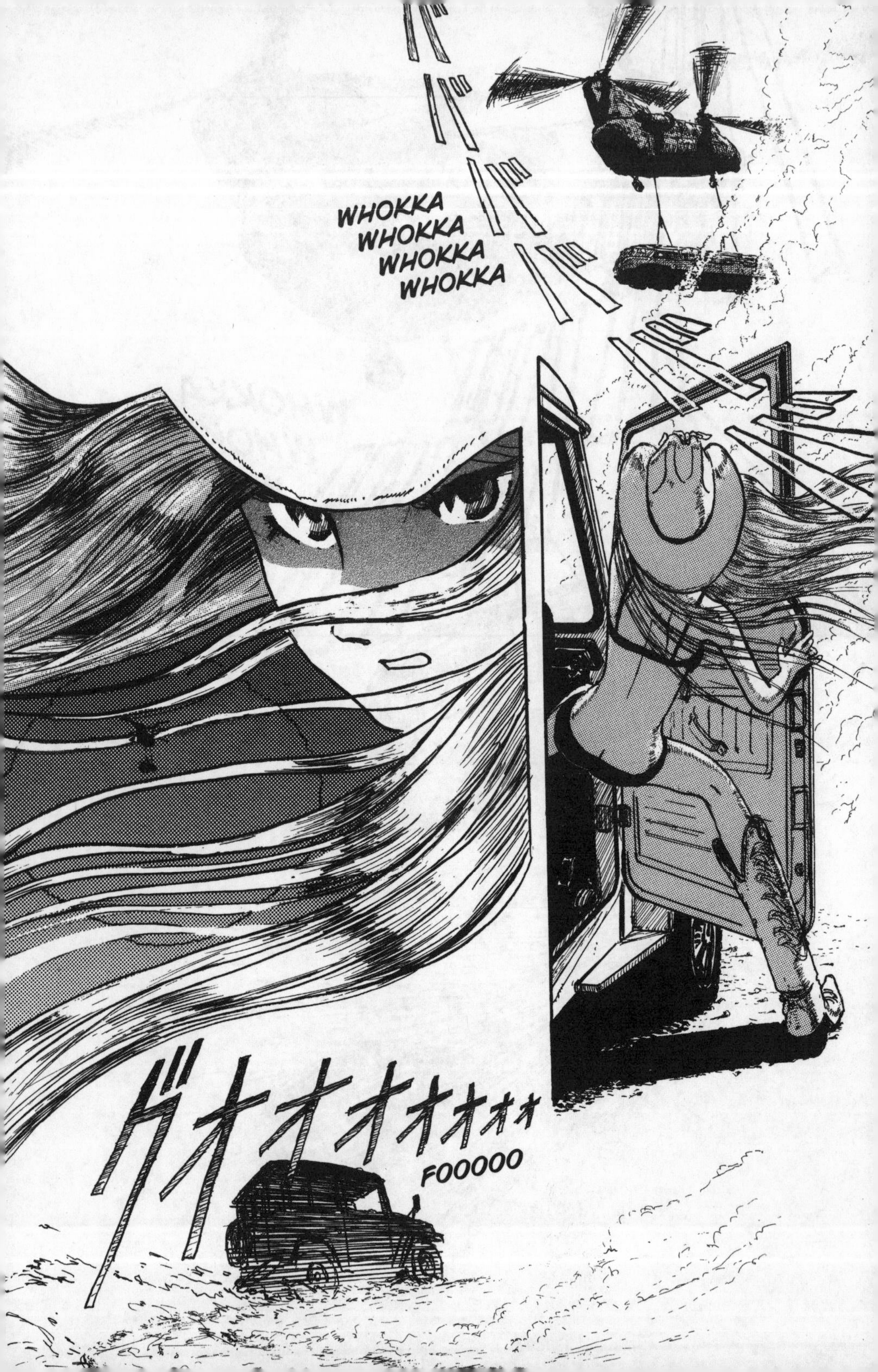
WHOKKA
WHOKKA
WHOKKA
WHOKKA
FOOOOO

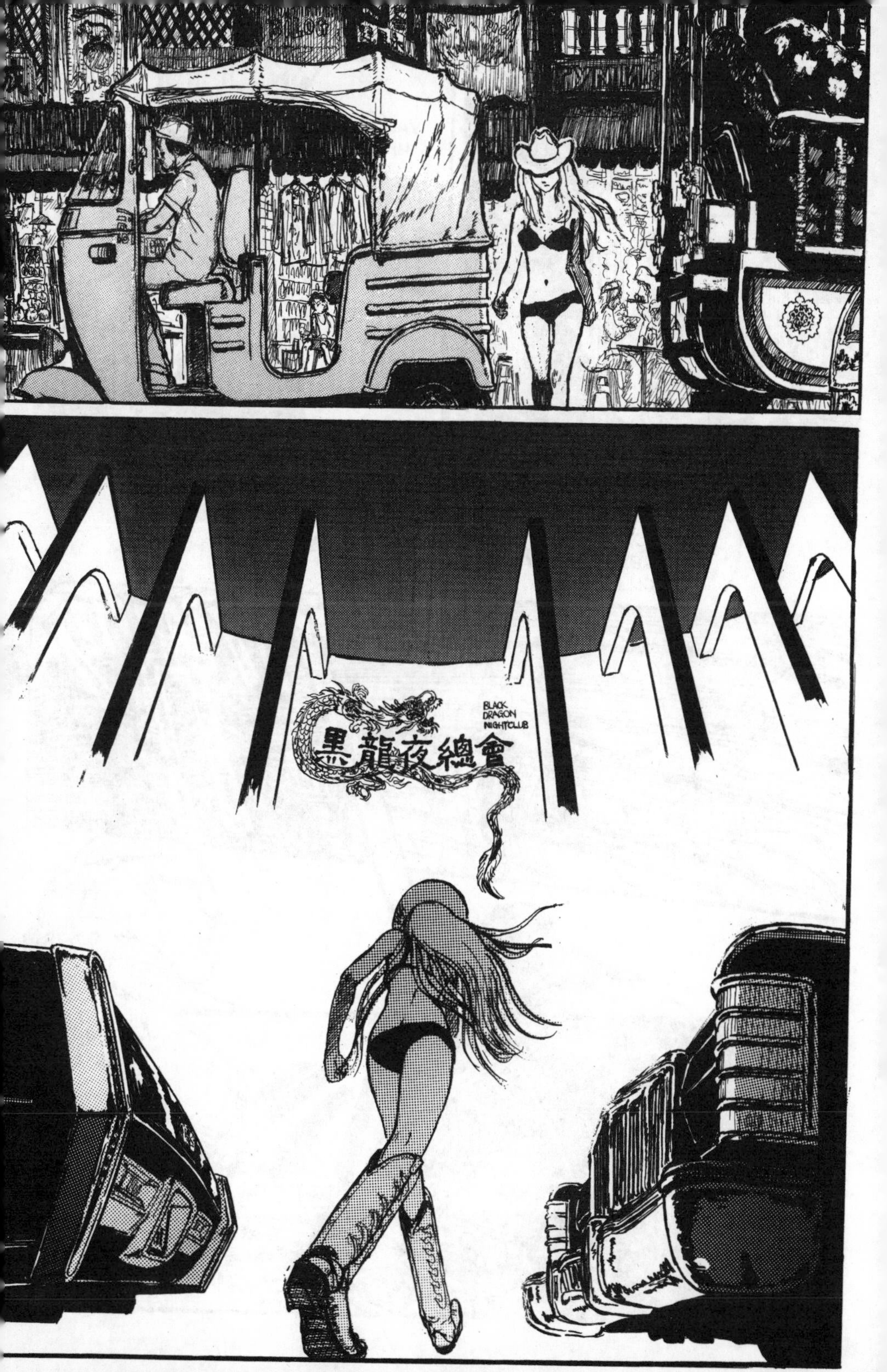
BLACK
DRAGON
NIGHTCLUB
黑龍夜總會

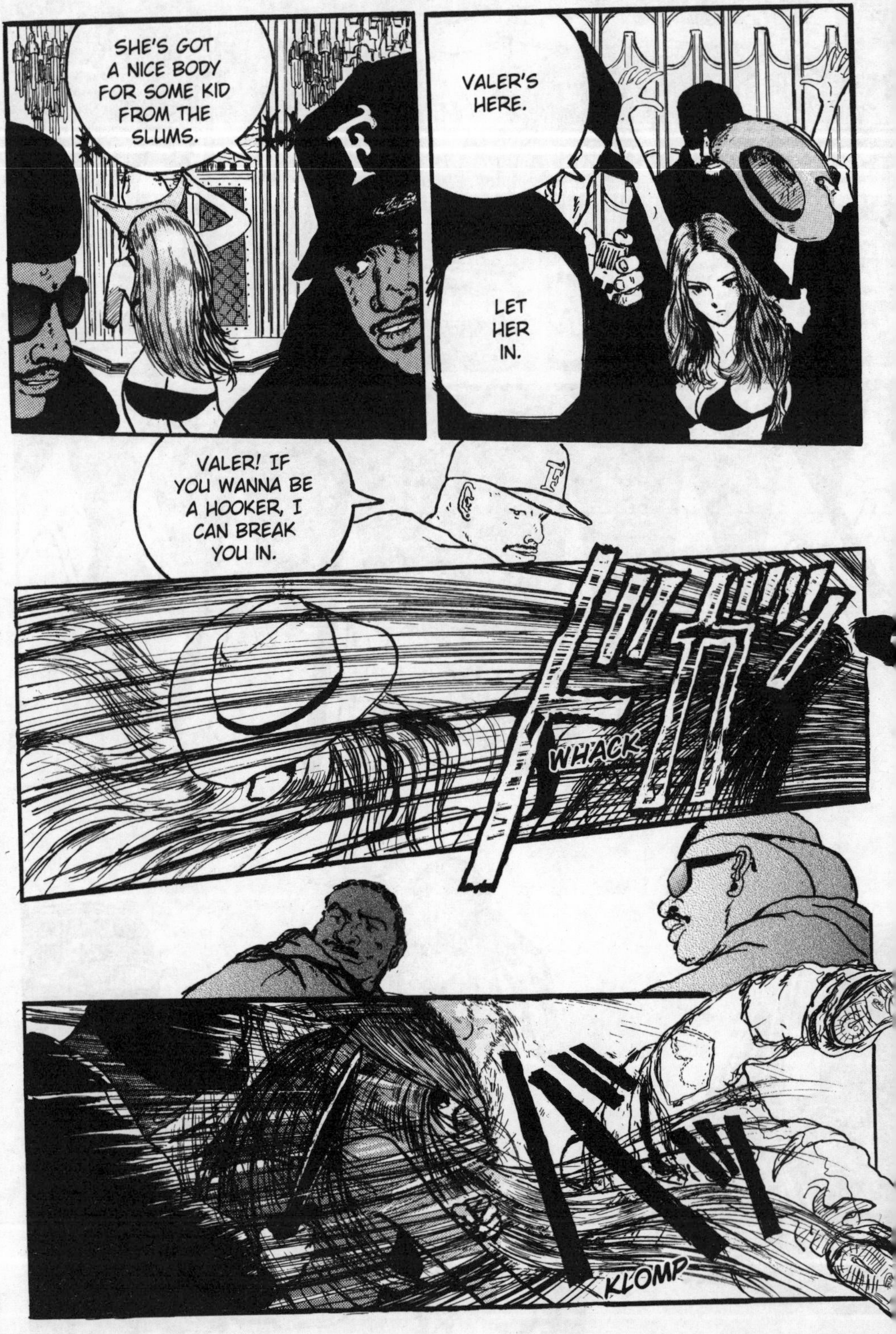
VALER'S HERE.
LET HER IN.
SHE'S GOT A NICE BODY FOR SOME KID FROM THE SLUMS.
VALER! IF YOU WANNA BE A HOOKER, I CAN BREAK YOU IN.
WHACK
KLOMP

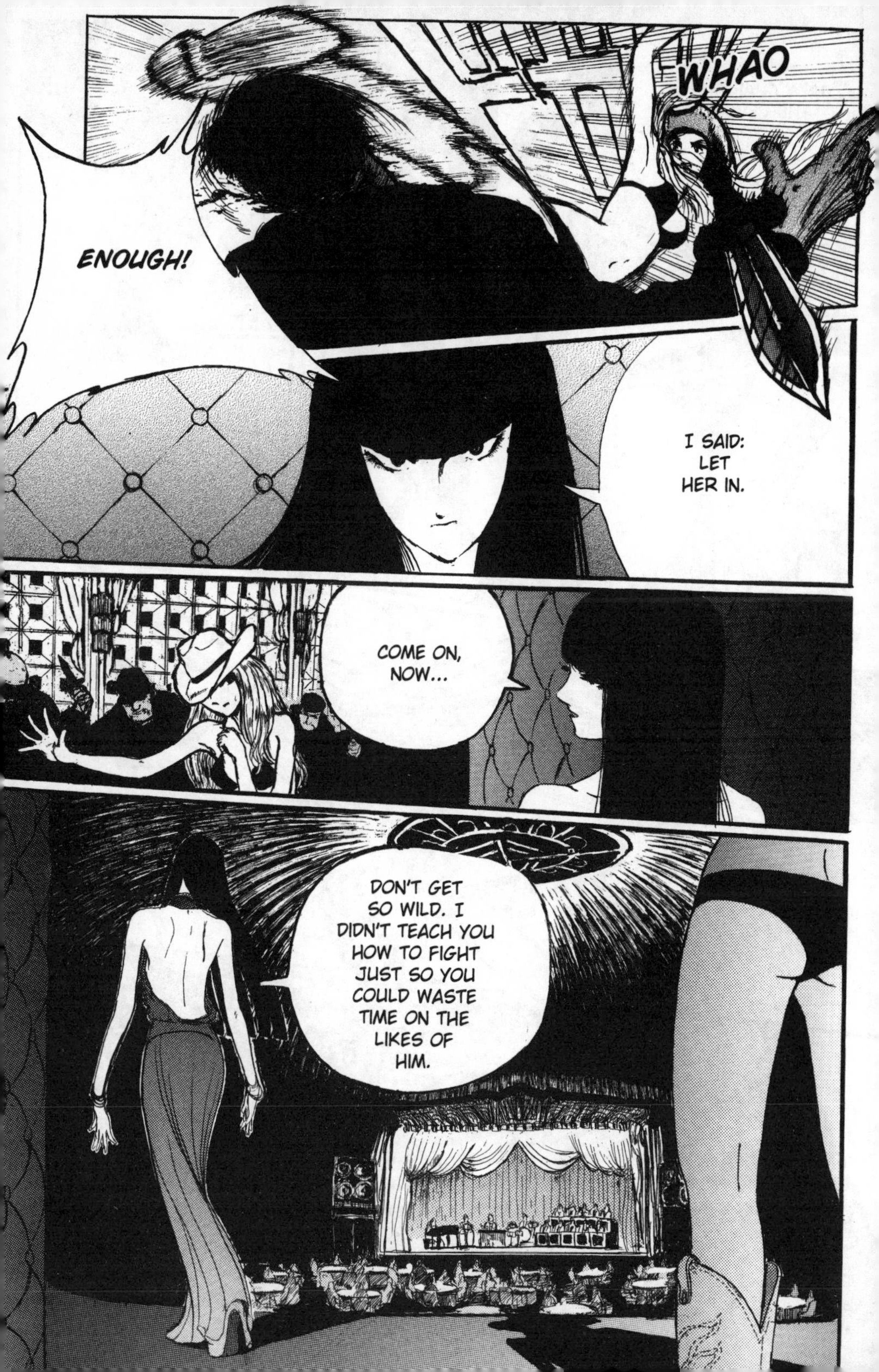
WHAO
ENOUGH!
I SAID: LET HER IN.
COME ON, NOW...
DON'T GET SO WILD. I DIDN'T TEACH YOU HOW TO FIGHT JUST SO YOU COULD WASTE TIME ON THE LIKES OF HIM.

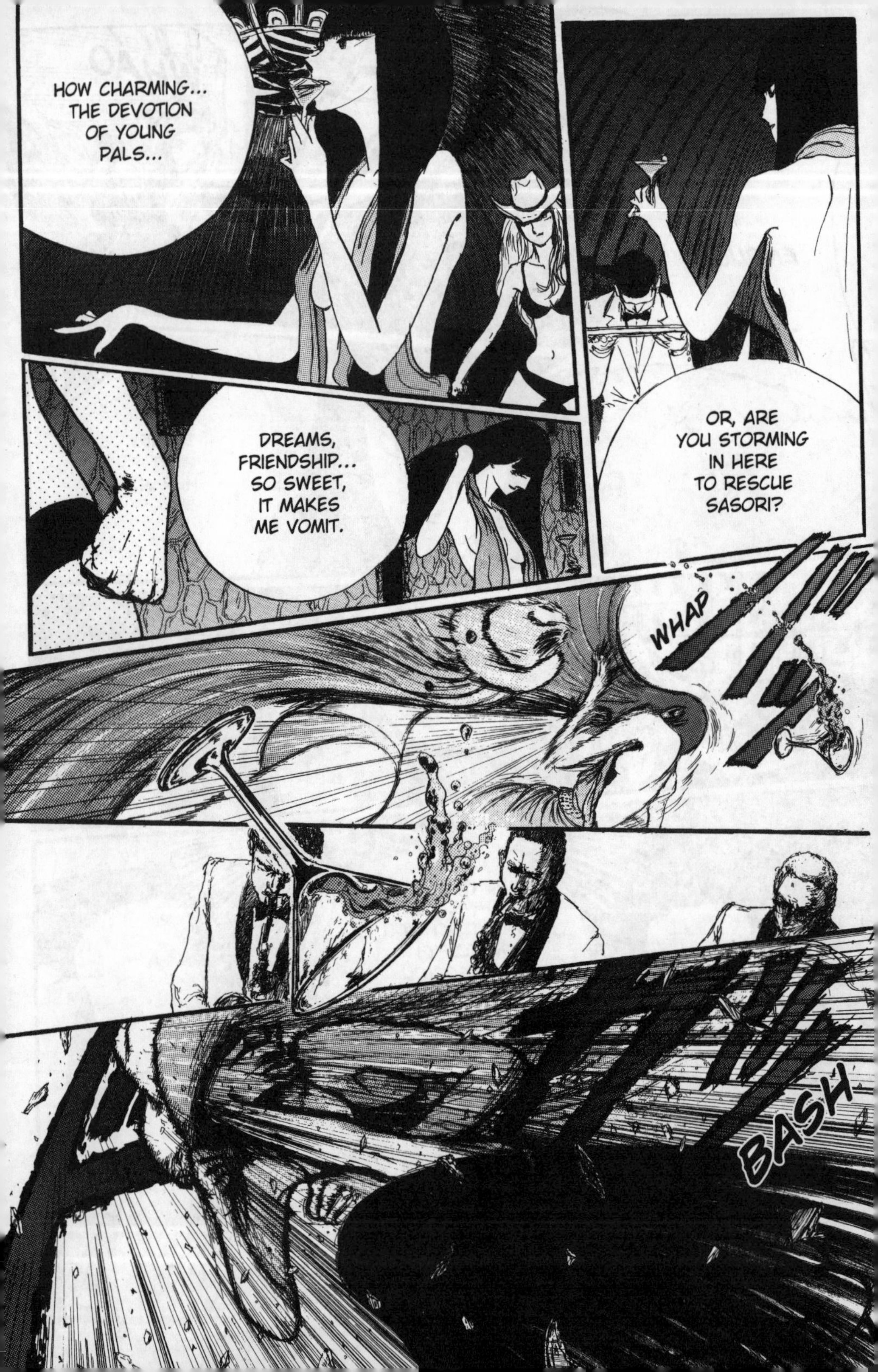
HOW CHARMING... THE DEVOTION OF YOUNG PALS...
DREAMS, FRIENDSHIP... SO SWEET, IT MAKES ME VOMIT.
OR, ARE YOU STORMING IN HERE TO RESCUE SASORI?
WHAP
BASH

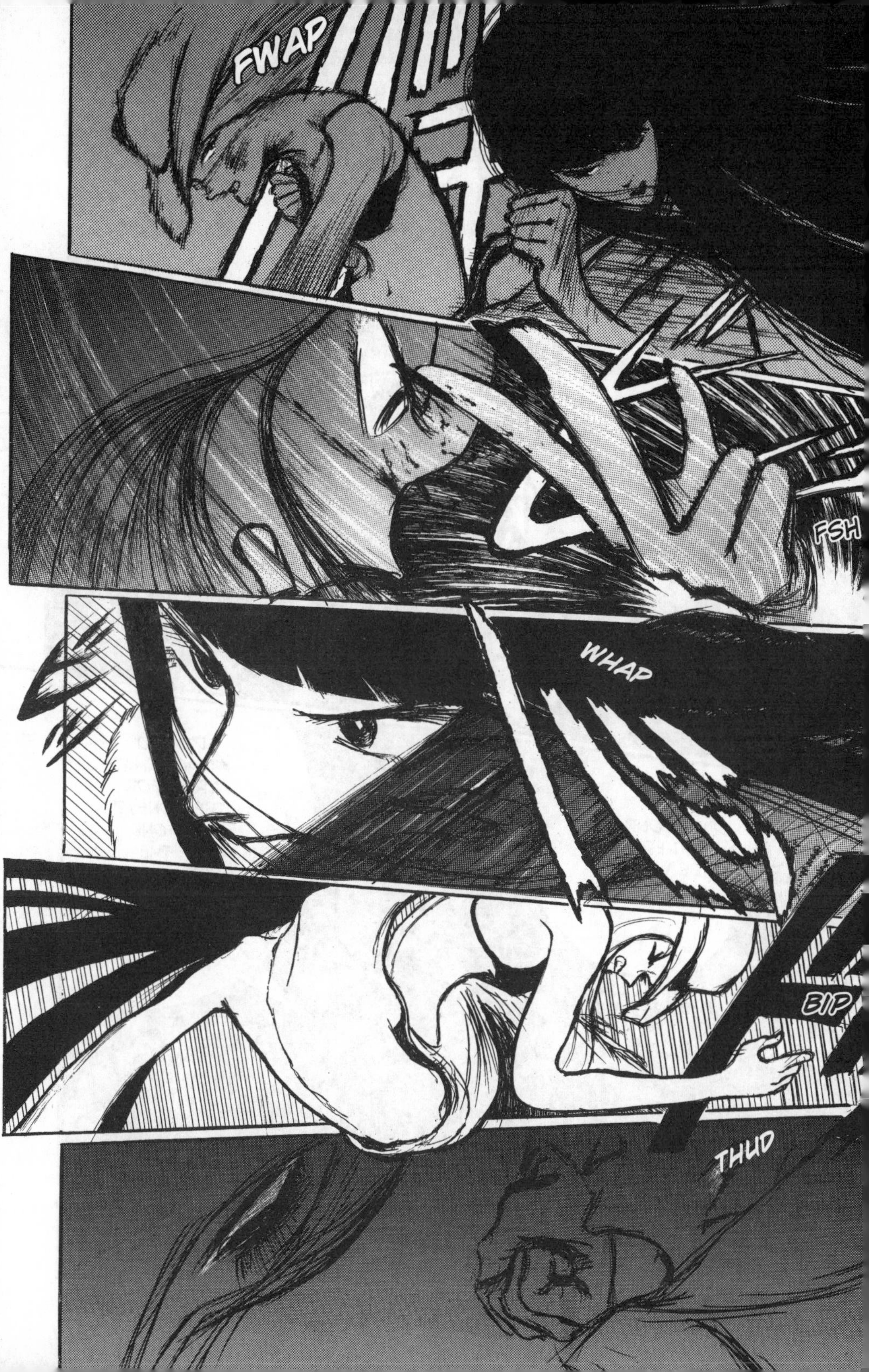
FWAP
FSH
WHAP
BIP
THUD

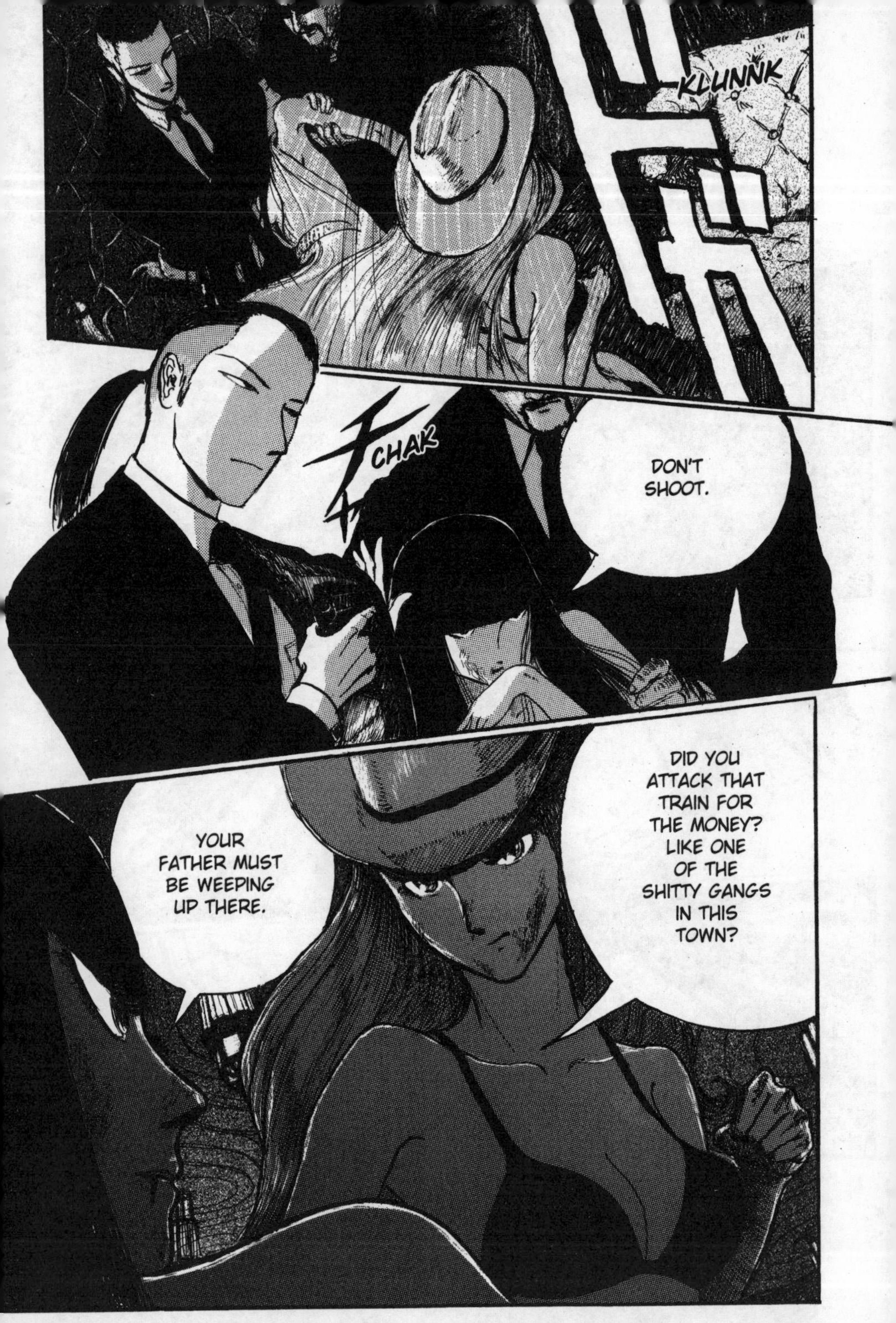
KLUNNK
DON'T SHOOT.
CHAK
DID YOU ATTACK THAT TRAIN FOR THE MONEY? LIKE ONE OF THE SHITTY GANGS IN THIS TOWN?
YOUR FATHER MUST BE WEEPING UP THERE.

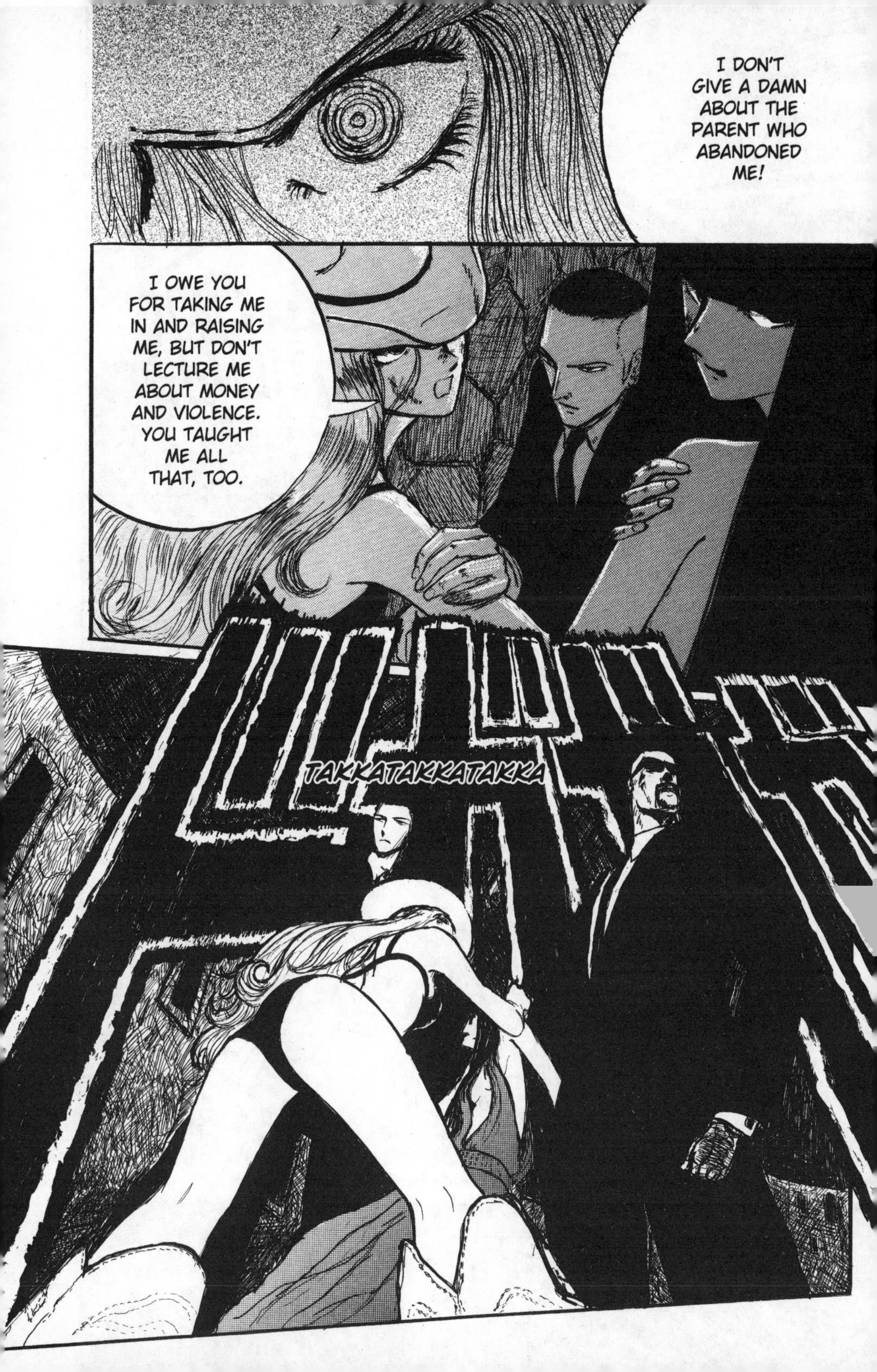
I DON'T GIVE A DAMN ABOUT THE PARENT WHO ABANDONED ME!
I OWE YOU FOR TAKING ME IN AND RAISING ME, BUT DON'T LECTURE ME ABOUT MONEY AND VIOLENCE. YOU TAUGHT ME ALL THAT, TOO.
TAKKATAKKATAKKA

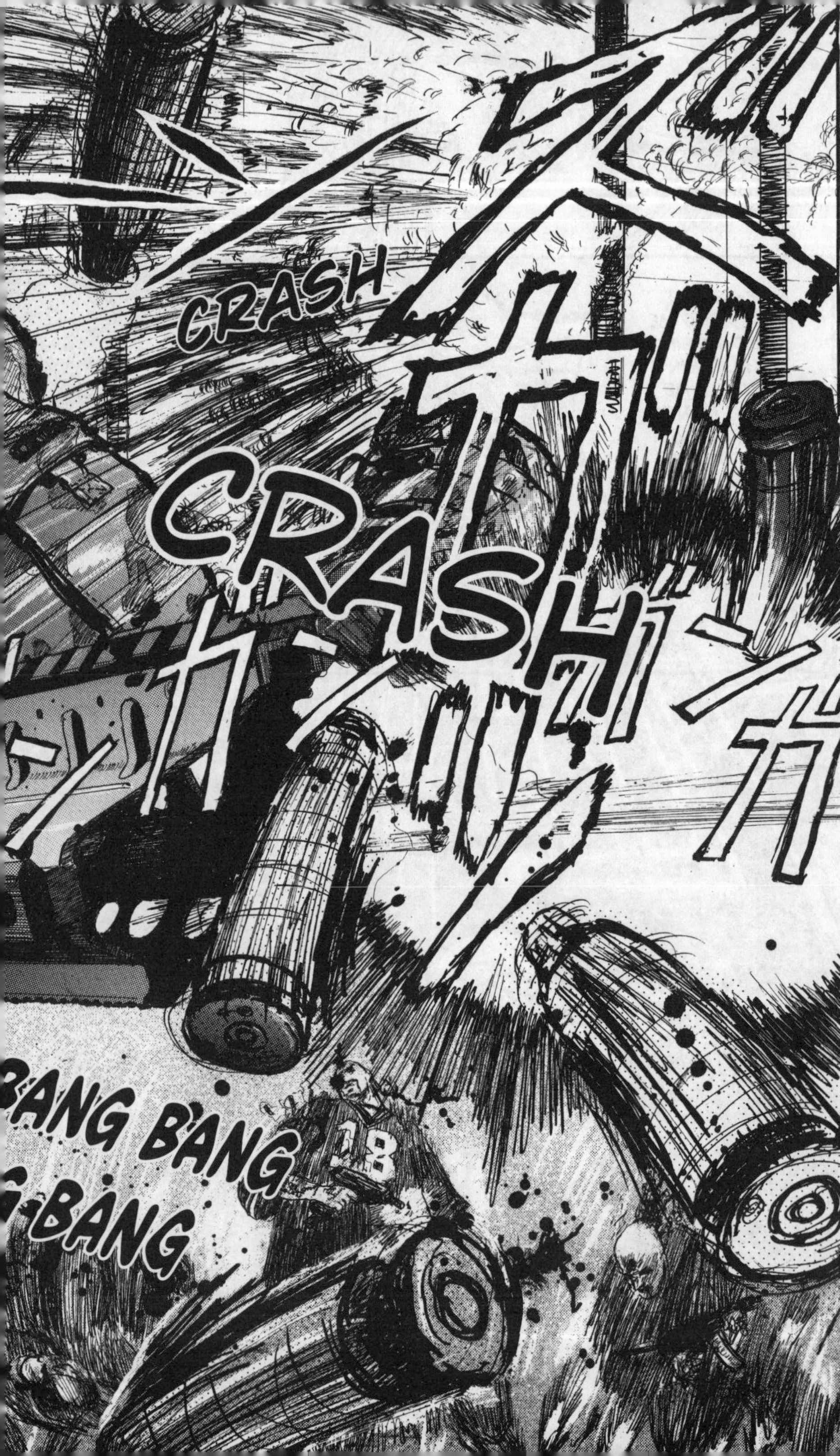
CRASH
CRASH
BANG BANG
G-BANG

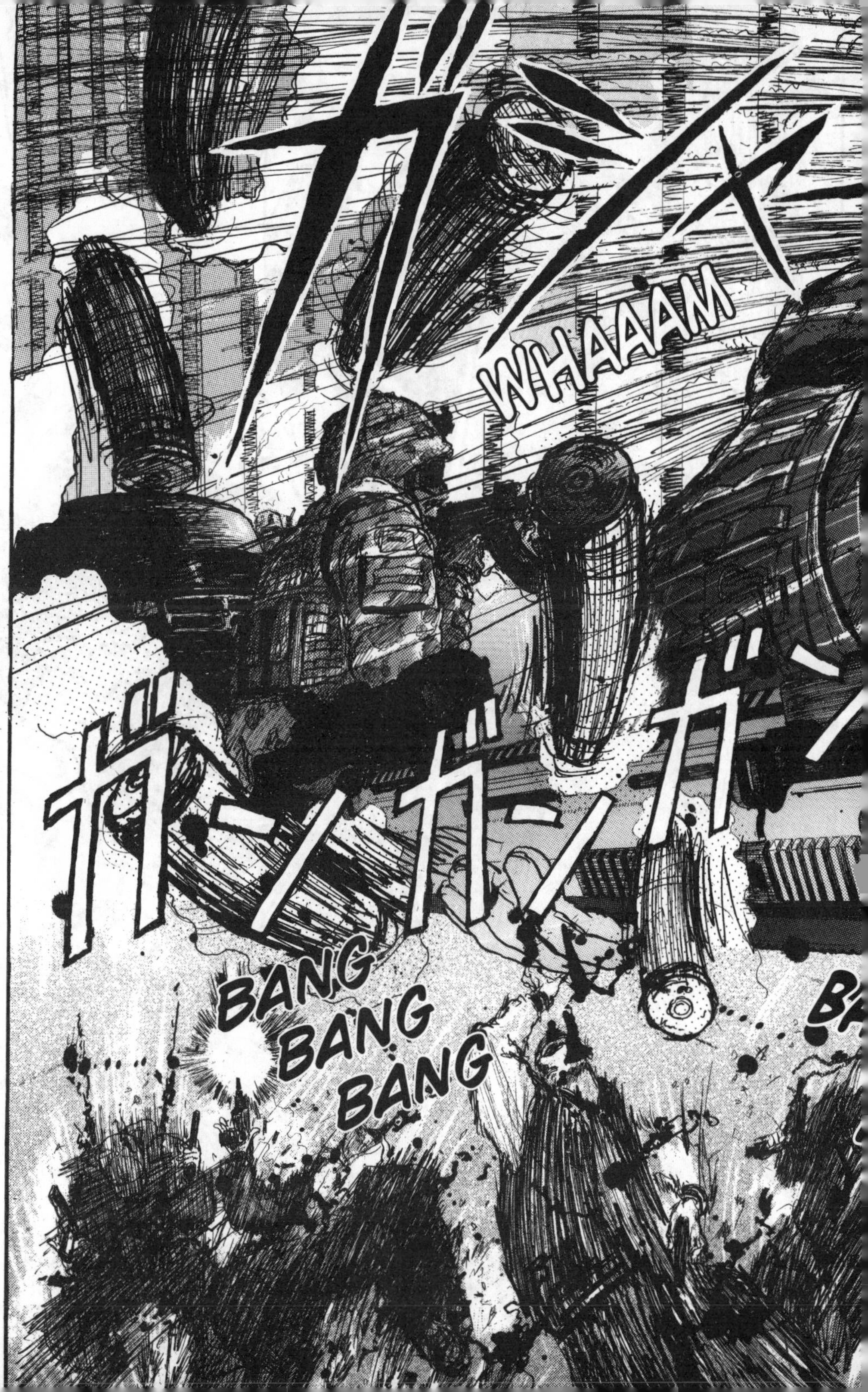
WHAAAM
BANG
BANG
BANG

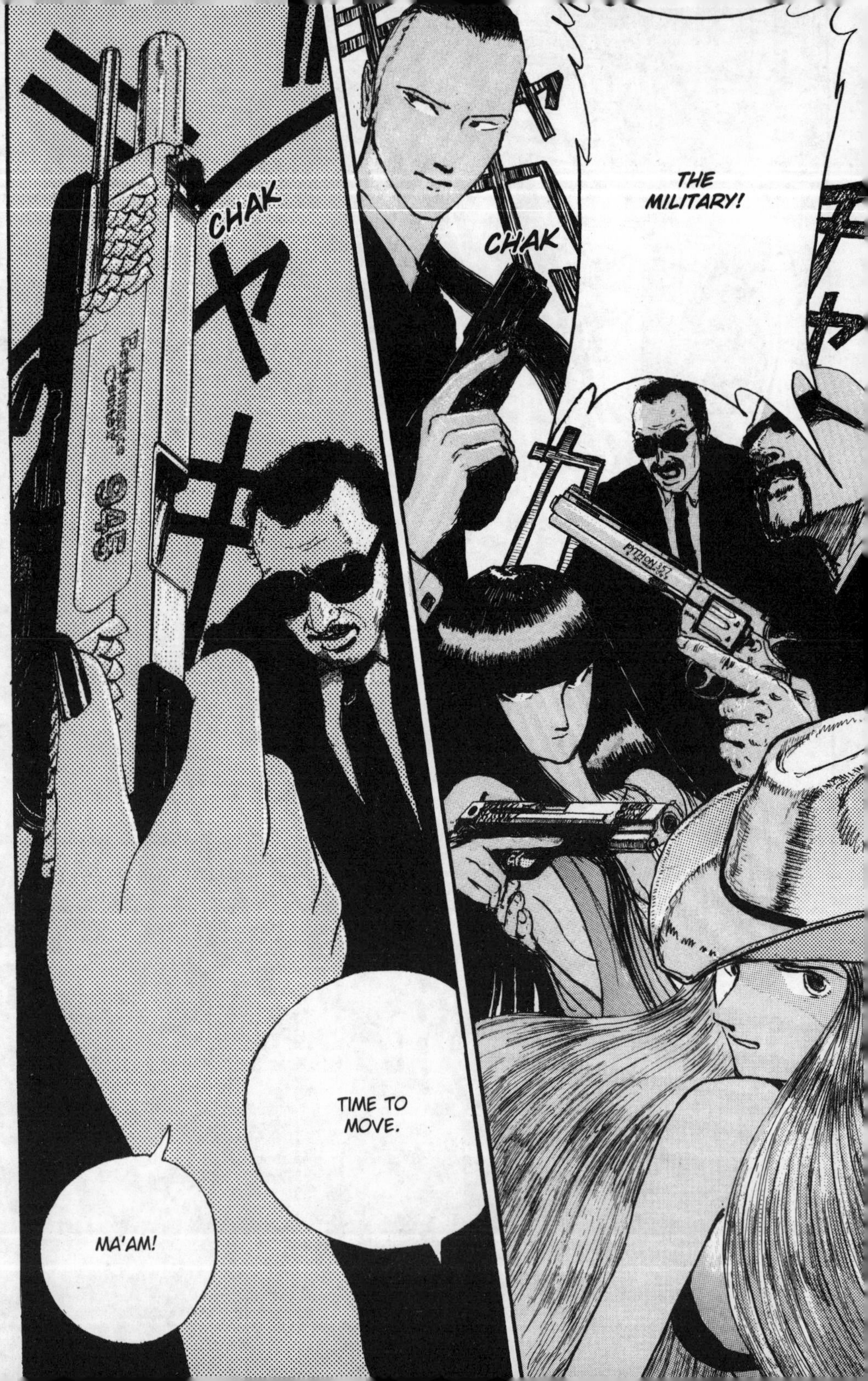
THE MILITARY!
CHAK
CHAK
TIME TO MOVE.
MA'AM!

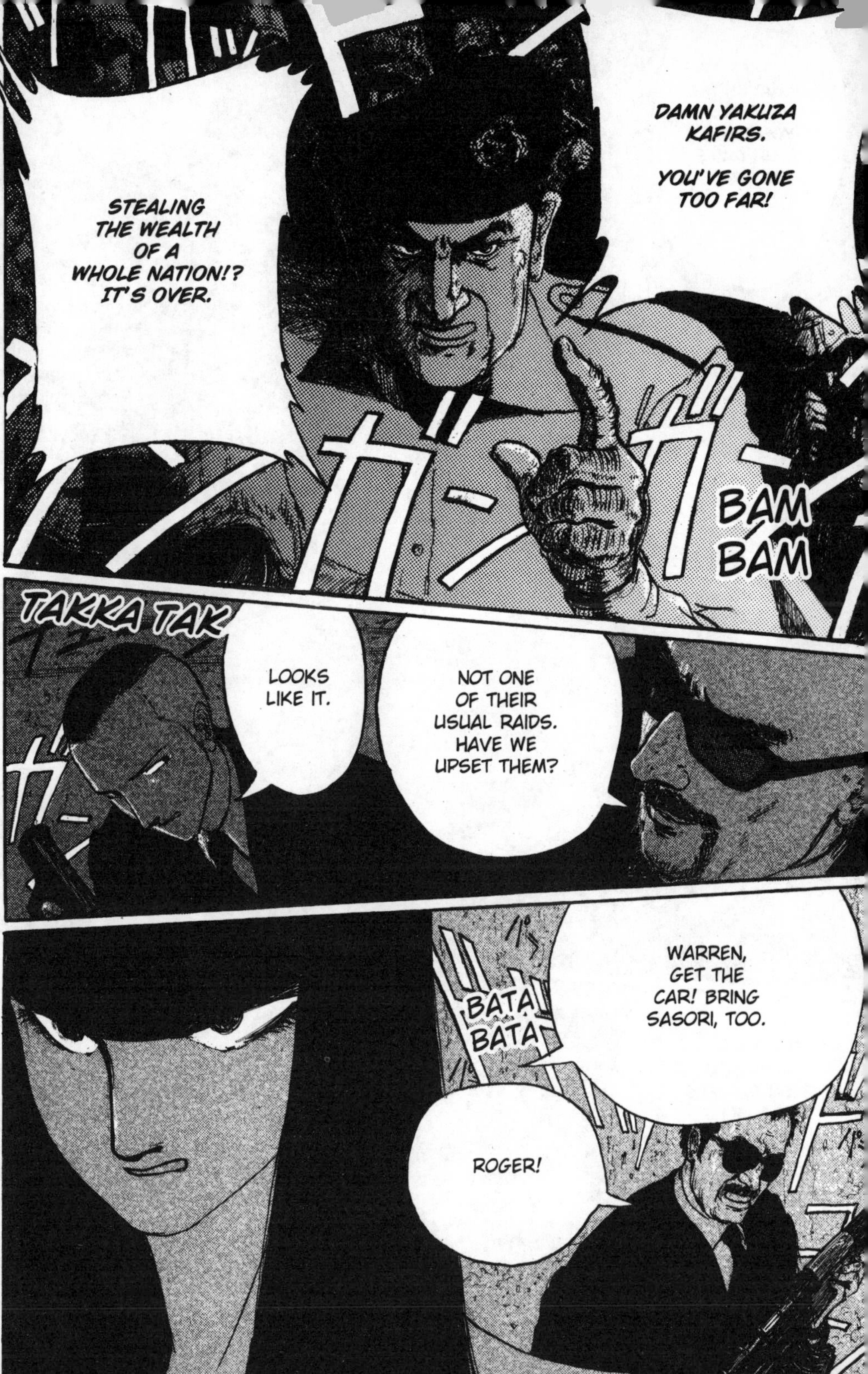
DAMN YAKUZA KAFIRS.
YOU'VE GONE TOO FAR!
STEALING THE WEALTH OF A WHOLE NATION!? IT'S OVER.
BAM BAM
NOT ONE OF THEIR USUAL RAIDS. HAVE WE UPSET THEM?
LOOKS LIKE IT.
TAKKA TAK
WARREN, GET THE CAR! BRING SASORI, TOO.
BATA BATA
ROGER!

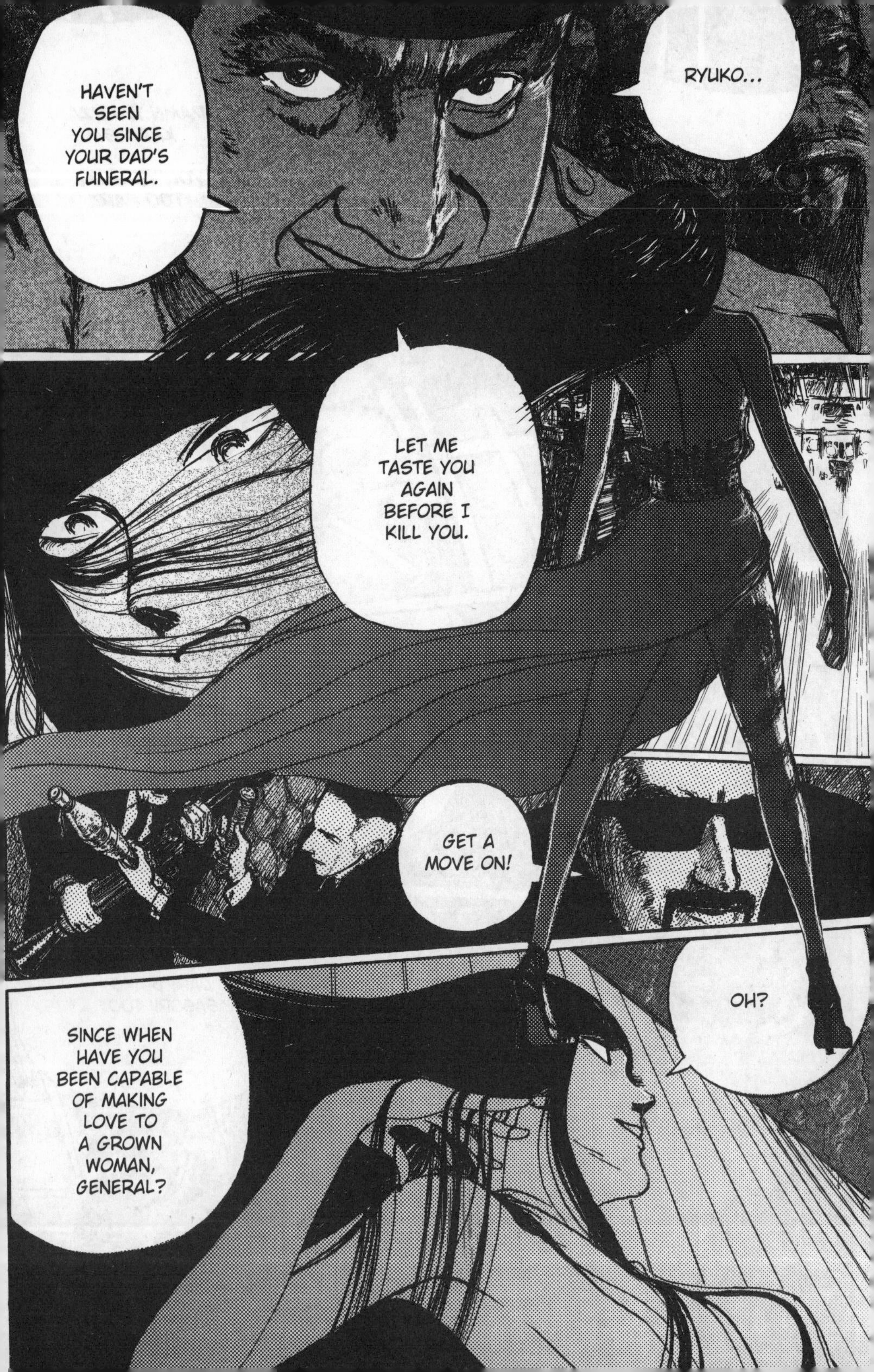
RYUKO...
HAVEN'T SEEN YOU SINCE YOUR DAD'S FUNERAL.
LET ME TASTE YOU AGAIN BEFORE I KILL YOU.
GET A MOVE ON!
OH?
SINCE WHEN HAVE YOU BEEN CAPABLE OF MAKING LOVE TO A GROWN WOMAN, GENERAL?

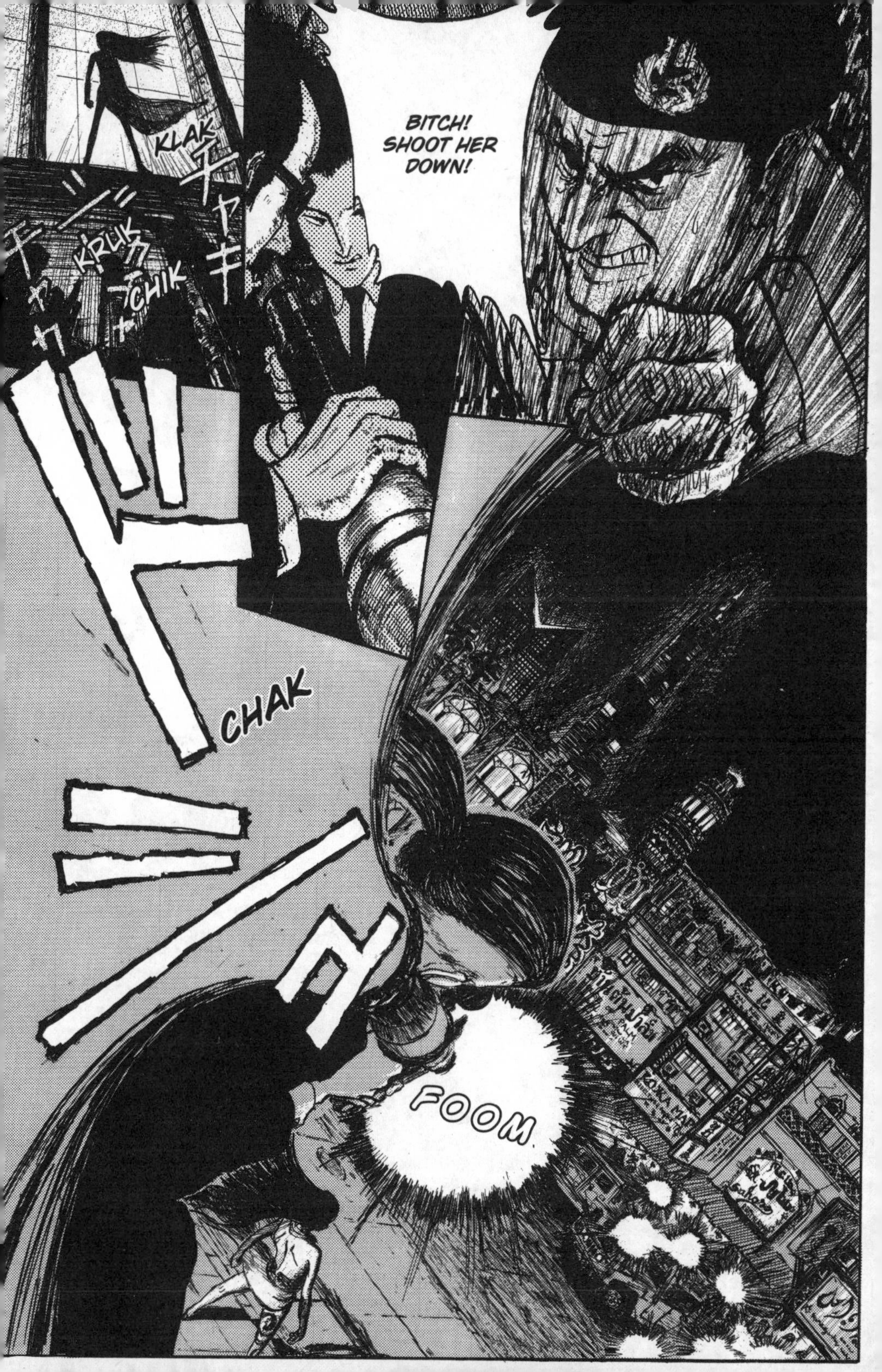
BITCH! SHOOT HER DOWN!
KLAK
KRUK
CHIK
CHAK
FOOM

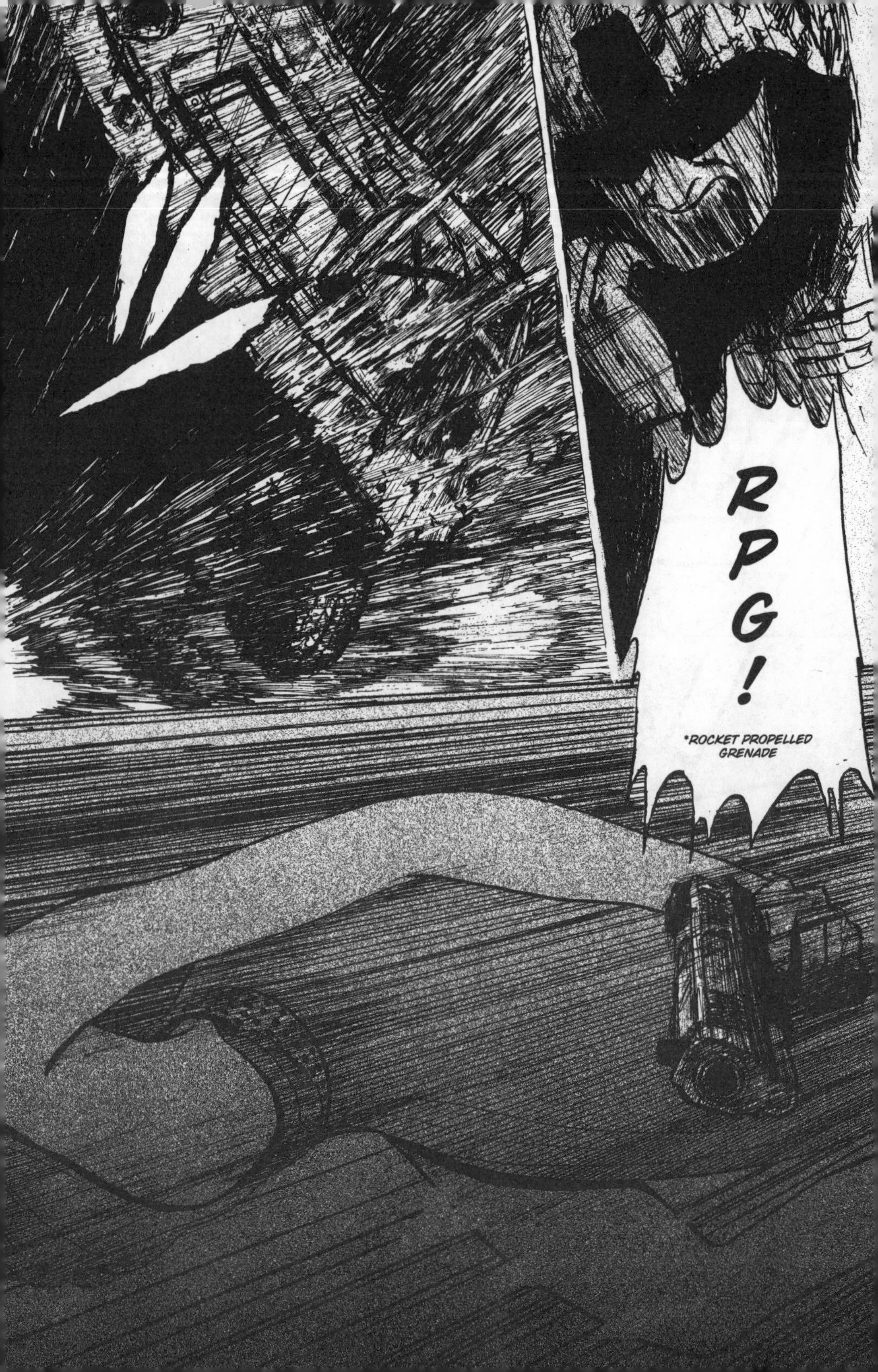
RPG!
*ROCKET PROPELLED GRENADE

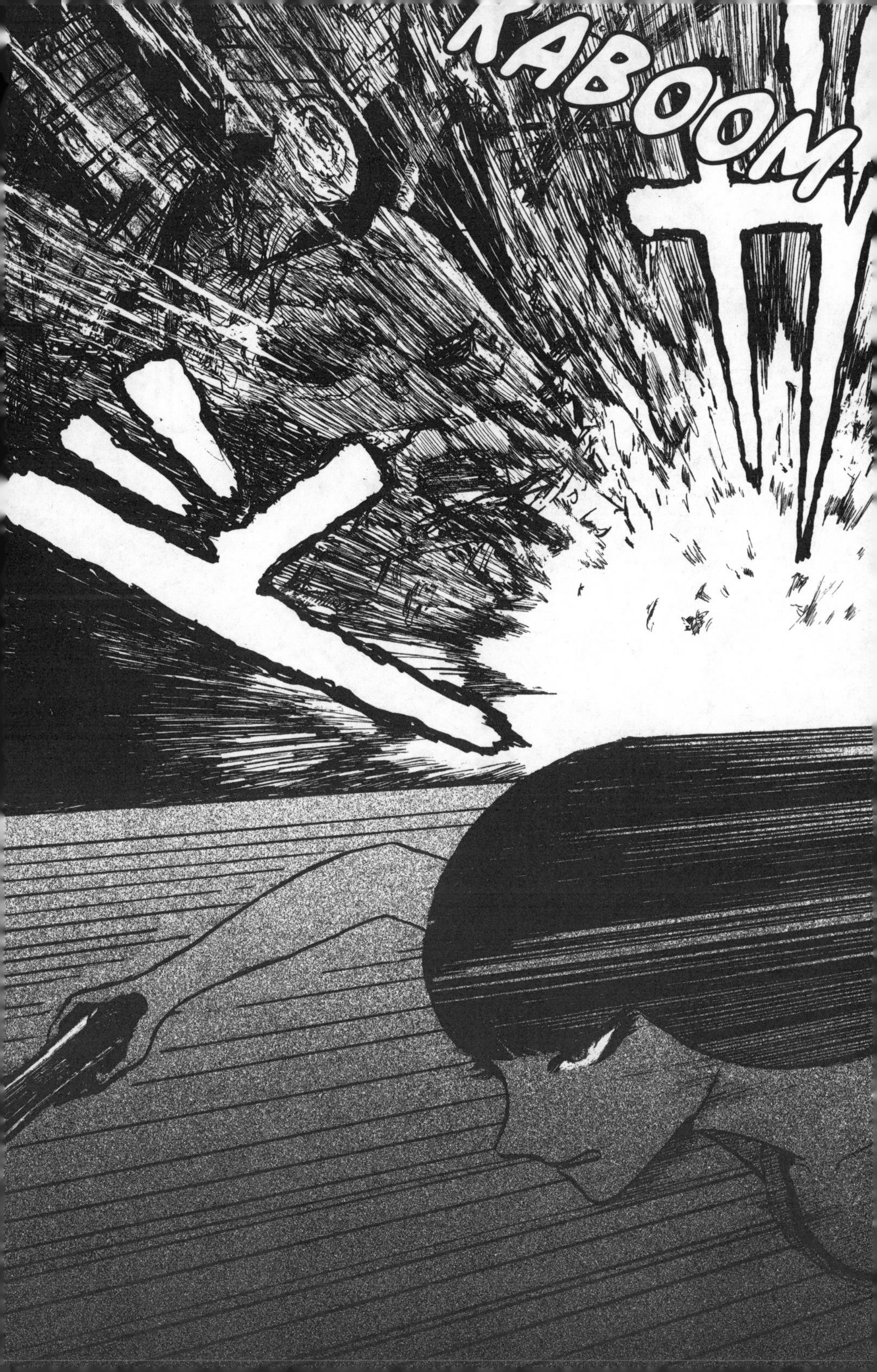
KABOOM

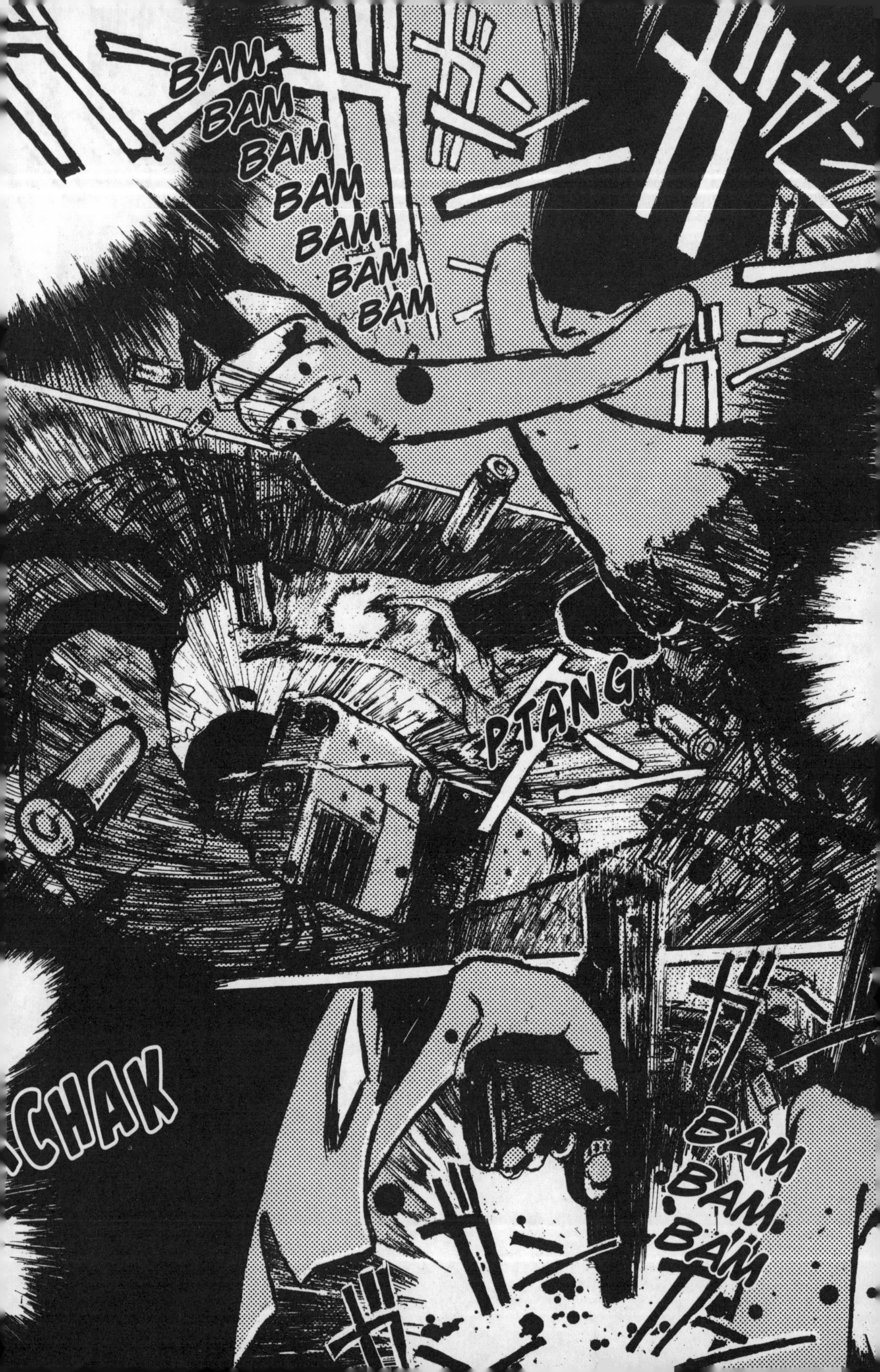
BAM
BAM
BAM
BAM
BAM
BAM
BAM
PTANG
BAM
BAM
BAM
CHAK

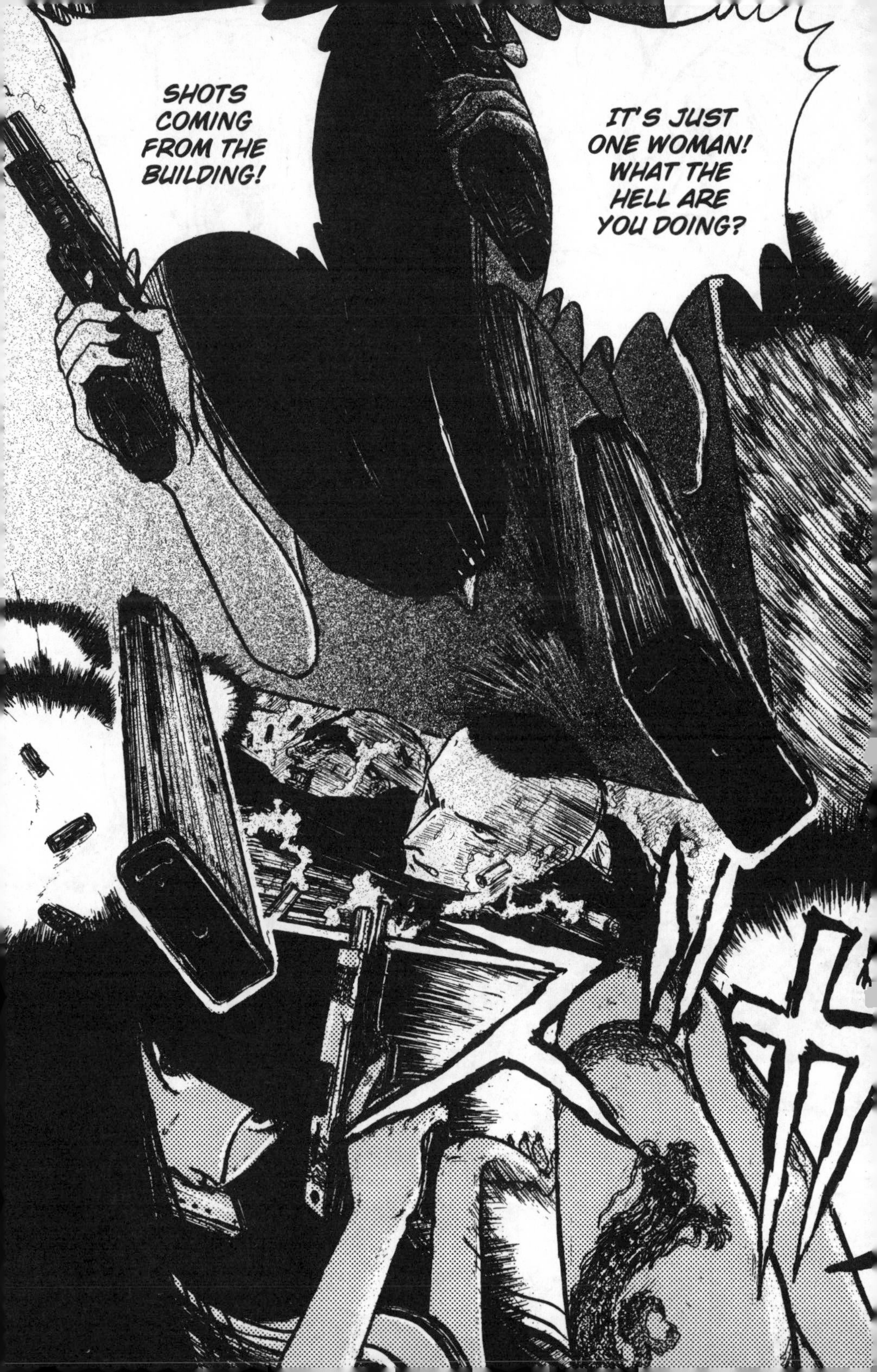
IT'S JUST ONE WOMAN! WHAT THE HELL ARE YOU DOING?
SHOTS COMING FROM THE BUILDING!

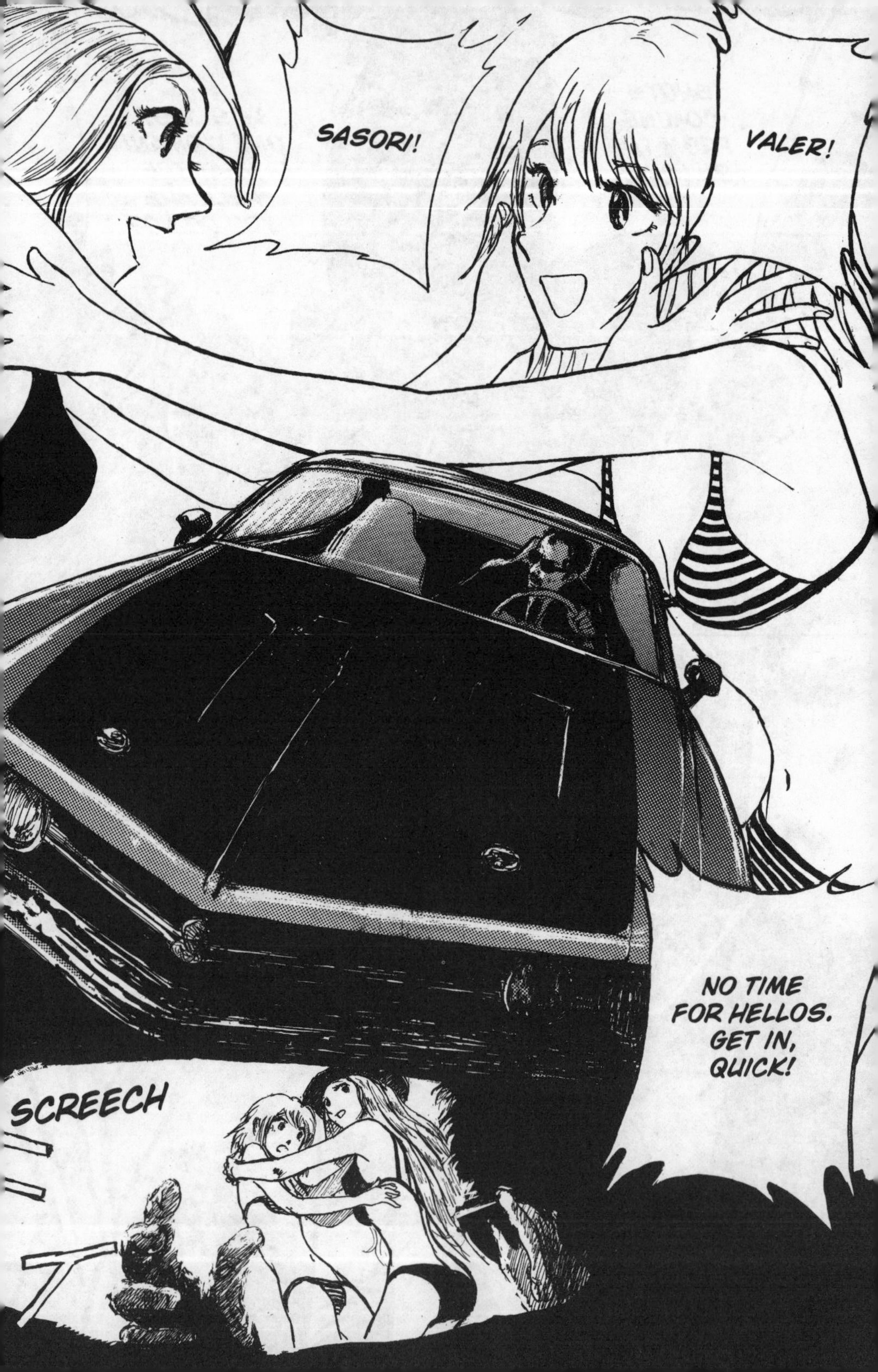
VALER!
SASORI!
NO TIME FOR HELLOS. GET IN, QUICK!
SCREECH

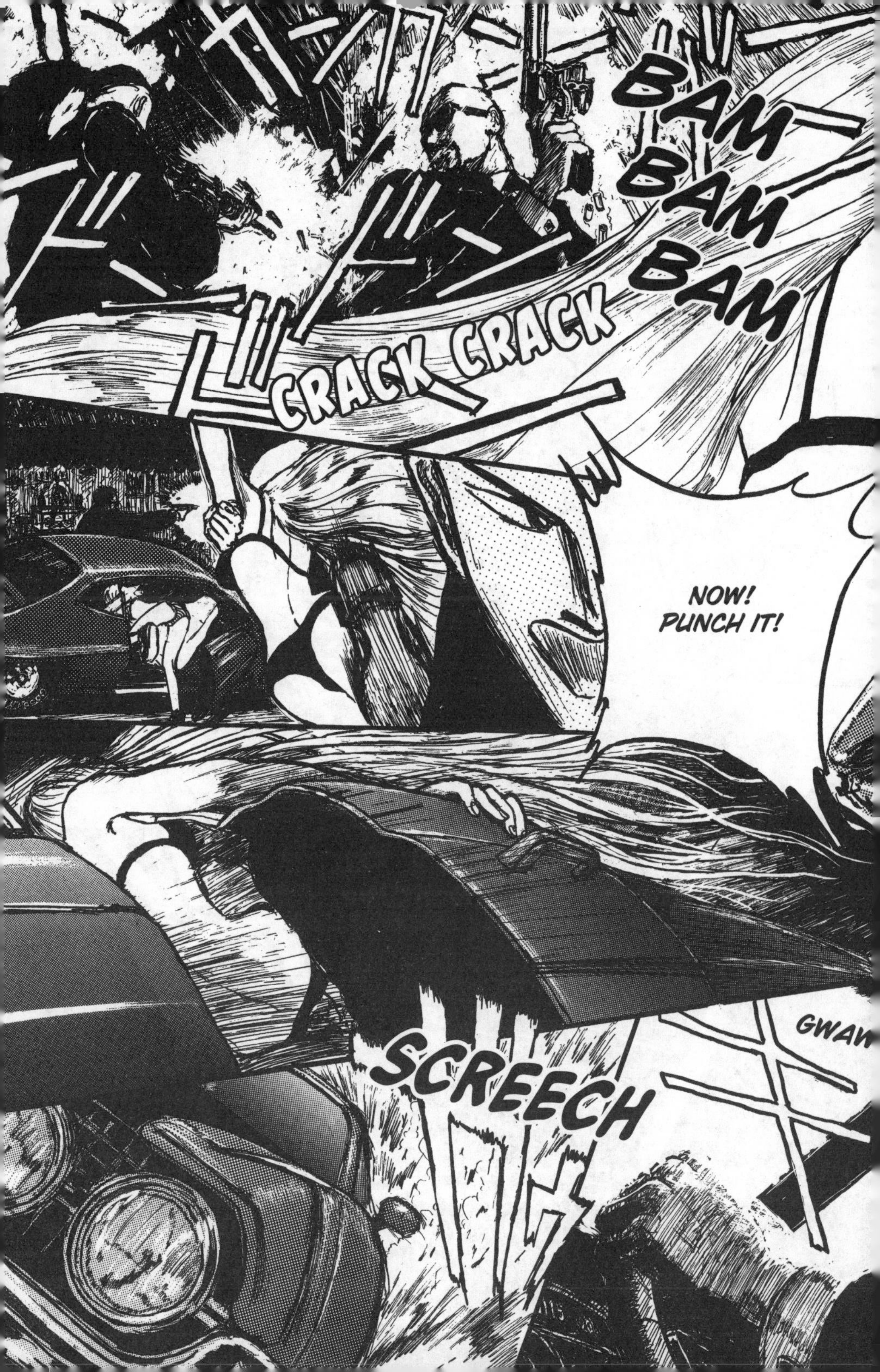
BAM BAM BAM
CRACK CRACK
NOW! PUNCH IT!
GWAW
SCREECH

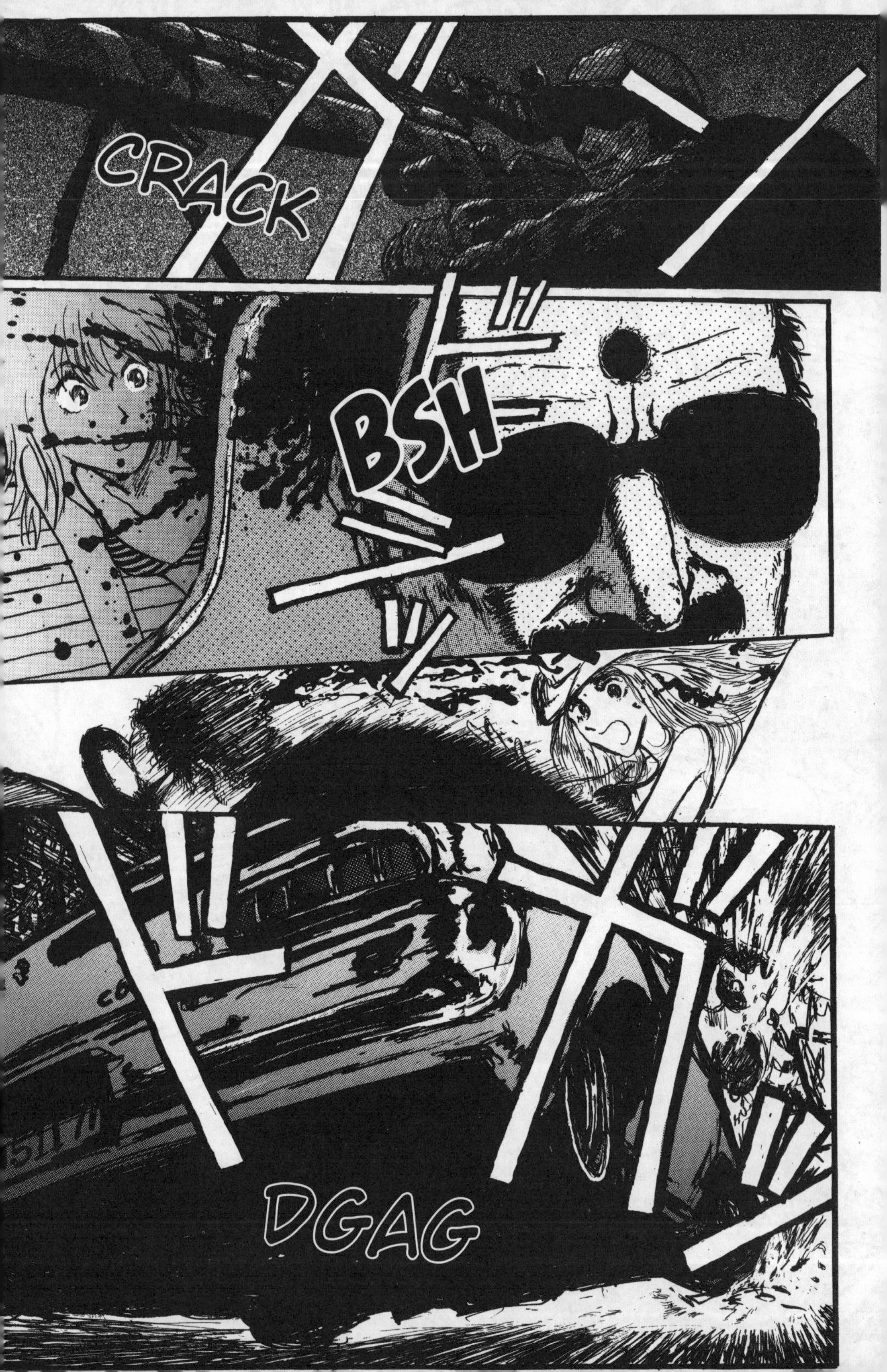
CRACK
BSH
DGAG

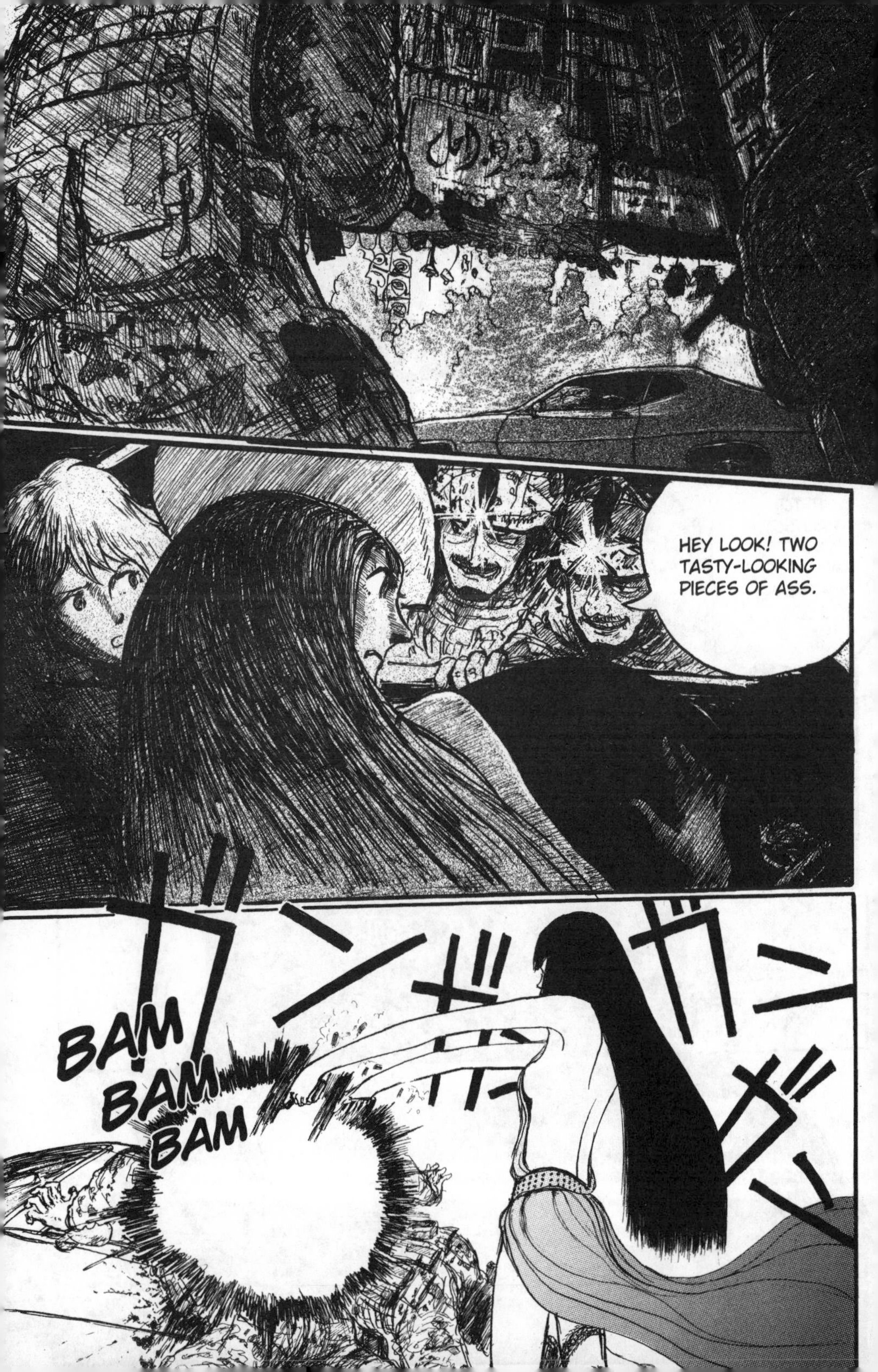
HEY LOOK! TWO TASTY-LOOKING PIECES OF ASS.
BAM BAM BAM

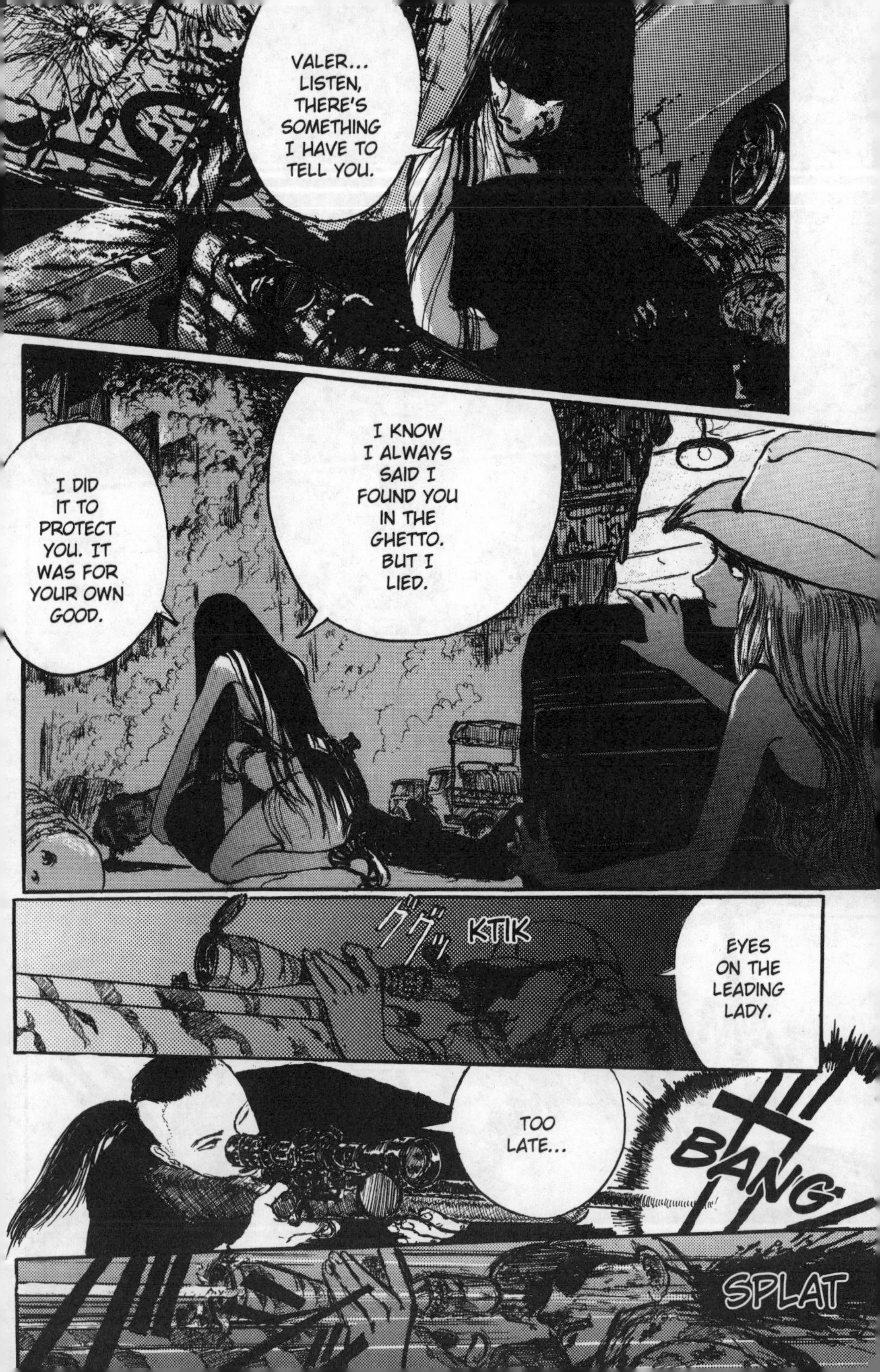
VALER... LISTEN, THERE'S SOMETHING I HAVE TO TELL YOU.
I KNOW I ALWAYS SAID I FOUND YOU IN THE GHETTO. BUT I LIED.
I DID IT TO PROTECT YOU. IT WAS FOR YOUR OWN GOOD.
EYES ON THE LEADING LADY.
ググッ
KTIK
BANG
TOO LATE...
SPLAT

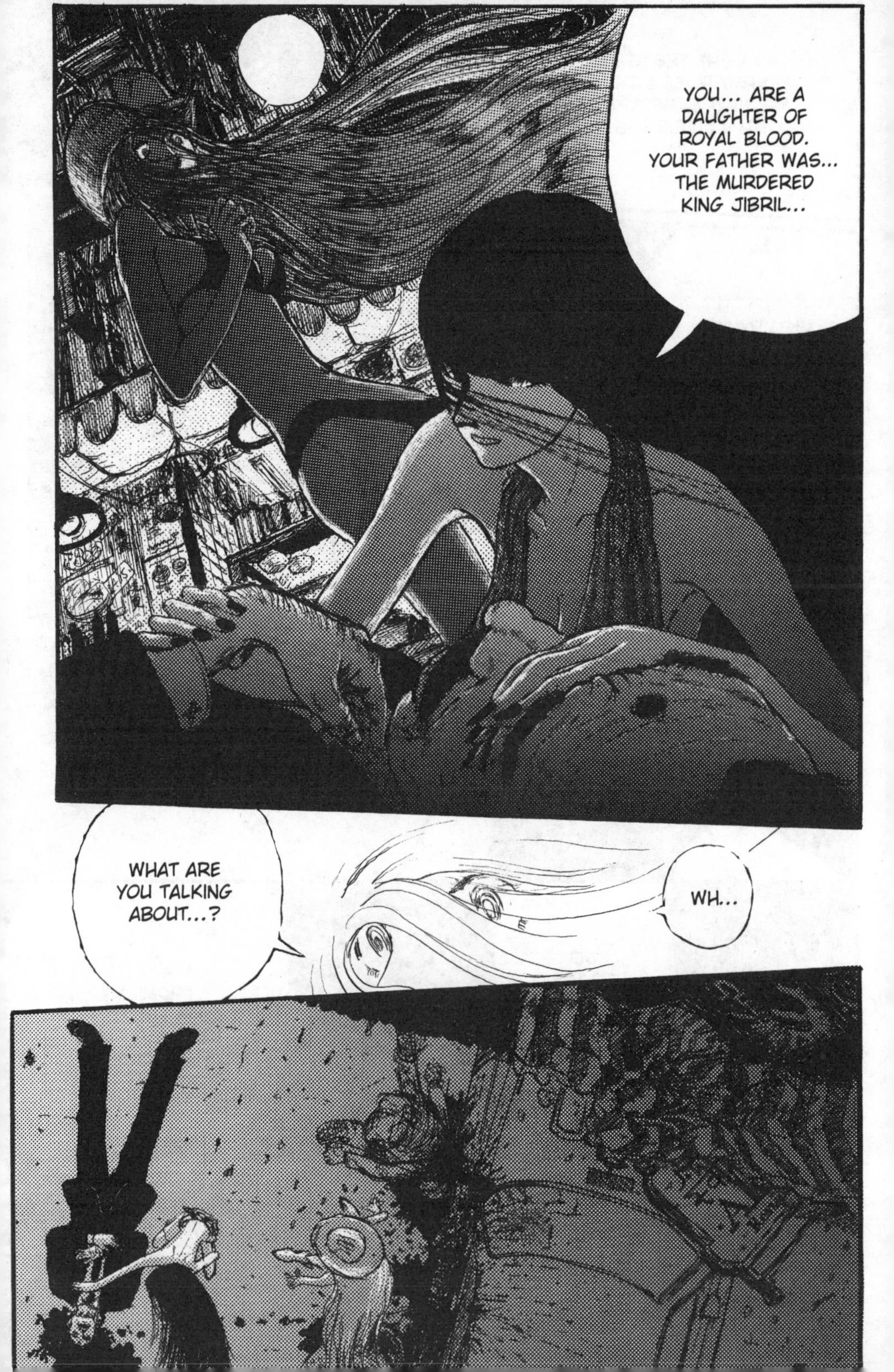
YOU... ARE A DAUGHTER OF ROYAL BLOOD. YOUR FATHER WAS... THE MURDERED KING JIBRIL...
WH...
WHAT ARE YOU TALKING ABOUT...?

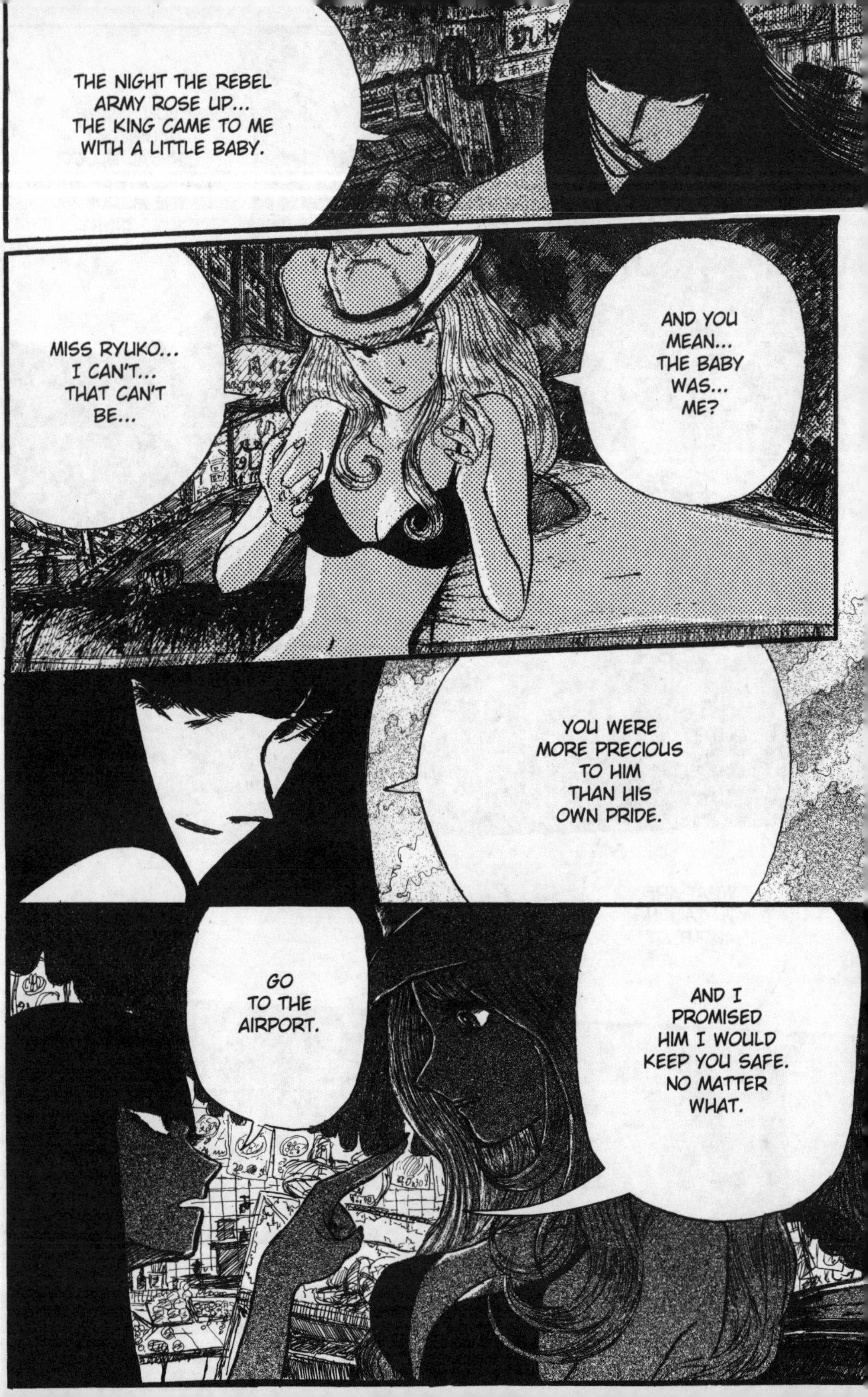
THE NIGHT THE REBEL ARMY ROSE UP... THE KING CAME TO ME WITH A LITTLE BABY.
AND YOU MEAN... THE BABY WAS... ME?
MISS RYUKO... I CAN'T... THAT CAN'T BE...
YOU WERE MORE PRECIOUS TO HIM THAN HIS OWN PRIDE.
AND I PROMISED HIM I WOULD KEEP YOU SAFE. NO MATTER WHAT.
GO TO THE AIRPORT.

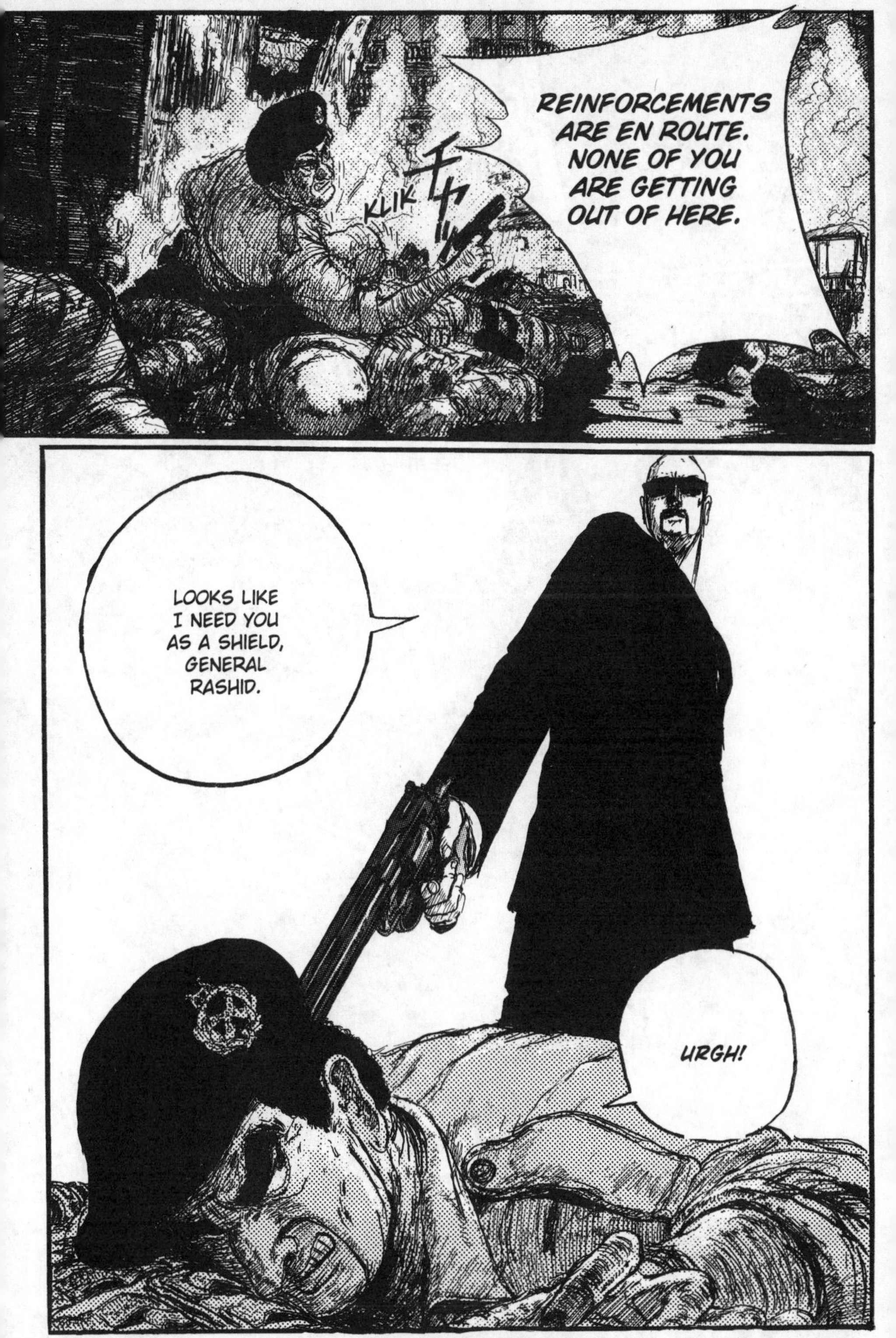
REINFORCEMENTS ARE EN ROUTE. NONE OF YOU ARE GETTING OUT OF HERE.
KLIK
LOOKS LIKE I NEED YOU AS A SHIELD, GENERAL RASHID.
URGH!

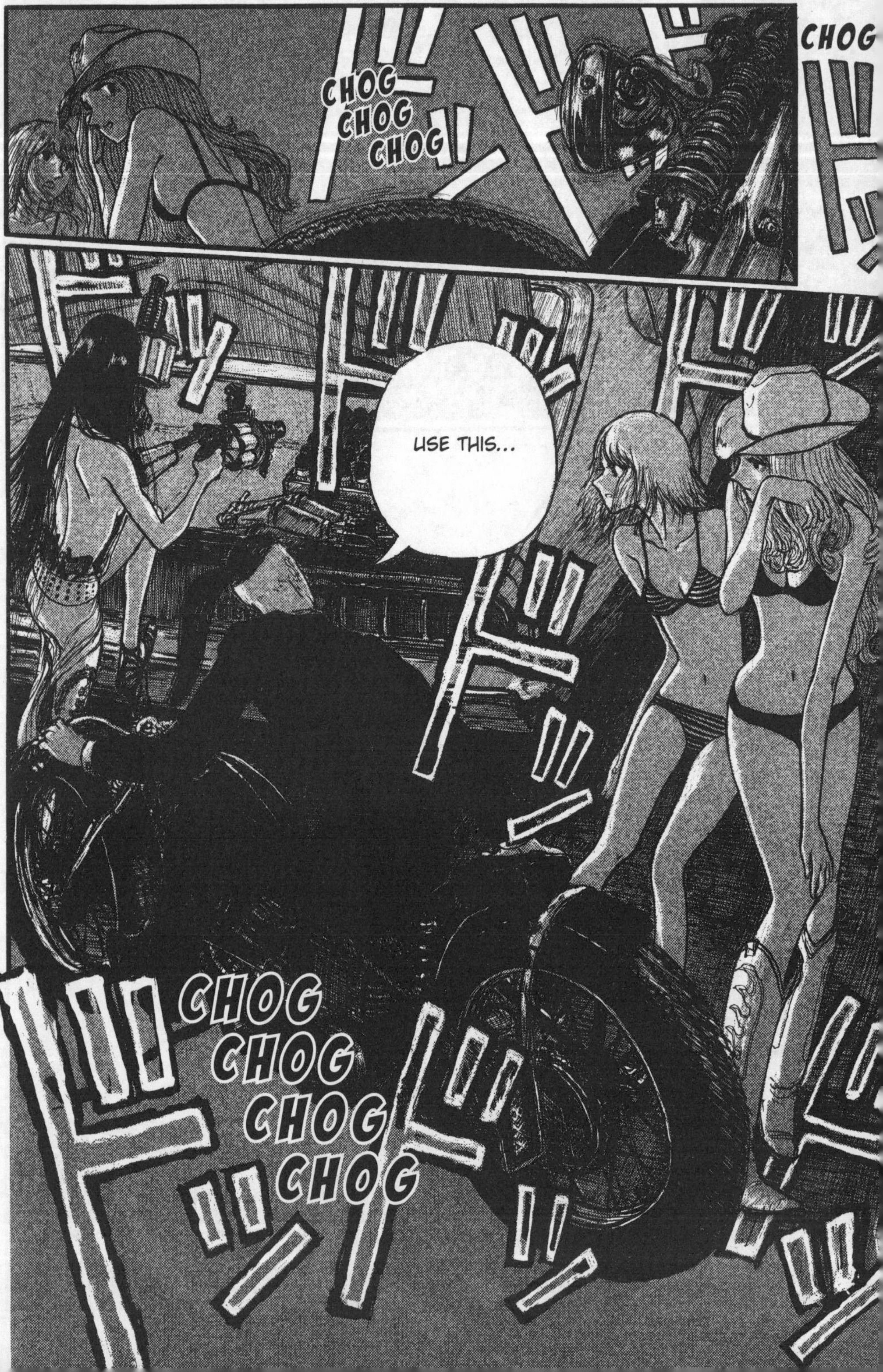
CHOG
CHOG CHOG CHOG
USE THIS...
CHOG CHOG CHOG CHOG

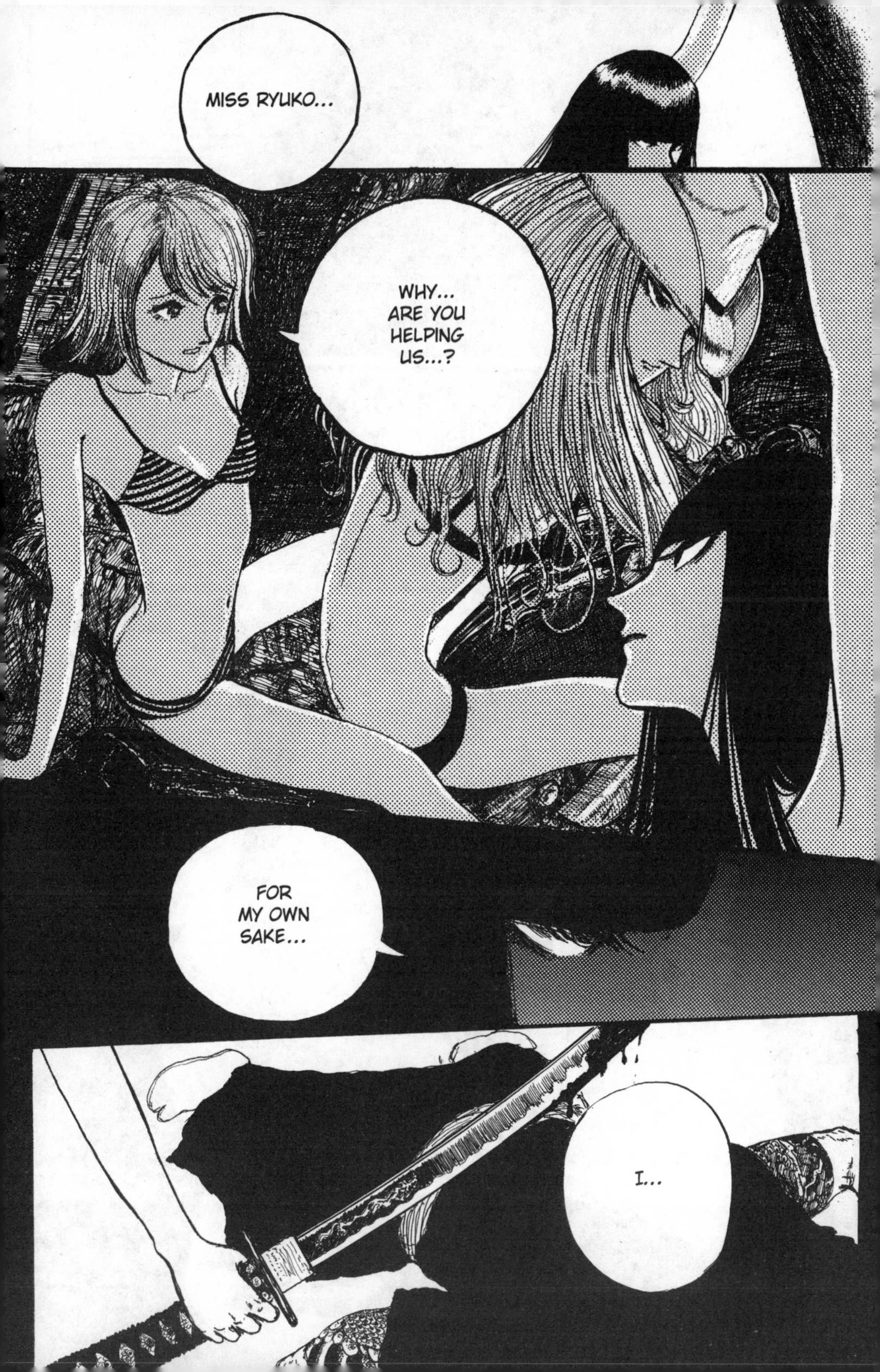
MISS RYUKO...
WHY... ARE YOU HELPING US...?
FOR MY OWN SAKE...
I...

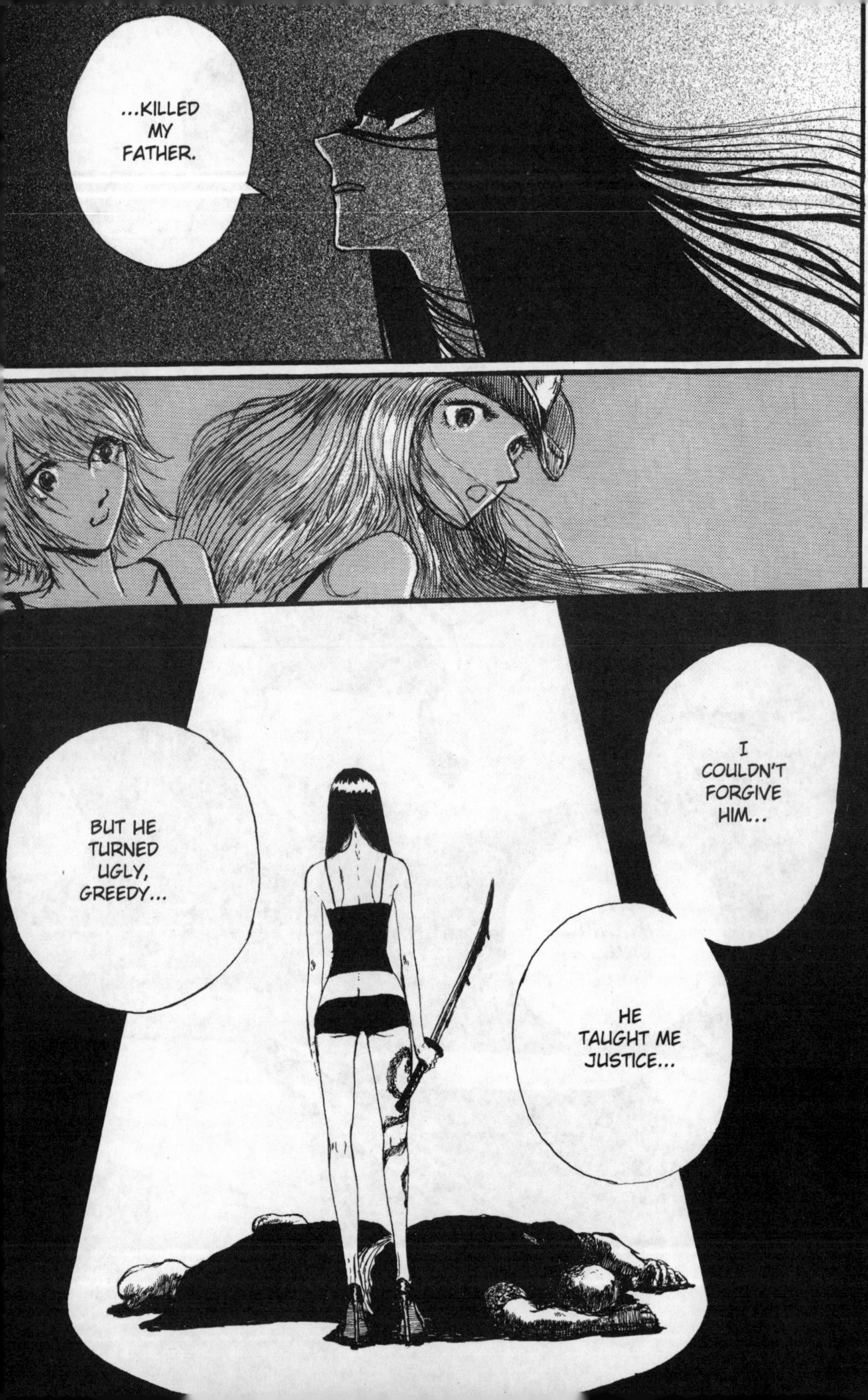
...KILLED MY FATHER.
I COULDN'T FORGIVE HIM...
BUT HE TURNED UGLY, GREEDY...
HE TAUGHT ME JUSTICE...

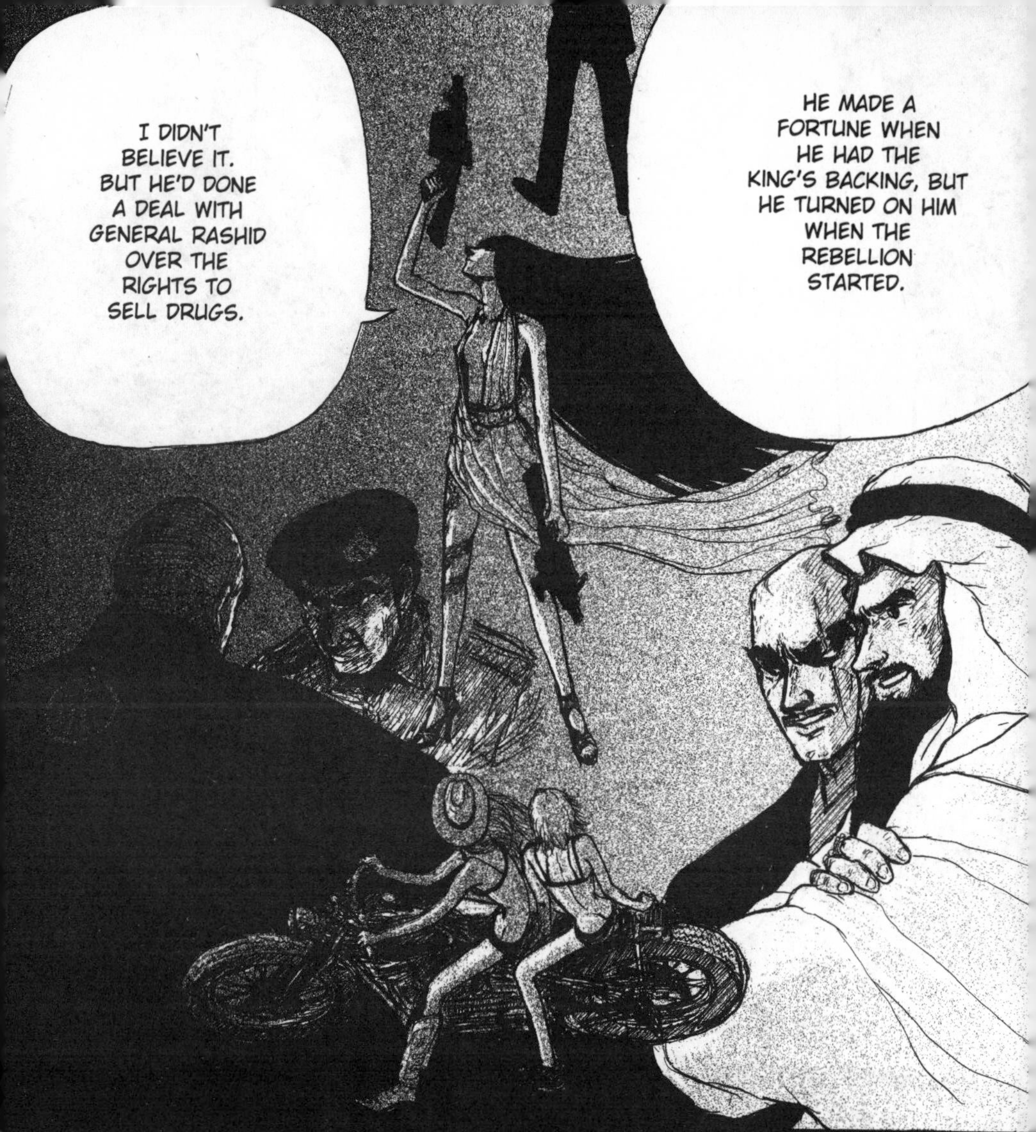
HE MADE A FORTUNE WHEN HE HAD THE KING'S BACKING, BUT HE TURNED ON HIM WHEN THE REBELLION STARTED.
I DIDN'T BELIEVE IT. BUT HE'D DONE A DEAL WITH GENERAL RASHID OVER THE RIGHTS TO SELL DRUGS.

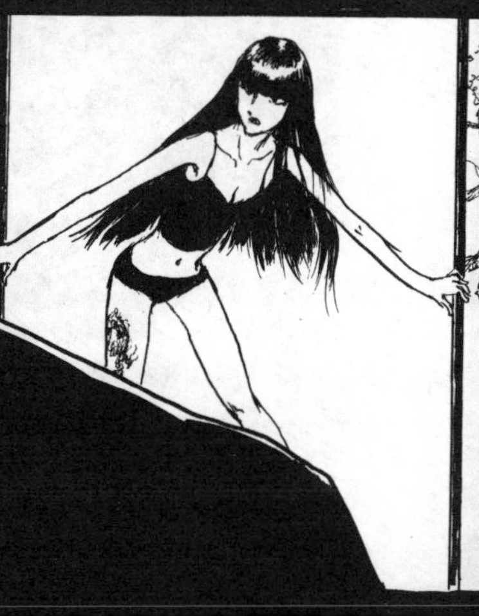

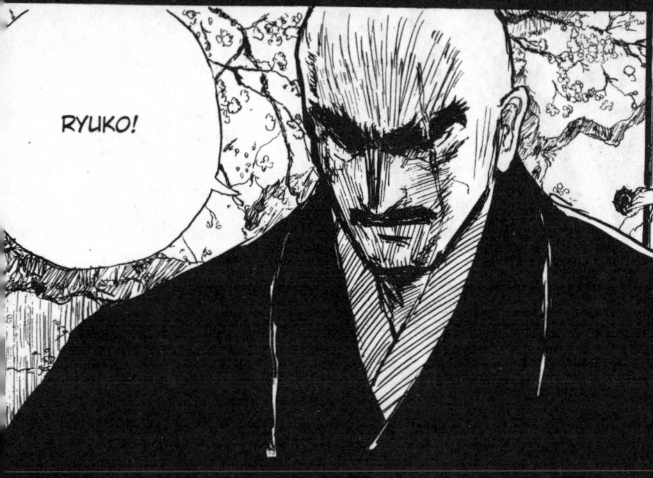
RYUKO!

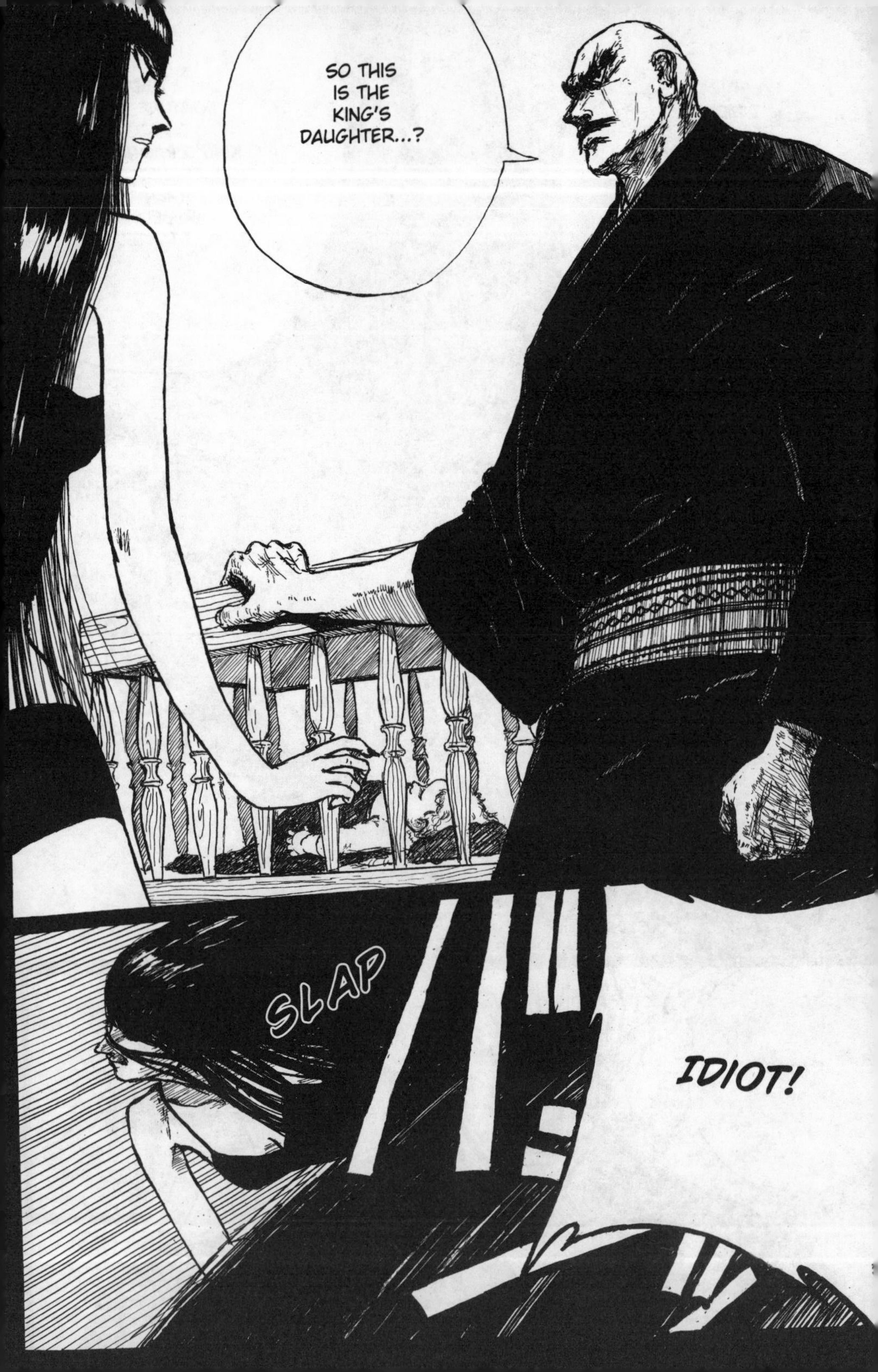
SO THIS IS THE KING'S DAUGHTER...?
SLAP
IDIOT!

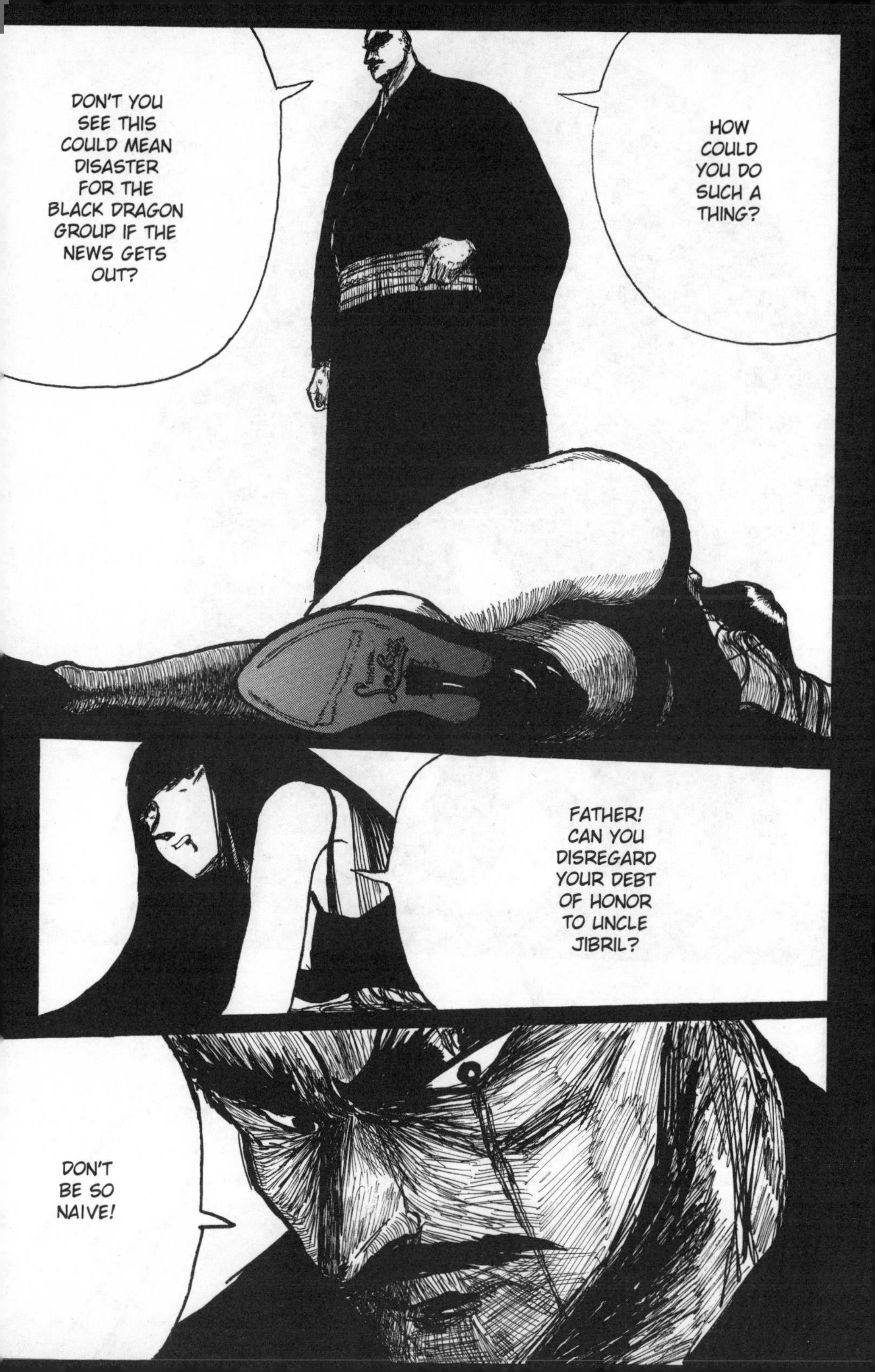
HOW COULD YOU DO SUCH A THING?
DON'T YOU SEE THIS COULD MEAN DISASTER FOR THE BLACK DRAGON GROUP IF THE NEWS GETS OUT?
FATHER! CAN YOU DISREGARD YOUR DEBT OF HONOR TO UNCLE JIBRIL?
DON'T BE SO NAIVE!

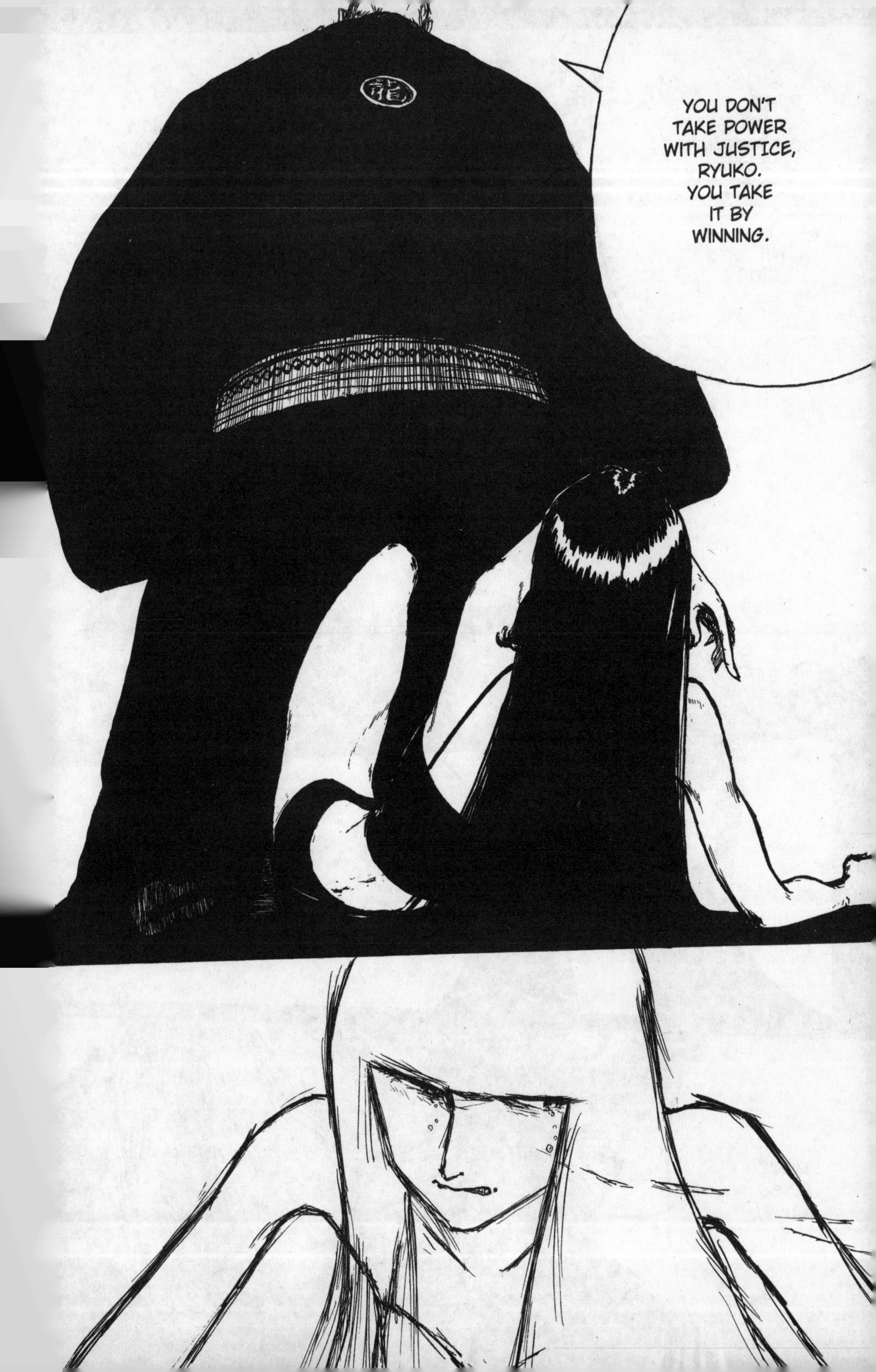
YOU DON'T TAKE POWER WITH JUSTICE, RYUKO. YOU TAKE IT BY WINNING.

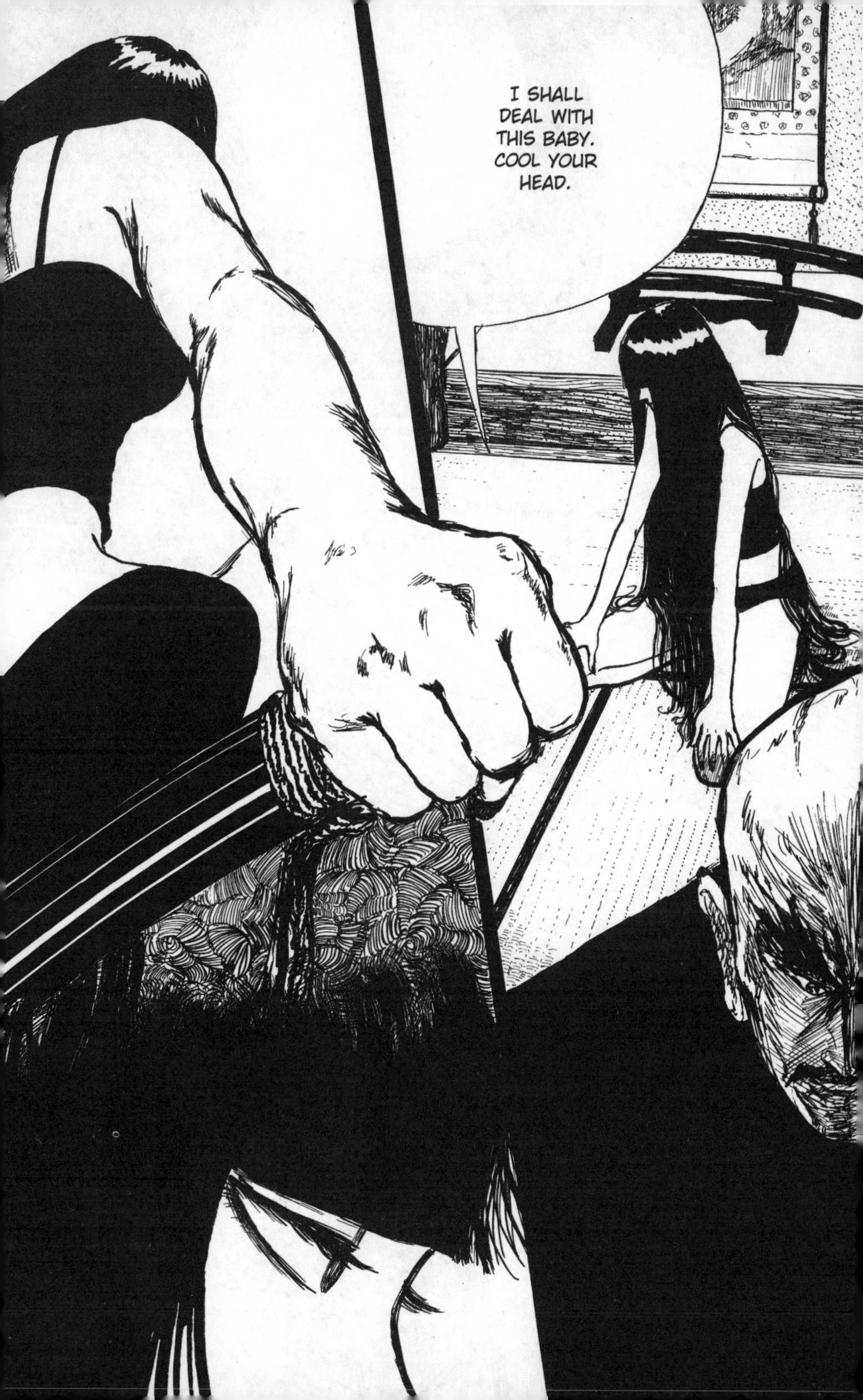
I SHALL DEAL WITH THIS BABY. COOL YOUR HEAD.

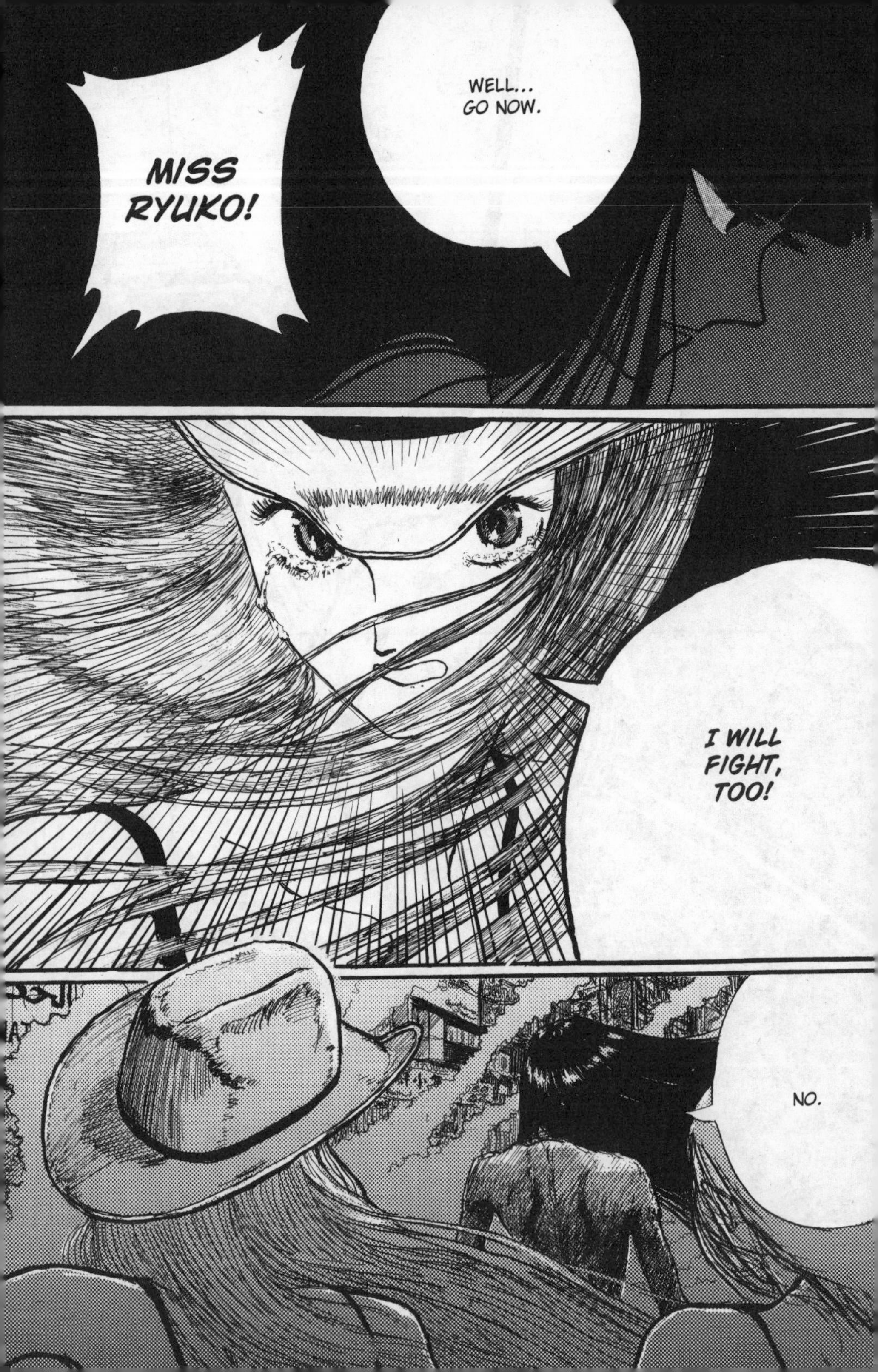
WELL... GO NOW.
MISS RYUKO!
I WILL FIGHT, TOO!
NO.

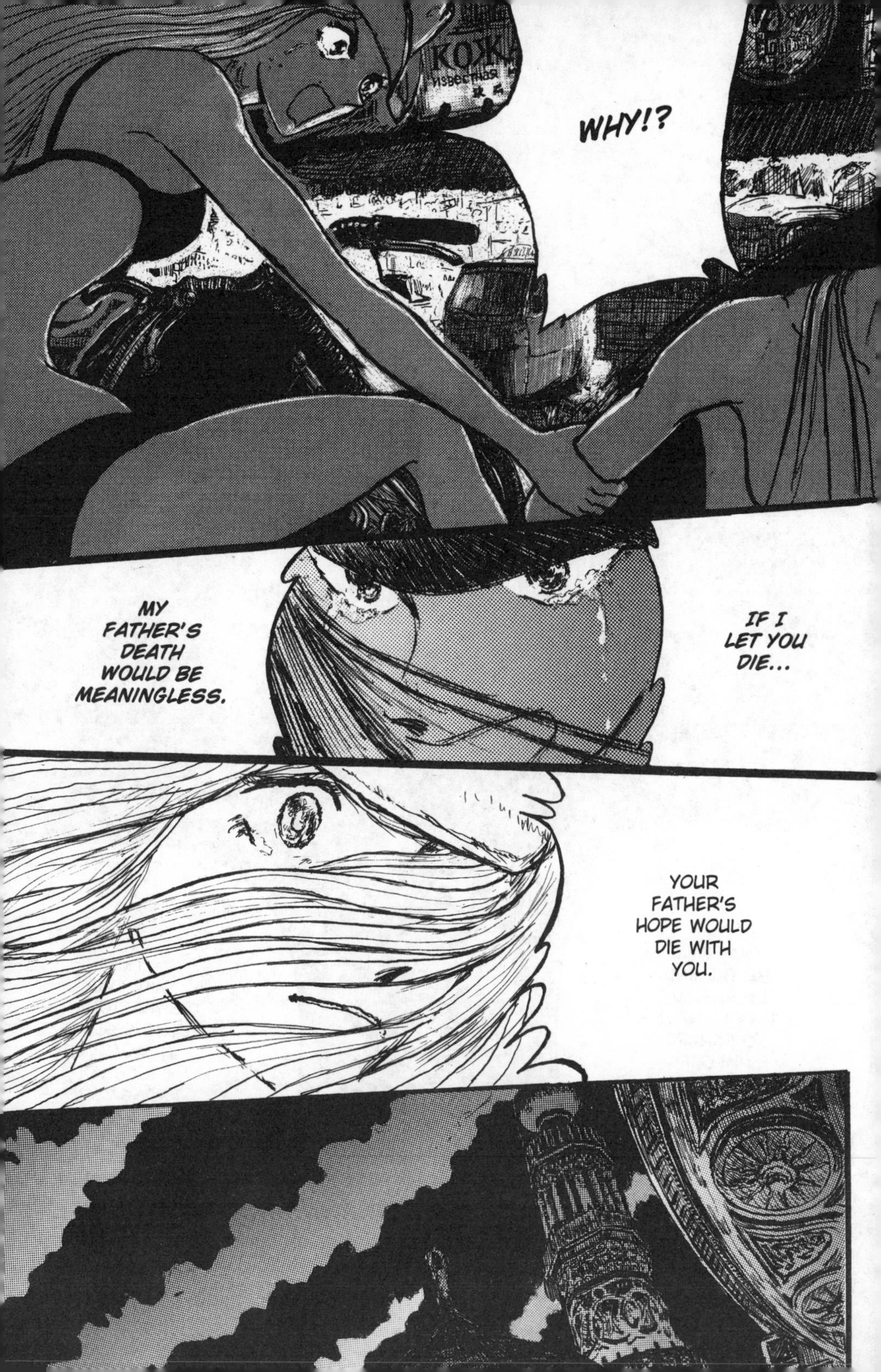
WHY!?
IF I LET YOU DIE...
MY FATHER'S DEATH WOULD BE MEANINGLESS.
YOUR FATHER'S HOPE WOULD DIE WITH YOU.

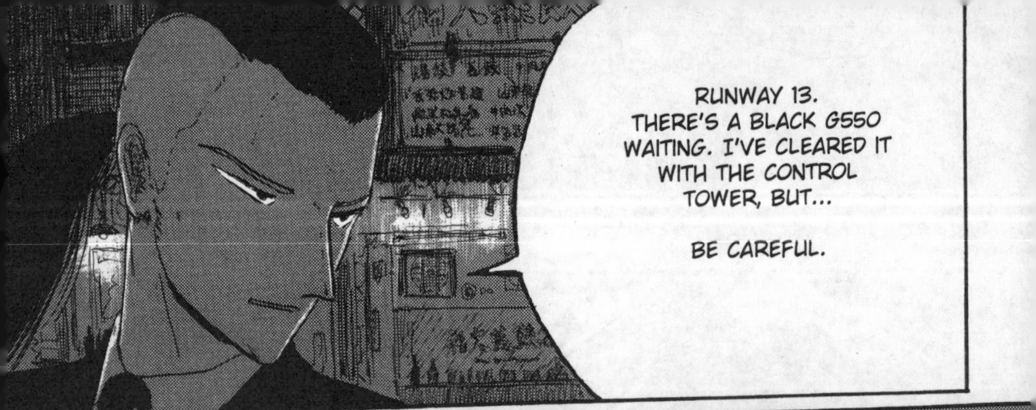
RUNWAY 13. THERE'S A BLACK G550 WAITING. I'VE CLEARED IT WITH THE CONTROL TOWER, BUT...
BE CAREFUL.

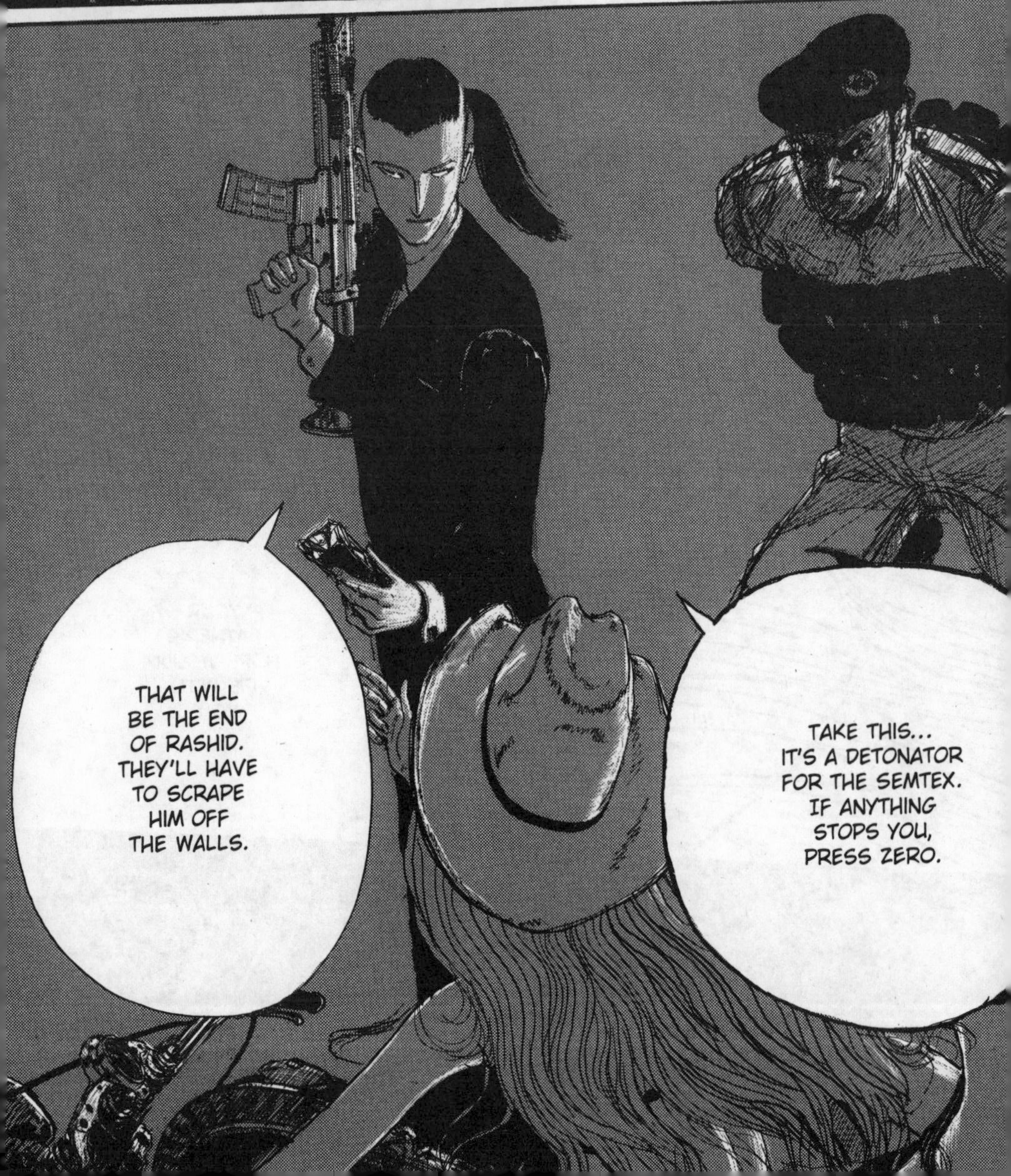
TAKE THIS... IT'S A DETONATOR FOR THE SEMTEX. IF ANYTHING STOPS YOU, PRESS ZERO.
THAT WILL BE THE END OF RASHID. THEY'LL HAVE TO SCRAPE HIM OFF THE WALLS.

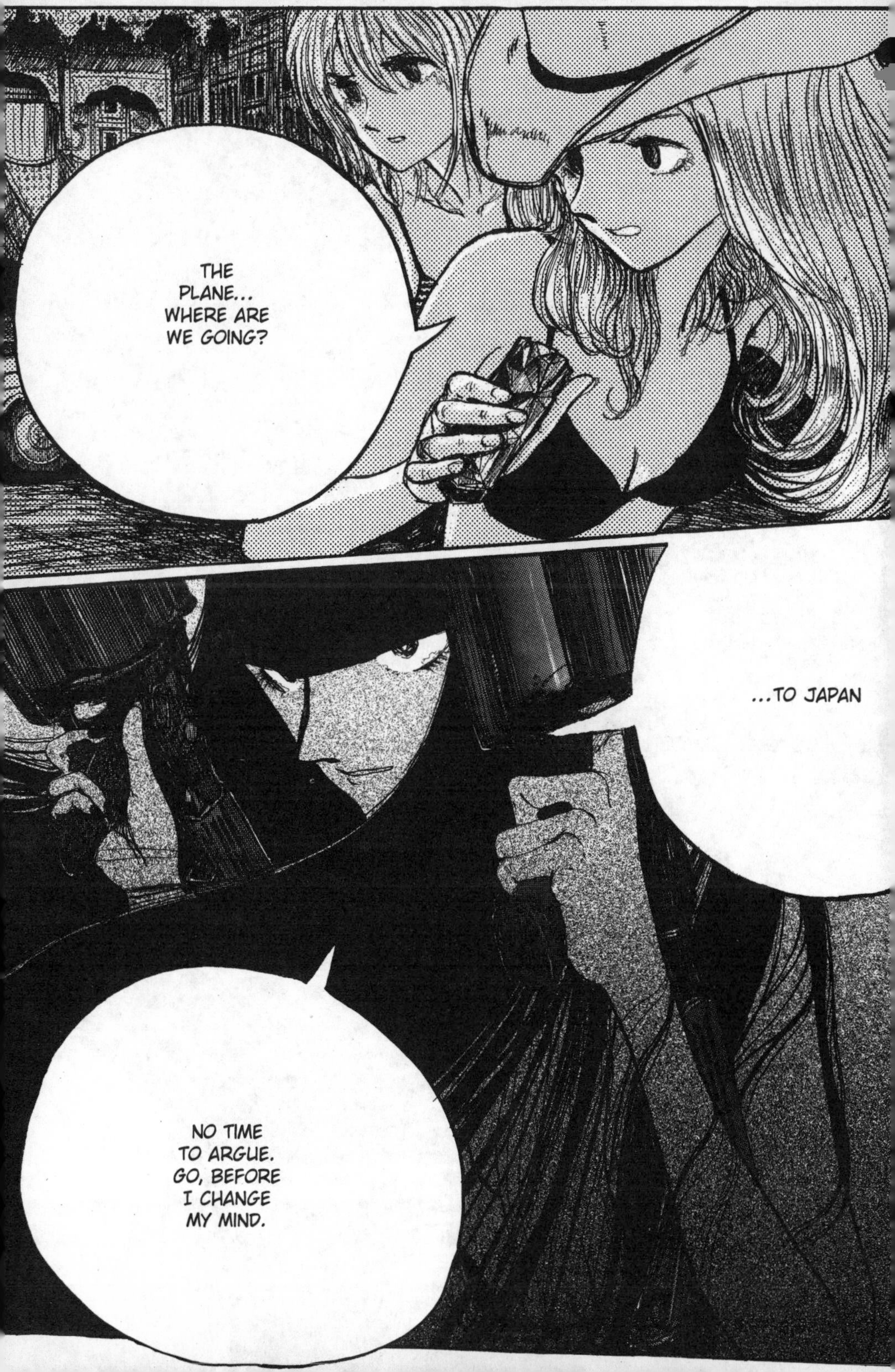
THE PLANE... WHERE ARE WE GOING?
...TO JAPAN
NO TIME TO ARGUE. GO, BEFORE I CHANGE MY MIND.

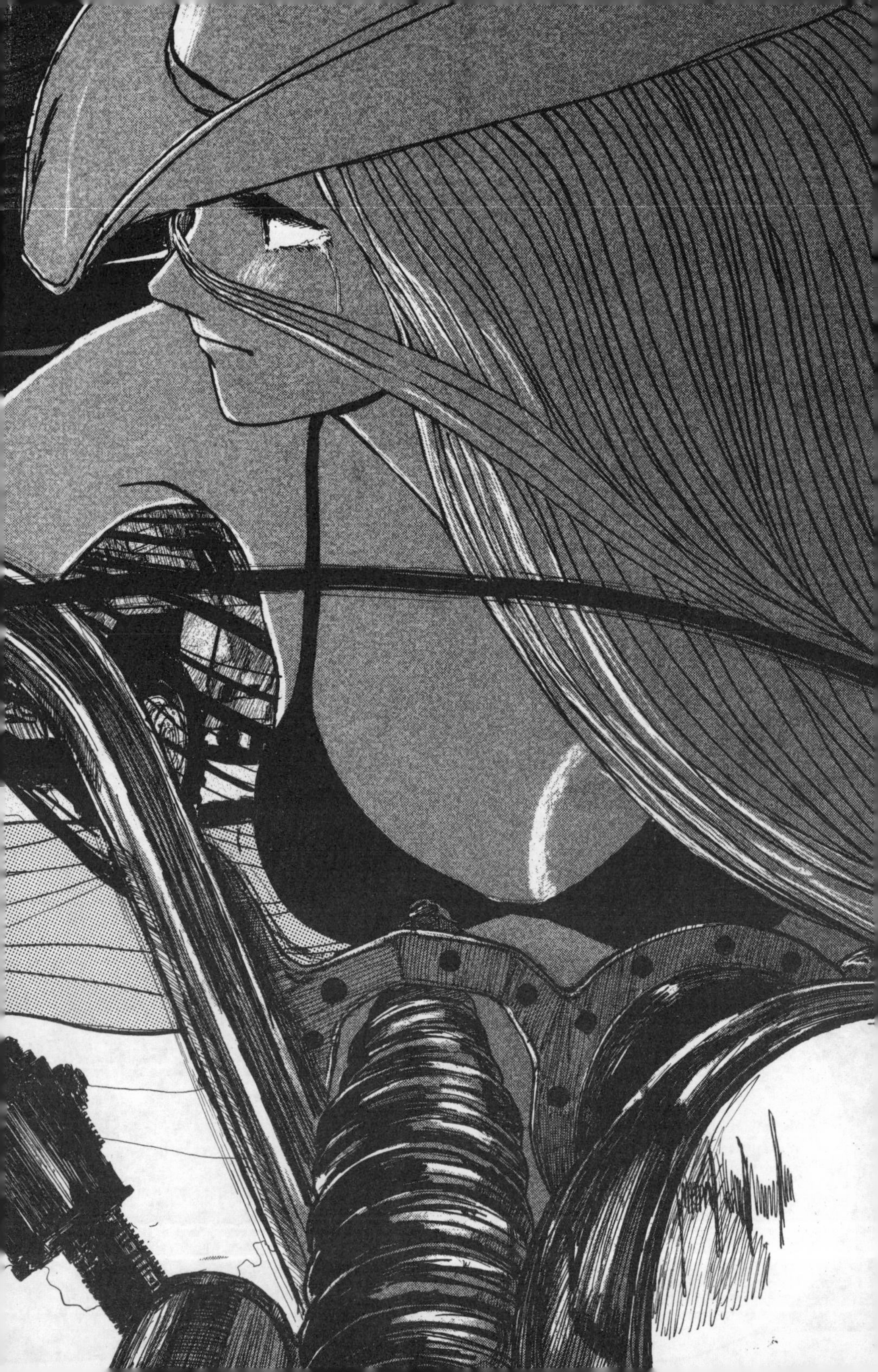

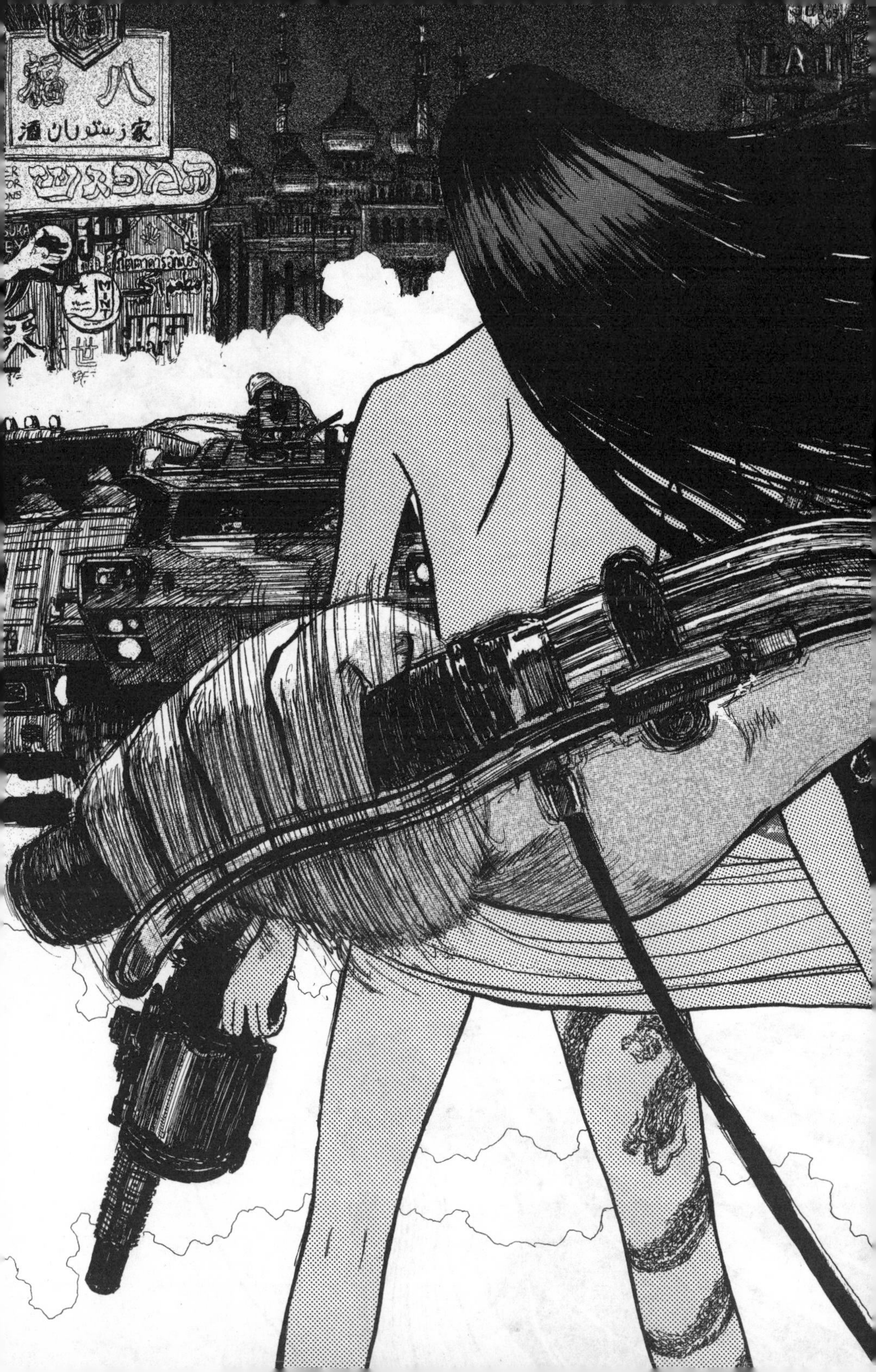
八
MINT
世

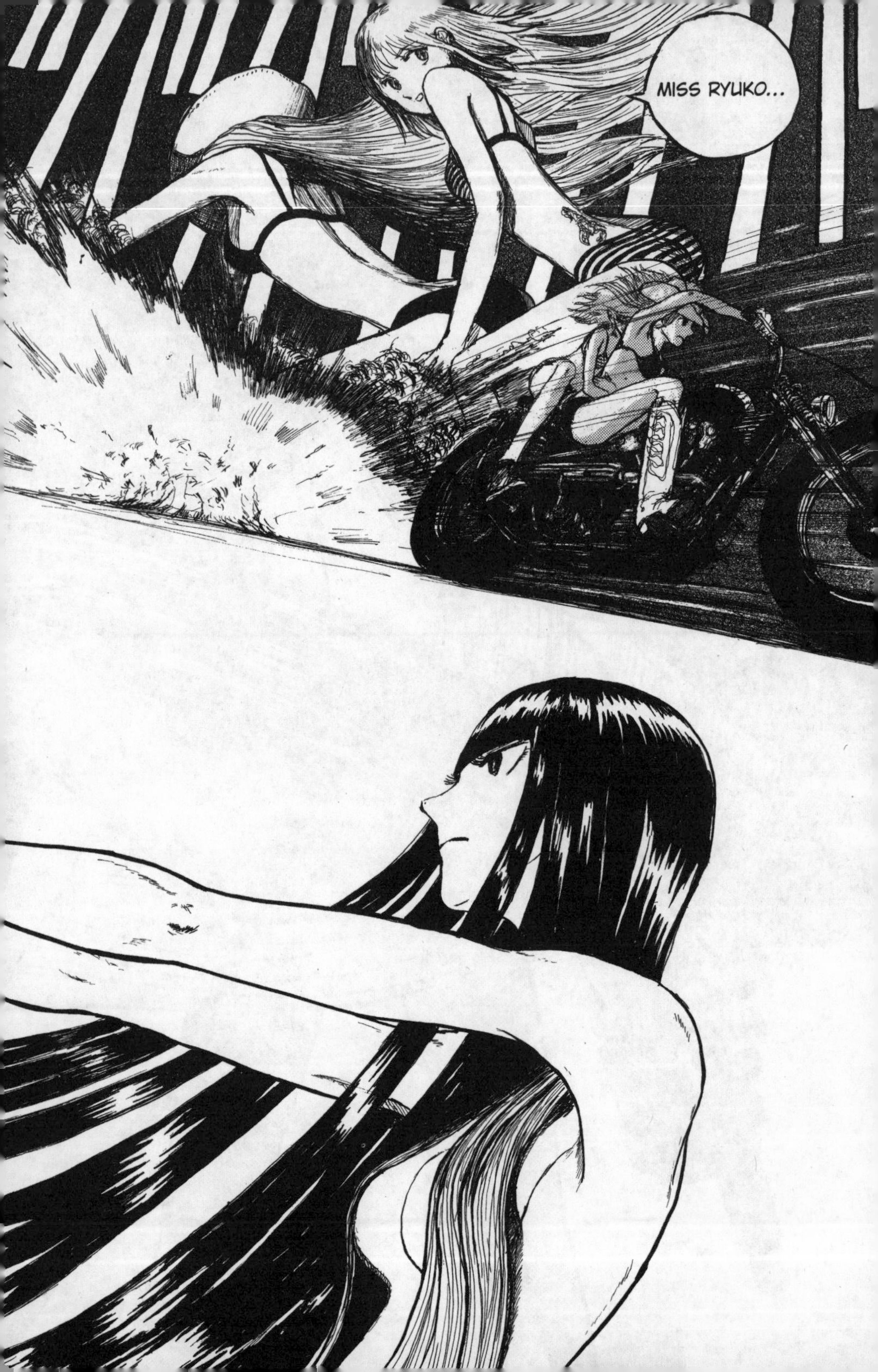
MISS RYUKO...

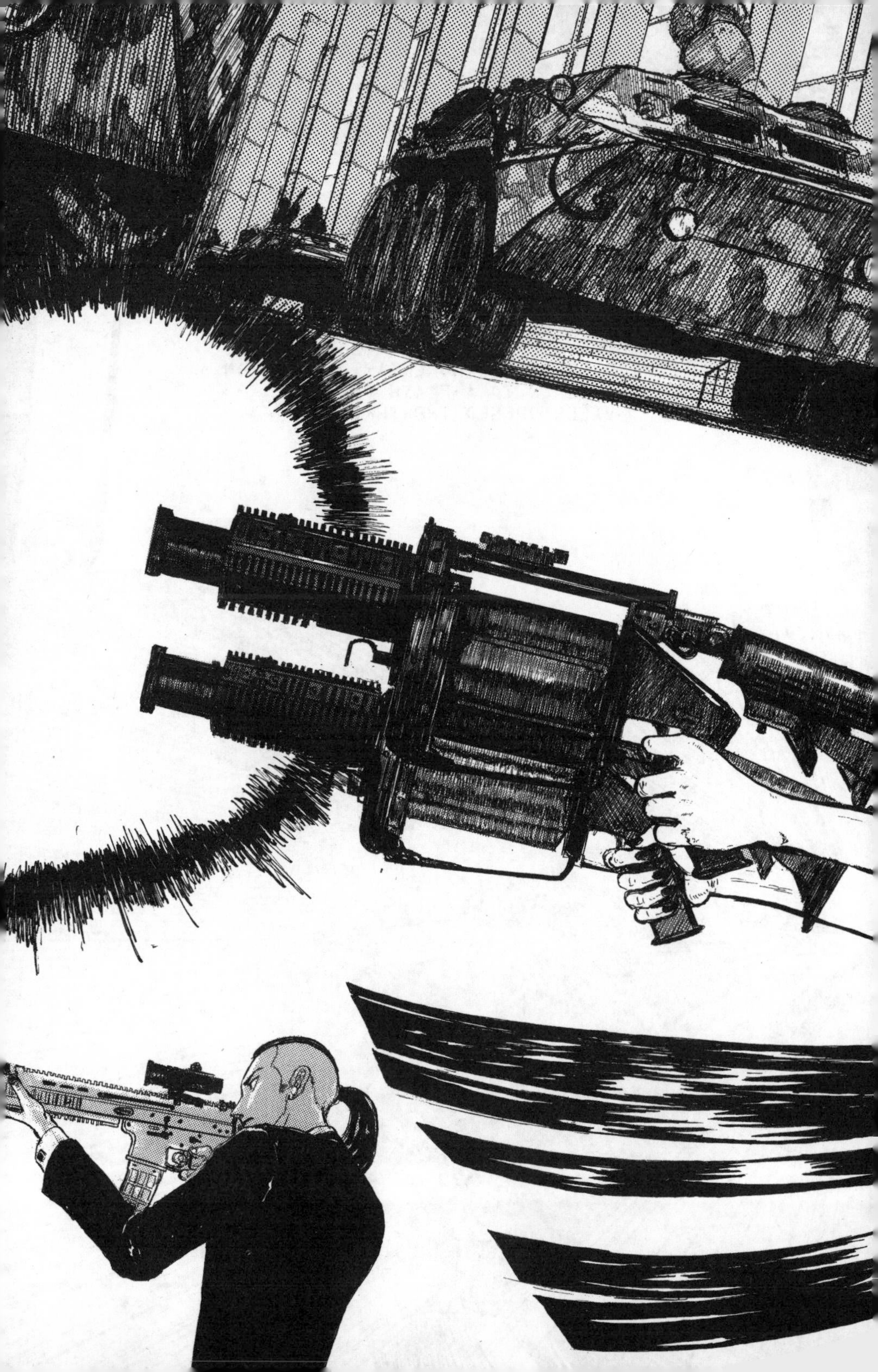

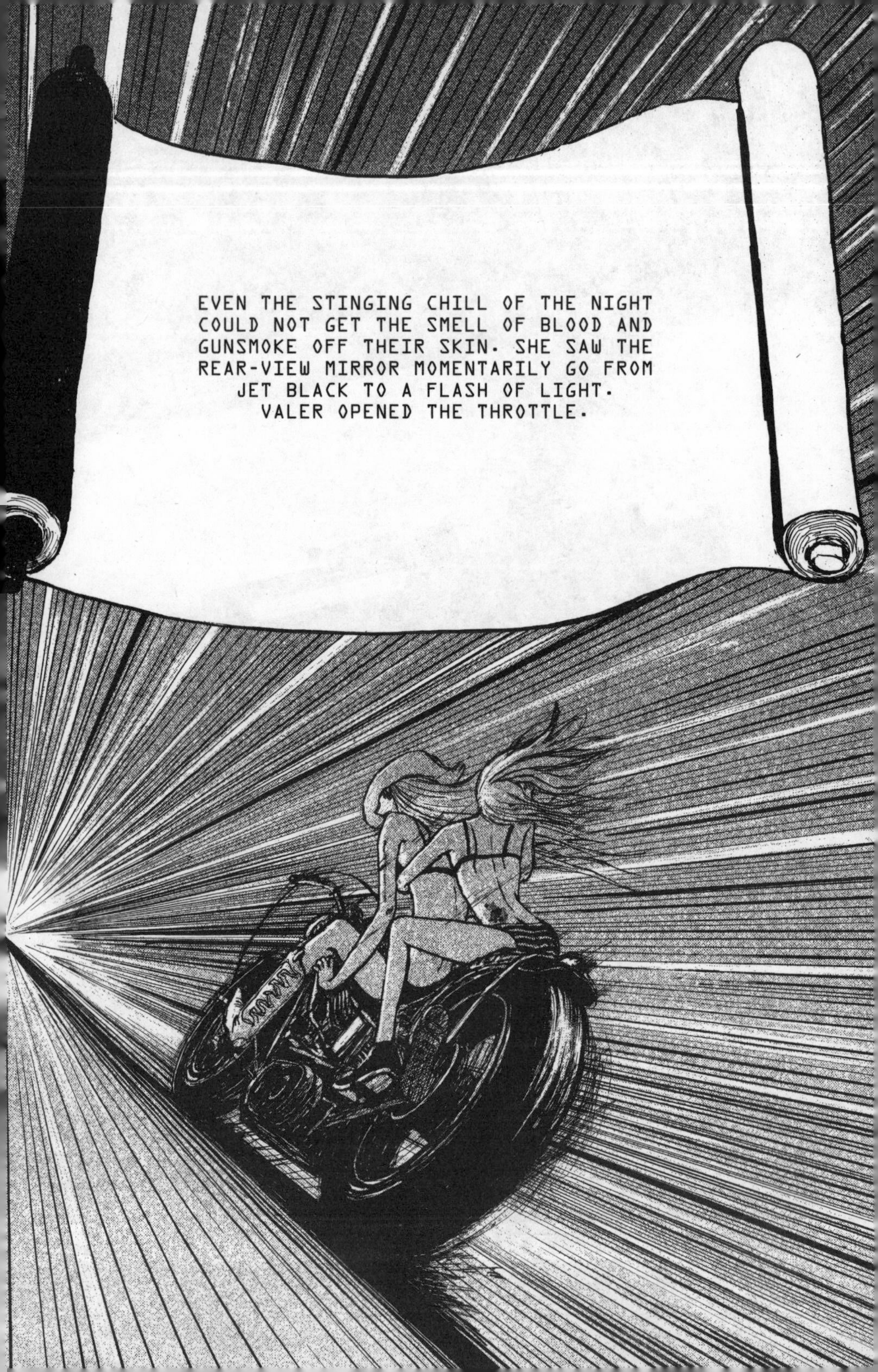
EVEN THE STINGING CHILL OF THE NIGHT COULD NOT GET THE SMELL OF BLOOD AND GUNSMOKE OFF THEIR SKIN. SHE SAW THE REAR-VIEW MIRROR MOMENTARILY GO FROM JET BLACK TO A FLASH OF LIGHT. VALER OPENED THE THROTTLE.

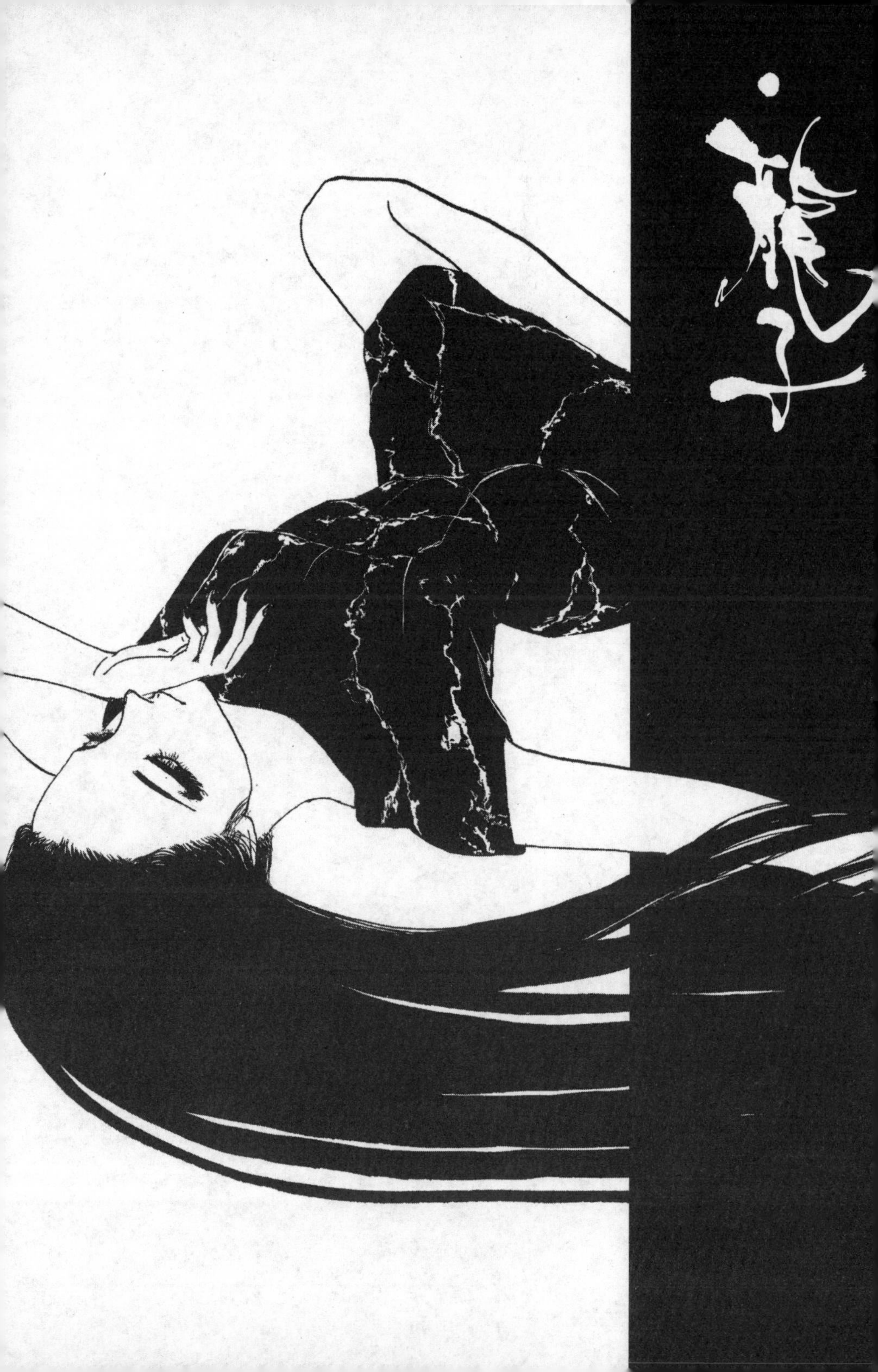
・龍子

CHAPTER 2:
STORM OF SAND

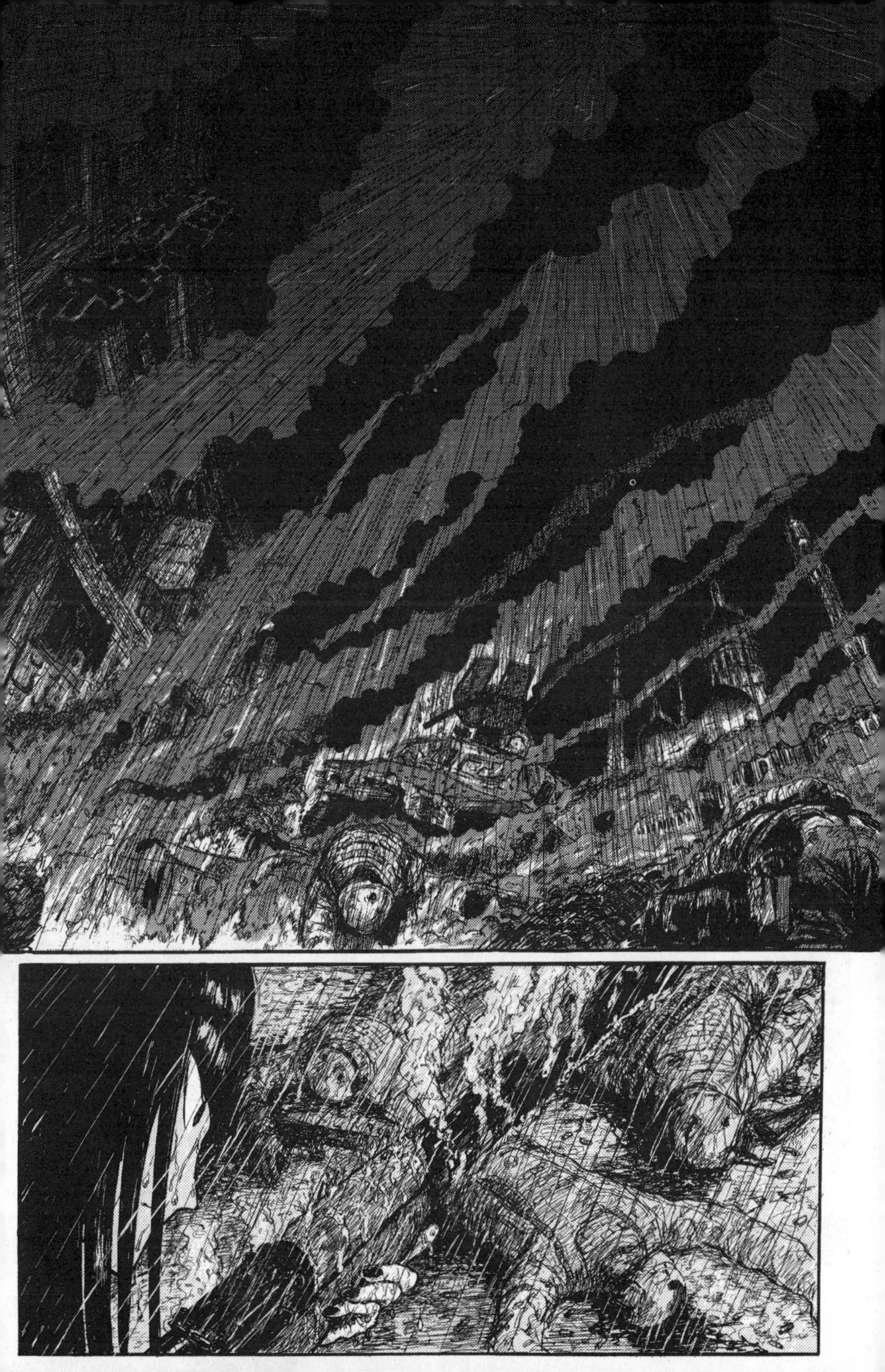

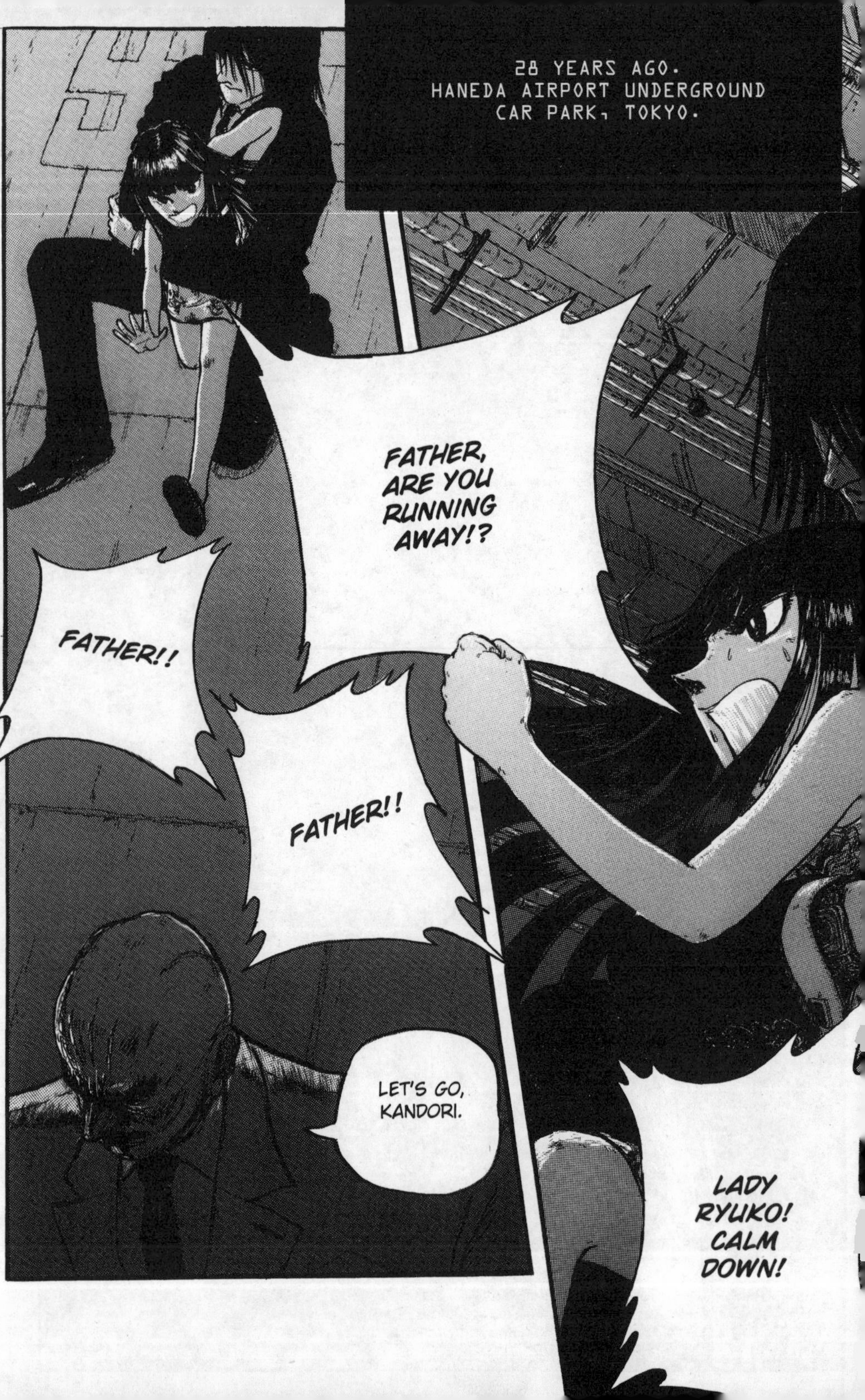
28 YEARS AGO.
HANEDA AIRPORT UNDERGROUND CAR PARK, TOKYO.
FATHER, ARE YOU RUNNING AWAY!?
FATHER!!
FATHER!!
LADY RYUKO! CALM DOWN!
LET'S GO, KANDORI.

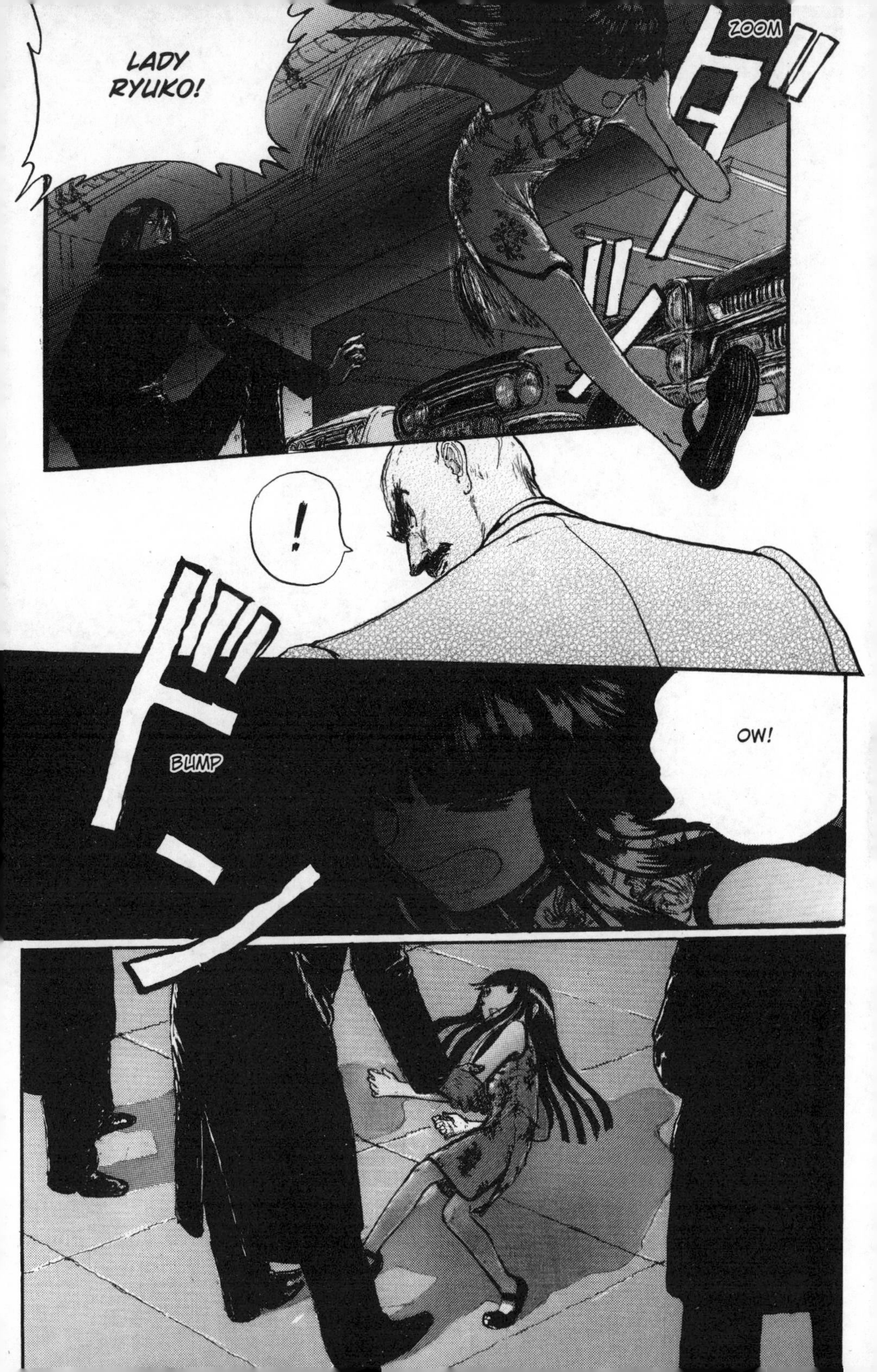
ZOOM
LADY RYUKO!
!
BUMP
OW!

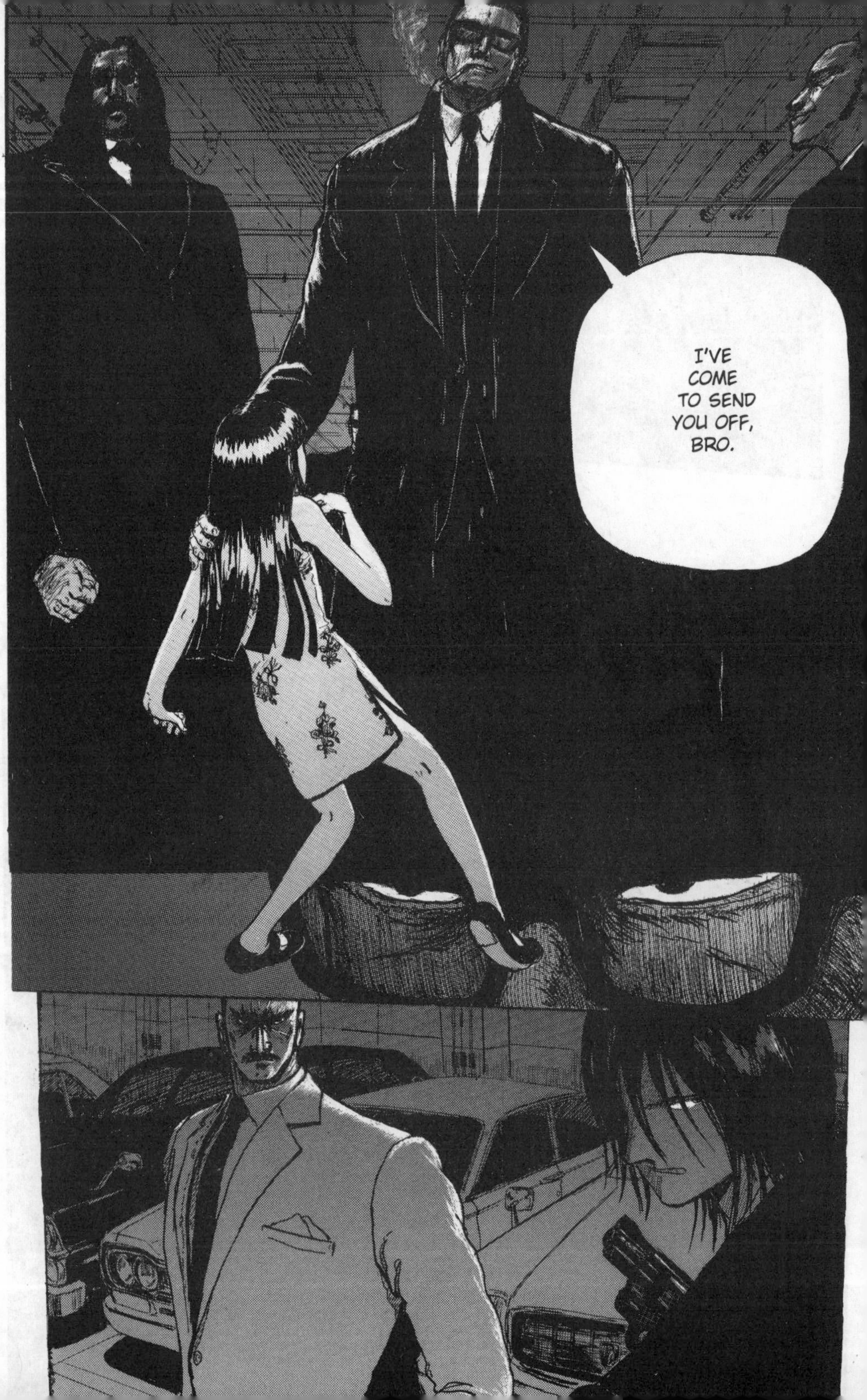
I'VE COME TO SEND YOU OFF, BRO.

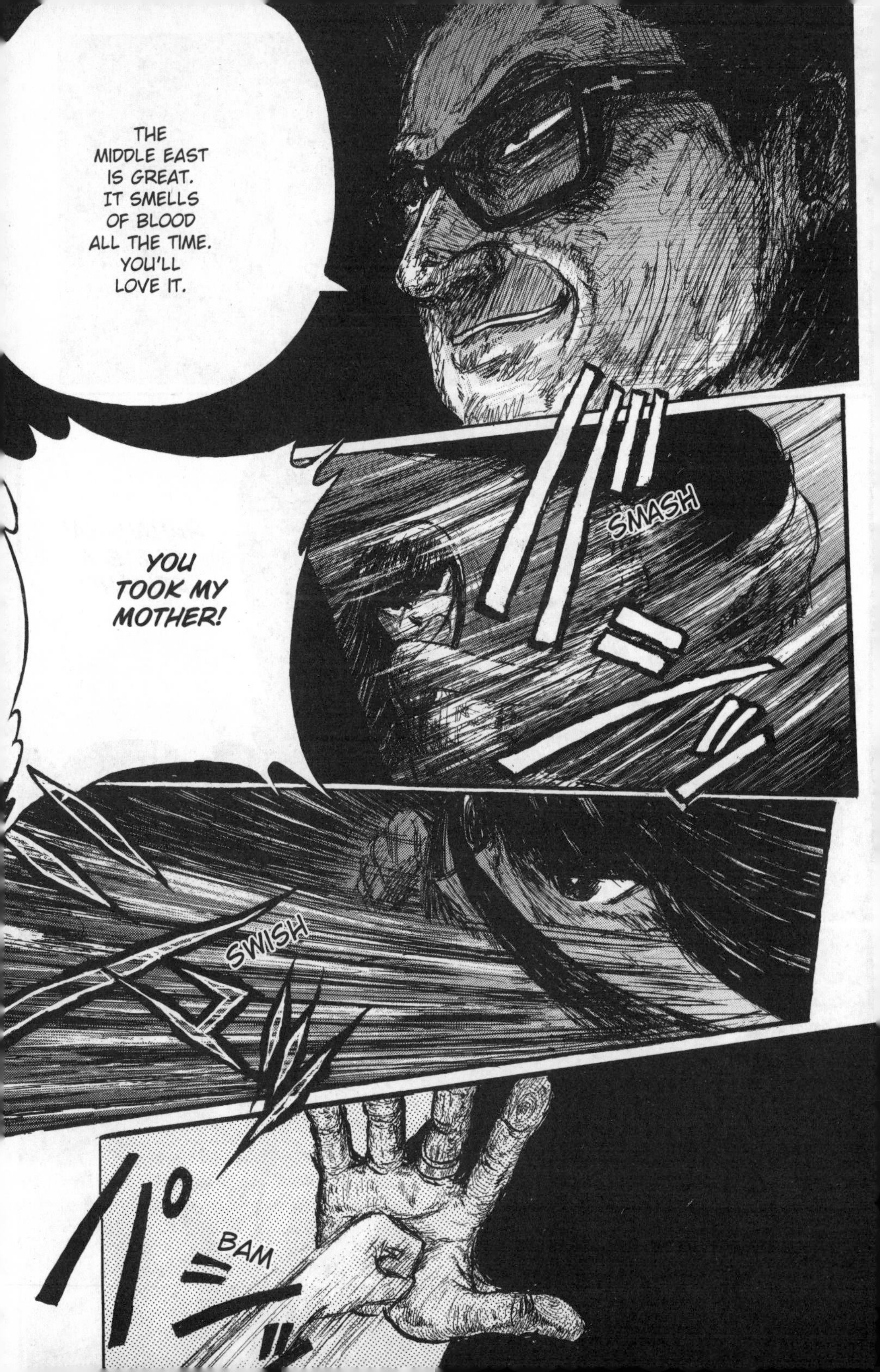
THE MIDDLE EAST IS GREAT. IT SMELLS OF BLOOD ALL THE TIME. YOU'LL LOVE IT.
SMASH
YOU TOOK MY MOTHER!
SWISH
BAM

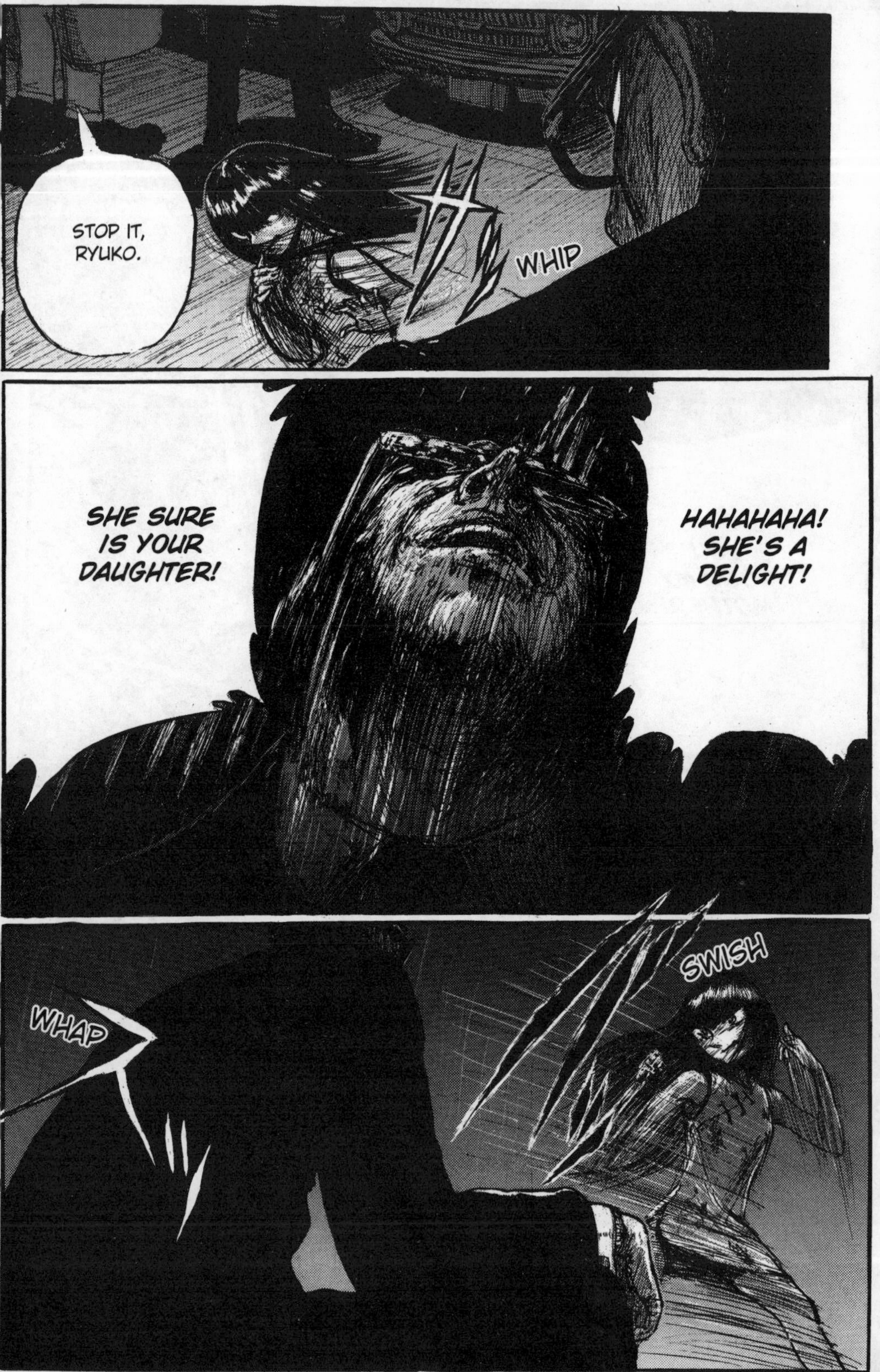
WHIP
STOP IT, RYUKO.
HAHAHAHA! SHE'S A DELIGHT!
SHE SURE IS YOUR DAUGHTER!
SWISH
WHAP

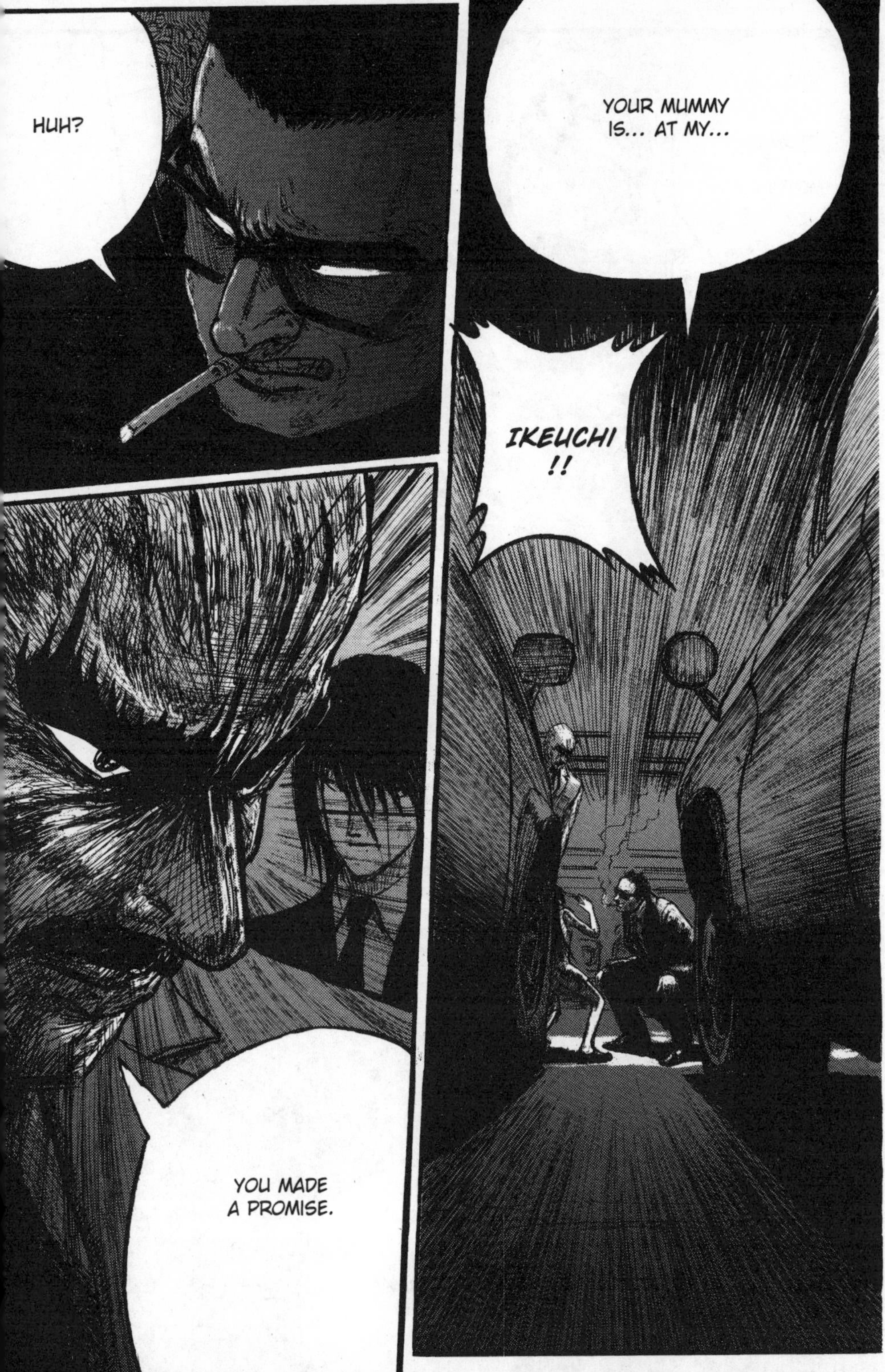
YOUR MUMMY IS... AT MY...
IKEUCHI !!
HUH?
YOU MADE A PROMISE.

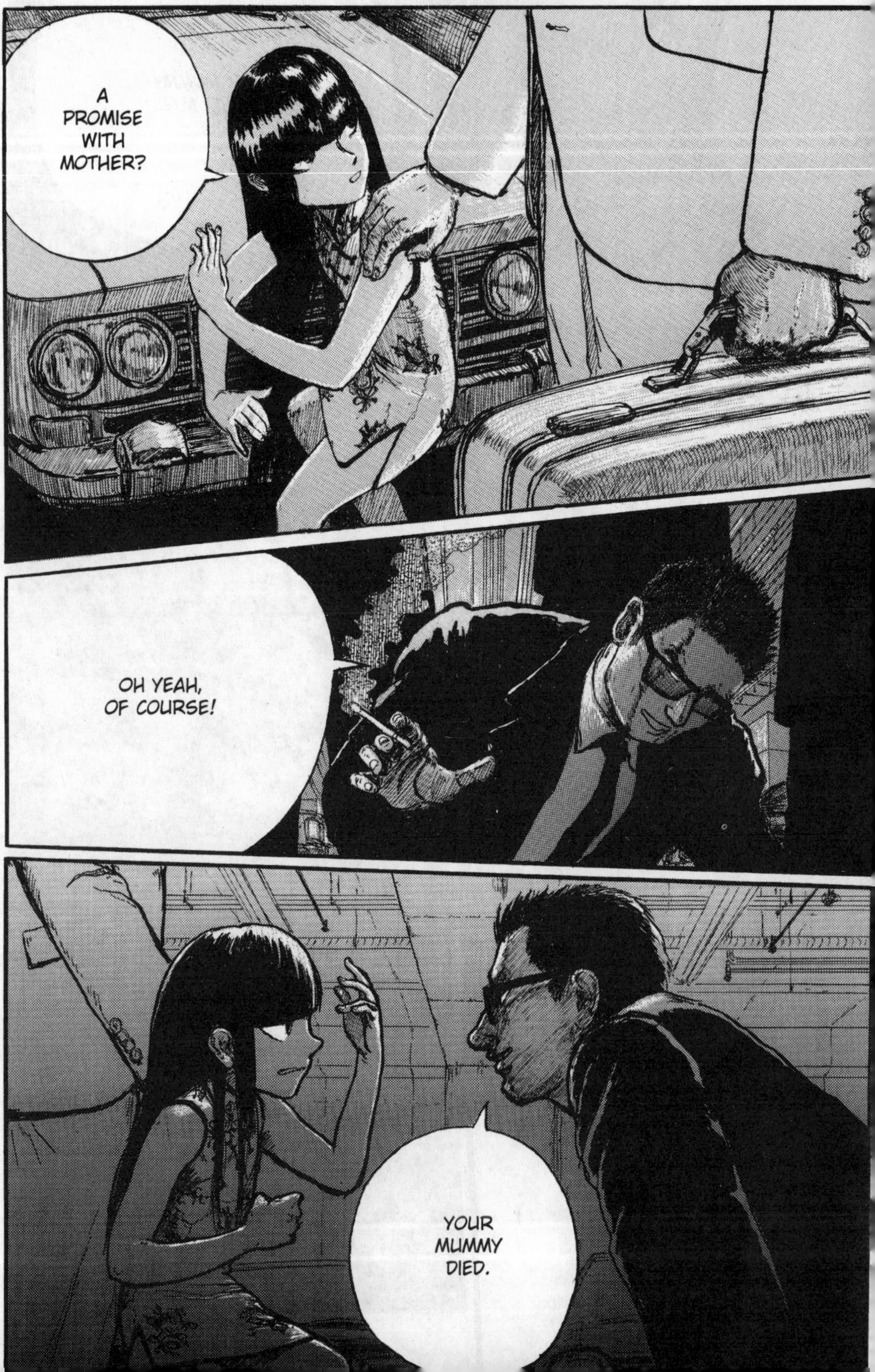
A PROMISE WITH MOTHER?
OH YEAH, OF COURSE!
YOUR MUMMY DIED.

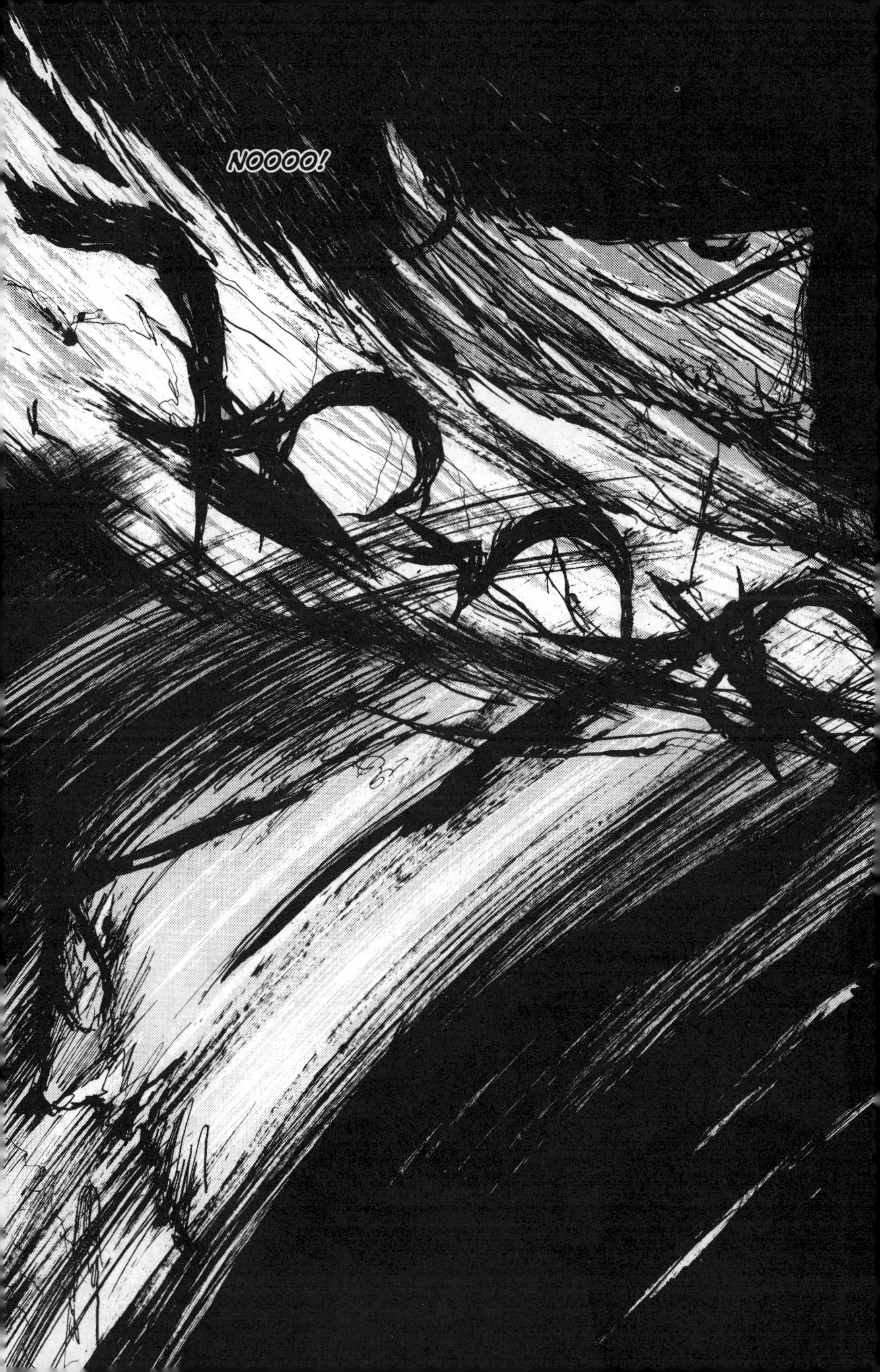
NOOOO!

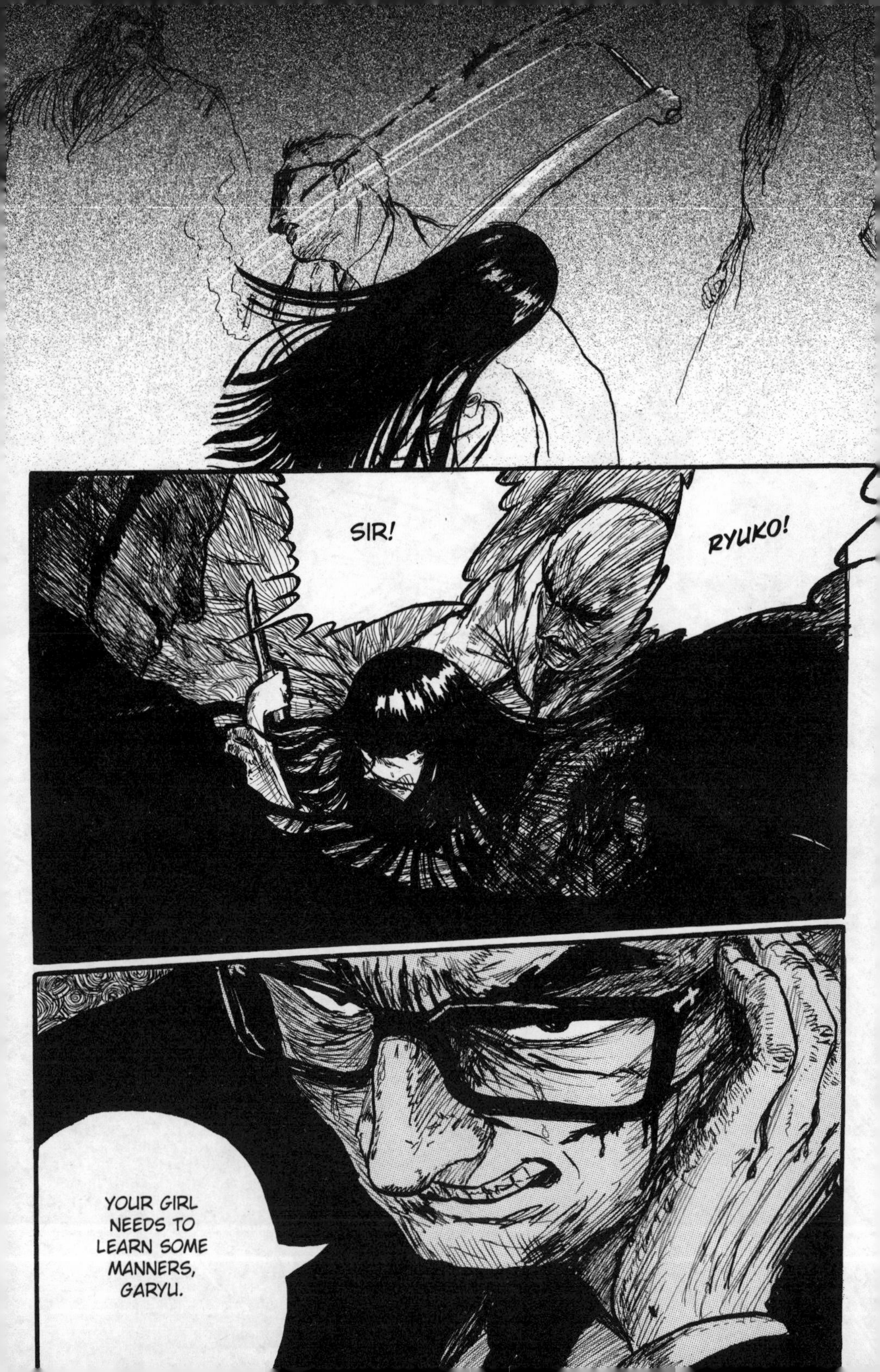
RYUKO!
SIR!
YOUR GIRL NEEDS TO LEARN SOME MANNERS, GARYU.

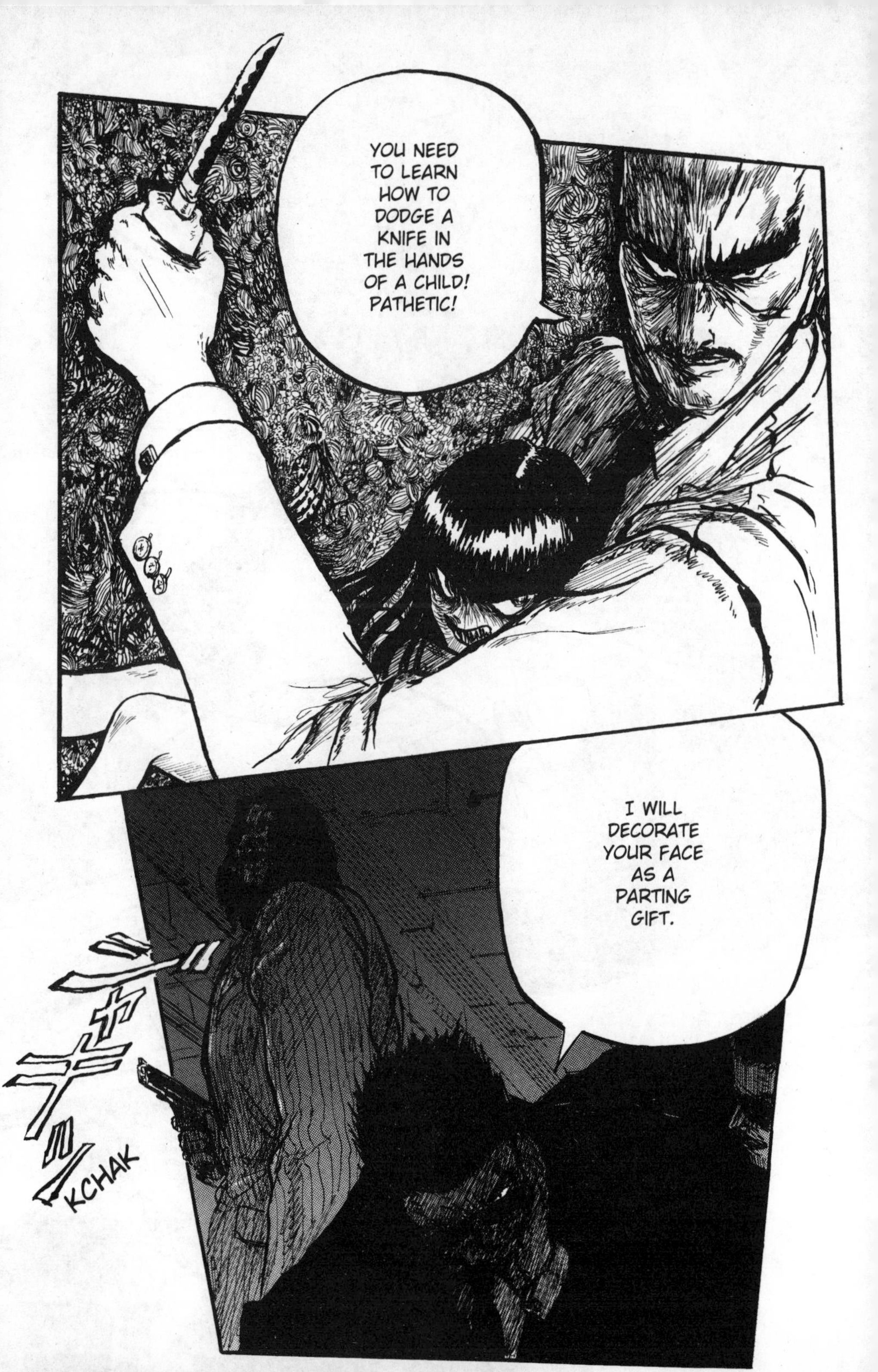
YOU NEED TO LEARN HOW TO DODGE A KNIFE IN THE HANDS OF A CHILD! PATHETIC!
I WILL DECORATE YOUR FACE AS A PARTING GIFT.
KCHAK

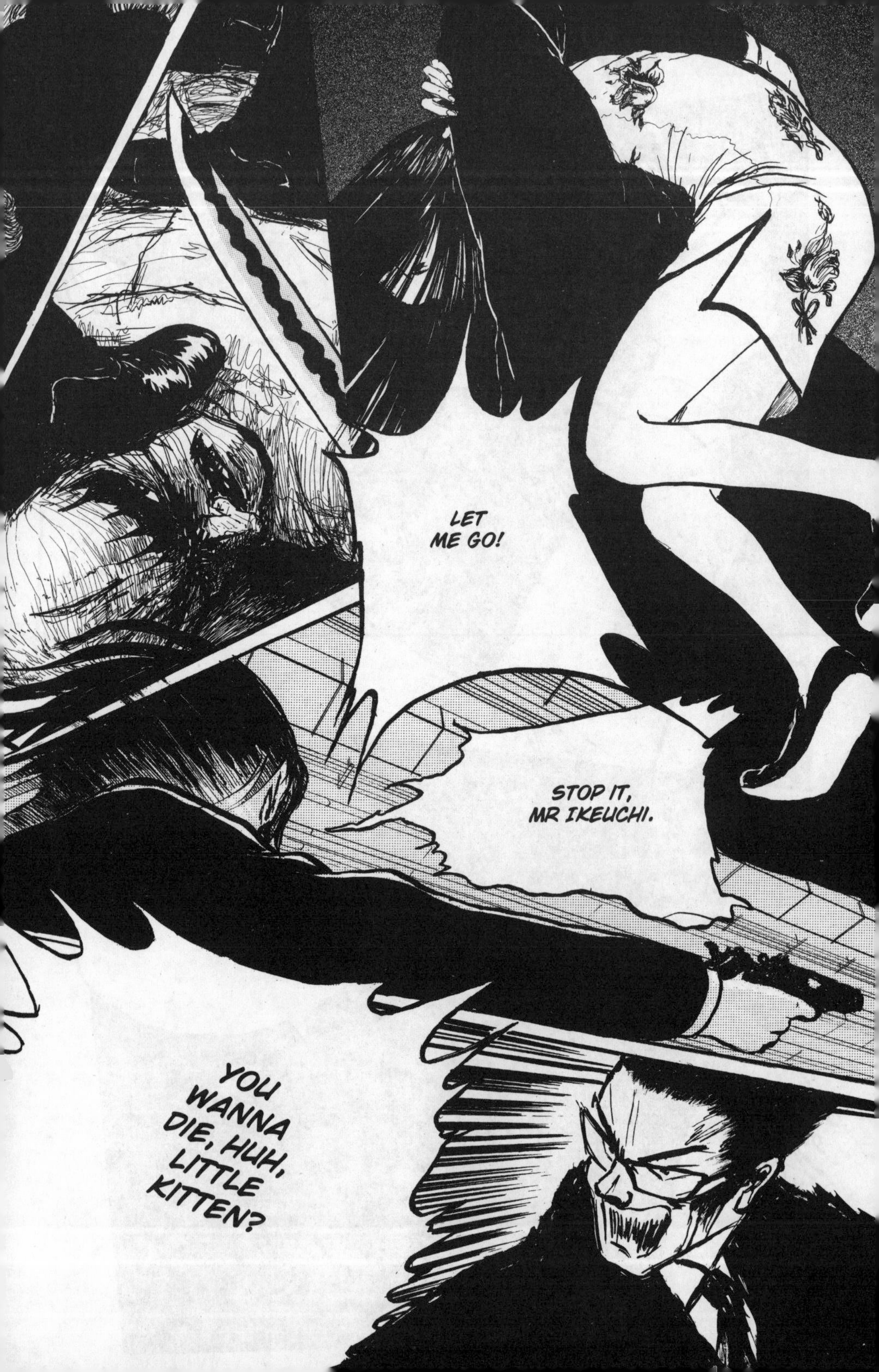
LET ME GO!
STOP IT, MR IKEUCHI.
YOU WANNA DIE, HUH, LITTLE KITTEN?

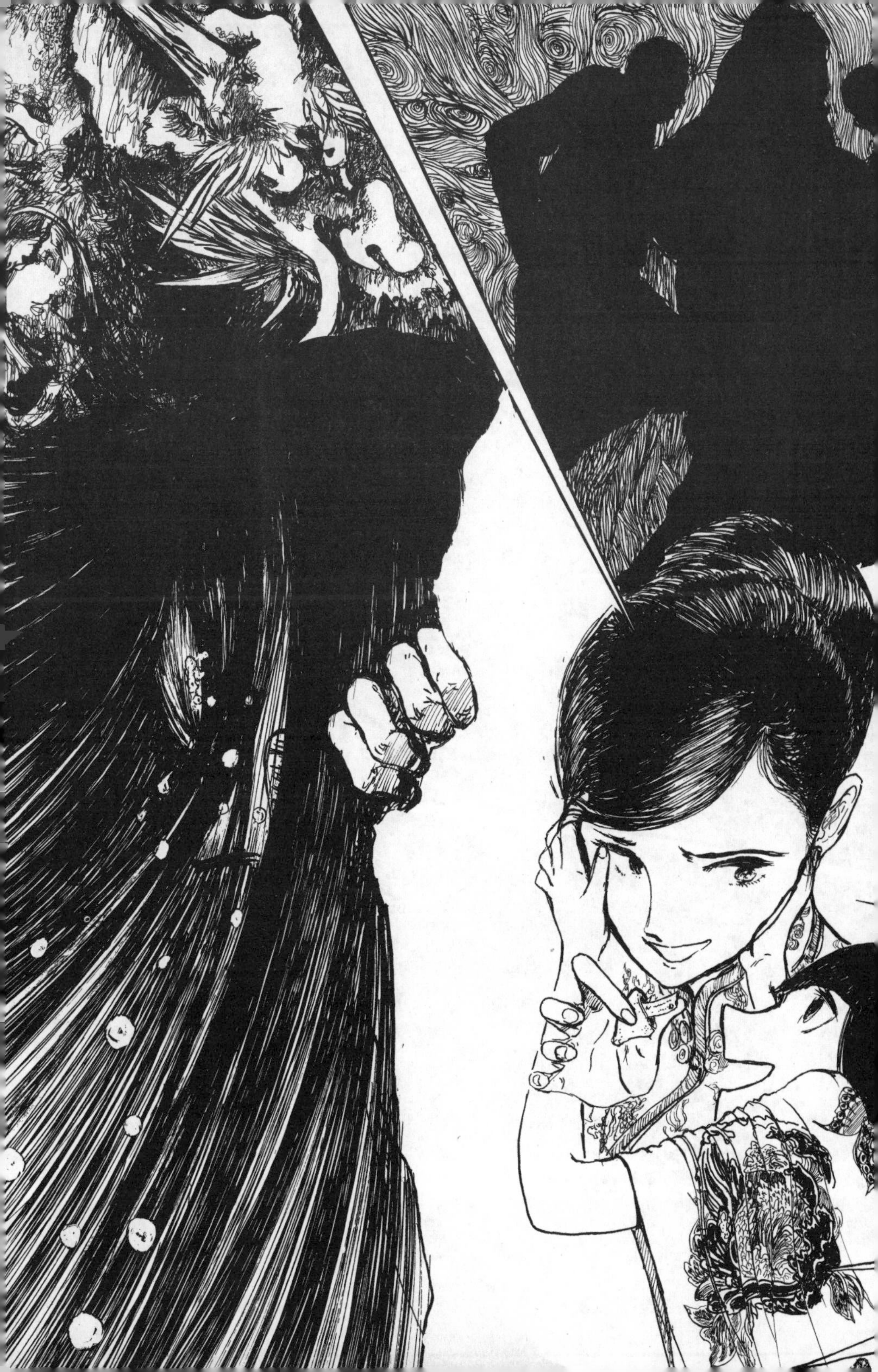

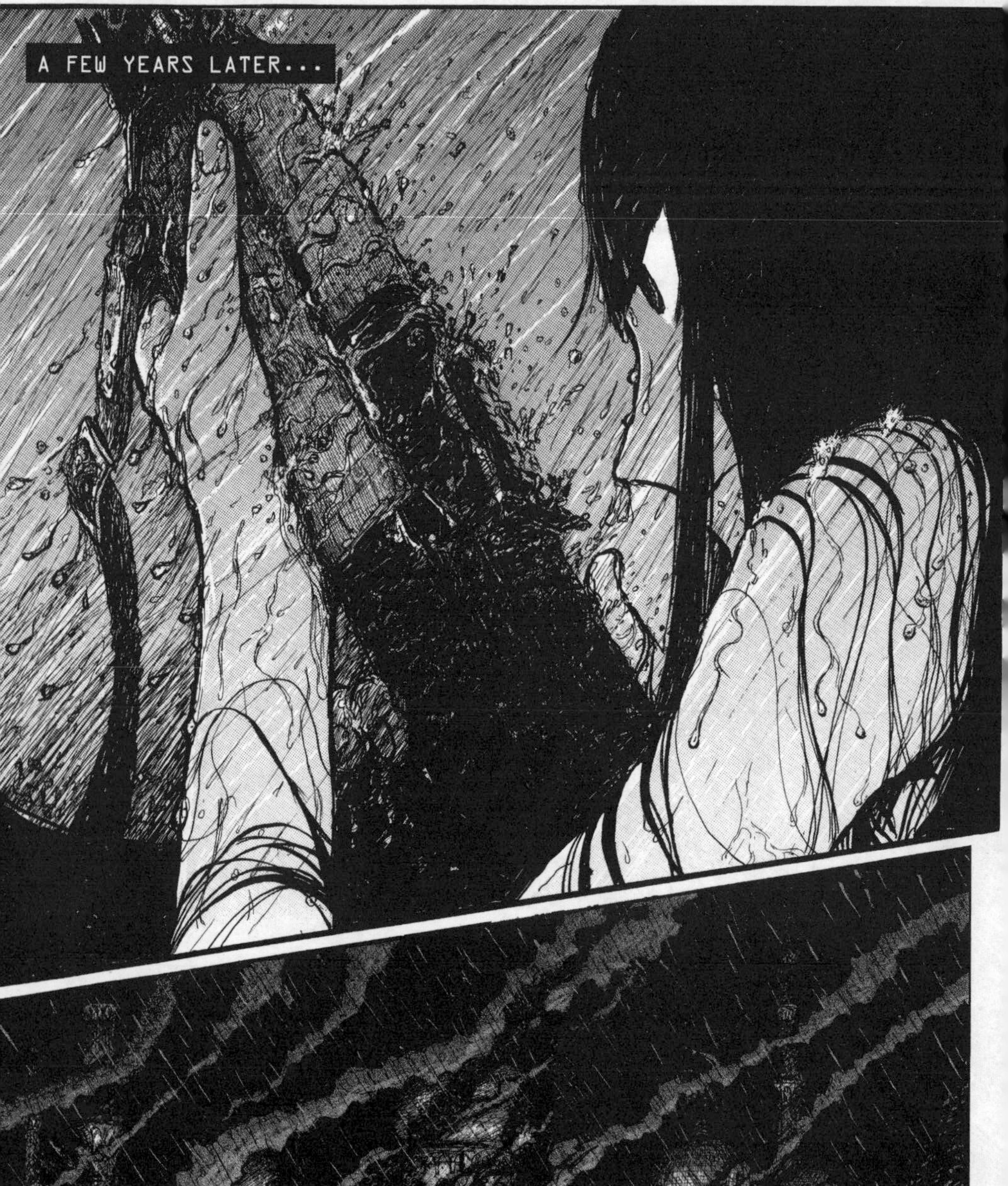
A FEW YEARS LATER...
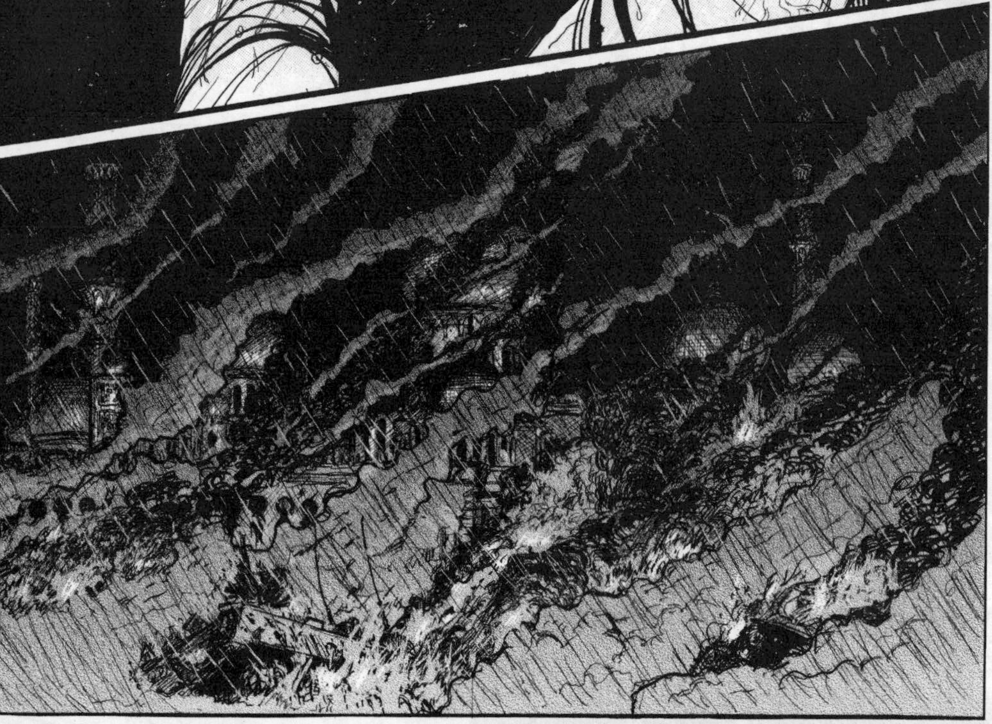

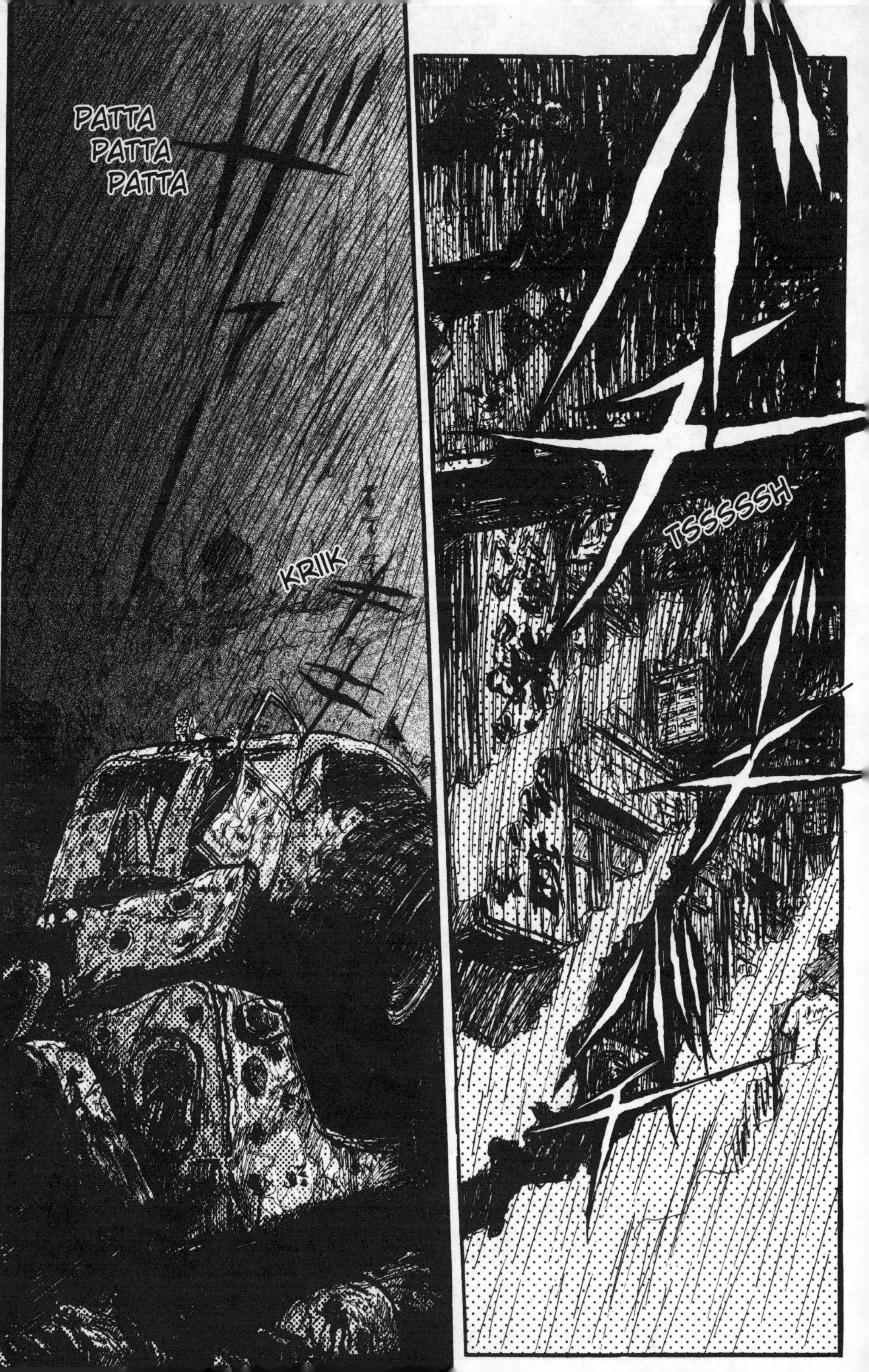
TSSSSSH
PATTA
PATTA
PATTA
KRIIK

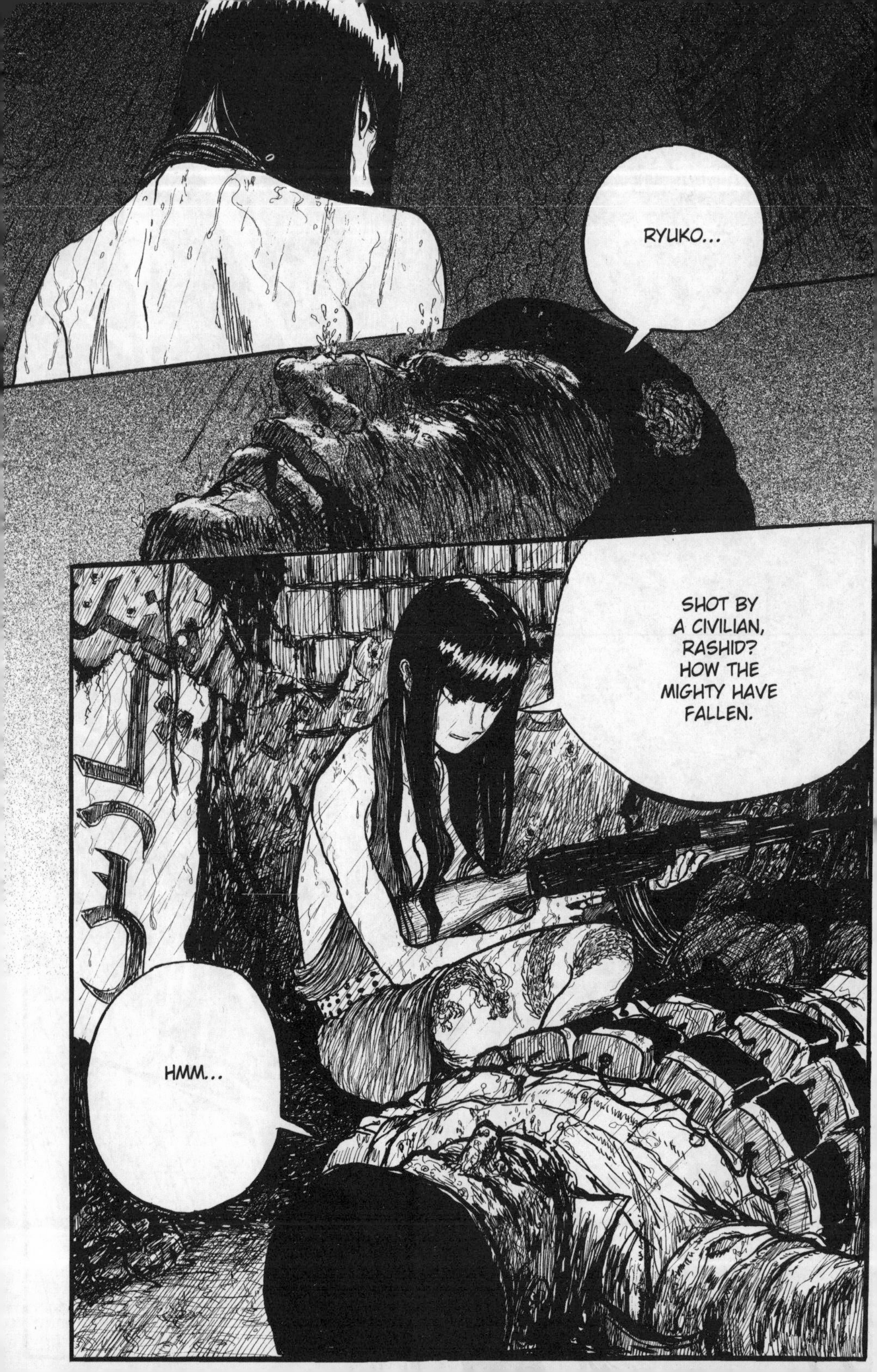
RYUKO...
SHOT BY A CIVILIAN, RASHID? HOW THE MIGHTY HAVE FALLEN.
HMM...

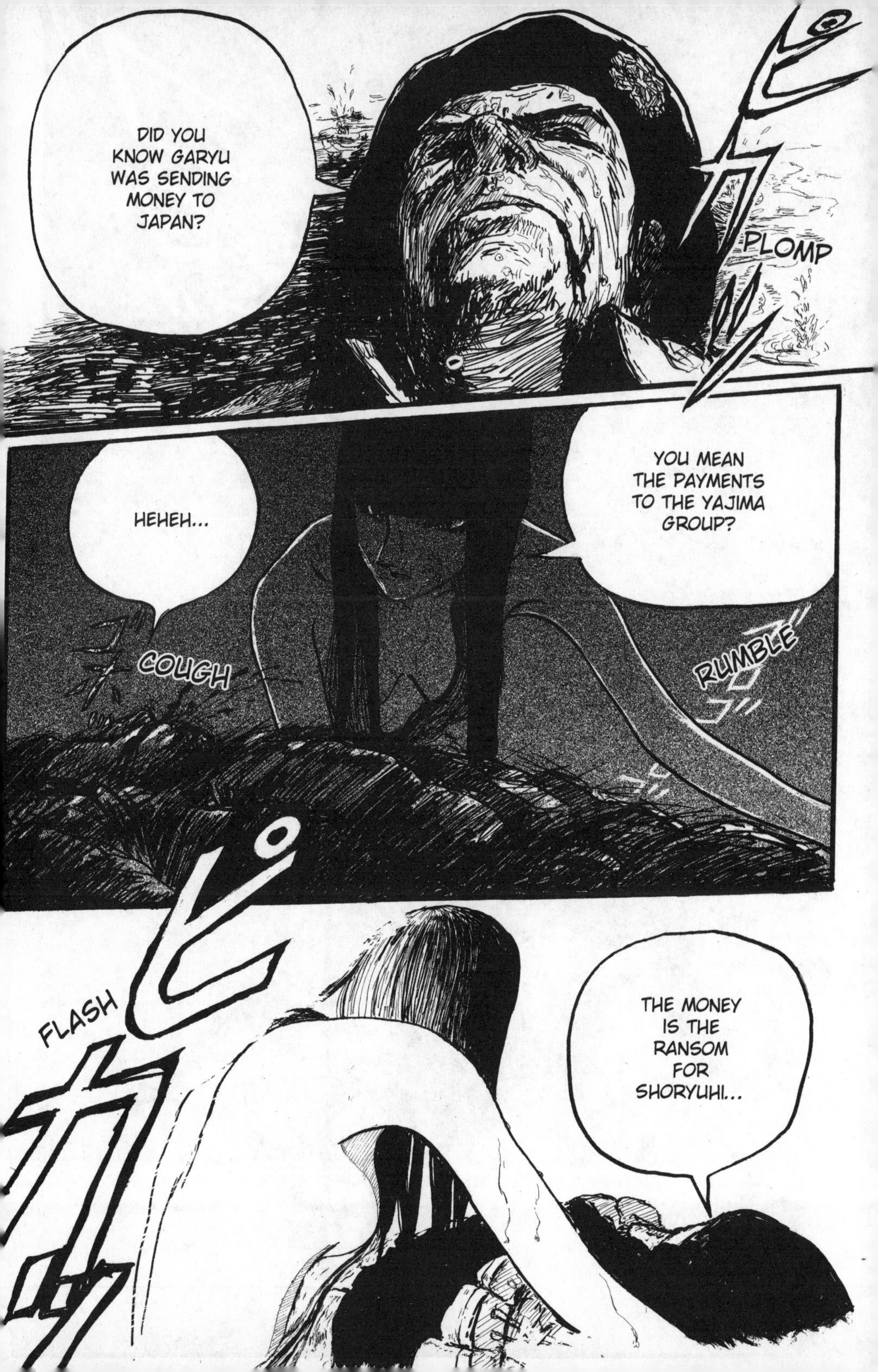
DID YOU KNOW GARYU WAS SENDING MONEY TO JAPAN?
PLOMP
YOU MEAN THE PAYMENTS TO THE YAJIMA GROUP?
HEHEH...
RUMBLE
COUGH
THE MONEY IS THE RANSOM FOR SHORYUHI...
FLASH

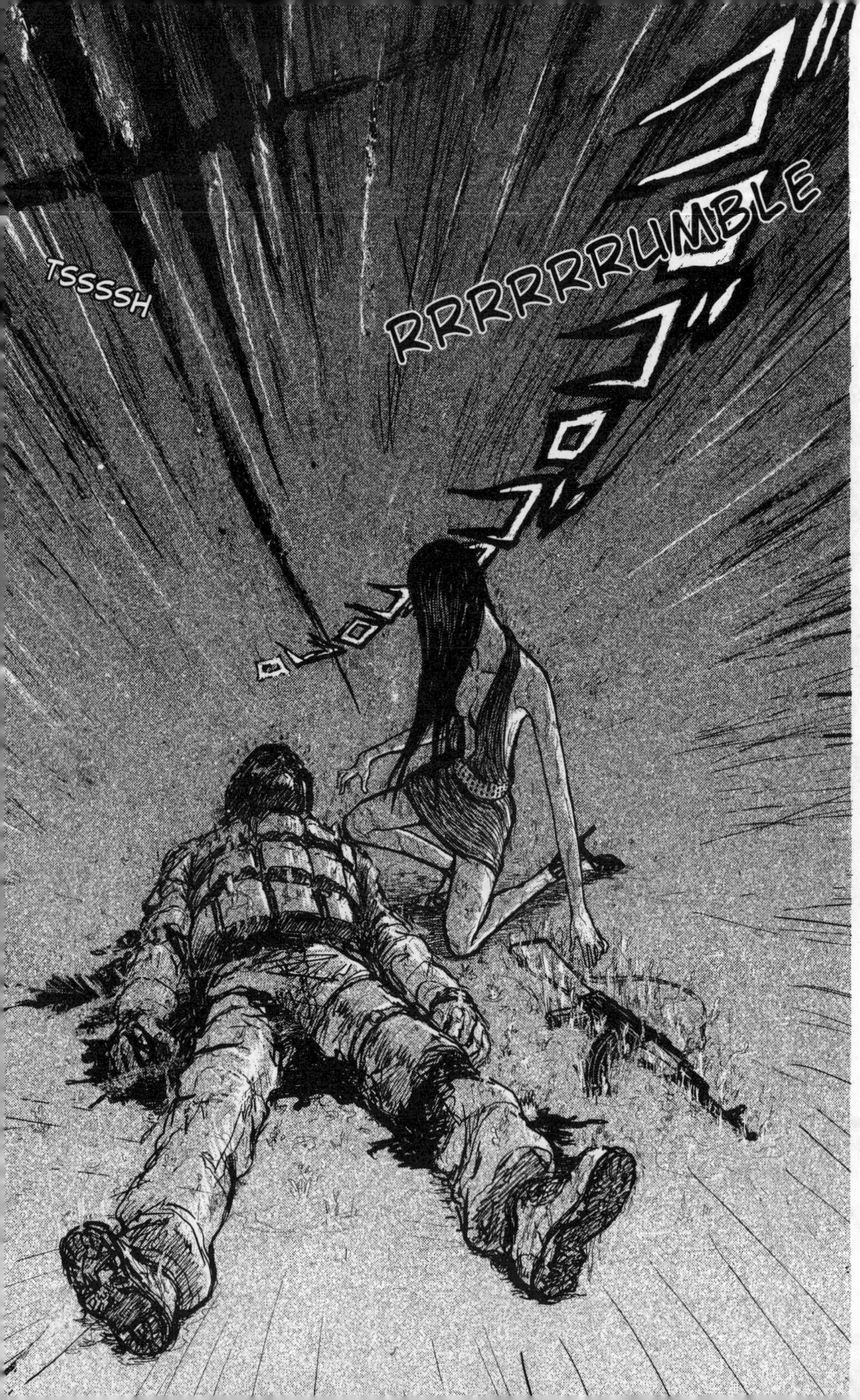
RRRRRRUMBLE
TSSSSH

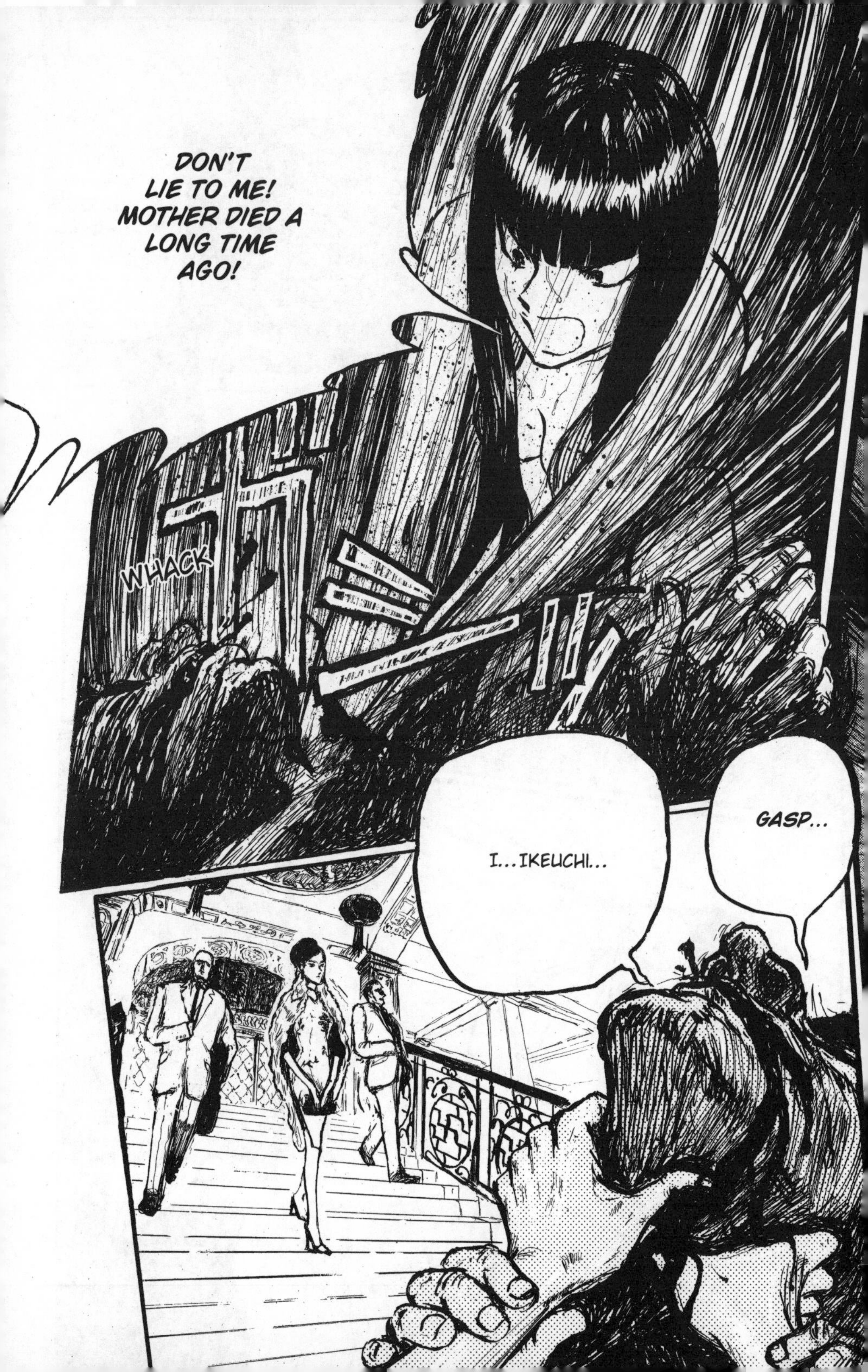
DON'T LIE TO ME! MOTHER DIED A LONG TIME AGO!
WHACK
GASP...
I...IKEUCHI...

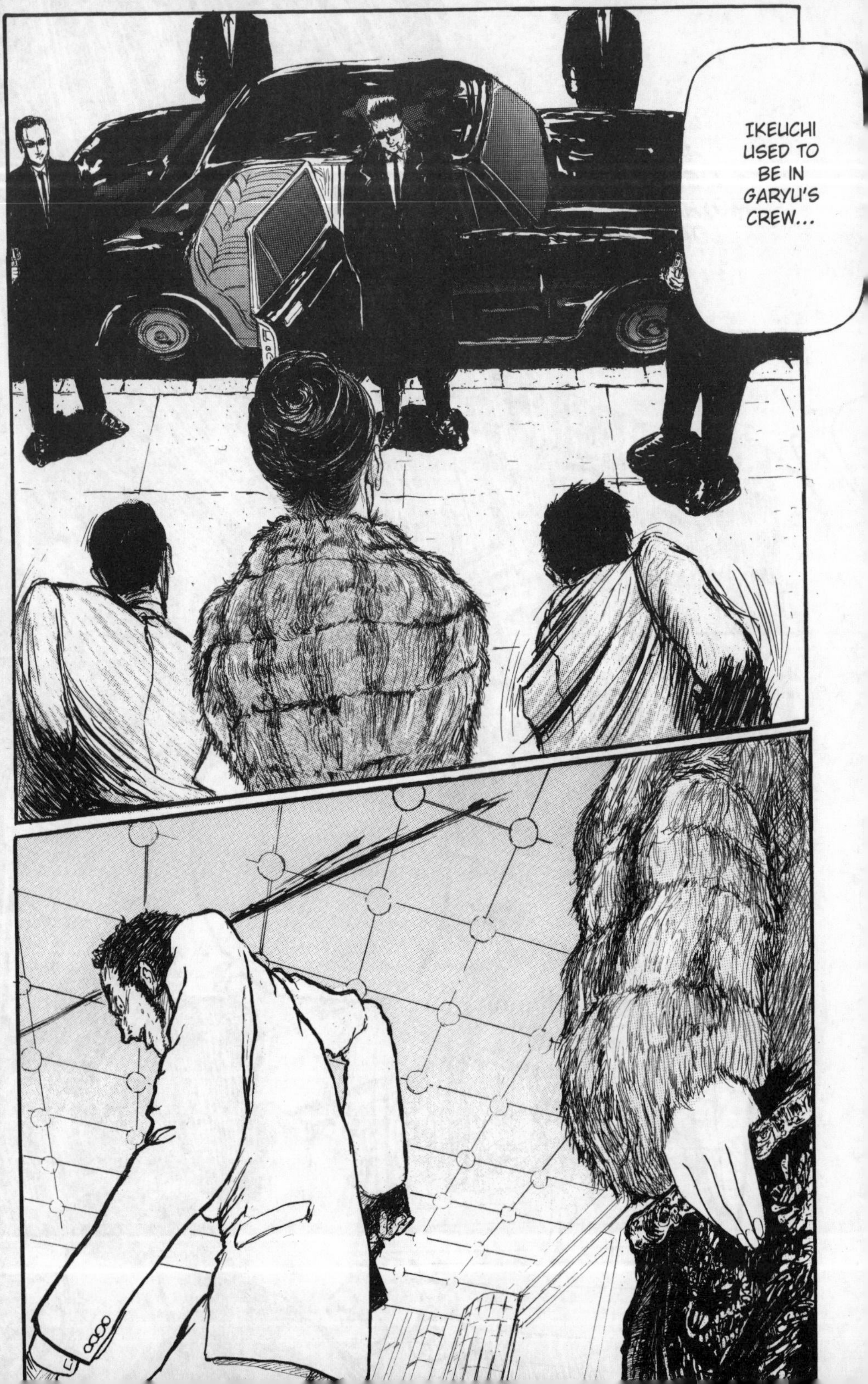
IKEUCHI USED TO BE IN GARYU'S CREW...

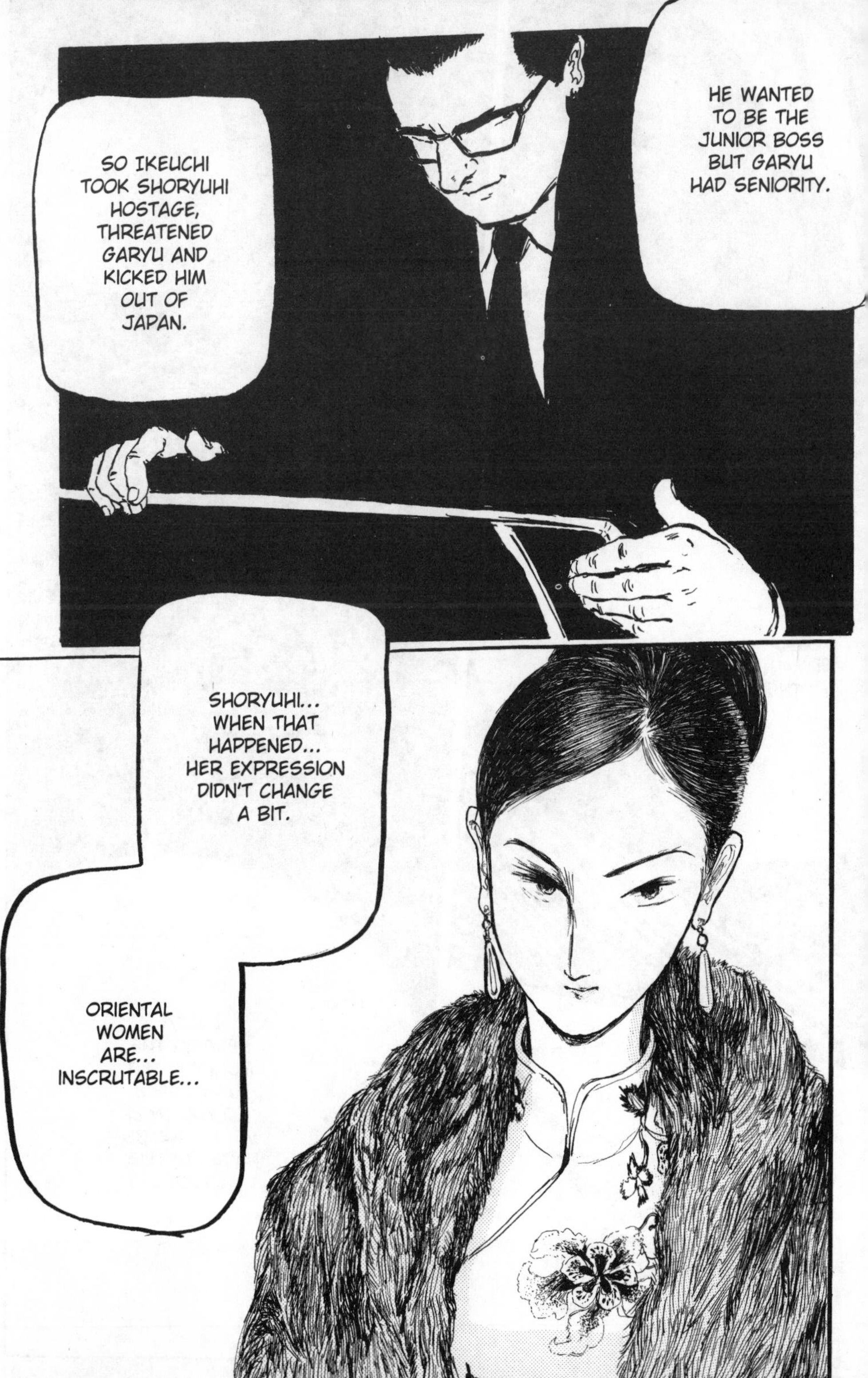
HE WANTED TO BE THE JUNIOR BOSS BUT GARYU HAD SENIORITY.
SO IKEUCHI TOOK SHORYUHI HOSTAGE, THREATENED GARYU AND KICKED HIM OUT OF JAPAN.
SHORYUHI... WHEN THAT HAPPENED... HER EXPRESSION DIDN'T CHANGE A BIT.
ORIENTAL WOMEN ARE... INSCRUTABLE...

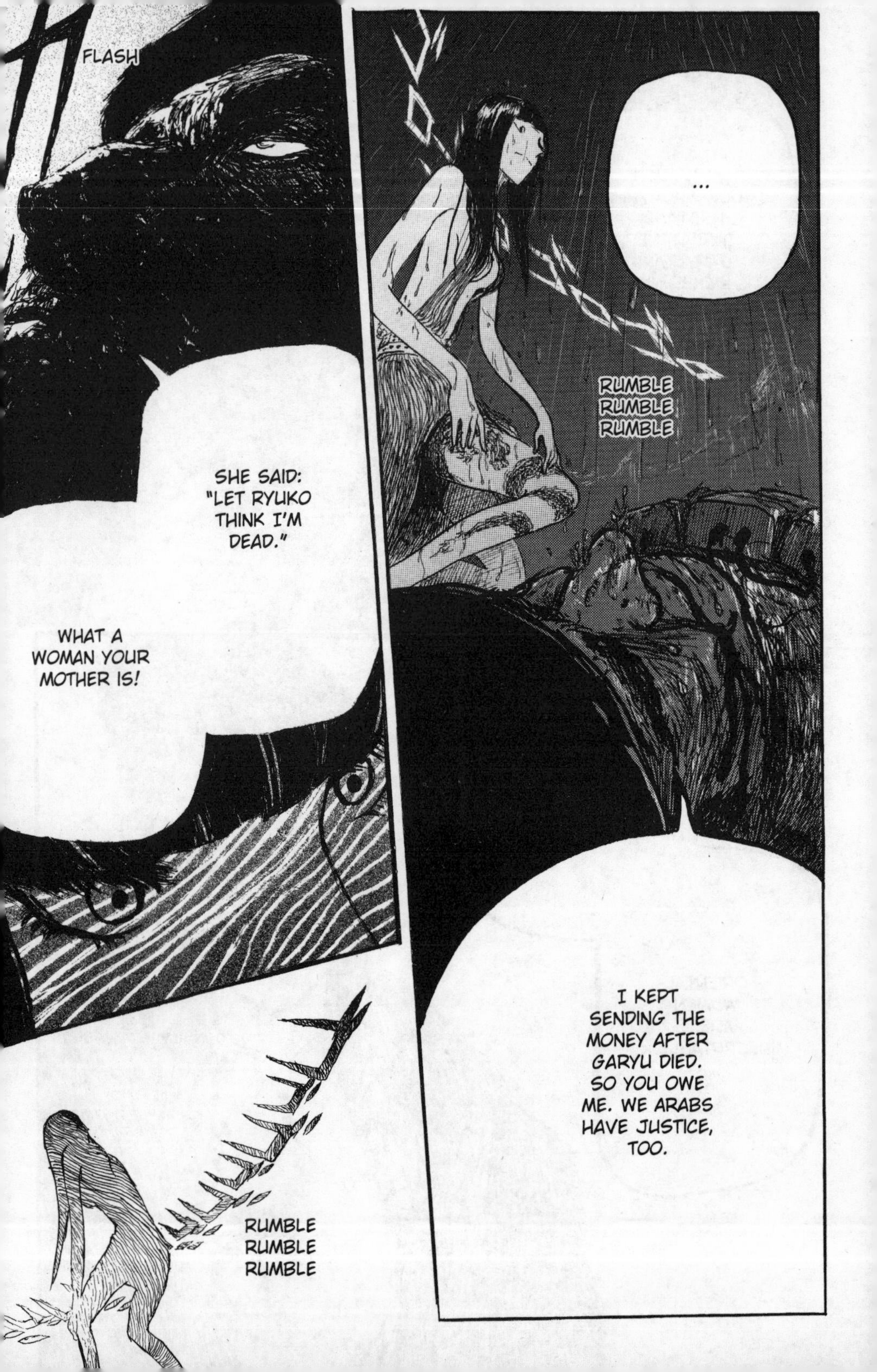
...
RUMBLE RUMBLE RUMBLE
I KEPT SENDING THE MONEY AFTER GARYU DIED. SO YOU OWE ME. WE ARABS HAVE JUSTICE, TOO.
FLASH
SHE SAID: "LET RYUKO THINK I'M DEAD."
WHAT A WOMAN YOUR MOTHER IS!
RUMBLE RUMBLE RUMBLE

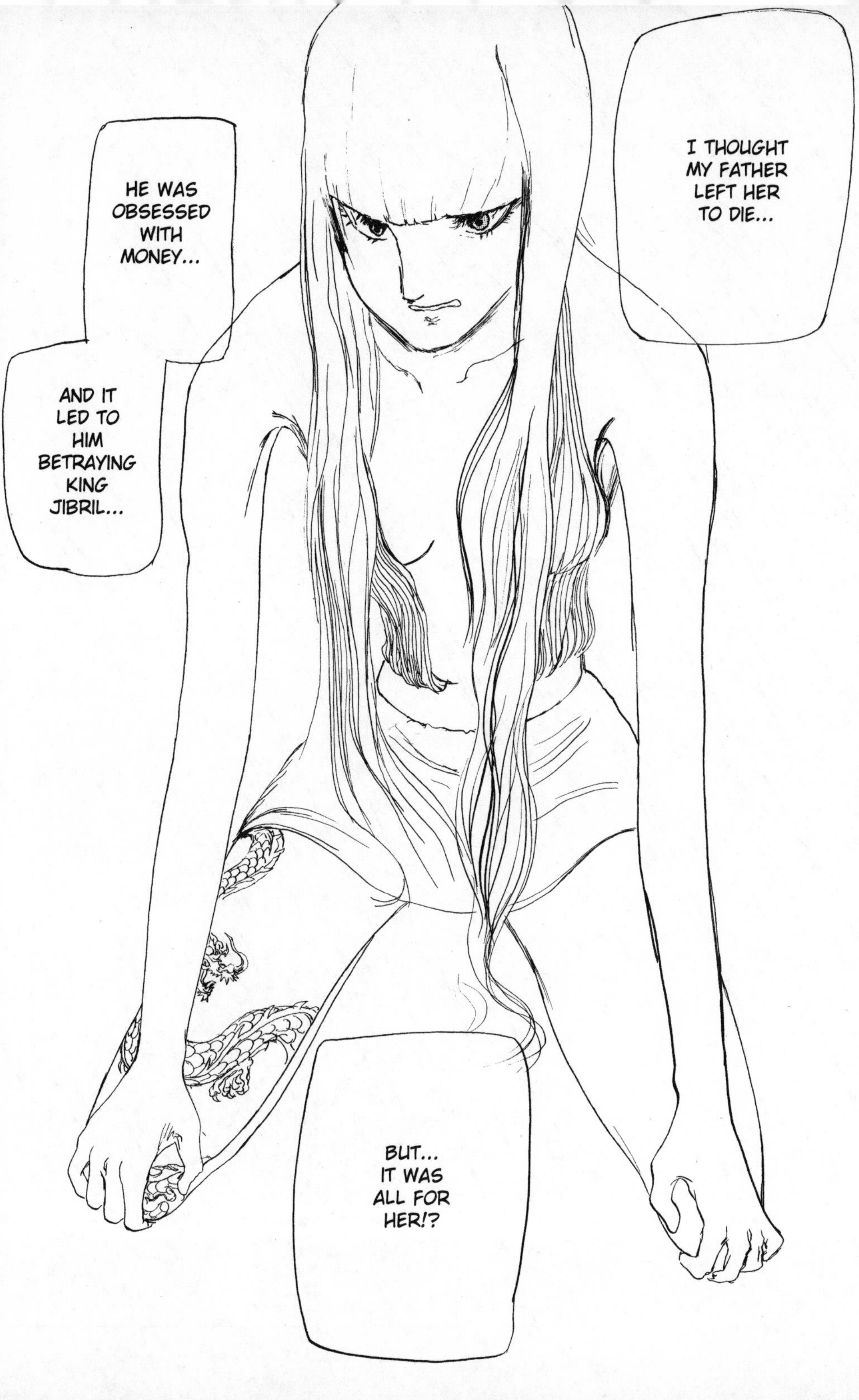
I THOUGHT MY FATHER LEFT HER TO DIE...
HE WAS OBSESSED WITH MONEY...
AND IT LED TO HIM BETRAYING KING JIBRIL...
BUT... IT WAS ALL FOR HER!?

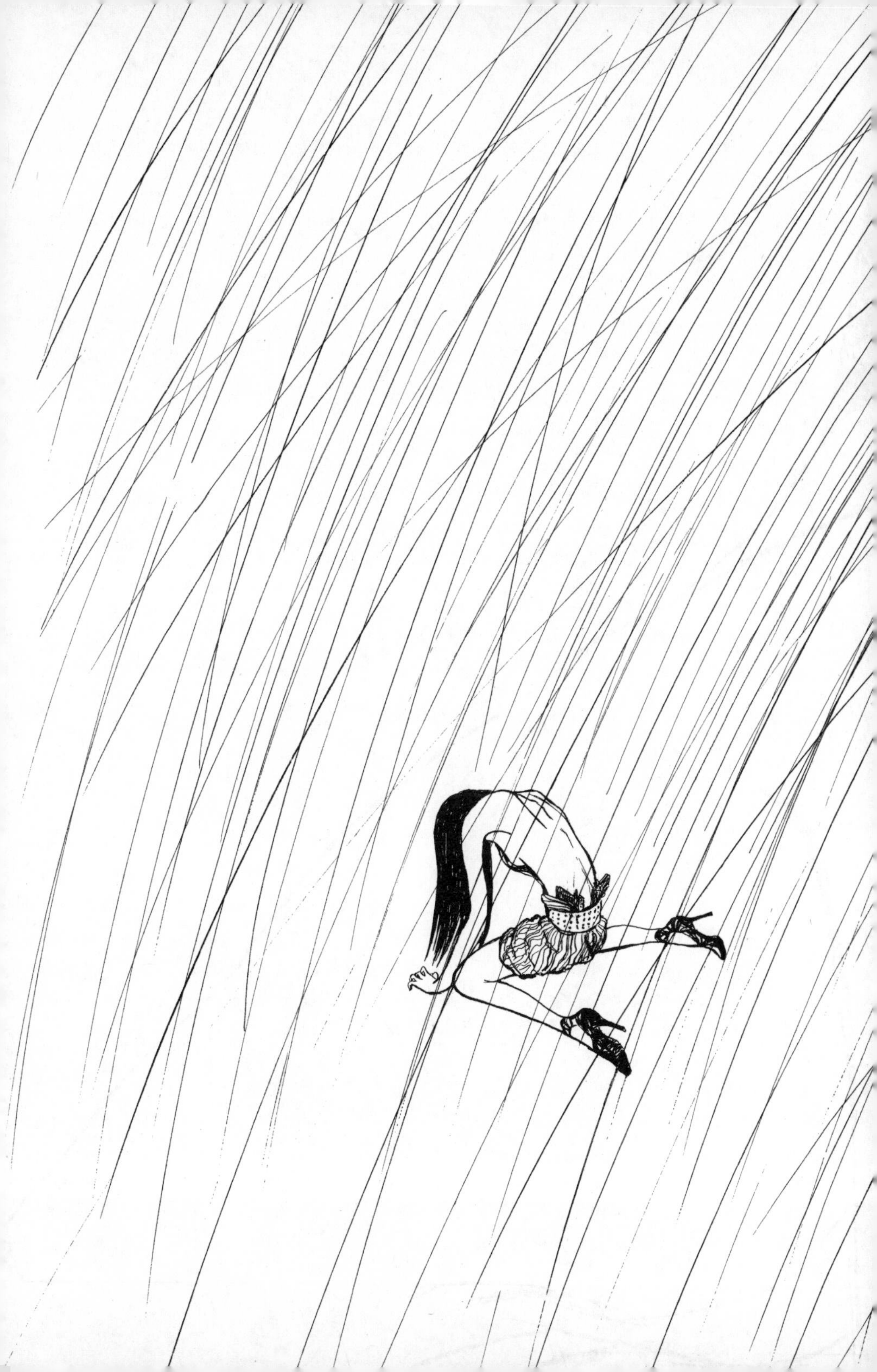

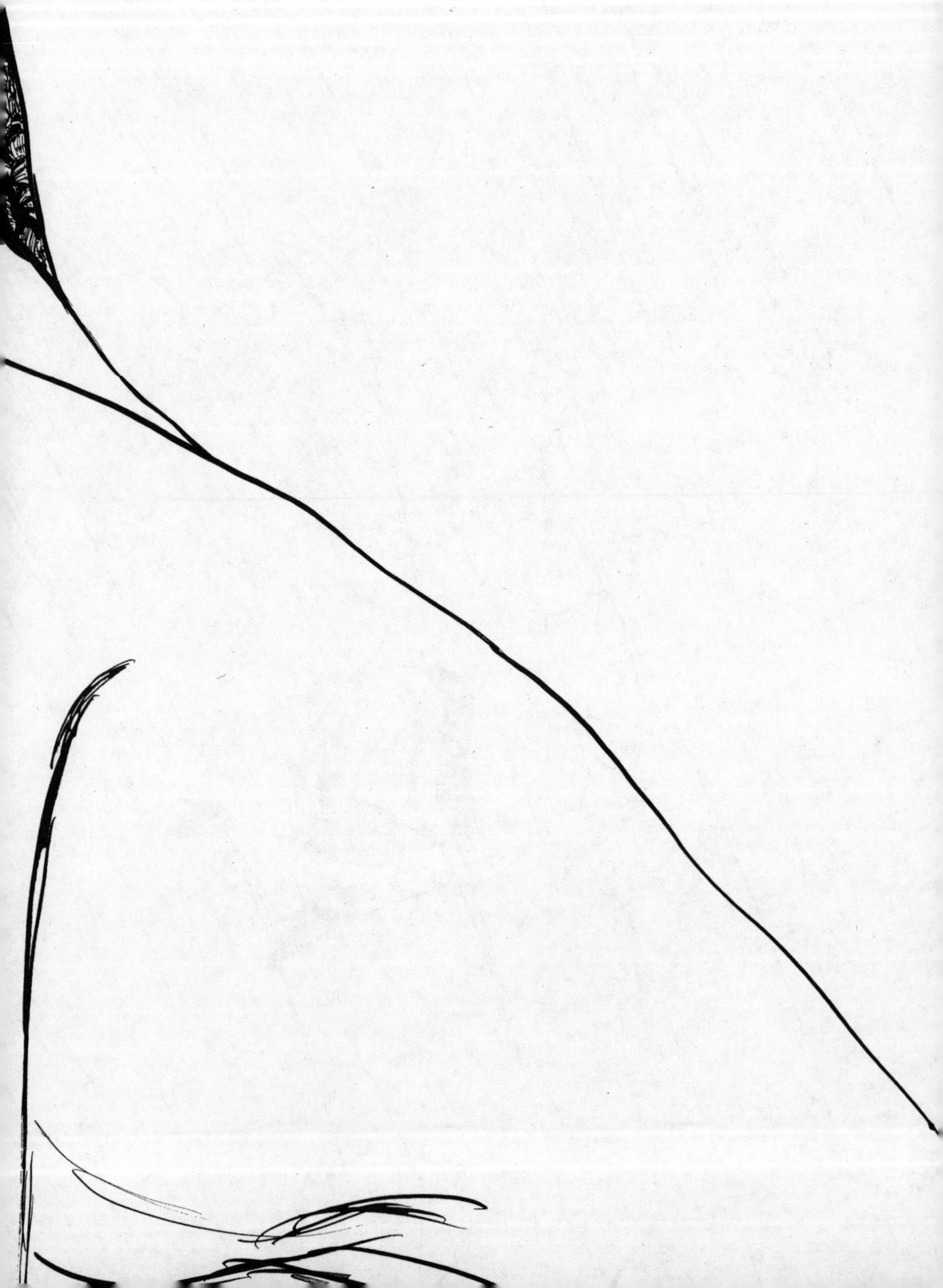

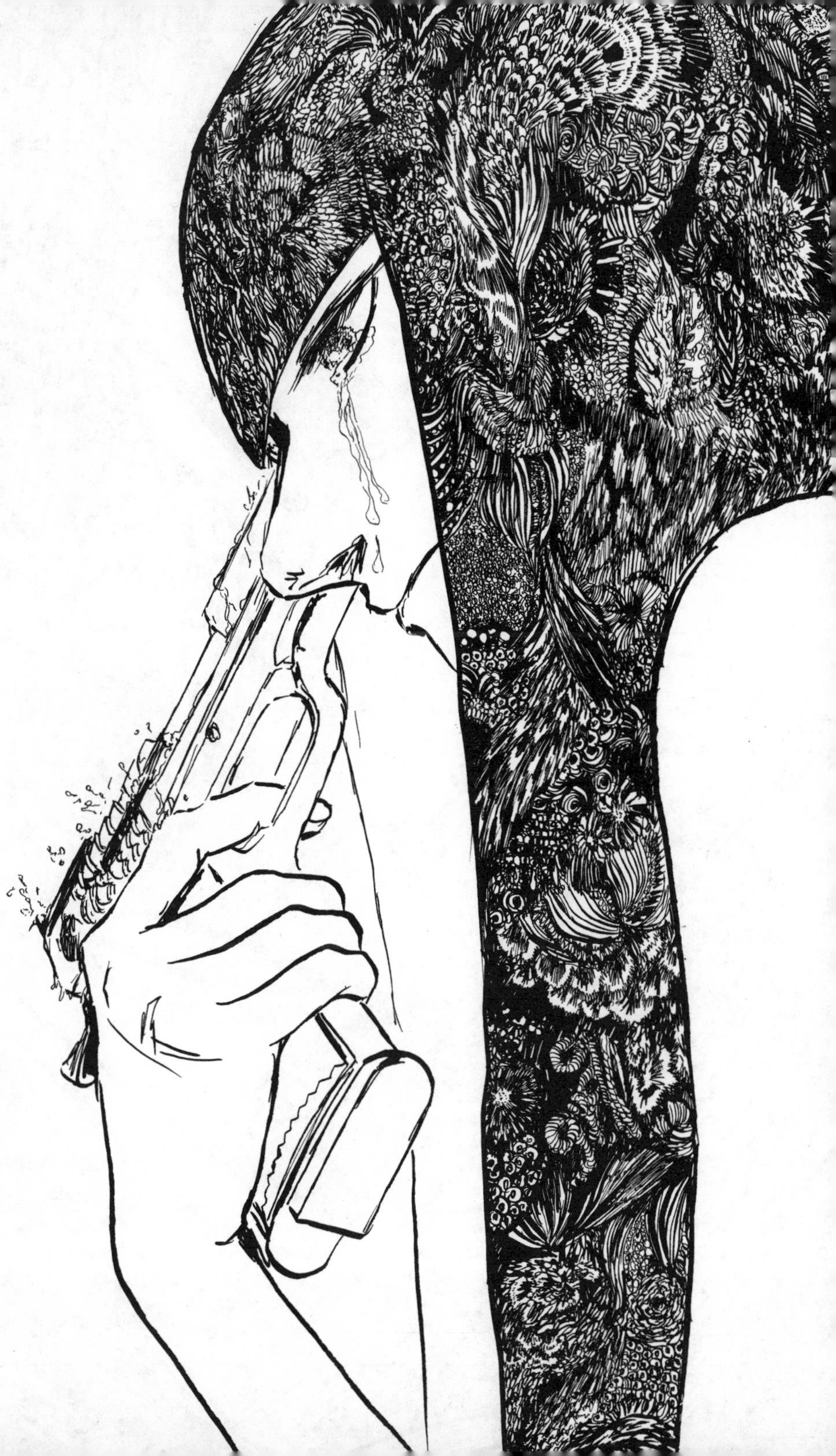

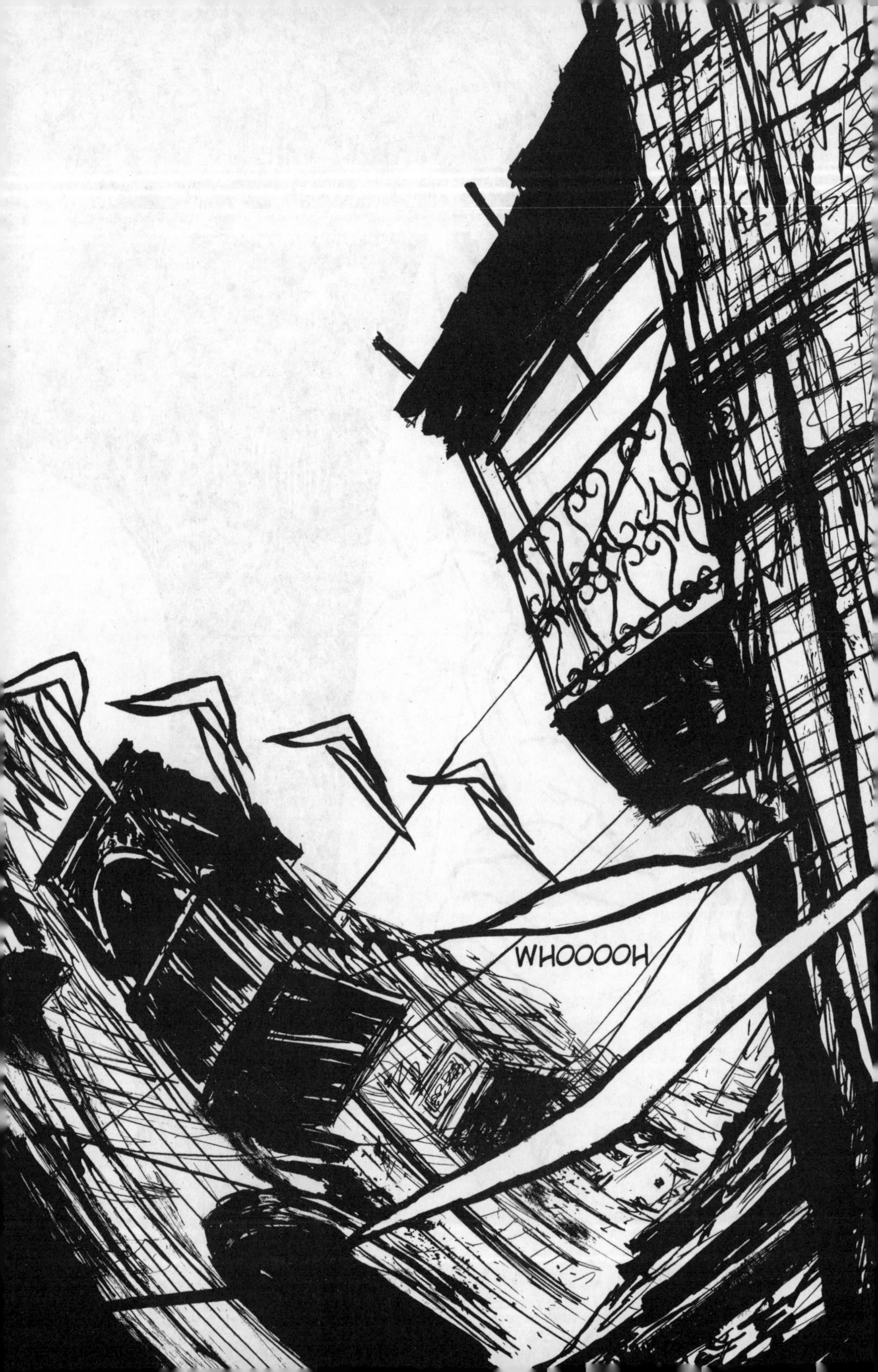
WHOOOOH

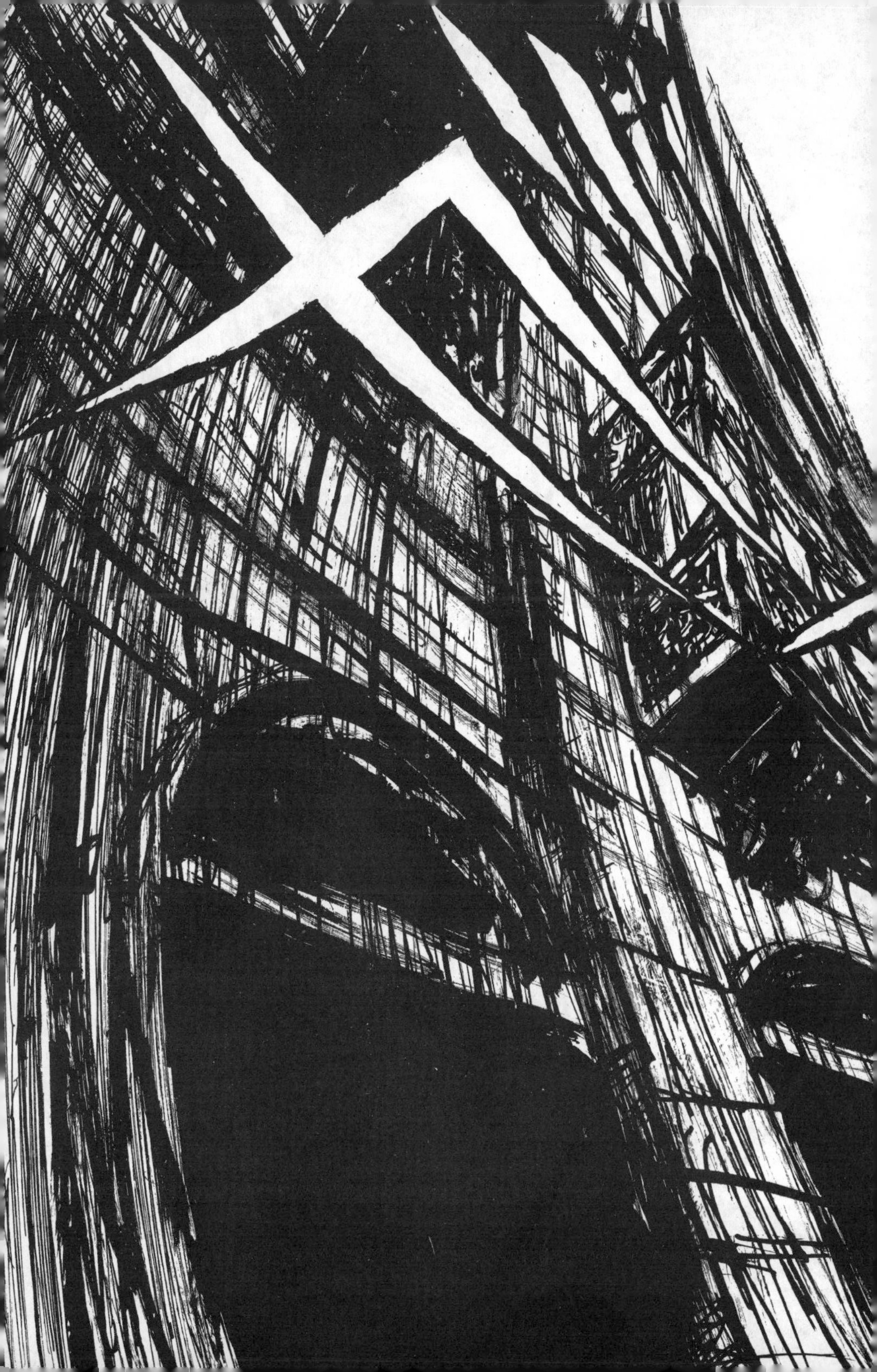

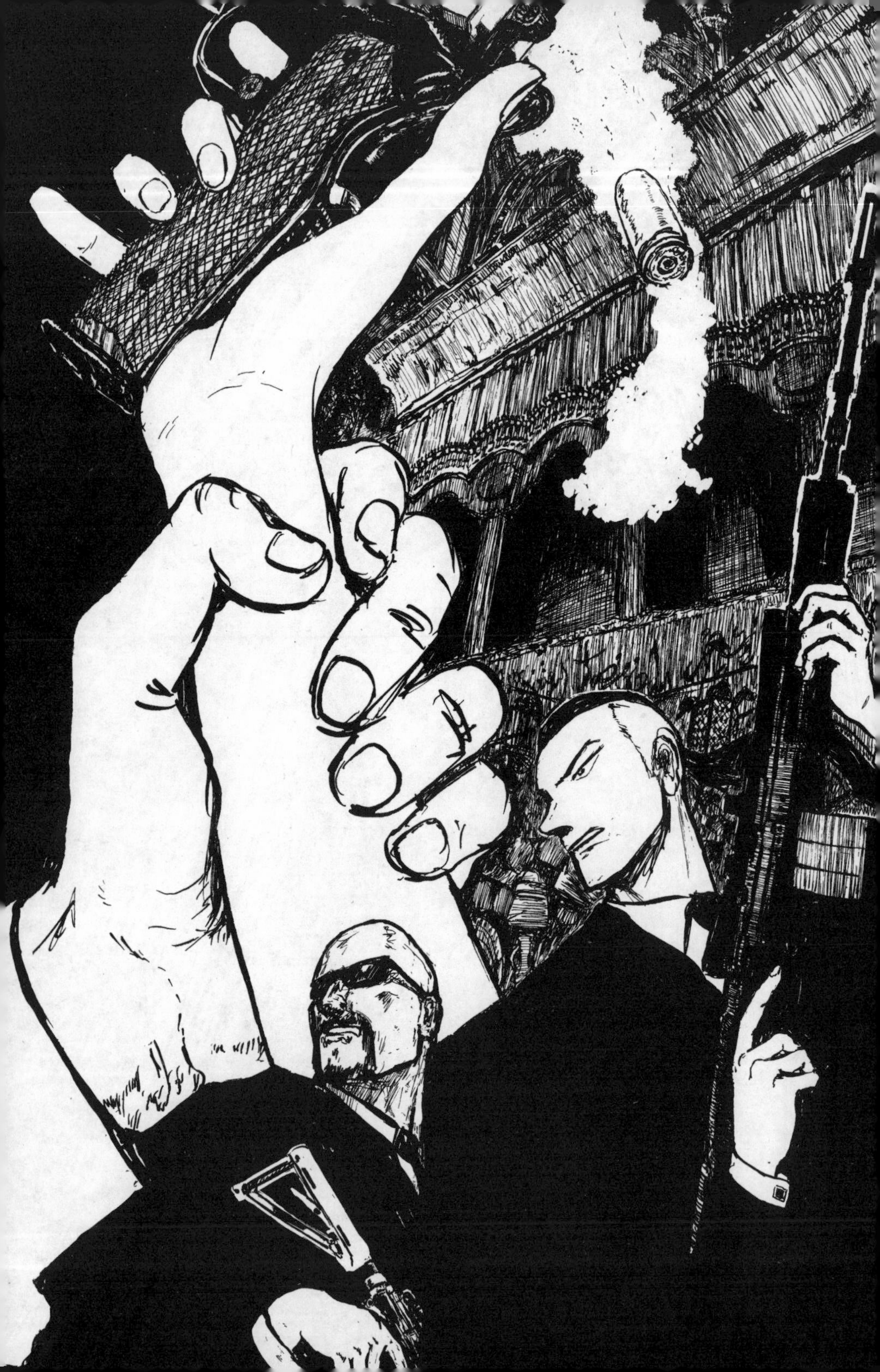

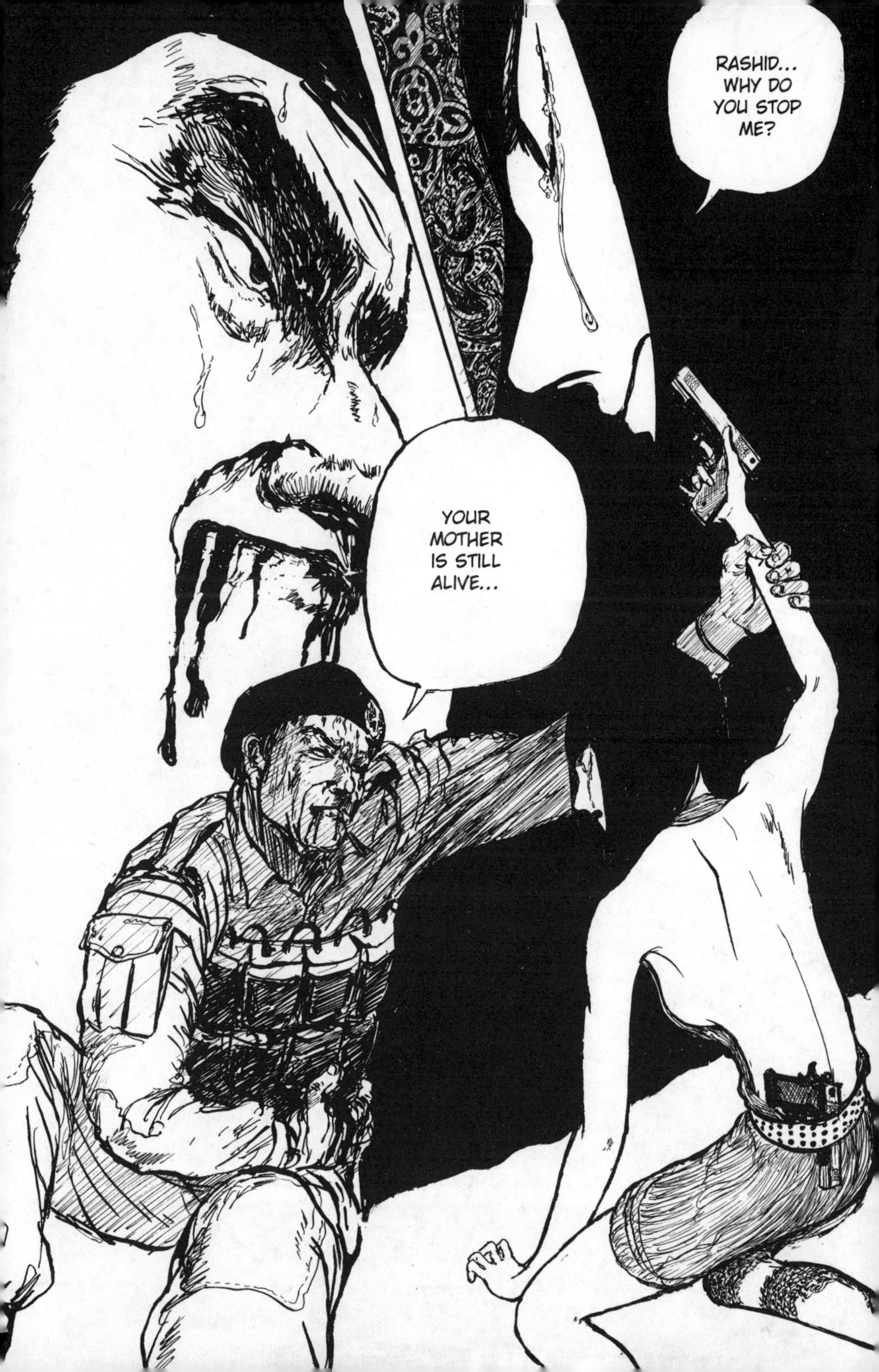
RASHID... WHY DO YOU STOP ME?
YOUR MOTHER IS STILL ALIVE...

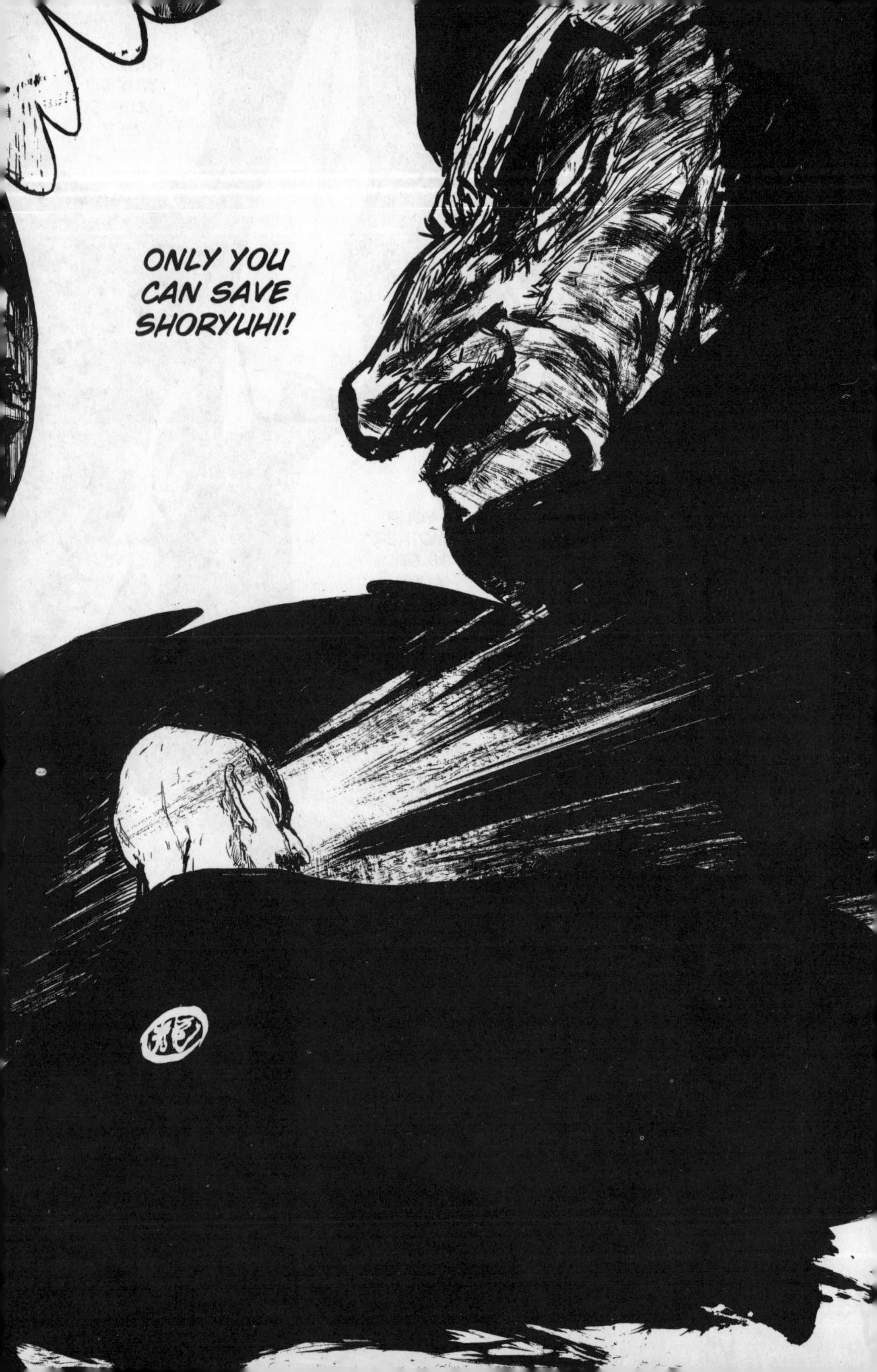
ONLY YOU CAN SAVE SHORYUHI!

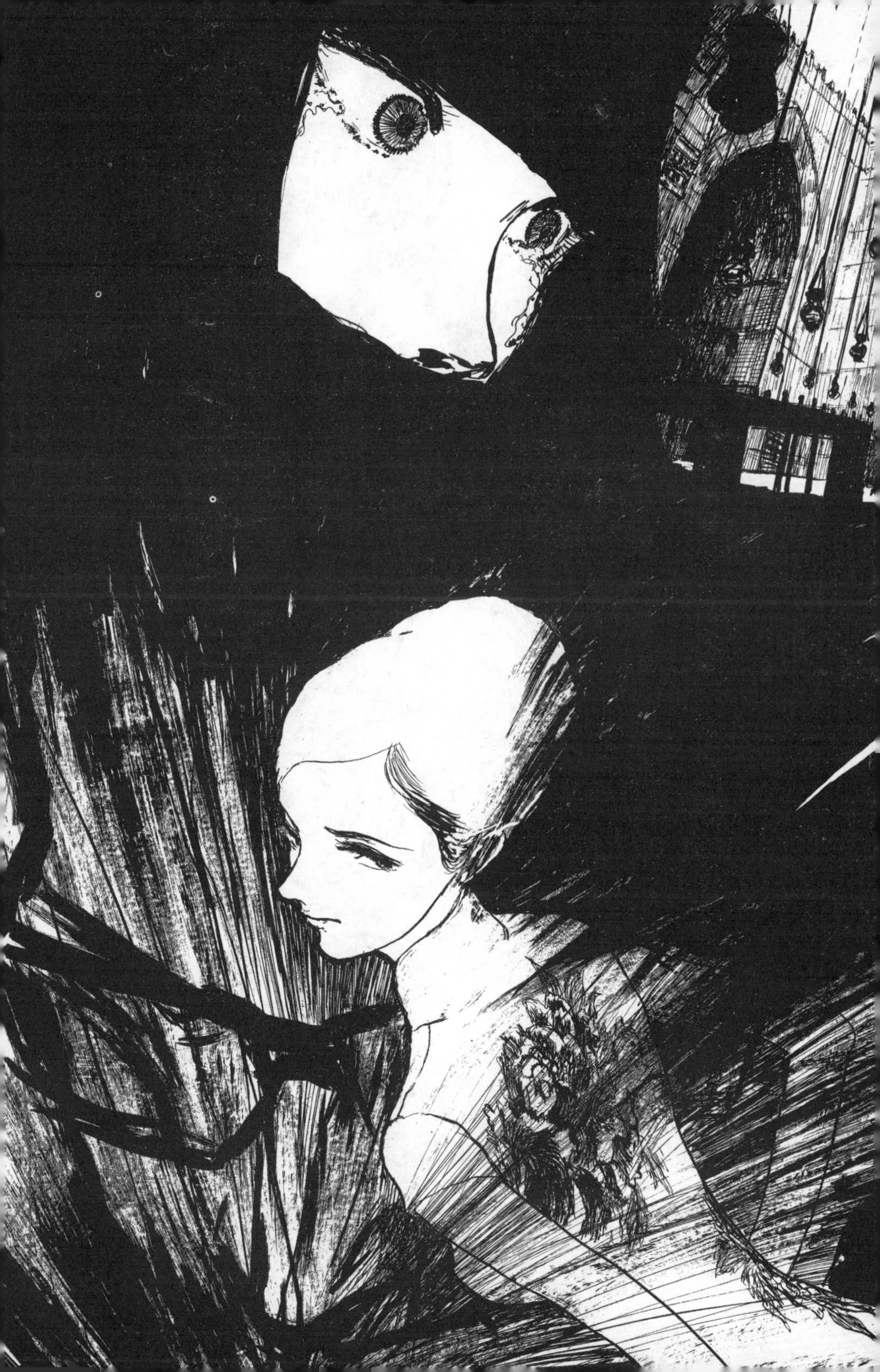

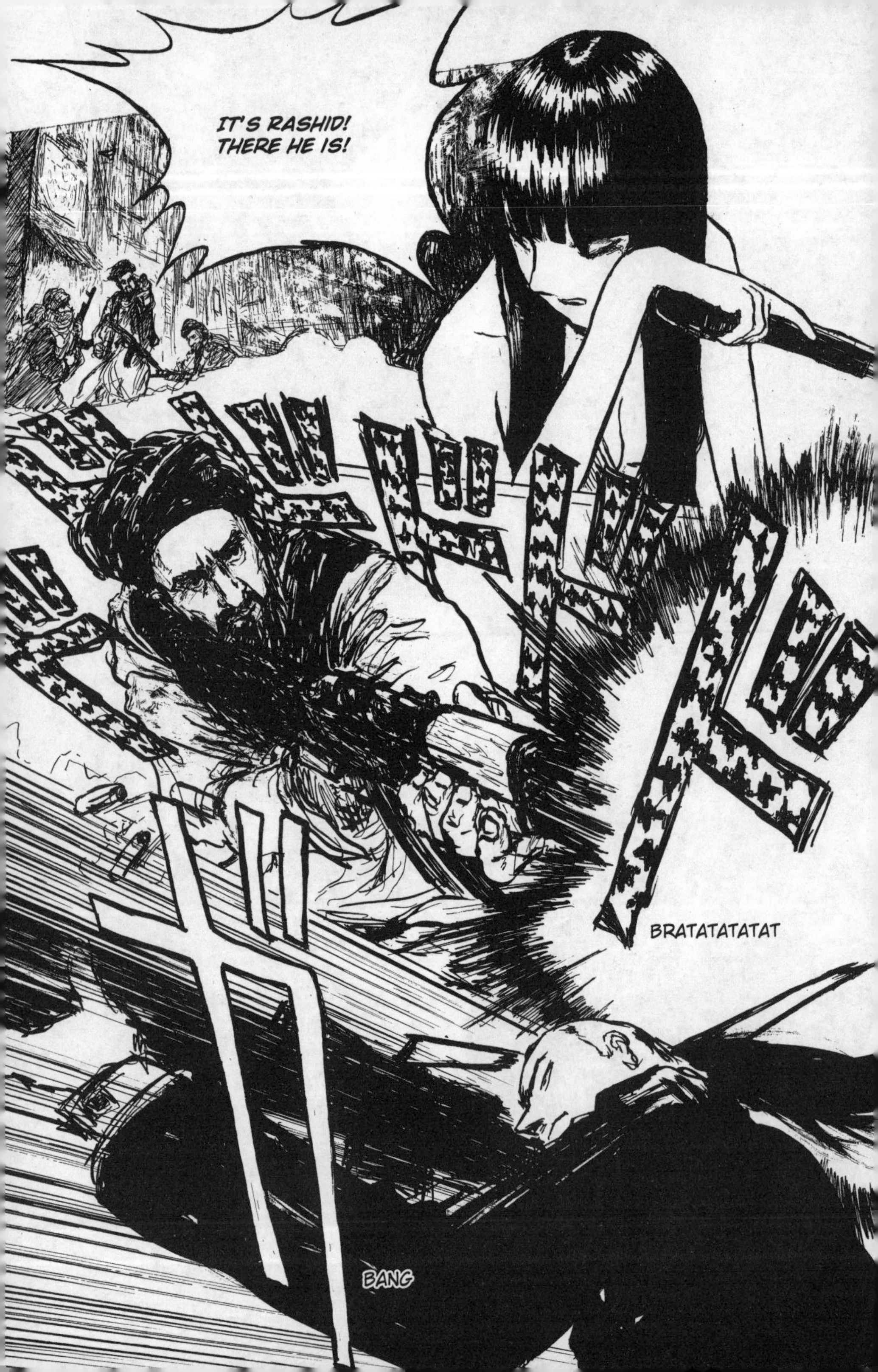
IT'S RASHID! THERE HE IS!
BRATATATATAT
BANG

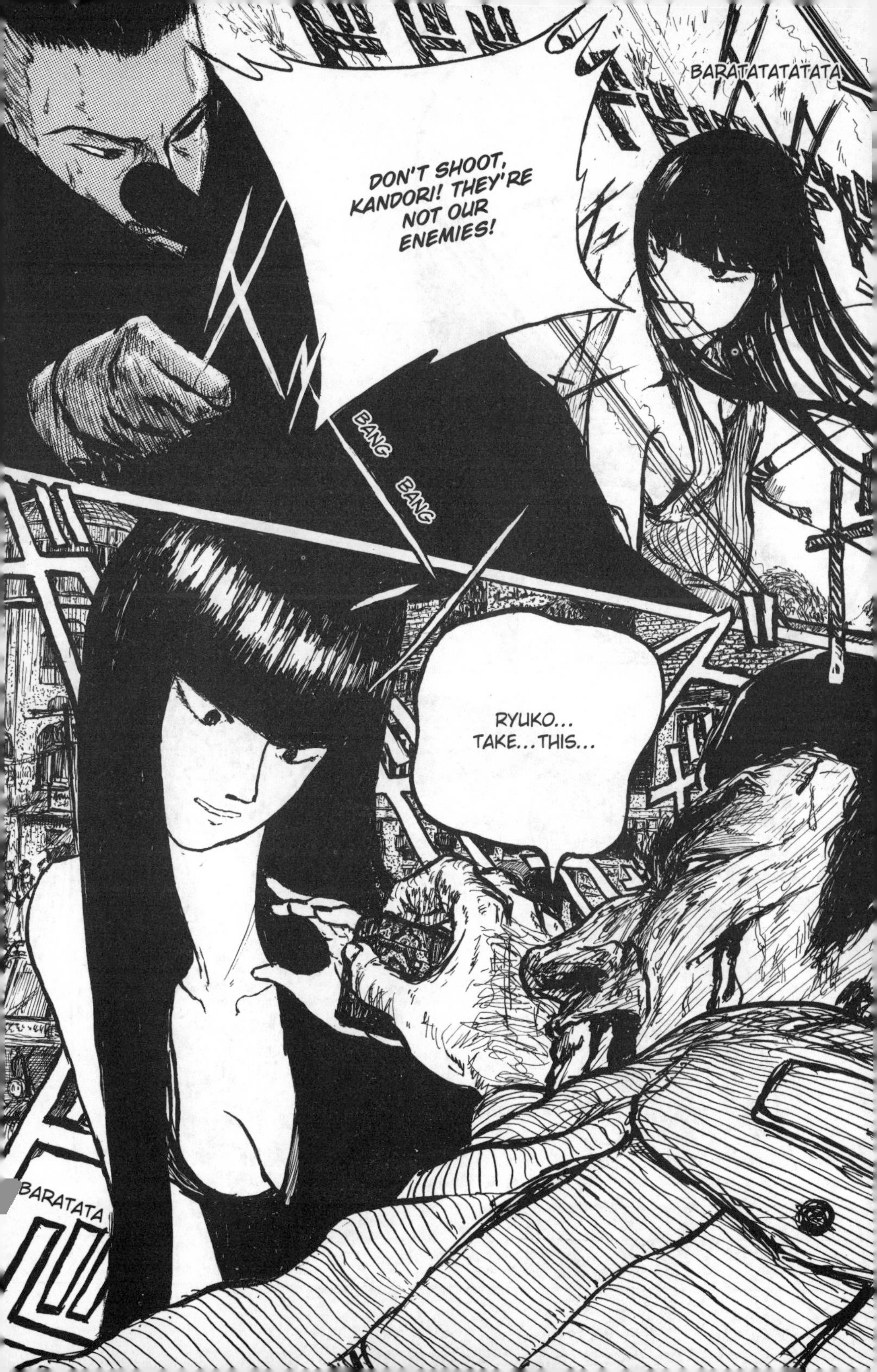
BARATATATATATA
DON'T SHOOT, KANDORI! THEY'RE NOT OUR ENEMIES!
BANG
BANG
RYUKO... TAKE... THIS...
BARATATA

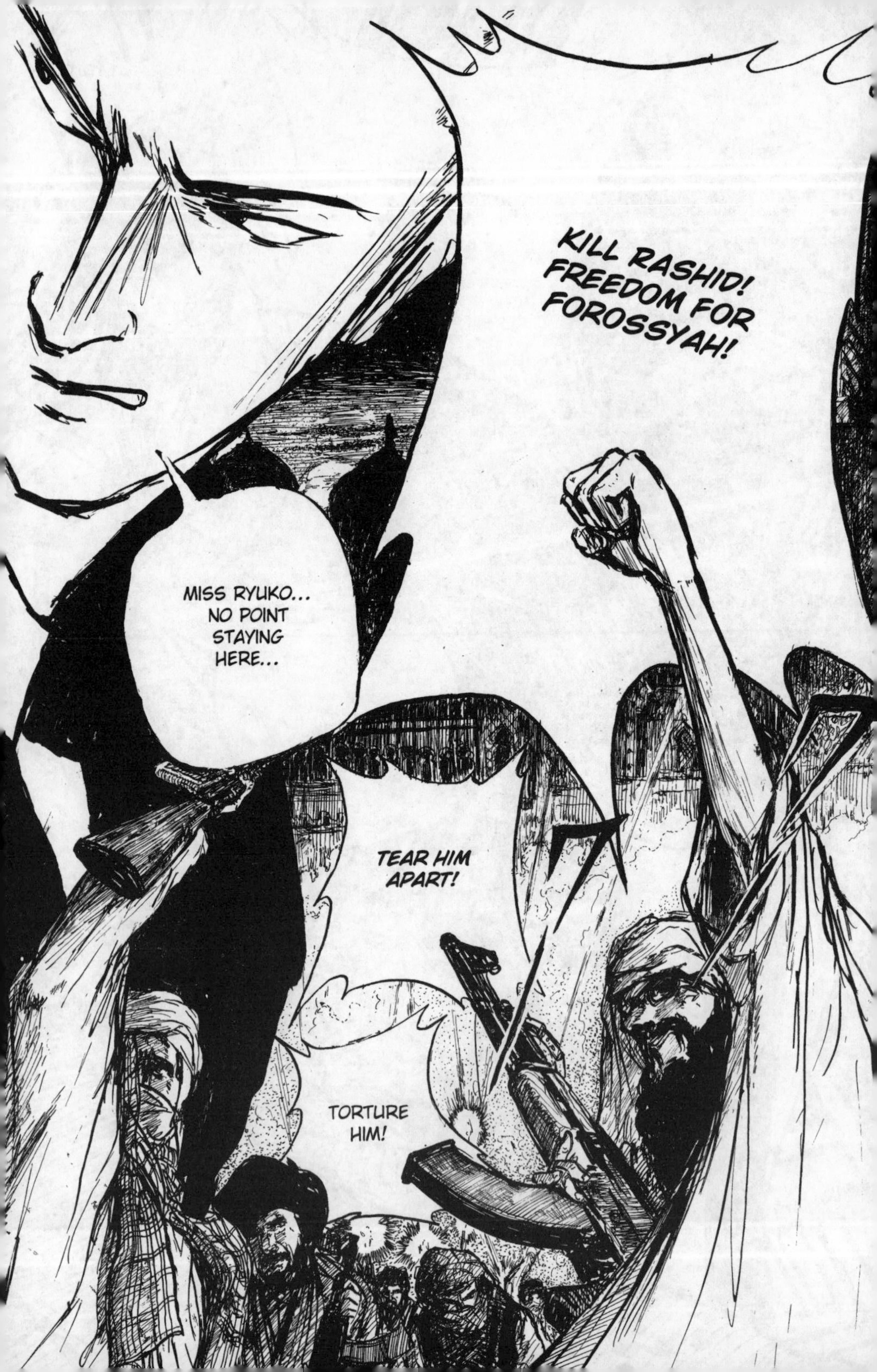
KILL RASHID! FREEDOM FOR FOROSSYAH!
MISS RYUKO... NO POINT STAYING HERE...
TEAR HIM APART!
TORTURE HIM!

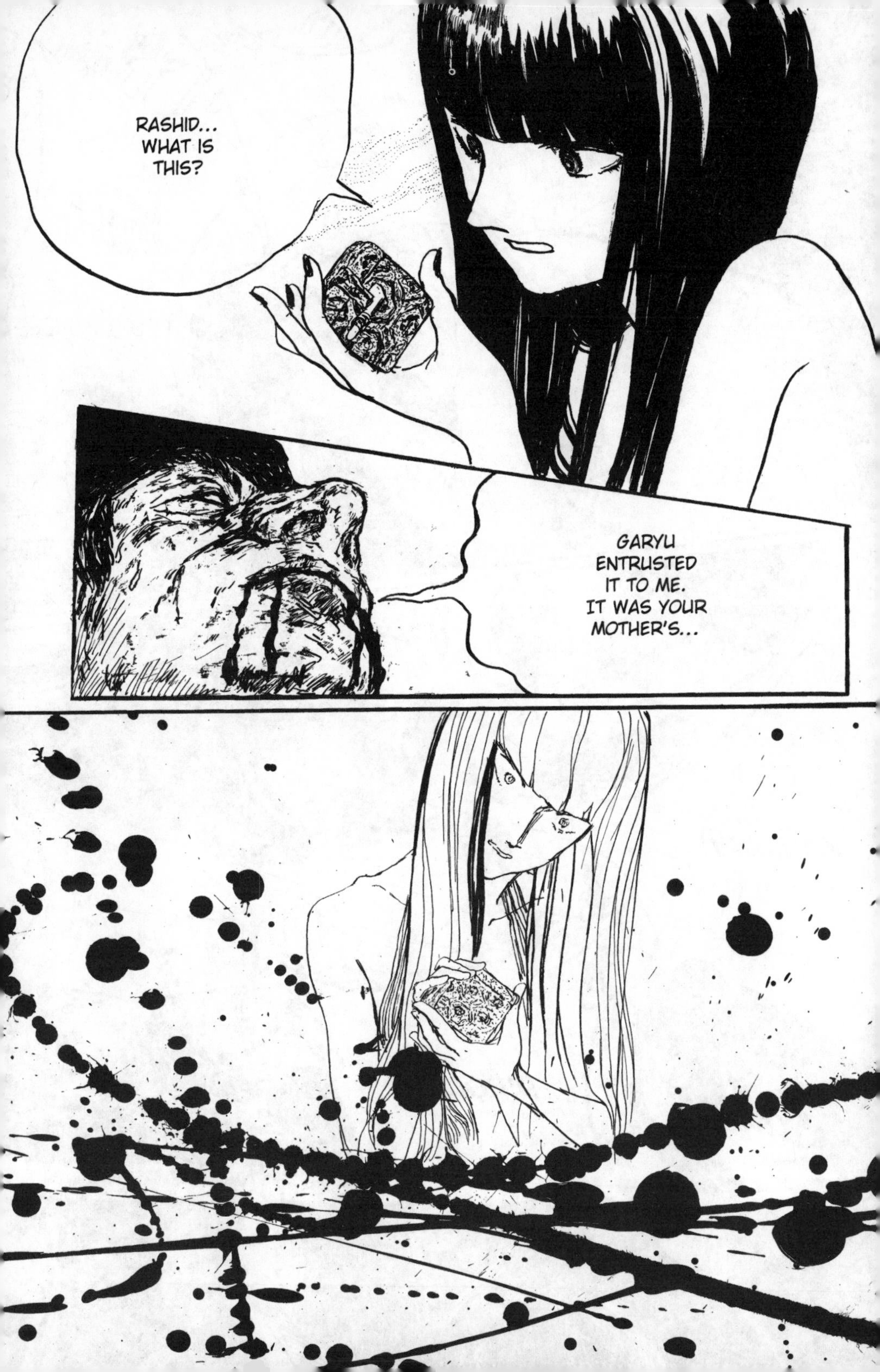
RASHID... WHAT IS THIS?
GARYU ENTRUSTED IT TO ME. IT WAS YOUR MOTHER'S...

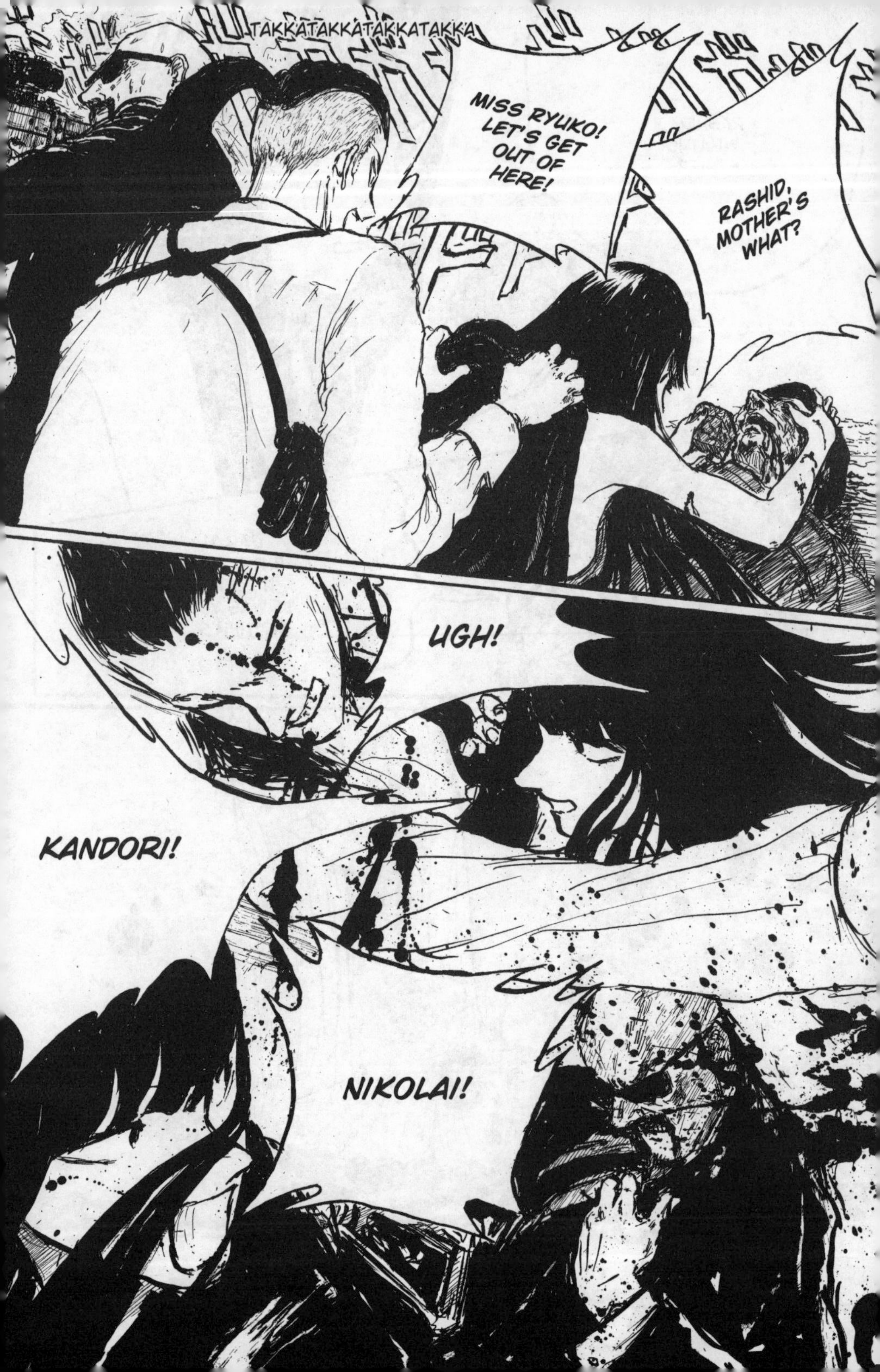
TAKKATAKKATAKKATAKKA
RASHID, MOTHER'S WHAT?
MISS RYUKO! LET'S GET OUT OF HERE!
UGH!
KANDORI!
NIKOLAI!

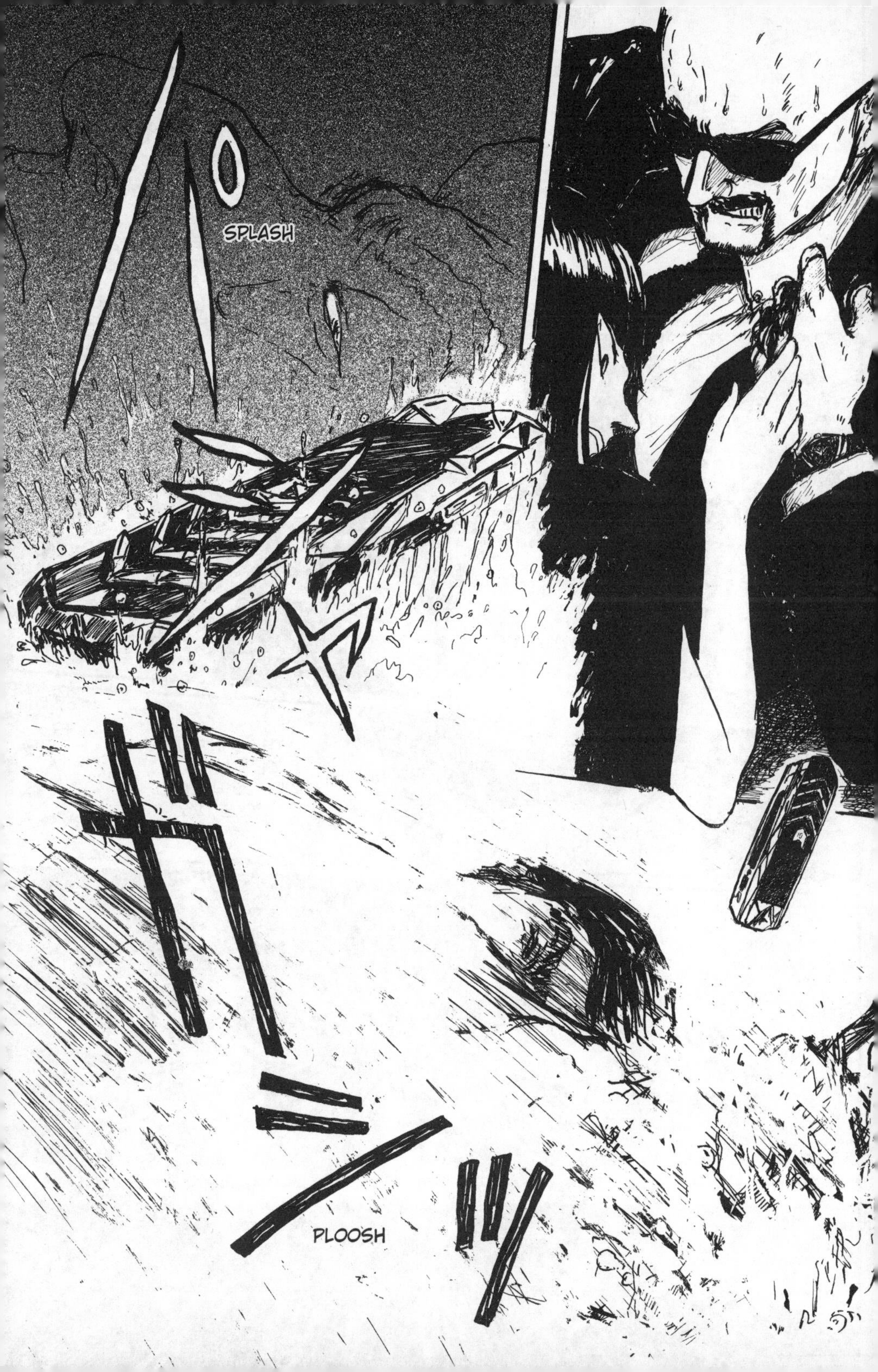
SPLASH
PLOOSH

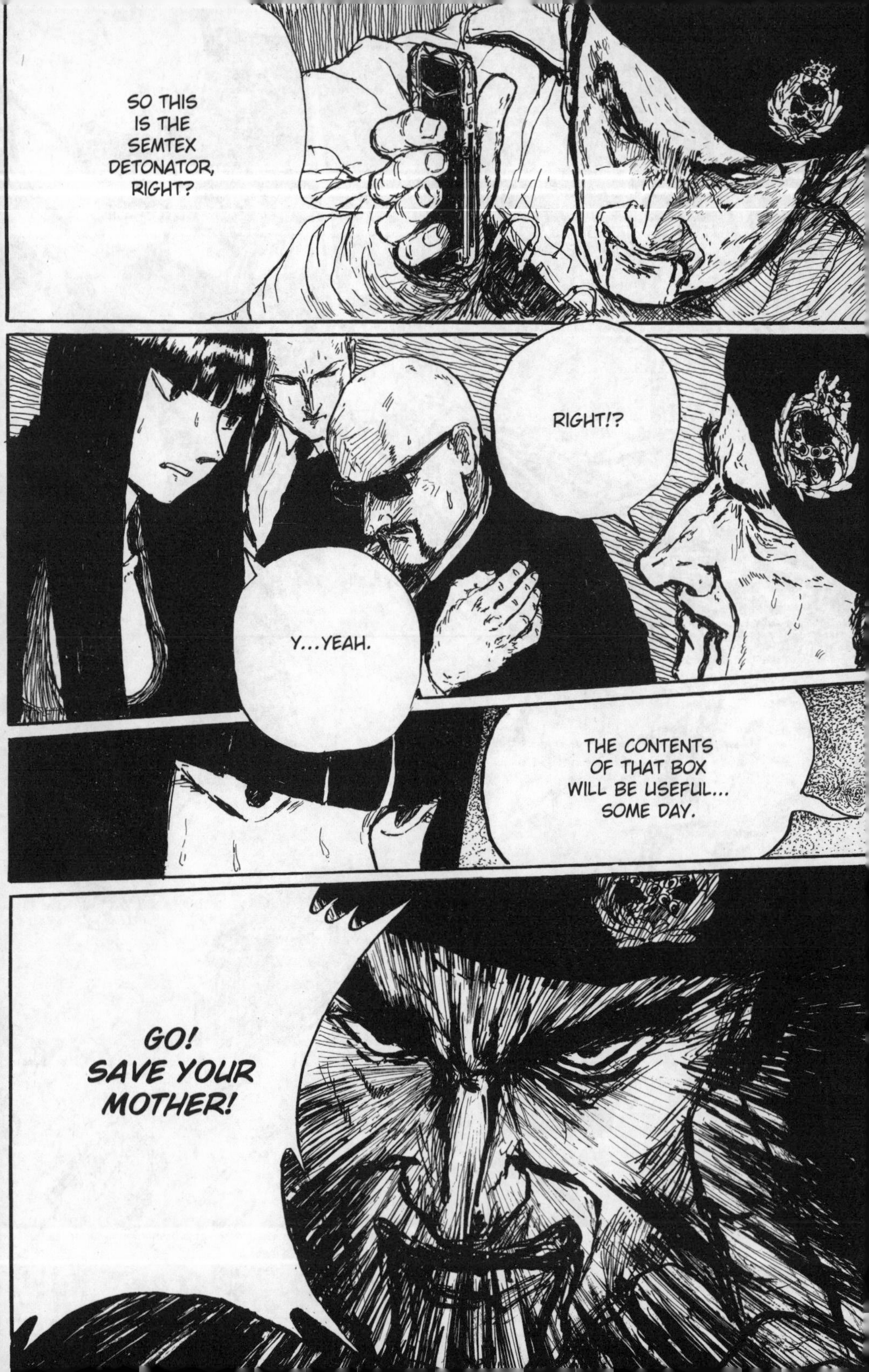
SO THIS IS THE SEMTEX DETONATOR, RIGHT?
RIGHT!?
Y...YEAH.
THE CONTENTS OF THAT BOX WILL BE USEFUL... SOME DAY.
GO! SAVE YOUR MOTHER!

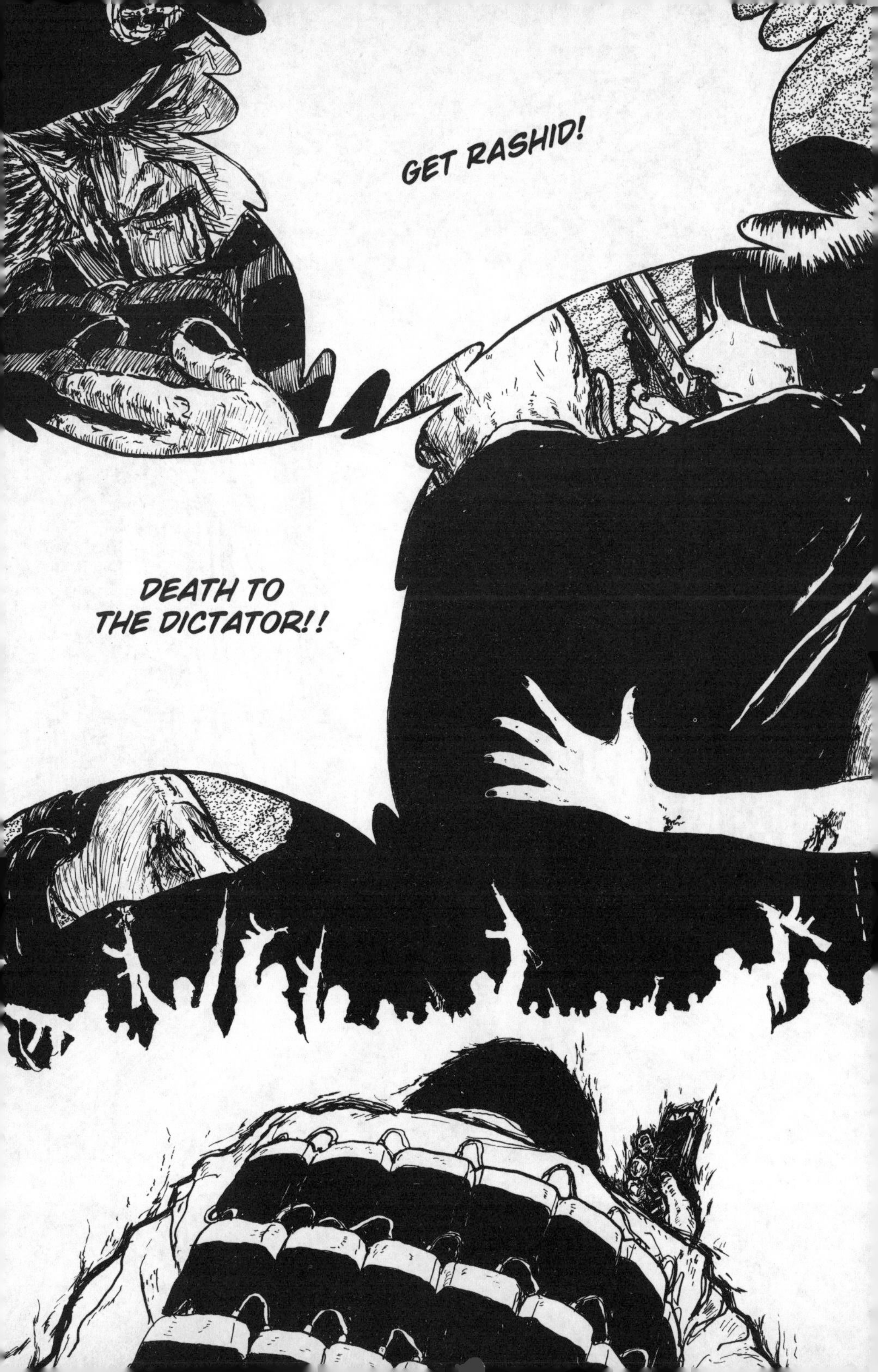
GET RASHID!
DEATH TO THE DICTATOR!!

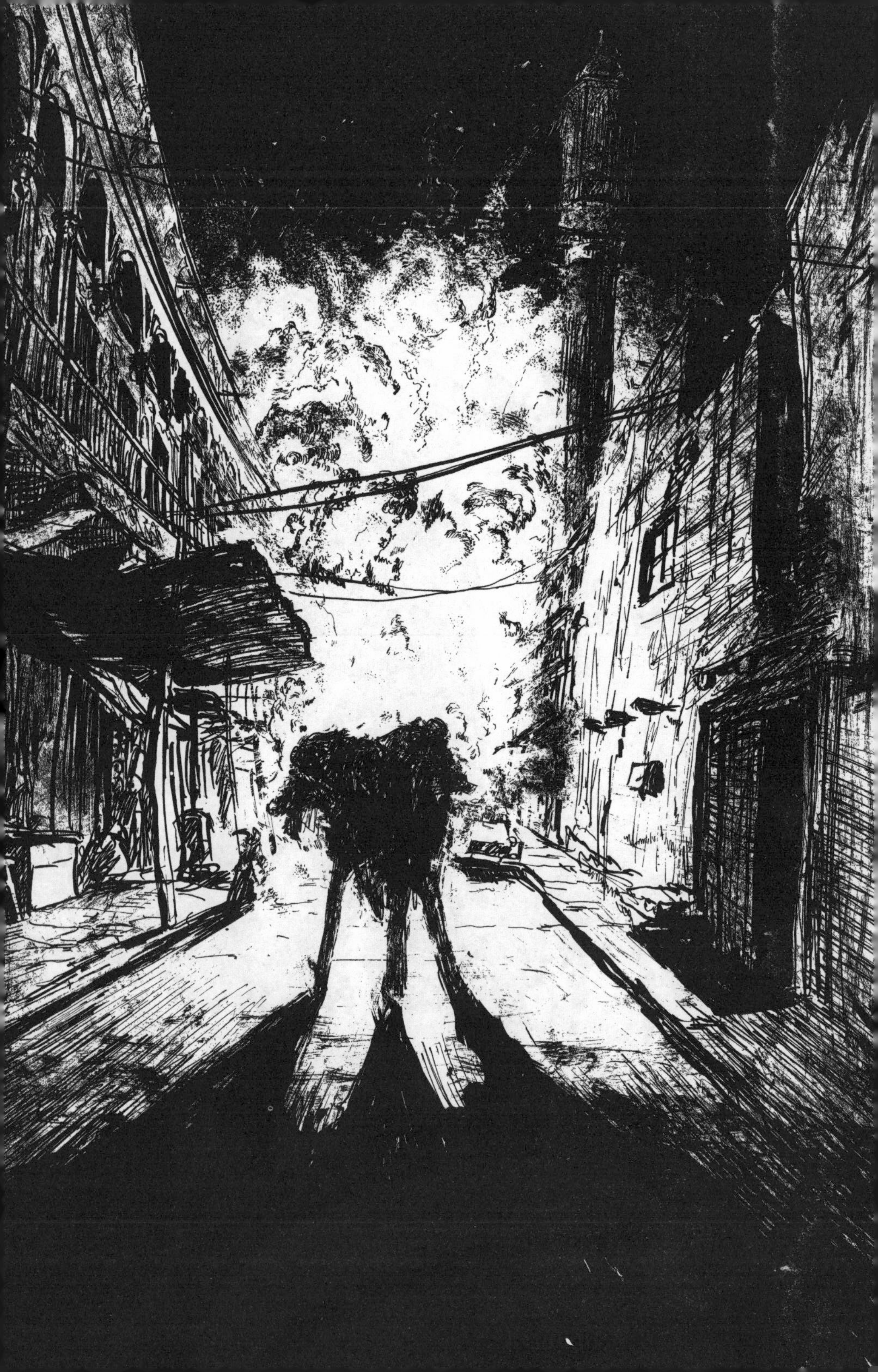

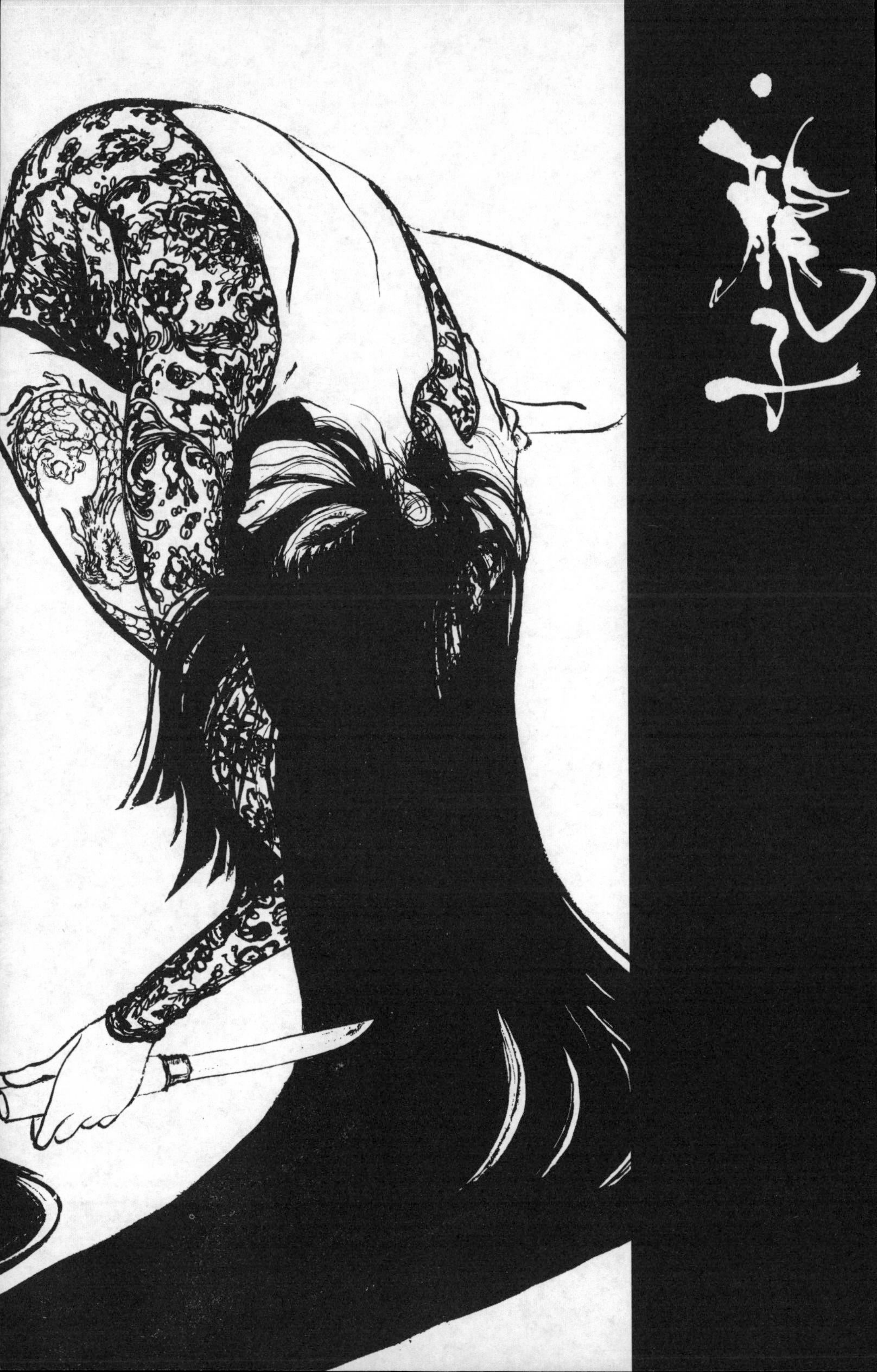
龍子

CHAPTER 3:
SEA SPARKLE

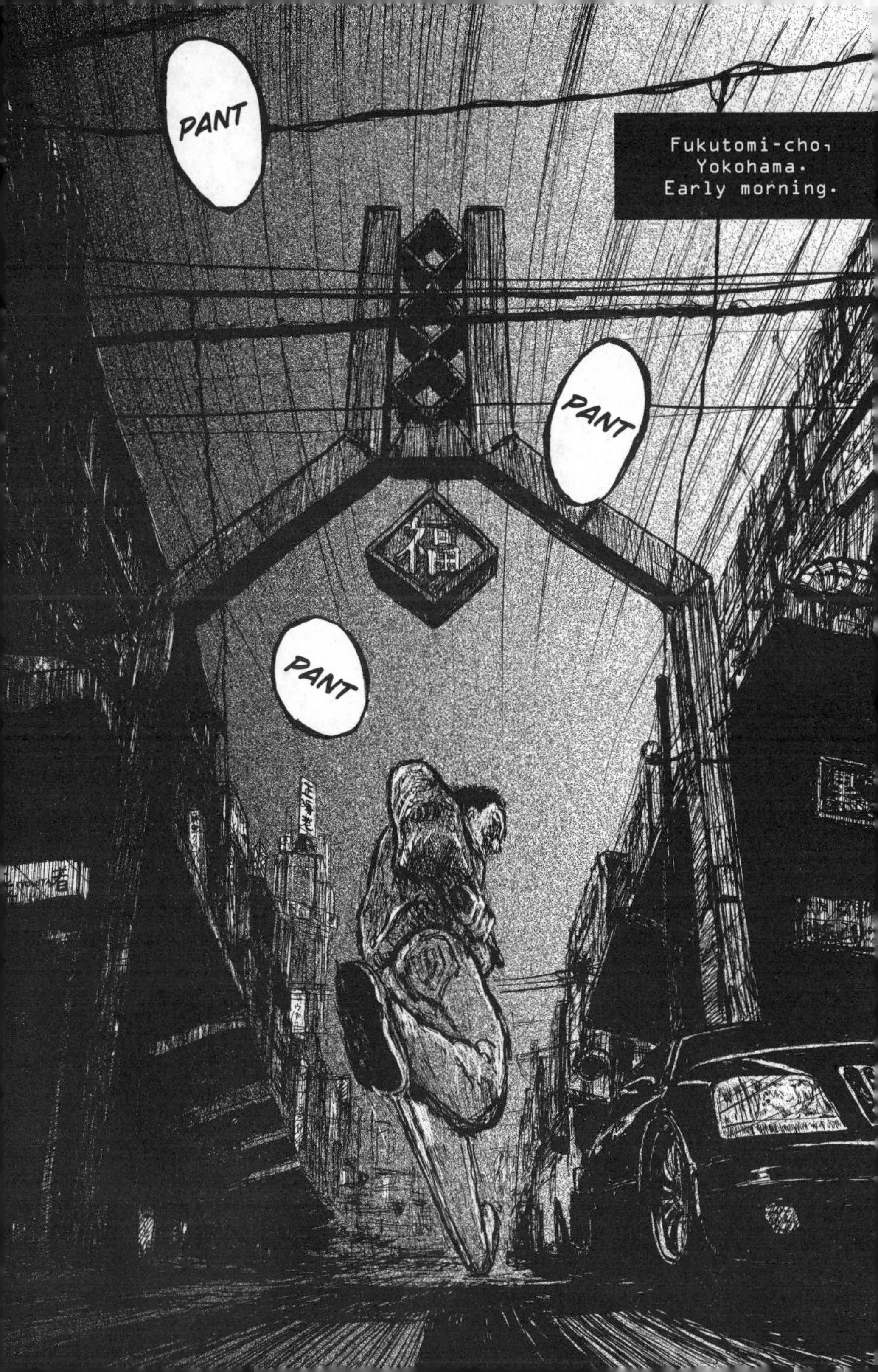
Fukutomi-cho, Yokohama. Early morning.
PANT
PANT
PANT

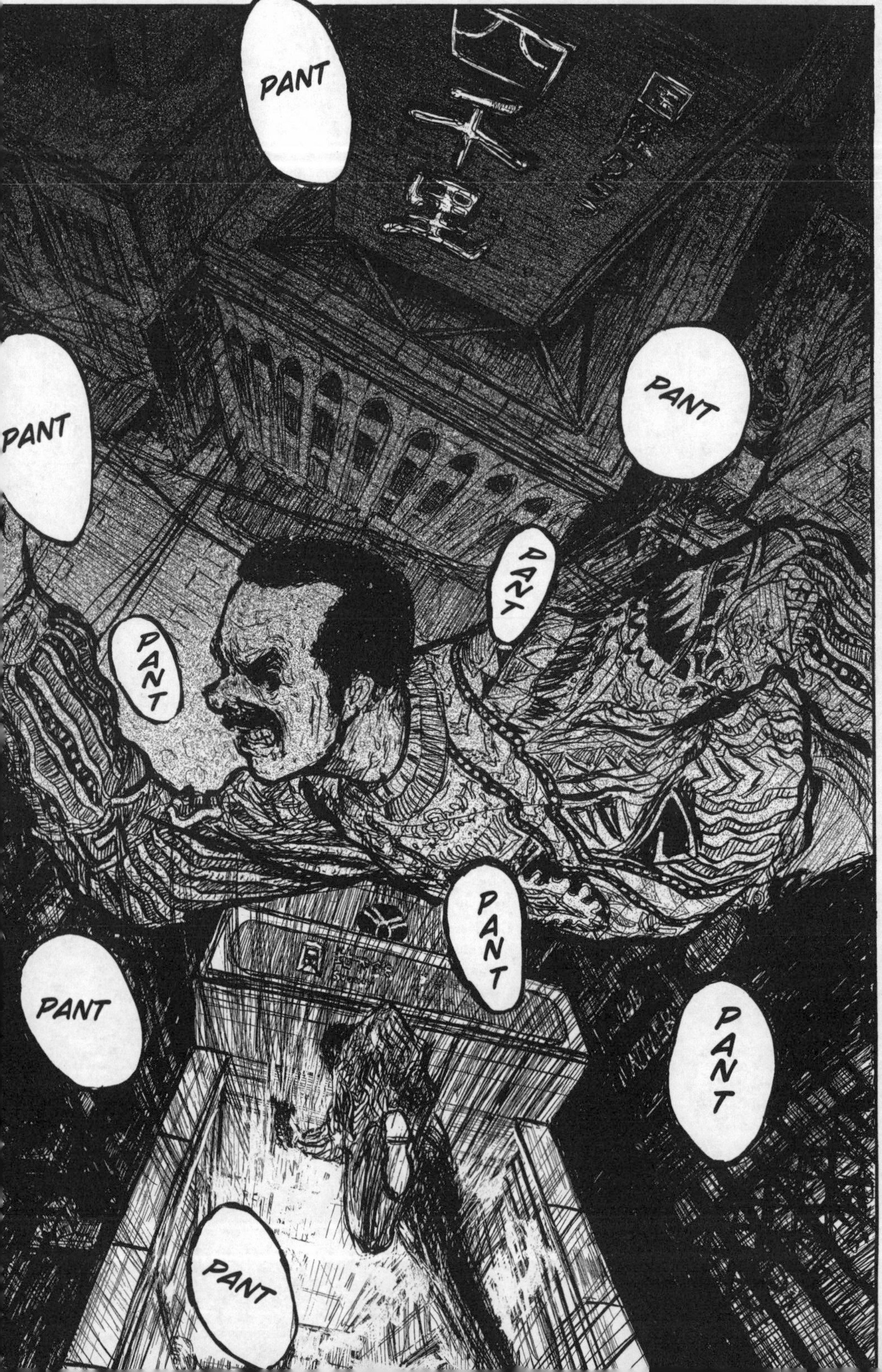
PANT
PANT
PANT
PANT
PANT
PANT
PANT
PANT
PANT

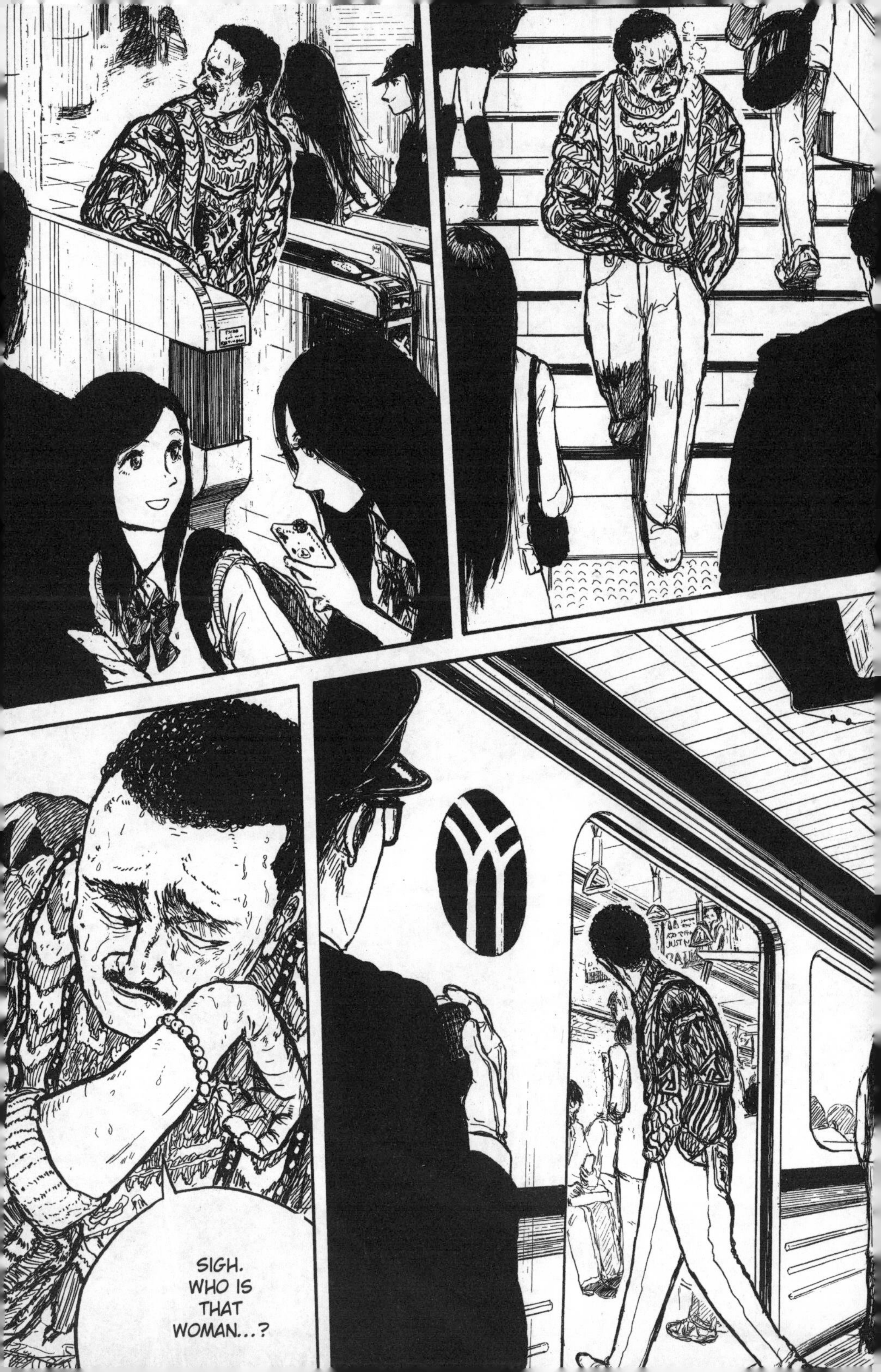
SIGH. WHO IS THAT WOMAN...?

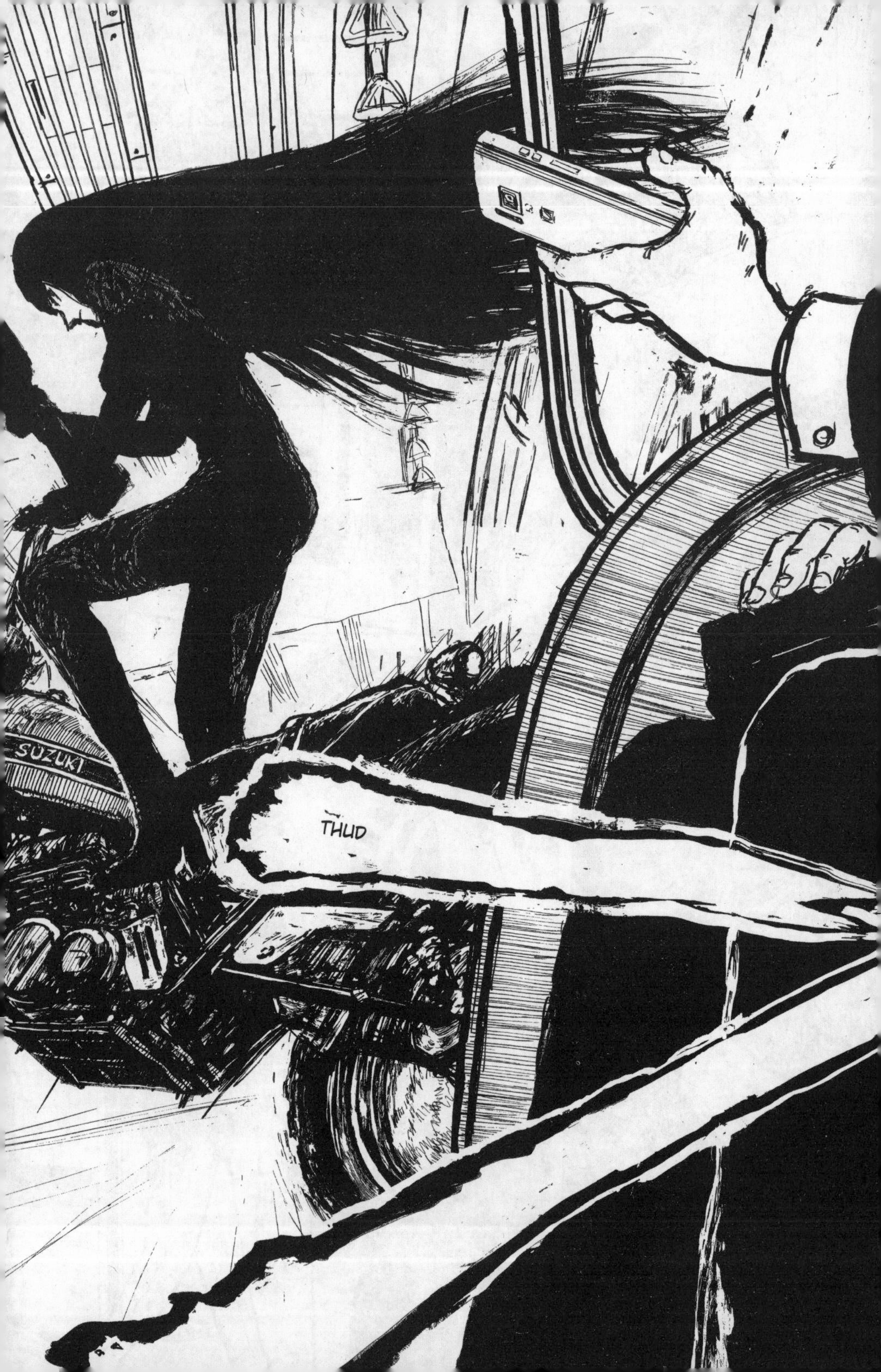
SUZUKI
THUD

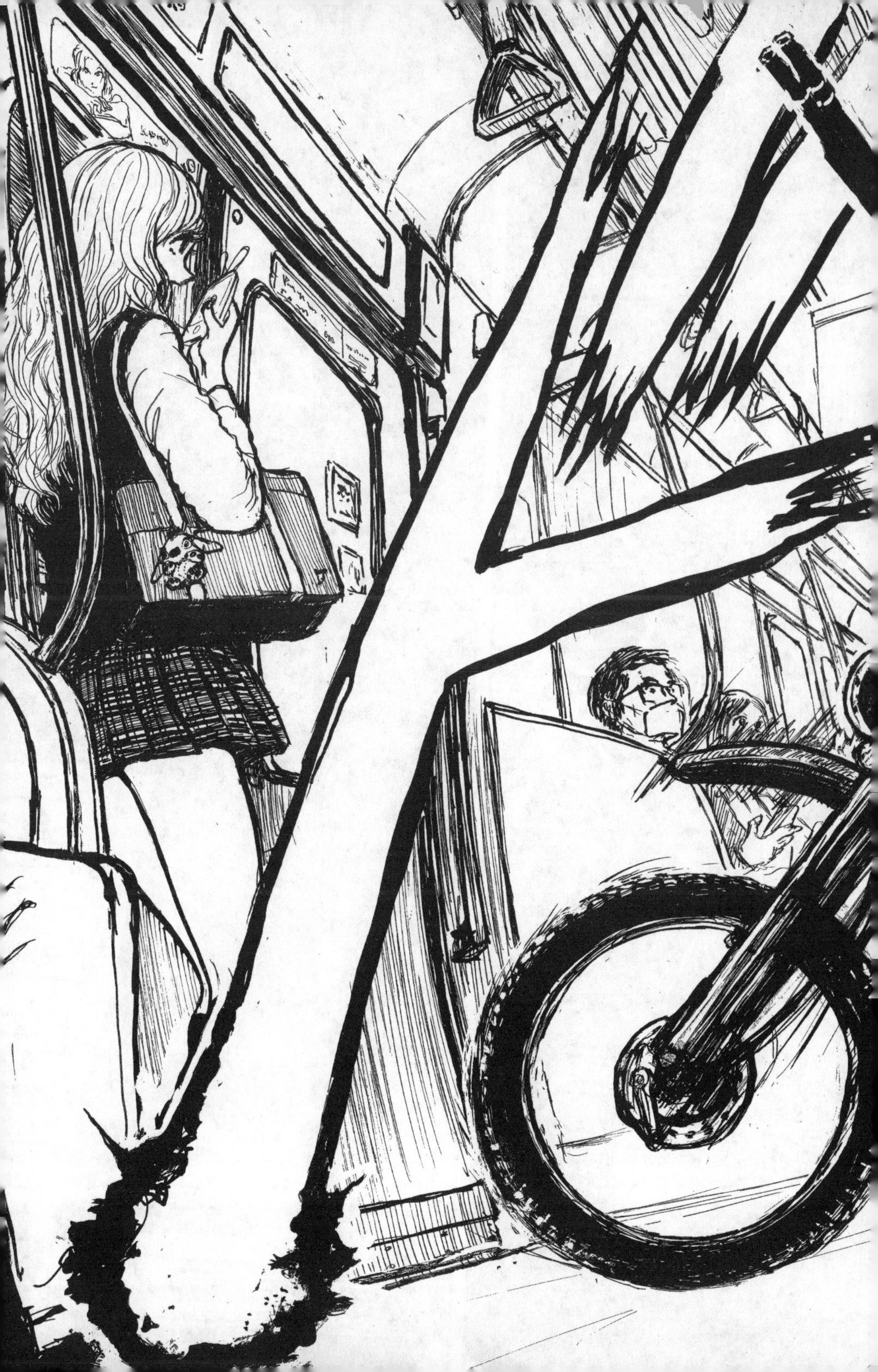

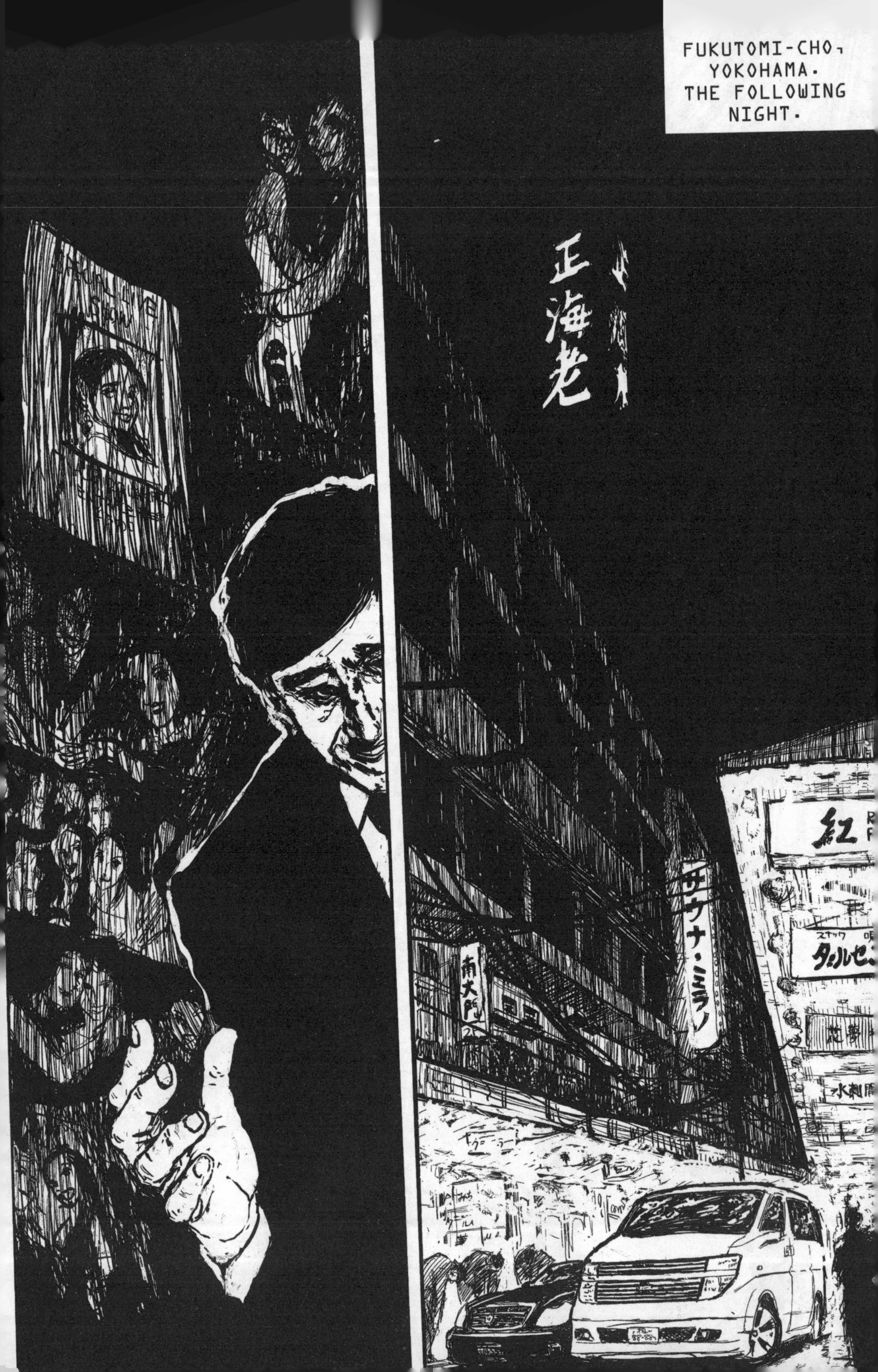
FUKUTOMI-CHO, YOKOHAMA. THE FOLLOWING NIGHT.
正海老
サウナ・ミラノ
南大門
紅

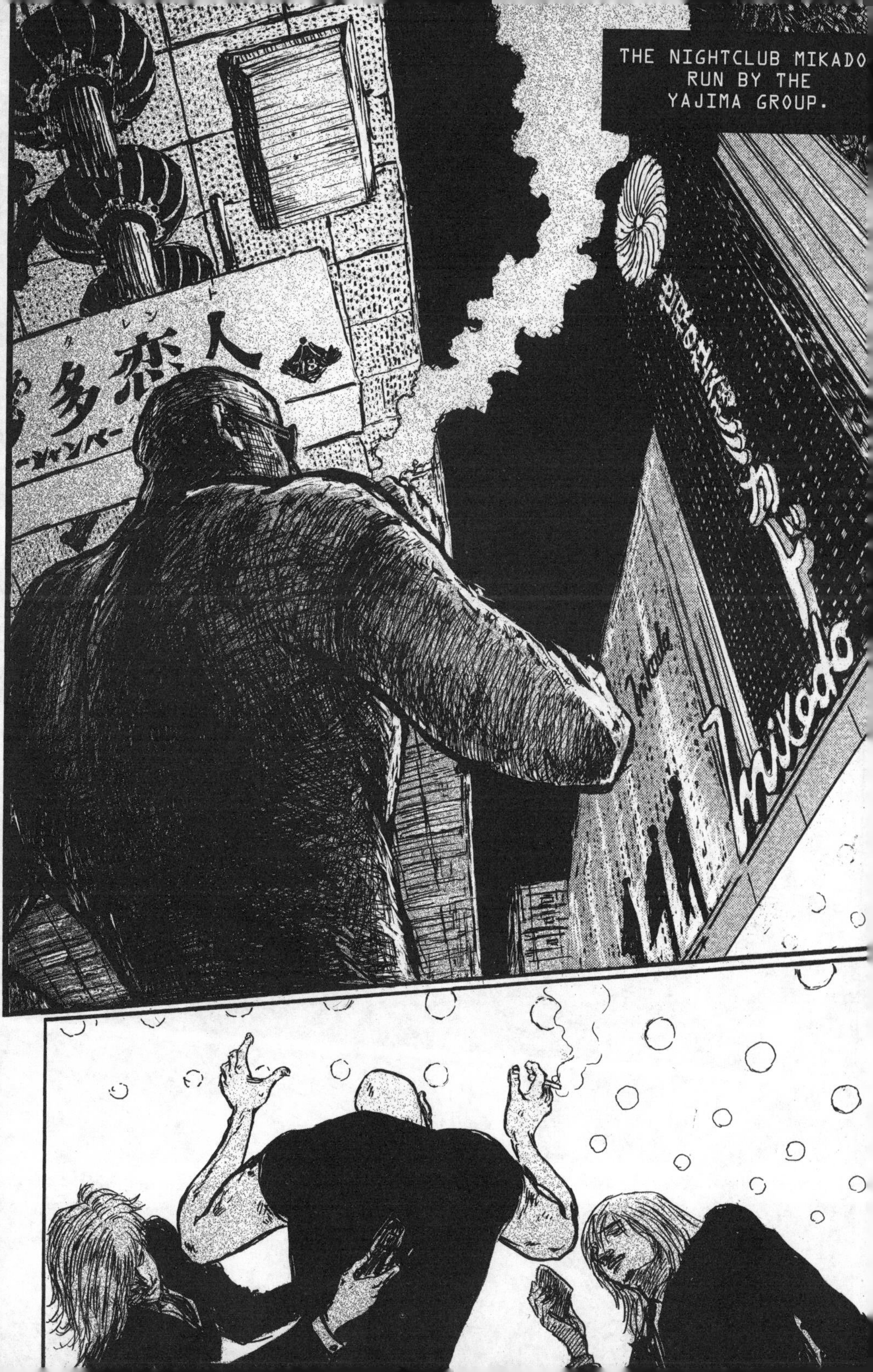
THE NIGHTCLUB MIKADO RUN BY THE YAJIMA GROUP.
多恋人
Mikado

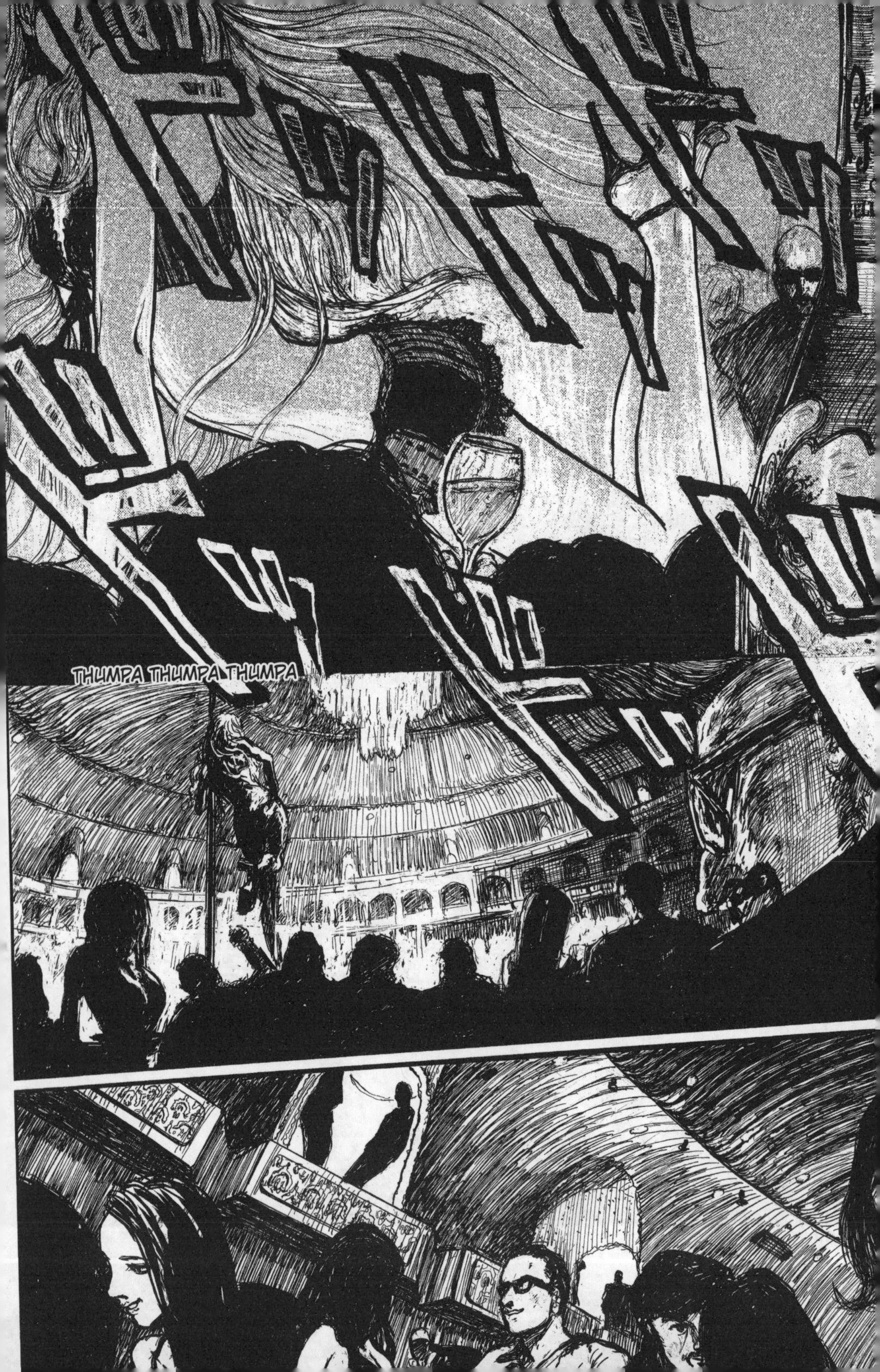
THUMPA THUMPA THUMPA

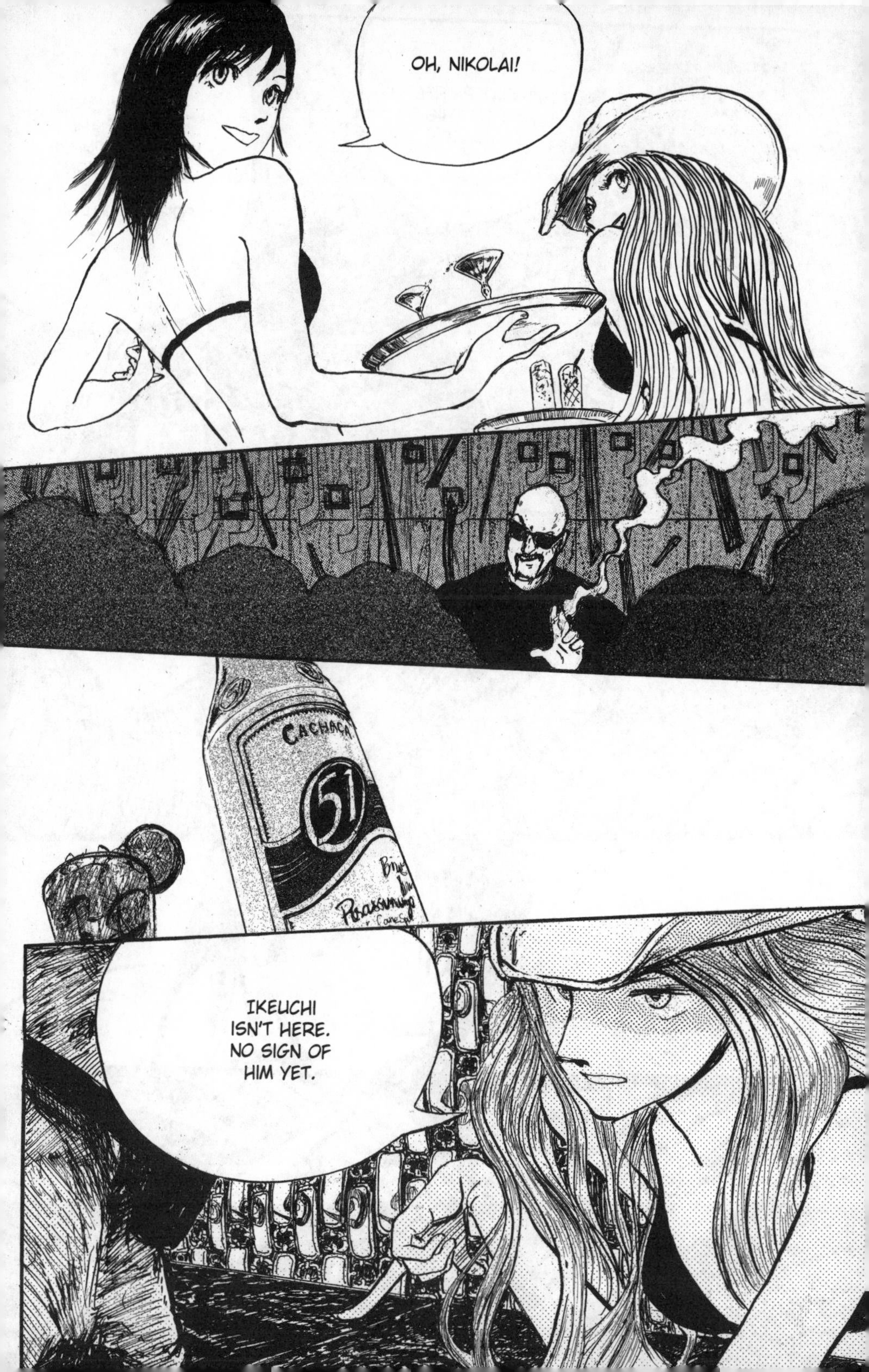
OH, NIKOLAI!
CACHACA
51
IKEUCHI ISN'T HERE. NO SIGN OF HIM YET.

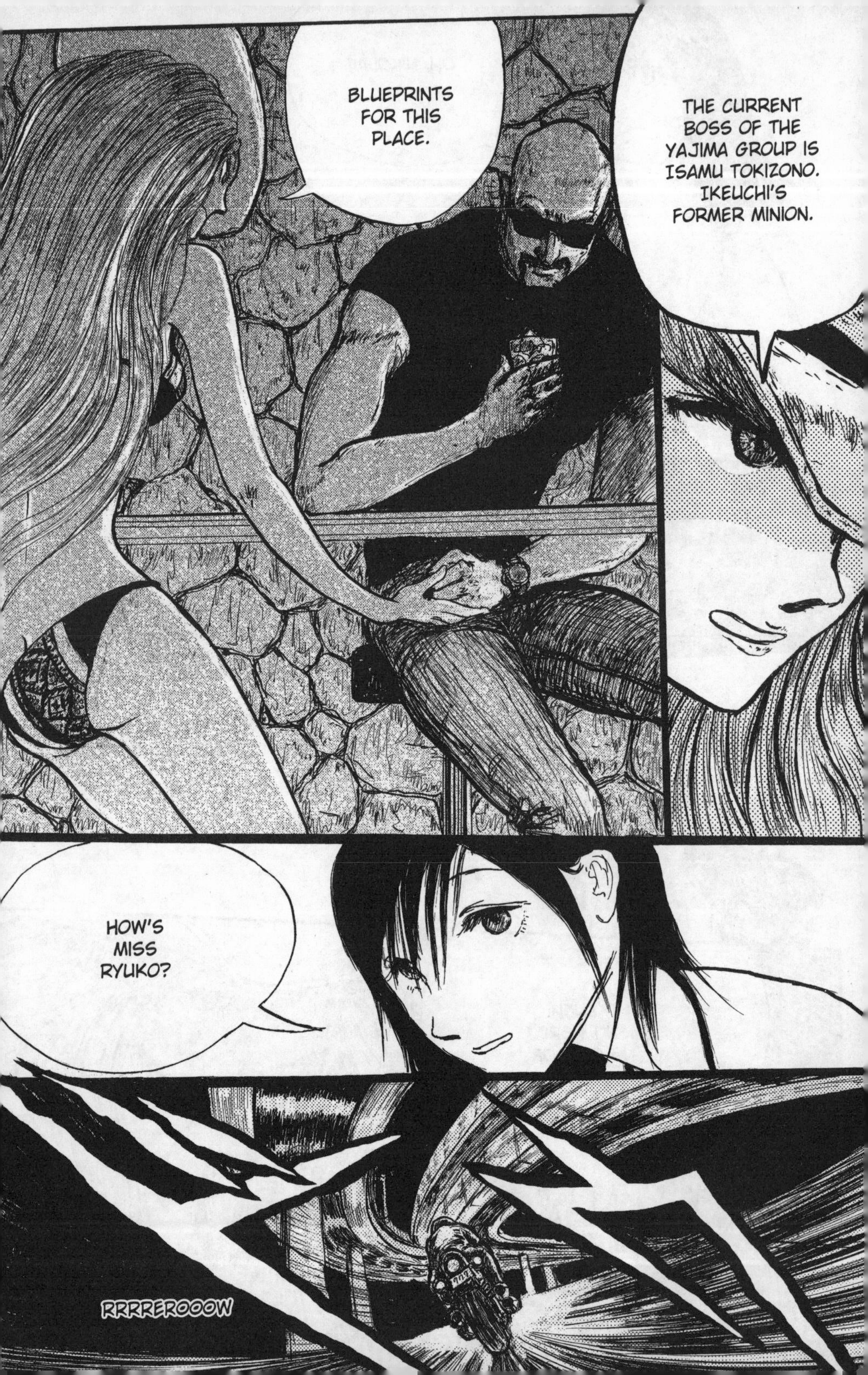
THE CURRENT BOSS OF THE YAJIMA GROUP IS ISAMU TOKIZONO. IKEUCHI'S FORMER MINION.
BLUEPRINTS FOR THIS PLACE.
HOW'S MISS RYUKO?
RRRREROOOW

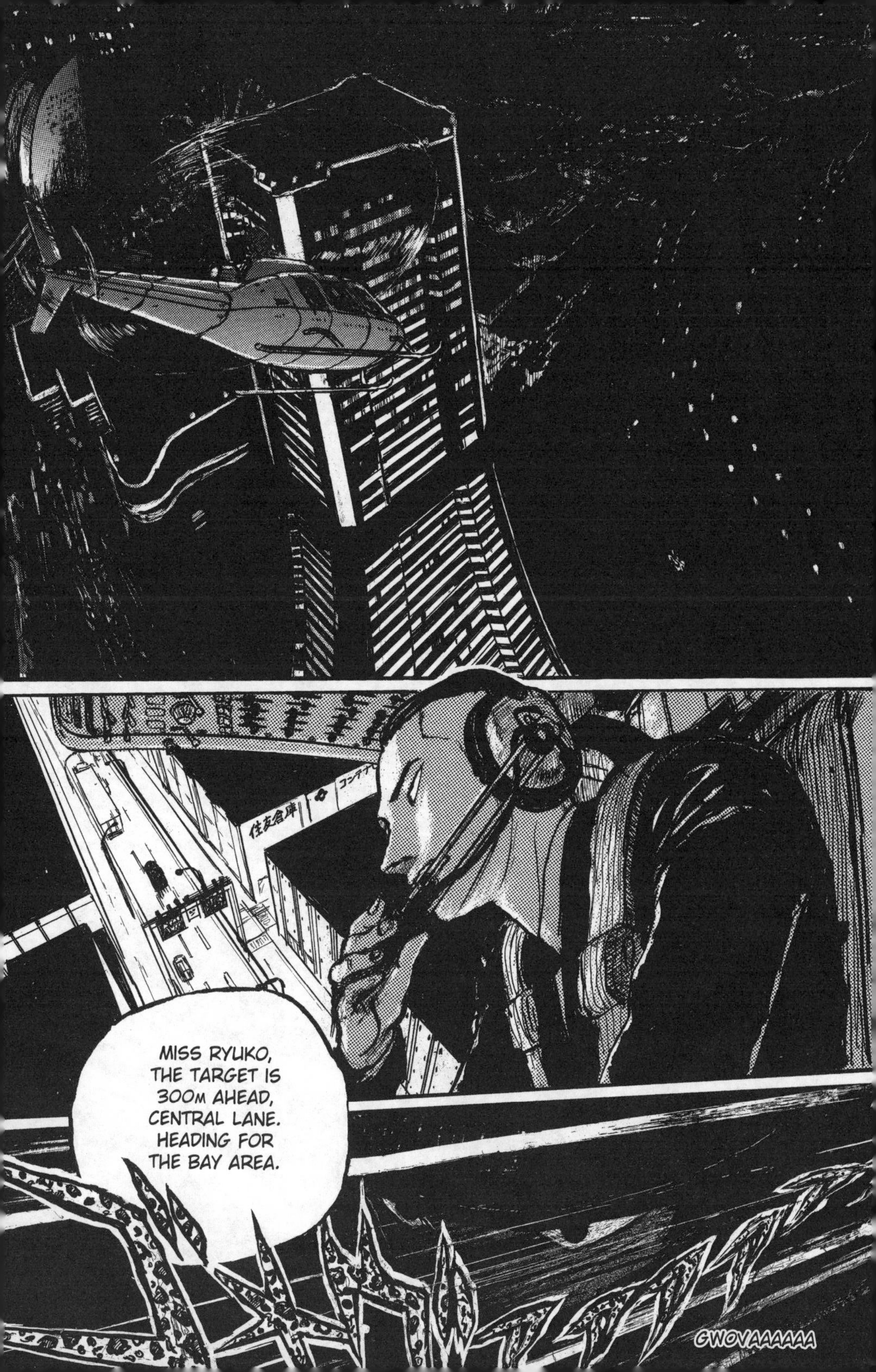
住友倉庫
MISS RYUKO, THE TARGET IS 300M AHEAD, CENTRAL LANE. HEADING FOR THE BAY AREA.
GWOVAAAAAA

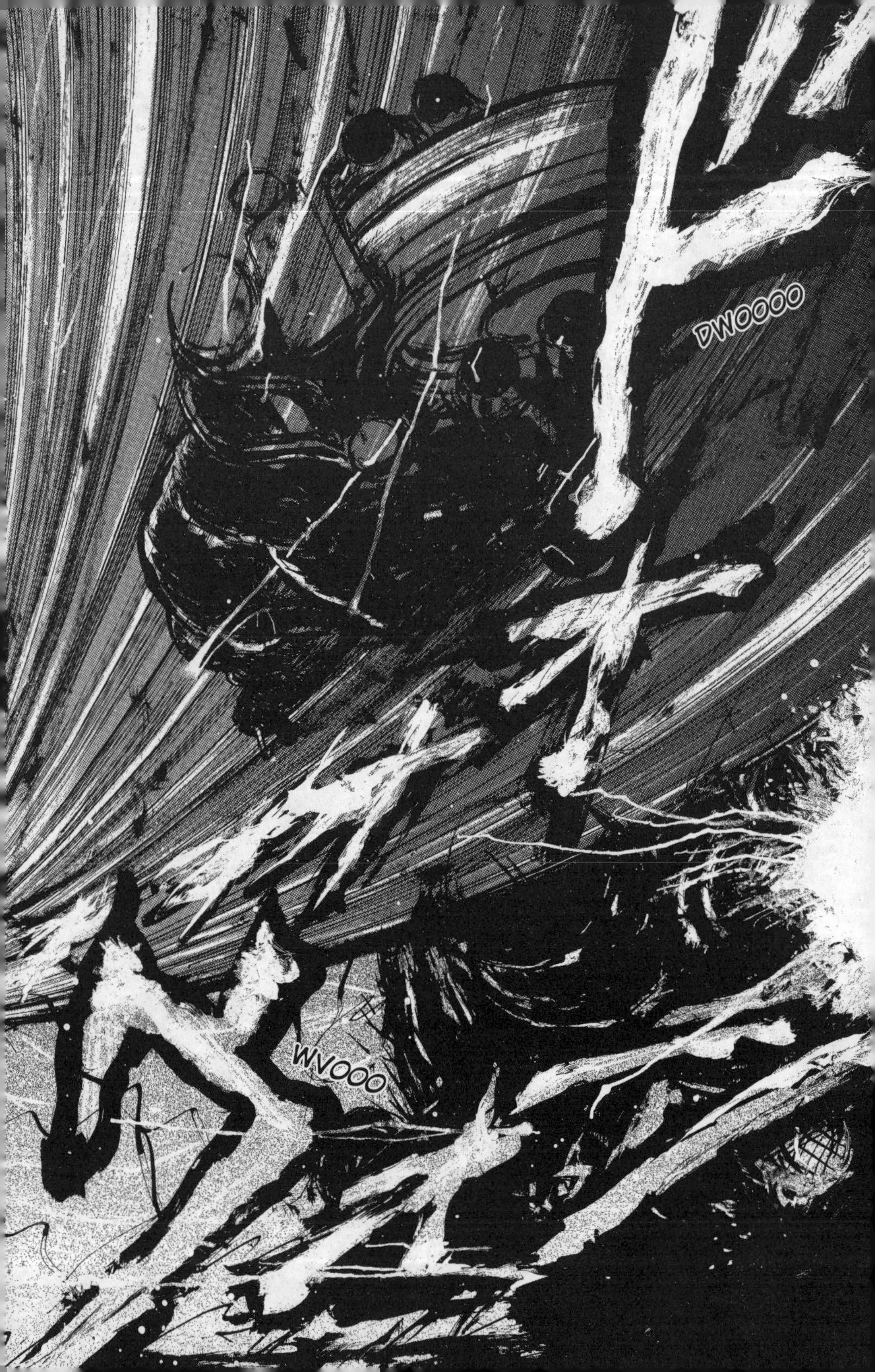
DWOOOO
WVOOO

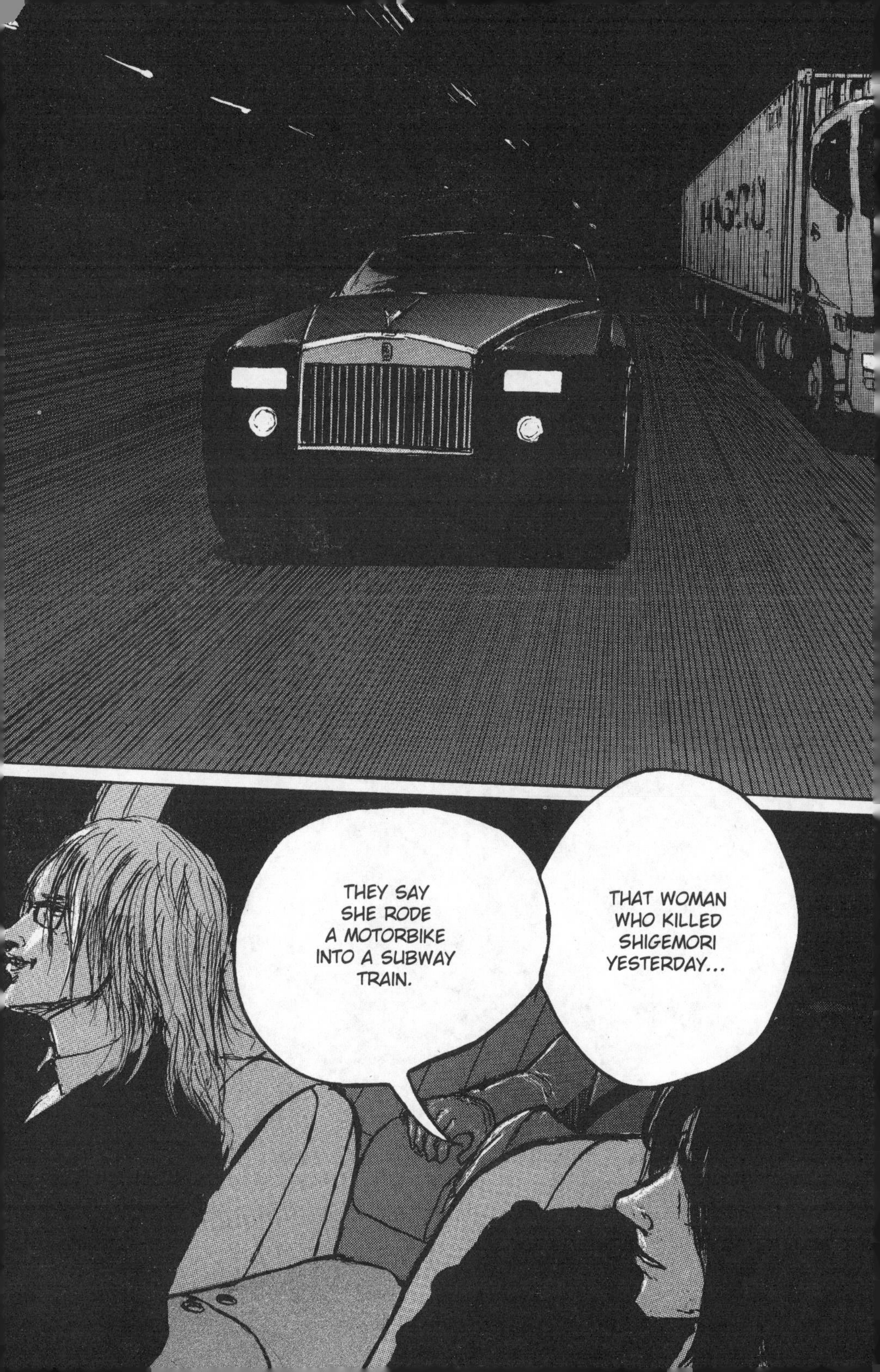
THAT WOMAN WHO KILLED SHIGEMORI YESTERDAY...
THEY SAY SHE RODE A MOTORBIKE INTO A SUBWAY TRAIN.

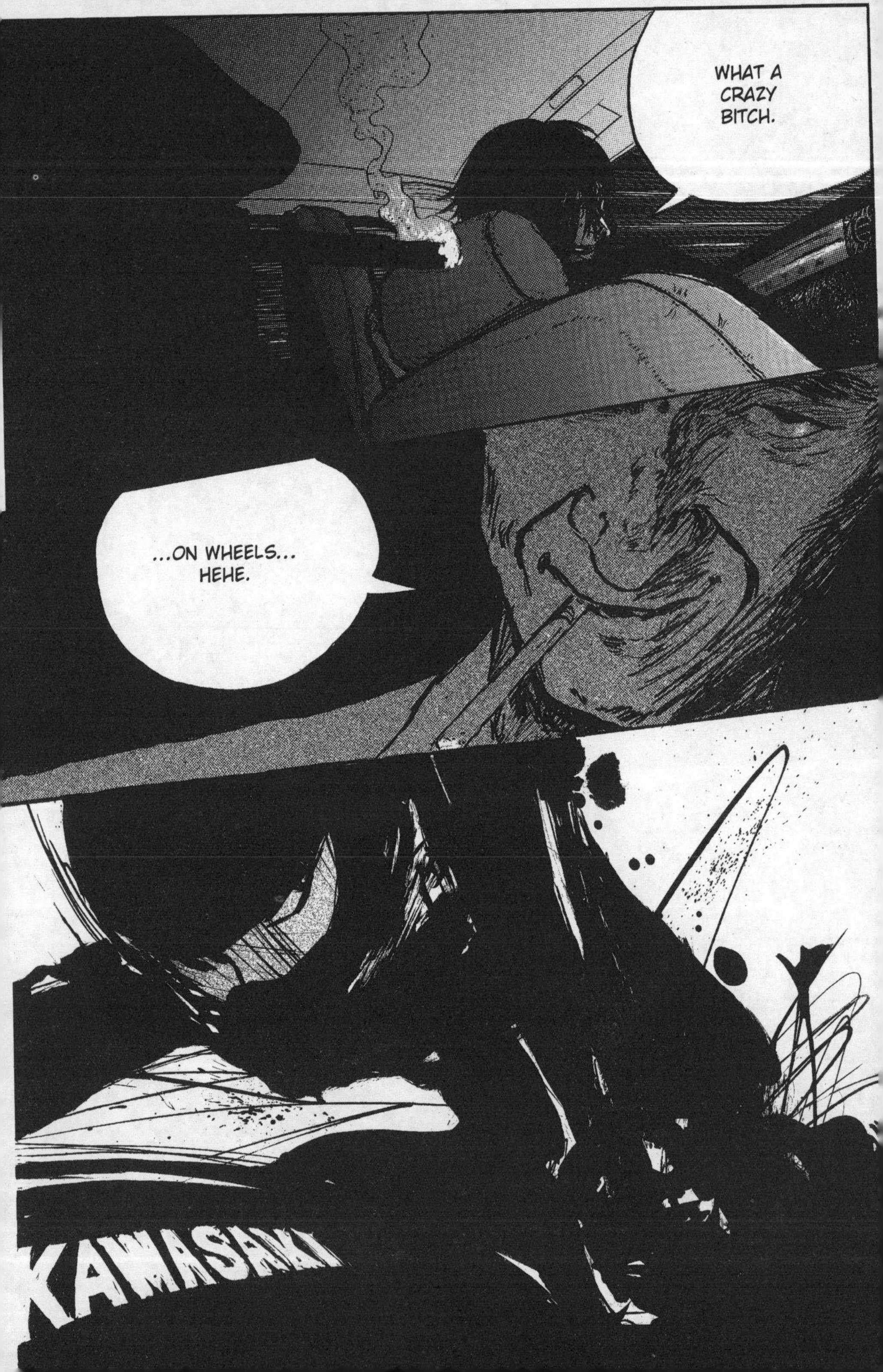
WHAT A CRAZY BITCH.
...ON WHEELS... HEHE.
KAWASAKI

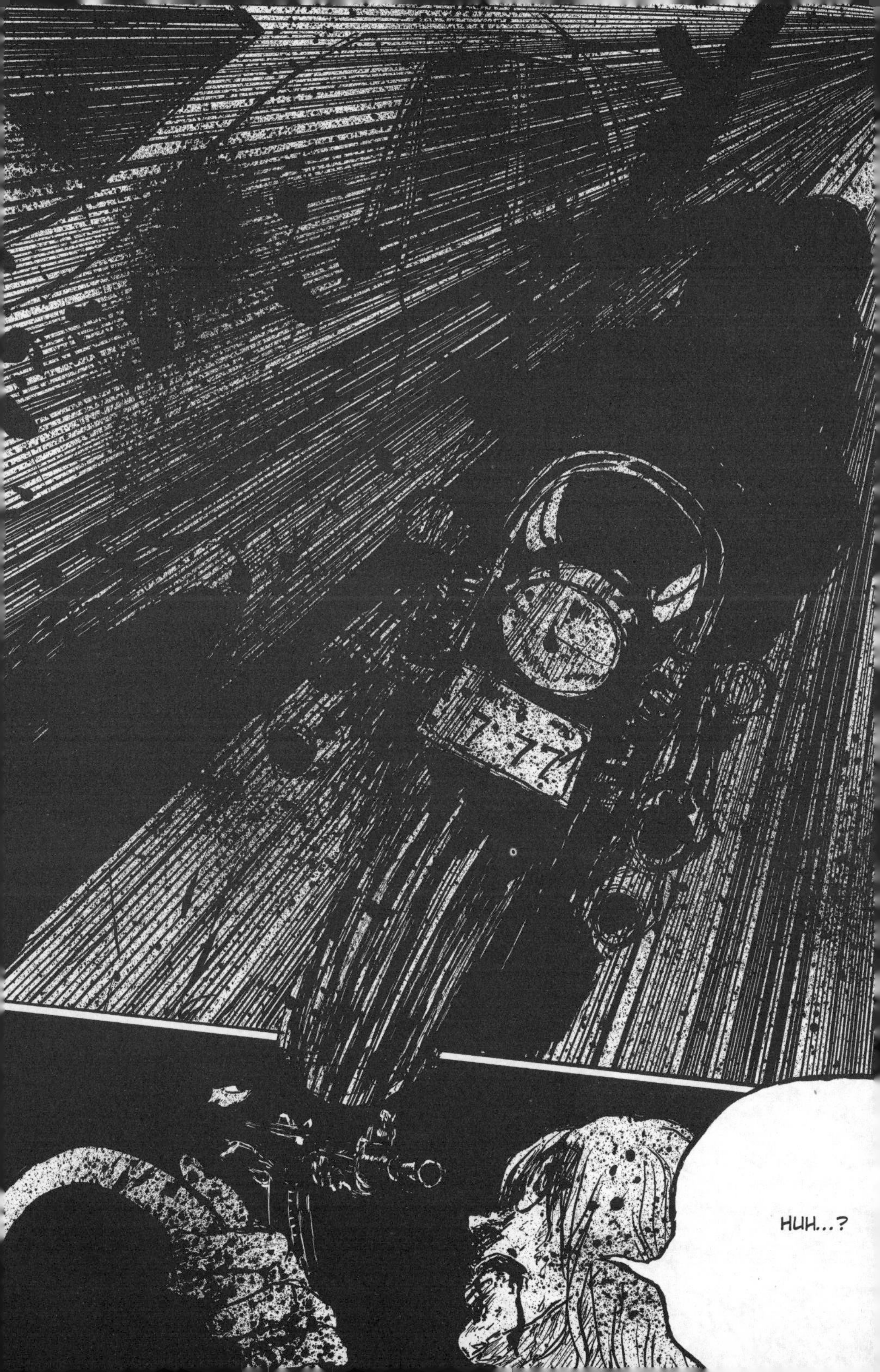
HUH...?

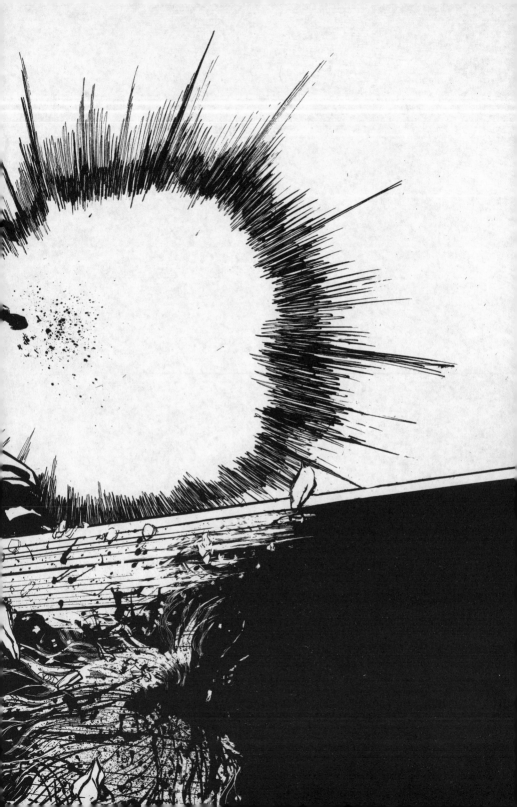

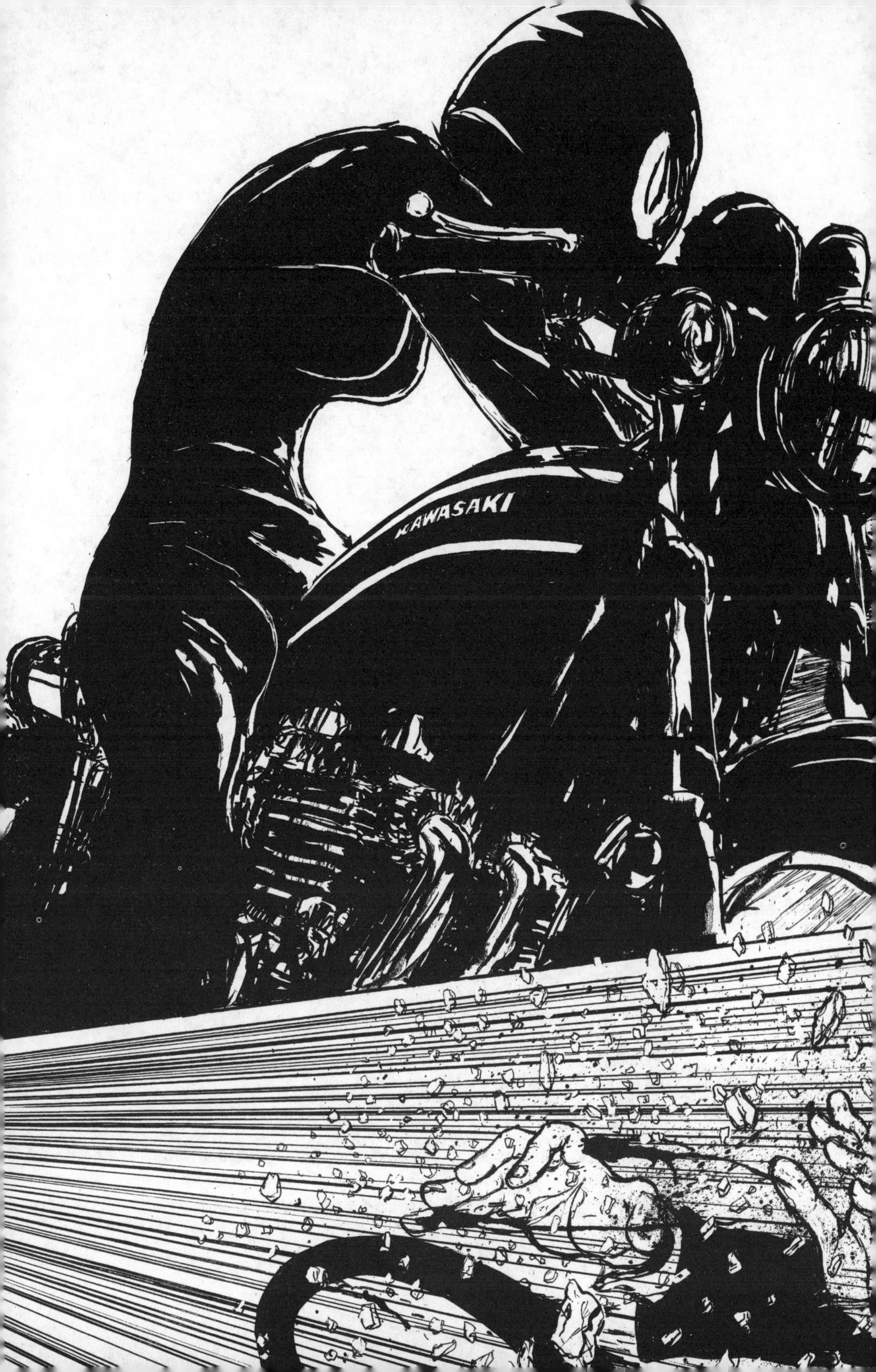
KAWASAKI

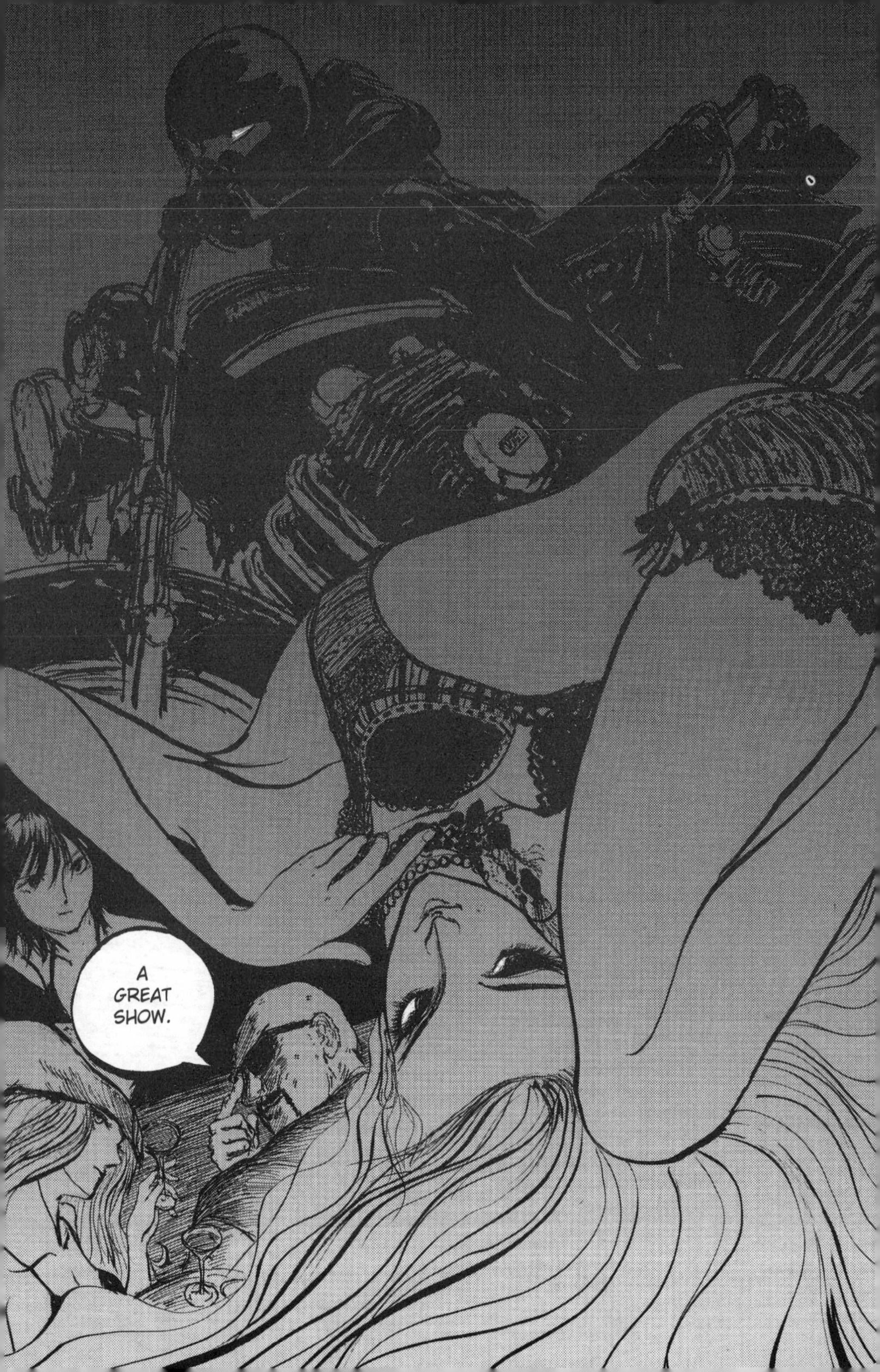
A GREAT SHOW.

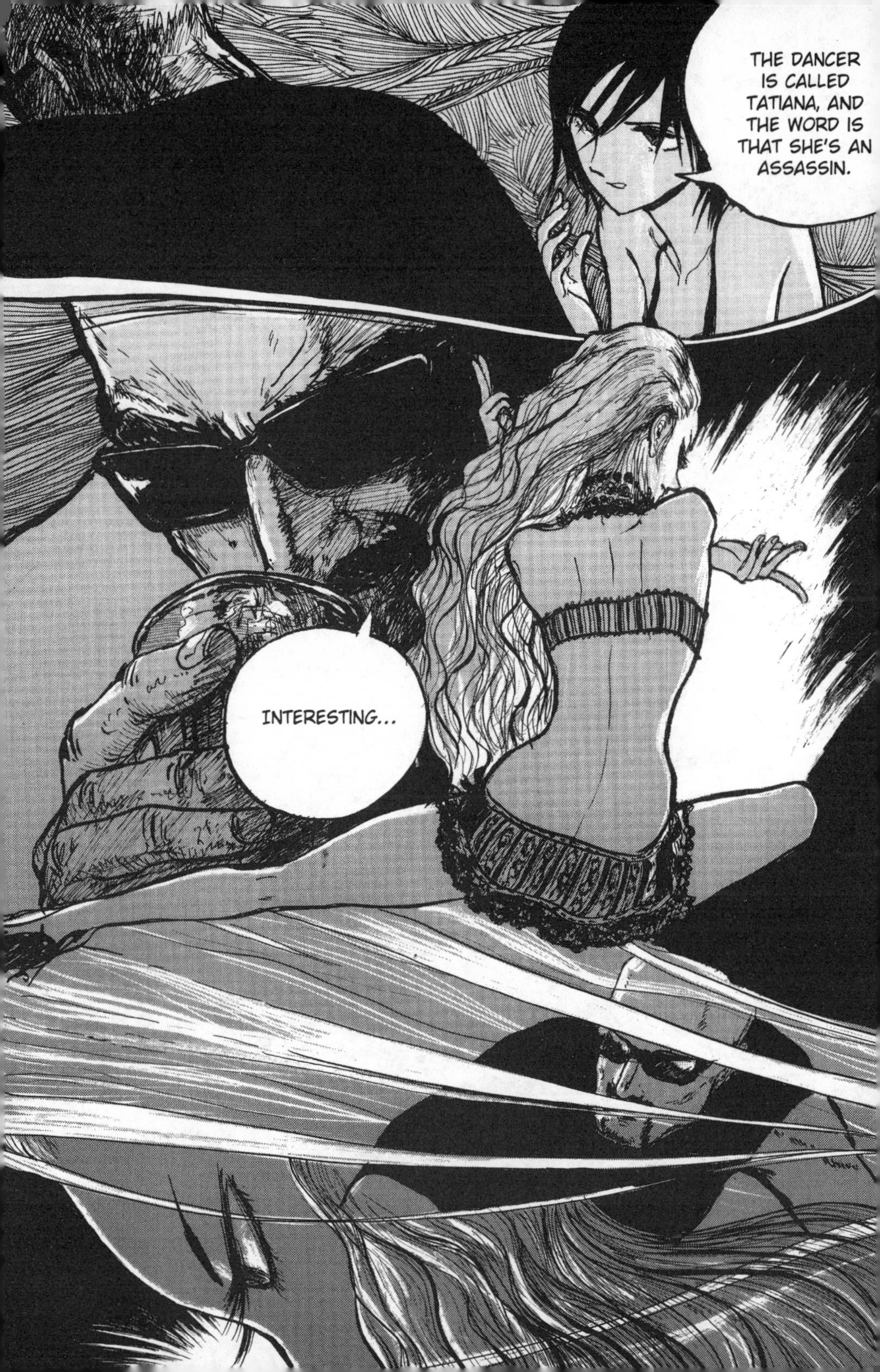
THE DANCER IS CALLED TATIANA, AND THE WORD IS THAT SHE'S AN ASSASSIN.
INTERESTING...

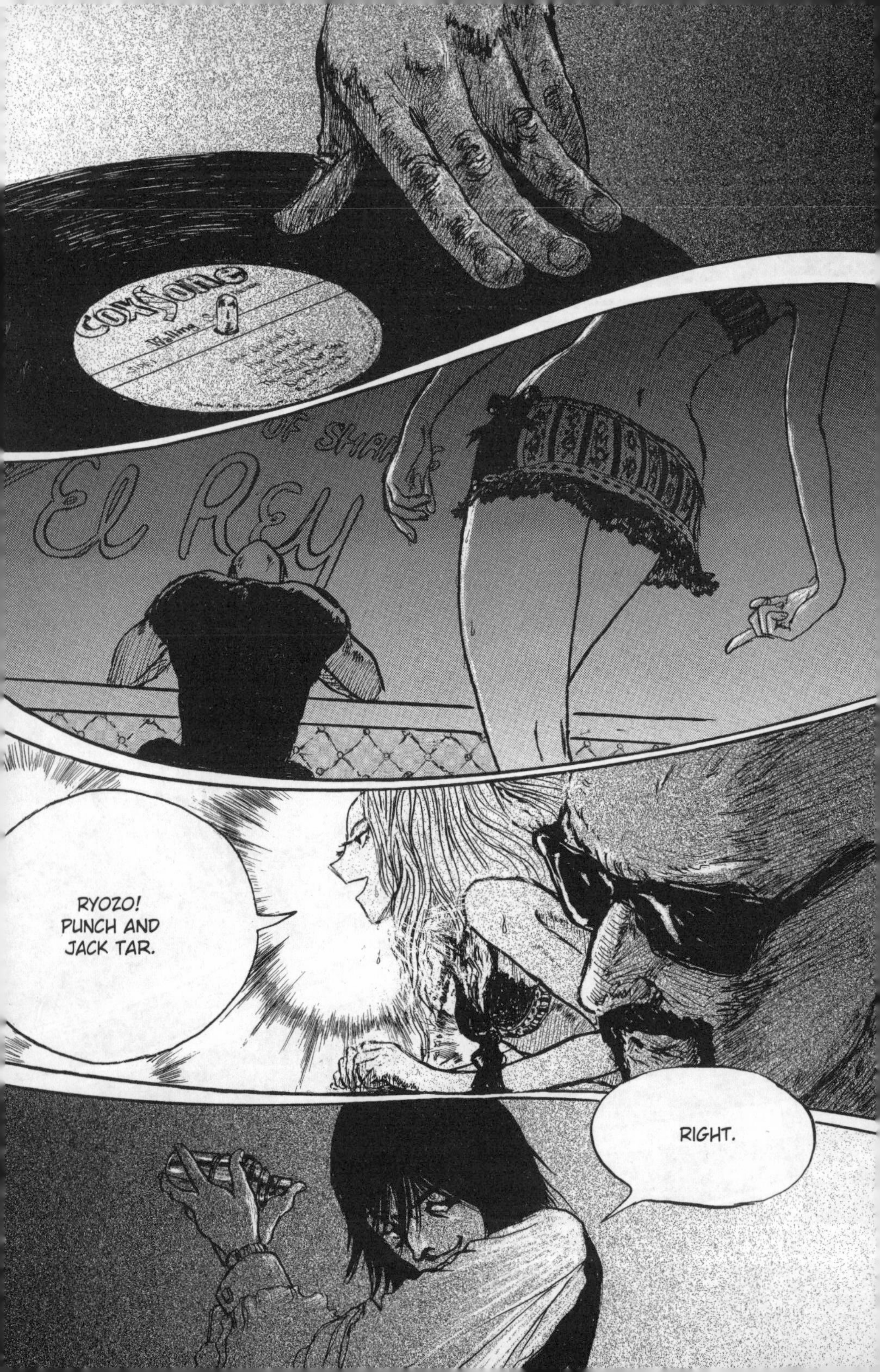
COXSONE
El Rey
RYOZO! PUNCH AND JACK TAR.
RIGHT.

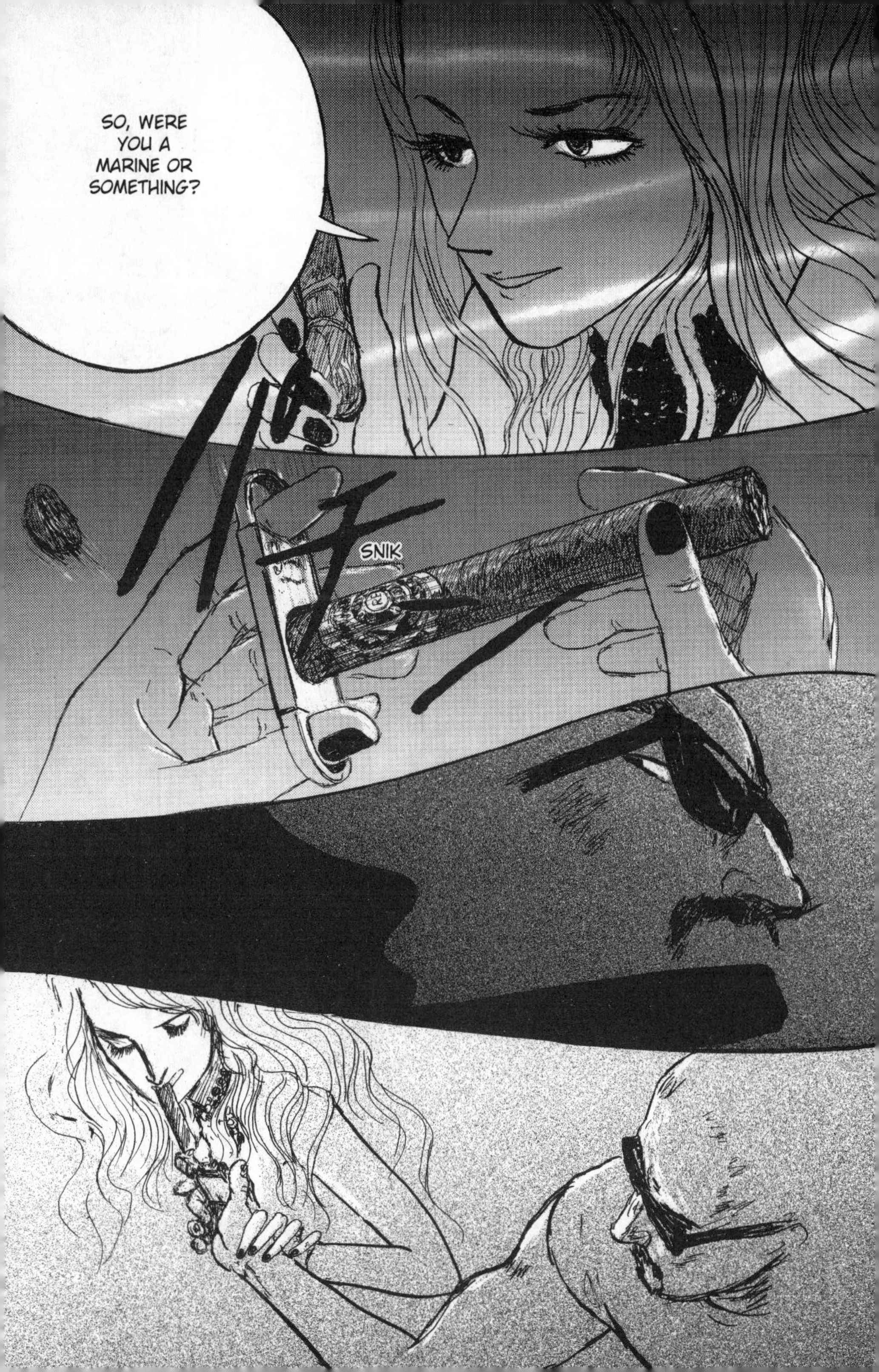
SO, WERE YOU A MARINE OR SOMETHING?
SNIK

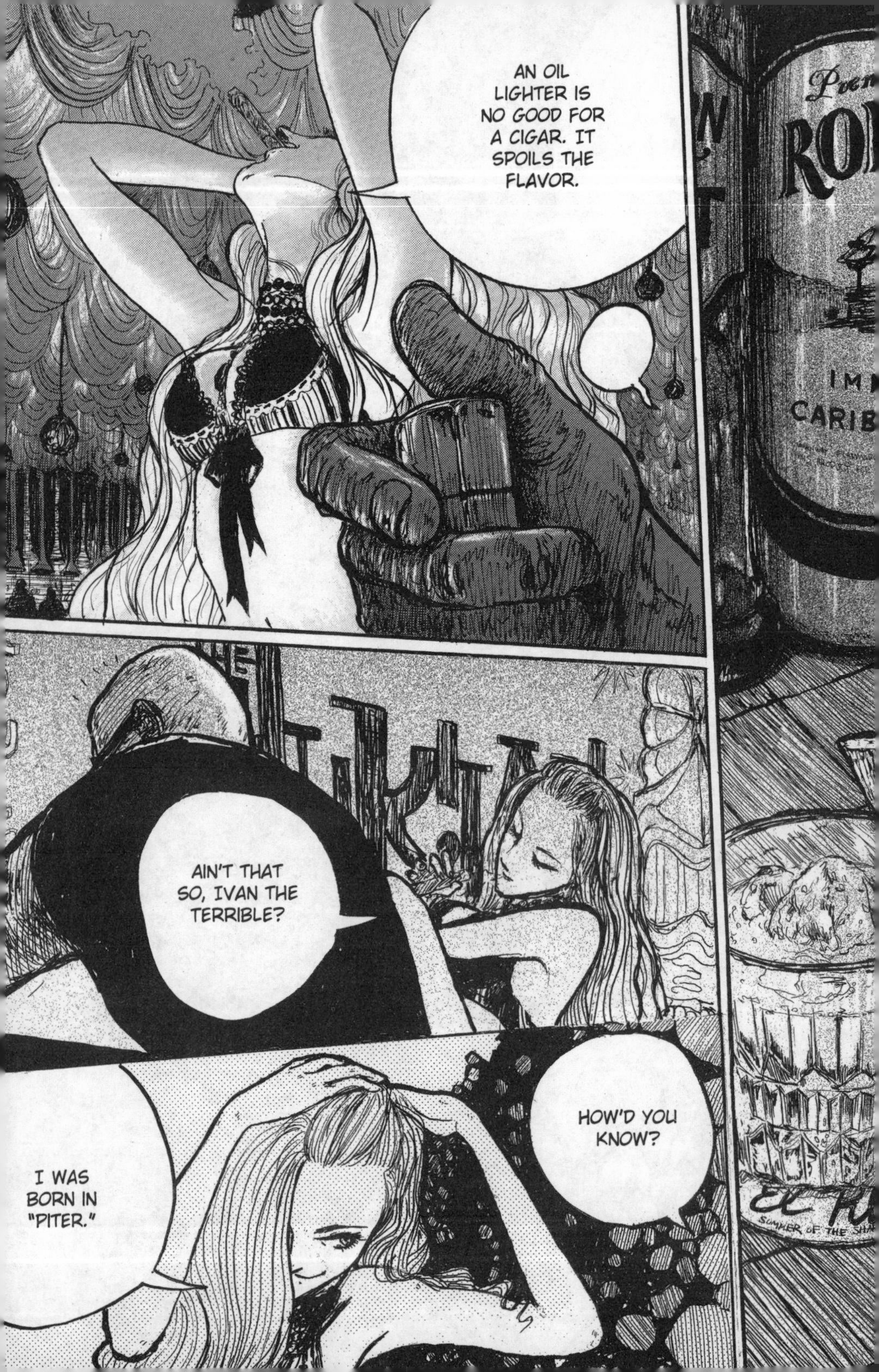
AN OIL LIGHTER IS NO GOOD FOR A CIGAR. IT SPOILS THE FLAVOR.
AIN'T THAT SO, IVAN THE TERRIBLE?
HOW'D YOU KNOW?
I WAS BORN IN "PITER."

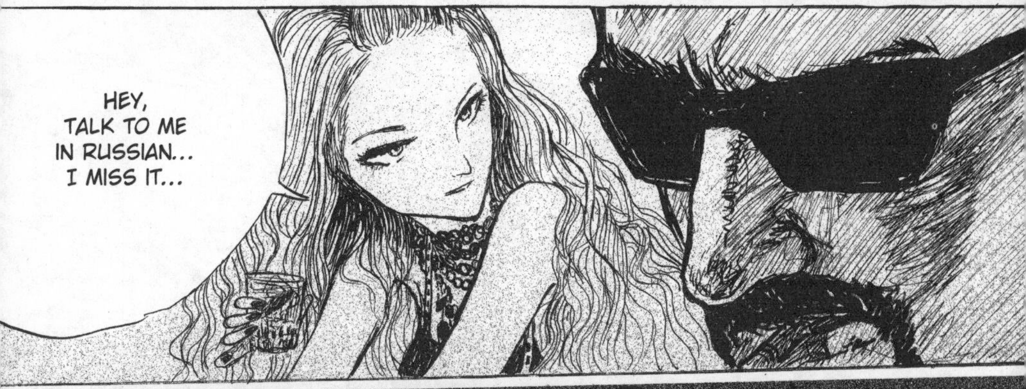
HEY, TALK TO ME IN RUSSIAN... I MISS IT...
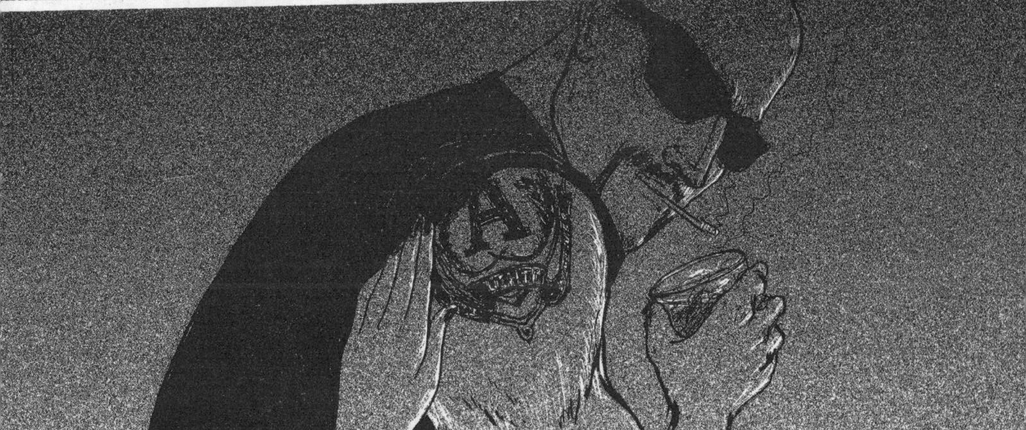
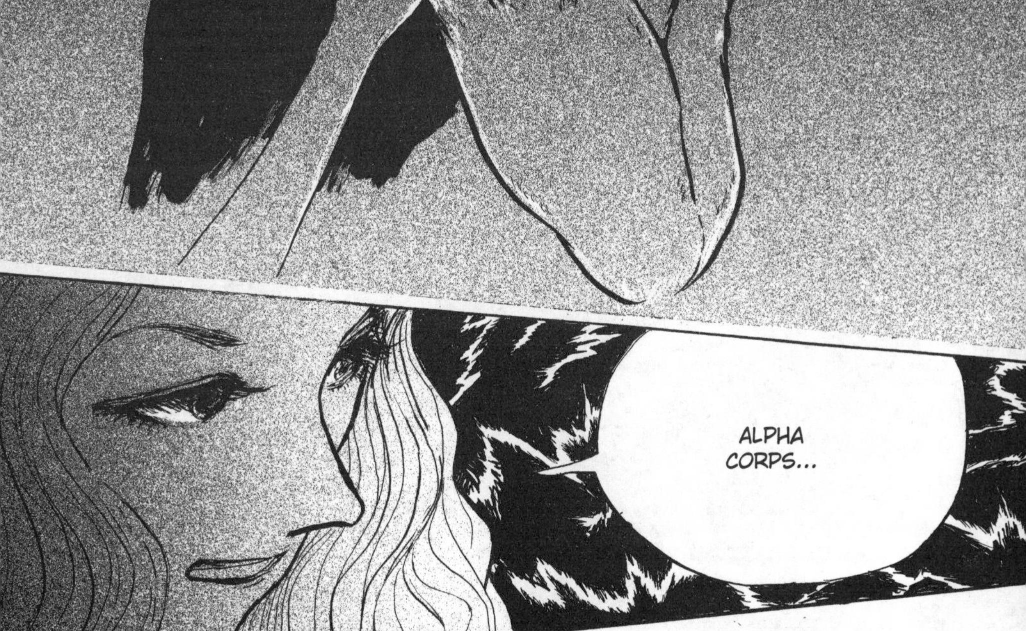
ALPHA CORPS...

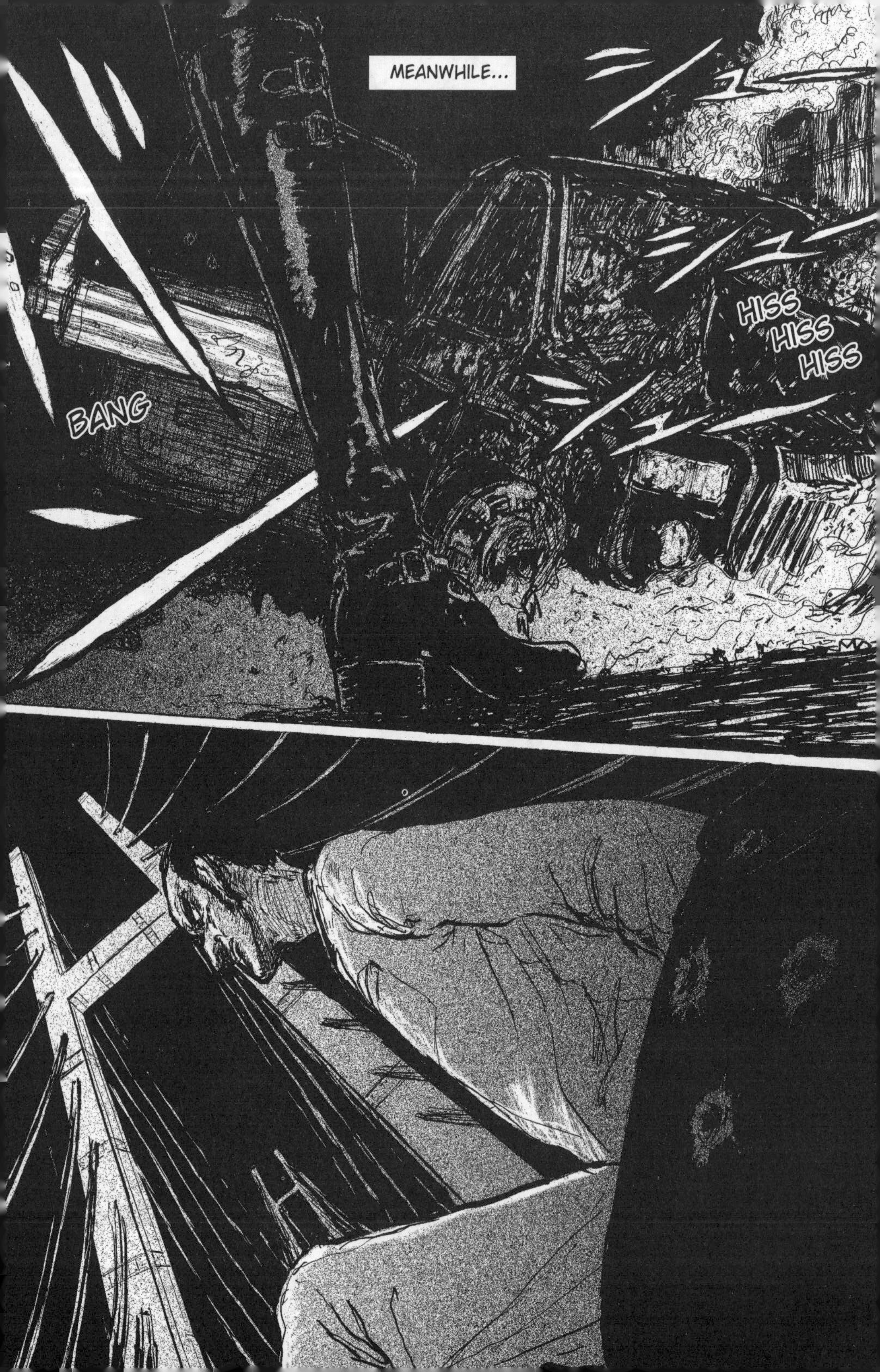
MEANWHILE...
HISS
HISS
HISS
BANG

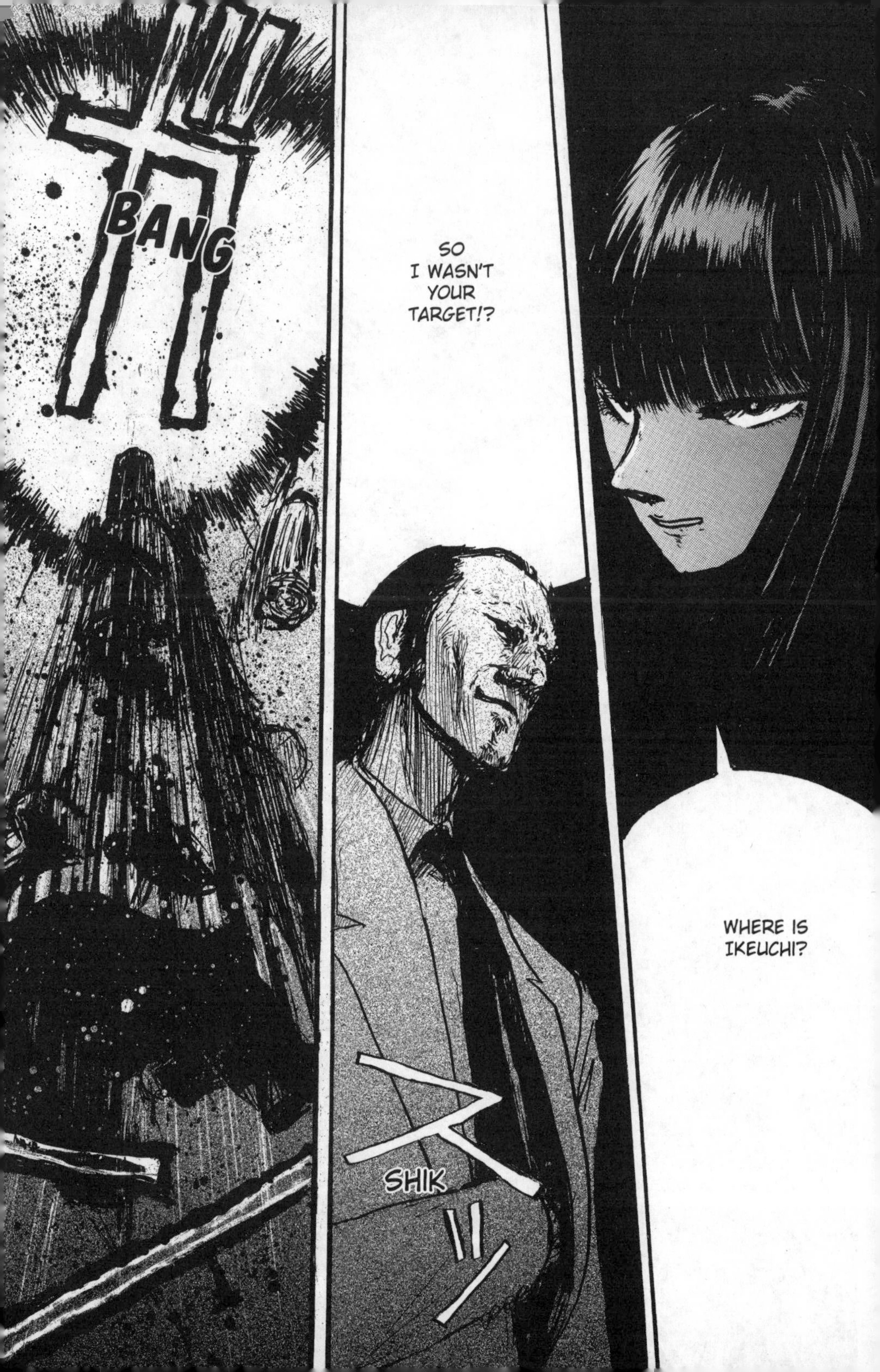
WHERE IS IKEUCHI?
SO I WASN'T YOUR TARGET!?
SHIK
BANG

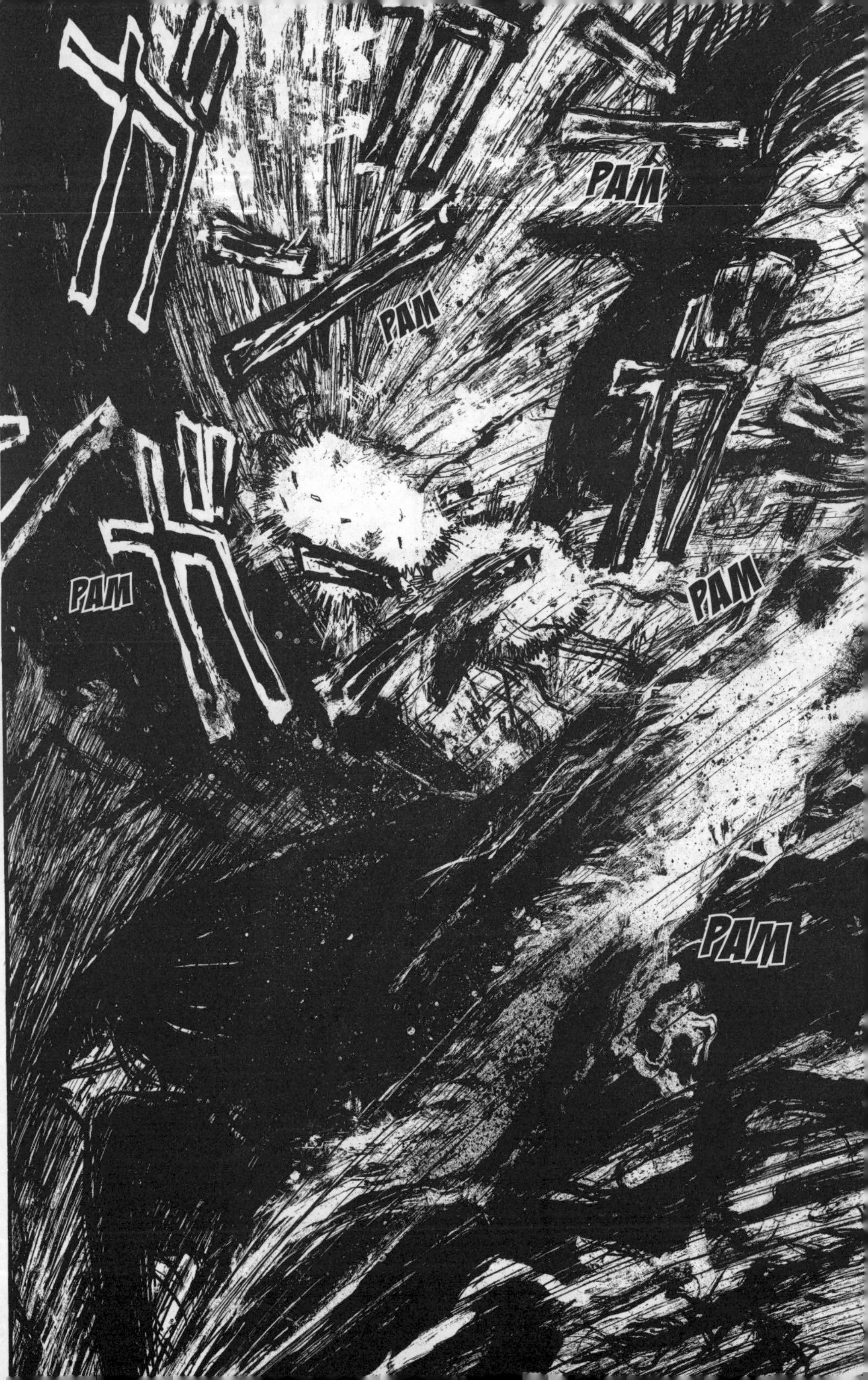
PAM
PAM
PAM
PAM
PAM

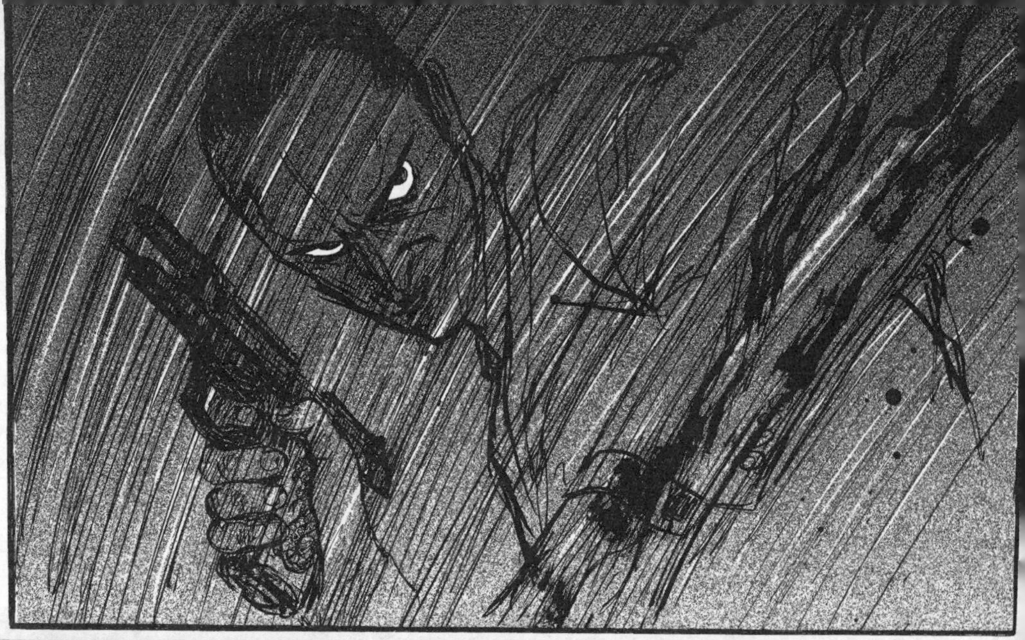
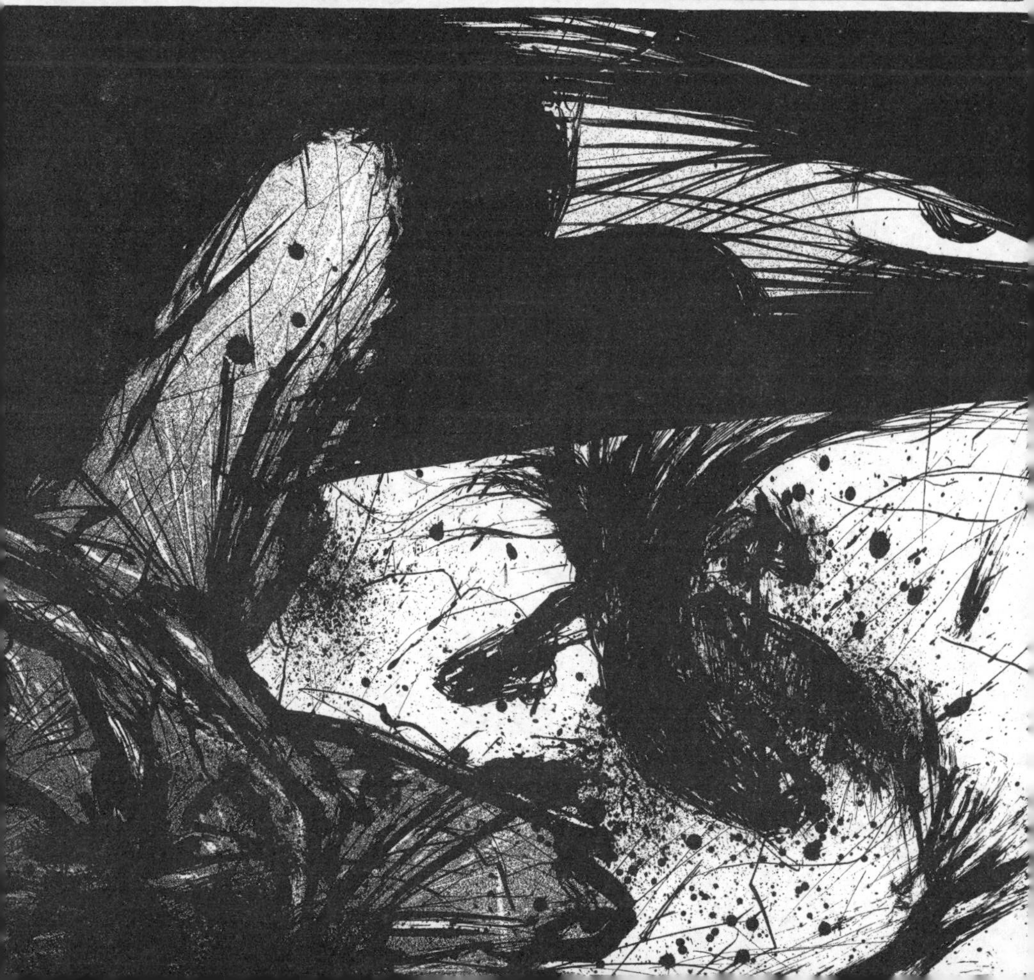

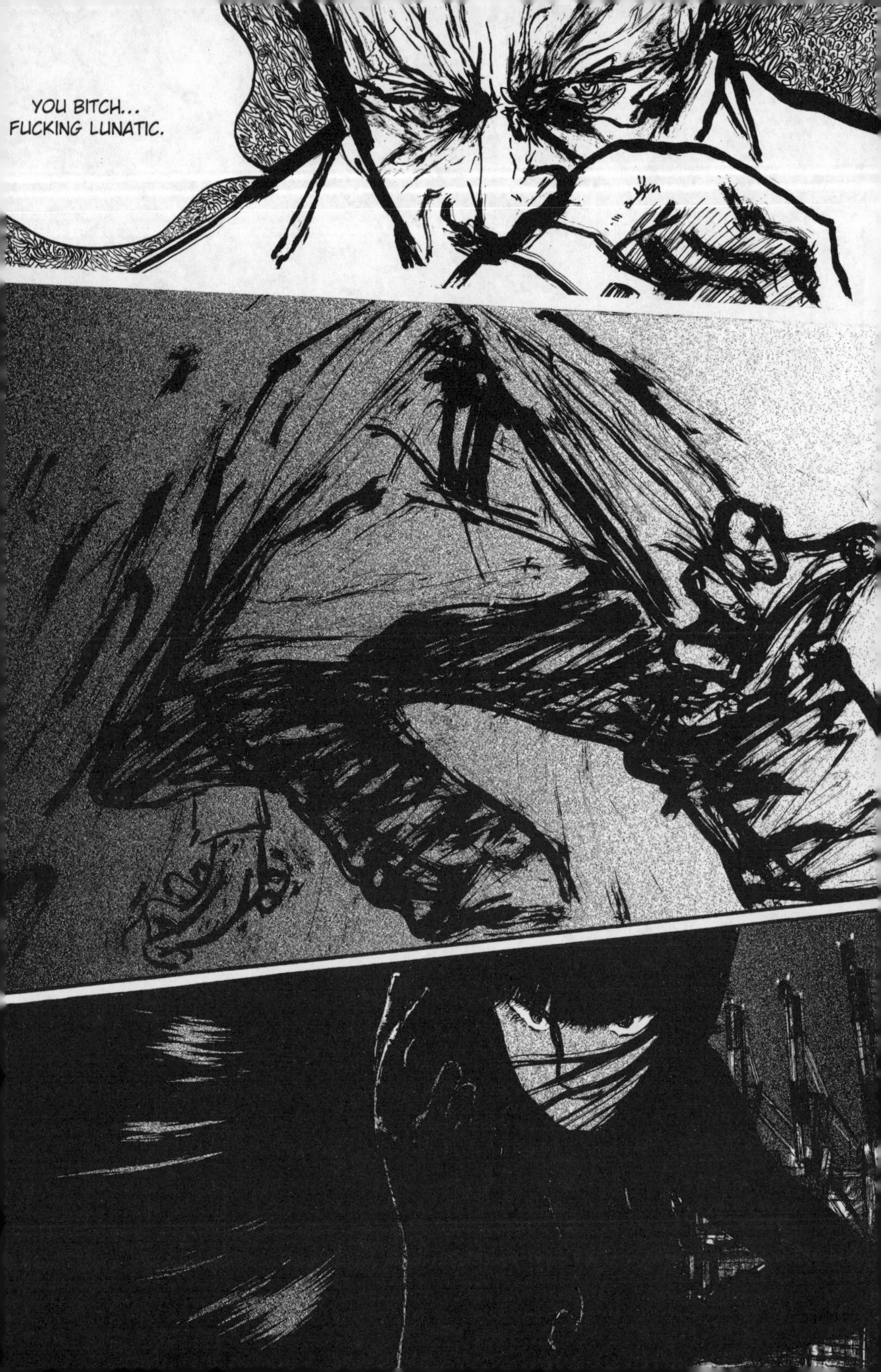
YOU BITCH... FUCKING LUNATIC.

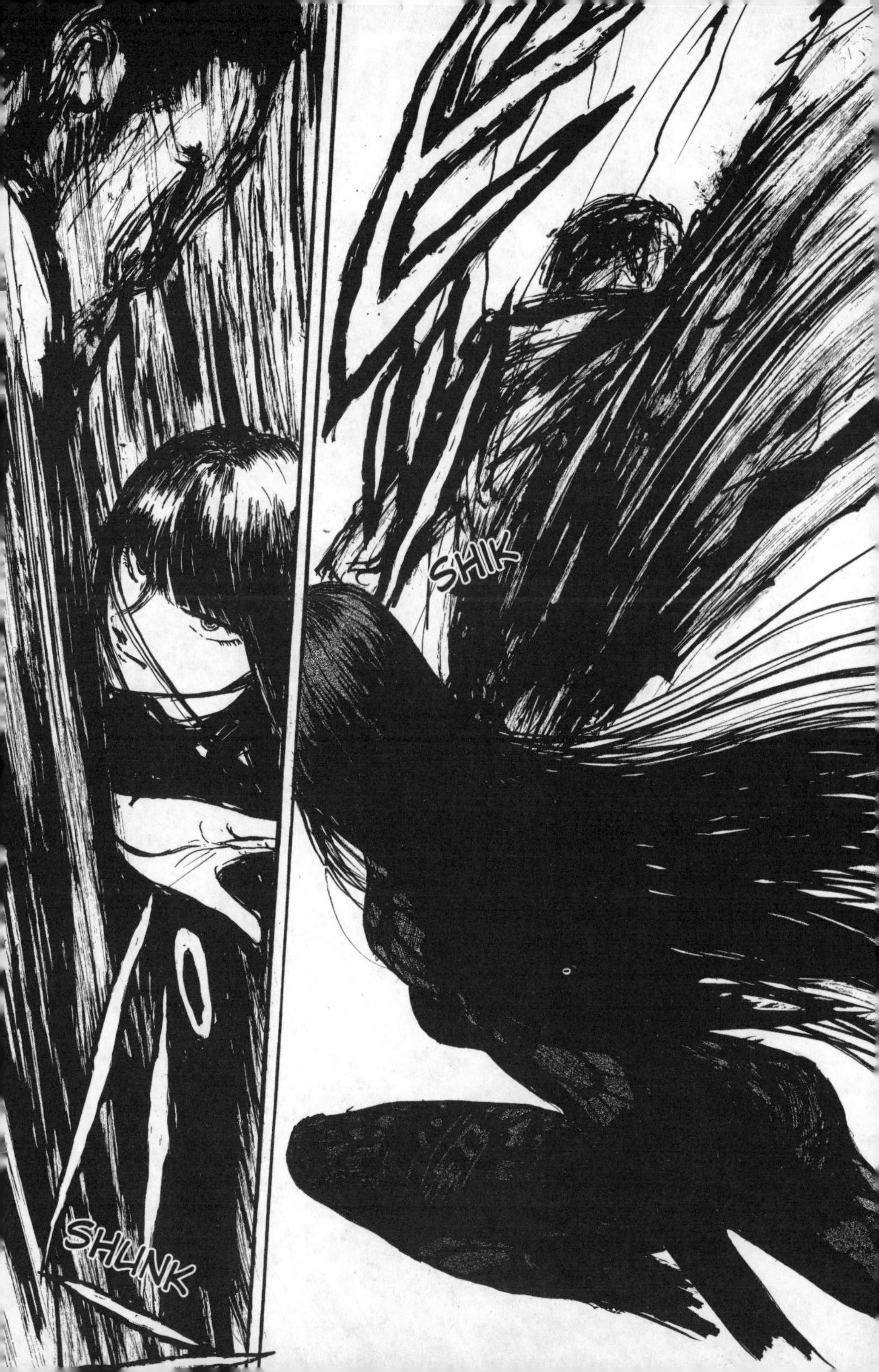
SHIK
SHLINK

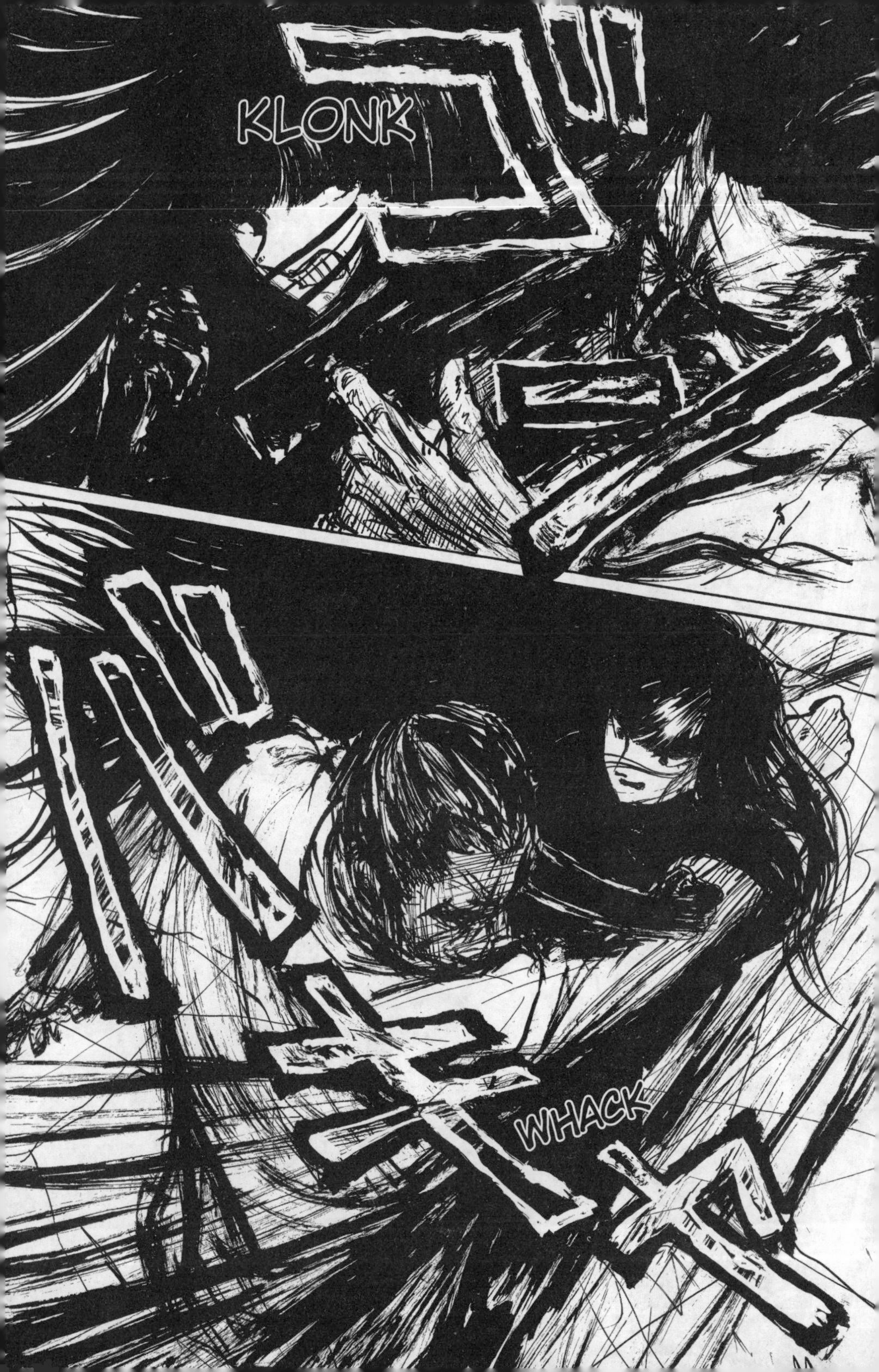
KLONK
WHACK

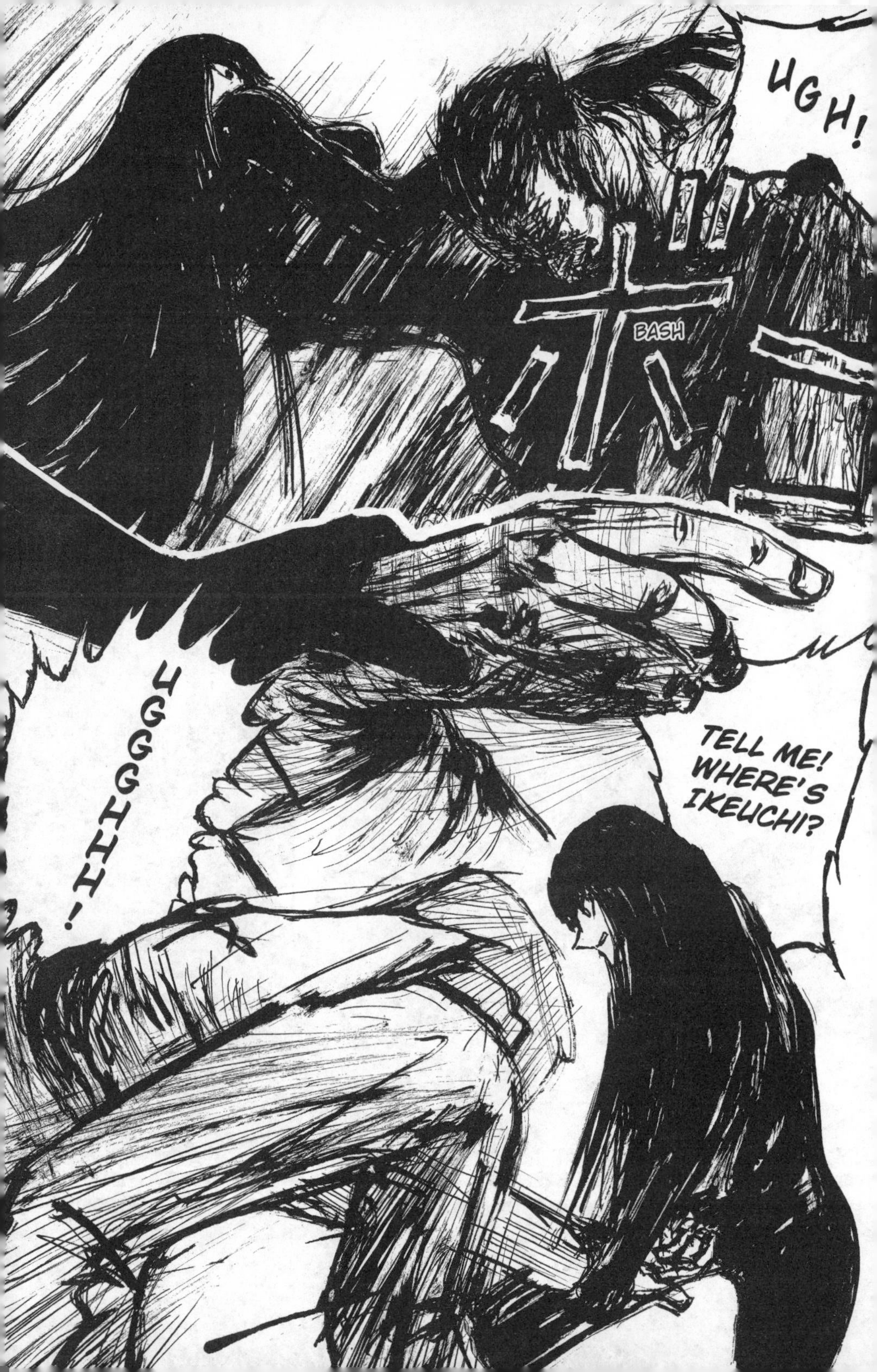
UGH!
BASH
TELL ME! WHERE'S IKEUCHI?
UGGGHHH!

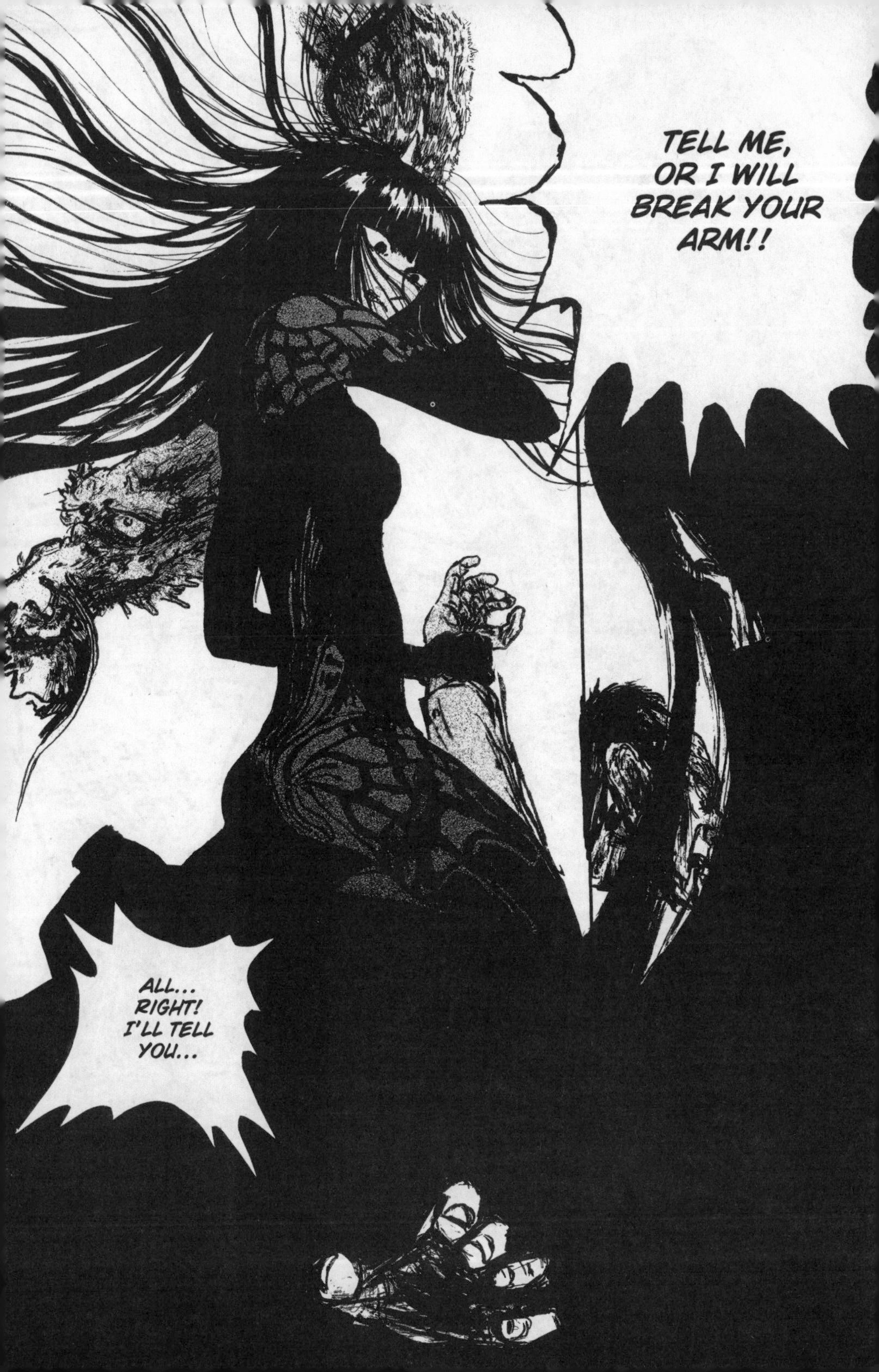
TELL ME, OR I WILL BREAK YOUR ARM!!
ALL... RIGHT! I'LL TELL YOU...

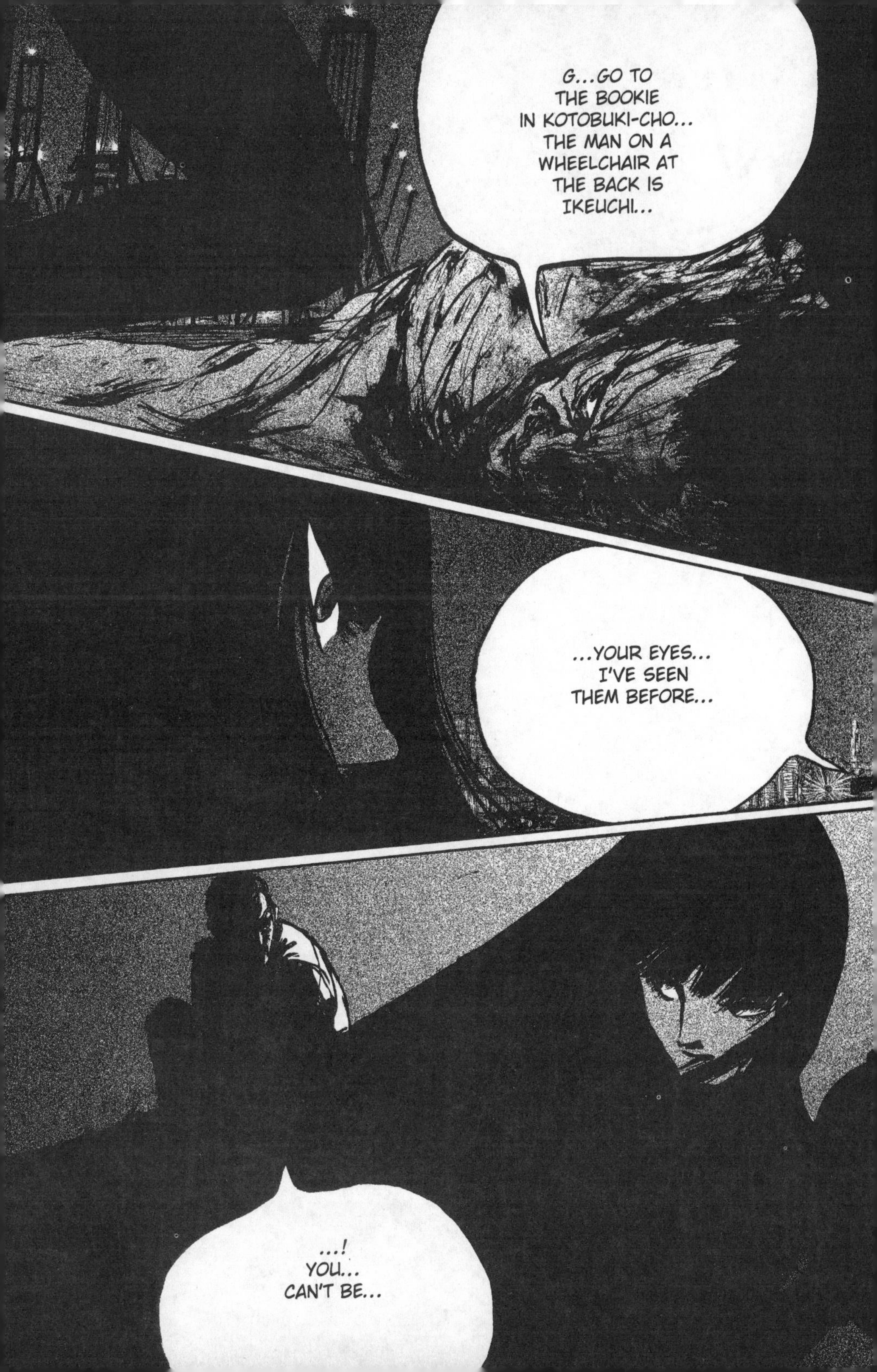
G...GO TO THE BOOKIE IN KOTOBUKI-CHO... THE MAN ON A WHEELCHAIR AT THE BACK IS IKEUCHI...
...YOUR EYES... I'VE SEEN THEM BEFORE...
...! YOU... CAN'T BE...

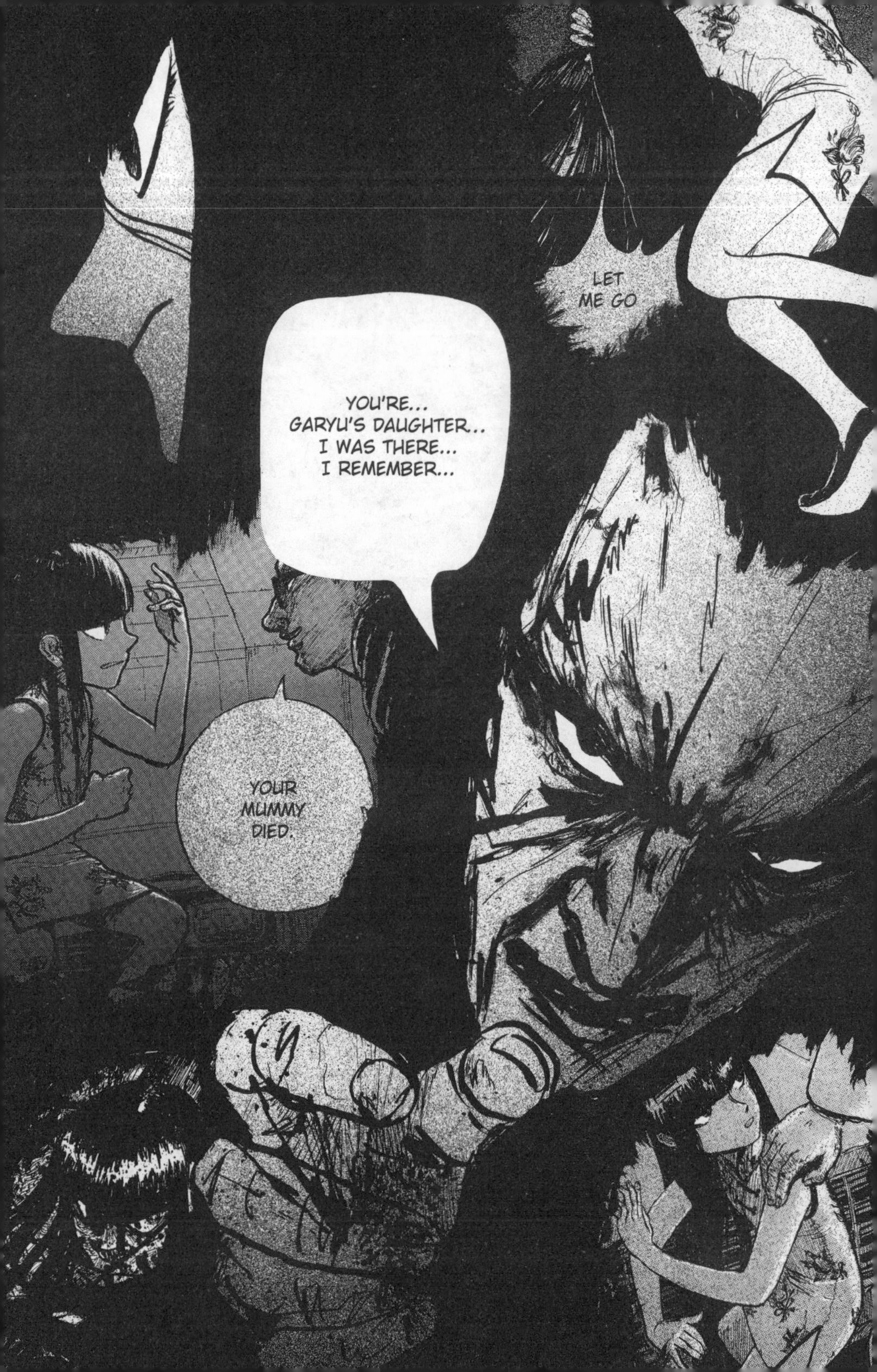
LET ME GO
YOU'RE... GARYU'S DAUGHTER... I WAS THERE... I REMEMBER...
YOUR MUMMY DIED.

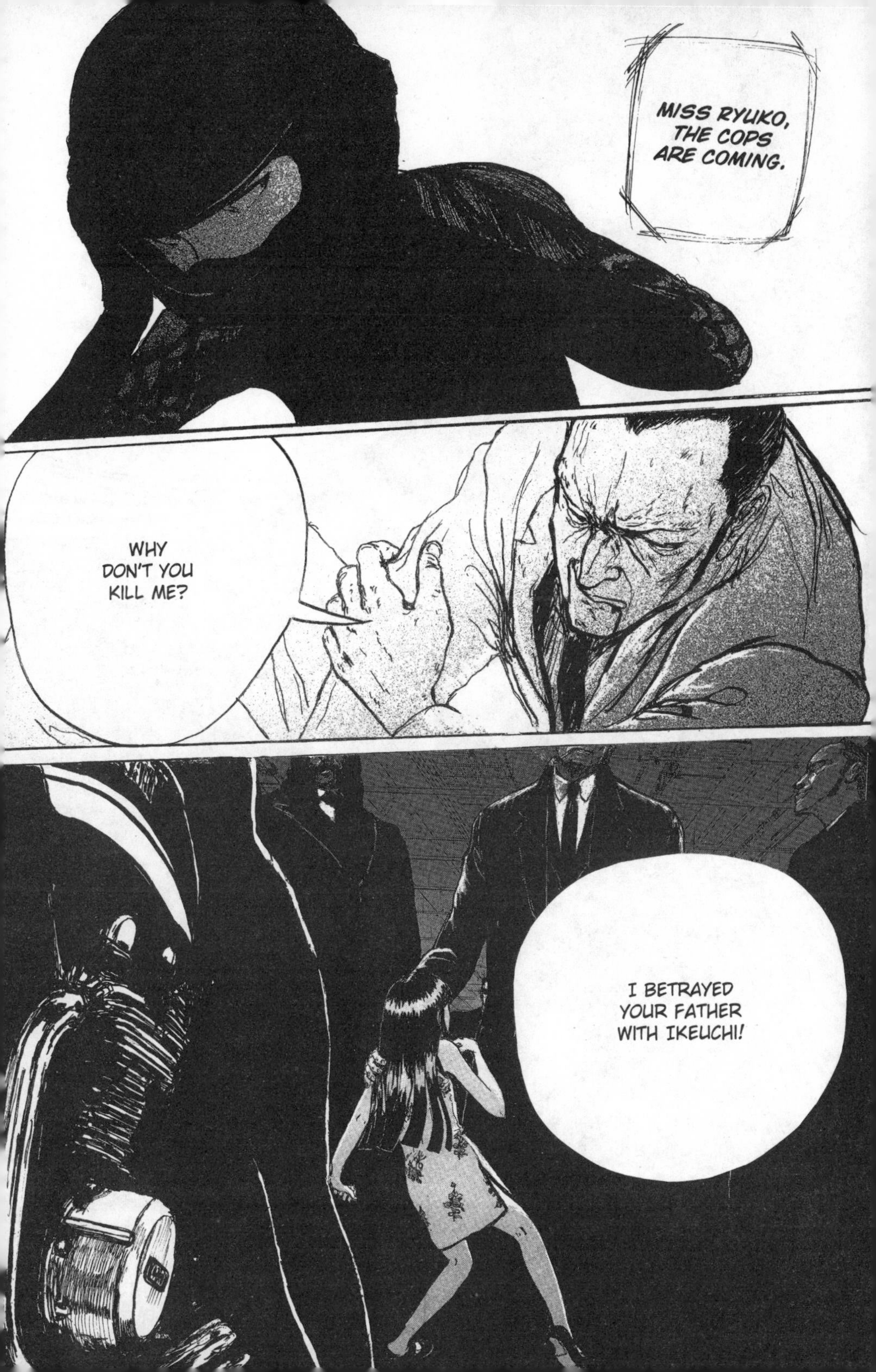
MISS RYUKO, THE COPS ARE COMING.
WHY DON'T YOU KILL ME?
I BETRAYED YOUR FATHER WITH IKEUCHI!

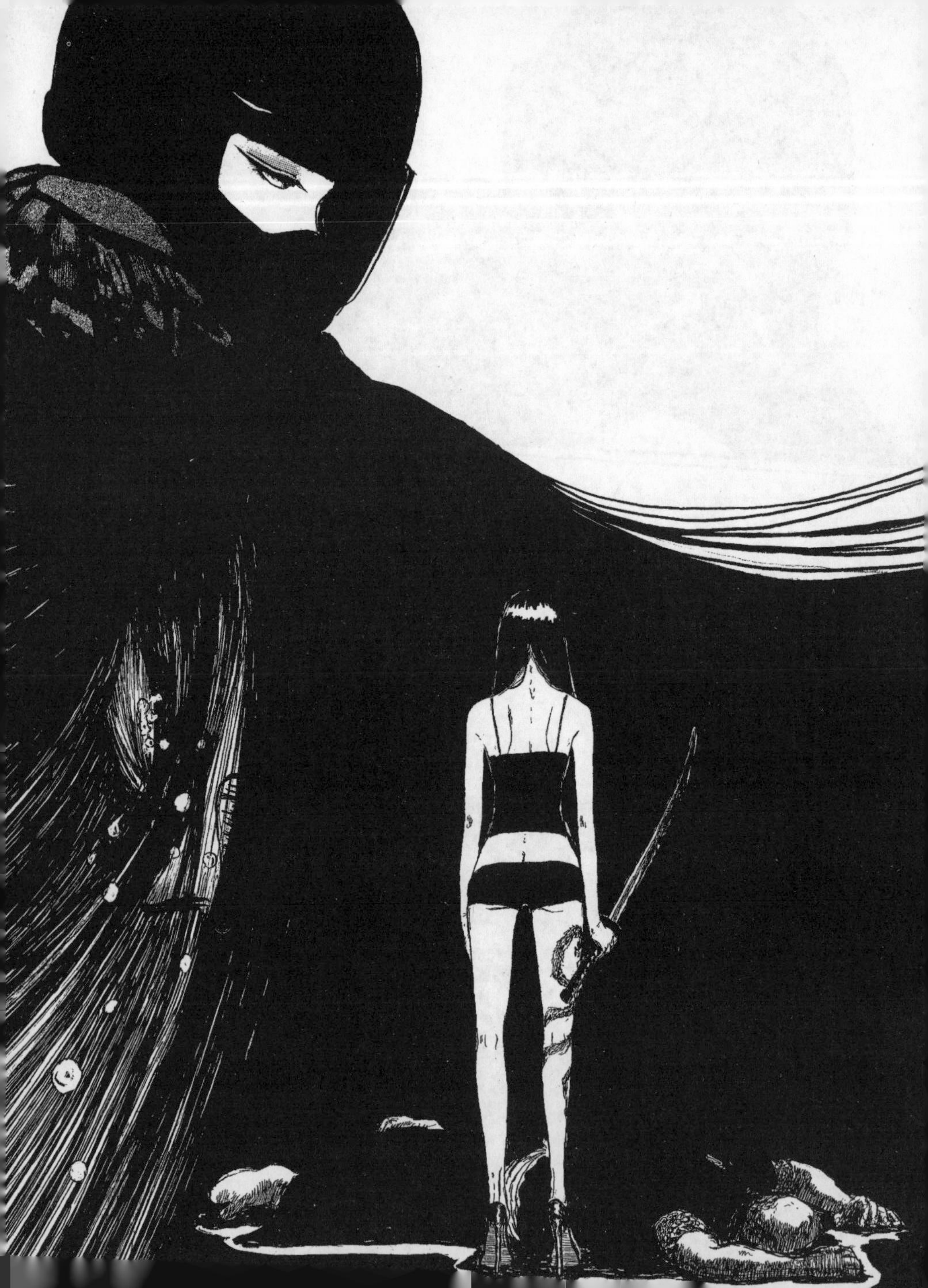

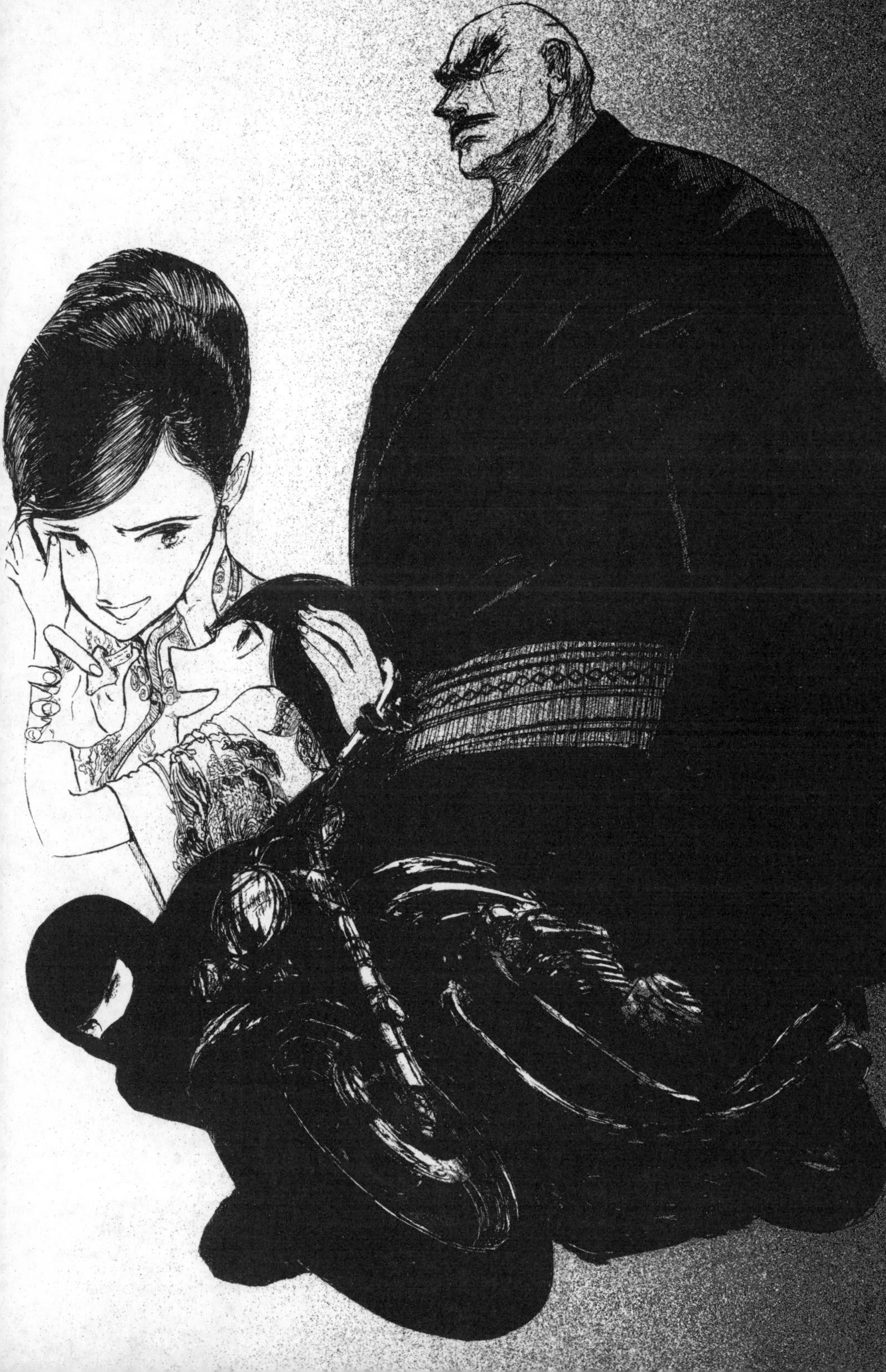

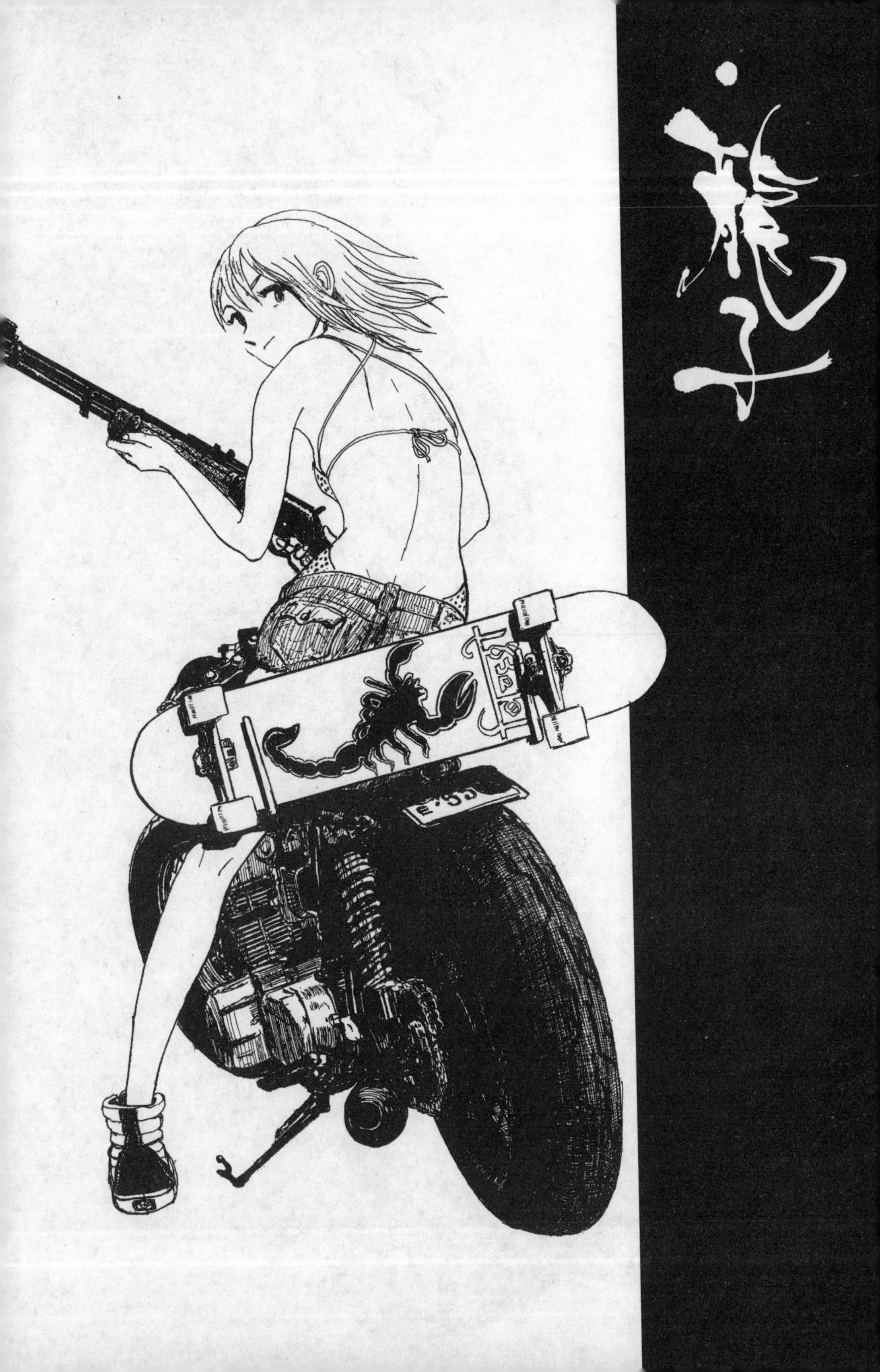

CHAPTER 4:
OLD WOUNDS

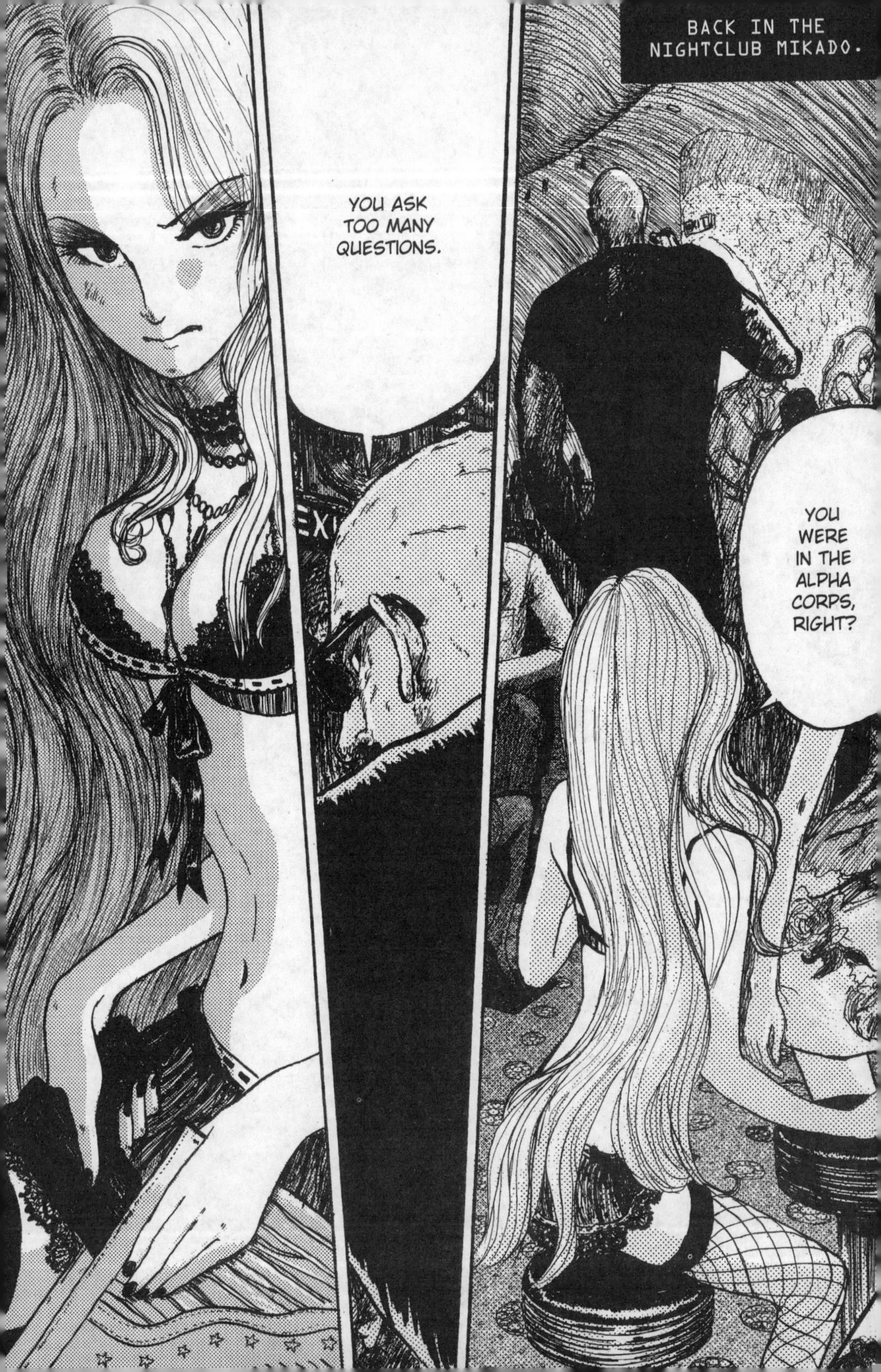
BACK IN THE NIGHTCLUB MIKADO.
YOU WERE IN THE ALPHA CORPS, RIGHT?
YOU ASK TOO MANY QUESTIONS.

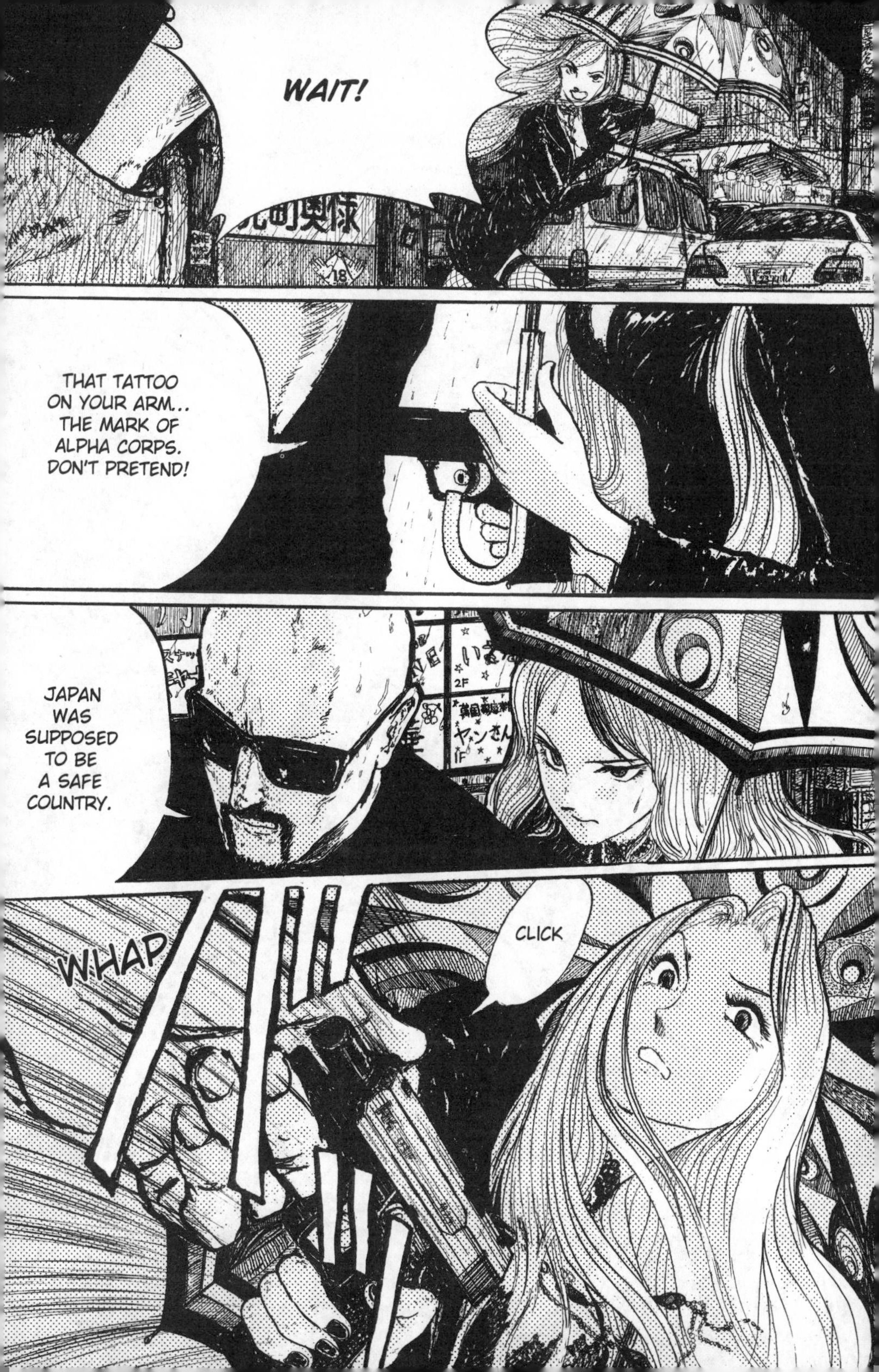
WAIT!
THAT TATTOO ON YOUR ARM... THE MARK OF ALPHA CORPS. DON'T PRETEND!
JAPAN WAS SUPPOSED TO BE A SAFE COUNTRY.
CLICK
WHAP

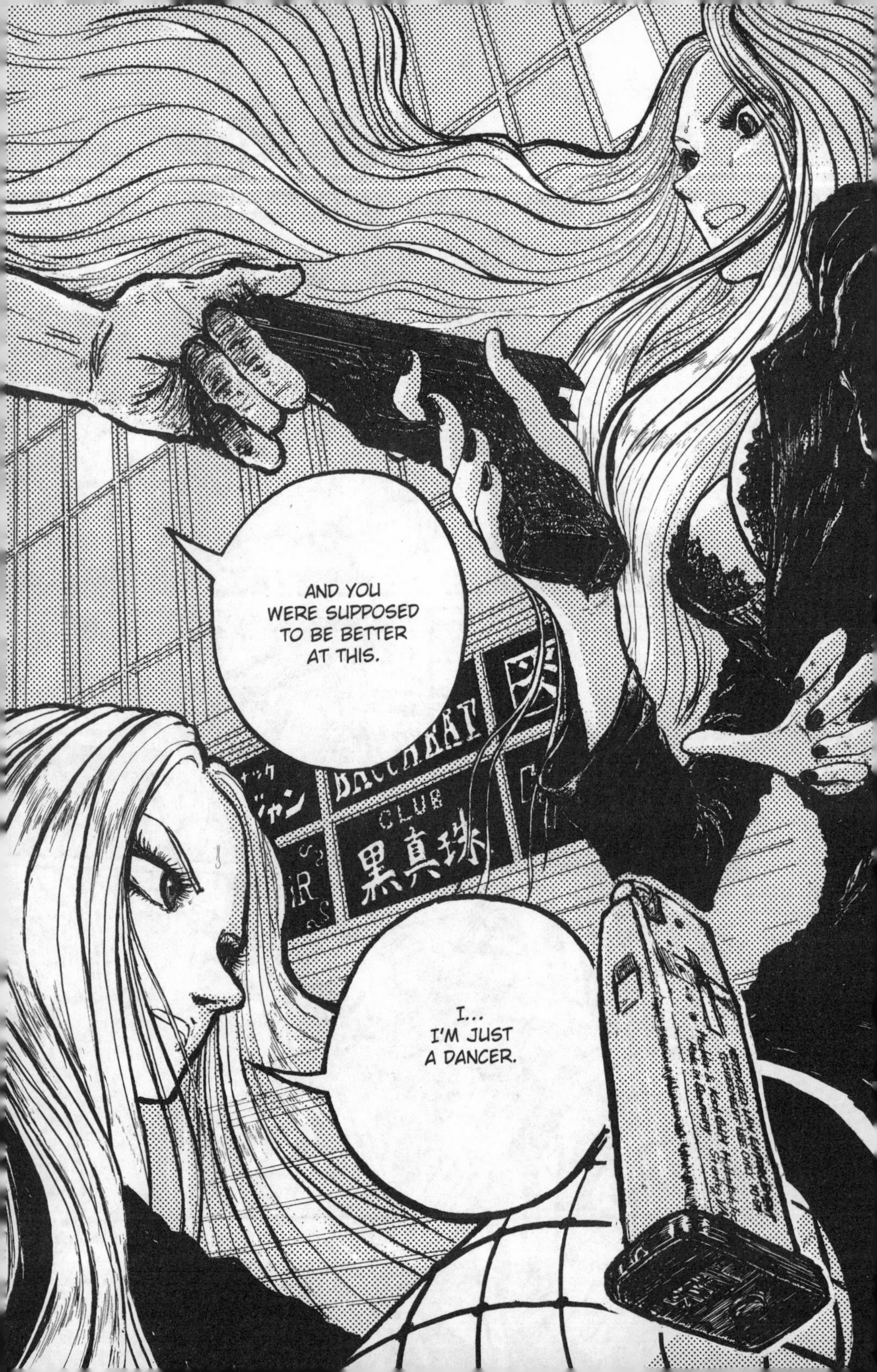
AND YOU WERE SUPPOSED TO BE BETTER AT THIS.
CLUB
黒真珠
I... I'M JUST A DANCER.

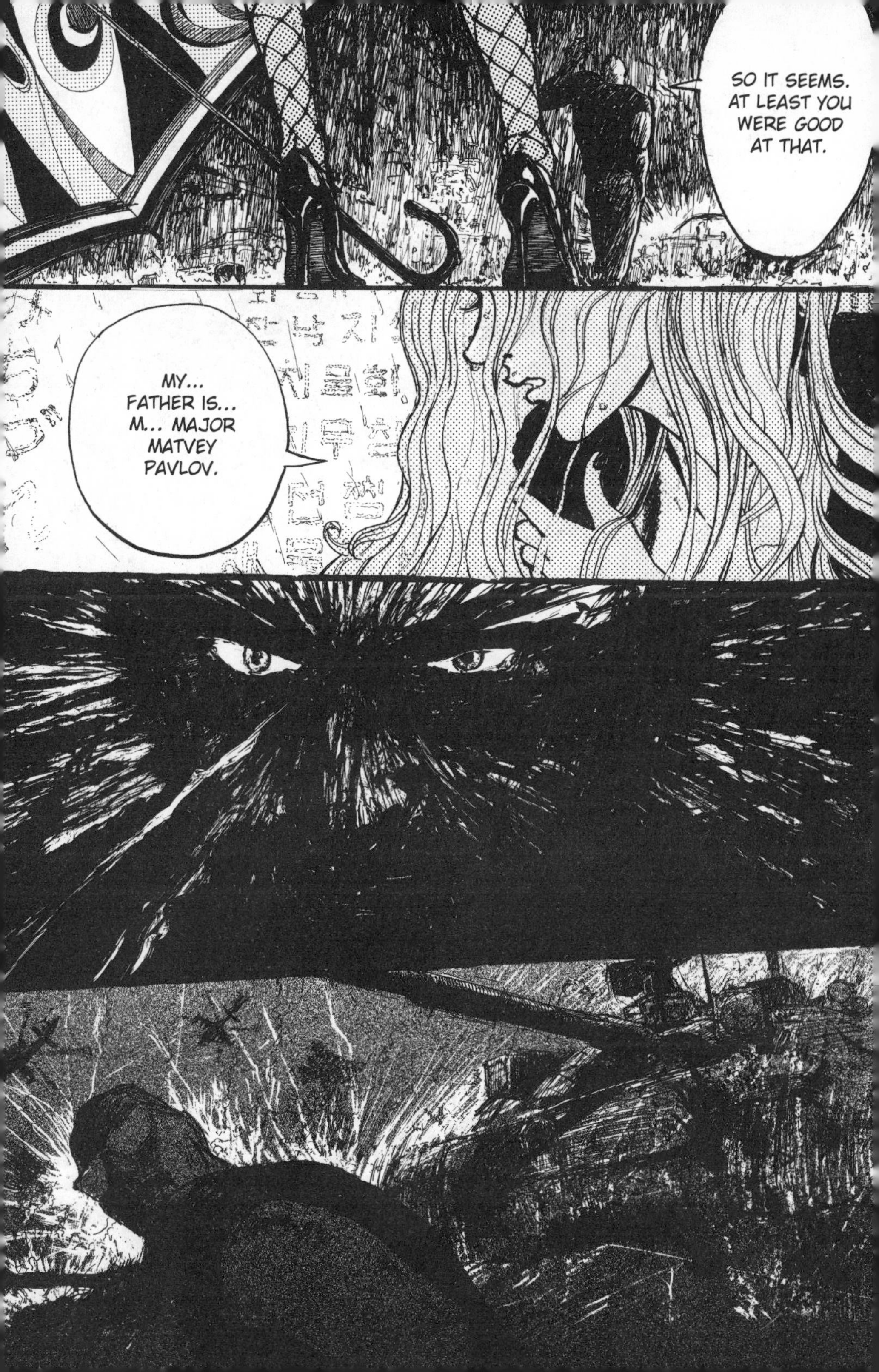
SO IT SEEMS. AT LEAST YOU WERE GOOD AT THAT.
MY... FATHER IS... M... MAJOR MATVEY PAVLOV.

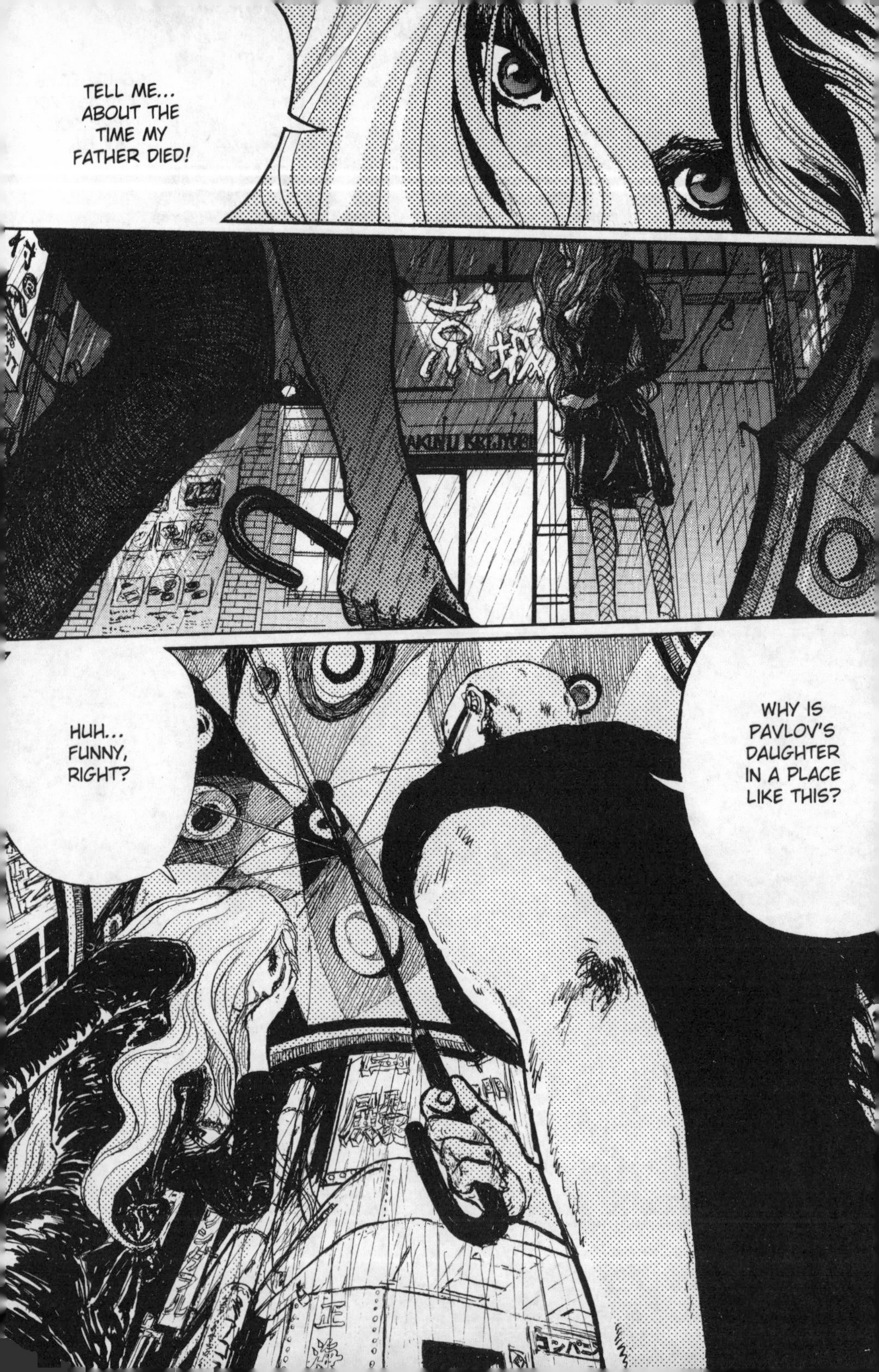
TELL ME... ABOUT THE TIME MY FATHER DIED!
WHY IS PAVLOV'S DAUGHTER IN A PLACE LIKE THIS?
HUH... FUNNY, RIGHT?

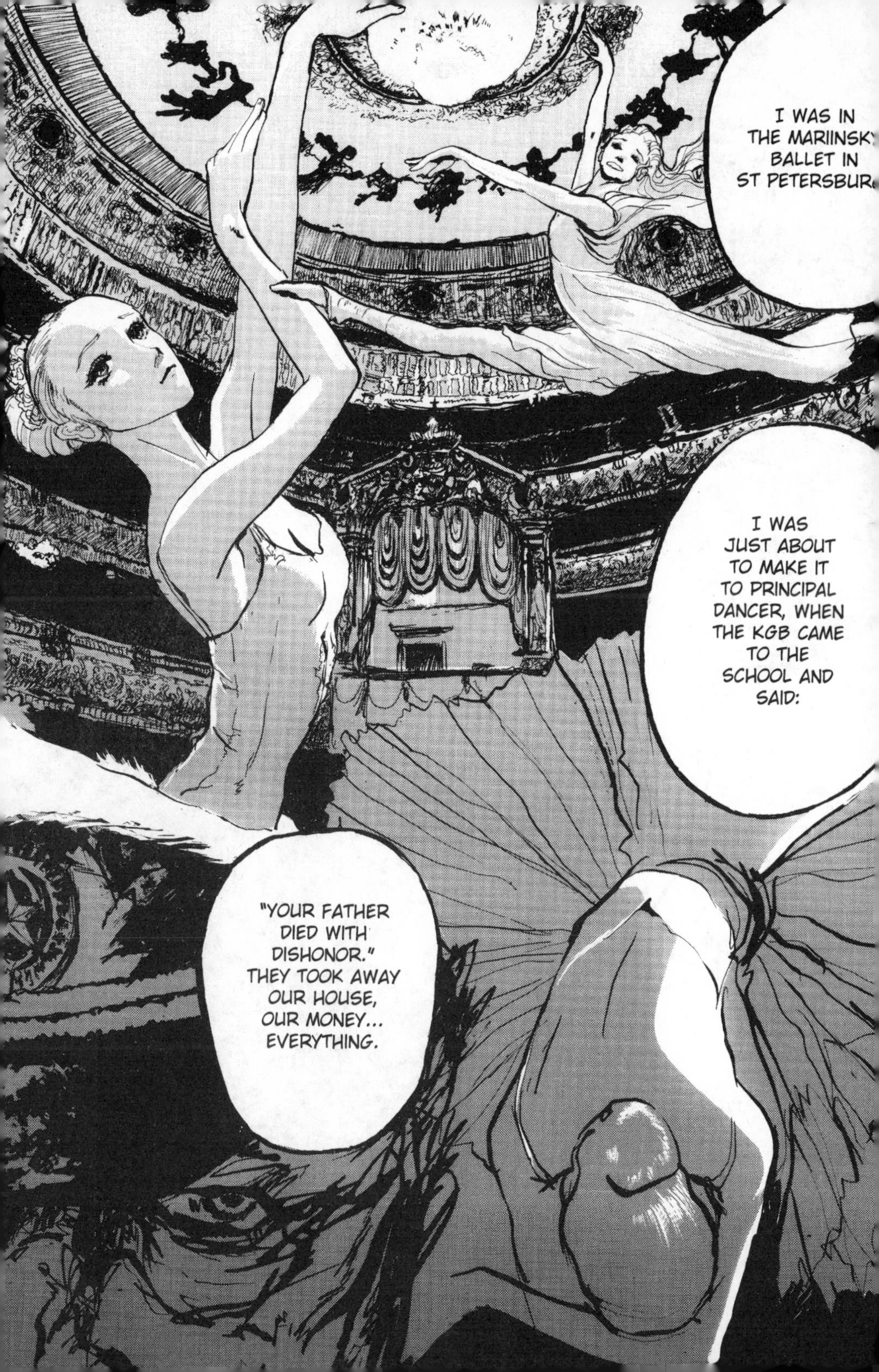
I WAS IN THE MARIINSKY BALLET IN ST PETERSBUR
I WAS JUST ABOUT TO MAKE IT TO PRINCIPAL DANCER, WHEN THE KGB CAME TO THE SCHOOL AND SAID:
"YOUR FATHER DIED WITH DISHONOR." THEY TOOK AWAY OUR HOUSE, OUR MONEY... EVERYTHING.

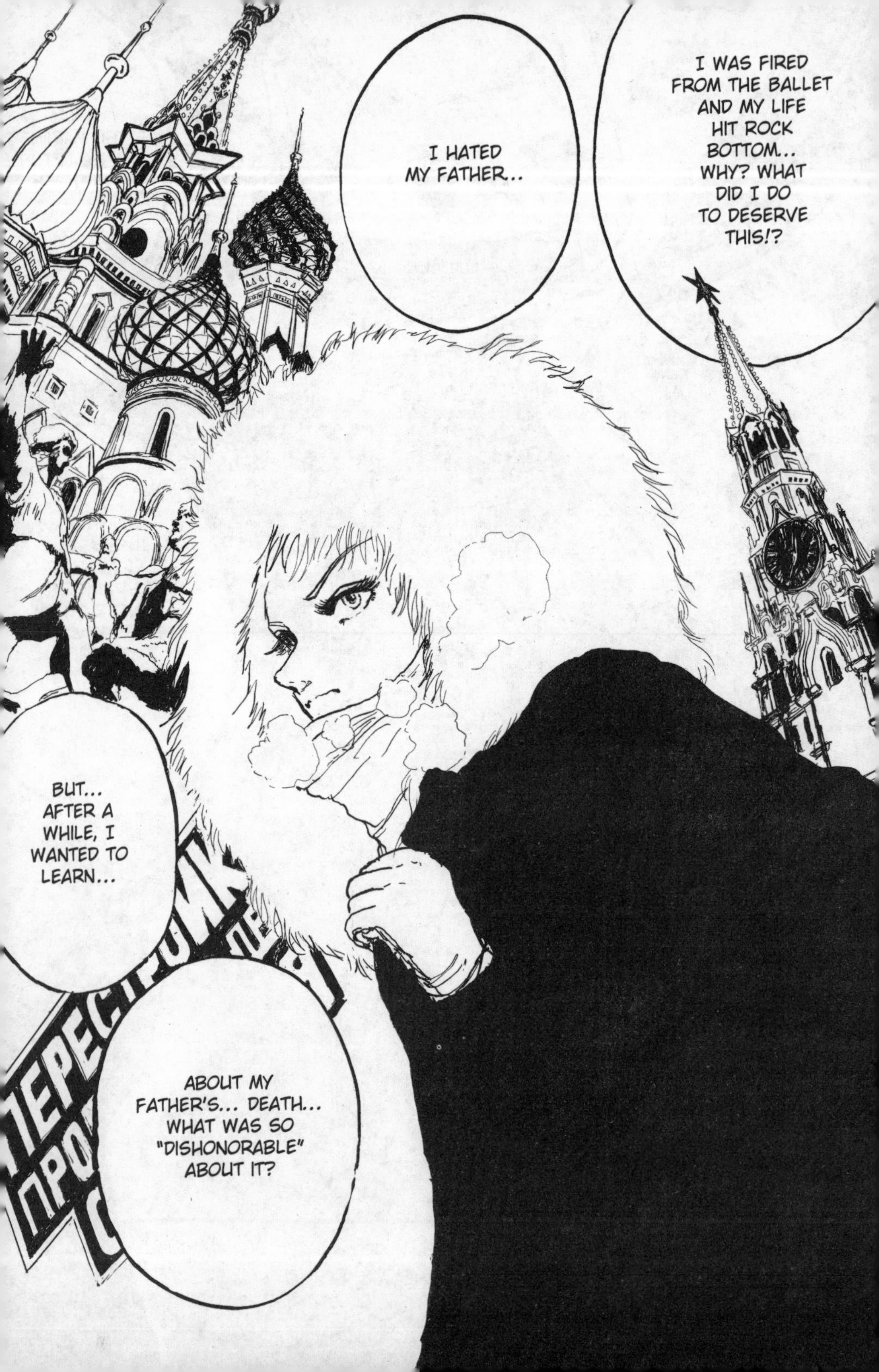
I WAS FIRED FROM THE BALLET AND MY LIFE HIT ROCK BOTTOM... WHY? WHAT DID I DO TO DESERVE THIS!?
I HATED MY FATHER...
BUT... AFTER A WHILE, I WANTED TO LEARN...
ABOUT MY FATHER'S... DEATH... WHAT WAS SO "DISHONORABLE" ABOUT IT?

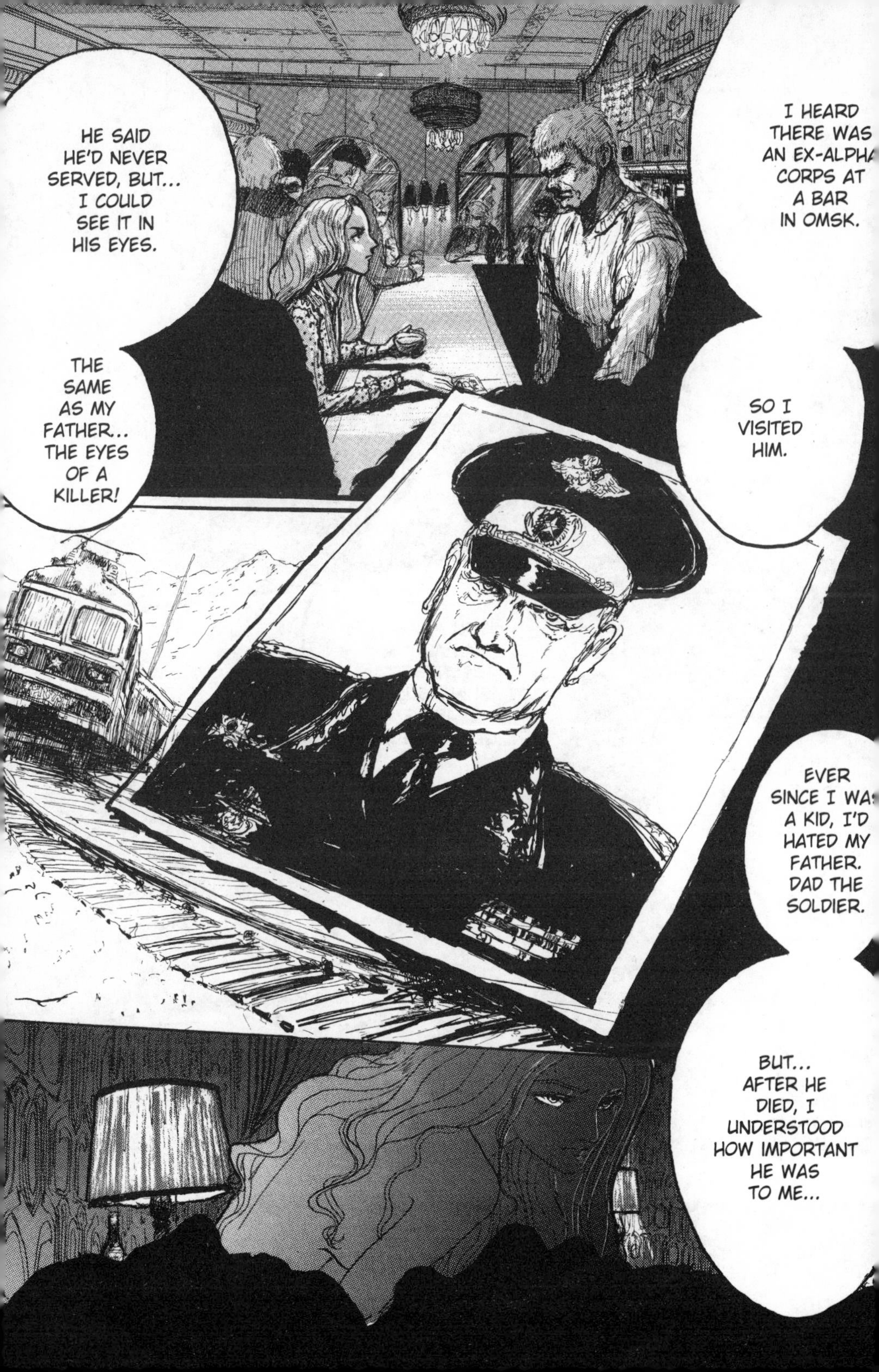
I HEARD THERE WAS AN EX-ALPHA CORPS AT A BAR IN OMSK.
SO I VISITED HIM.
HE SAID HE'D NEVER SERVED, BUT... I COULD SEE IT IN HIS EYES.
THE SAME AS MY FATHER... THE EYES OF A KILLER!
EVER SINCE I WAS A KID, I'D HATED MY FATHER. DAD THE SOLDIER.
BUT... AFTER HE DIED, I UNDERSTOOD HOW IMPORTANT HE WAS TO ME...

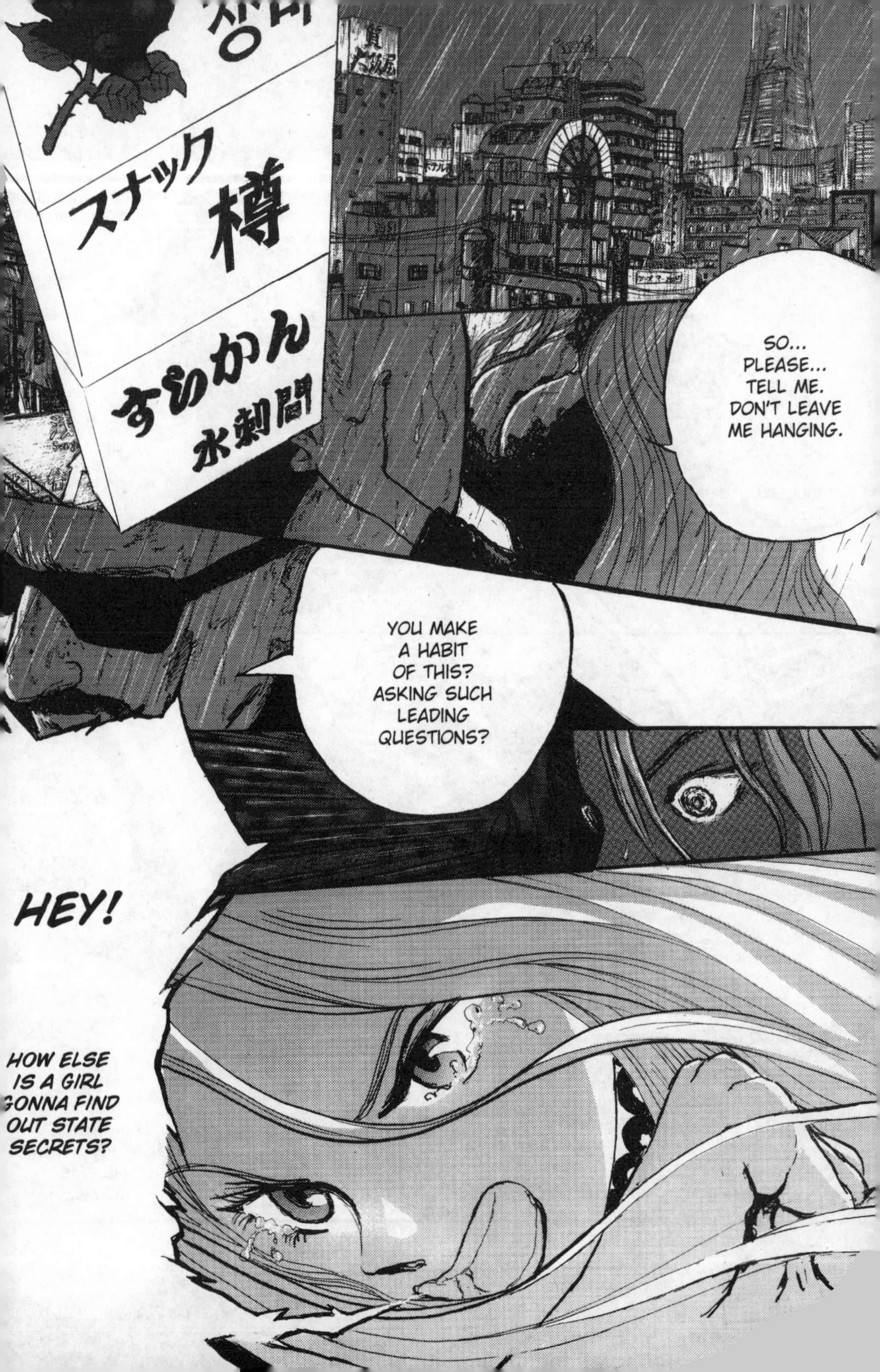
SO... PLEASE... TELL ME. DON'T LEAVE ME HANGING.
スナック
樽
YOU MAKE A HABIT OF THIS? ASKING SUCH LEADING QUESTIONS?
HEY!
HOW ELSE IS A GIRL GONNA FIND OUT STATE SECRETS?

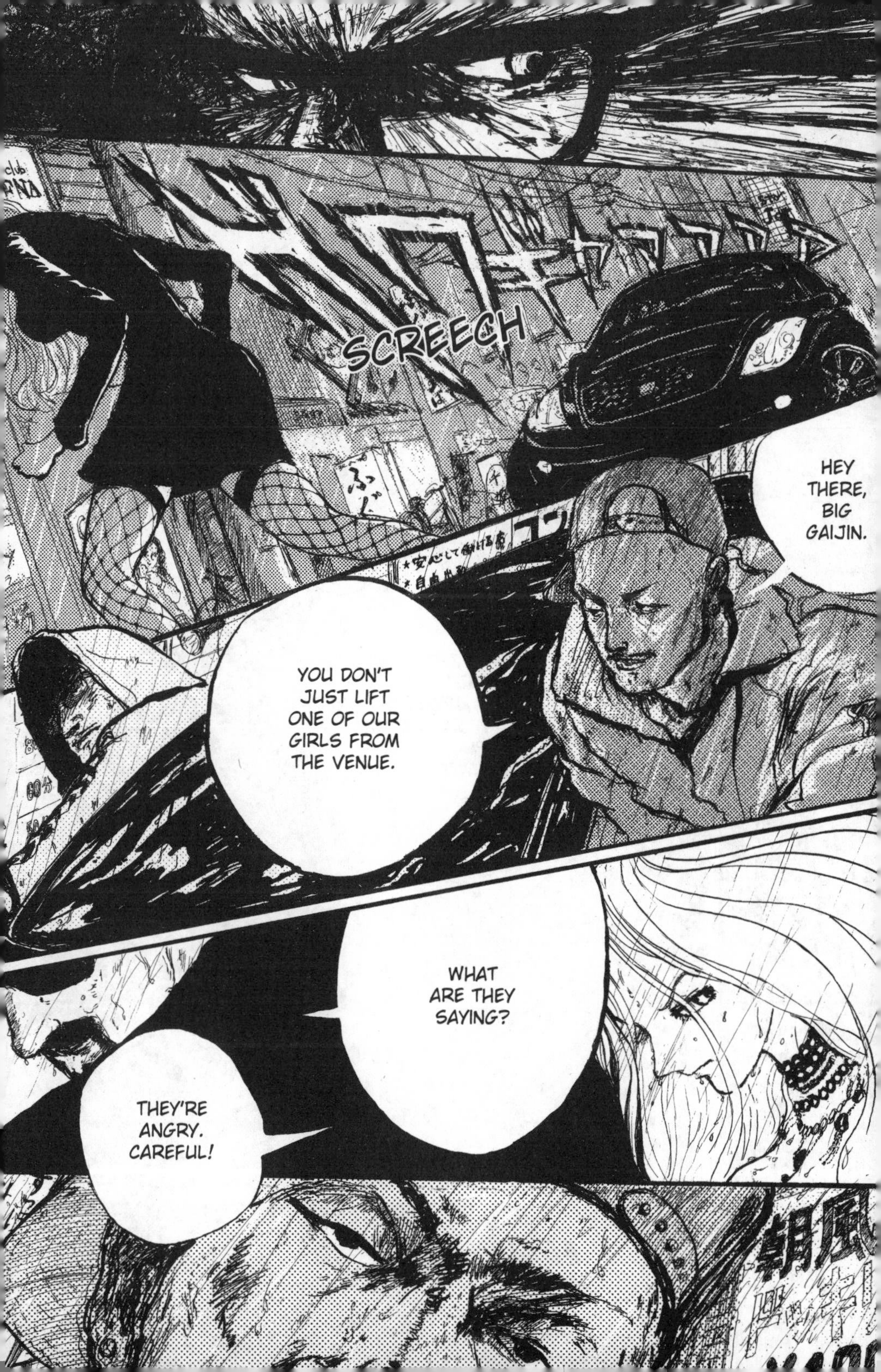
SCREECH
HEY THERE, BIG GAIJIN.
YOU DON'T JUST LIFT ONE OF OUR GIRLS FROM THE VENUE.
WHAT ARE THEY SAYING?
THEY'RE ANGRY. CAREFUL!

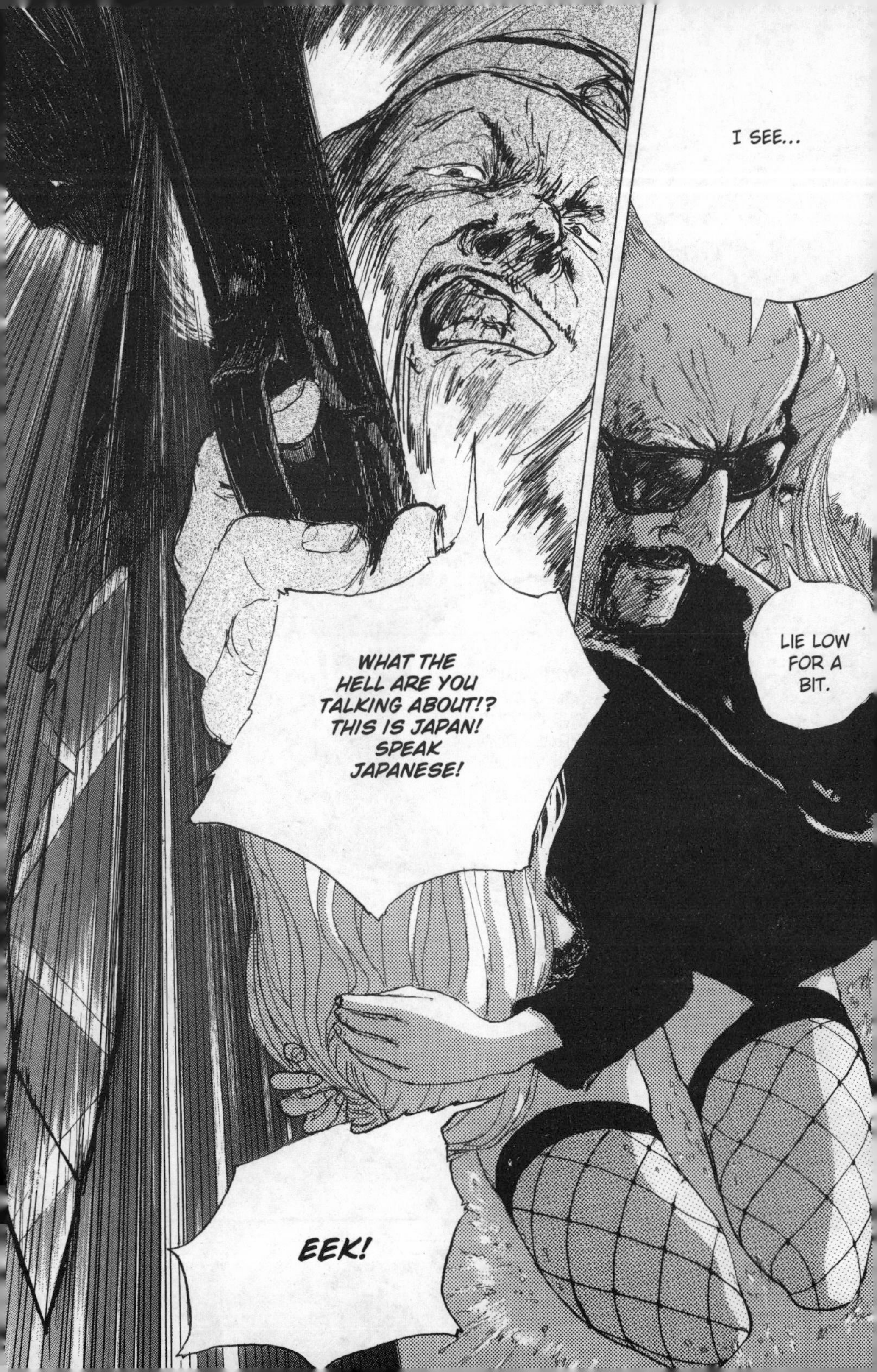
I SEE...
LIE LOW FOR A BIT.
WHAT THE HELL ARE YOU TALKING ABOUT!? THIS IS JAPAN! SPEAK JAPANESE!
EEK!

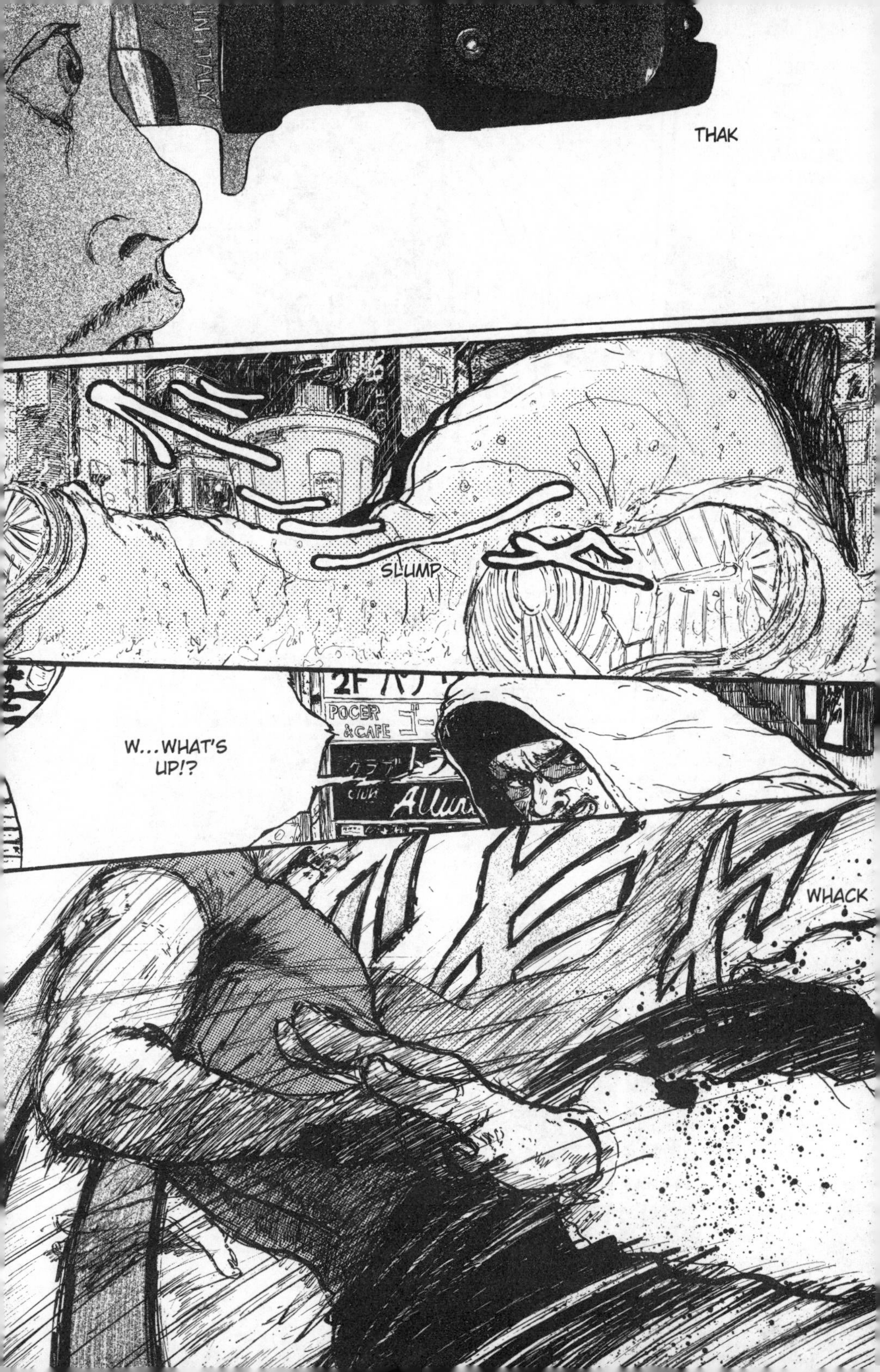
IN ITALY
THAK
SLUMP
2F
POCER
&CAFE
W...WHAT'S
UP!?
club
WHACK

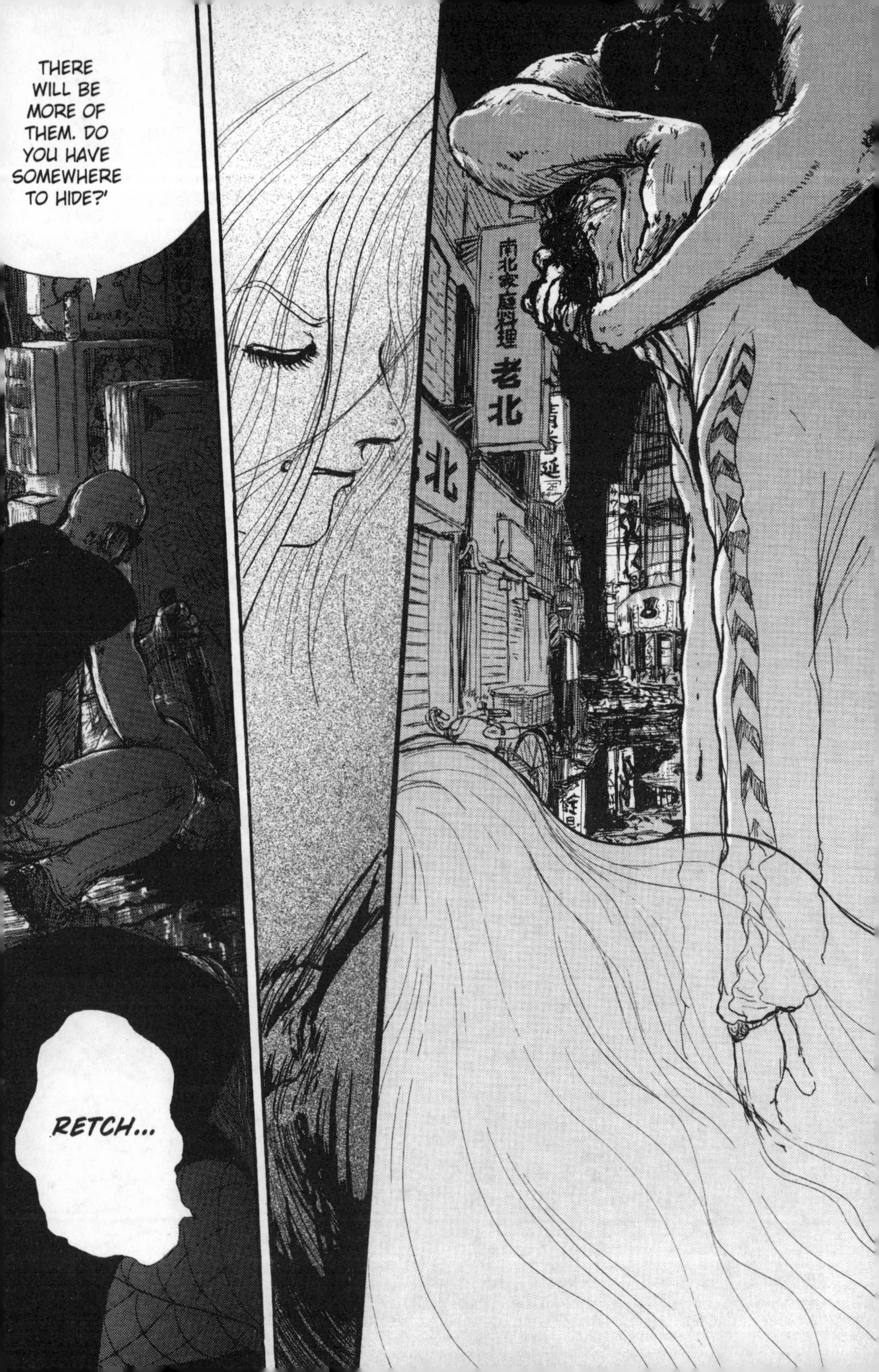
南北家庭料理
老北
THERE WILL BE MORE OF THEM. DO YOU HAVE SOMEWHERE TO HIDE?'
RETCH...

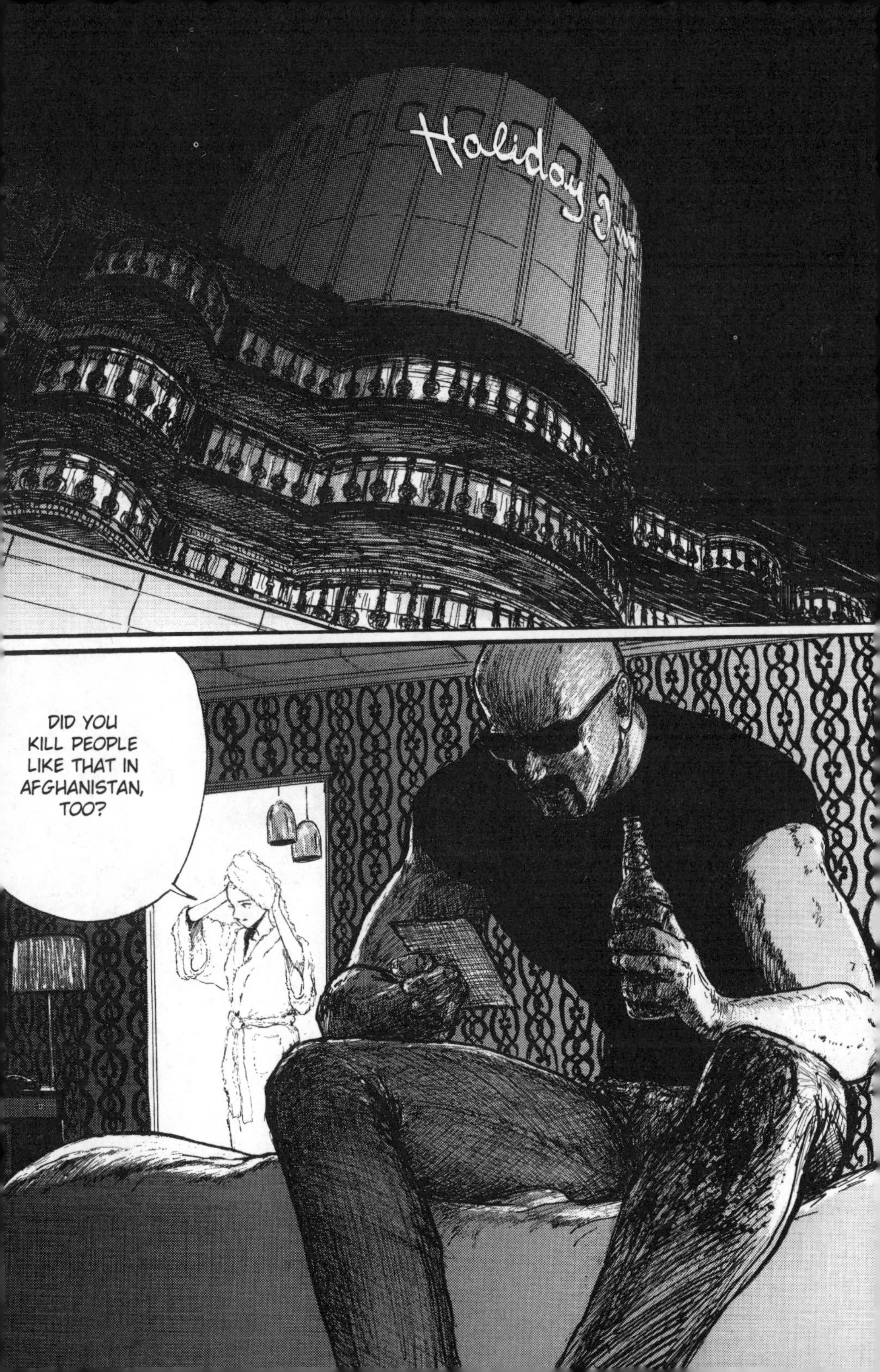
DID YOU KILL PEOPLE LIKE THAT IN AFGHANISTAN, TOO?

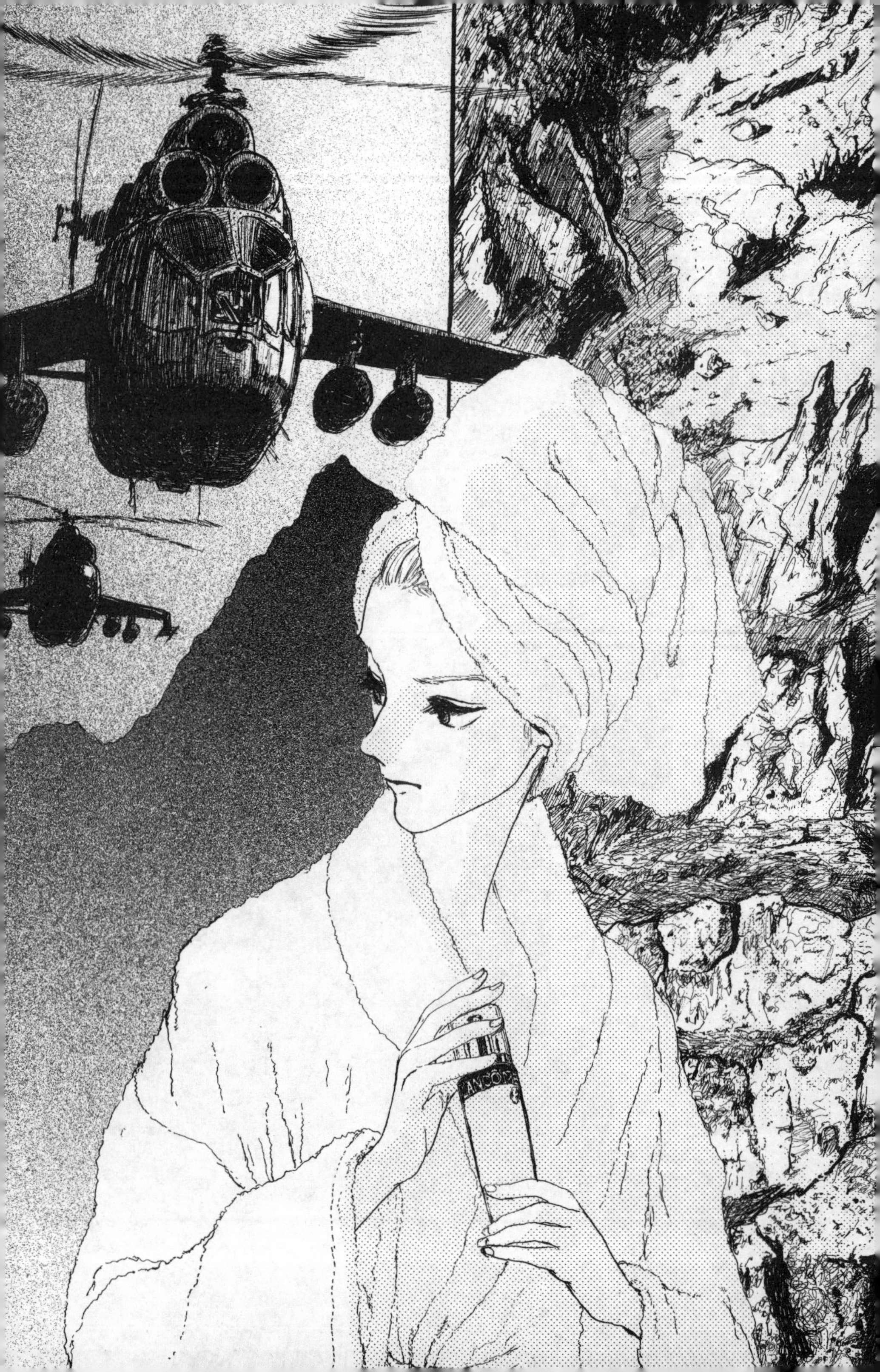

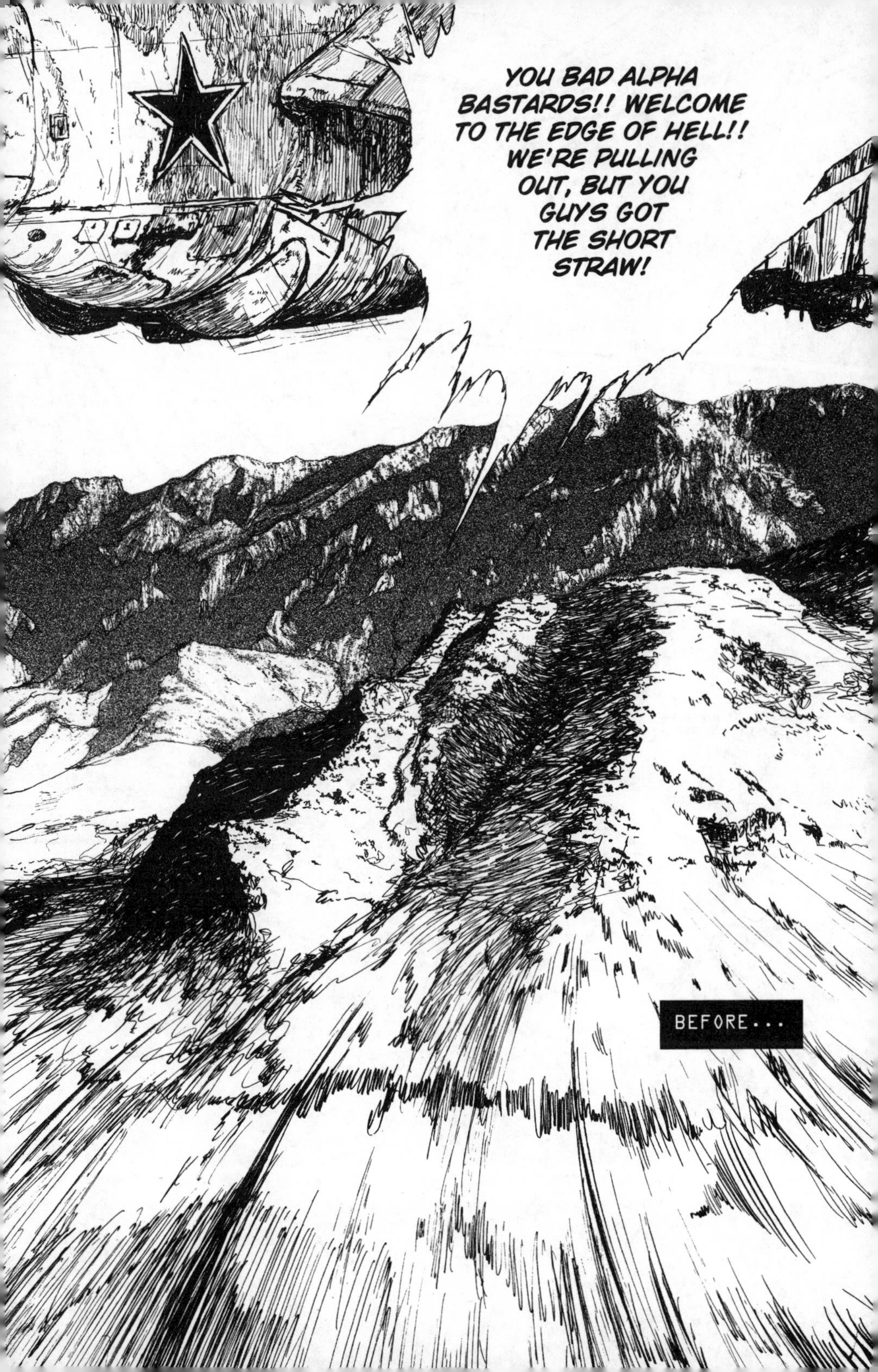
YOU BAD ALPHA BASTARDS!! WELCOME TO THE EDGE OF HELL!! WE'RE PULLING OUT, BUT YOU GUYS GOT THE SHORT STRAW!
BEFORE...

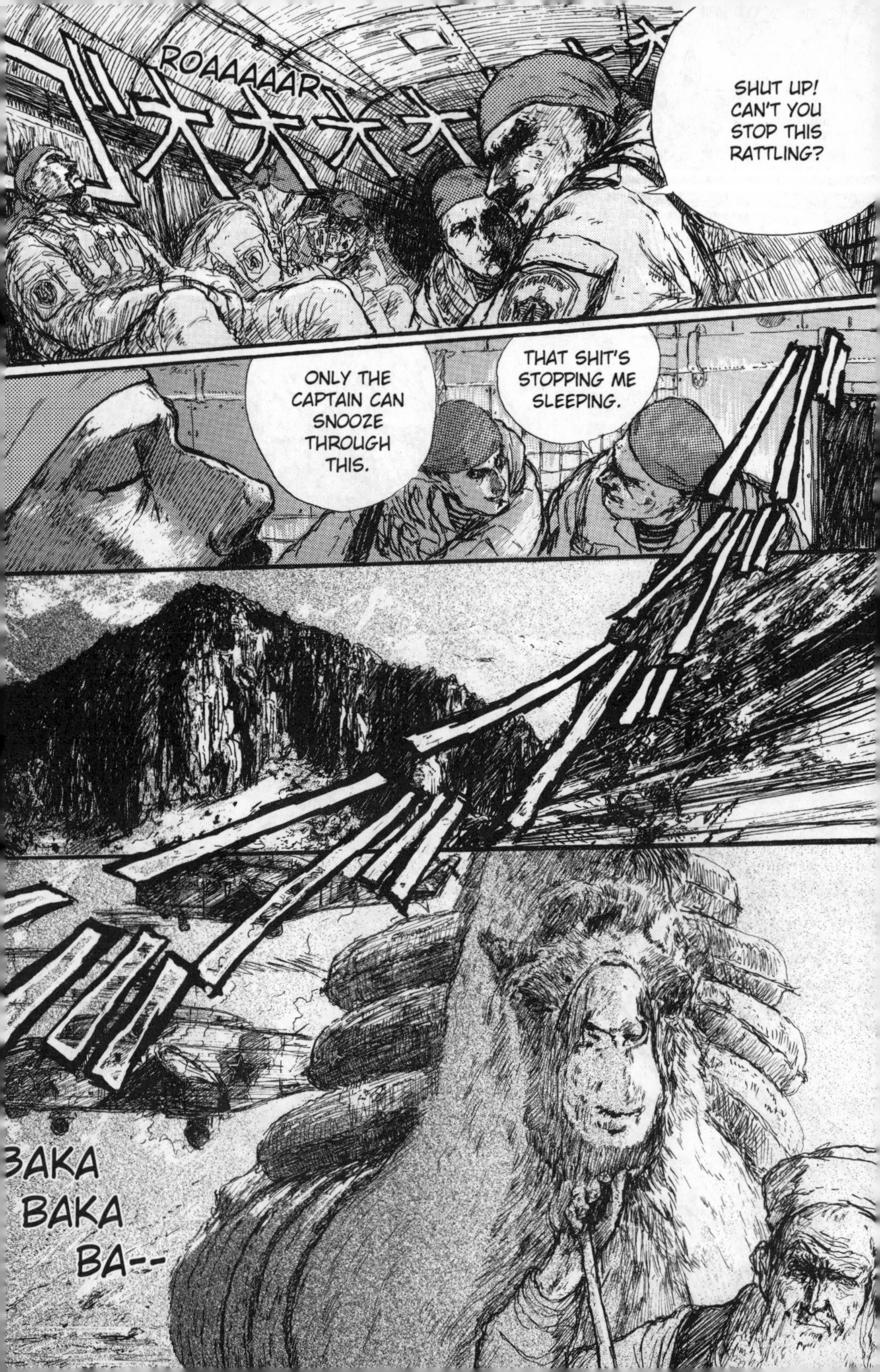
SHUT UP! CAN'T YOU STOP THIS RATTLING?
ROAAAAAR
THAT SHIT'S STOPPING ME SLEEPING.
ONLY THE CAPTAIN CAN SNOOZE THROUGH THIS.
BAKA BAKA BA--

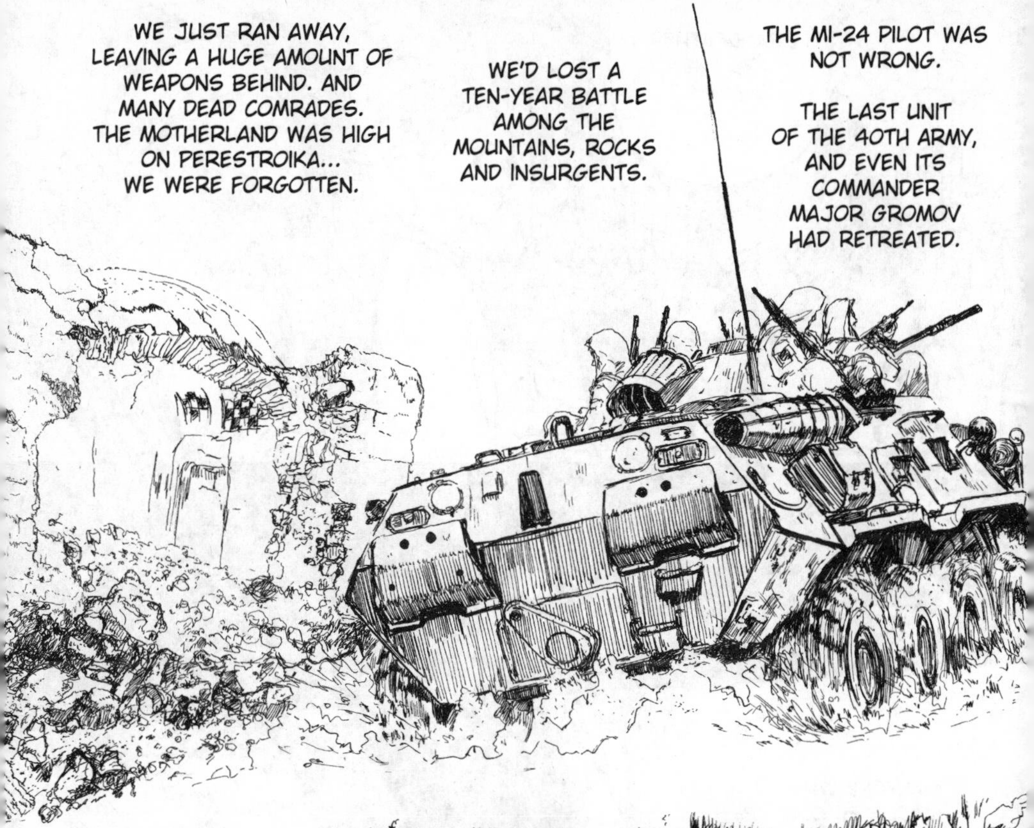
THE MI-24 PILOT WAS NOT WRONG.
THE LAST UNIT OF THE 40TH ARMY, AND EVEN ITS COMMANDER MAJOR GROMOV HAD RETREATED.
WE'D LOST A TEN-YEAR BATTLE AMONG THE MOUNTAINS, ROCKS AND INSURGENTS.
WE JUST RAN AWAY, LEAVING A HUGE AMOUNT OF WEAPONS BEHIND. AND MANY DEAD COMRADES. THE MOTHERLAND WAS HIGH ON PERESTROIKA... WE WERE FORGOTTEN.
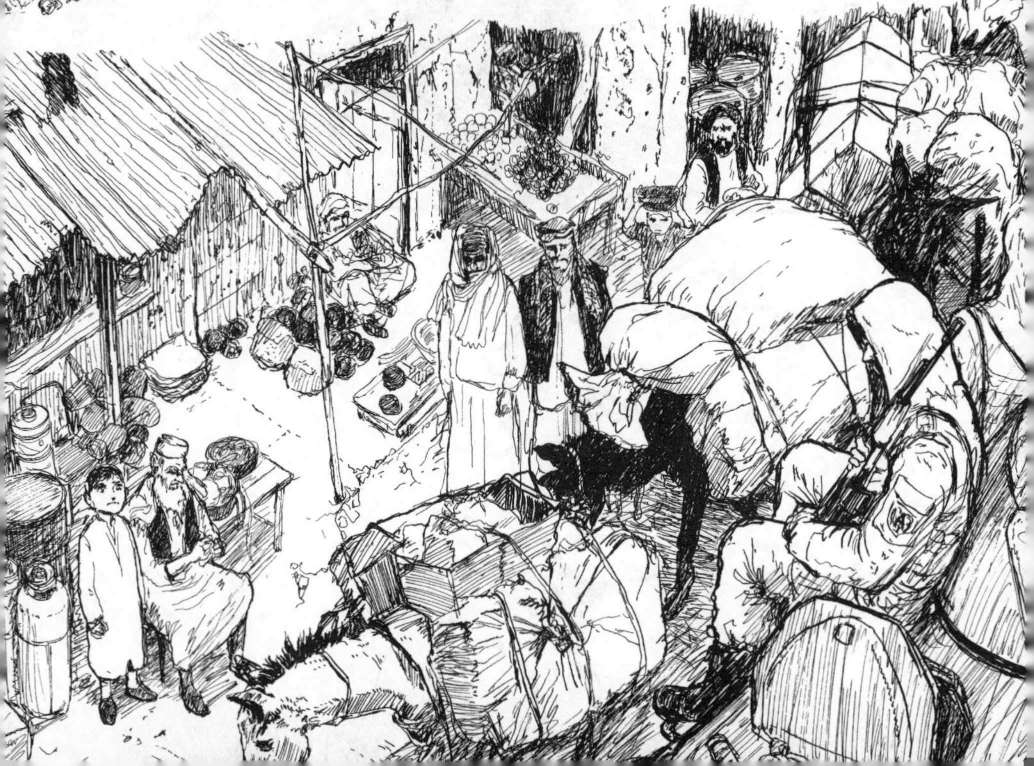

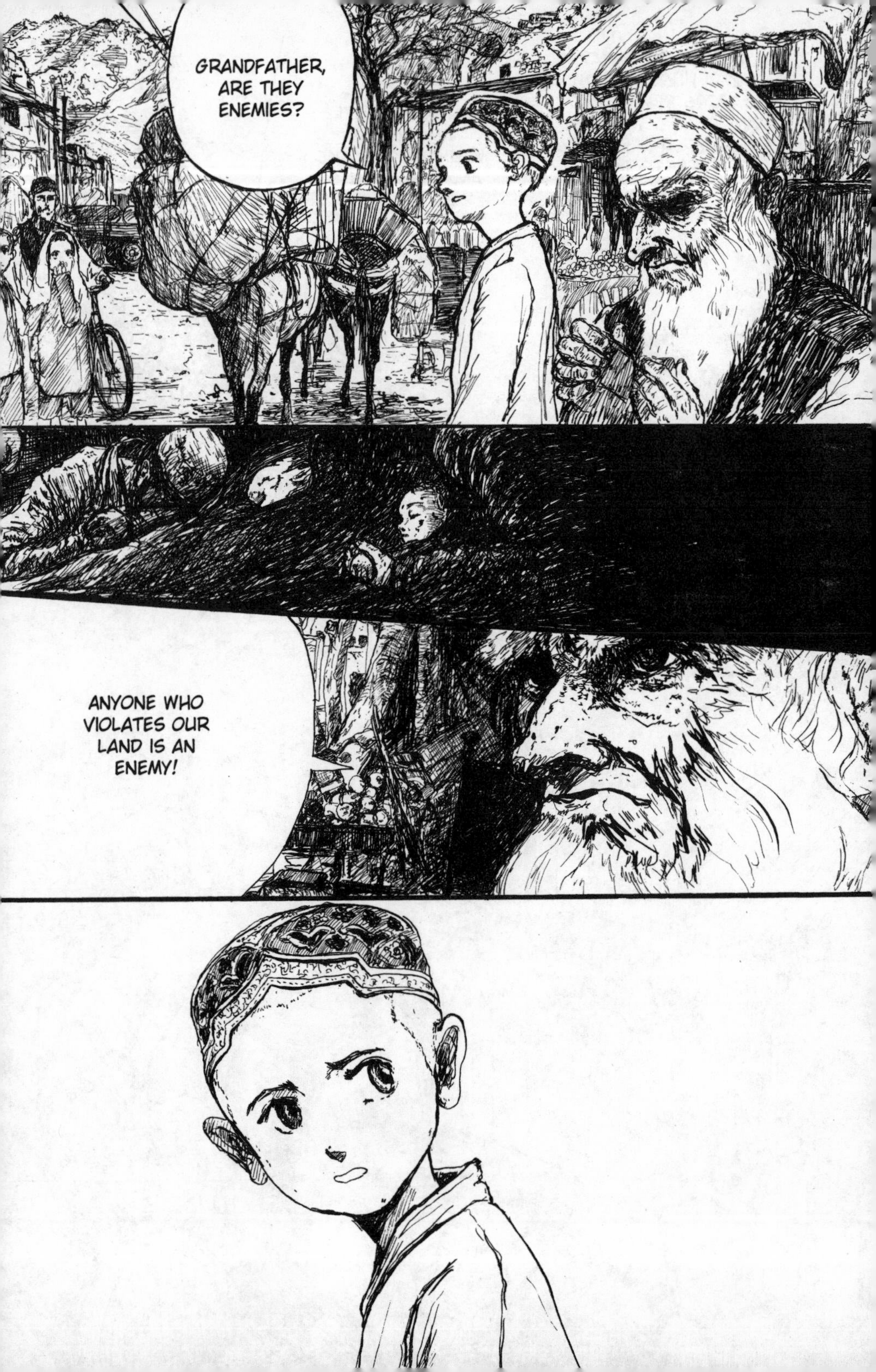
GRANDFATHER, ARE THEY ENEMIES?
ANYONE WHO VIOLATES OUR LAND IS AN ENEMY!

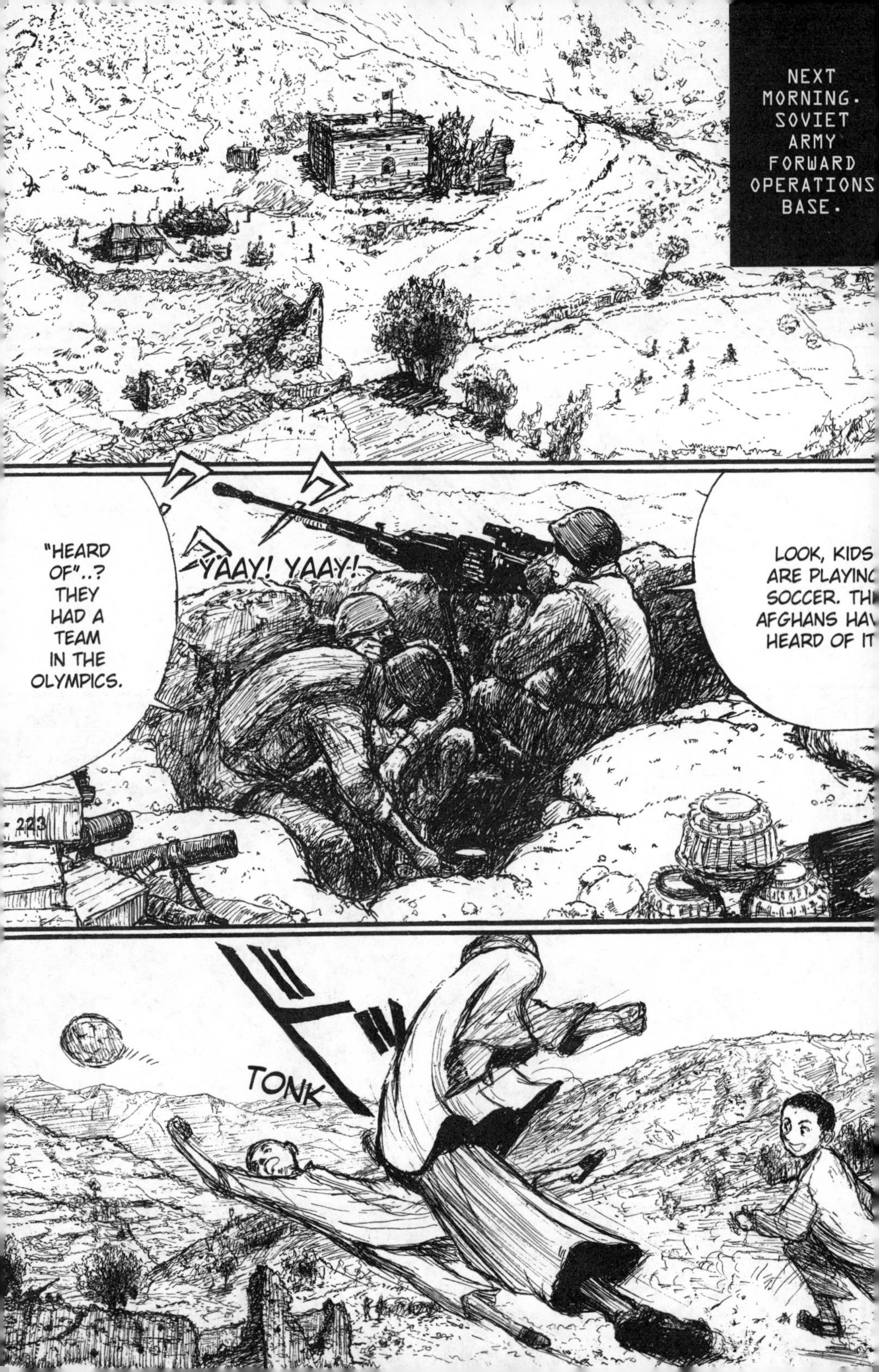
NEXT MORNING. SOVIET ARMY FORWARD OPERATIONS BASE.
LOOK, KIDS ARE PLAYING SOCCER. TH AFGHANS HAV HEARD OF IT
YAAY! YAAY!
"HEARD OF"..? THEY HAD A TEAM IN THE OLYMPICS.
223
TONK

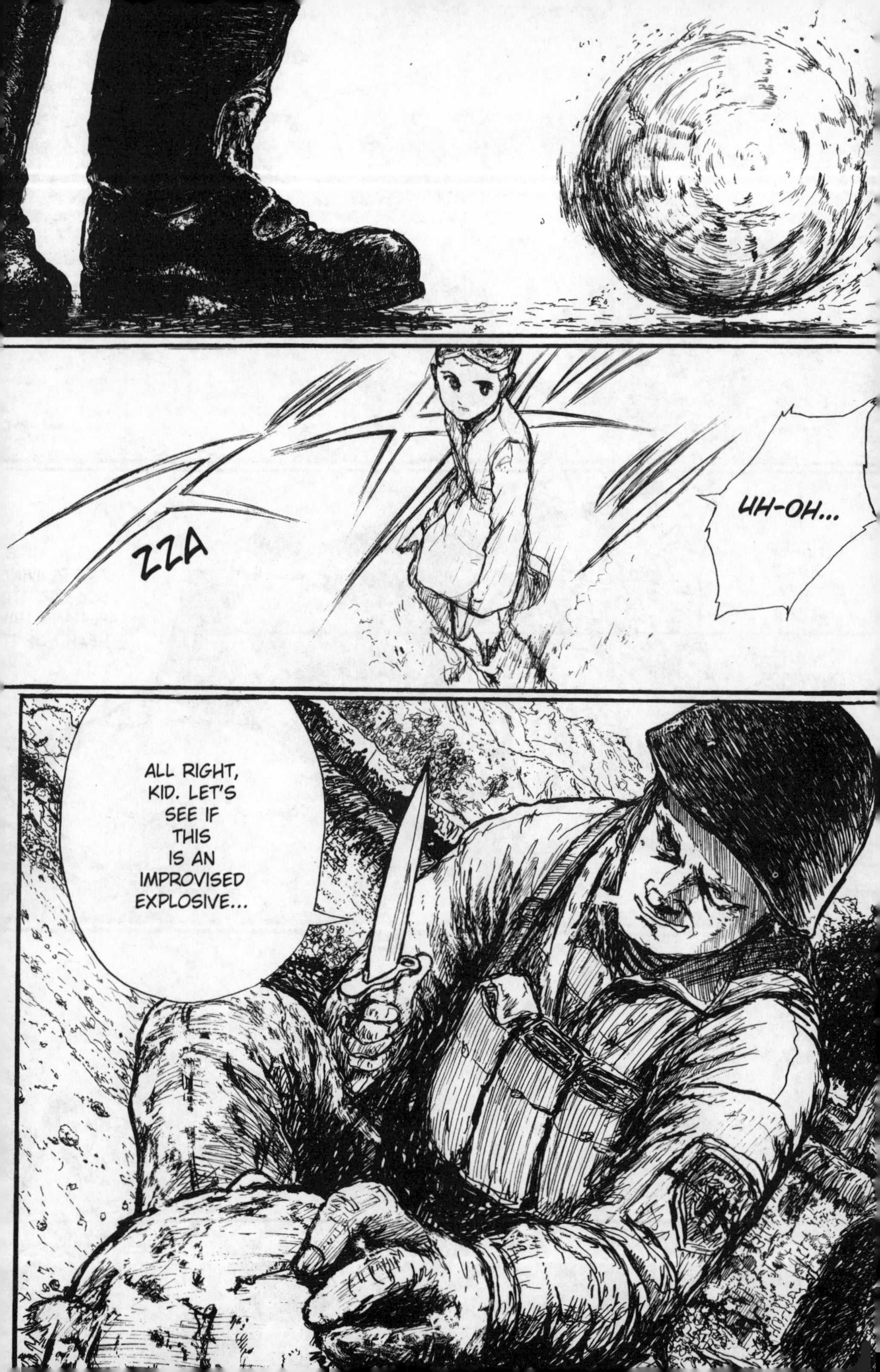
UH-OH...
ZZA
ALL RIGHT, KID. LET'S SEE IF THIS IS AN IMPROVISED EXPLOSIVE...

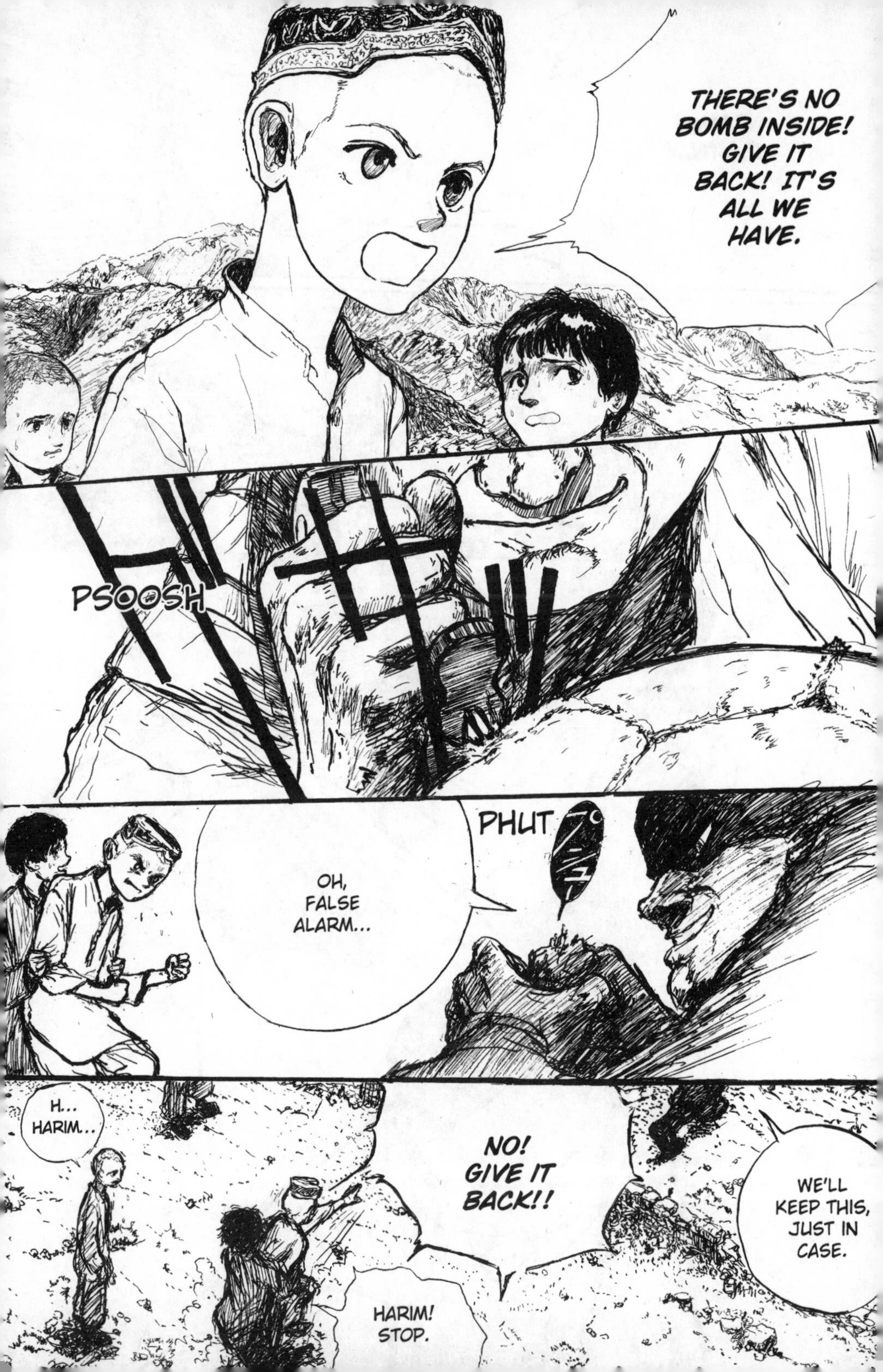
THERE'S NO BOMB INSIDE! GIVE IT BACK! IT'S ALL WE HAVE.
PSOOSH
PHUT
OH, FALSE ALARM...
WE'LL KEEP THIS, JUST IN CASE.
NO! GIVE IT BACK!!
H... HARIM...
HARIM! STOP.

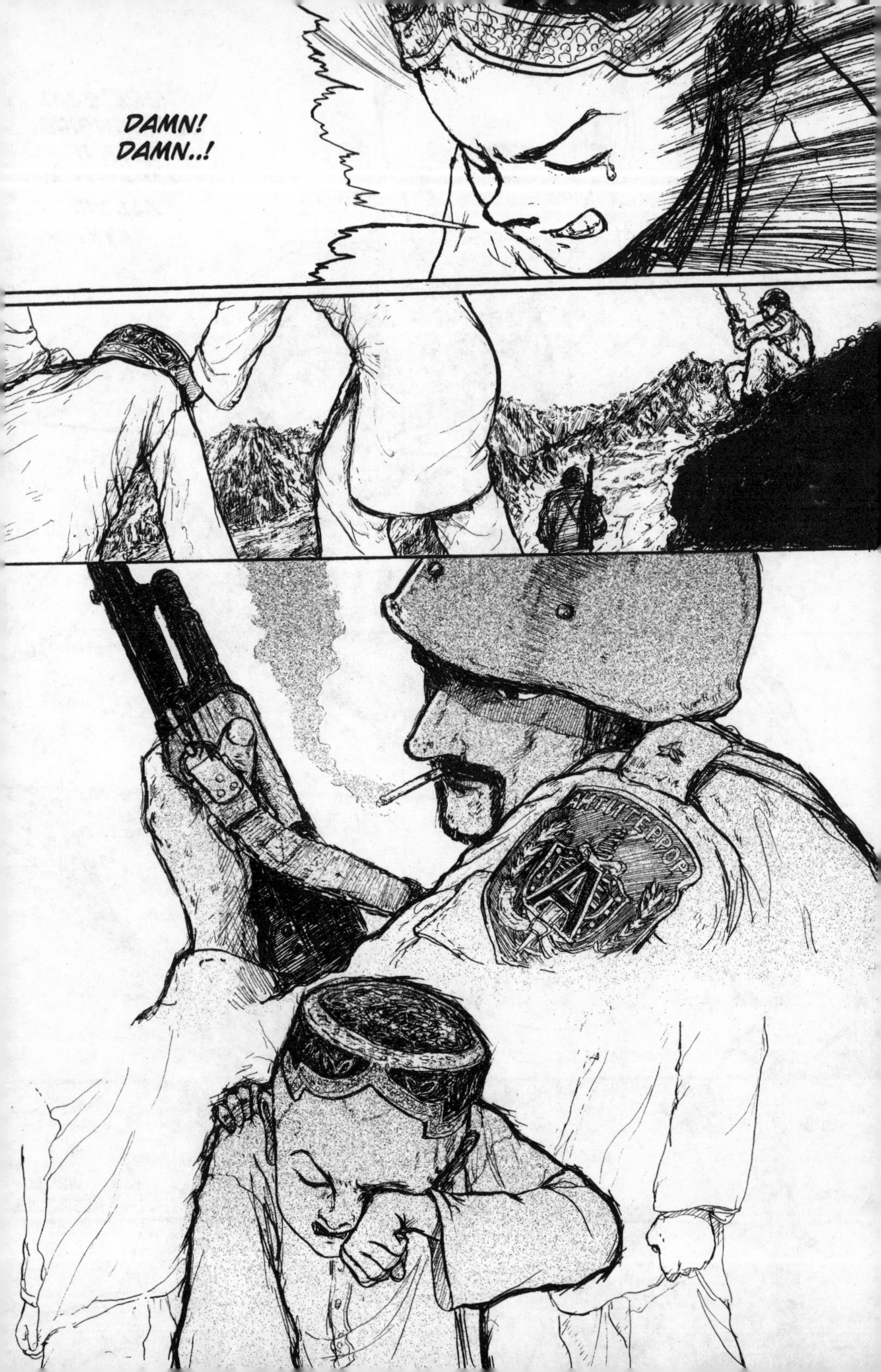
DAMN!
DAMN..!

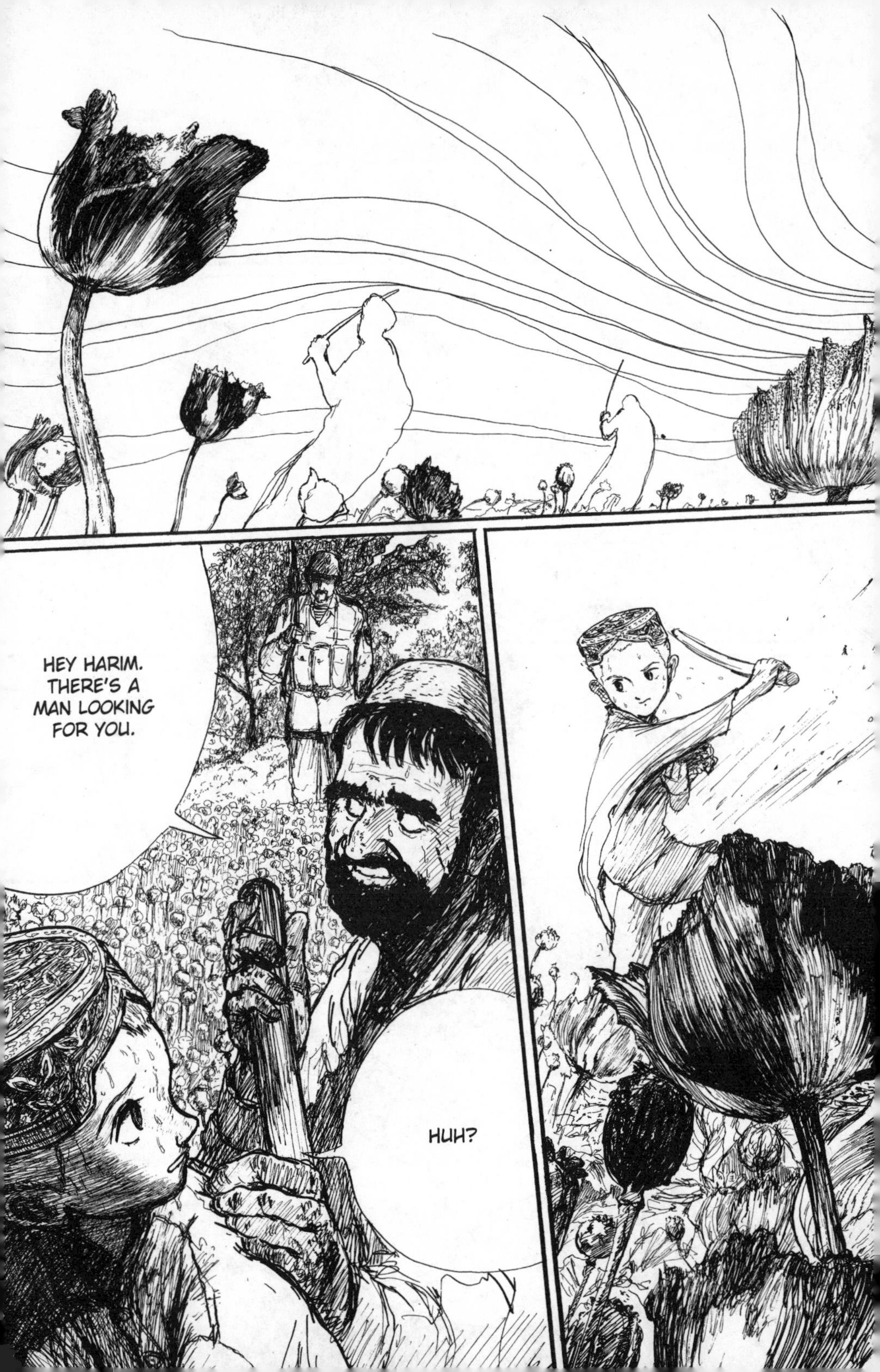
HEY HARIM. THERE'S A MAN LOOKING FOR YOU.
HUH?

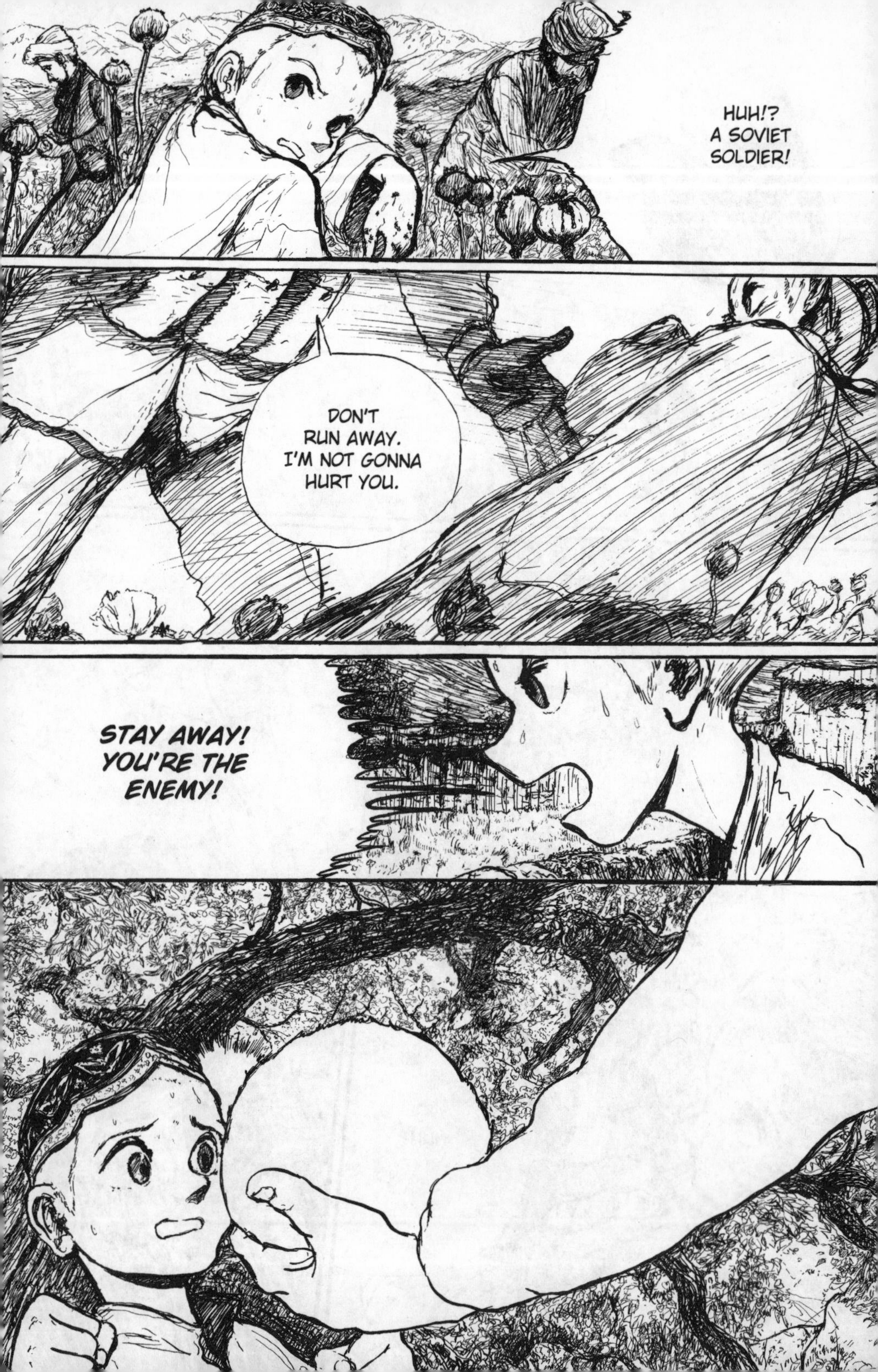
HUH!? A SOVIET SOLDIER!
DON'T RUN AWAY. I'M NOT GONNA HURT YOU.
STAY AWAY! YOU'RE THE ENEMY!

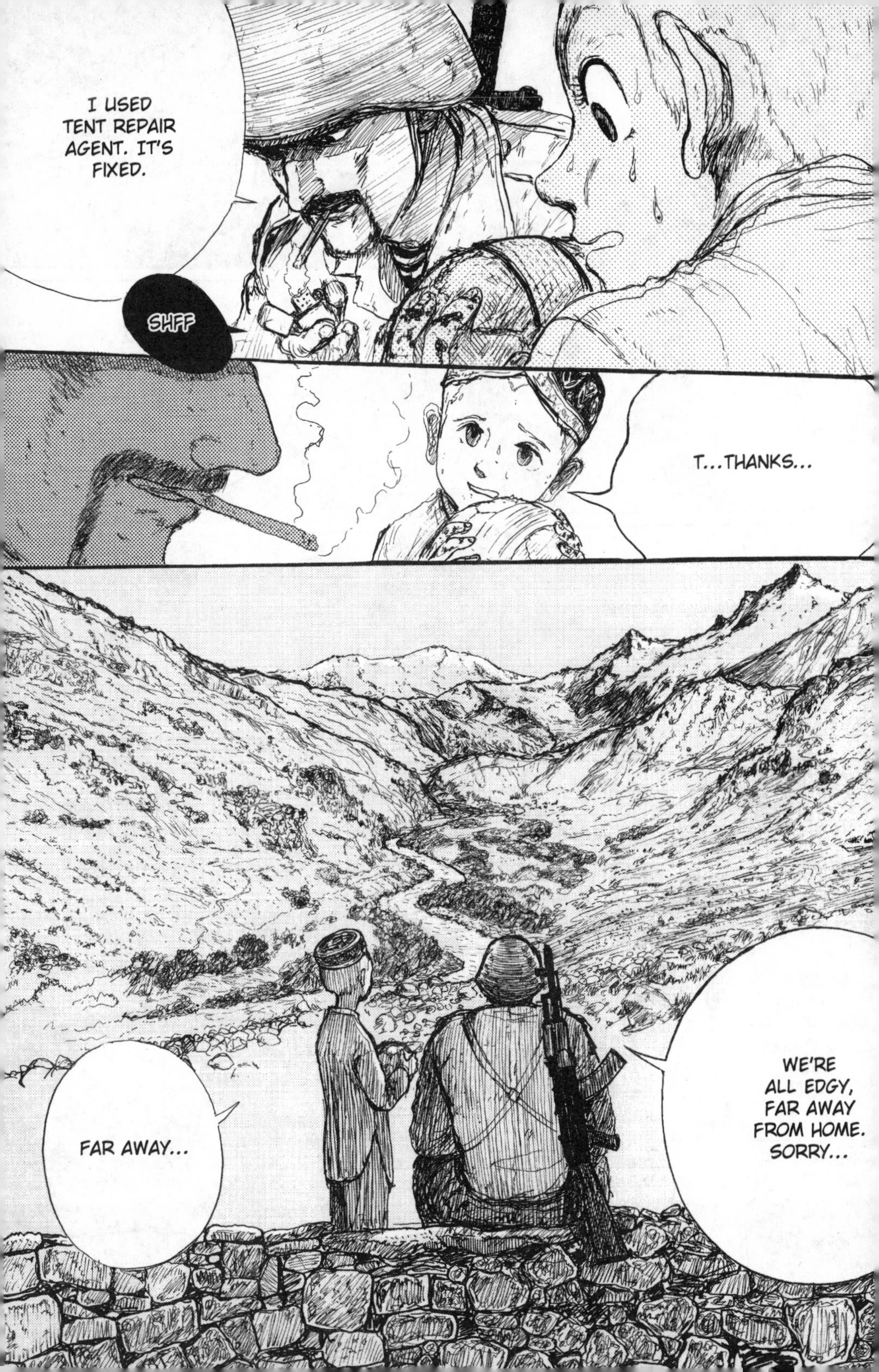

I USED TENT REPAIR AGENT. IT'S FIXED.
SHFF
T...THANKS...
WE'RE ALL EDGY, FAR AWAY FROM HOME. SORRY...
FAR AWAY...

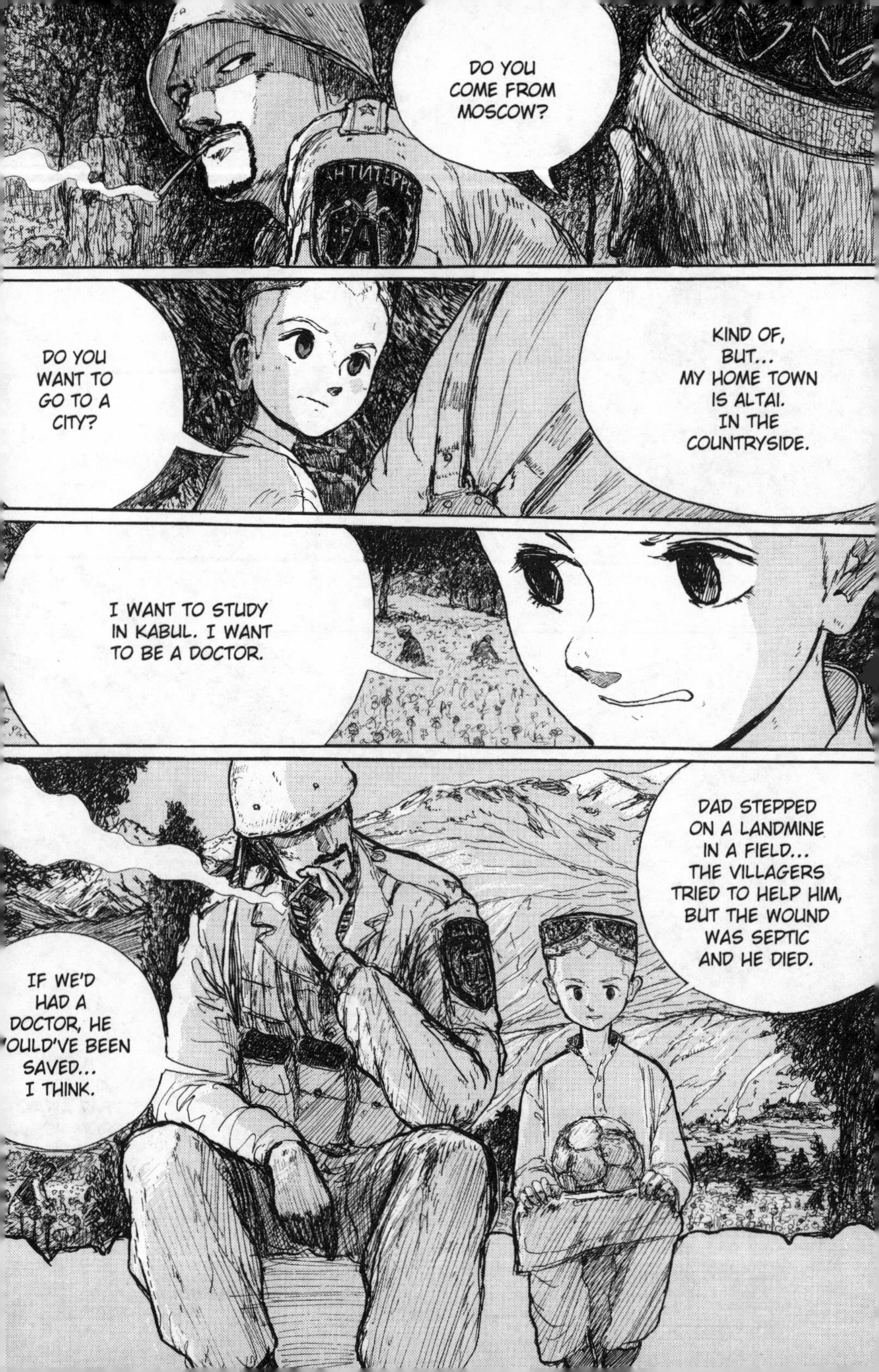
DO YOU COME FROM MOSCOW?
KIND OF, BUT... MY HOME TOWN IS ALTAI. IN THE COUNTRYSIDE.
DO YOU WANT TO GO TO A CITY?
I WANT TO STUDY IN KABUL. I WANT TO BE A DOCTOR.
DAD STEPPED ON A LANDMINE IN A FIELD... THE VILLAGERS TRIED TO HELP HIM, BUT THE WOUND WAS SEPTIC AND HE DIED.
IF WE'D HAD A DOCTOR, HE 'OULD'VE BEEN SAVED... I THINK.

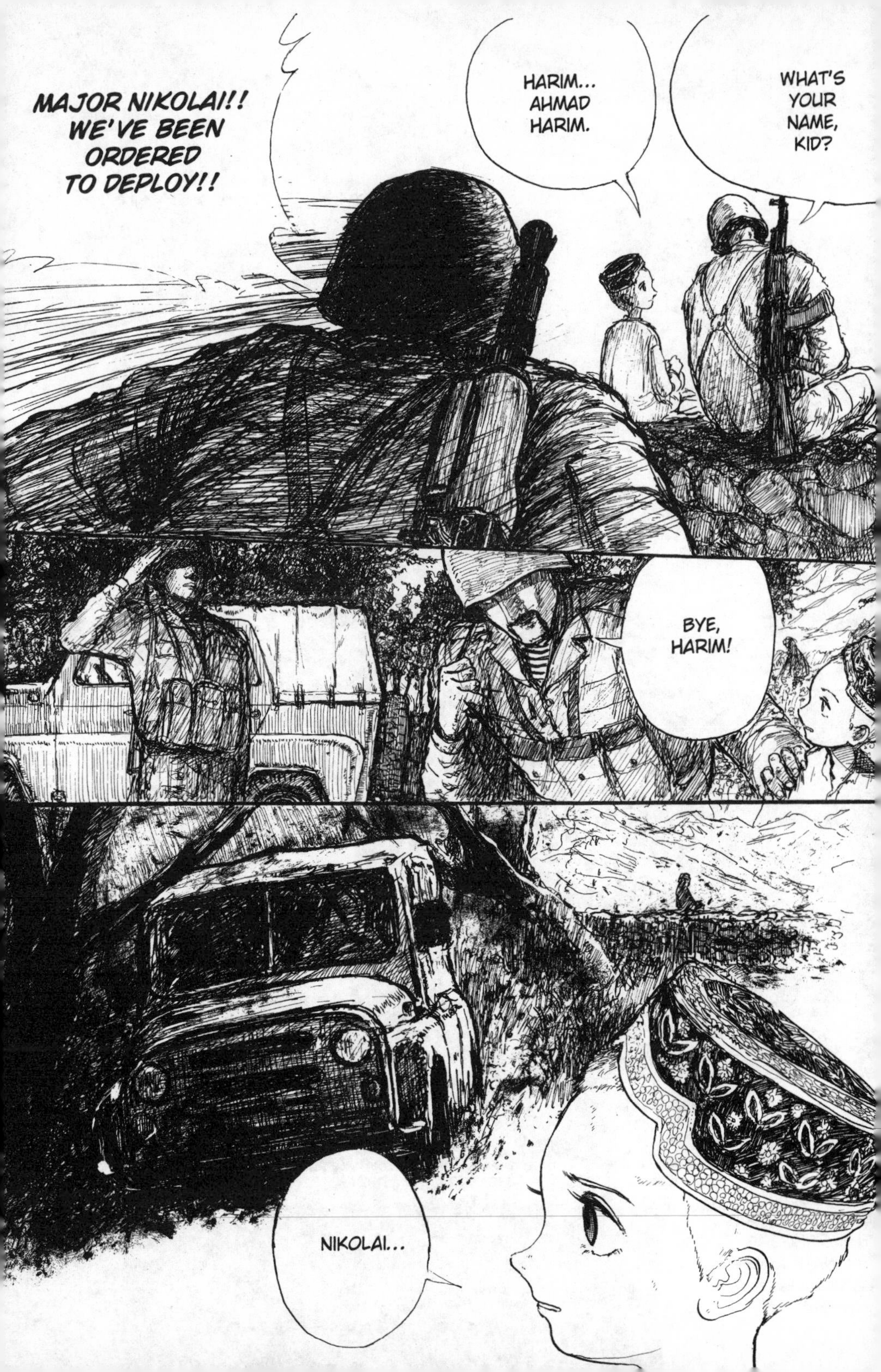
WHAT'S YOUR NAME, KID?
HARIM... AHMAD HARIM.
MAJOR NIKOLAI!! WE'VE BEEN ORDERED TO DEPLOY!!
BYE, HARIM!
NIKOLAI...

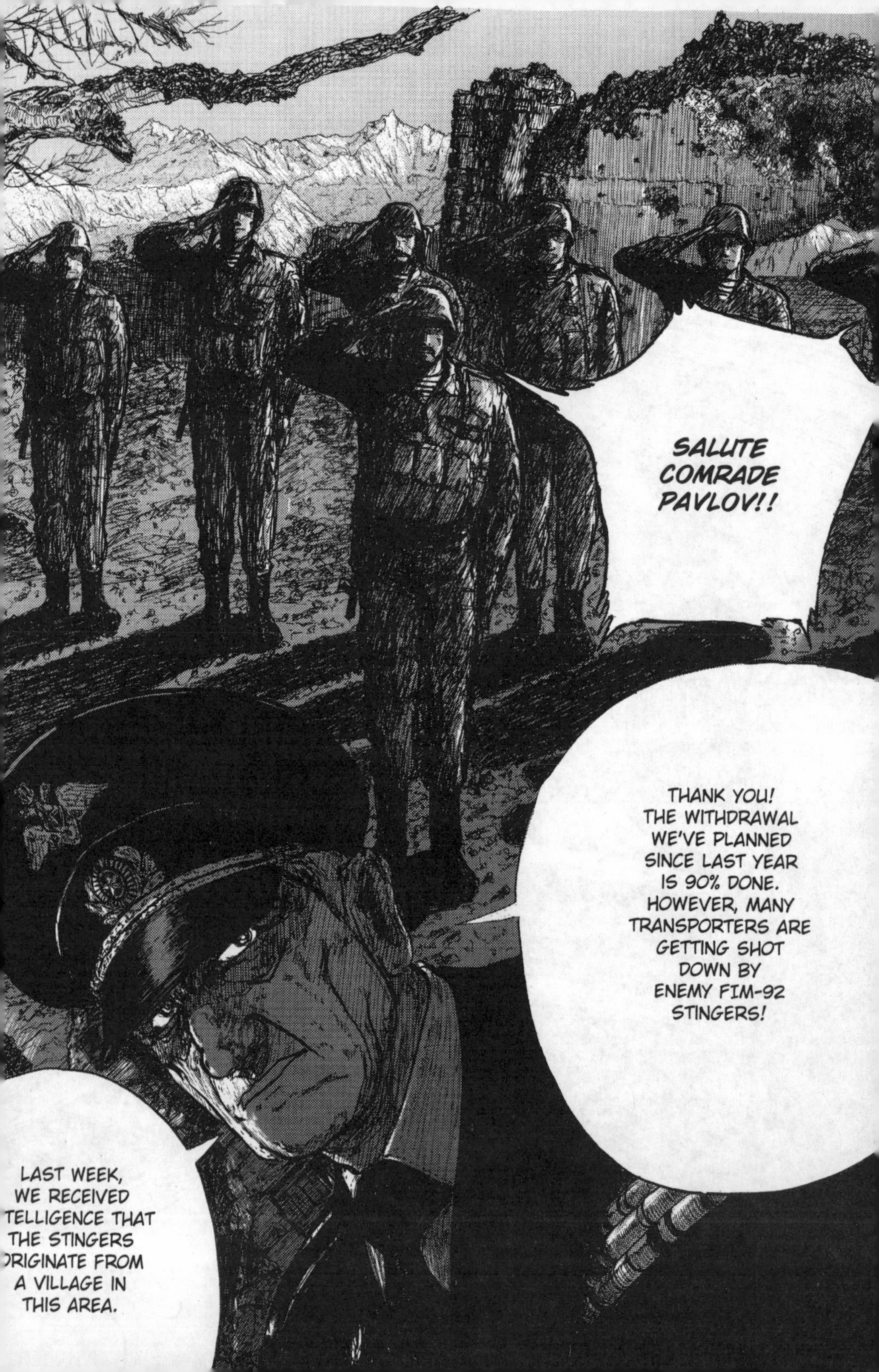
SALUTE COMRADE PAVLOV!!
THANK YOU! THE WITHDRAWAL WE'VE PLANNED SINCE LAST YEAR IS 90% DONE. HOWEVER, MANY TRANSPORTERS ARE GETTING SHOT DOWN BY ENEMY FIM-92 STINGERS!
LAST WEEK, WE RECEIVED TELLIGENCE THAT THE STINGERS RIGINATE FROM A VILLAGE IN THIS AREA.

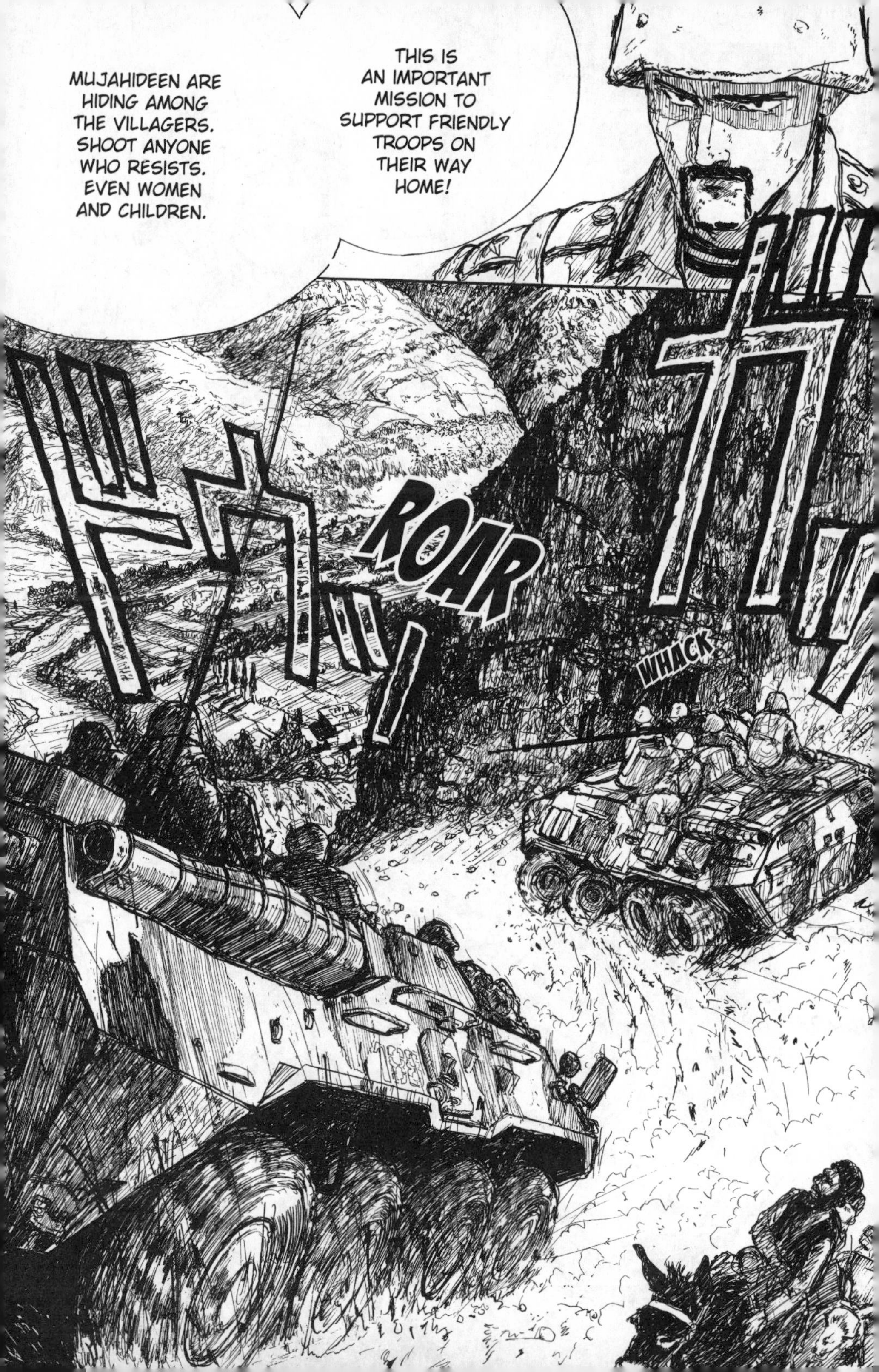
THIS IS AN IMPORTANT MISSION TO SUPPORT FRIENDLY TROOPS ON THEIR WAY HOME!
MUJAHIDEEN ARE HIDING AMONG THE VILLAGERS. SHOOT ANYONE WHO RESISTS. EVEN WOMEN AND CHILDREN.
ROAR
WHACK

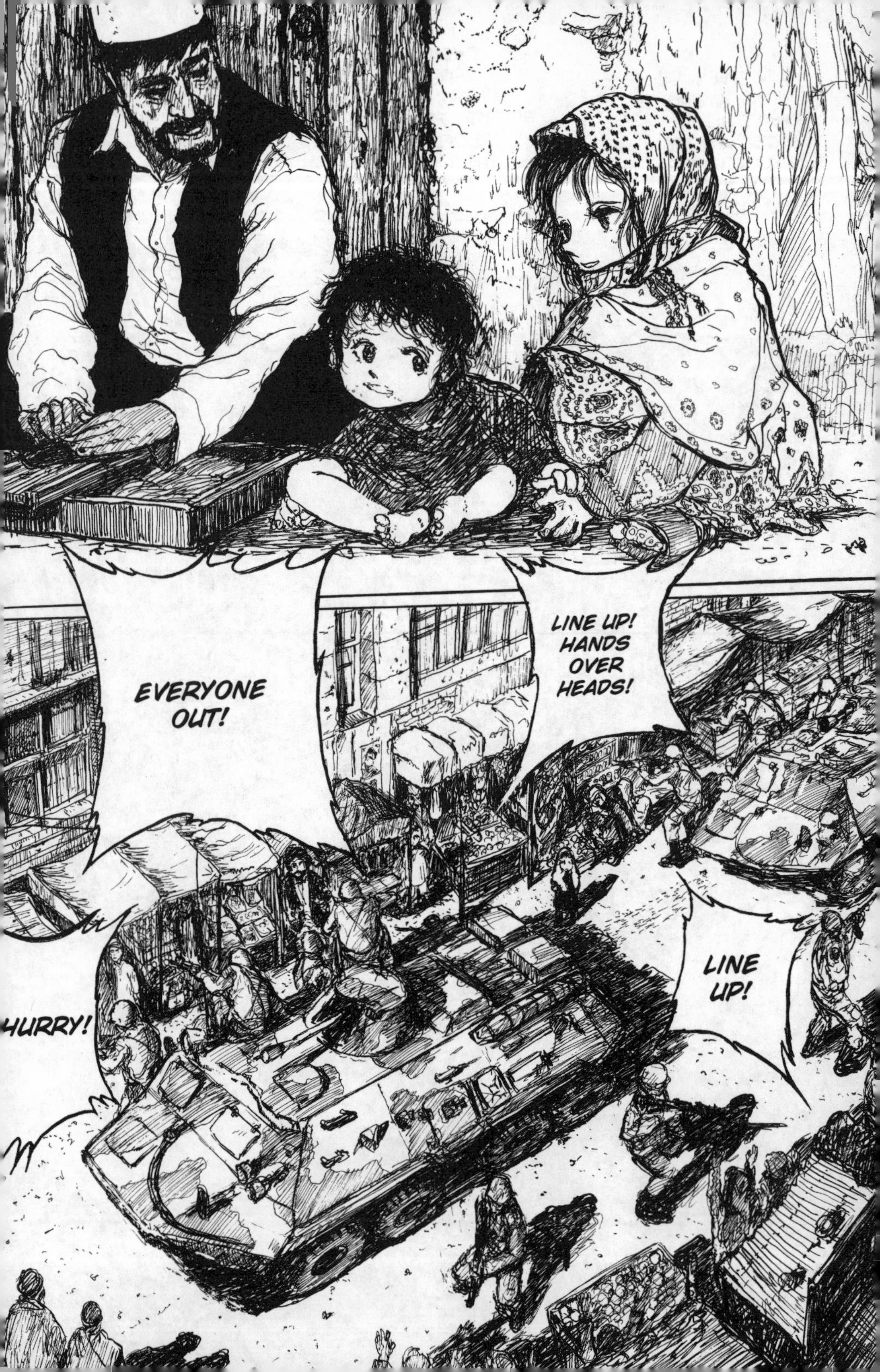
LINE UP! HANDS OVER HEADS!
EVERYONE OUT!
LINE UP!
HURRY!

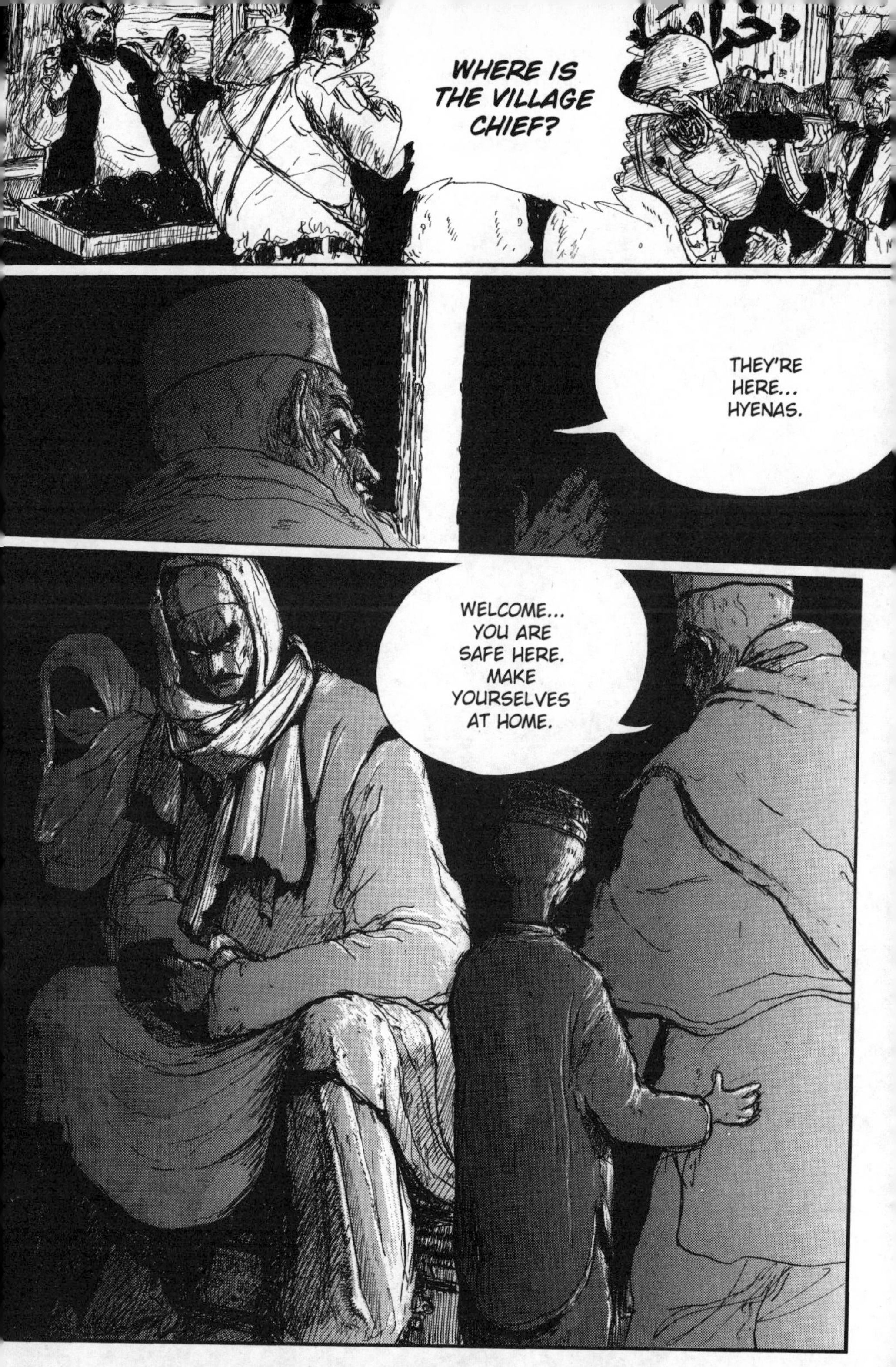
WHERE IS THE VILLAGE CHIEF?
THEY'RE HERE... HYENAS.
WELCOME... YOU ARE SAFE HERE. MAKE YOURSELVES AT HOME.

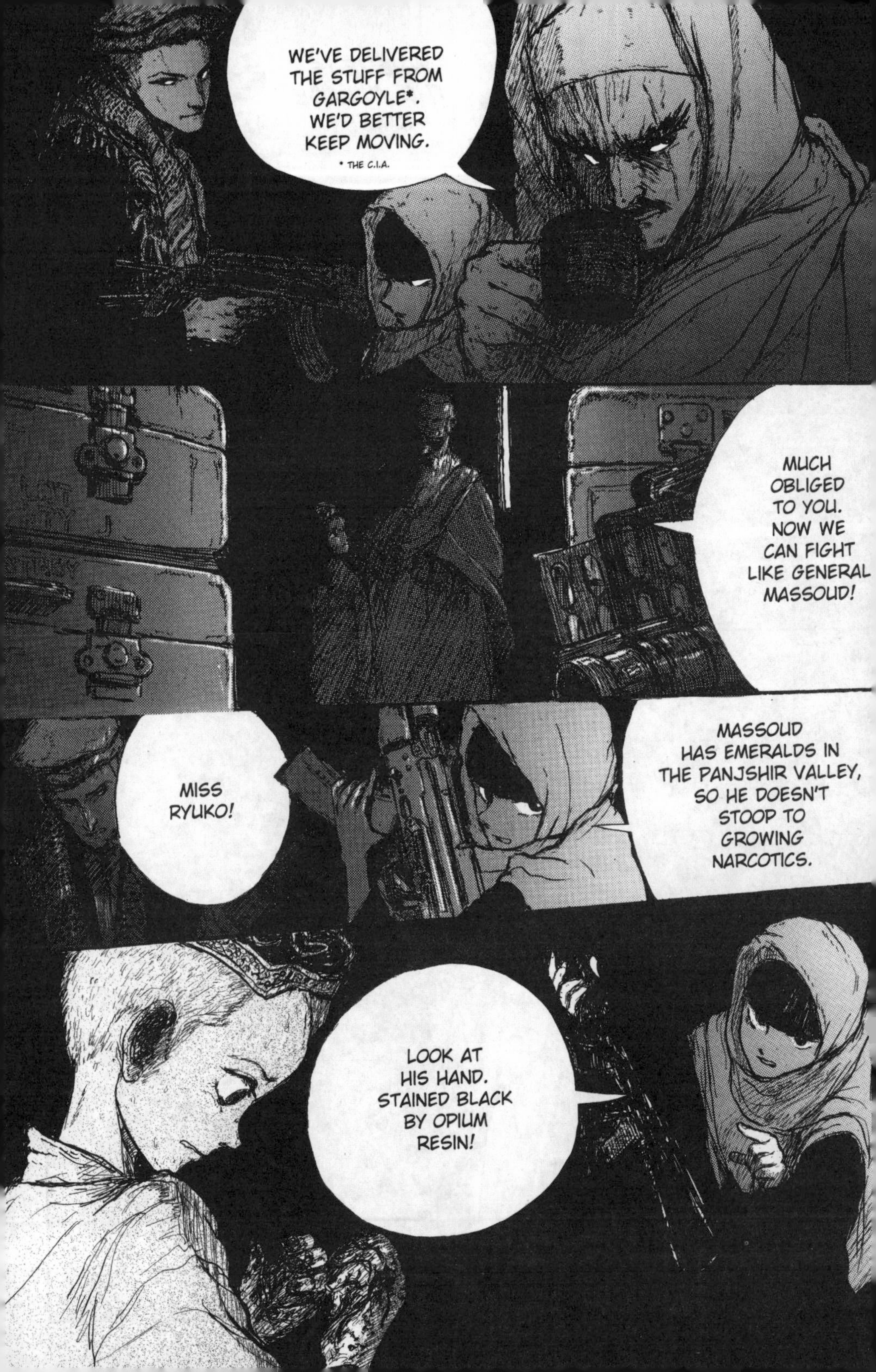
WE'VE DELIVERED THE STUFF FROM GARGOYLE*. WE'D BETTER KEEP MOVING.
* THE C.I.A.
MUCH OBLIGED TO YOU. NOW WE CAN FIGHT LIKE GENERAL MASSOUD!
MASSOUD HAS EMERALDS IN THE PANJSHIR VALLEY, SO HE DOESN'T STOOP TO GROWING NARCOTICS.
MISS RYUKO!
LOOK AT HIS HAND. STAINED BLACK BY OPIUM RESIN!

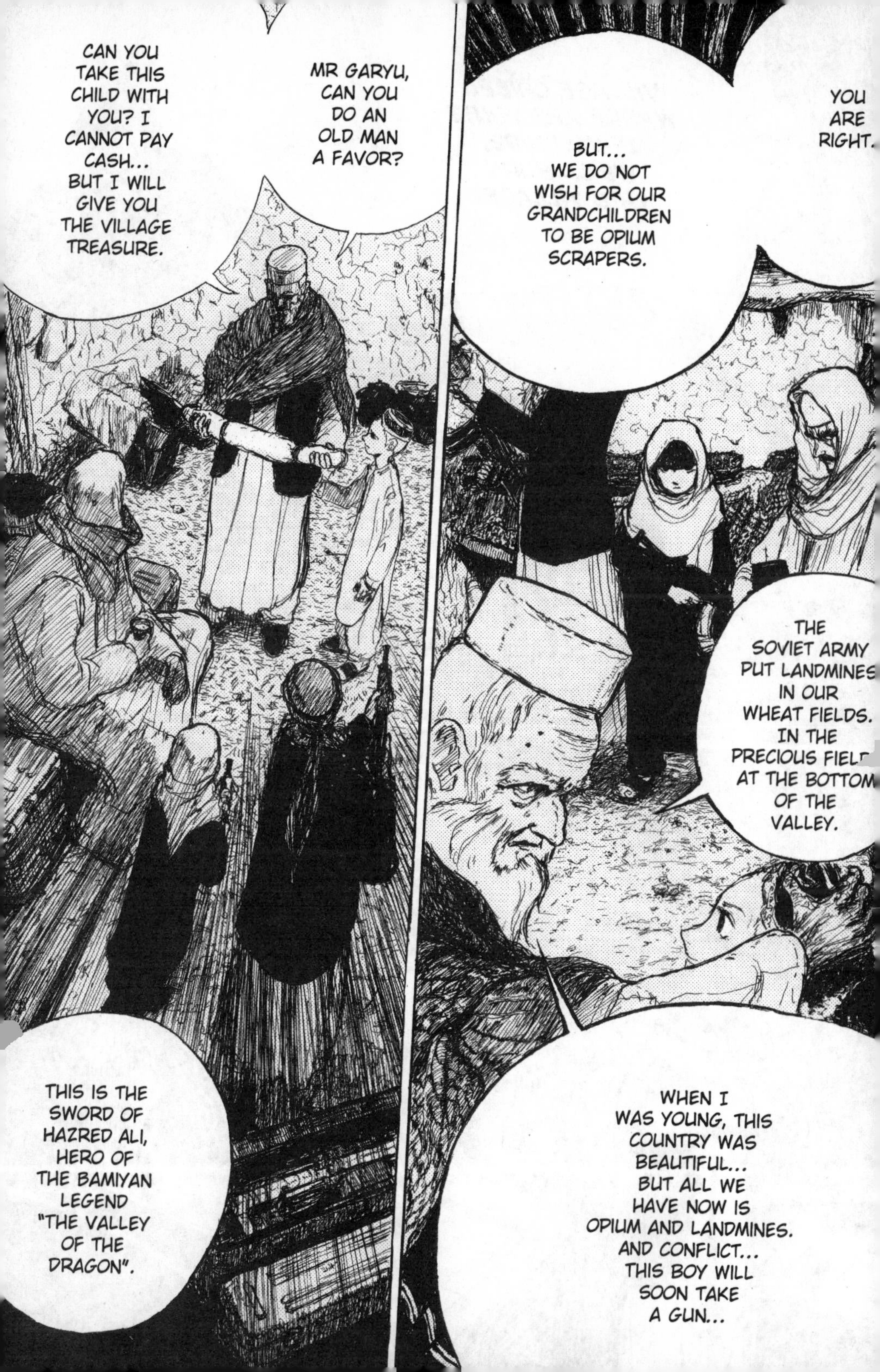
YOU ARE RIGHT.
BUT... WE DO NOT WISH FOR OUR GRANDCHILDREN TO BE OPIUM SCRAPERS.
THE SOVIET ARMY PUT LANDMINES IN OUR WHEAT FIELDS. IN THE PRECIOUS FIELD AT THE BOTTOM OF THE VALLEY.
WHEN I WAS YOUNG, THIS COUNTRY WAS BEAUTIFUL... BUT ALL WE HAVE NOW IS OPIUM AND LANDMINES. AND CONFLICT... THIS BOY WILL SOON TAKE A GUN...
MR GARYU, CAN YOU DO AN OLD MAN A FAVOR?
CAN YOU TAKE THIS CHILD WITH YOU? I CANNOT PAY CASH... BUT I WILL GIVE YOU THE VILLAGE TREASURE.
THIS IS THE SWORD OF HAZRED ALI, HERO OF THE BAMIYAN LEGEND "THE VALLEY OF THE DRAGON".

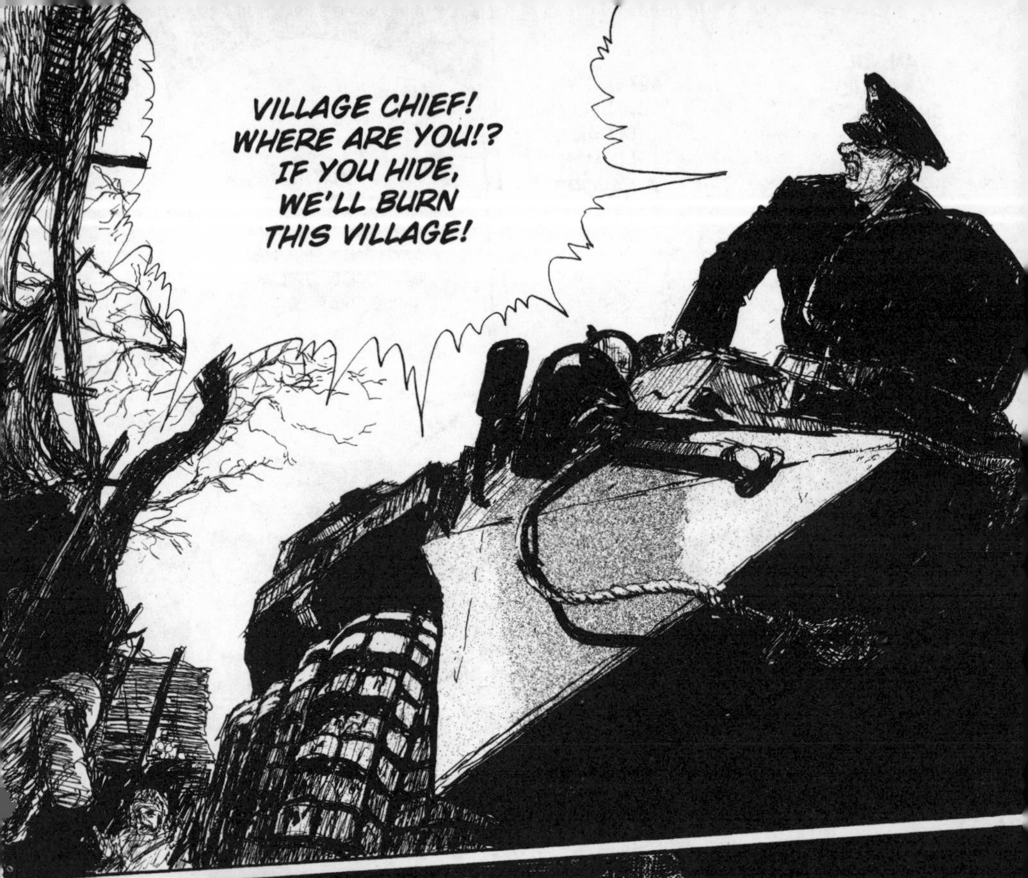
VILLAGE CHIEF! WHERE ARE YOU!? IF YOU HIDE, WE'LL BURN THIS VILLAGE!
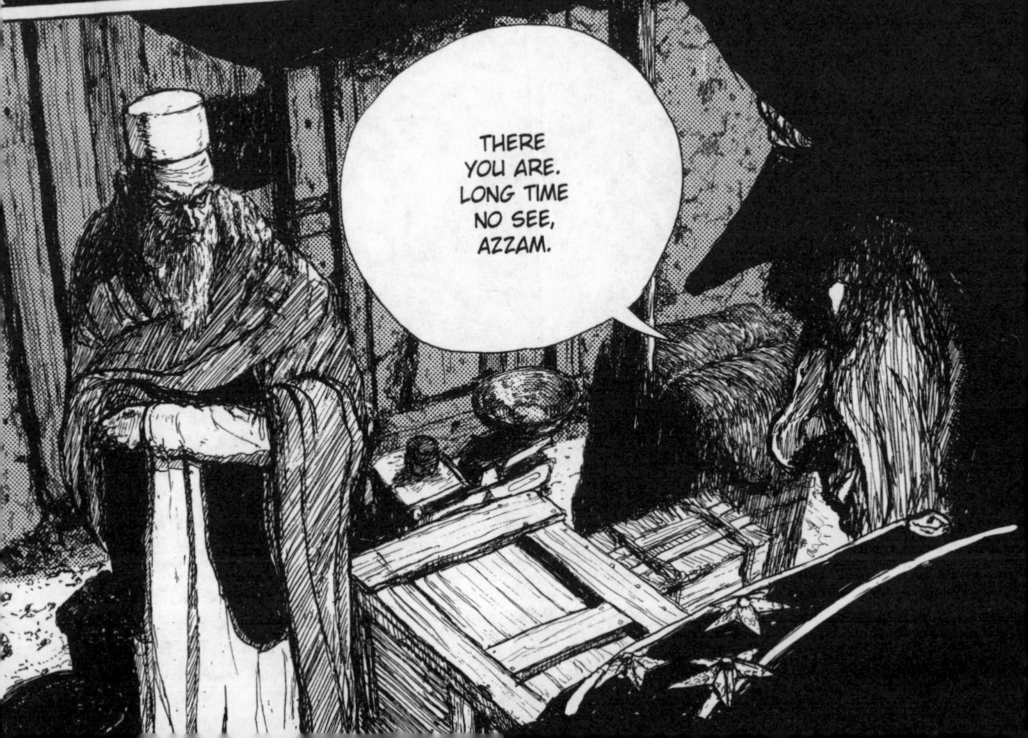
THERE YOU ARE. LONG TIME NO SEE, AZZAM.

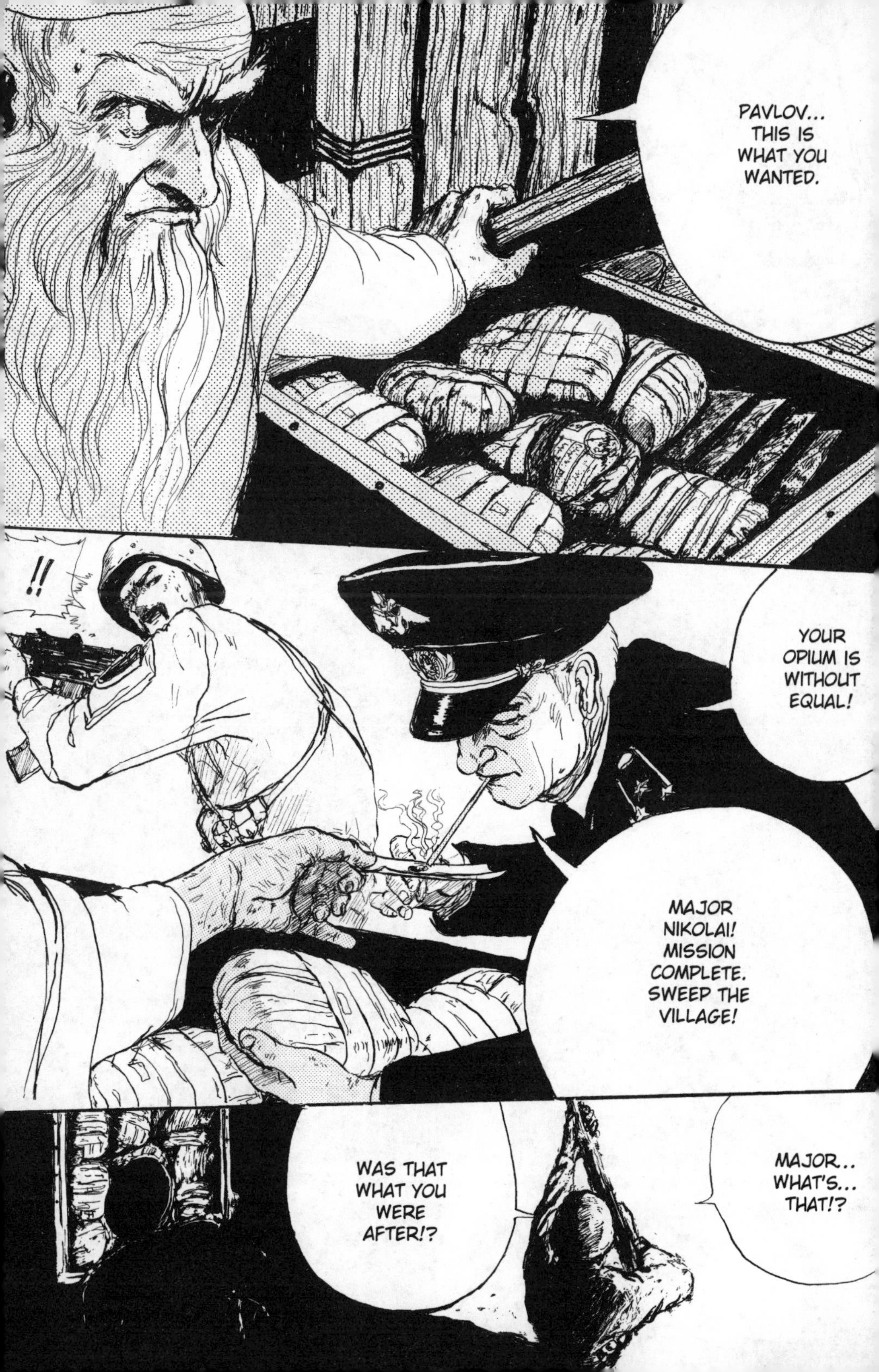
PAVLOV... THIS IS WHAT YOU WANTED.
YOUR OPIUM IS WITHOUT EQUAL!
MAJOR NIKOLAI! MISSION COMPLETE. SWEEP THE VILLAGE!
!!
MAJOR.. WHAT'S... THAT!?
WAS THAT WHAT YOU WERE AFTER!?

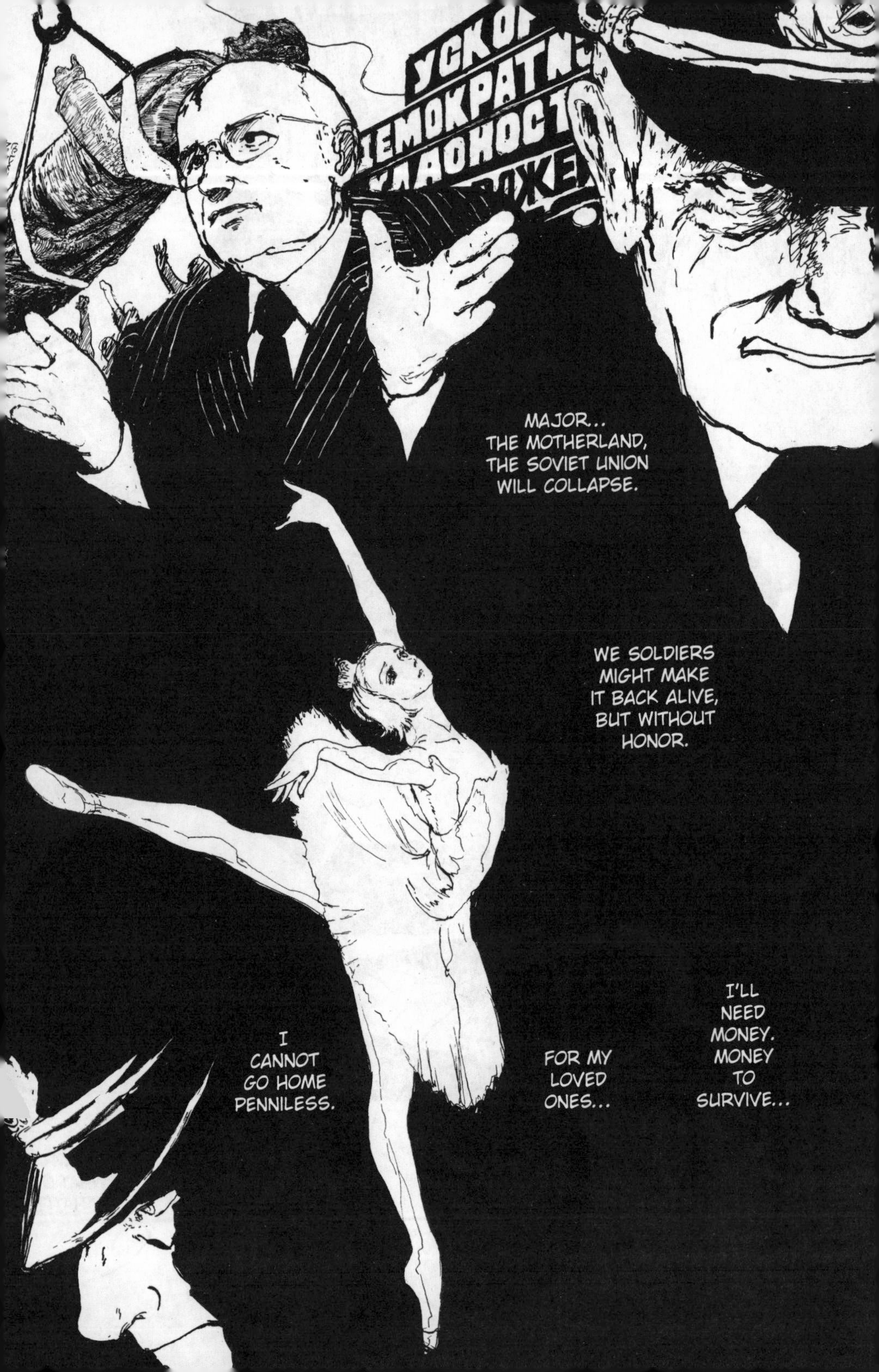
MAJOR.. THE MOTHERLAND, THE SOVIET UNION WILL COLLAPSE.
WE SOLDIERS MIGHT MAKE IT BACK ALIVE, BUT WITHOUT HONOR.
I'LL NEED MONEY. MONEY TO SURVIVE...
FOR MY LOVED ONES...
I CANNOT GO HOME PENNILESS.

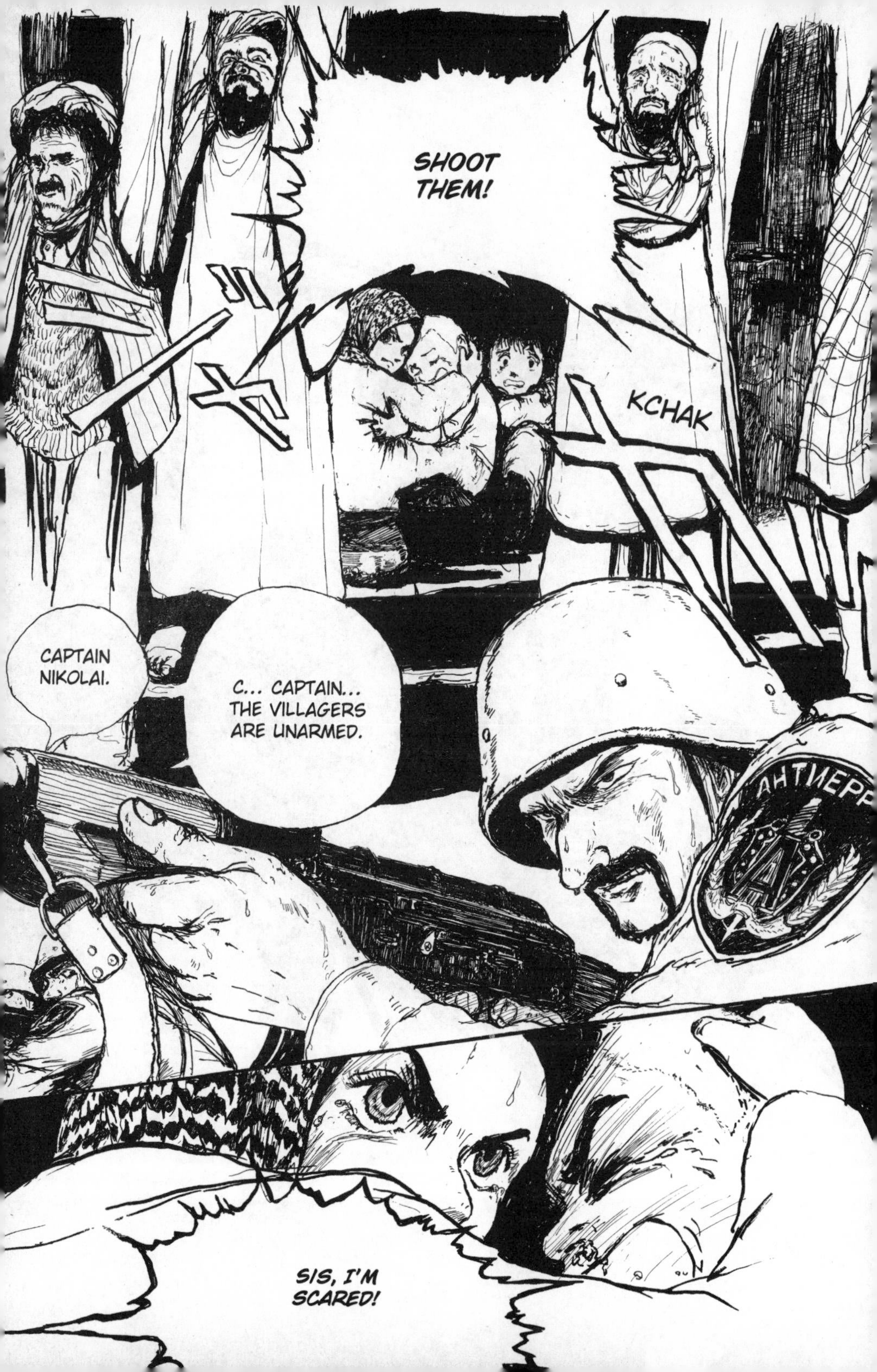
SHOOT THEM!
KCHAK
C... CAPTAIN... THE VILLAGERS ARE UNARMED.
CAPTAIN NIKOLAI.
SIS, I'M SCARED!

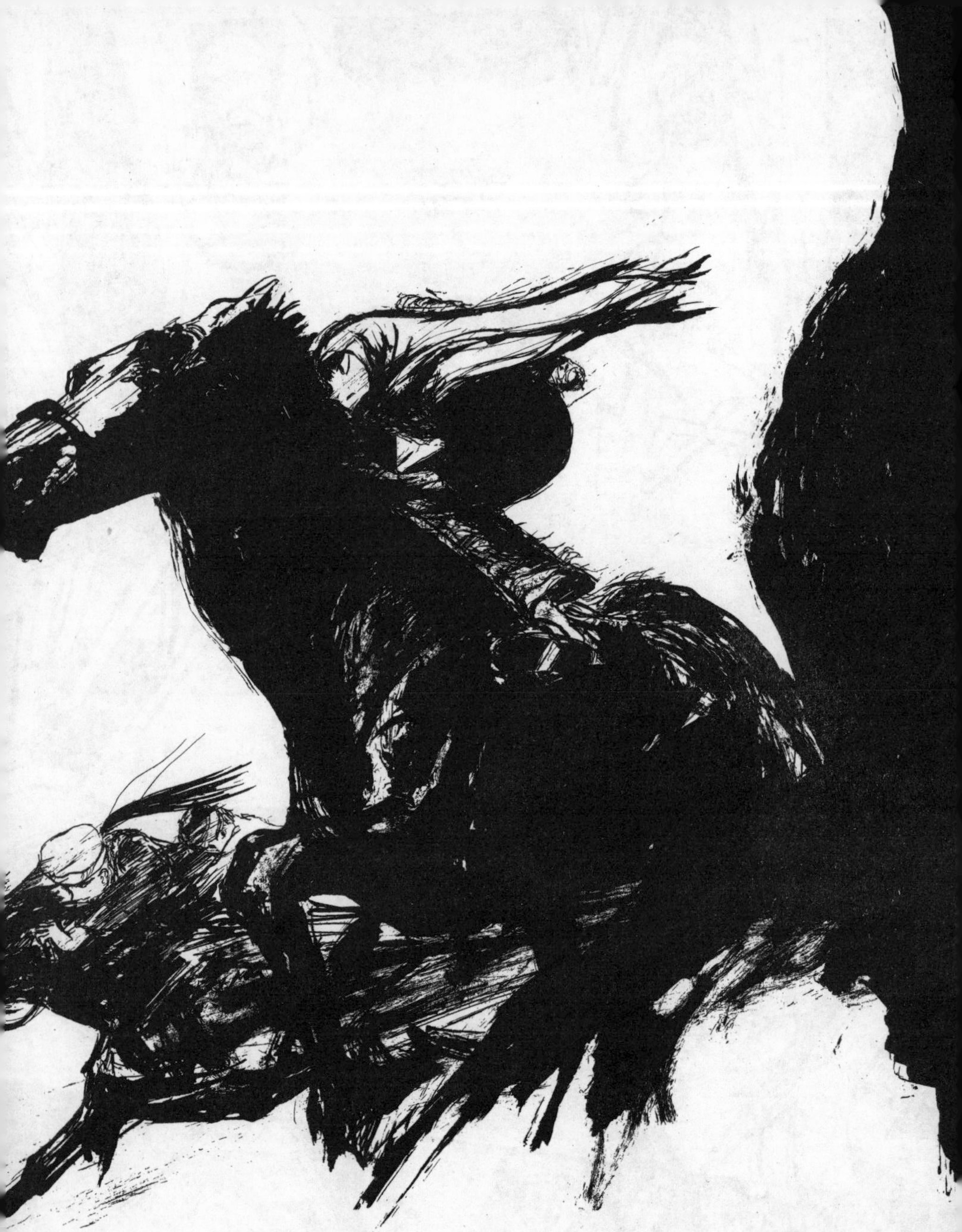

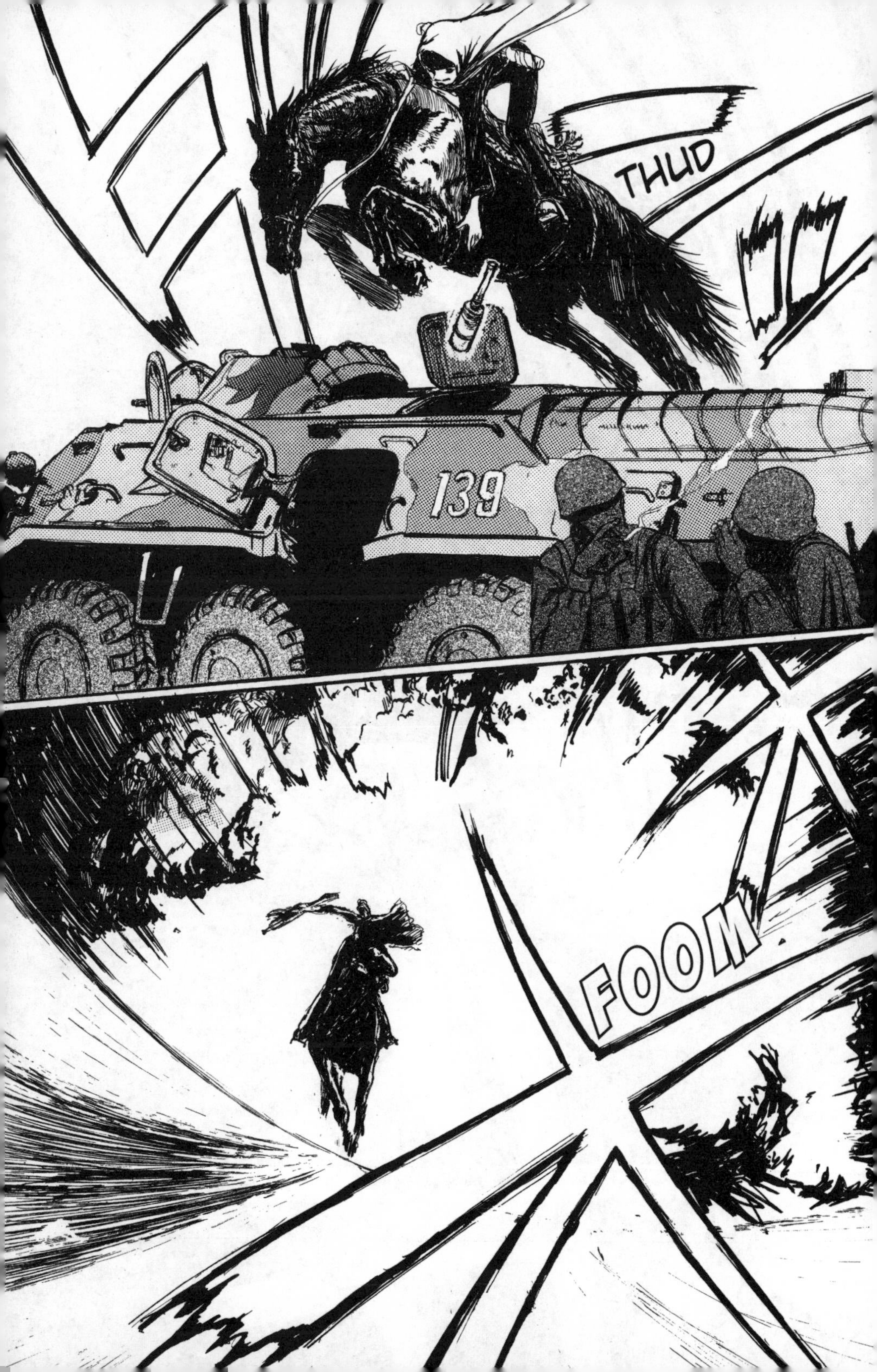
THUD
139
FOOM

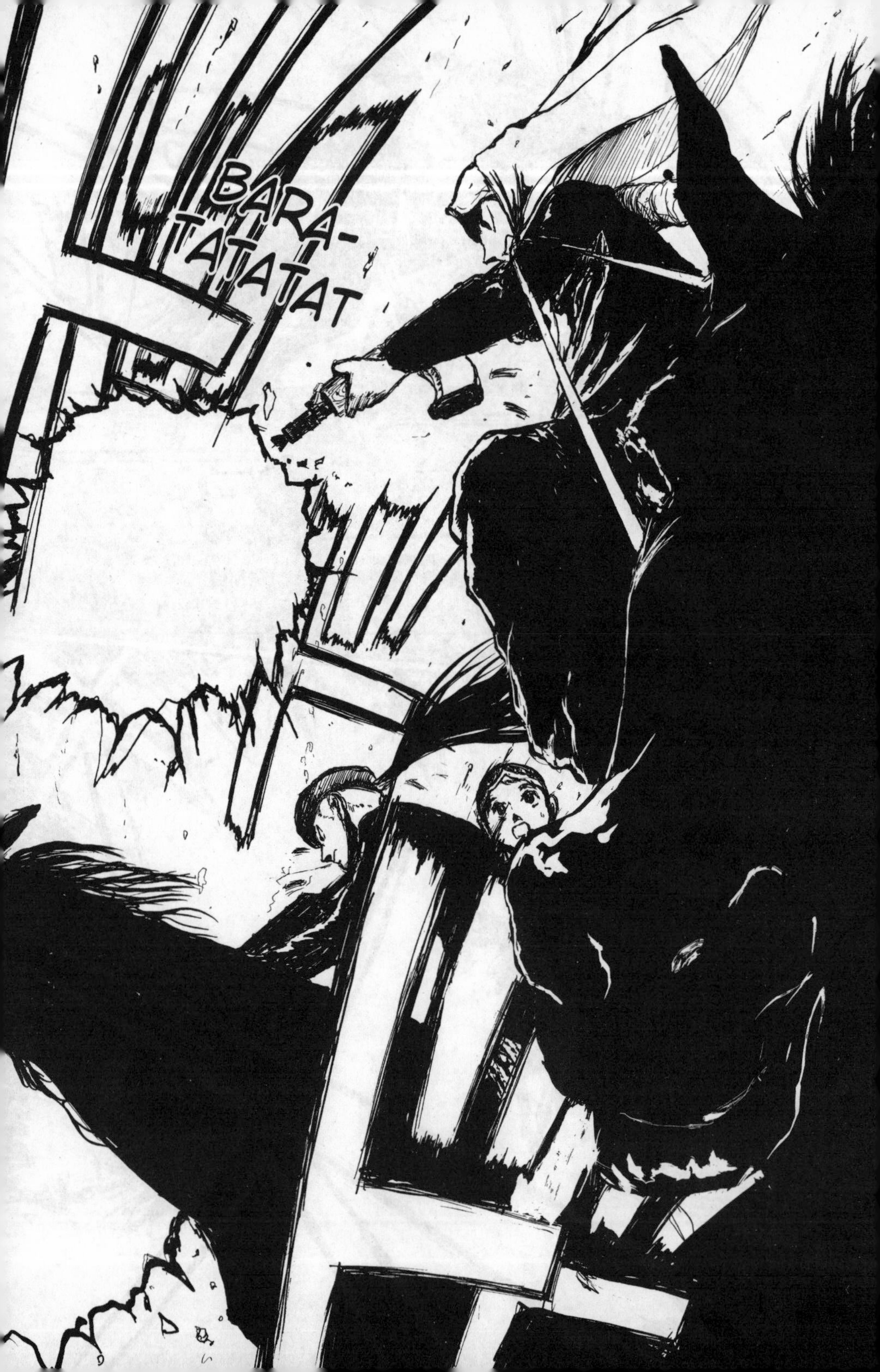
BARA-
TATATAT

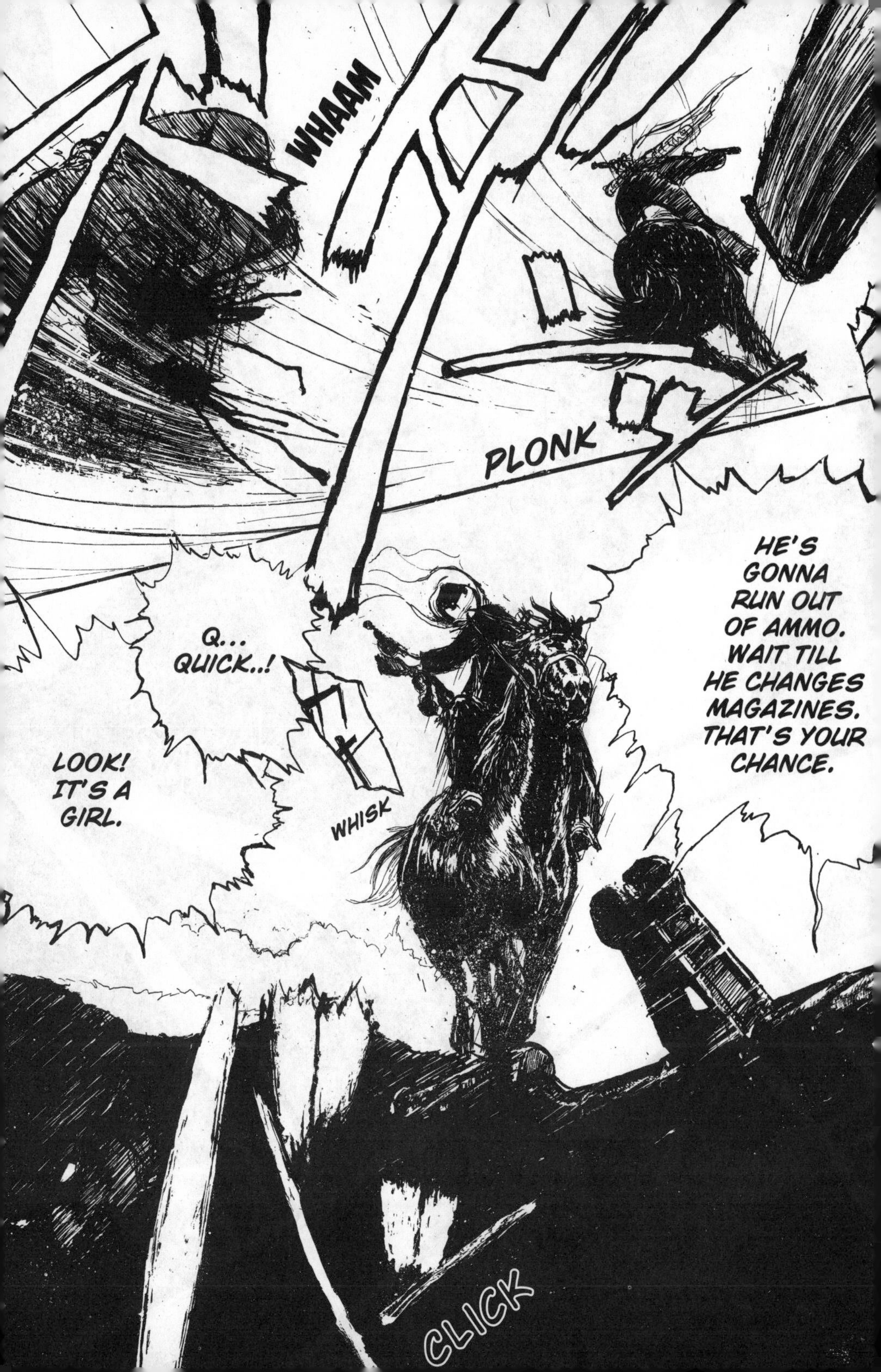
WHAAM
PLONK
HE'S GONNA RUN OUT OF AMMO. WAIT TILL HE CHANGES MAGAZINES. THAT'S YOUR CHANCE.
Q... QUICK..!
LOOK! IT'S A GIRL.
WHISK
CLICK

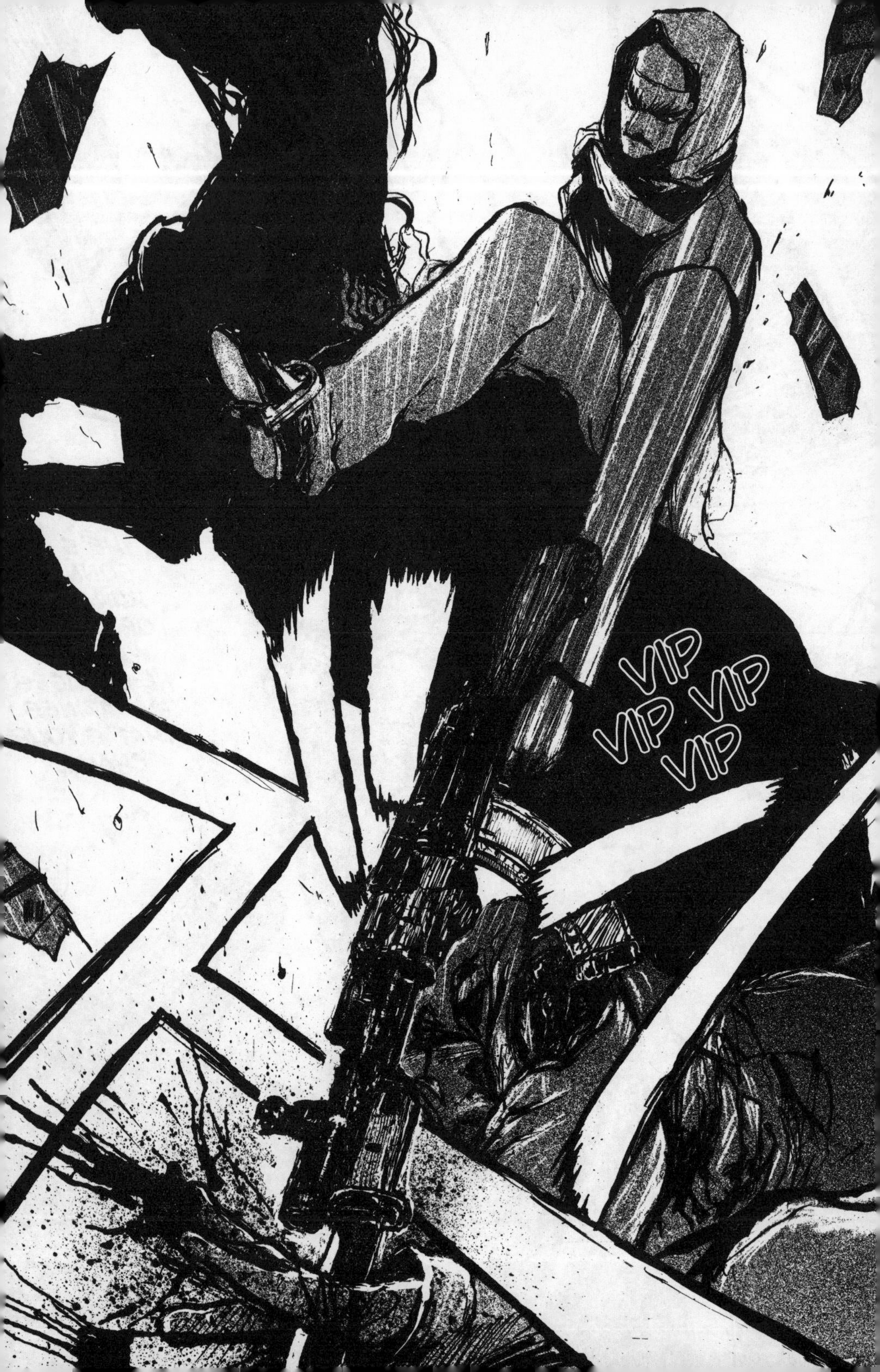
VIP
VIP VIP
VIP

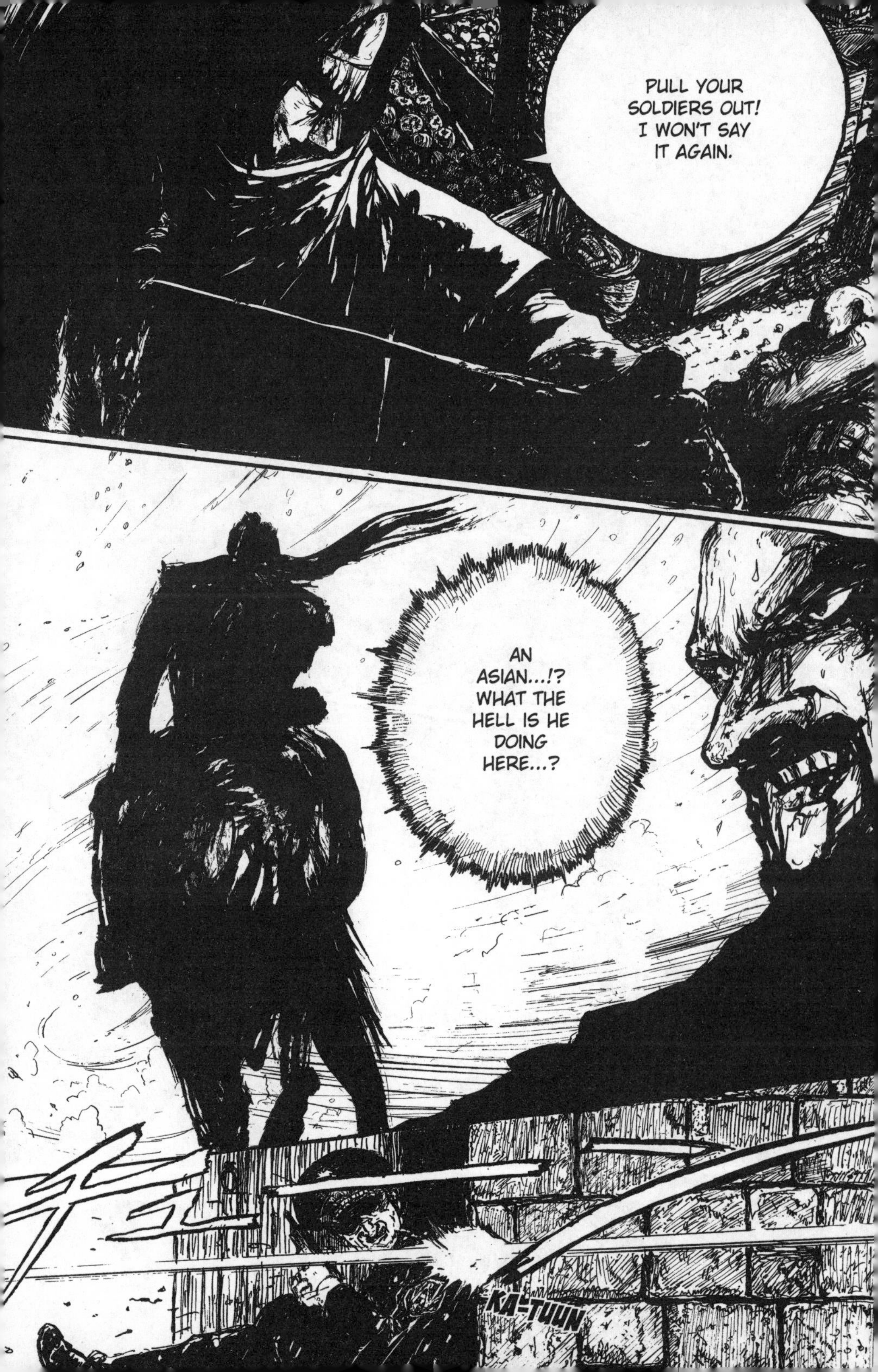
PULL YOUR SOLDIERS OUT! I WON'T SAY IT AGAIN.
AN ASIAN...!? WHAT THE HELL IS HE DOING HERE...?
KA-TUUN

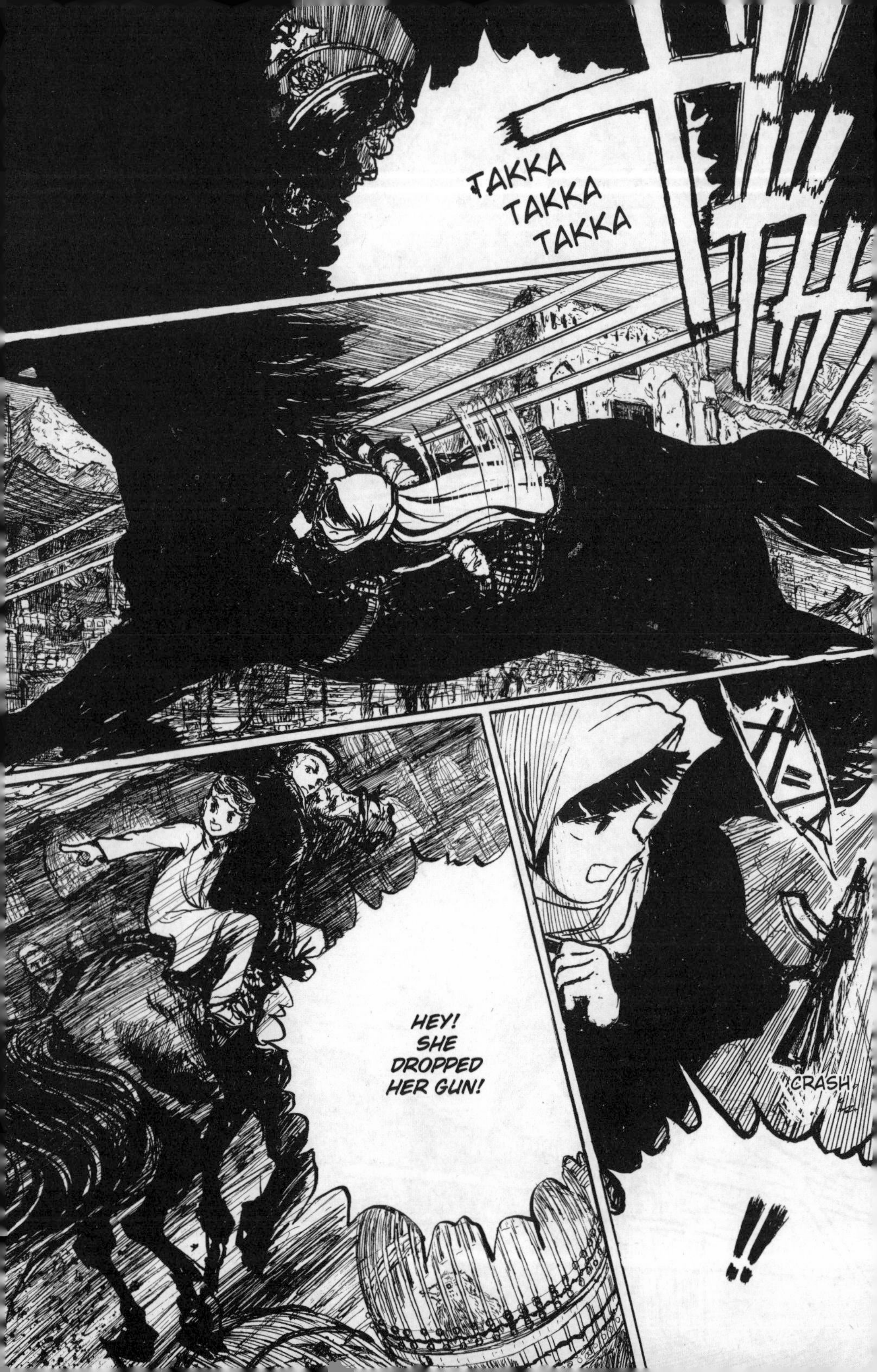
TAKKA
TAKKA
TAKKA
CRASH
!!
HEY! SHE DROPPED HER GUN!

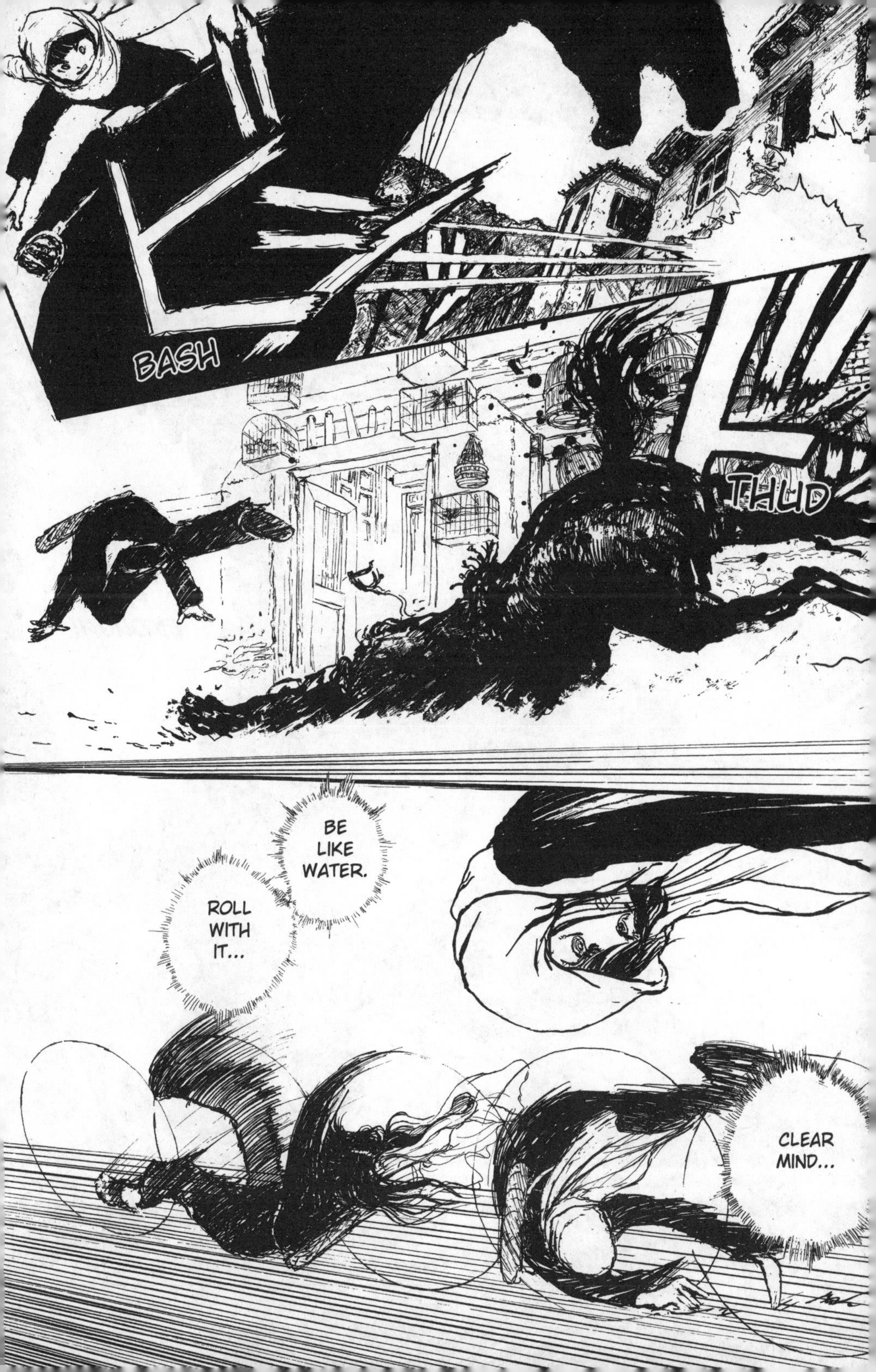
BASH
THUD
BE LIKE WATER.
ROLL WITH IT...
CLEAR MIND...

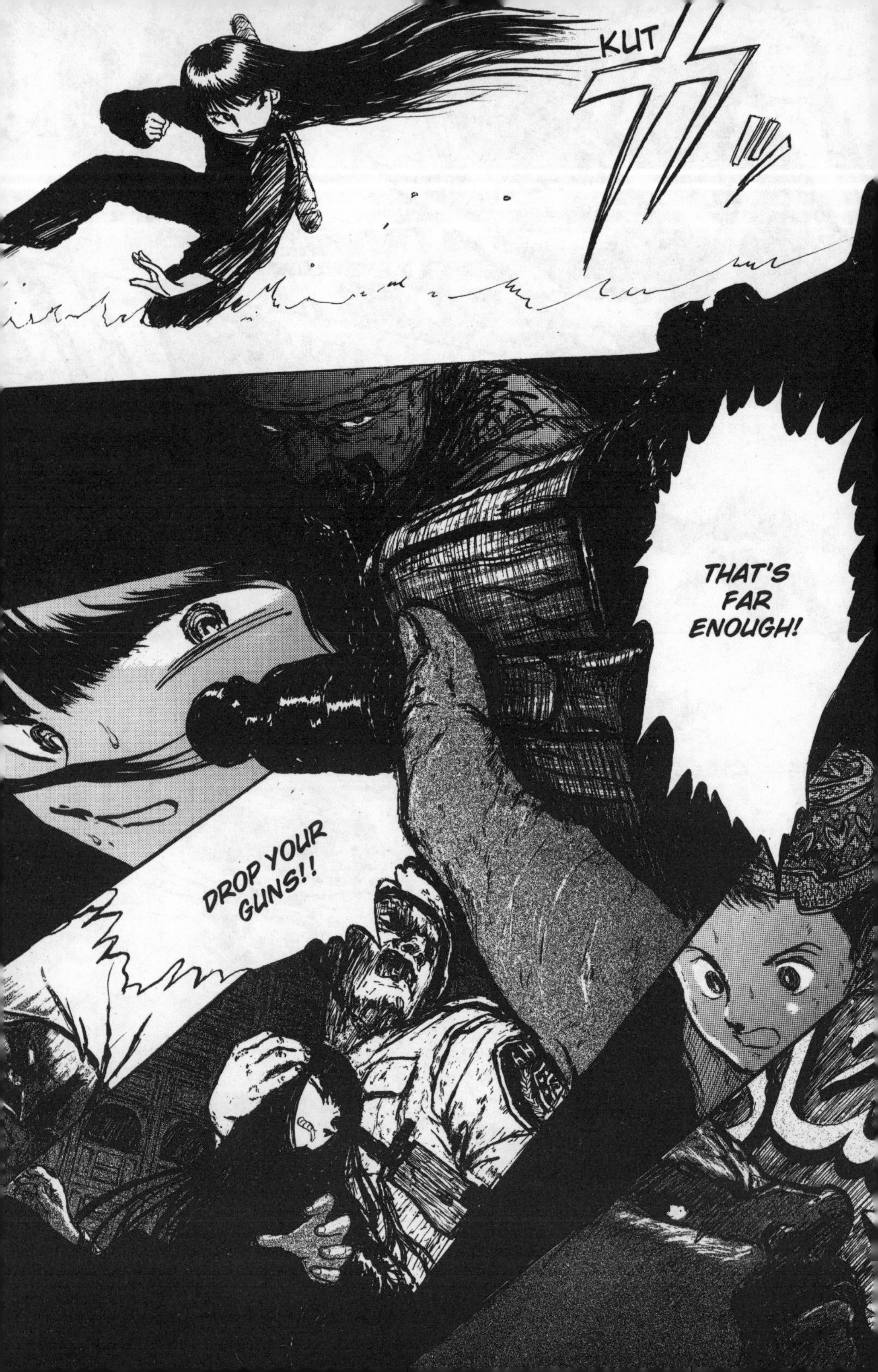
KUT
THAT'S FAR ENOUGH!
DROP YOUR GUNS!!

CHAPTER 5:
ENMITY

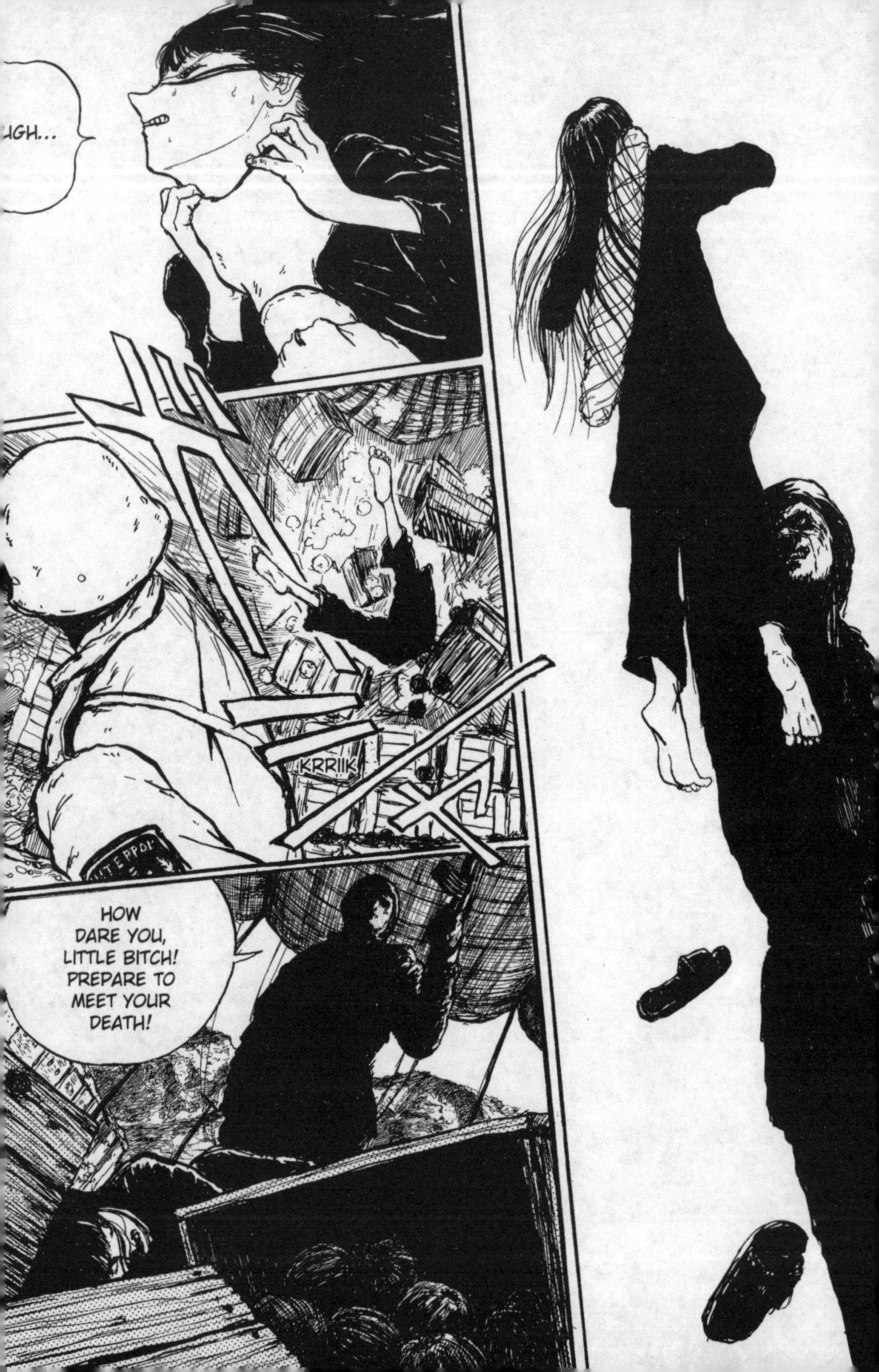
UGH...
KRRIIK
HOW DARE YOU, LITTLE BITCH! PREPARE TO MEET YOUR DEATH!

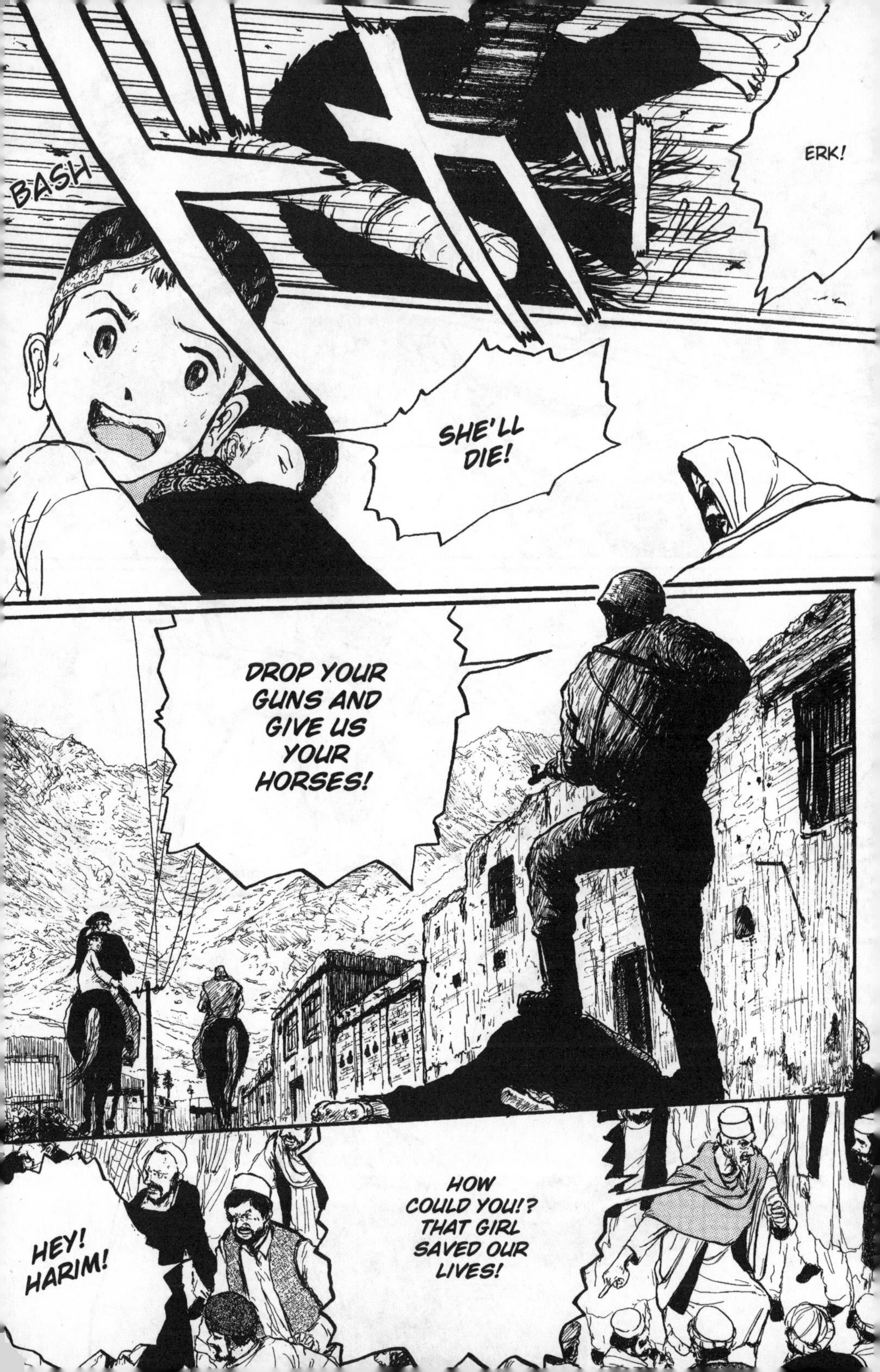
ERK!
BASH
SHE'LL DIE!
DROP YOUR GUNS AND GIVE US YOUR HORSES!
HOW COULD YOU!? THAT GIRL SAVED OUR LIVES!
HEY! HARIM!

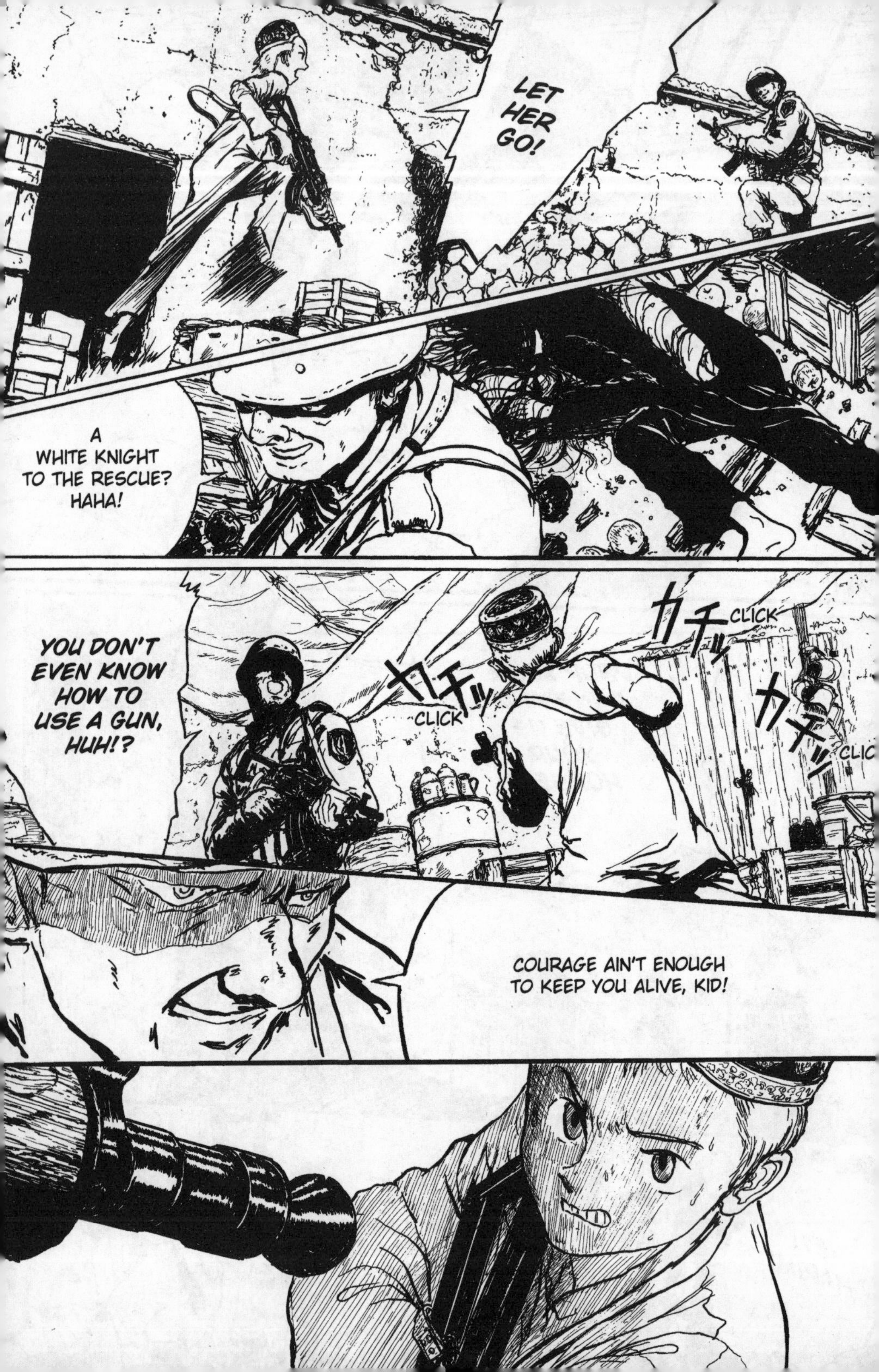
LET HER GO!
A WHITE KNIGHT TO THE RESCUE? HAHA!
カチッ
CLICK
カチッ
CLIC
カチッ
CLICK
YOU DON'T EVEN KNOW HOW TO USE A GUN, HUH!?
COURAGE AIN'T ENOUGH TO KEEP YOU ALIVE, KID!

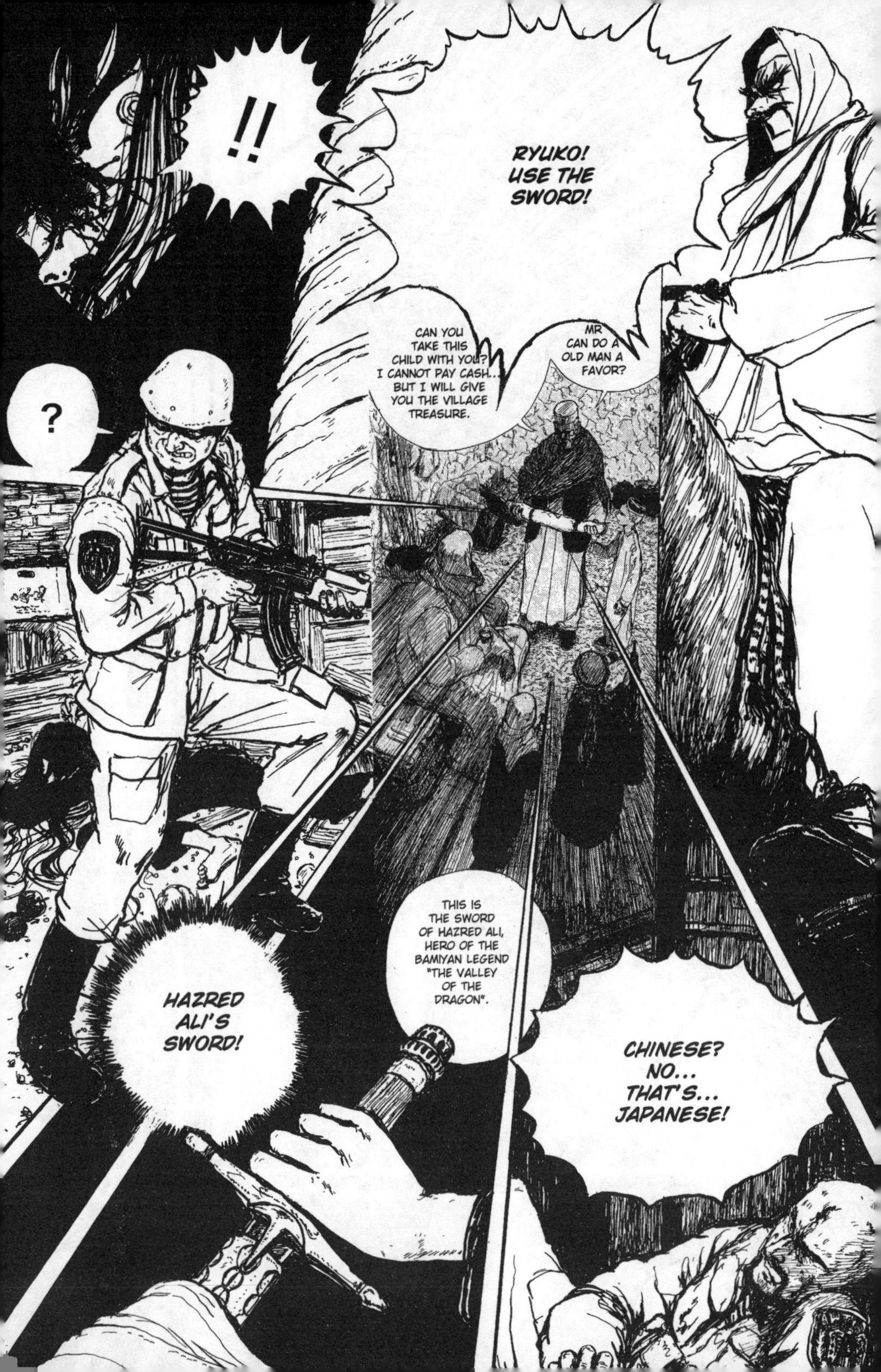
RYUKO! USE THE SWORD!
!!
MR CAN DO A OLD MAN A FAVOR?
CAN YOU TAKE THIS CHILD WITH YOU? I CANNOT PAY CASH... BUT I WILL GIVE YOU THE VILLAGE TREASURE.
THIS IS THE SWORD OF HAZRED ALI, HERO OF THE BAMIYAN LEGEND "THE VALLEY OF THE DRAGON".
?
CHINESE? NO... THAT'S... JAPANESE!
HAZRED ALI'S SWORD!

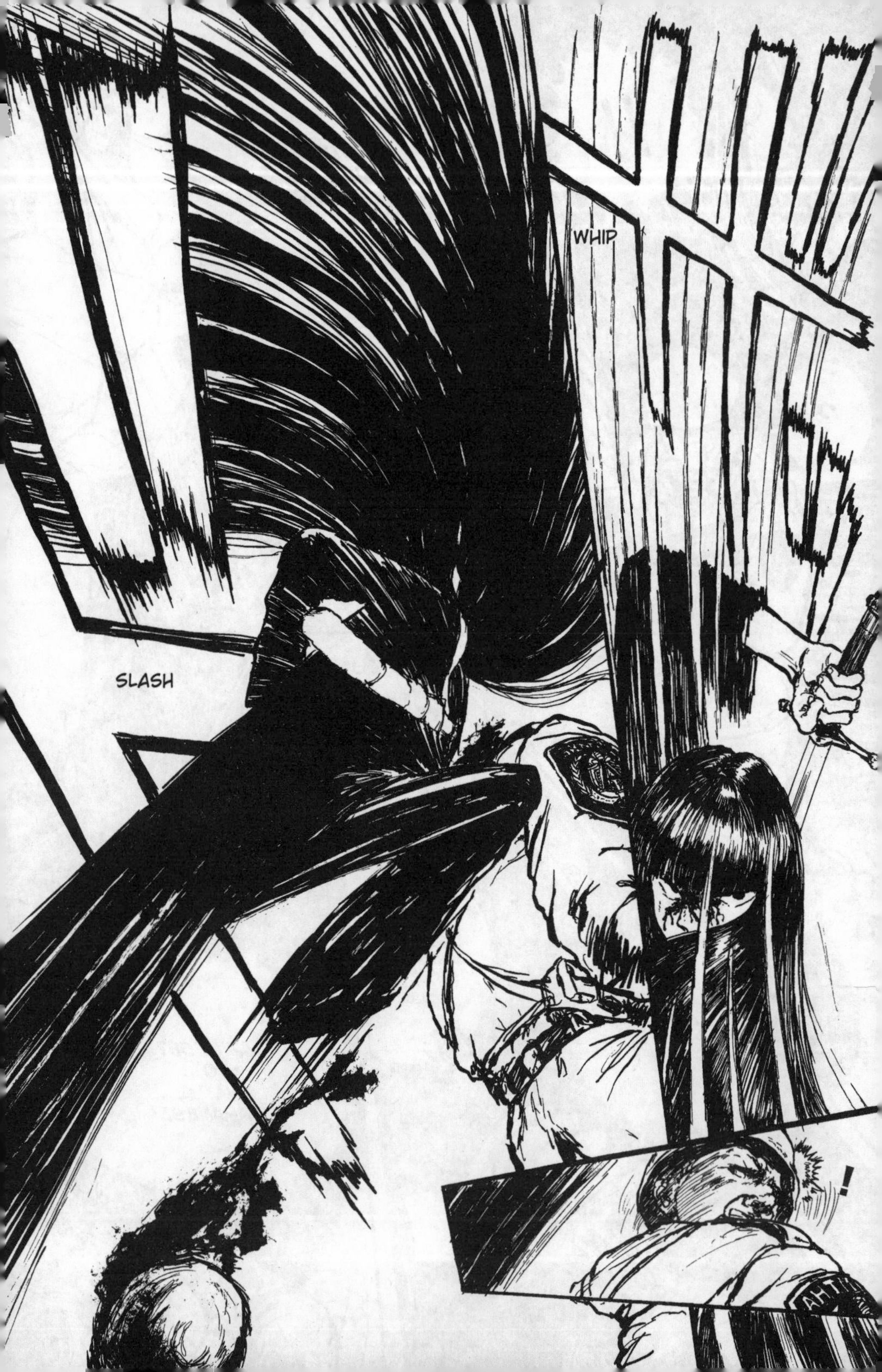
WHIP
SLASH
!

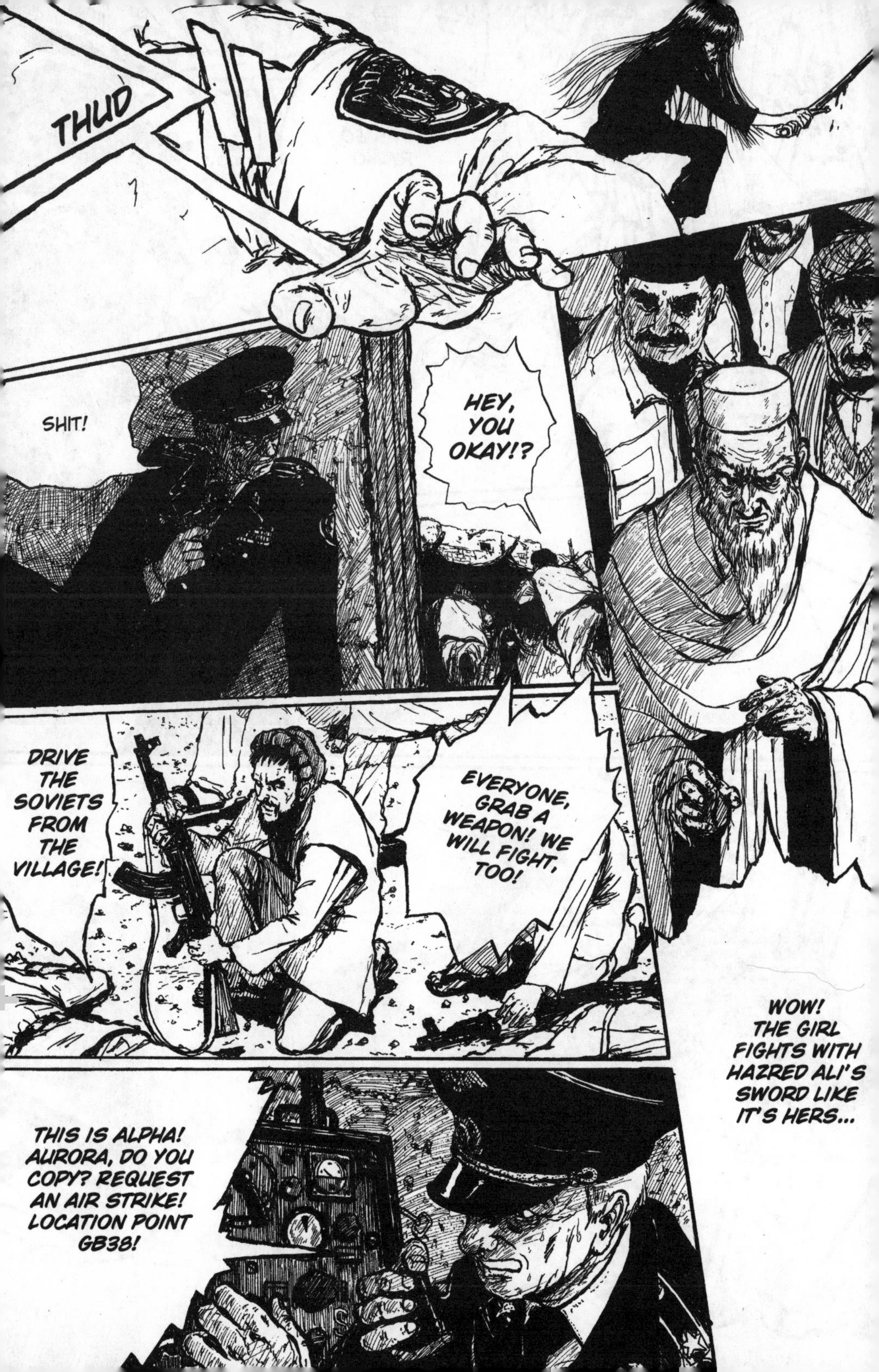
THUD
WOW! THE GIRL FIGHTS WITH HAZRED ALI'S SWORD LIKE IT'S HERS...
HEY, YOU OKAY!?
SHIT!
EVERYONE, GRAB A WEAPON! WE WILL FIGHT, TOO!
DRIVE THE SOVIETS FROM THE VILLAGE!
THIS IS ALPHA! AURORA, DO YOU COPY? REQUEST AN AIR STRIKE! LOCATION POINT GB38!

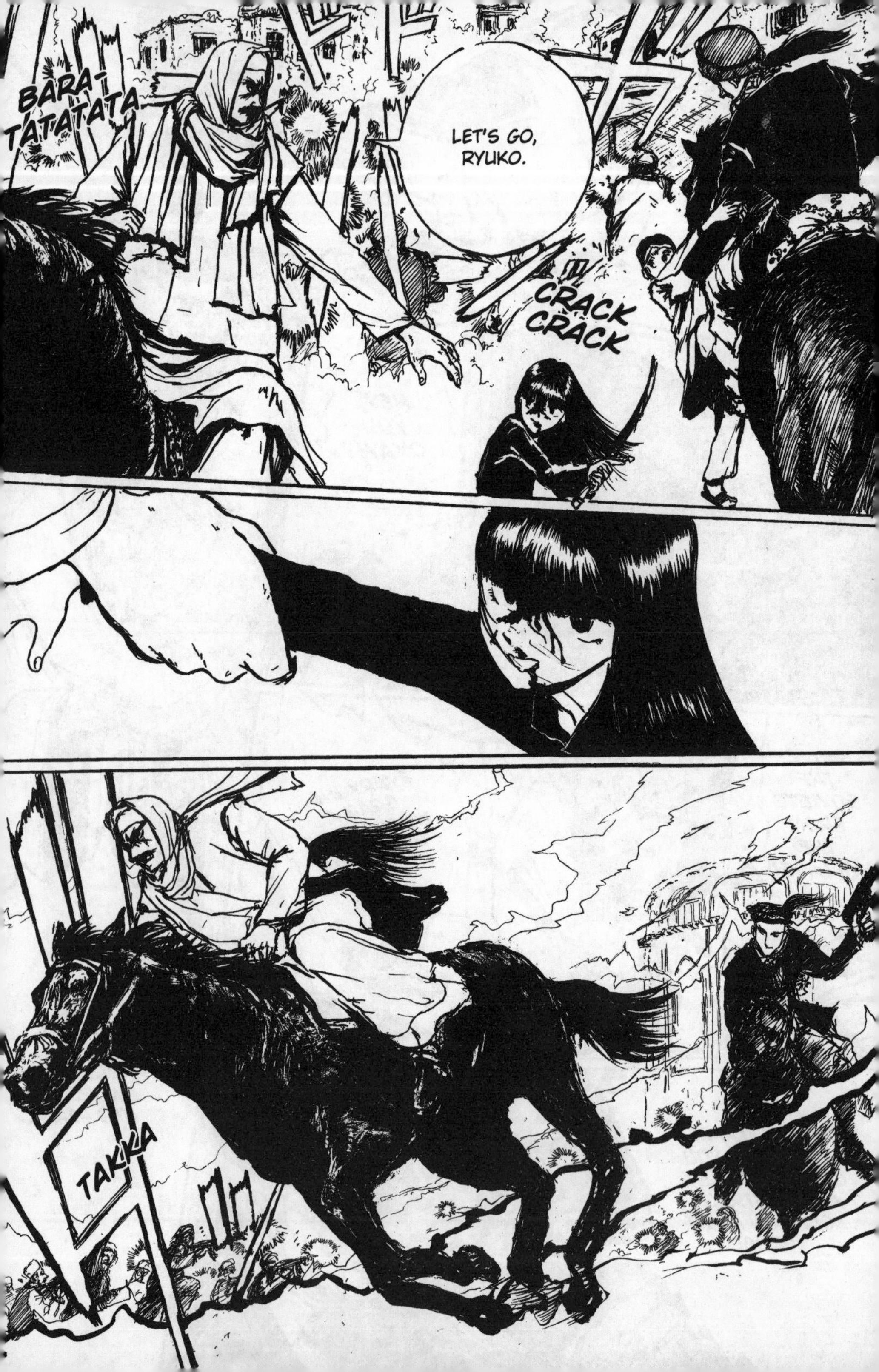
LET'S GO, RYUKO.
CRACK CRACK
BARA-TATATATA
TAKKA

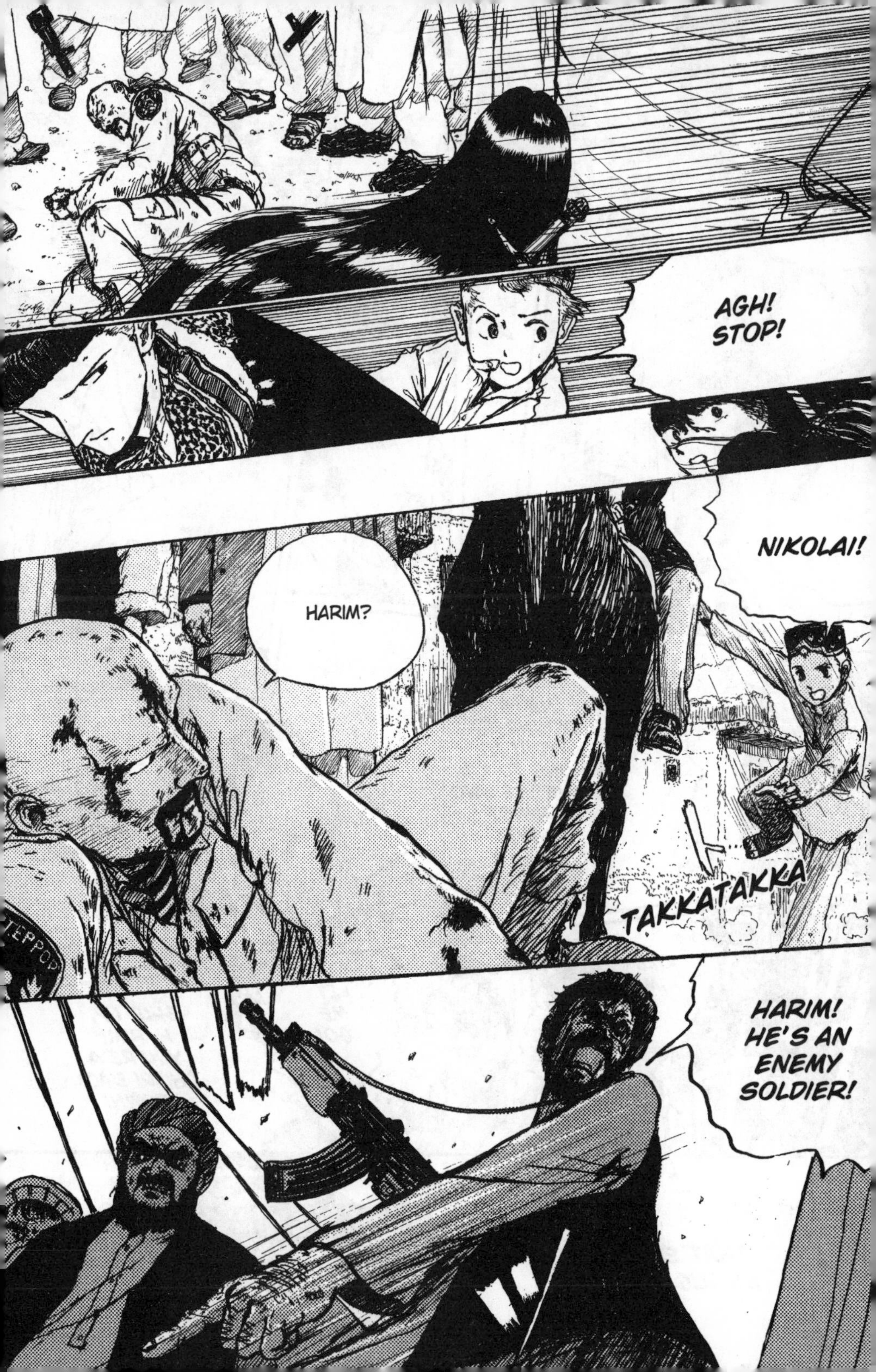
AGH! STOP!
NIKOLAI!
HARIM?
TAKKATAKKA
HARIM! HE'S AN ENEMY SOLDIER!

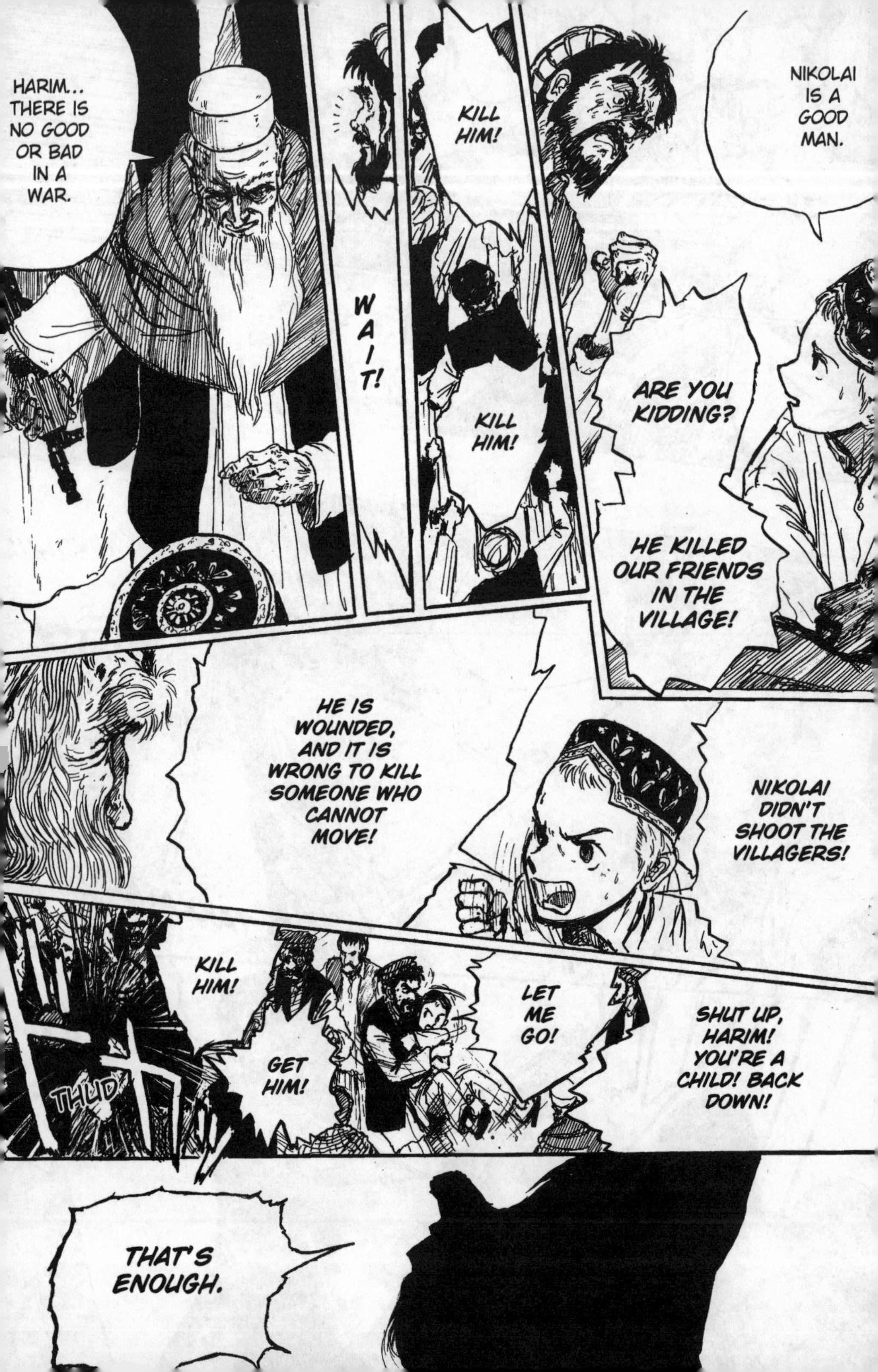
NIKOLAI IS A GOOD MAN.
ARE YOU KIDDING?
HE KILLED OUR FRIENDS IN THE VILLAGE!
KILL HIM!
WAIT!
KILL HIM!
HARIM... THERE IS NO GOOD OR BAD IN A WAR.
NIKOLAI DIDN'T SHOOT THE VILLAGERS!
HE IS WOUNDED, AND IT IS WRONG TO KILL SOMEONE WHO CANNOT MOVE!
SHUT UP, HARIM! YOU'RE A CHILD! BACK DOWN!
LET ME GO!
GET HIM!
KILL HIM!
THUD
THAT'S ENOUGH.

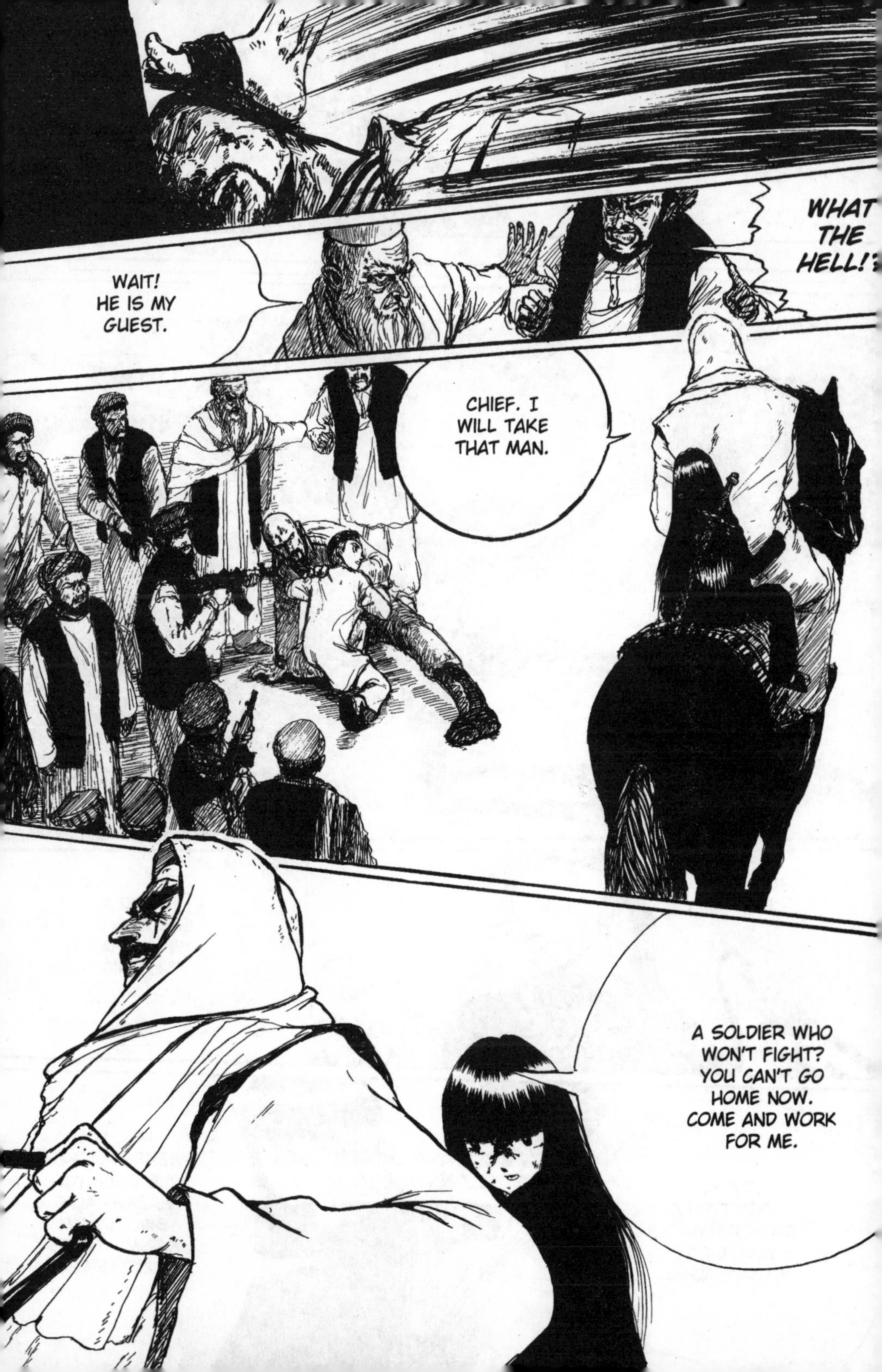
WHAT THE HELL!?
WAIT! HE IS MY GUEST.
CHIEF. I WILL TAKE THAT MAN.
A SOLDIER WHO WON'T FIGHT? YOU CAN'T GO HOME NOW. COME AND WORK FOR ME.

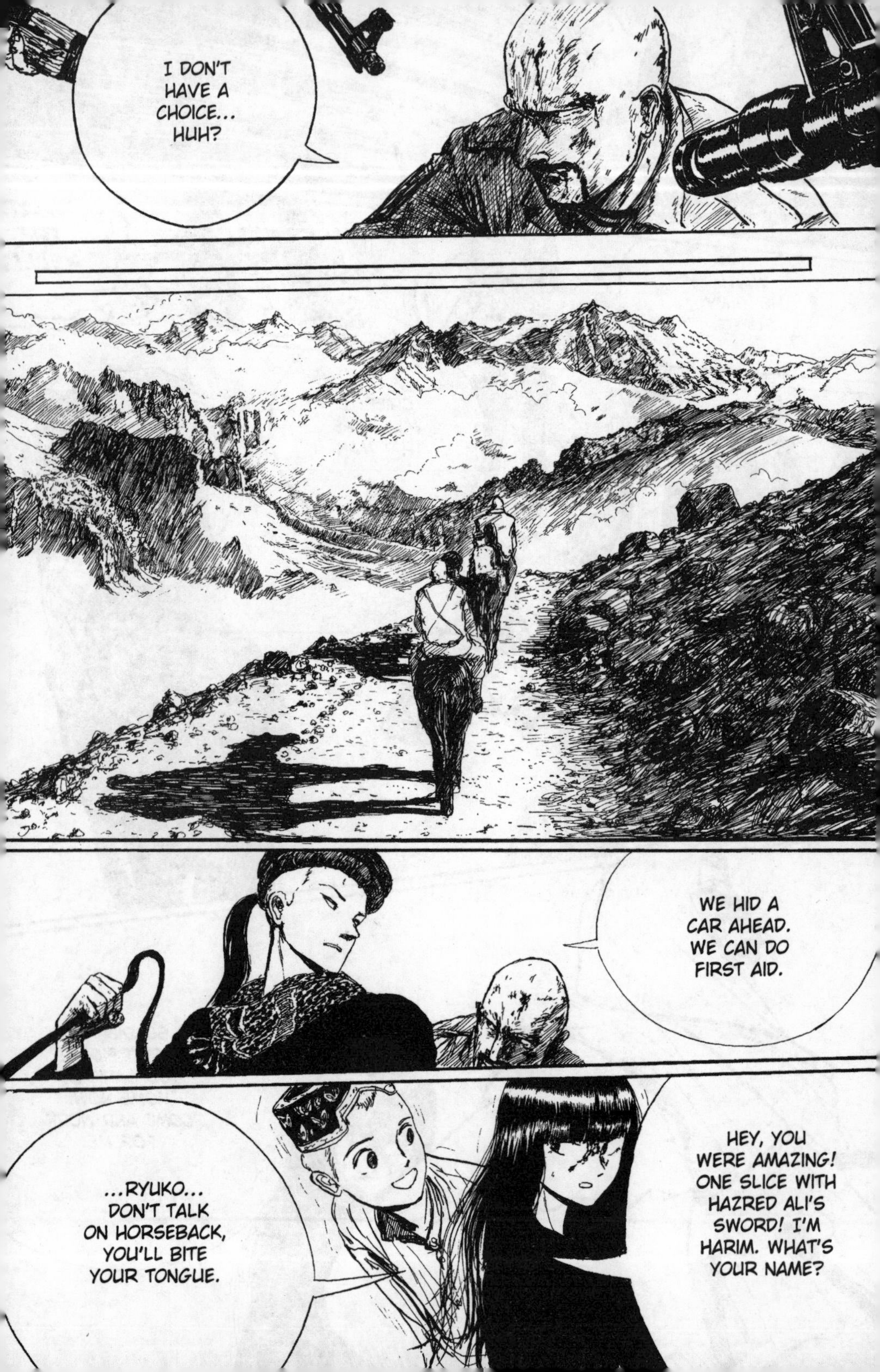
I DON'T HAVE A CHOICE... HUH?
WE HID A CAR AHEAD. WE CAN DO FIRST AID.
HEY, YOU WERE AMAZING! ONE SLICE WITH HAZRED ALI'S SWORD! I'M HARIM. WHAT'S YOUR NAME?
...RYUKO... DON'T TALK ON HORSEBACK, YOU'LL BITE YOUR TONGUE.

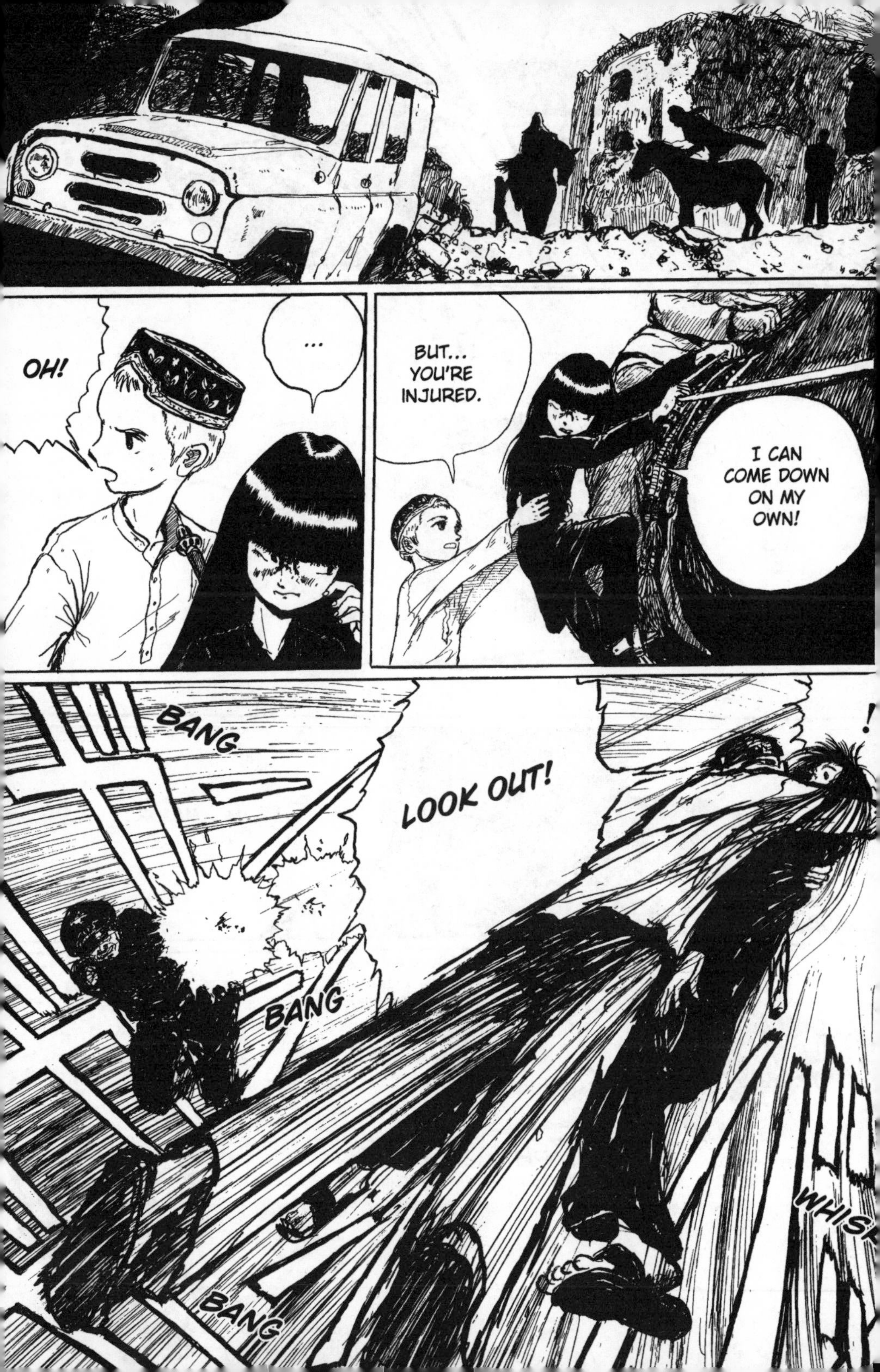
I CAN COME DOWN ON MY OWN!
BUT... YOU'RE INJURED.
...
OH!
!
LOOK OUT!
BANG
WHIS
BANG
BANG

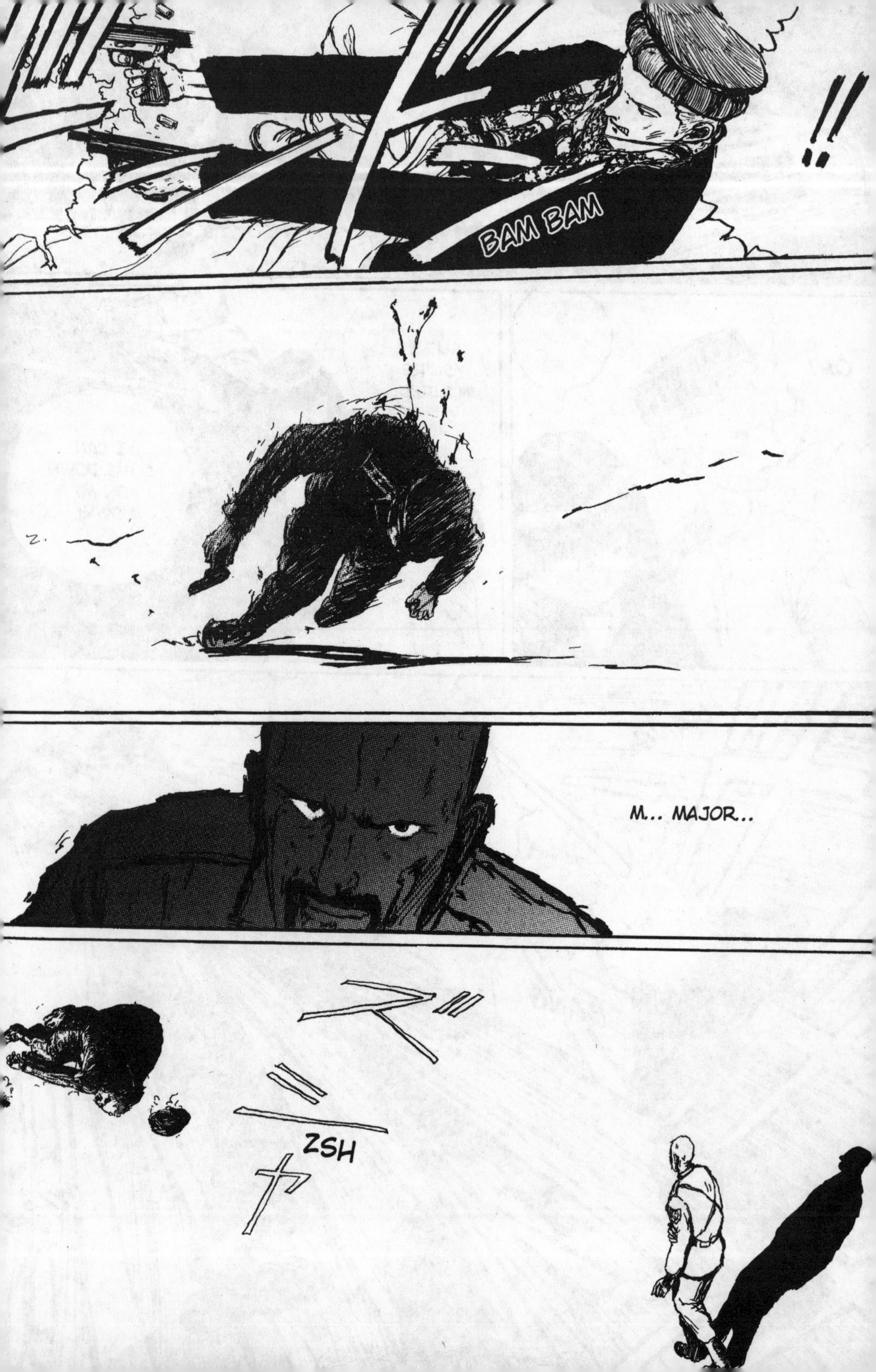
!!
BAM BAM
M... MAJOR..
ZSH

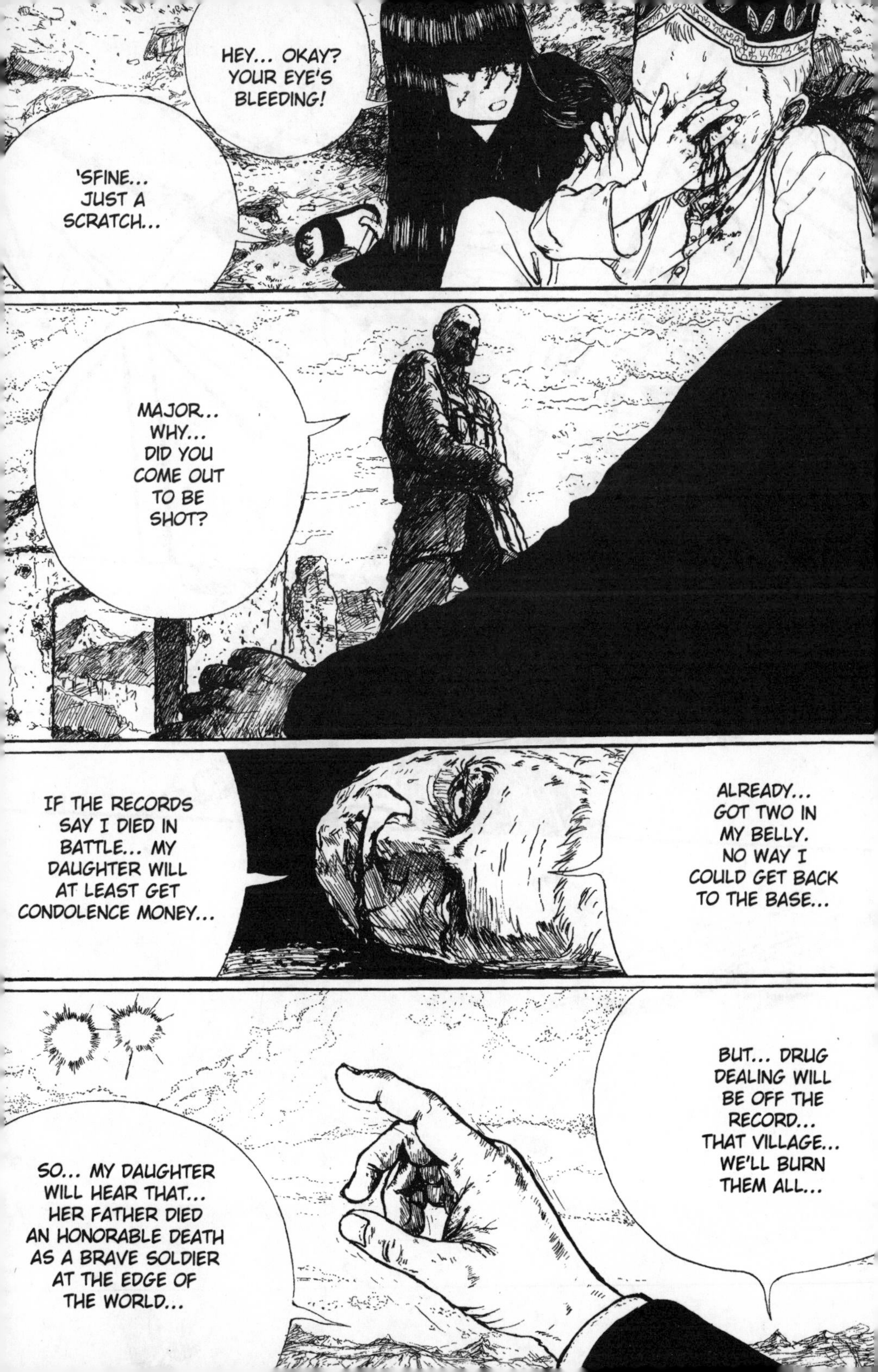
HEY... OKAY? YOUR EYE'S BLEEDING!
'SFINE... JUST A SCRATCH...
MAJOR... WHY... DID YOU COME OUT TO BE SHOT?
ALREADY... GOT TWO IN MY BELLY. NO WAY I COULD GET BACK TO THE BASE...
IF THE RECORDS SAY I DIED IN BATTLE... MY DAUGHTER WILL AT LEAST GET CONDOLENCE MONEY...
BUT... DRUG DEALING WILL BE OFF THE RECORD... THAT VILLAGE... WE'LL BURN THEM ALL...
SO... MY DAUGHTER WILL HEAR THAT... HER FATHER DIED AN HONORABLE DEATH AS A BRAVE SOLDIER AT THE EDGE OF THE WORLD...

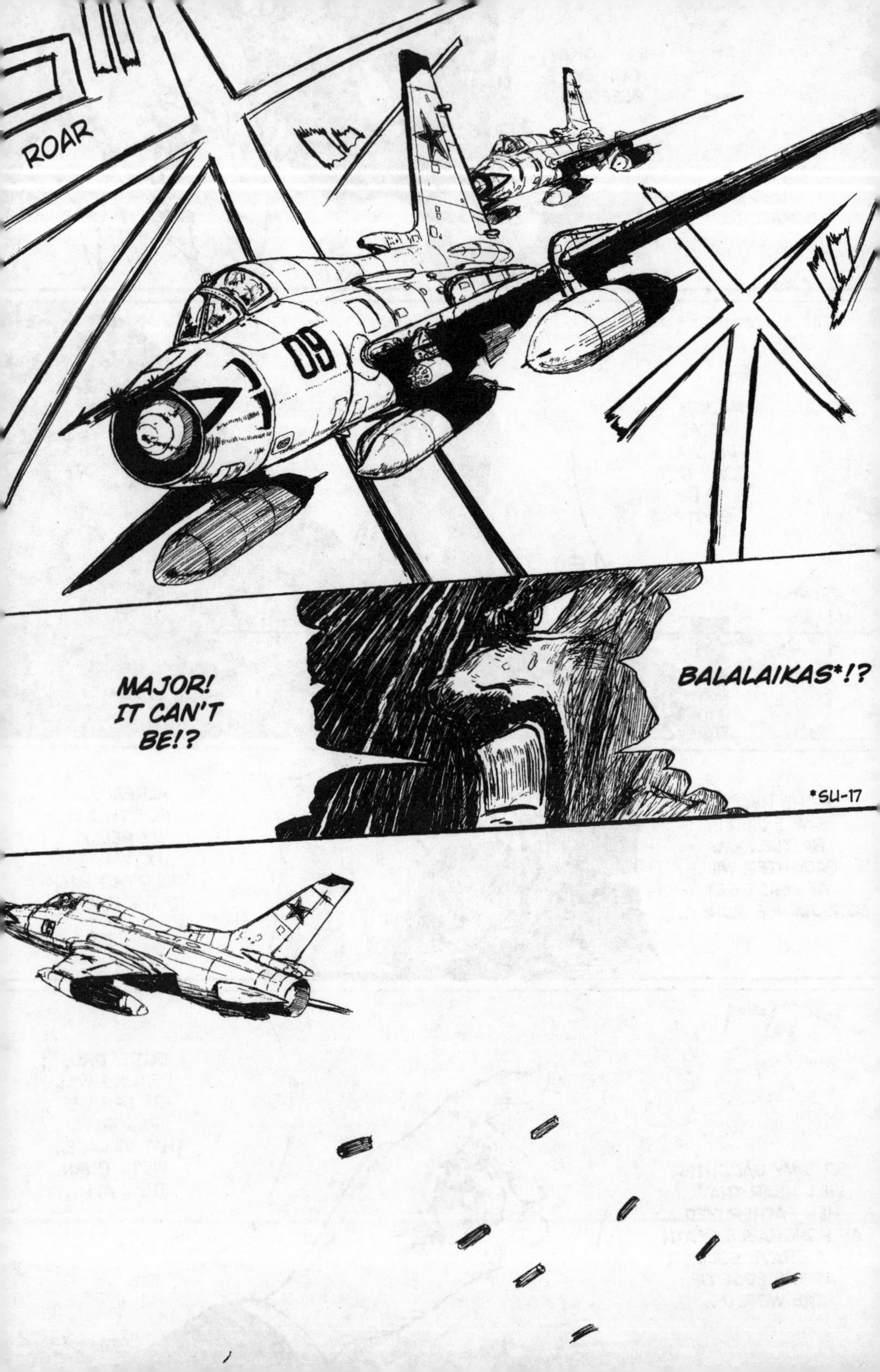
ROAR
BALALAIKAS*!?
MAJOR! IT CAN'T BE!?
*SU-17

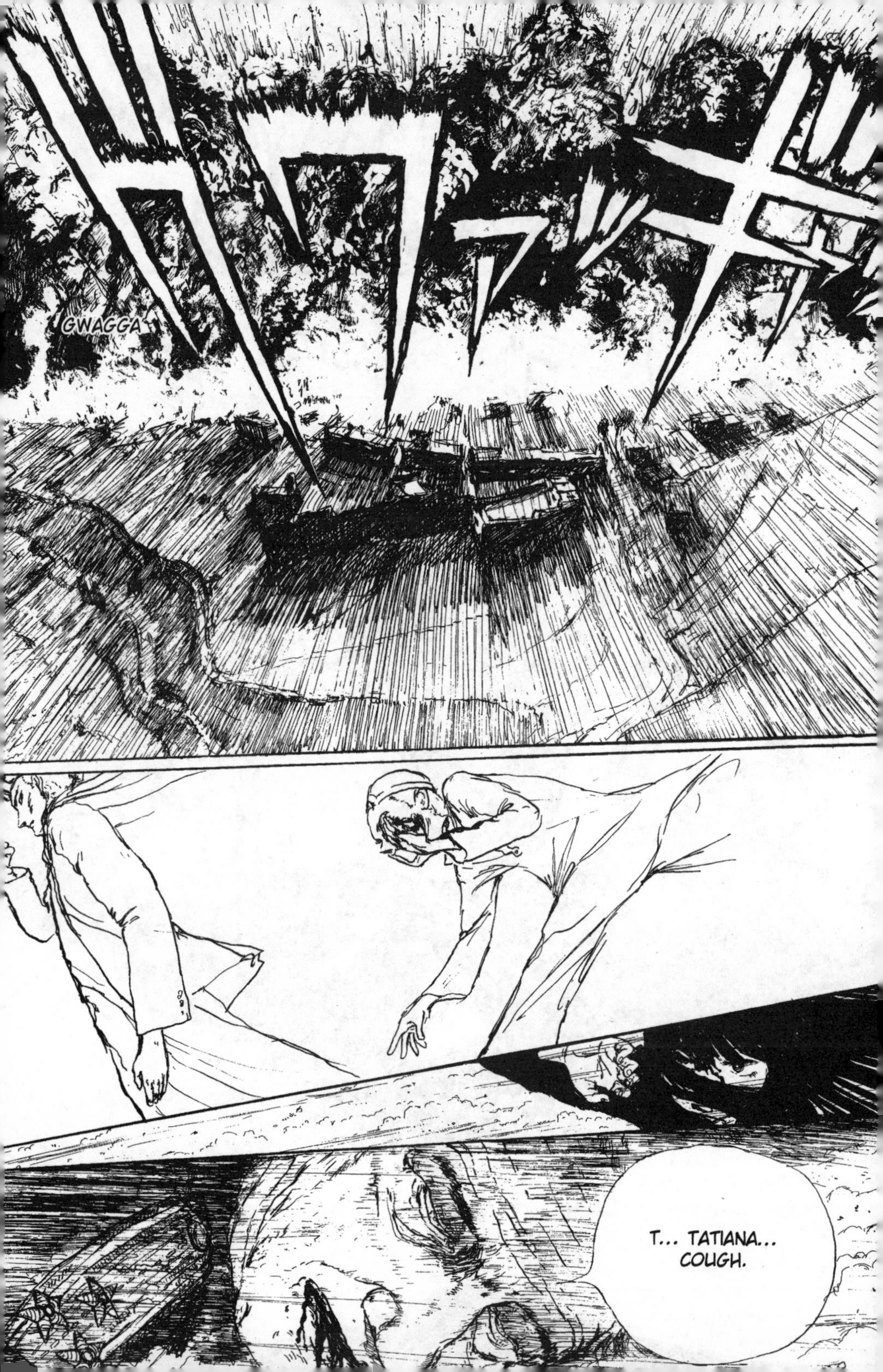
GWAGGA
T... TATIANA... COUGH.

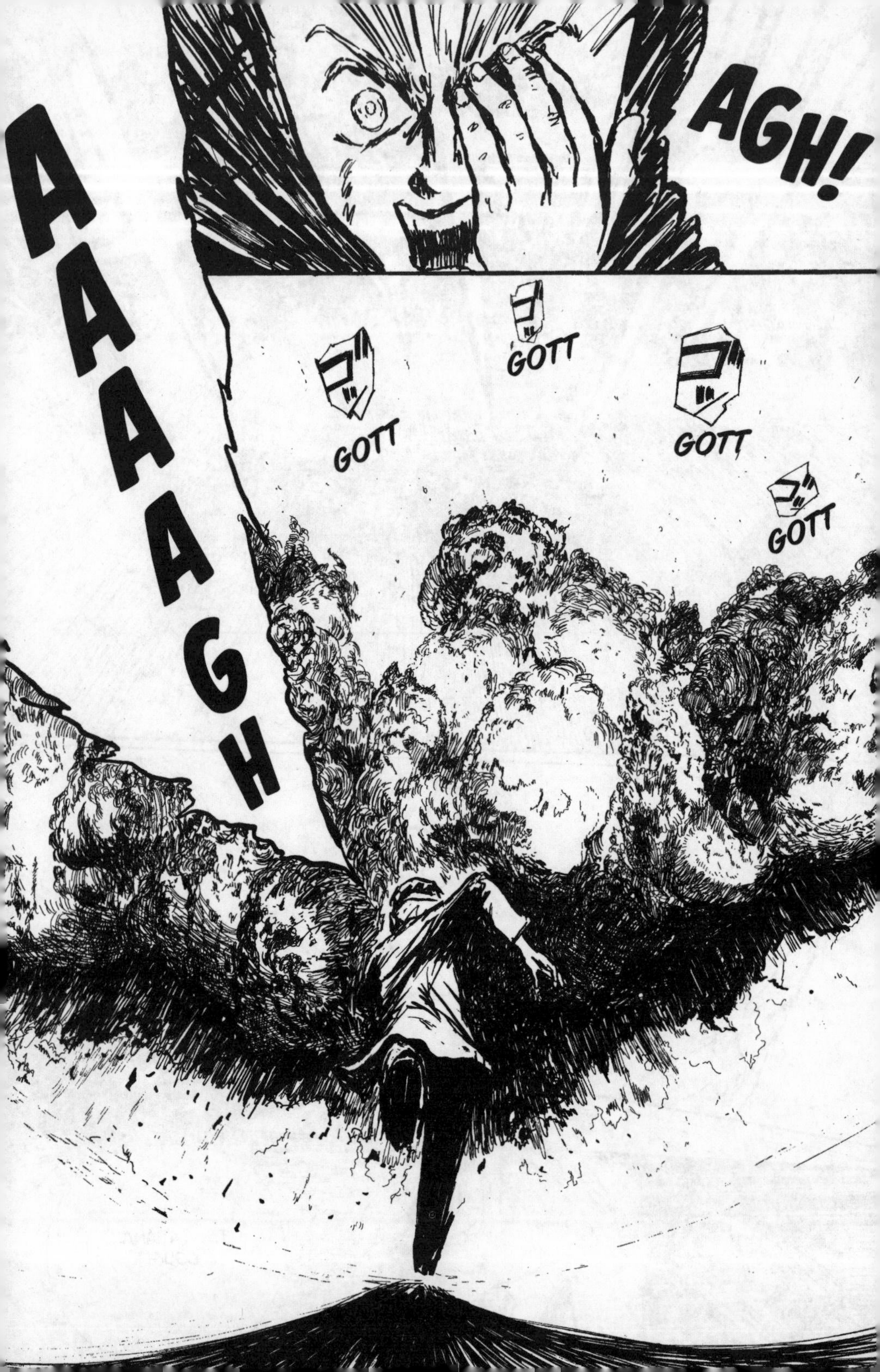
AGH!
AAAAGH
ゴッ
GOTT
ゴッ
GOTT
ゴッ
GOTT
ゴッ
GOTT

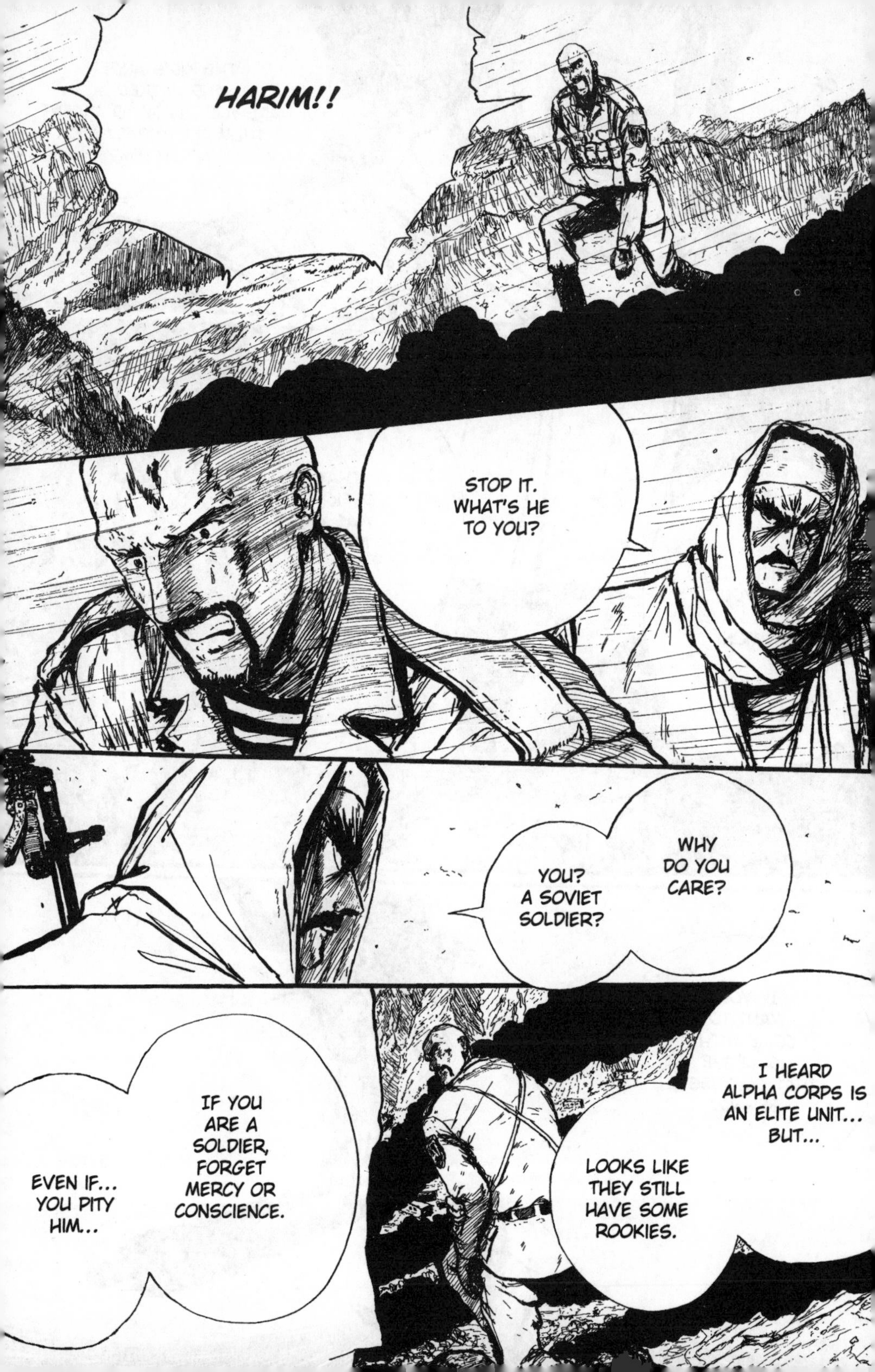
HARIM!!
STOP IT. WHAT'S HE TO YOU?
WHY DO YOU CARE?
YOU? A SOVIET SOLDIER?
I HEARD ALPHA CORPS IS AN ELITE UNIT... BUT...
LOOKS LIKE THEY STILL HAVE SOME ROOKIES.
IF YOU ARE A SOLDIER, FORGET MERCY OR CONSCIENCE.
EVEN IF... YOU PITY HIM...

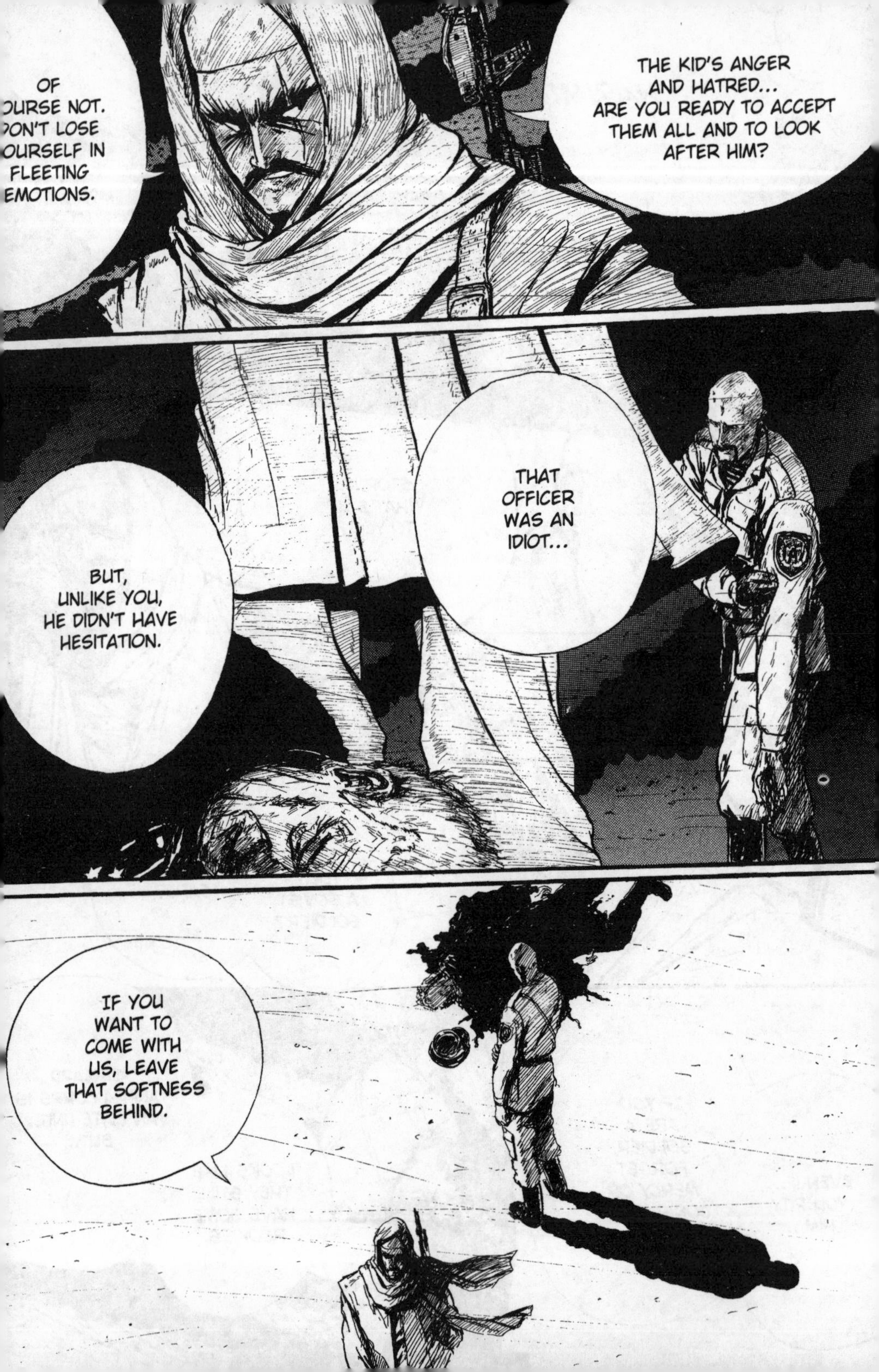
THE KID'S ANGER AND HATRED... ARE YOU READY TO ACCEPT THEM ALL AND TO LOOK AFTER HIM?
OF OURSE NOT. ON'T LOSE OURSELF IN FLEETING EMOTIONS.
THAT OFFICER WAS AN IDIOT...
BUT, UNLIKE YOU, HE DIDN'T HAVE HESITATION.
IF YOU WANT TO COME WITH US, LEAVE THAT SOFTNESS BEHIND.

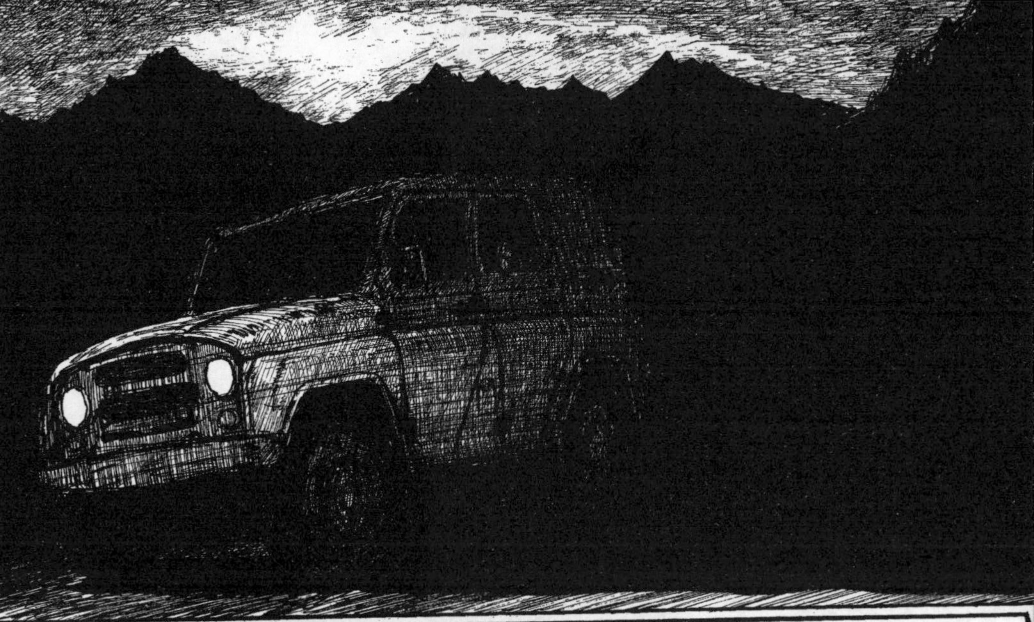

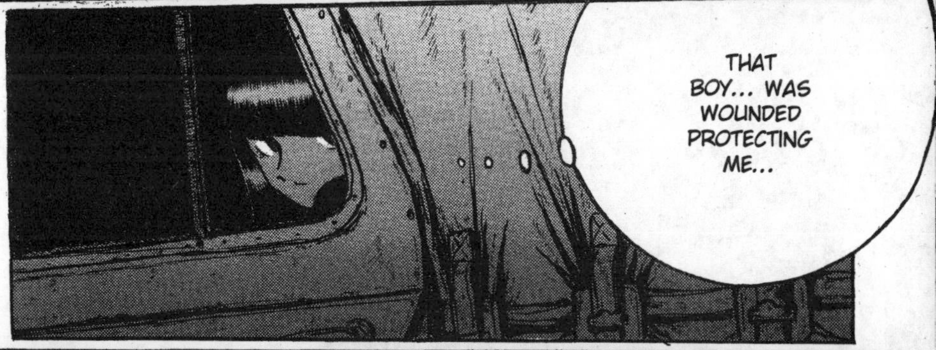
THAT BOY... WAS WOUNDED PROTECTING ME...

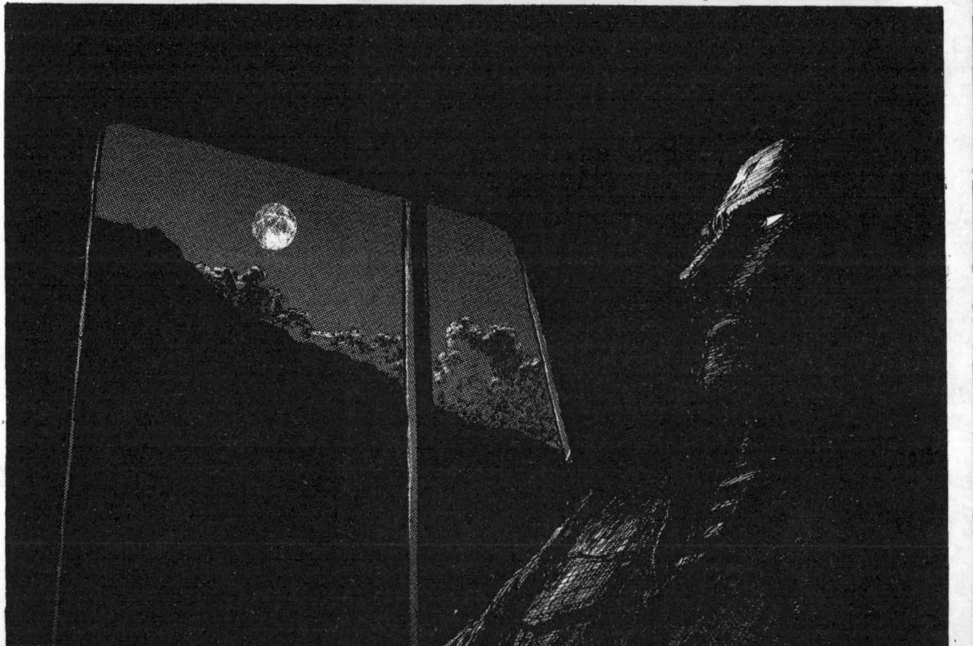

PRESENT DAY.
YAMASHITA-CHO,
YOKOHAMA.

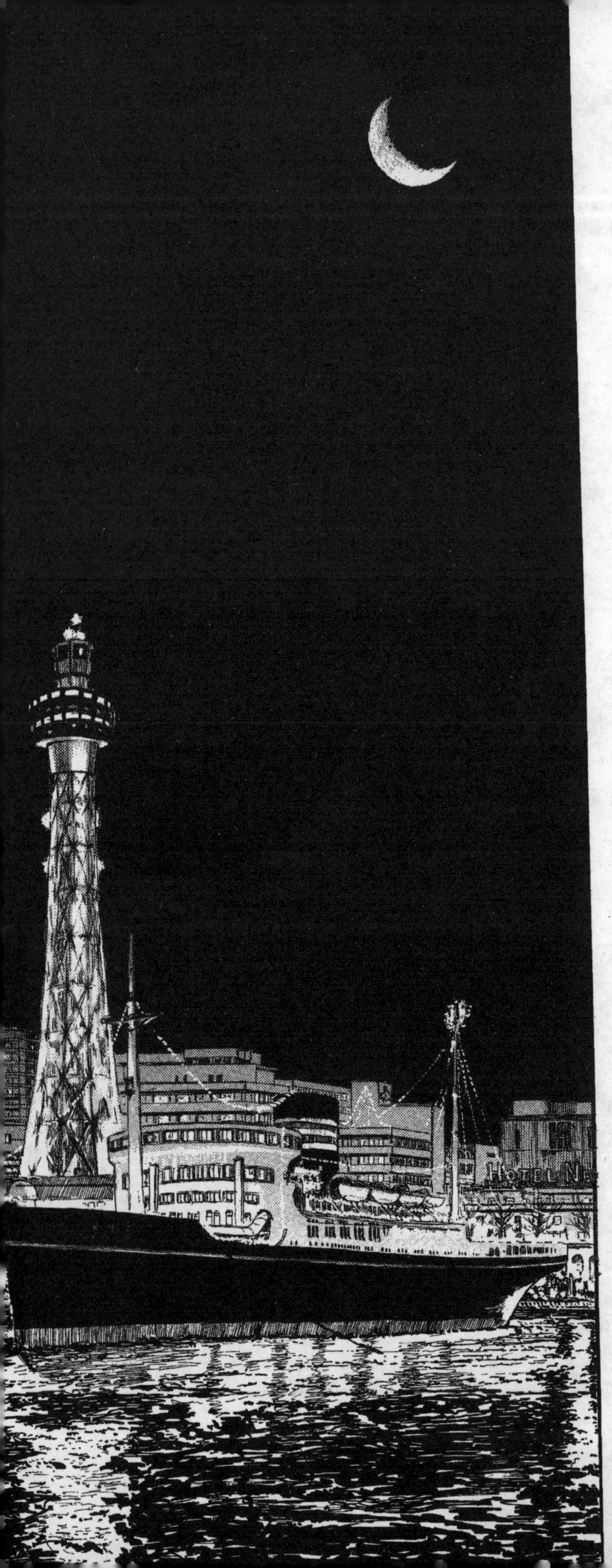

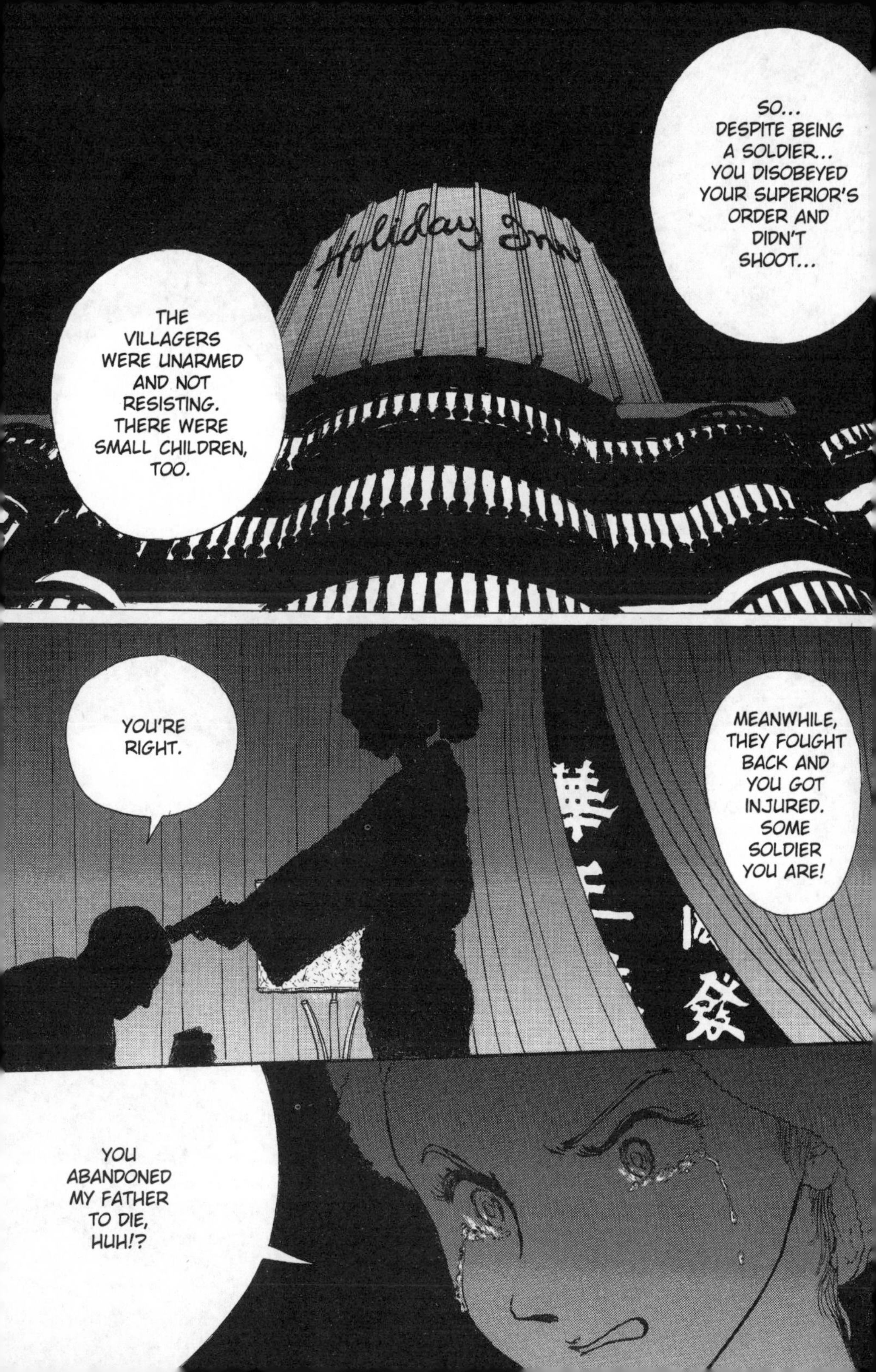
SO... DESPITE BEING A SOLDIER... YOU DISOBEYED YOUR SUPERIOR'S ORDER AND DIDN'T SHOOT...
Holiday Inn
THE VILLAGERS WERE UNARMED AND NOT RESISTING. THERE WERE SMALL CHILDREN, TOO.
MEANWHILE, THEY FOUGHT BACK AND YOU GOT INJURED. SOME SOLDIER YOU ARE!
YOU'RE RIGHT.
YOU ABANDONED MY FATHER TO DIE, HUH!?

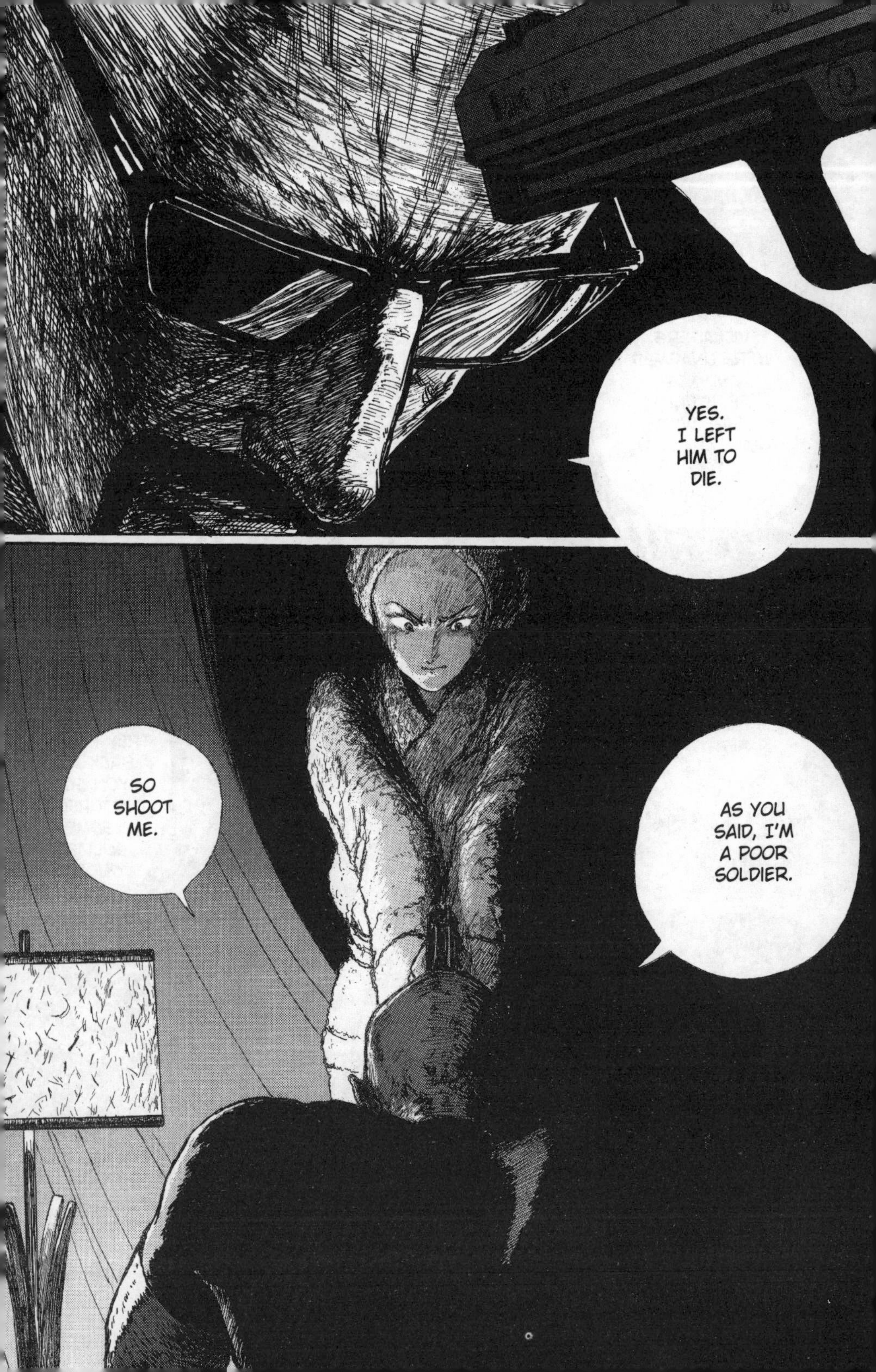
YES. I LEFT HIM TO DIE.
AS YOU SAID, I'M A POOR SOLDIER.
SO SHOOT ME.

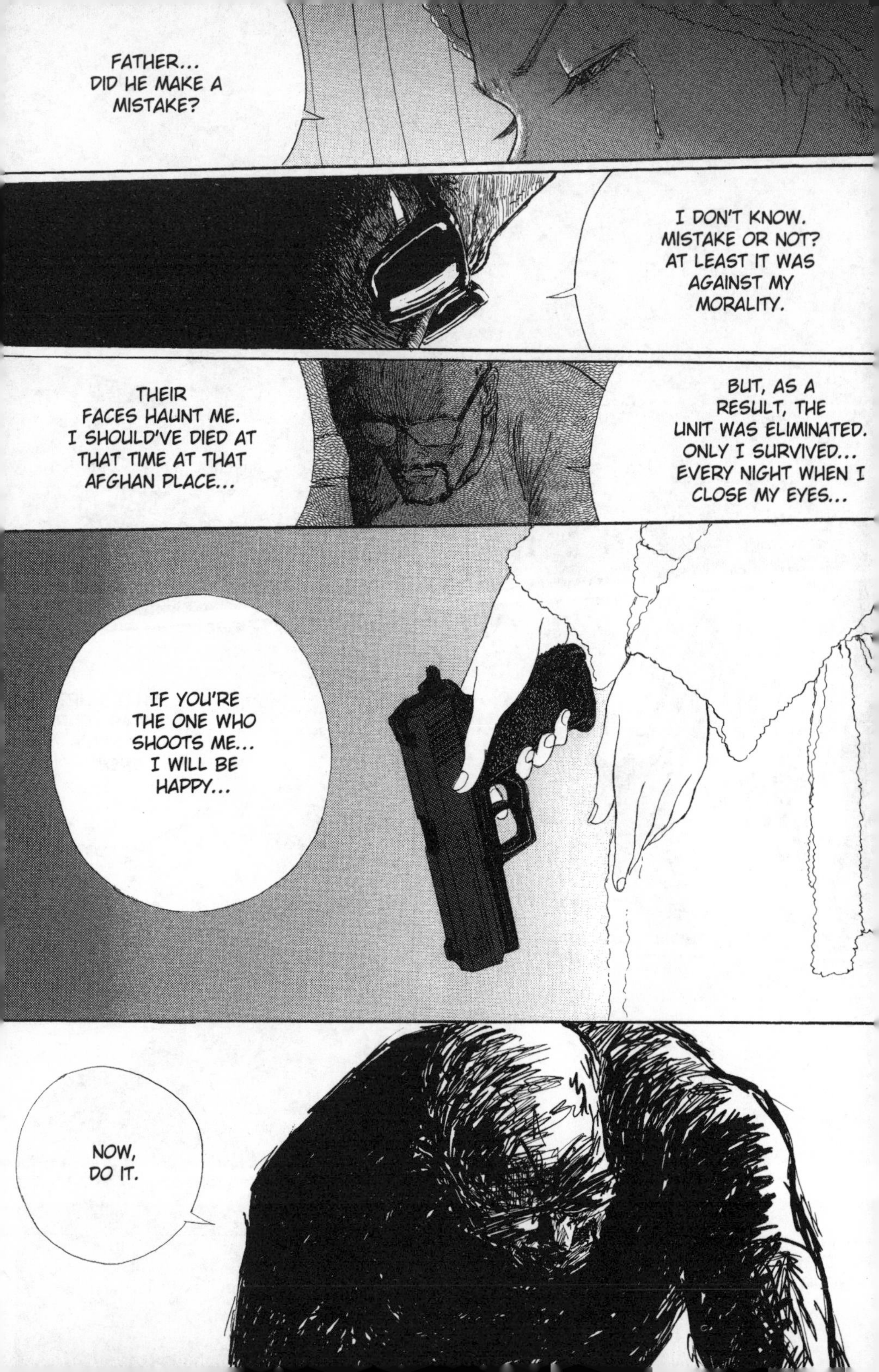
FATHER... DID HE MAKE A MISTAKE?
I DON'T KNOW. MISTAKE OR NOT? AT LEAST IT WAS AGAINST MY MORALITY.
BUT, AS A RESULT, THE UNIT WAS ELIMINATED. ONLY I SURVIVED... EVERY NIGHT WHEN I CLOSE MY EYES...
THEIR FACES HAUNT ME. I SHOULD'VE DIED AT THAT TIME AT THAT AFGHAN PLACE...
IF YOU'RE THE ONE WHO SHOOTS ME... I WILL BE HAPPY...
NOW, DO IT.

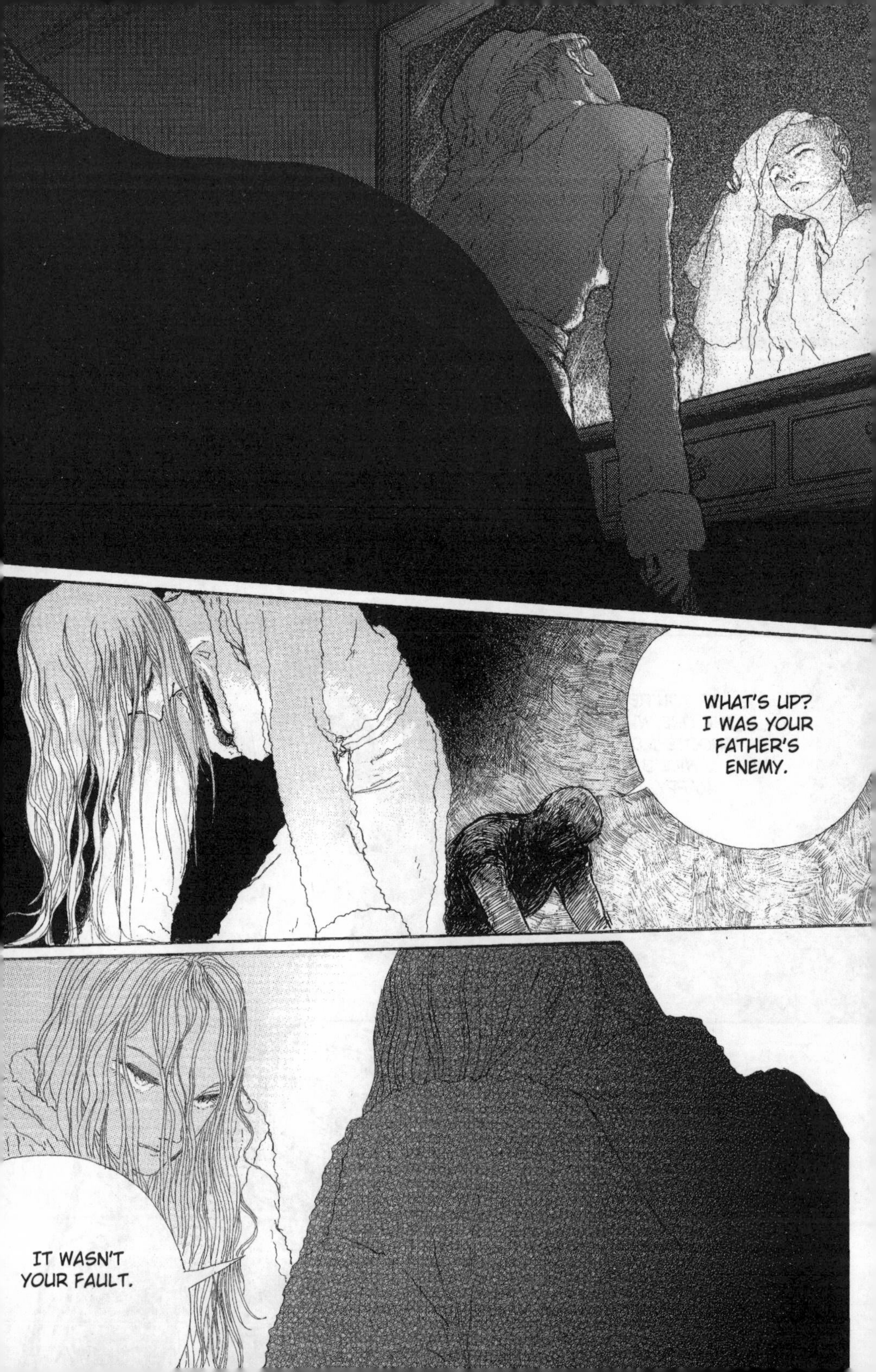
WHAT'S UP? I WAS YOUR FATHER'S ENEMY.
IT WASN'T YOUR FAULT.

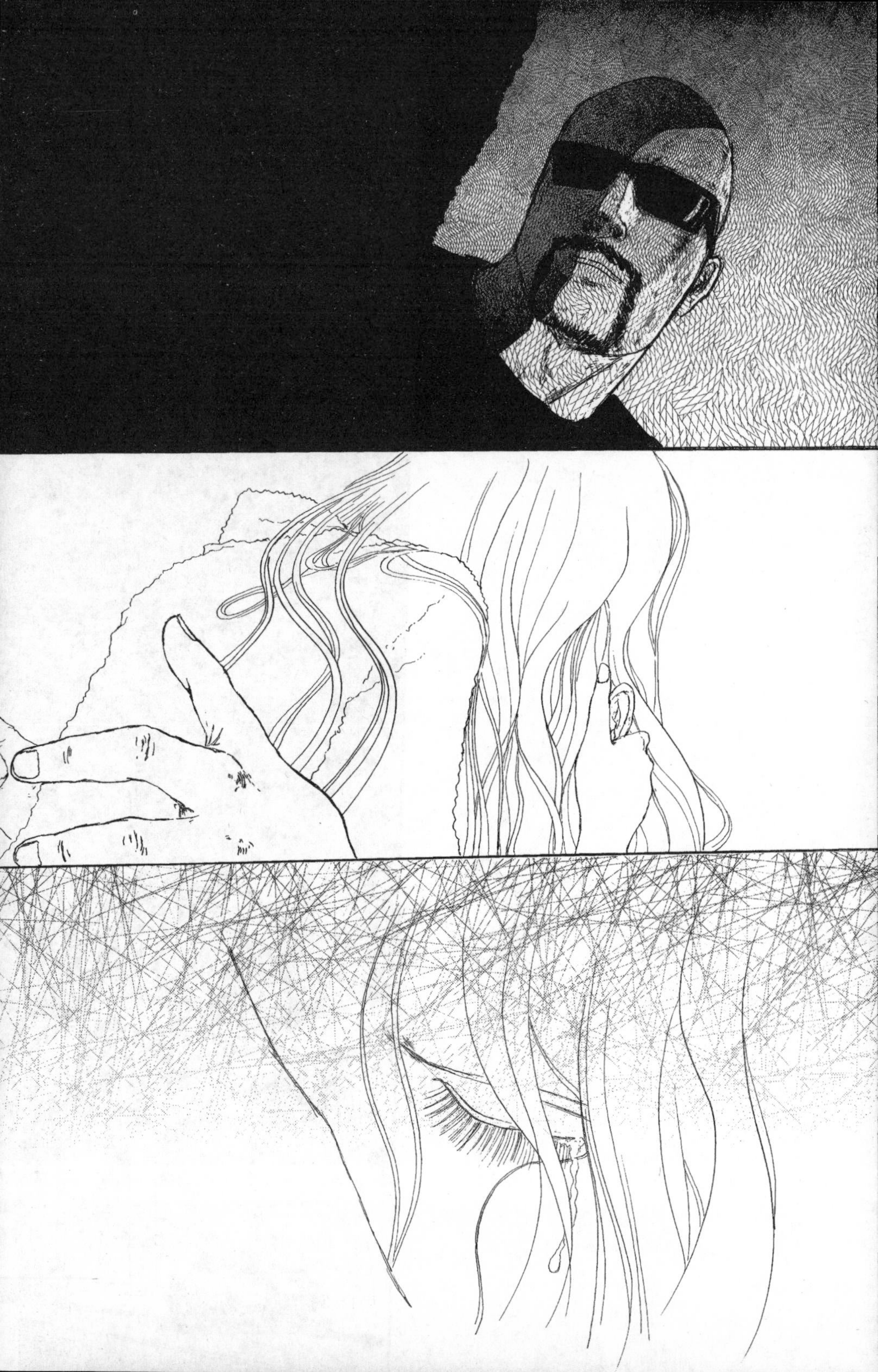

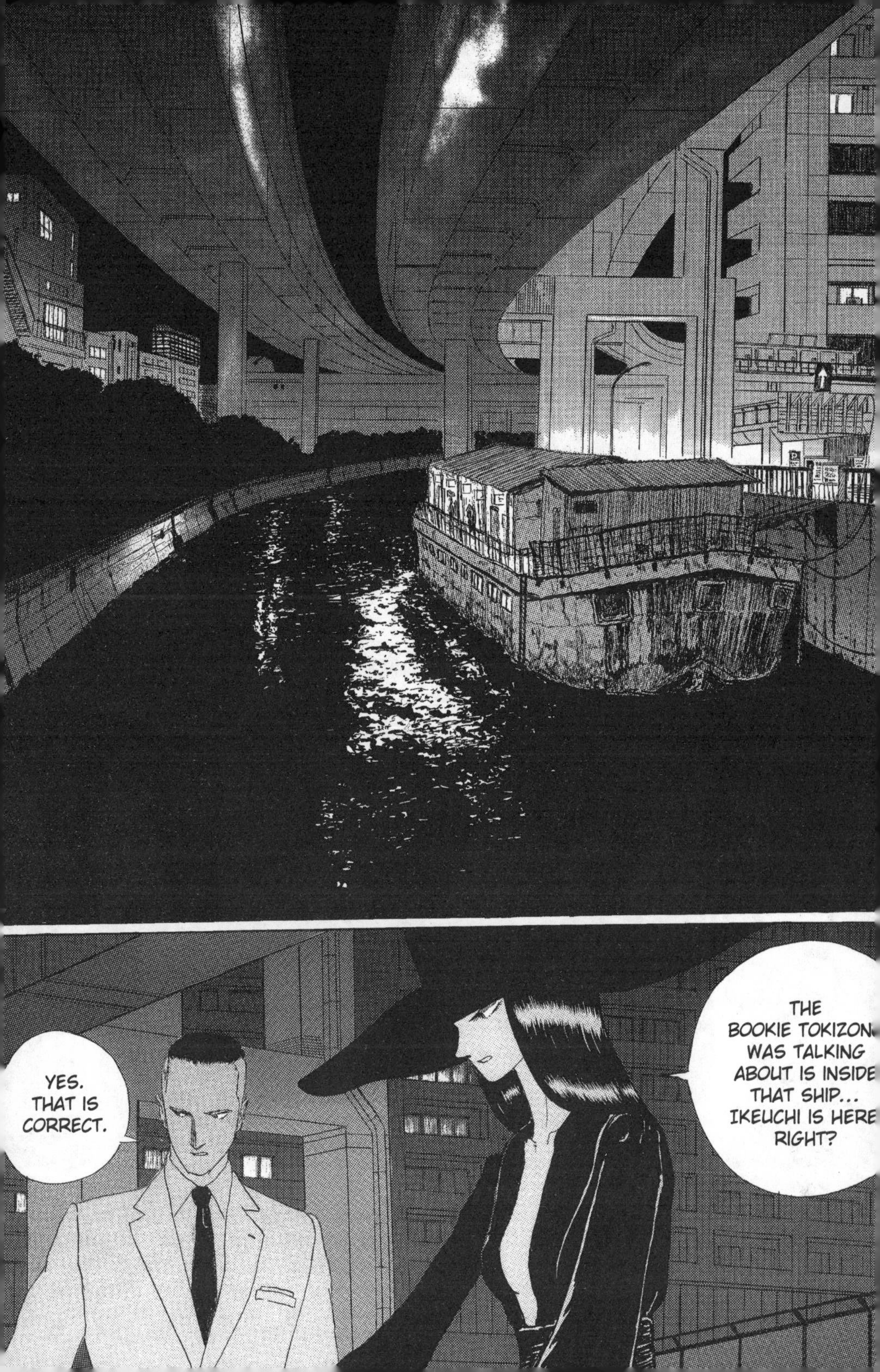
THE BOOKIE TOKIZON WAS TALKING ABOUT IS INSIDE THAT SHIP... IKEUCHI IS HERE RIGHT?
YES. THAT IS CORRECT.

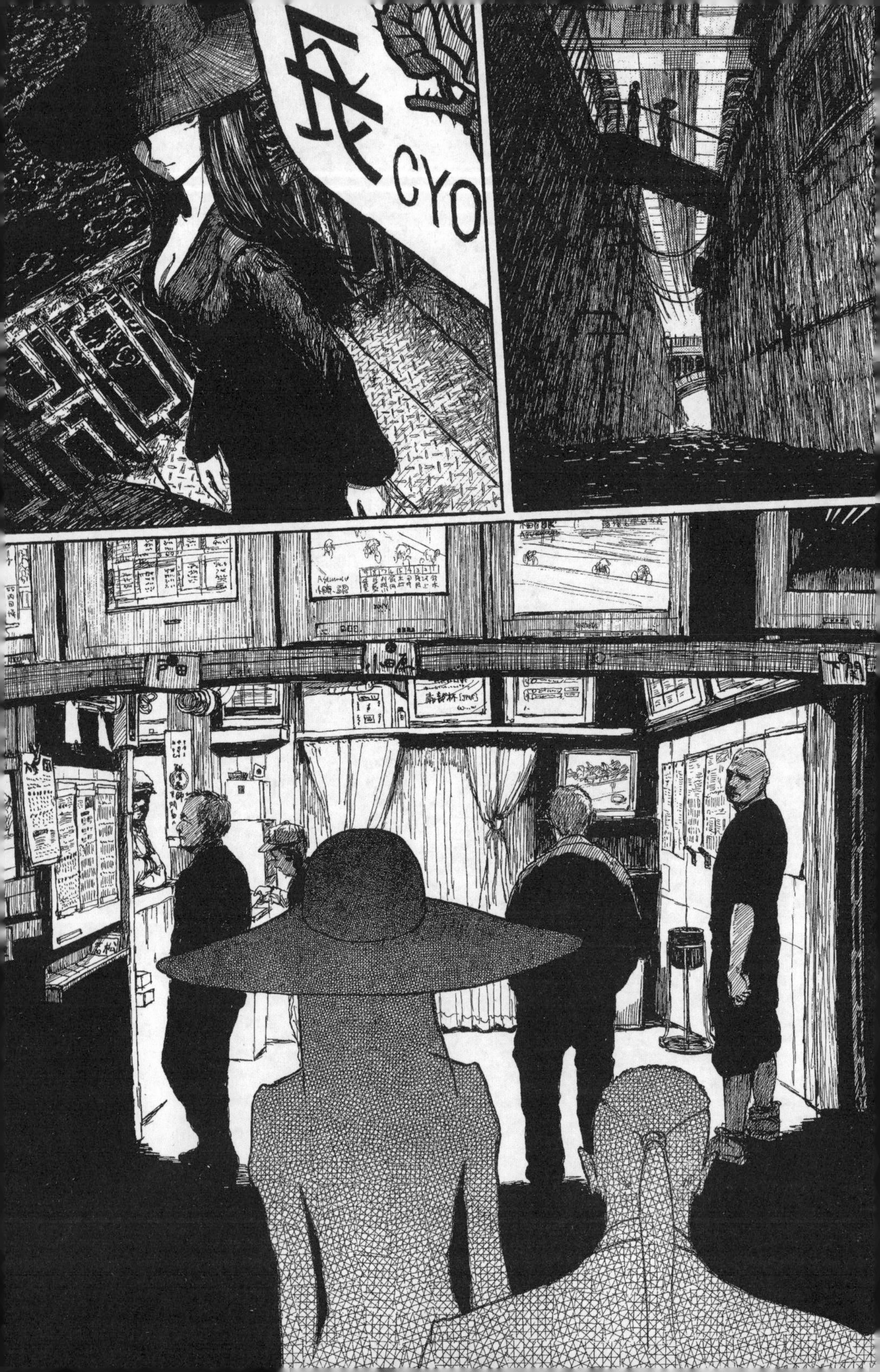
CYO

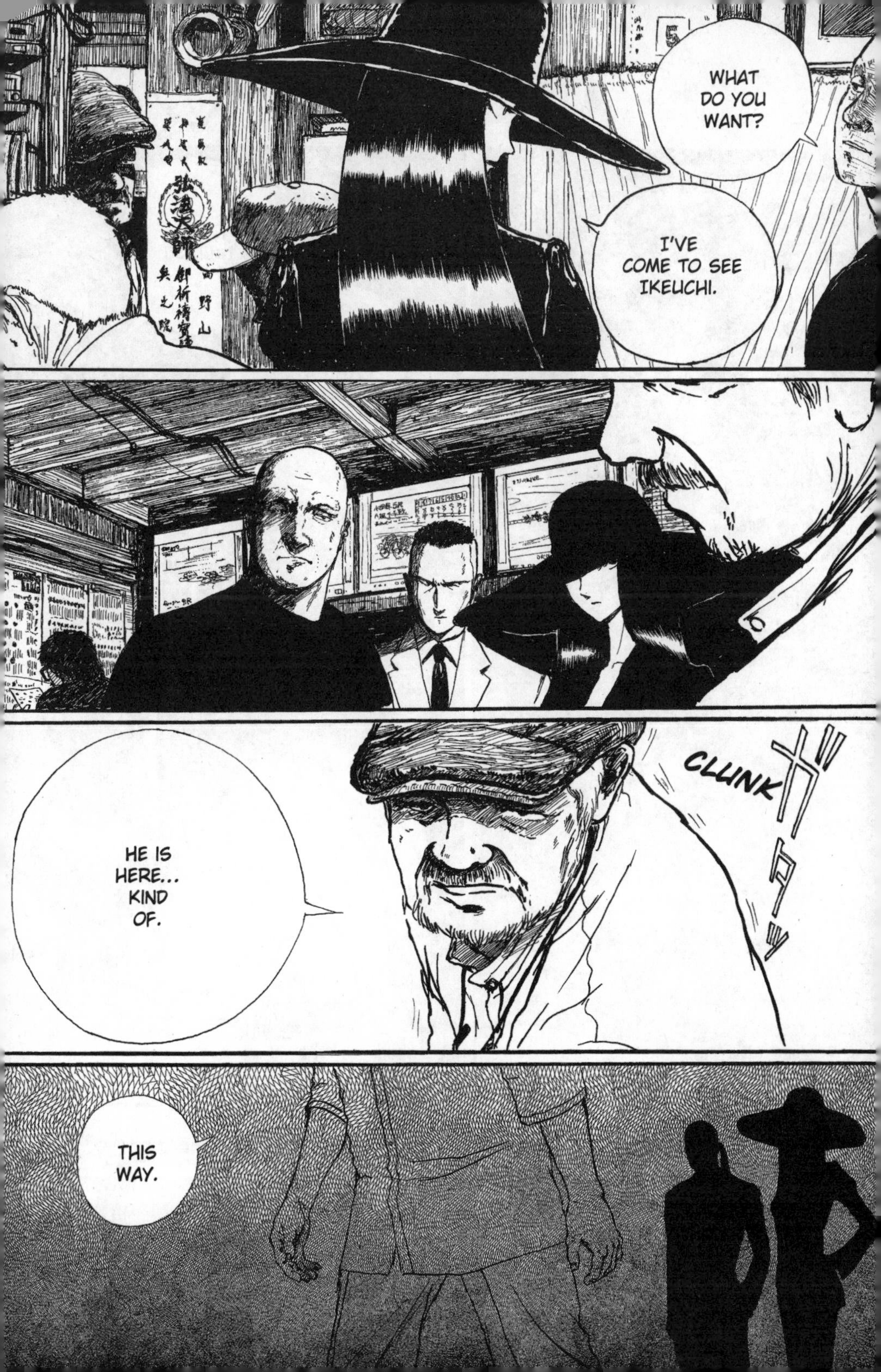
WHAT DO YOU WANT?
I'VE COME TO SEE IKEUCHI.
CLUNK
HE IS HERE... KIND OF.
THIS WAY.

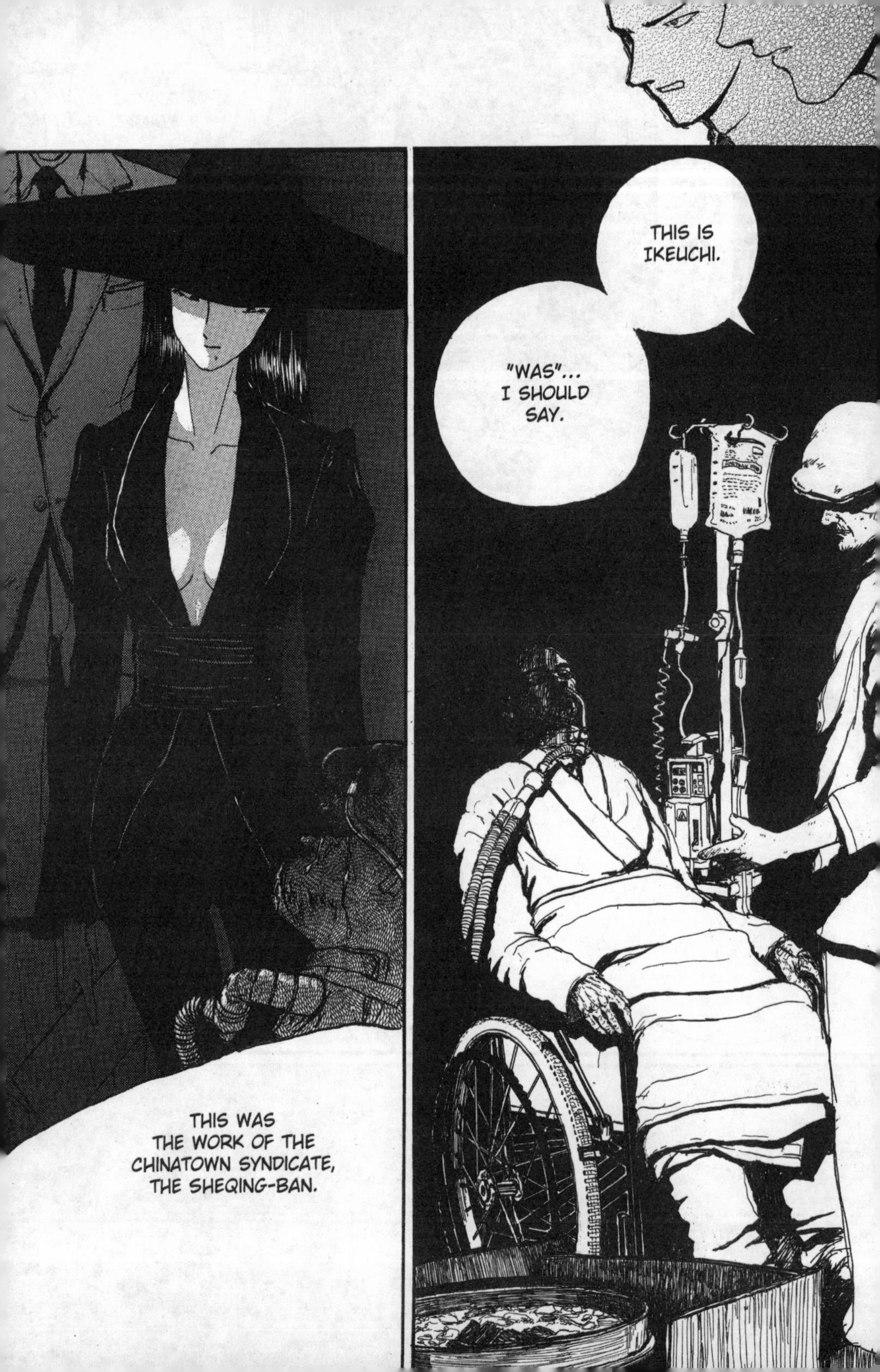
THIS IS IKEUCHI.
"WAS"... I SHOULD SAY.
THIS WAS THE WORK OF THE CHINATOWN SYNDICATE, THE SHEQING-BAN.

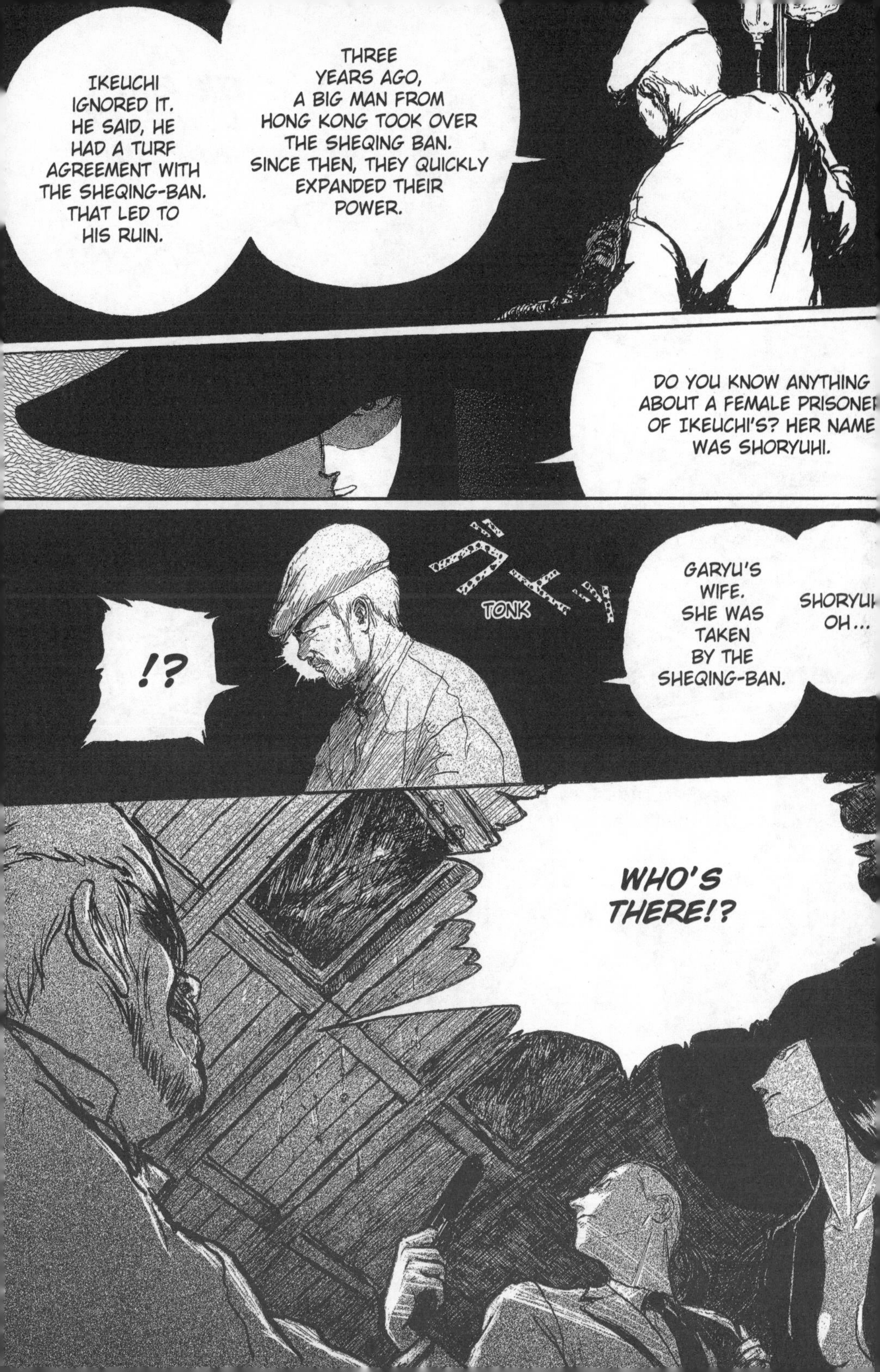
THREE YEARS AGO, A BIG MAN FROM HONG KONG TOOK OVER THE SHEQING BAN. SINCE THEN, THEY QUICKLY EXPANDED THEIR POWER.
IKEUCHI IGNORED IT. HE SAID, HE HAD A TURF AGREEMENT WITH THE SHEQING-BAN. THAT LED TO HIS RUIN.
DO YOU KNOW ANYTHING ABOUT A FEMALE PRISONE OF IKEUCHI'S? HER NAME WAS SHORYUHI.
SHORYU OH...
GARYU'S WIFE. SHE WAS TAKEN BY THE SHEQING-BAN.
TONK
!?
WHO'S THERE!?

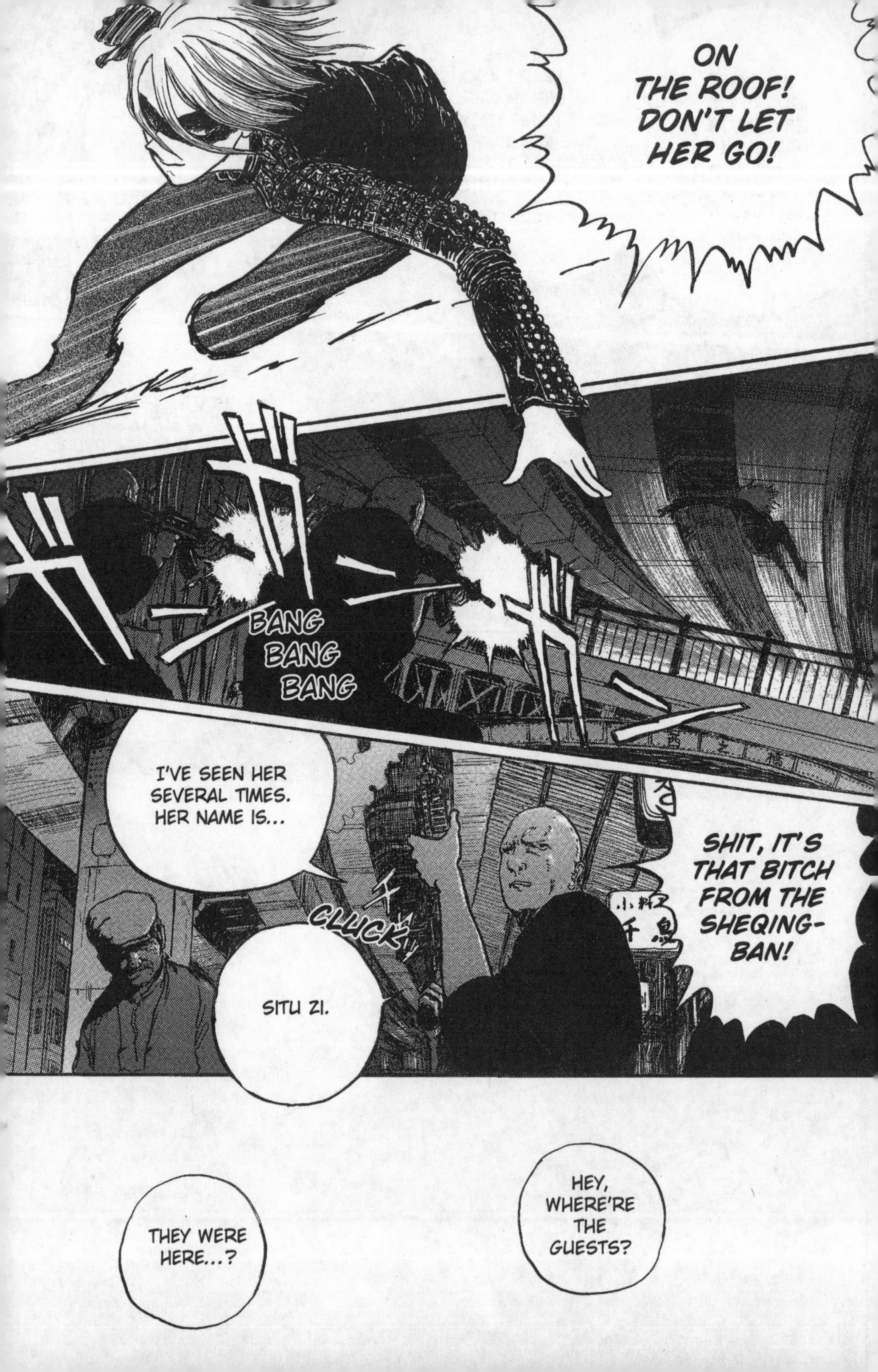
ON THE ROOF! DON'T LET HER GO!
BANG BANG BANG
SHIT, IT'S THAT BITCH FROM THE SHEQING-BAN!
I'VE SEEN HER SEVERAL TIMES. HER NAME IS...
CLUCK
SITU ZI.
HEY, WHERE'RE THE GUESTS?
THEY WERE HERE...?

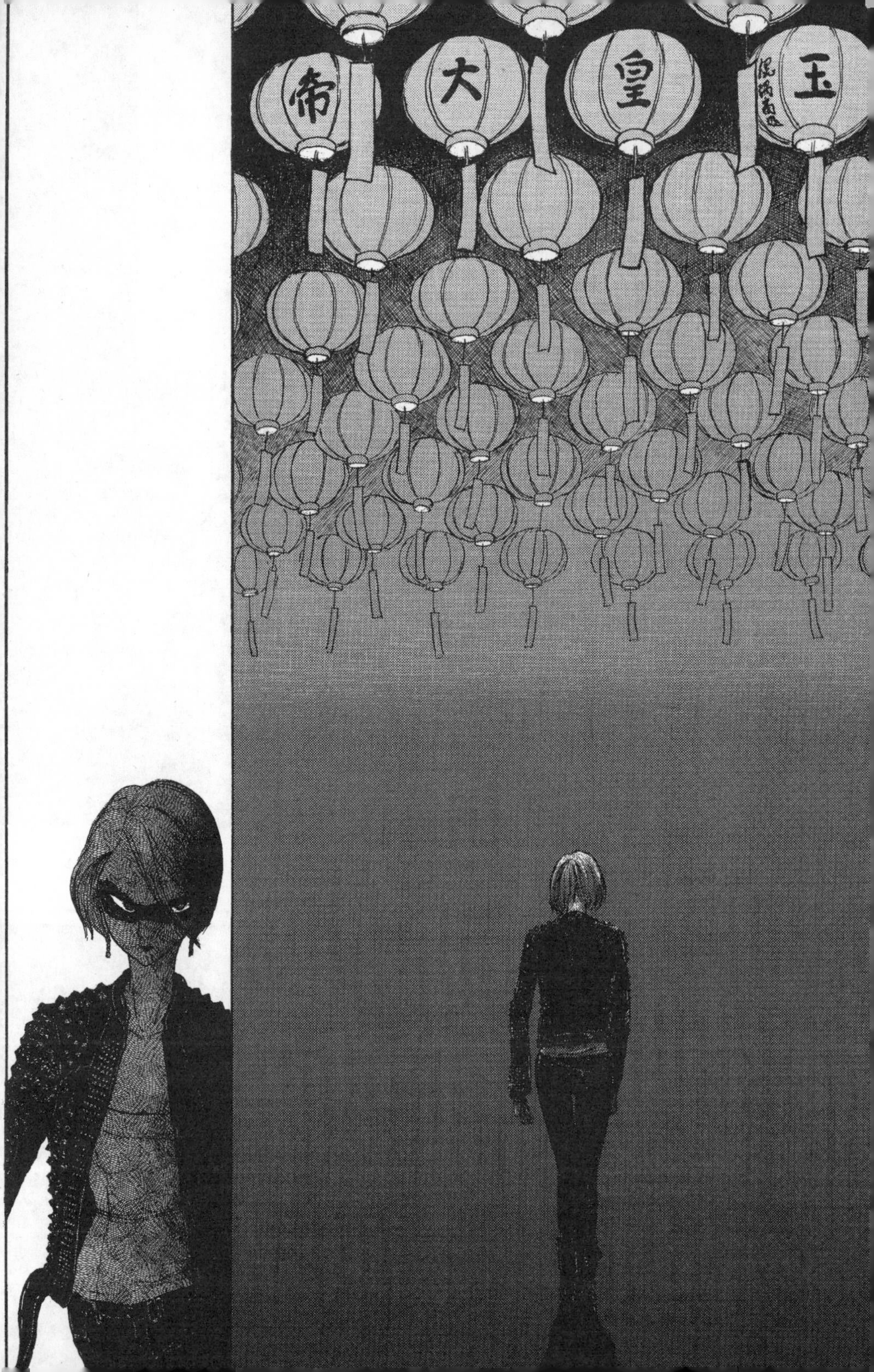
玉
皇
大
帝

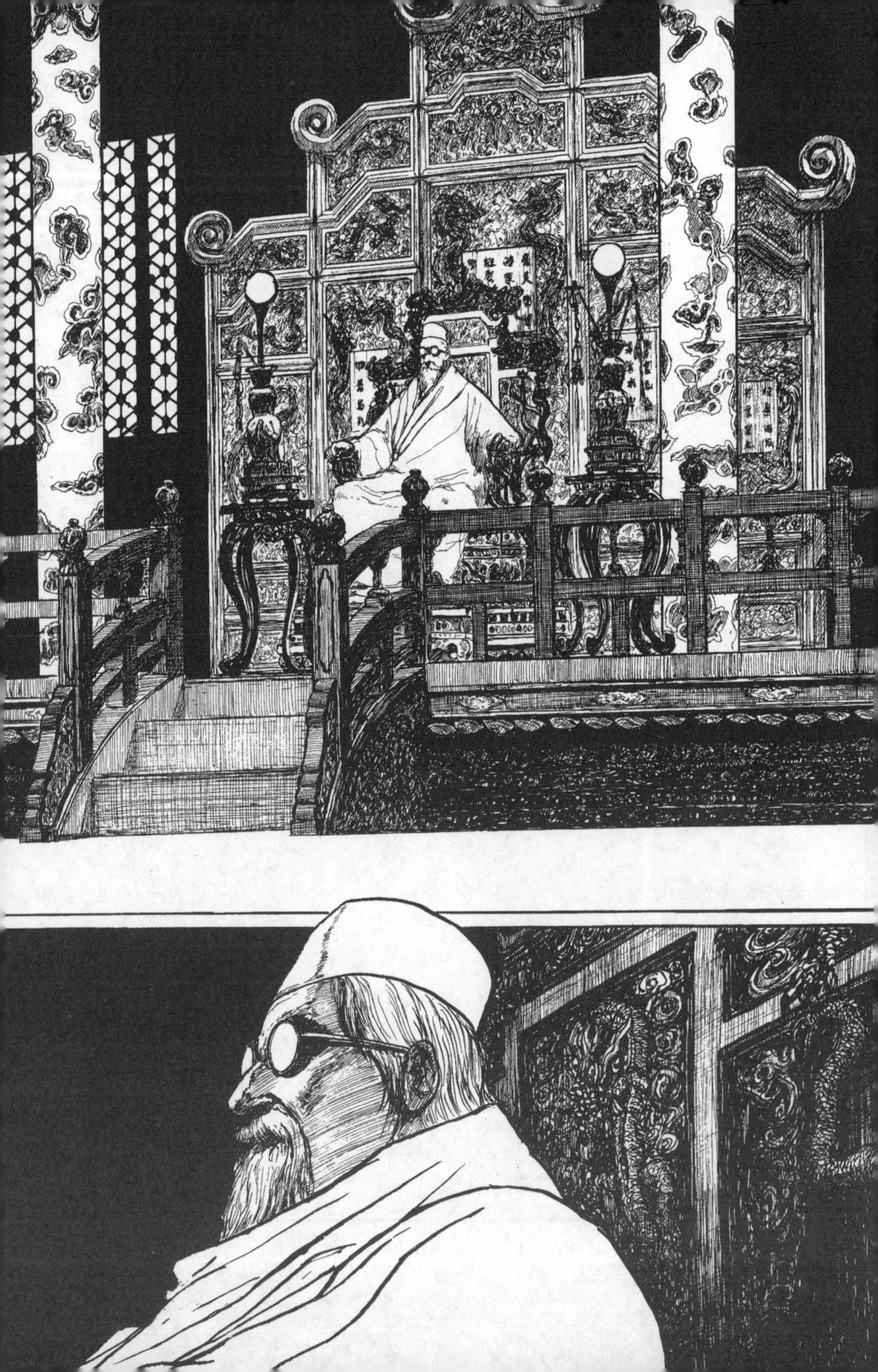

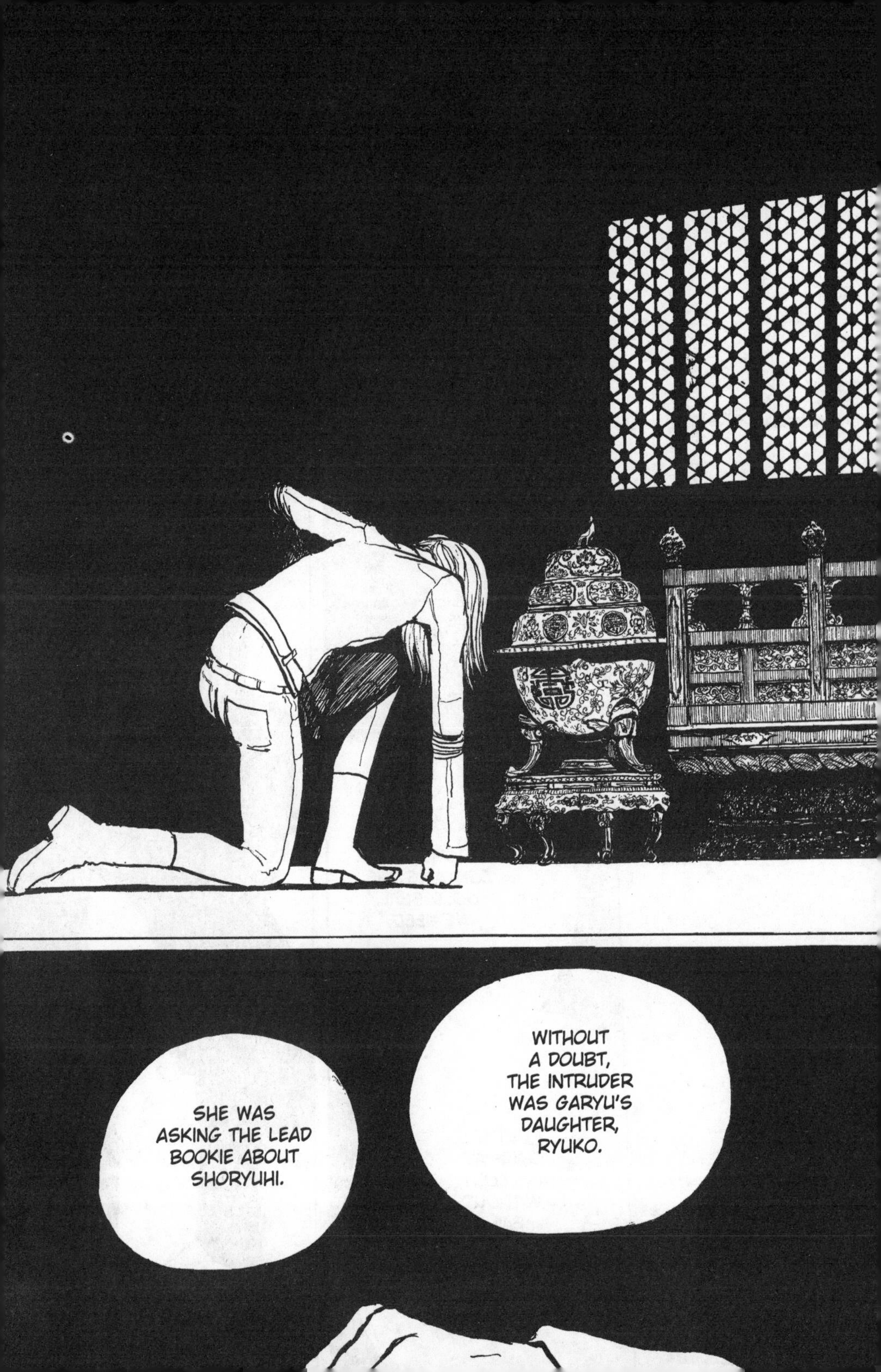
WITHOUT A DOUBT, THE INTRUDER WAS GARYU'S DAUGHTER, RYUKO.
SHE WAS ASKING THE LEAD BOOKIE ABOUT SHORYUHI.

THE REPORT FROM FOROSSYAH SAID RASHID HANDED A SMALL BOX TO RYUKO JUST BEFORE HE BLEW HIMSELF UP.

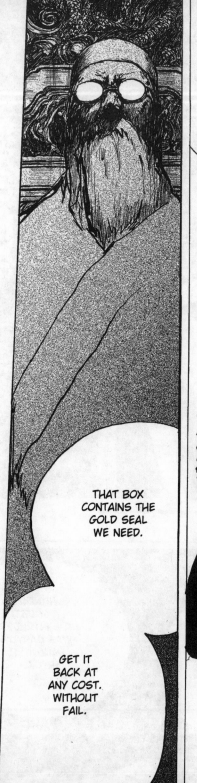

YES SIR!

THAT BOX CONTAINS THE GOLD SEAL WE NEED.

GET IT BACK AT ANY COST. WITHOUT FAIL.

CHAPTER 6:
TRIPLE THREAT

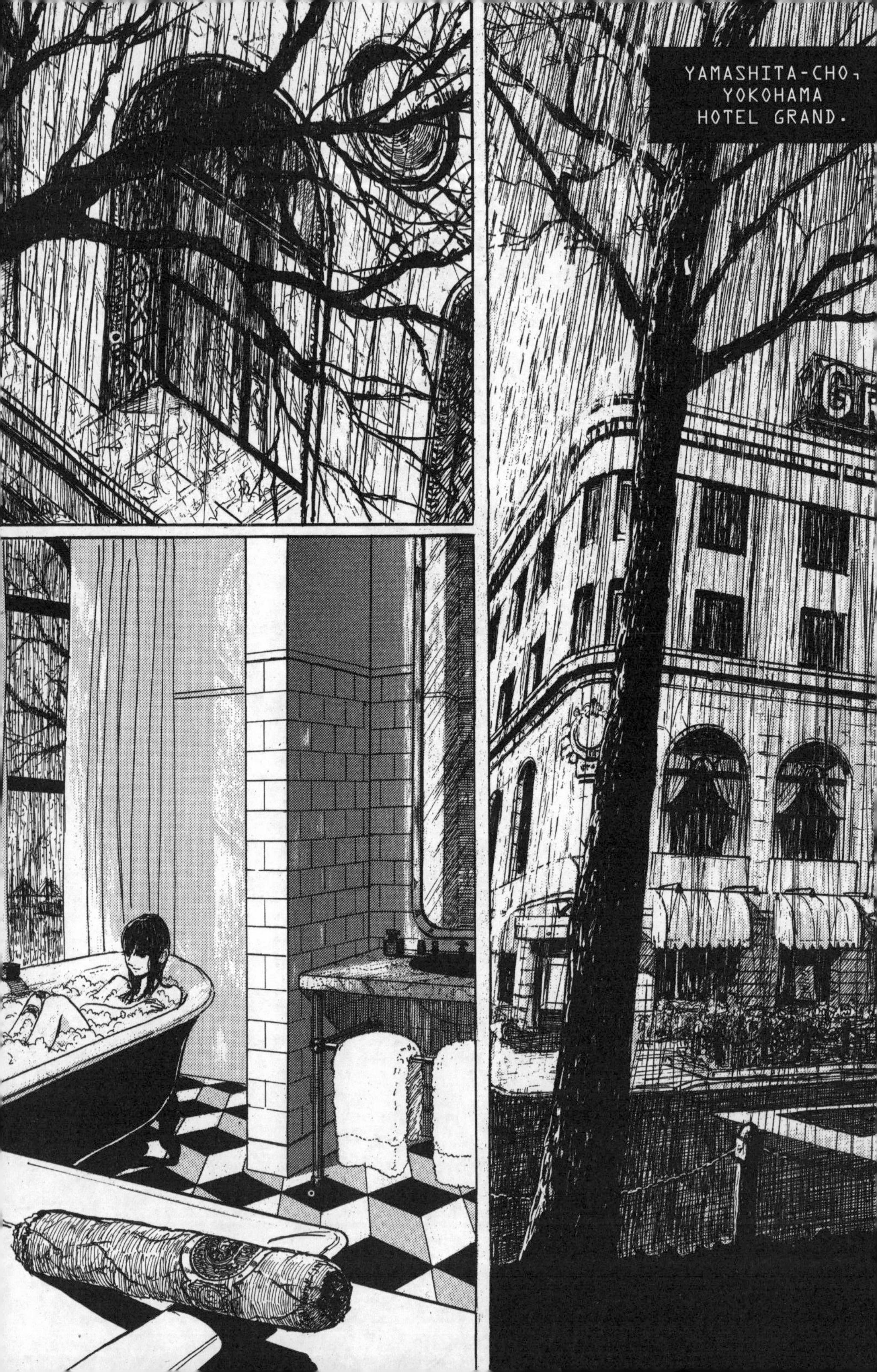
YAMASHITA-CHO, YOKOHAMA
HOTEL GRAND.

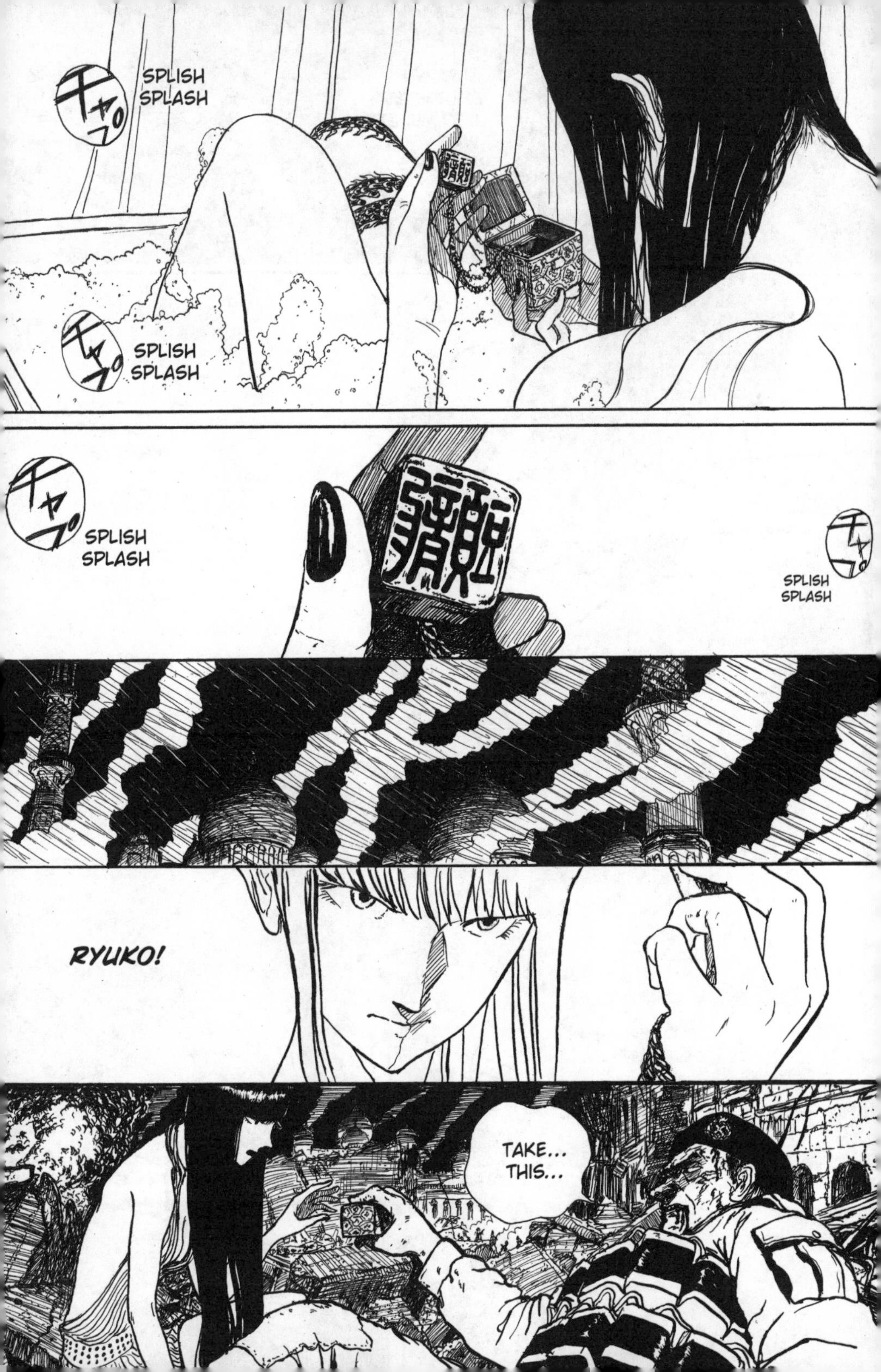
SPLISH SPLASH
チャプ
SPLISH SPLASH
チャプ
チャプ
SPLISH SPLASH
チャプ
SPLISH SPLASH
RYUKO!
TAKE... THIS...

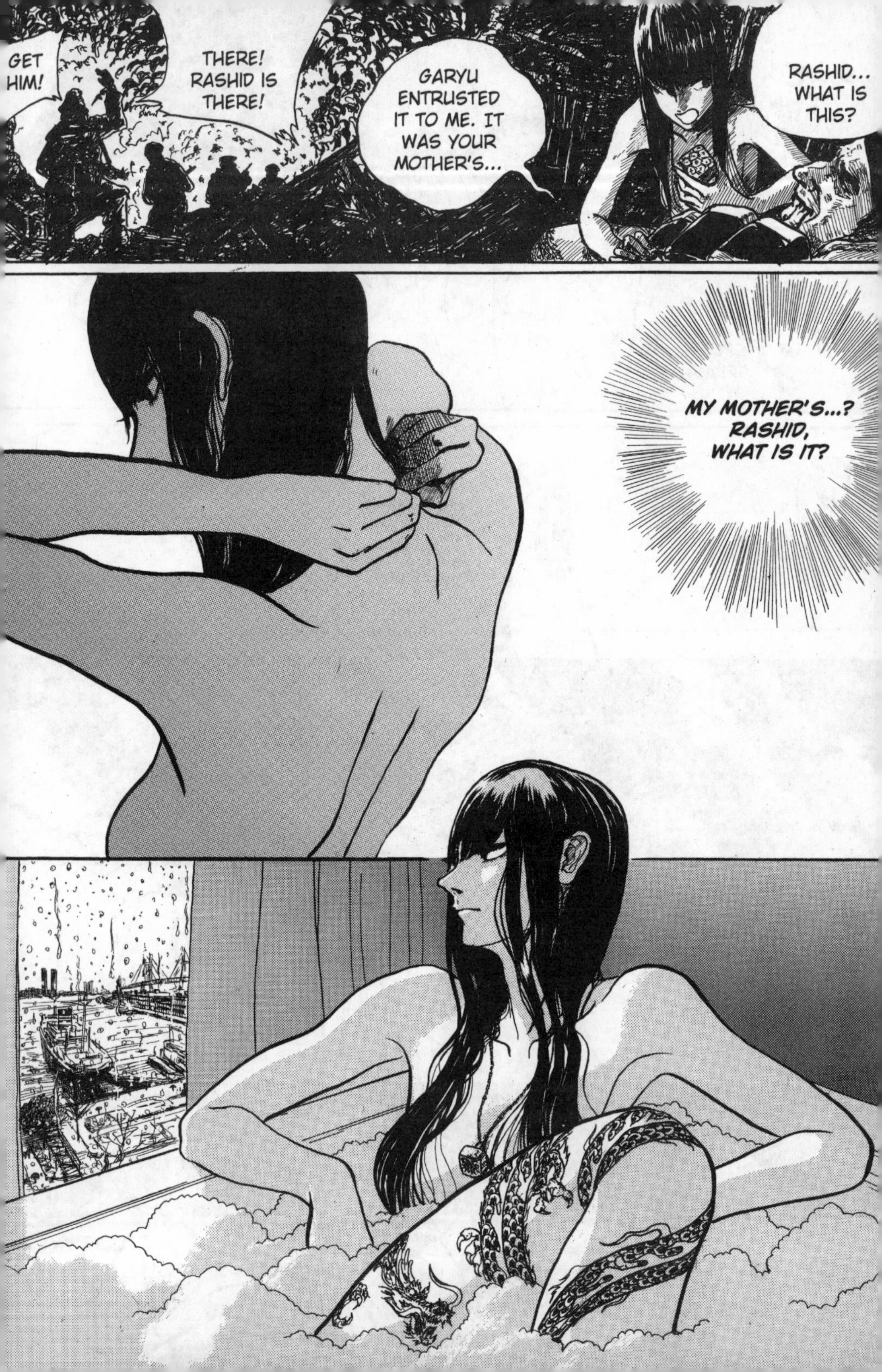
RASHID... WHAT IS THIS?
GARYU ENTRUSTED IT TO ME. IT WAS YOUR MOTHER'S...
THERE! RASHID IS THERE!
GET HIM!
MY MOTHER'S...? RASHID, WHAT IS IT?

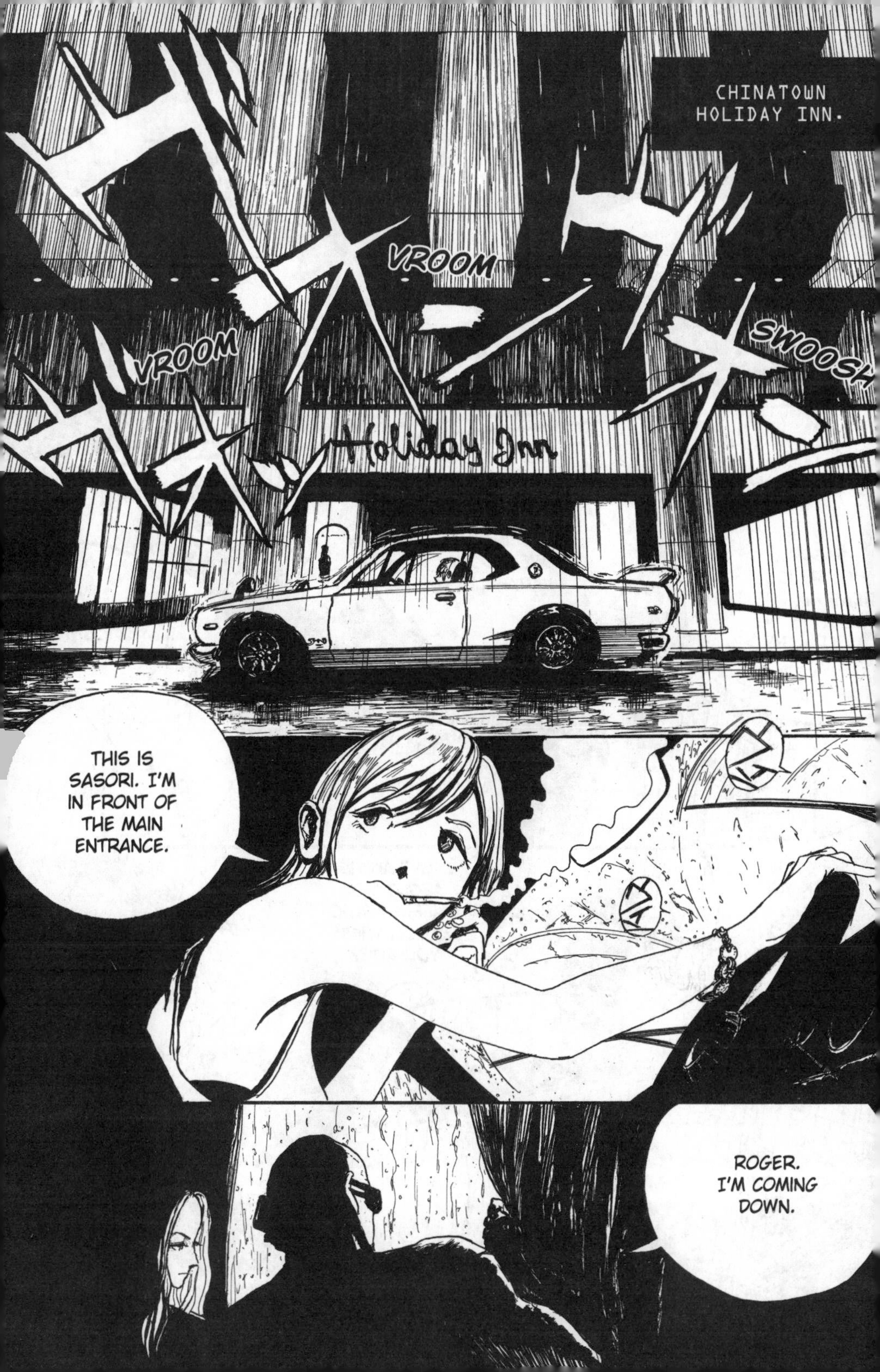
CHINATOWN
HOLIDAY INN.
SWOOSH
VROOM
VROOM
Holiday Inn
THIS IS SASORI. I'M IN FRONT OF THE MAIN ENTRANCE.
ROGER. I'M COMING DOWN.

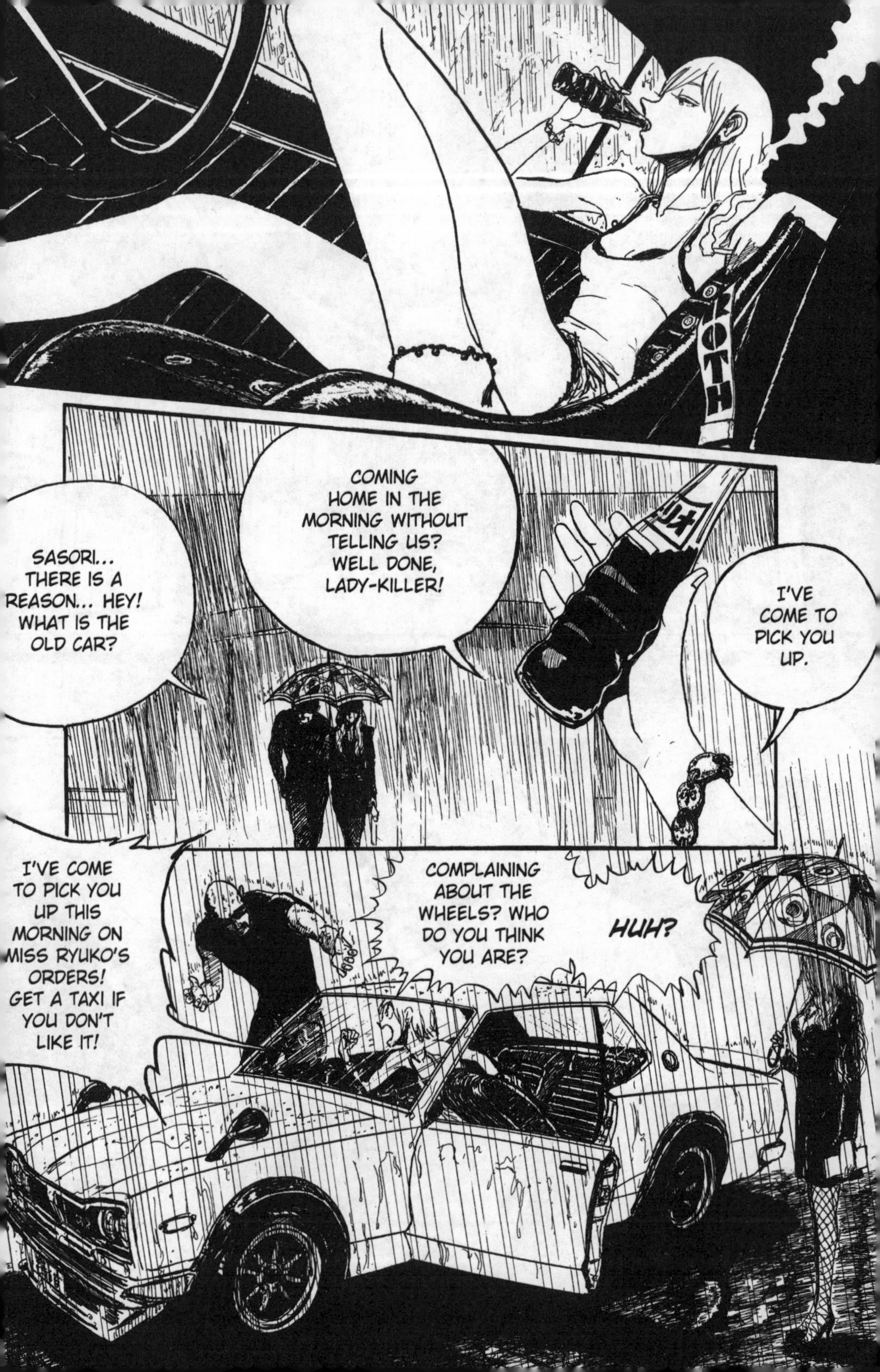
I'VE COME TO PICK YOU UP.
COMING HOME IN THE MORNING WITHOUT TELLING US? WELL DONE, LADY-KILLER!
SASORI... THERE IS A REASON... HEY! WHAT IS THE OLD CAR?
HUH?
COMPLAINING ABOUT THE WHEELS? WHO DO YOU THINK YOU ARE?
I'VE COME TO PICK YOU UP THIS MORNING ON MISS RYUKO'S ORDERS! GET A TAXI IF YOU DON'T LIKE IT!

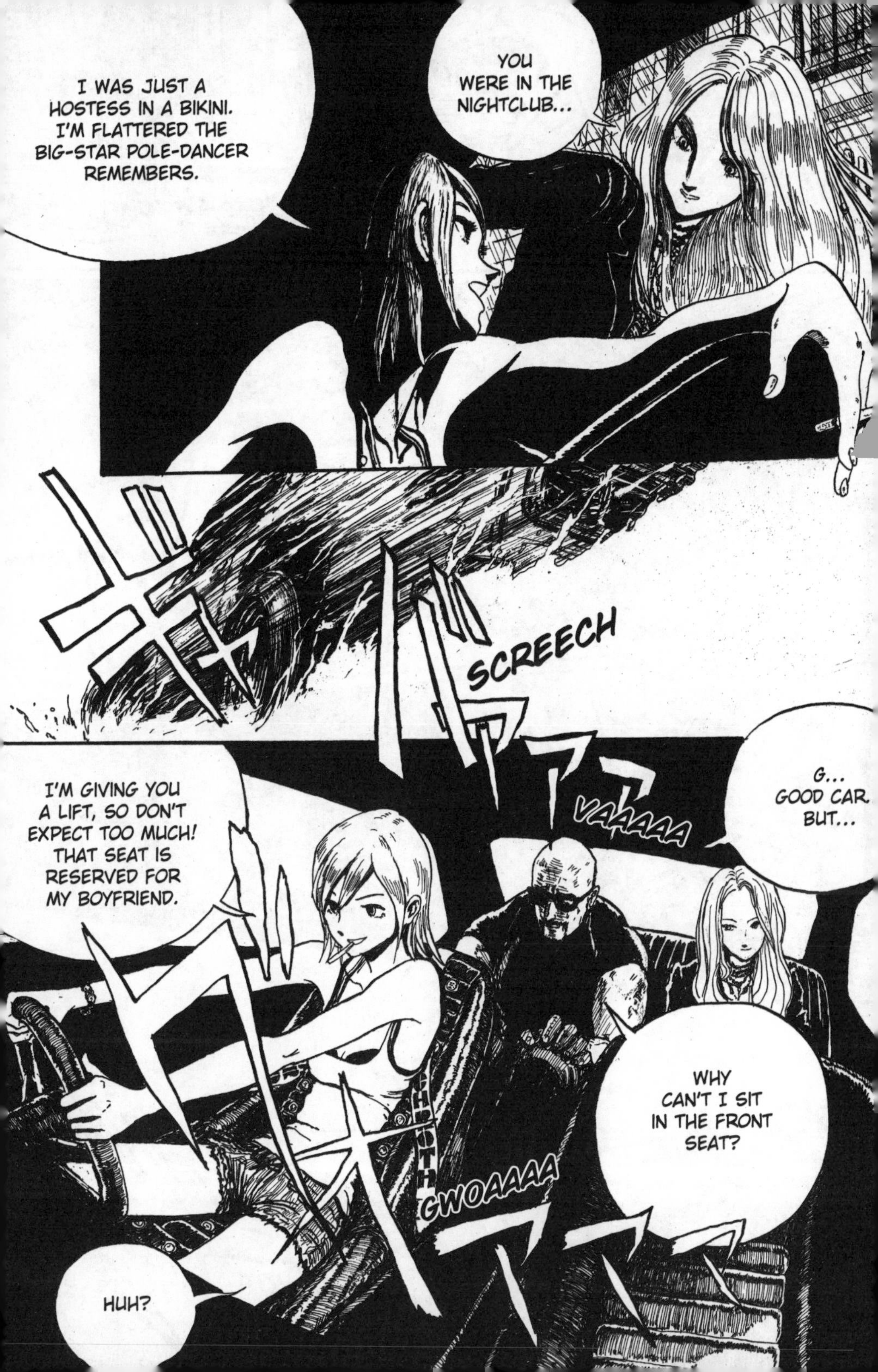
YOU WERE IN THE NIGHTCLUB...
I WAS JUST A HOSTESS IN A BIKINI. I'M FLATTERED THE BIG-STAR POLE-DANCER REMEMBERS.
SCREECH
G... GOOD CAR BUT...
VAAAAA
WHY CAN'T I SIT IN THE FRONT SEAT?
GWOAAAA
HUH?
I'M GIVING YOU A LIFT, SO DON'T EXPECT TOO MUCH! THAT SEAT IS RESERVED FOR MY BOYFRIEND.

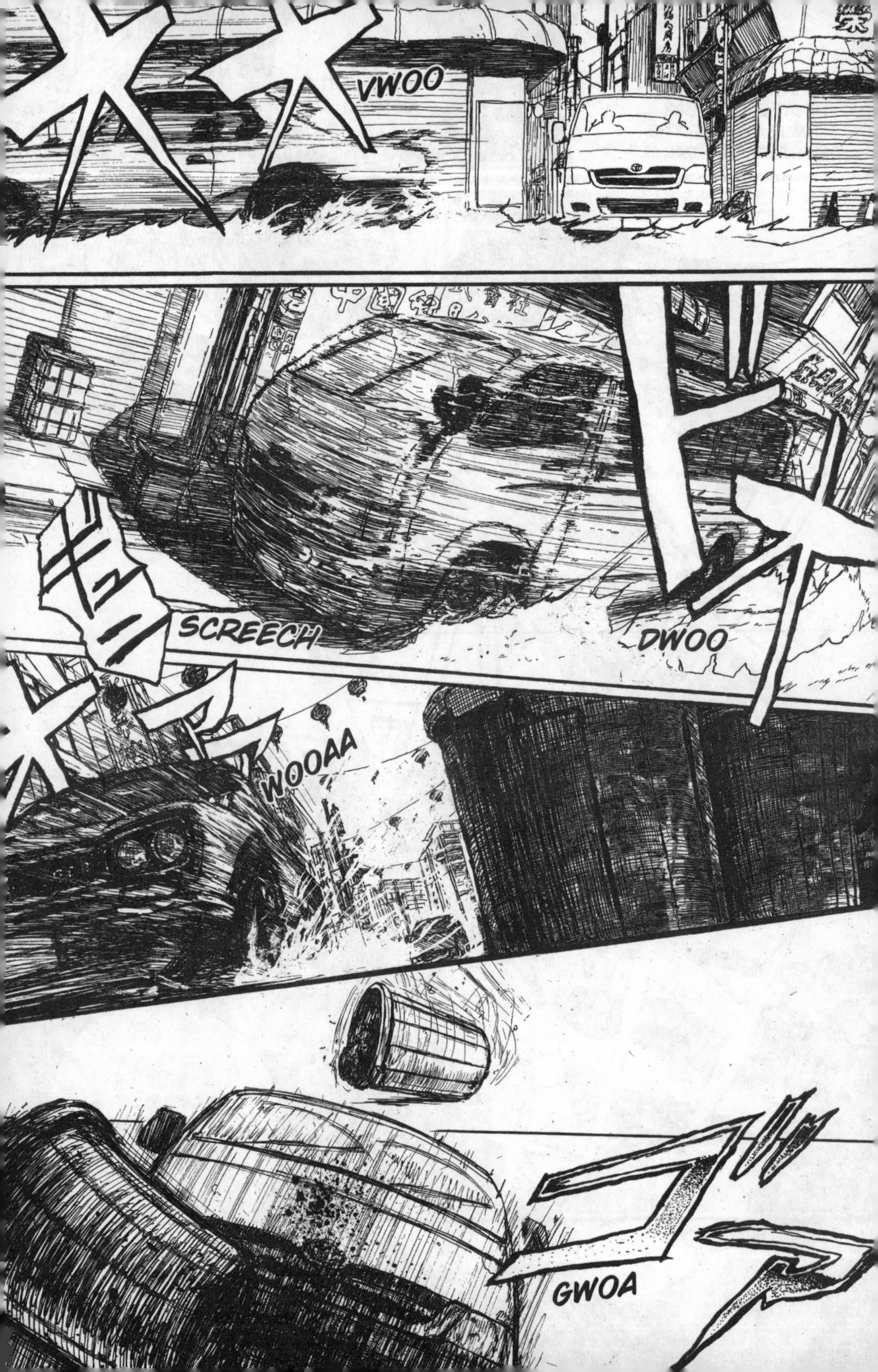
VWOO
DWOO
SCREECH
WOOAA
GWOA

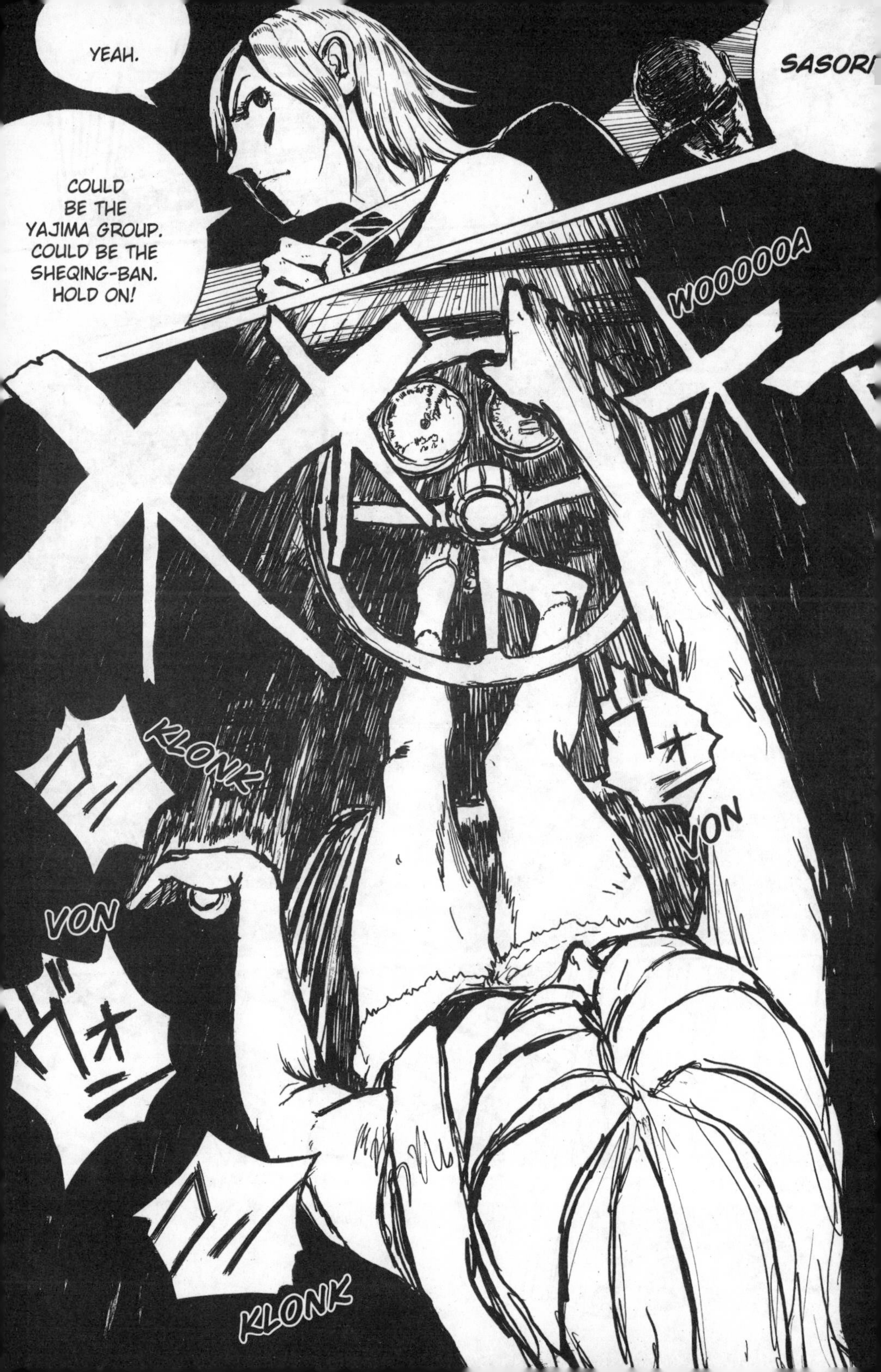
SASORI
YEAH.
COULD BE THE YAJIMA GROUP. COULD BE THE SHEQING-BAN. HOLD ON!
WOOOOOA
VON
KLONK
VON
KLONK

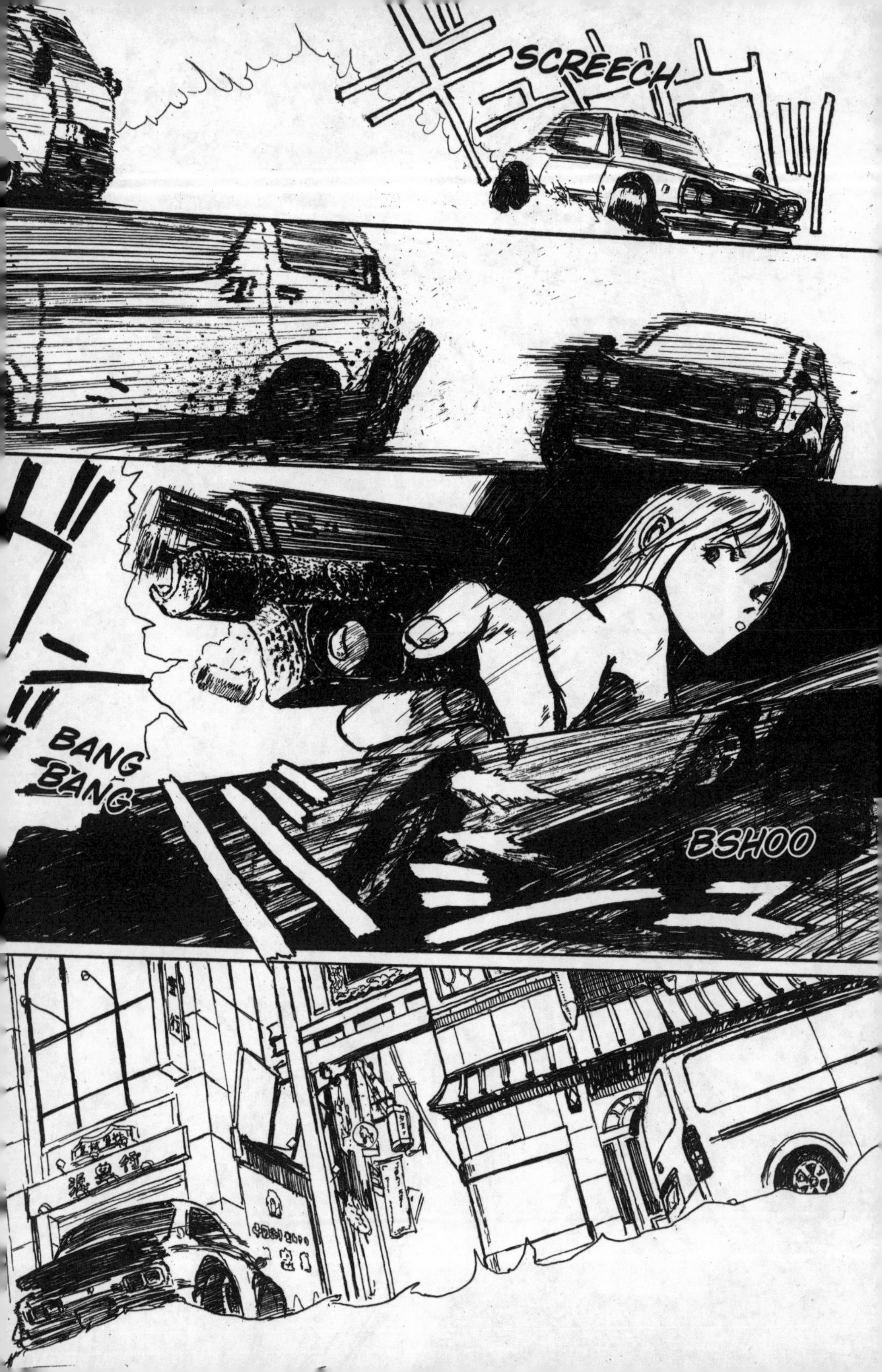
SCREECH
BANG BANG
BSHOO

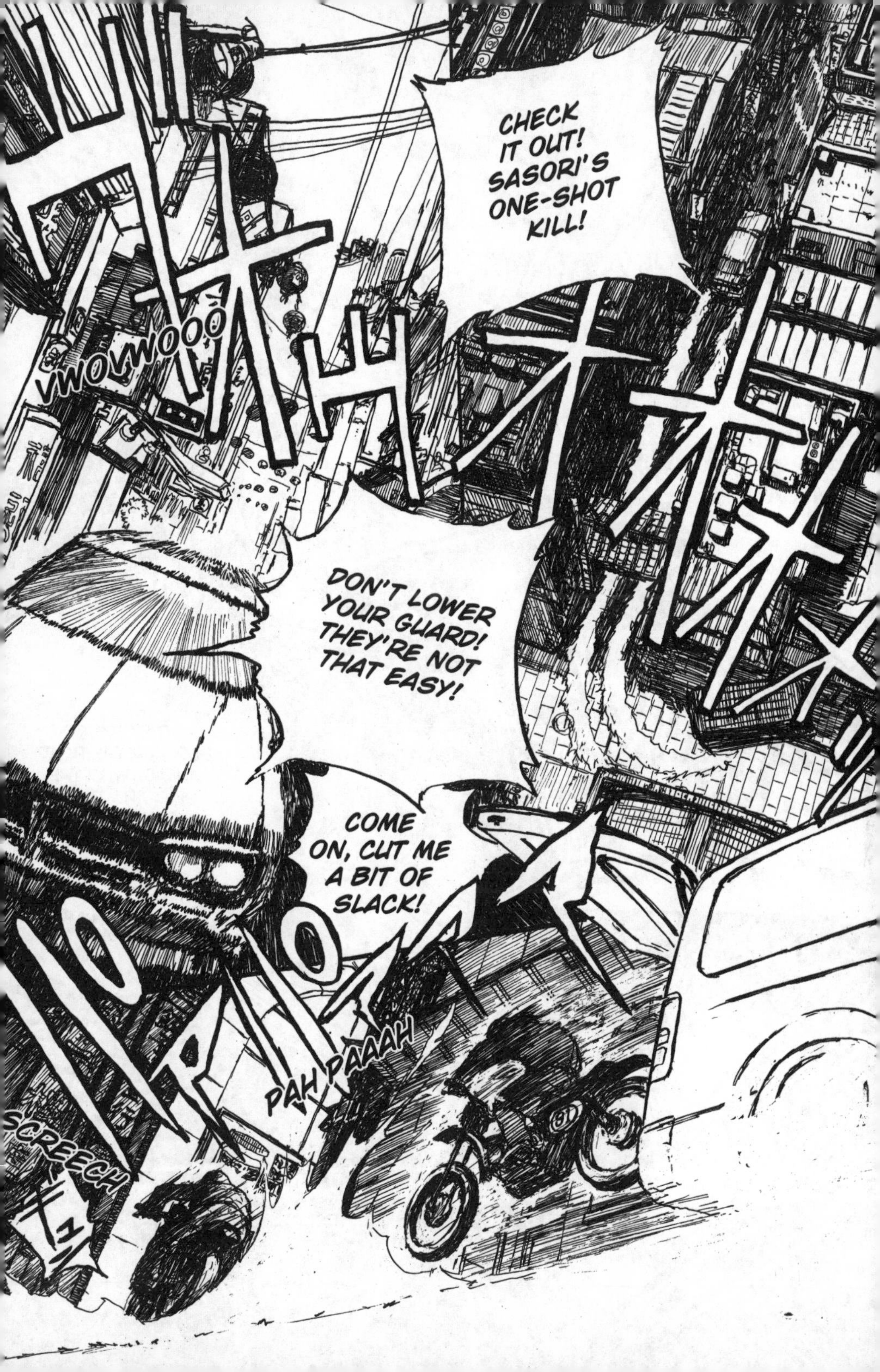
CHECK IT OUT! SASORI'S ONE-SHOT KILL!
VWOVWOOO
DON'T LOWER YOUR GUARD! THEY'RE NOT THAT EASY!
COME ON, CUT ME A BIT OF SLACK!
PAH PAAAH
SCREECH

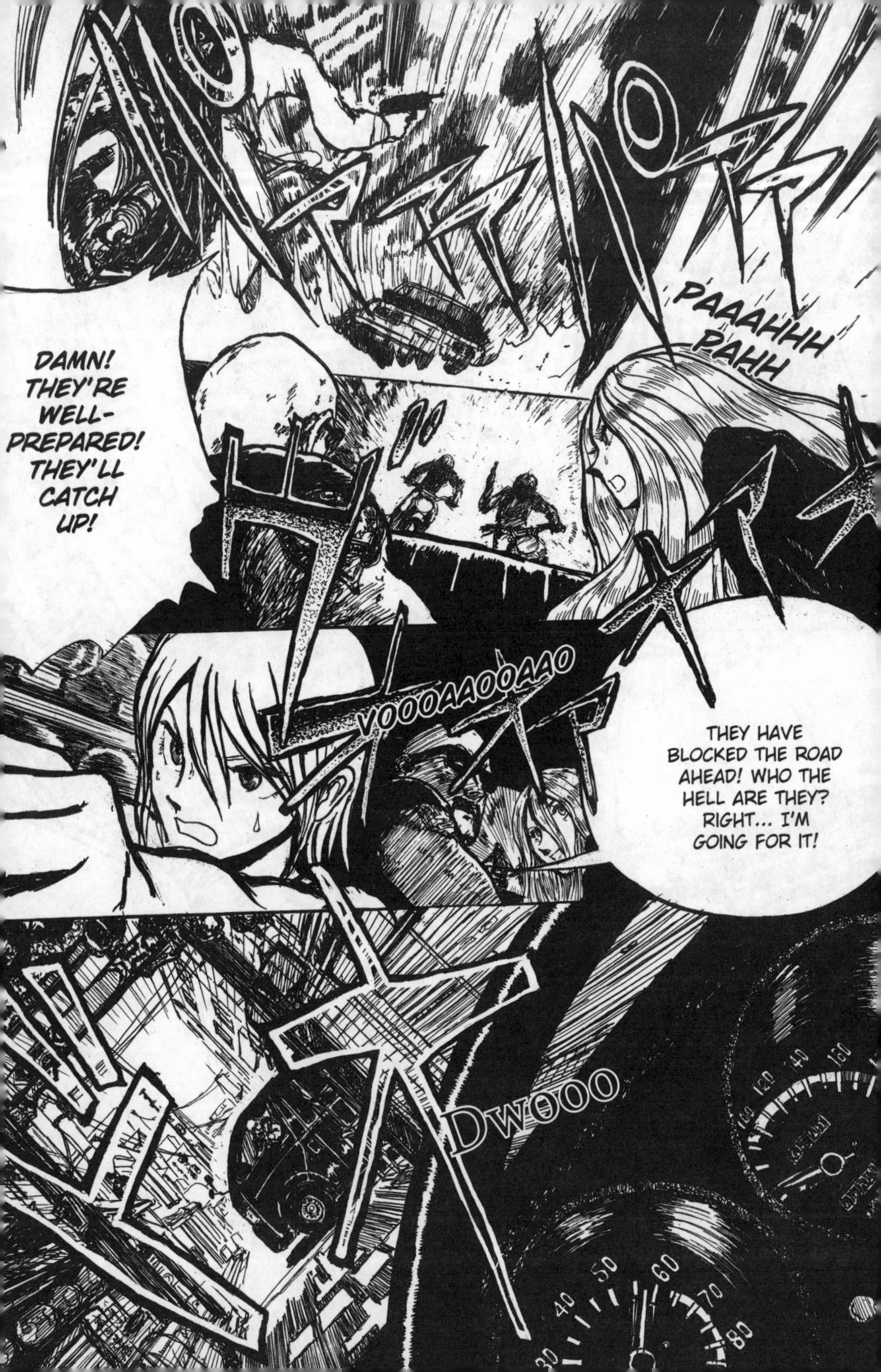
PAAAHHH PAHH
DAMN! THEY'RE WELL-PREPARED! THEY'LL CATCH UP!
THEY HAVE BLOCKED THE ROAD AHEAD! WHO THE HELL ARE THEY? RIGHT... I'M GOING FOR IT!
VOOOAAOOAAO
Dwooo

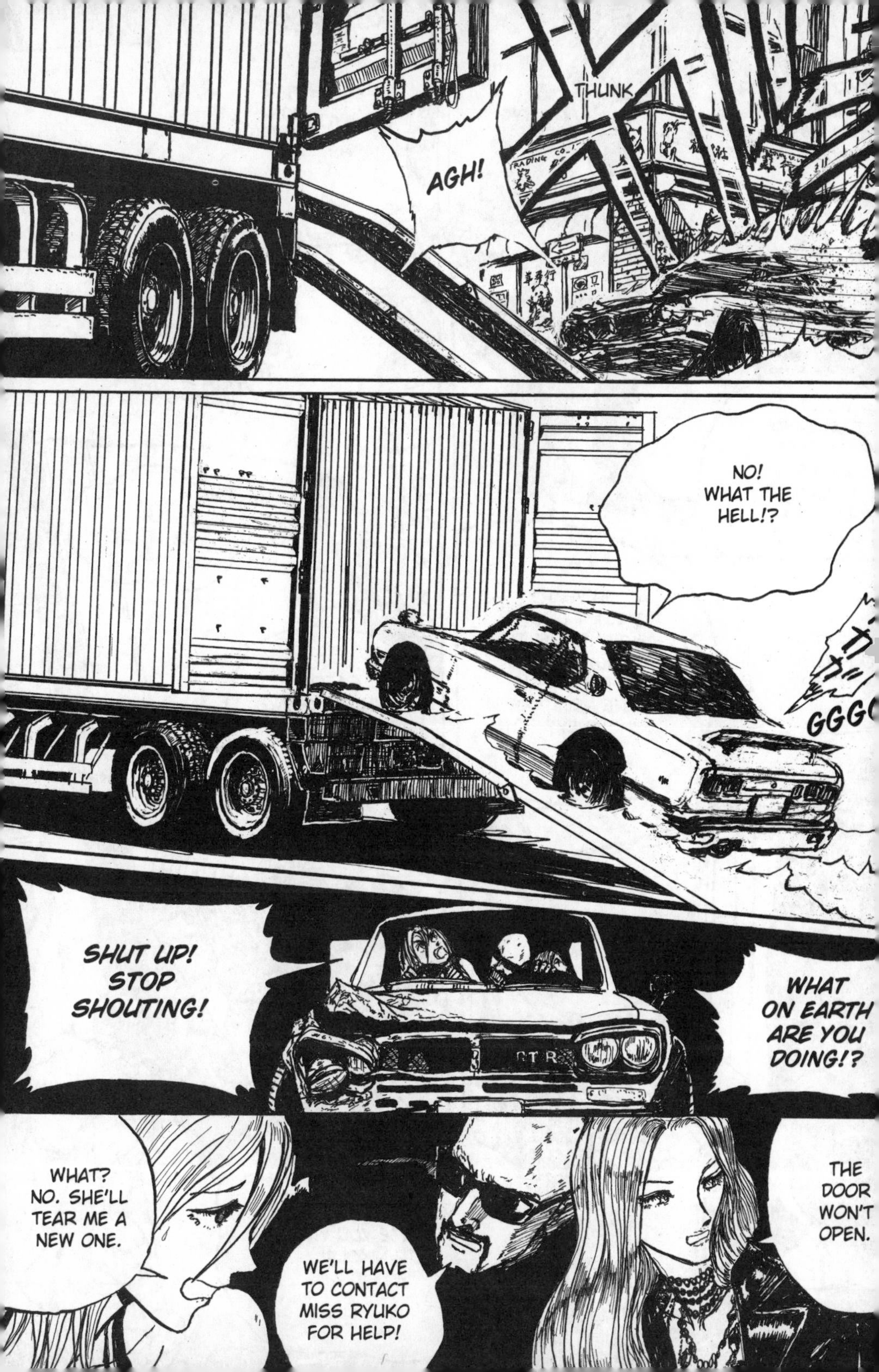
THUNK
AGH!
NO! WHAT THE HELL!?
GGG
WHAT ON EARTH ARE YOU DOING!?
SHUT UP! STOP SHOUTING!
THE DOOR WON'T OPEN.
WE'LL HAVE TO CONTACT MISS RYUKO FOR HELP!
WHAT? NO. SHE'LL TEAR ME A NEW ONE.

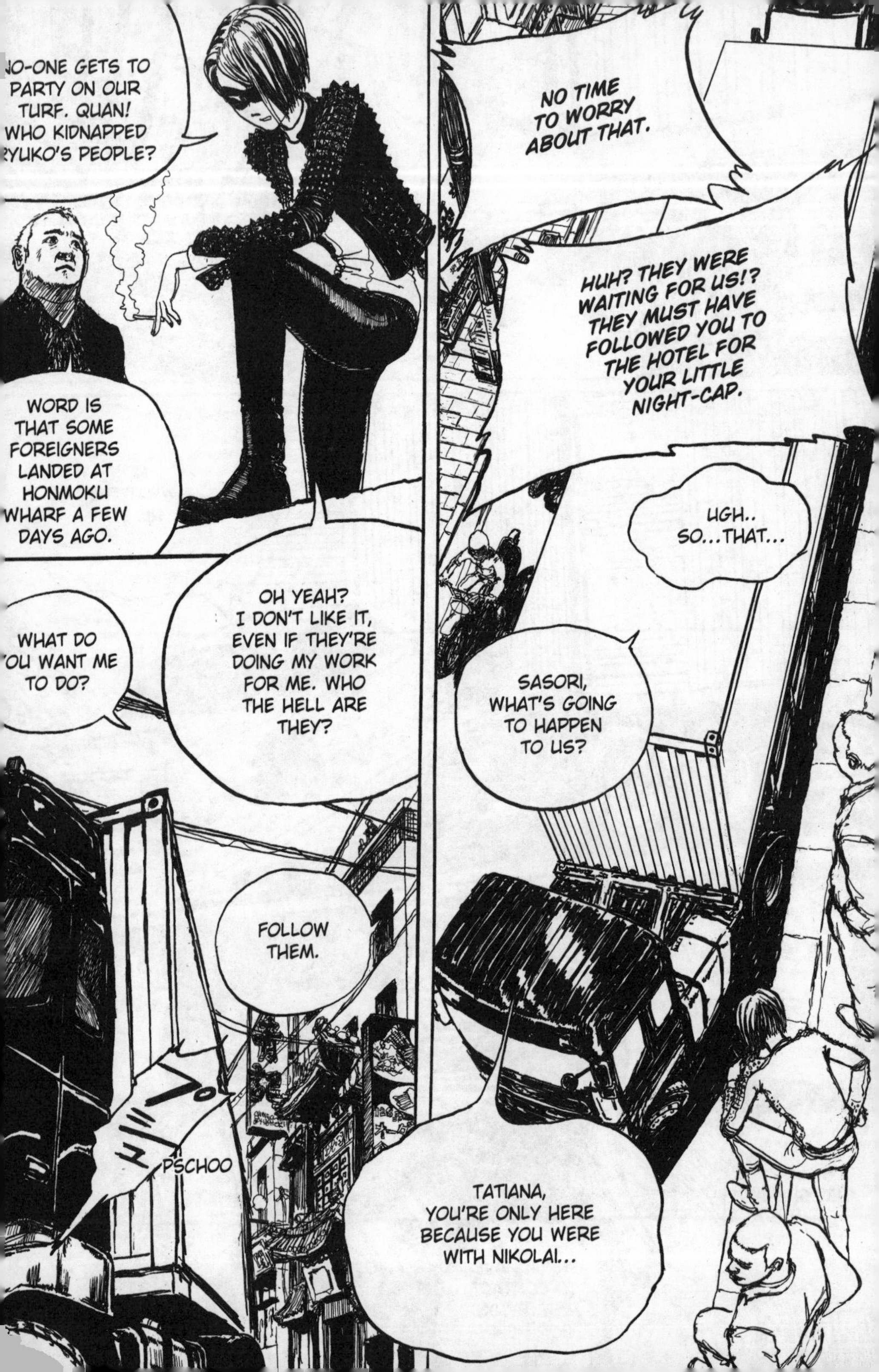
NO TIME TO WORRY ABOUT THAT.
HUH? THEY WERE WAITING FOR US!? THEY MUST HAVE FOLLOWED YOU TO THE HOTEL FOR YOUR LITTLE NIGHT-CAP.
UGH.. SO...THAT...
SASORI, WHAT'S GOING TO HAPPEN TO US?
TATIANA, YOU'RE ONLY HERE BECAUSE YOU WERE WITH NIKOLAI...
NO-ONE GETS TO PARTY ON OUR TURF. QUAN! WHO KIDNAPPED RYUKO'S PEOPLE?
WORD IS THAT SOME FOREIGNERS LANDED AT HONMOKU WHARF A FEW DAYS AGO.
OH YEAH? I DON'T LIKE IT, EVEN IF THEY'RE DOING MY WORK FOR ME. WHO THE HELL ARE THEY?
WHAT DO YOU WANT ME TO DO?
FOLLOW THEM.
PSCHOO

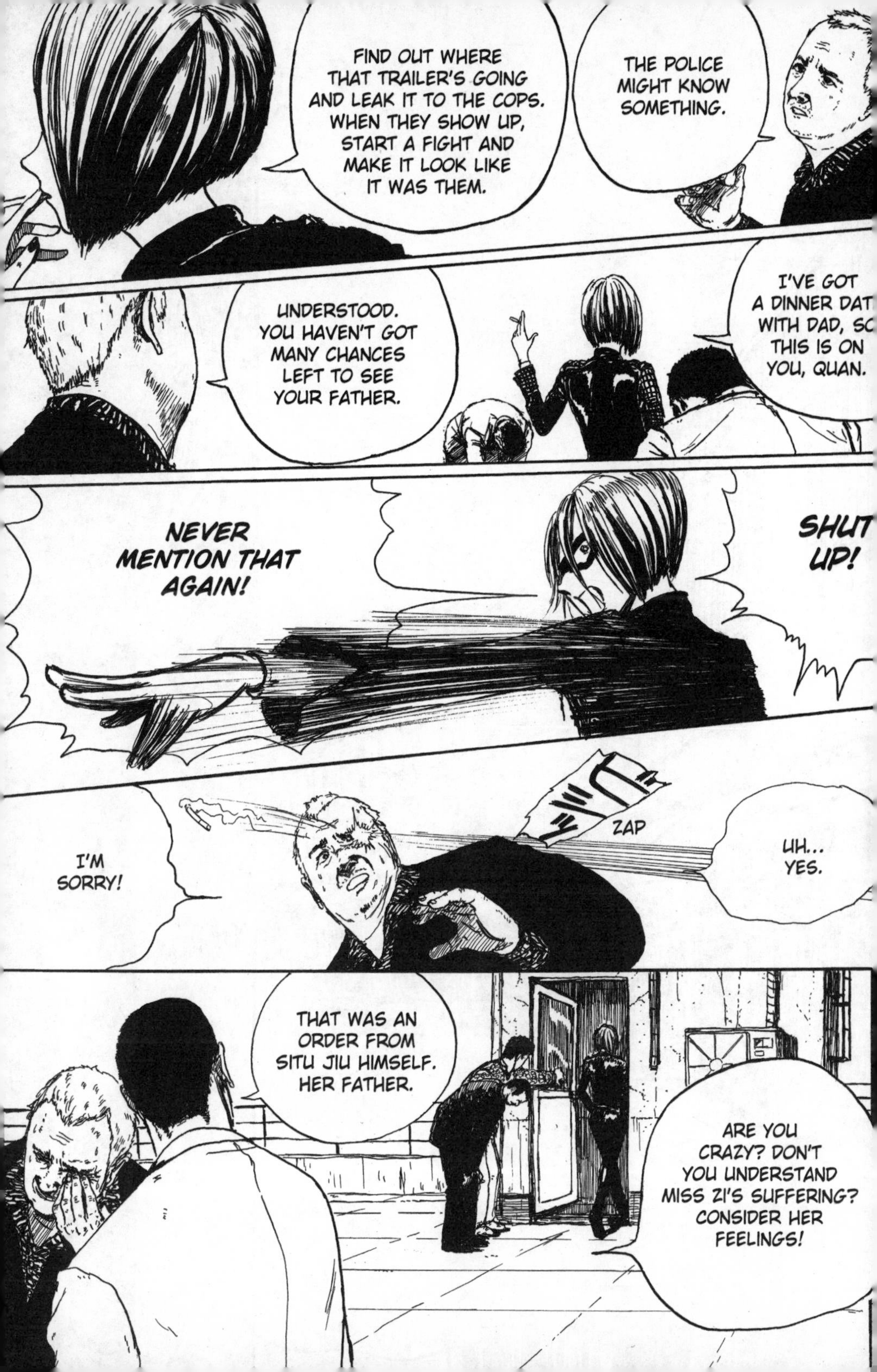
THE POLICE MIGHT KNOW SOMETHING.
FIND OUT WHERE THAT TRAILER'S GOING AND LEAK IT TO THE COPS. WHEN THEY SHOW UP, START A FIGHT AND MAKE IT LOOK LIKE IT WAS THEM.
I'VE GOT A DINNER DAT WITH DAD, SC THIS IS ON YOU, QUAN.
UNDERSTOOD. YOU HAVEN'T GOT MANY CHANCES LEFT TO SEE YOUR FATHER.
SHUT UP!
NEVER MENTION THAT AGAIN!
UH... YES.
ZAP
I'M SORRY!
ARE YOU CRAZY? DON'T YOU UNDERSTAND MISS ZI'S SUFFERING? CONSIDER HER FEELINGS!
THAT WAS AN ORDER FROM SITU JIU HIMSELF. HER FATHER.

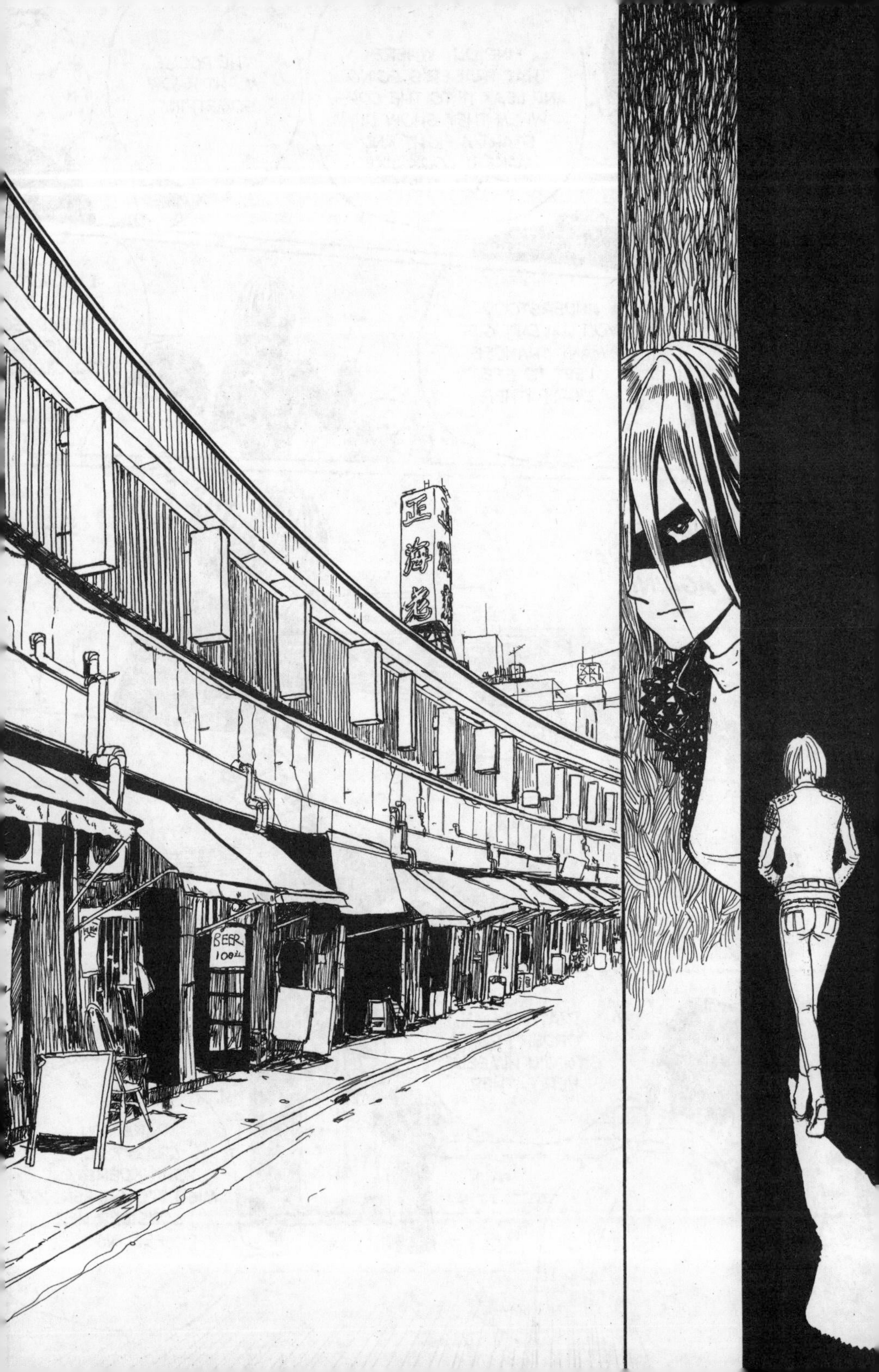

正海老
BEER
100

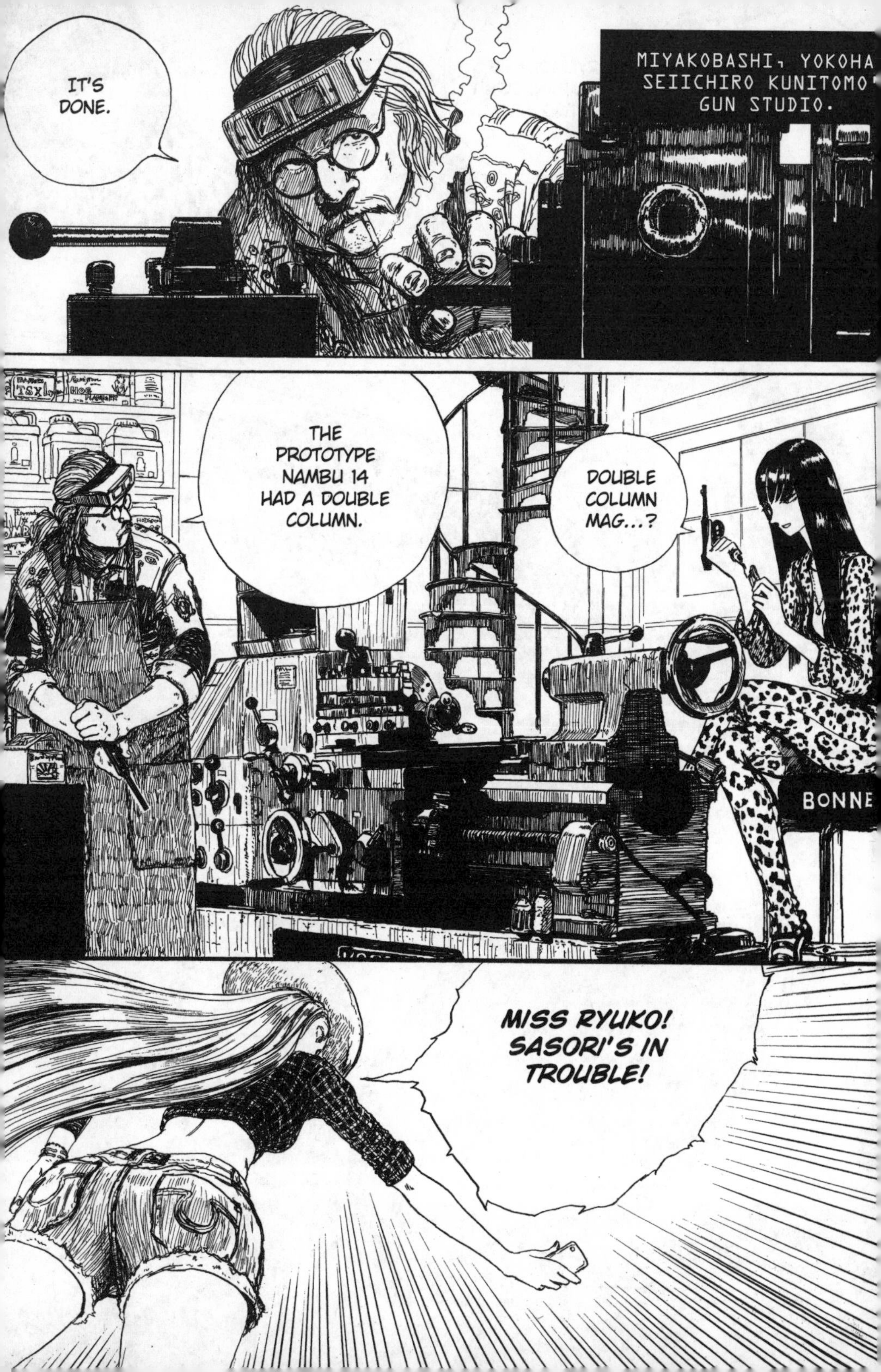
MIYAKOBASHI, YOKOHA
SEIICHIRO KUNITOMO'S
GUN STUDIO.
IT'S DONE.
THE PROTOTYPE NAMBU 14 HAD A DOUBLE COLUMN.
DOUBLE COLUMN MAG...?
BONNE
MISS RYUKO! SASORI'S IN TROUBLE!

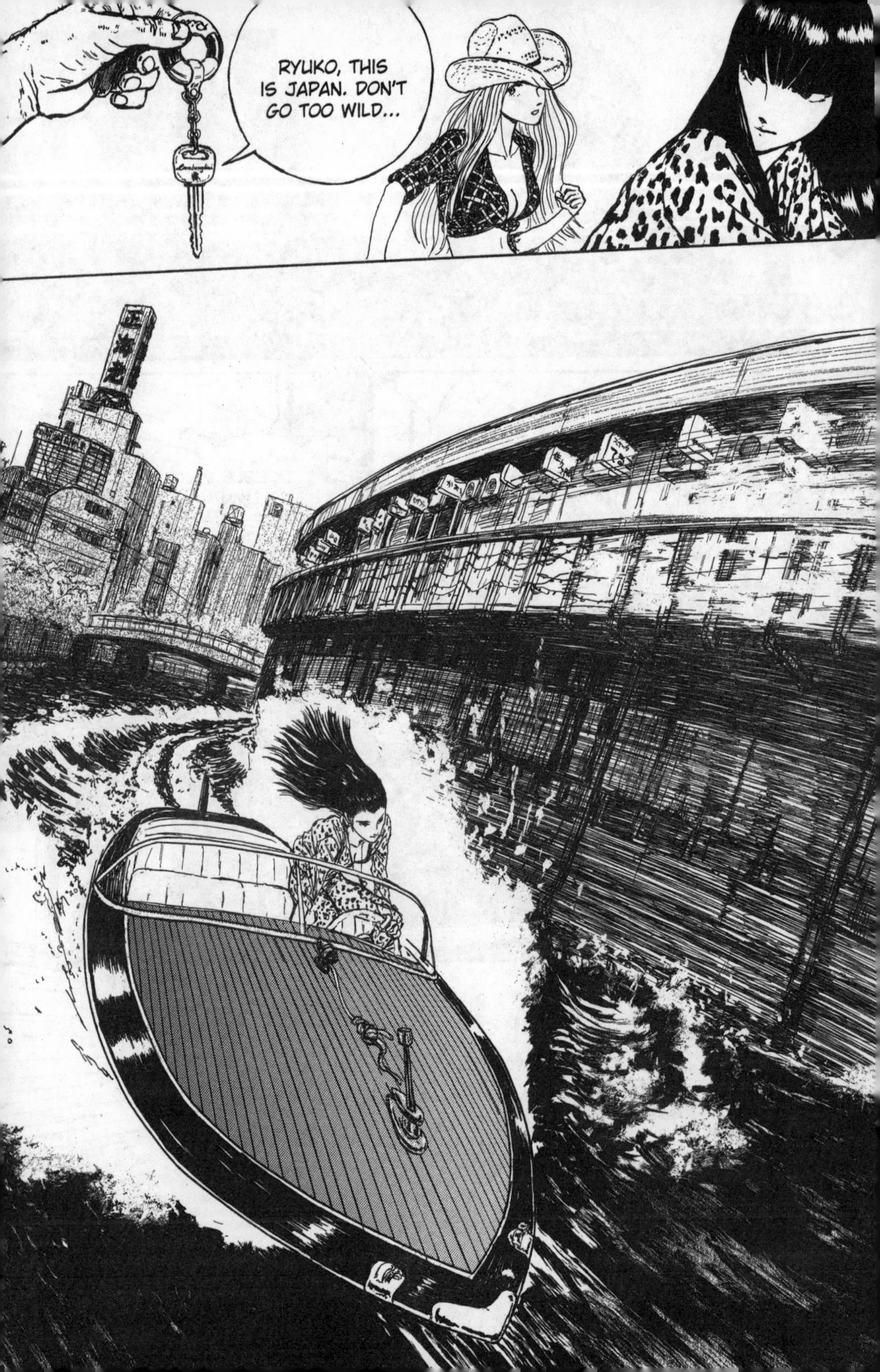
RYUKO, THIS IS JAPAN. DON'T GO TOO WILD...

END OF PART ONE

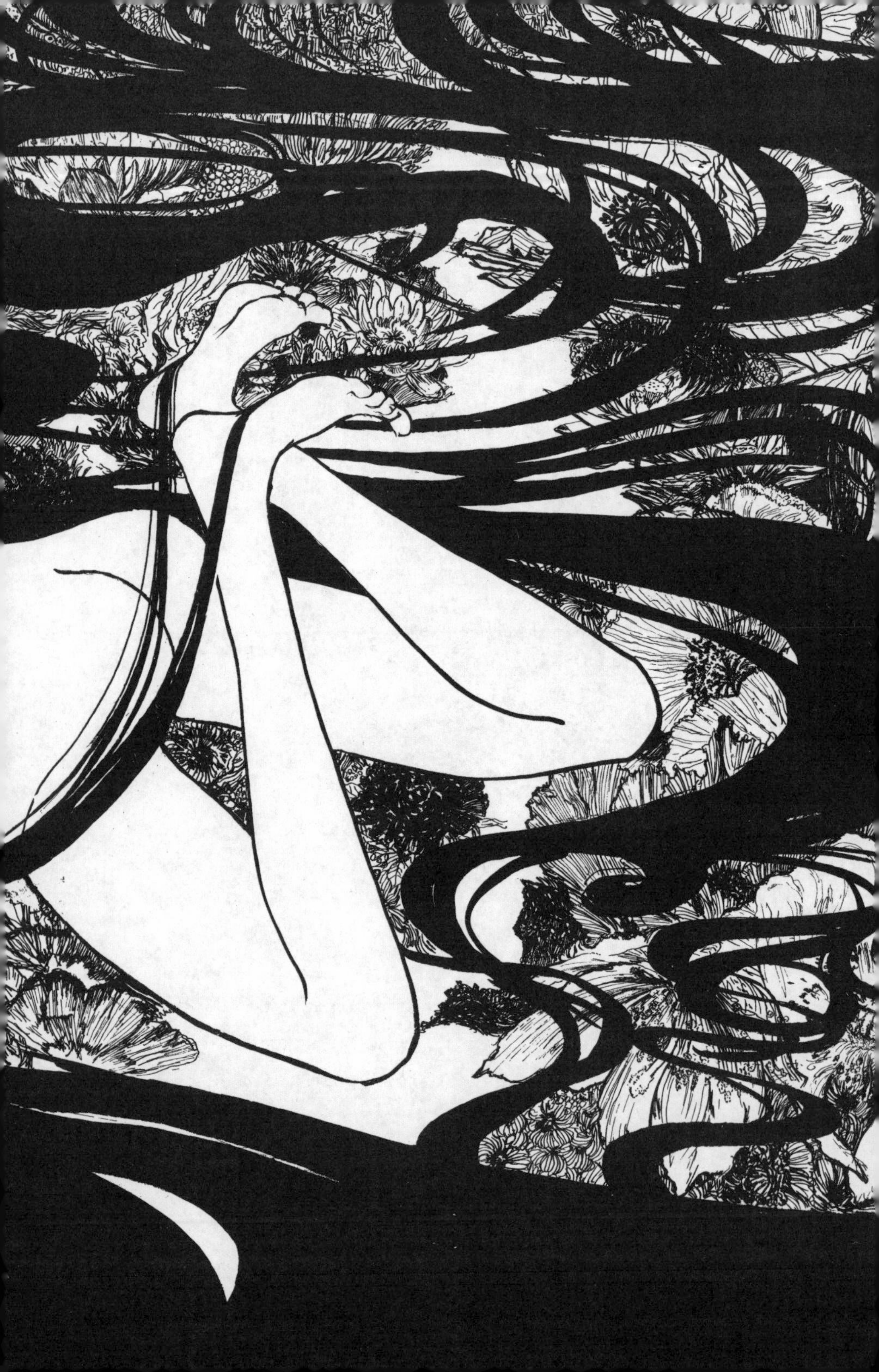

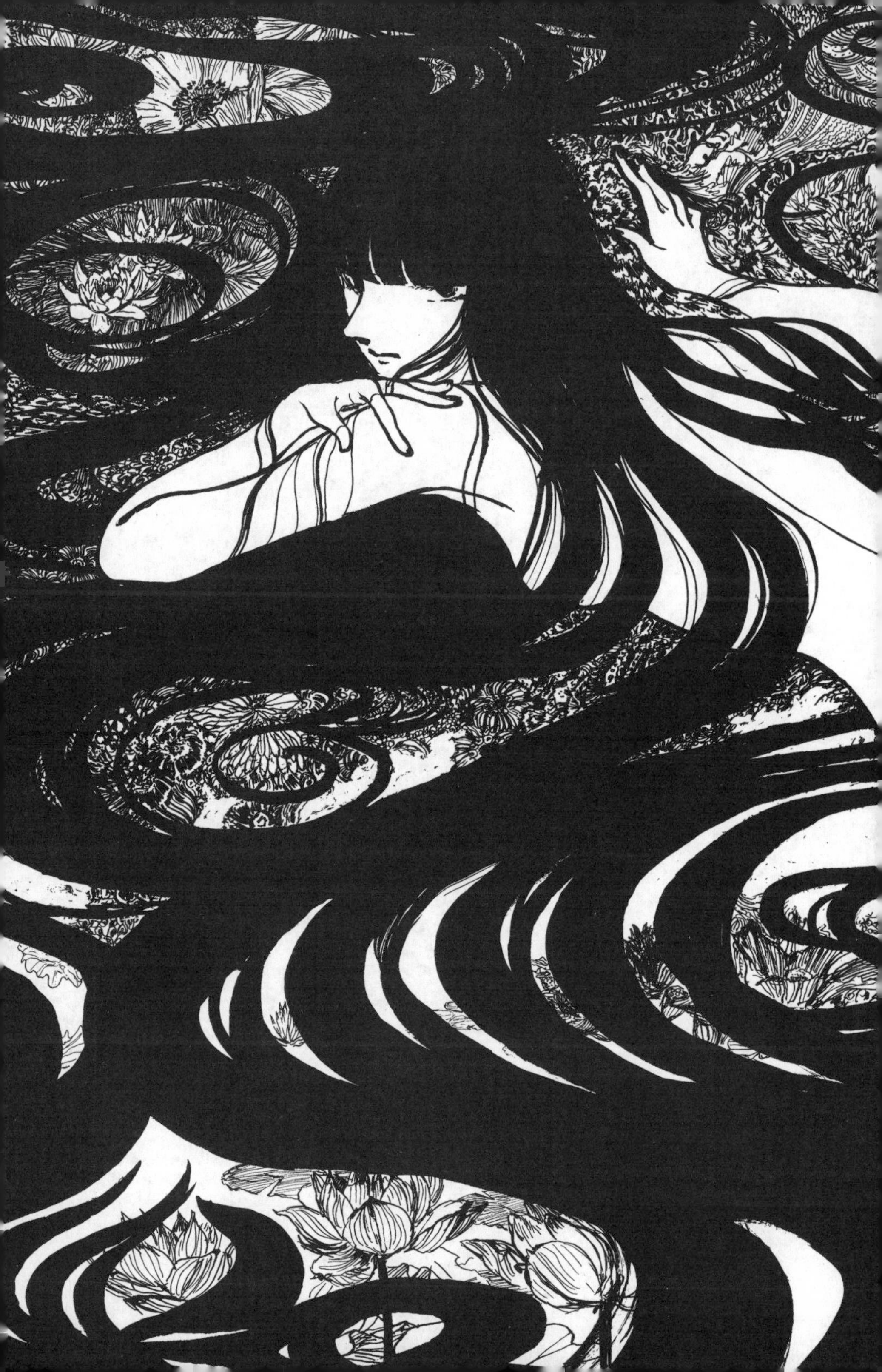

ELDO YOSHIMIZU
BIOGRAPHY

Born in Tokyo, Eldo Yoshimizu is an artist,
sculptor, musician, and photographer.

As a sculptor, Yoshimizu creates vast, jewel-like
shapes and sinuous, vivid outlines which are
among Japan's most significant pieces of public
art. His work has been exhibited in galleries all
over the world, and he has held positions as an
artist in residence in Italy, France and New York.

Yoshimizu's character of Ryuko has appeared in
art galleries around Japan and Europe and has
now made her jump to manga.

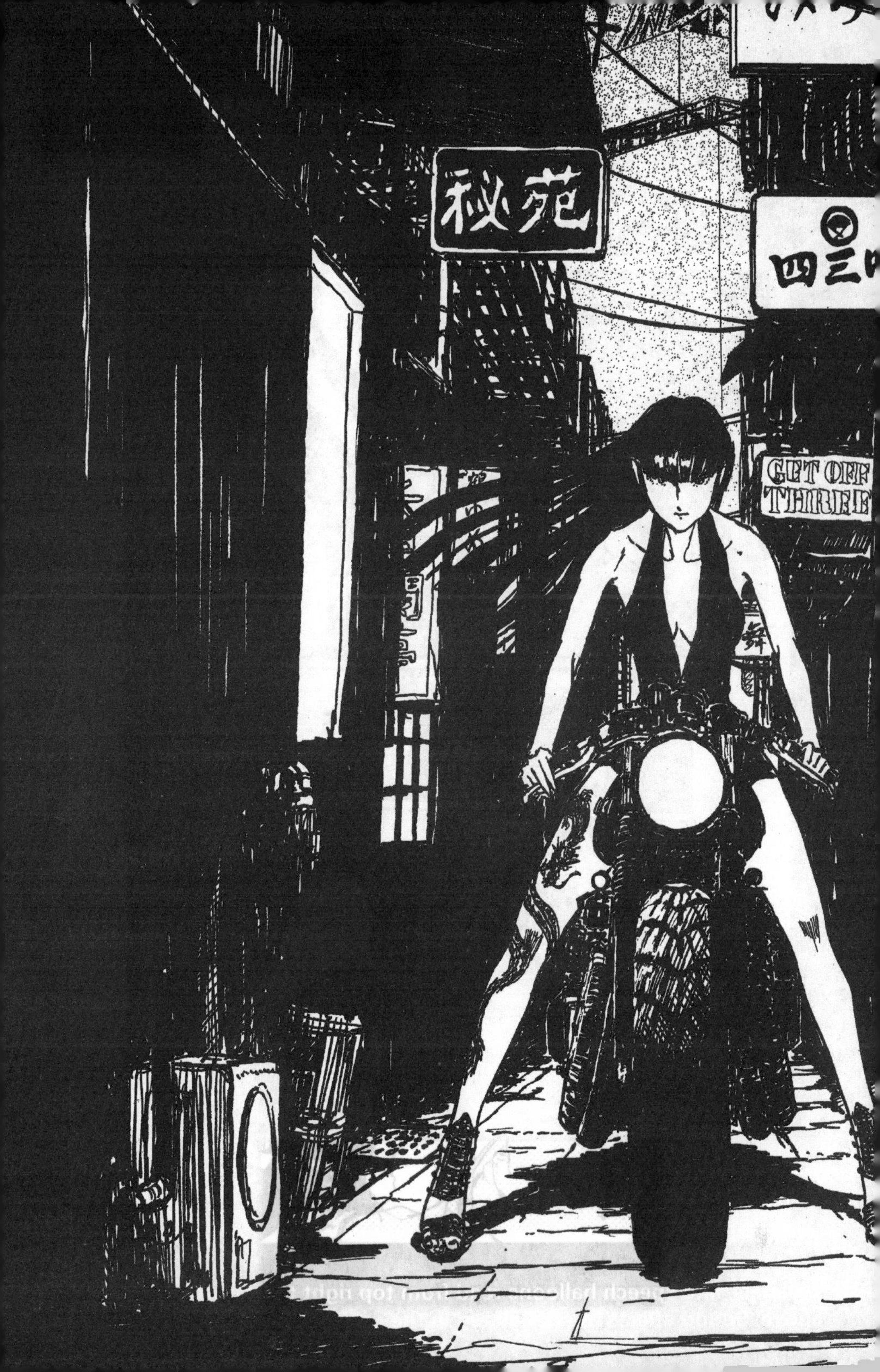
秘苑
GET OFF
THREE

STOP!

This manga is presented in its original right-to-left reading format. This is the back of the book!

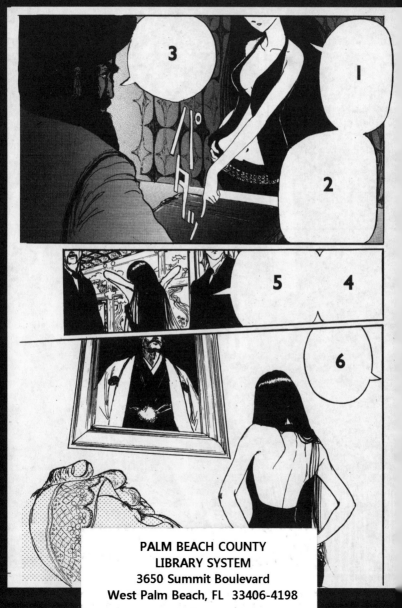

Pages, panels, and s... ...bottom left, a... above. Sound effects are translated in the gutters between the pa...